Drama for Composition

Bert C. Bach
Millikin University

Gordon Browning
Eastern Kentucky University

Drama for Composition

Scott, Foresman and Company
Glenview, Illinois   Brighton, England

Library of Congress Catalog Card Number: 78-173635

ISBN: 0-673-07640-7

Copyright © 1973 Scott, Foresman and Company, Glenview, Illinois.
Philippines Copyright 1973 Scott, Foresman and Company.
All Rights Reserved.
Printed in the United States of America.

Regional offices of Scott, Foresman and Company are located in Dallas, Texas; Glenview, Illinois; Oakland, New Jersey; Palo Alto, California; Tucker, Georgia; and Brighton, England.

Acknowledgments

Everyman. From the book *Everyman and Medieval Miracle Plays.* Edited by A. C. Cawley. Dutton paperback edition published 1959 by E. P. Dutton & Co., Inc. Reprinted by permission of E. P. Dutton & Co., Inc. and J. M. Dent & Sons Ltd.

The School for Scandal by Richard Brinsley Sheridan. *British Dramatists from Dryden to Sheridan.* Copyright © 1969 by George Winchester Stone, Jr. Copyright 1939 by George H. Nettleton and Arthur E. Case. Reprinted by permission of the publisher, Houghton Mifflin Company.

Arms And The Man by George Bernard Shaw from *Seven Plays by Bernard Shaw.* Reprinted by permission of The Society of Authors for the Bernard Shaw Estate.

Hamlet by William Shakespeare from *An Introduction to Shakespeare,* edited by Hardin Craig. Reprinted by permission of Hardin Craig, Jr.

The Playboy of the Western World by John Millington Synge. Copyright 1907 and renewed 1952 by the Executors of the Estate of John M. Synge. Reprinted from *The Complete Plays of John M. Synge* by permission of Random House, Inc.

Day of Absence. Copyright, © 1966, by Douglas Turner Ward. Reprinted by permission of the author and of Dramatists Play Service, Inc.

CAUTION: *Day of Absence,* being duly copyrighted, is subject to a royalty. The amateur acting rights in the play are controlled exclusively by the Dramatists Play Service, Inc., 440 Park Avenue South, New York, N.Y. 10016. No amateur production of the play may be given without obtaining in advance the written permission of the Dramatists Play Service, Inc., and paying the requisite fee.

Volpone by Ben Jonson. Reprinted by permission from *English Drama 1580-1642* edited by C. F. Tucker Brooke and Nathaniel Burton Paradise. (Lexington, Mass.: D. C. Heath and Company, 1933).

Desire Under the Elms by Eugene O'Neill. Copyright 1924 and renewed 1952 by Eugene O'Neill. Reprinted from *Nine Plays by Eugene O'Neill* by permission of Random House, Inc.

A Phoenix Too Frequent by Christopher Fry. Copyright 1950 by Christopher Fry. Reprinted by permission of Oxford University Press, Inc. All rights of any kind, including performance and reproduction, are reserved.

Cover photograph by Bill McCartney.

Preface

Drama for Composition, like its companion anthology, *Fiction for Composition,* provides a coherent rationale for composition courses using literary genres as their subject matter. This aim prescribes, foremost, that both teacher and student recognize a relationship between the problems of the playwright and those of the composition student. For example, the dramatist—like the writer of expository prose—seeks to appeal to an audience, to convey a meaning, and to evoke a response. The relevance of such considerations to freshman English is developed in the individual section introductions. Given the similarities between writing a play and writing an essay, there is no reason why the composition student cannot profit from reading a collection of plays chosen to illustrate features of good writing and grouped according to the following characteristics: anticipating the audience (the beginning), maintaining credibility (the middle), and achieving resolution (the end).

This text is designed so that a teacher who finds the organization inappropriate to his methods will still find the book useful. We are aware, for instance, that the dramatist faces certain considerations of no concern to the student writer of prose. For example, descriptive details are embodied in the *presented play* but not in the *play as literature;* the author can present, but not overtly interpret, action; and action *must* have precedence over psychological probing. For those who wish to emphasize drama rather than composition, we have provided an alternate table of contents that—together with the material in the glossary—will permit the teacher to present the plays in a more conventional manner.

Finally, a well-written drama speaks for itself; the student may benefit from reading it and participating in class discussion—without the help (or hindrance) of editorial commentary. Since our intended focus is on elements of composition, however, we have selected only English-language plays. They are grouped chronologically within the individual sections. Textual notes, although obviously necessary for certain selections, have been kept to a minimum and even excluded altogether whenever possible.

We wish to acknowledge the editorial assistance of Mr. Verne Reaves and Ms. Sybil Sosin of Scott, Foresman, and also the assistance of Ms. Debbie Martin and Ms. Donna Cryer in preparing the manuscript.

> Bert C. Bach
> Millikin University
>
> Gordon Browning
> Eastern Kentucky University

Contents

I. ANTICIPATING THE AUDIENCE: THE BEGINNING 1

Anonymous	Everyman	5
Richard Brinsley Sheridan	The School for Scandal	26
George Bernard Shaw	Arms and the Man	89

II. MAINTAINING CREDIBILITY: THE MIDDLE 141

William Shakespeare	Hamlet	146
John Millington Synge	The Playboy of the Western World	251
Douglas Turner Ward	Day of Absence: A Satirical Fantasy	295

III. ACHIEVING RESOLUTION: THE END 321

Ben Jonson	Volpone; or, the Fox	326
Eugene O'Neill	Desire Under the Elms	426
Christopher Fry	A Phoenix Too Frequent	471

GLOSSARY 502

Alternate Table of Contents

I. MORALITY PLAY

Medieval

| Anonymous | Everyman | 5 |

II. TRAGEDIES

Romantic

| William Shakespeare | Hamlet | 146 |

Modern

| Eugene O'Neill | Desire Under the Elms | 426 |

III. COMEDIES

Comedy of Humors

| Ben Jonson | Volpone; or, the Fox | 326 |

Comedy of Manners

| Richard Brinsley Sheridan | The School for Scandal | 26 |

Burlesque Comedy

| George Bernard Shaw | Arms and the Man | 89 |

Modern Verse Comedy

| Christopher Fry | A Phoenix Too Frequent | 471 |

Farce

| John Millington Synge | The Playboy of the Western World | 251 |

Satirical Fantasy

| Douglas Turner Ward | Day of Absence: A Satirical Fantasy | 295 |

The Plays in Chronological Order

Anonymous	Everyman	5
William Shakespeare	Hamlet	146
Ben Jonson	Volpone; or, the Fox	326
Richard Brinsley Sheridan	The School for Scandal	26
George Bernard Shaw	Arms and the Man	89
John Millington Synge	The Playboy of the Western World	251
Eugene O'Neill	Desire Under the Elms	426
Christopher Fry	A Phoenix Too Frequent	471
Douglas Turner Ward	Day of Absence: A Satirical Fantasy	295

Part I

ANTICIPATING THE AUDIENCE: THE BEGINNING

Part I

ANTICIPATING THE AUDIENCE: THE BEGINNING

The playwright, like the theme writer, must anticipate an audience. If he correctly anticipates its nature, he will entertain its members by relating an action which—in serious drama—embodies a universal meaning. If he does not, he will fail to engage their interest, fail to communicate, and—on most occasions—bore them.

In whatever medium one writes, he must recognize the *level* of his audience. That is, he must ask such questions as these: Is the audience educated? Is it serious? Is it decidedly lowbrow or decidedly urbane? Is it serious or carefree, thoughtful or frequently inattentive? Even though it is passé these days to draw value judgments concerning the relative merits of different audiences, it is yet a truism that audience levels differ. Obviously, the evening crowd at Carnegie Hall is not the same as the daytime television audience, nor does the Wagnerian crowd—save in unusual circumstances—spend its Saturday evenings at psychedelic pop concerts.

In composition classes, most themes are written either on assigned topics (frequently related to reading assignments) or according to assigned rhetorical modes (e.g., description, narration, definition, argumentation). While these prescriptions limit possibilities, similar limitations are frequently placed upon dramatists by the nature of their audiences. Consider, for instance, the problems faced by the anonymous author of *Everyman* (pages 5ff.), intent upon communicating a moral purpose to a medieval audience increasingly concerned with secular matters. Like the playwright, the theme writer must involve his audience, clarify the relevancy of what he has to say, and develop a proper tone with no unnecessary fanfare.

Beginning writers characteristically find introductory sections or paragraphs difficult to write. This ought not to be so if the entire paper has been properly planned and if the potential audience has been thoroughly evaluated. But it should be obvious that nobody can adequately introduce something or someone he does not know; likewise, an introductory section cannot be written properly by one who neither knows what he is going to say nor understands the nature of the audience he wishes to address. While we hesitate to say that the introductory section should be written last, it certainly should be reread carefully and revised if the development of the paper warrants it.

The primary question is most apparent: What should the introductory section contain? If this question is answered first, the matter of *tone* (i.e., the writer's attitude toward his audience and his material) can be more easily confronted. For example, the opening dialogue of *The School for Scandal* (pages 27-28) and the ludicrous entrance of Bluntschli in the first act of *Arms and the Man* (pages 92 ff.) indicate the authors' comic intent, whereas the Messenger's foreshadowing in *Everyman* of an allegorical conflict between vice and virtue indicates that playwright's more serious purpose.

The following are some important considerations for student writers:

1. For expository or argumentative compositions, the introduction should contain a *thesis statement,* whether or not it is labeled as such. This statement should embody a particular observation or position taken in reference to the subject (see the Messenger's opening speech in *Everyman*). In writing a thesis statement, remember these details:

   a. Avoid including within any parallel structures an idea that will not be developed equally with other ideas included in the same parallel structures.
   b. Use the thesis statement as a tool for dividing the composition into logical segments. Of the following two statements, only the second does this: (1) "Marcella Sembrich was one of America's earliest great singers." (2) "Marcella Sembrich, the nineteenth-century American soprano, lacked the natural vocal capabilities possessed by many of her contemporaries, but she had greater virtuosity than most Americans of her time."
   c. Avoid a thesis that is unintentionally ambiguous, purposely equivocal, or needlessly cryptic.
   d. Cast the thesis statements so that they command attention. *Occasionally* a paradox, epigram, aphorism, or cleverly embraced allusion can draw immediate audience attention; much of the impact in Shaw's *Arms and the Man* is achieved by the early introduction of a paradoxically cowardly, chocolate-loving professional soldier. But be careful to avoid degenerating into mere cuteness.
   e. In stating the thesis, avoid rhetorically formal or mechanical diction (for example: "In this paper I shall demonstrate three valid reasons for abolishing capital punishment"). Many writers adopt such stereotyped beginnings, but they create a turgid effect that is difficult to overcome. This is especially true of mechanical sentences that appear first in a paragraph. For sake of clarity and emphasis, the thesis statement should frequently appear as the last sentence in an introductory section or paragraph.

2. If the body of the paper requires the reader's awareness of a critical term or principle (especially one not used in the usual sense), the introductory paragraph should provide a definition. At this point a warning is apropos: *Avoid using verbatim dictionary definitions,* since they probably will contain much that is irrelevant to your purposes.

3. Occasionally, the introductory passage may contain an interestingly related event that leads directly—either through explanation or illustration—to the thesis statement. When employing this technique, make sure that the relevance of the narrative to the thesis statement is explicitly clear.

4. If the subject of the paper requires that the reader be aware of a particular fact, the presentation of that fact is an important part of the introductory section. The presentation should be clear and its relevance to the entire composition thoroughly established.

5. A brief statement that will shock the reader is often an effective beginning for an introductory paragraph. Like similar devices, this one should be used infrequently, else it loses its effectiveness.

A dramatist is well aware that he must compose a play that can be presented in 2 or 2½ hours. This length restriction requires him to devise an introduction that will establish a proper mood and point directly to the central action of the play. Likewise, the theme writer must recognize that he is working within a certain length requirement. Hence, he must avoid common pitfalls that arise in writing introductory sections:

1. Avoid an embellished, wandering statement that delays executing the real business of the introduction.
2. Avoid apologizing or griping in the introduction.
3. Avoid writing an introduction that bears no relationship to the thesis statement.
4. Avoid writing an introductory paragraph that contains self-evident statements.
5. Avoid introducing the paper with a broad statement that cannot possibly be substantiated.
6. Avoid providing excessive background material in the introduction.

Anonymous

Everyman *(ca. 1470) is a morality play, or a sermon in dramatic form (see page 505). Though its authorship is unknown, it is very similar to a Dutch work, Petrus Dorlaudus'* Elckerlijc; *scholars have speculated that it may be a translation of that work. Some have suggested, on the other hand, that* Elckerlijc *might be a translation of the English play; others argue that both are taken from an earlier version that has not survived. In any case,* Everyman *is the most popular of the English morality plays, and it has been revived numerous times on the modern stage.*

Like many allegories, the morality play was frequently long and digressive. For example, the longest of the English moralities, The Castle of Perseverance, *contained over 3600 lines. On the other hand, the dramatic unity of* Everyman, *which contains only 900 lines, is easily apparent. Note that the play does not furnish specific details of Everyman's past life and, furthermore, that the introduction strictly delimits the kinds of details that will be relevant to the play's action.*

EVERYMAN

CHARACTERS

EVERYMAN
GOD: ADONAI
DEATH
MESSENGER
FELLOWSHIP
COUSIN
KINDRED
GOODS
GOOD-DEEDS

STRENGTH
DISCRETION
FIVE-WITS
BEAUTY
KNOWLEDGE
CONFESSION
ANGEL
DOCTOR

Here beginneth a treatise how the high father of heaven sendeth death to summon every creature to come and give account of their lives in this world and is in manner of a moral play.

MESSENGER. I pray you all give your audience,
   And hear this matter with reverence,
   By figure a moral play—
   The *Summoning of Everyman* called it is,
   That of our lives and ending shows
   How transitory we be all day.
   This matter is wondrous precious,
   But the intent of it is more gracious,
   And sweet to bear away.
   The story saith,—Man, in the beginning,   10
   Look well, and take good heed to the ending,
   Be you never so gay!
   Ye think sin in the beginning full sweet,
   Which in the end causeth thy soul to weep,
   When the body lieth in clay.
   Here shall you see how Fellowship and Jollity,
   Both Strength, Pleasure, and Beauty,
   Will fade from thee as flower in May.
   For ye shall hear, how our heaven king
   Calleth Everyman to a general reckoning: 20
   Give audience, and hear what he doth say.
GOD. I perceive here in my majesty,
   How that all creatures be to me unkind,
   Living without dread in worldly prosperity:
   Of ghostly sight the people be so blind,
   Drowned in sin, they know me not for their God;
   In worldly riches is all their mind,
   They fear not my rightwiseness, the sharp rod;
   My law that I shewed, when I for them died,
   They forget clean, and shedding of my blood red;   30
   I hanged between two, it cannot be denied;
   To get them life I suffered to be dead;
   I healed their feet, with thorns hurt was my head:
   I could do no more than I did truly,
   And now I see the people do clean forsake me.
   They use the seven deadly sins damnable;
   As pride, covetise, wrath, and lechery,
   Now in the world be made commendable;
   And thus they leave of angels the heavenly company;
   Everyman liveth so after his own pleasure,   40
   And yet of their life they be nothing sure:
   I see the more that I them forbear
   The worse they be from year to year;
   All that liveth appaireth fast,
   Therefore I will in all the haste
   Have a reckoning of Everyman's person
   For and I leave the people thus alone
   In their life and wicked tempests,
   Verily they will become much worse than beasts;
   For now one would by envy another up eat;   50

44. *appaireth:* is impaired.

Charity they all do clean forget.
I hoped well that Everyman
In my glory should make his mansion,
And thereto I had them all elect;
But now I see, like traitors deject,
They thank me not for the pleasure that I to them meant,
Nor yet for their being that I them have lent;
I proffered the people great multitude of mercy,
And few there be that asketh it heartily;
They be so cumbered with worldly riches,   60
That needs on them I must do justice,
On Everyman living without fear.
Where art thou, Death, thou mighty messenger?
DEATH.   Almighty God, I am here at your will,
  Your commandment to fulfil.
GOD.   Go thou to Everyman,
  And show him in my name
  A pilgrimage he must on him take,
  Which he in no wise may escape;
  And that he bring with him a sure reckoning   70
  Without delay or any tarrying.
DEATH.   Lord, I will in the world go run over all,
  And cruelly outsearch both great and small;
  Every man will I beset that liveth beastly
  Out of God's laws, and dreadeth not folly:
  He that loveth riches I will strike with my dart,
  His sight to blind, and from heaven to depart,
  Except that alms be his good friend,
  In hell for to dwell, world without end.
  Lo, yonder I see Everyman walking;   80
  Full little he thinketh on my coming;
  His mind is on fleshly lusts and his treasure,
  And great pain it shall cause him to endure
  Before the Lord Heaven King.
  Everyman, stand still; whither art thou going
  Thus gaily? Hast thou thy Maker forget?
EVERYMAN.   Why askst thou?
  Wouldest thou wete?
DEATH.   Yea, sir, I will show you;
  In great haste I am sent to thee   90
  From God out of his majesty.
EVERYMAN.   What, sent to me?
DEATH.   Yea, certainly.
  Though thou have forget him here,
  He thinketh on thee in the heavenly sphere,
  As, or we depart, thou shalt know.
EVERYMAN.   What desireth God of me?
DEATH.   That shall I show thee;
  A reckoning he will needs have
  Without any longer respite.   100

    88. *wete:* know.

EVERYMAN. To give a reckoning longer leisure I crave;
  This blind matter troubleth my wit.
DEATH.   On thee thou must take a long journey:
  Therefore thy book of count with thee thou bring;
  For turn again thou can not by no way,
  And look thou be sure of thy reckoning:
  For before God thou shalt answer, and show
  Thy many bad deeds and good but a few;
  How thou hast spent thy life, and in what wise,
  Before the chief lord of paradise.   110
  Have ado that we were in that way,
  For, wete thou well, thou shalt make none attournay.
EVERYMAN.   Full unready I am such reckoning to give.
  I know thee not: what messenger art thou?
DEATH.   I am Death, that no man dreadeth.
  For every man I rest and no man spareth;
  For it is God's commandment
  That all to me should be obedient.
EVERYMAN.   O Death, thou comest when I had thee least in mind;
  In thy power it lieth me to save,   120
  Yet of my good will I give thee, if ye will be kind,
  Yea, a thousand pound shalt thou have,
  And defer this matter till another day.
DEATH.   Everyman, it may not be by no way;
  I set not by gold, silver, nor riches,
  Ne by pope, emperor, king, duke, ne princes.
  For and I would receive gifts great,
  All the world I might get;
  But my custom is clean contrary.
  I give thee no respite: come hence, and not tarry.   130
EVERYMAN.   Alas, shall I have no longer respite?
  I may say Death giveth no warning:
  To think on thee, it maketh my heart sick,
  For all unready is my book of reckoning.
  But twelve year and I might have abiding,
  My counting book I would make so clear,
  That my reckoning I should not need to fear.
  Wherefore, Death, I pray thee, for God's mercy,
  Spare me till I be provided of remedy.
DEATH.   Thee availeth not to cry, weep, and pray: 140
  But haste thee lightly that you were gone the journey,
  And prove thy friends if thou can.
  For, wete thou well, the tide abideth no man,
  And in the world each living creature
  For Adam's sin must die of nature.
EVERYMAN.   Death, if I should this pilgrimage take,
  And my reckoning surely make,
  Show me, for saint charity,
  Should I not come again shortly?

112. *attournay:* mediator.

DEATH. No, Everyman; and thou be once there, 150
  Thou mayst nevermore come here,
  Trust me verily.
EVERYMAN. O gracious God, in the high seat celestial,
  Have mercy on me in this most need;
  Shall I have no company from this vale terrestrial
  Of mine acquaintance that way me to lead?
DEATH. Yea, if any be so hardy,
  That would go with thee and bear thee company.
  Hie thee that you were gone to God's magnificence,
  Thy reckoning to give before his presence. 160
  What, weenest thou thy life is given thee,
  And thy worldly goods also?
EVERYMAN. I had wend so, verily.
DEATH. Nay, nay; it was but lent thee;
  For as soon as thou art go,
  Another awhile shall have it, and then go therefro
  Even as thou hast done.
  Everyman, thou art mad; thou hast thy wits five,
  And here on earth will not amend thy life,
  For suddenly I do come. 170
EVERYMAN. O wretched caitiff, whither shall I flee,
  That I might scape this endless sorrow!
  Now, gentle Death, spare me till to-morrow,
  That I may amend me
  With good advisement.
DEATH. Nay, thereto I will not consent,
  Nor no man will I respite,
  But to the heart suddenly I shall smite
  Without any advisement.
  And now out of thy sight I will me hie; 180
  See thou make thee ready shortly,
  For thou mayst say this is the day
  That no man living may scape away.
EVERYMAN. Alas, I may well weep with sighs deep;
  Now have I no manner of company
  To help me in my journey, and me to keep;
  And also my writing is full unready.
  How shall I do now for to excuse me?
  I would to God I had never be gete!
  To my soul a full great profit it had be; 190
  For now I fear pains huge and great.
  The time passeth; Lord, help that all wrought;
  For though I mourn it availeth nought.
  The day passeth, and is almost a-go;
  I wot not well what for to do.
  To whom were I best my complaint to make?
  What, and I to Fellowship thereof spake,
  And showed him of this sudden chance?
  For in him is all mine affiance;

189. *gete:* been gotten, been born.

We have in the world so many a day   200
Be on good friends in sport and play.
I see him yonder, certainly;
I trust that he will bear me company;
Therefore to him will I speak to ease my sorrow.
Well met, good Fellowship, and good morrow!

FELLOWSHIP *speaketh.*   Everyman, good morrow by this day.
Sir, why lookest thou so piteously?
If any thing be amiss, I pray thee, me say,
That I may help to remedy.

EVERYMAN.   Yea, good Fellowship, yea,   210
I am in great jeopardy.

FELLOWSHIP.   My true friend, show to me your mind;
I will not forsake thee, unto my life's end,
In the way of good company.

EVERYMAN.   That was well spoken, and lovingly.

FELLOWSHIP.   Sir, I must needs know your heaviness;
I have pity to see you in any distress;
If any have you wronged ye shall revenged be,
Though I on the ground be slain for thee,—
Though that I know before that I should die.   220

EVERYMAN.   Verily, Fellowship, gramercy.

FELLOWSHIP.   Tush! by thy thanks I set not a straw.
Show me your grief, and say no more.

EVERYMAN.   If I my heart should to you break,
And then you to turn your mind from me,
And would not me comfort, when you hear me speak,
Then should I ten times sorrier be.

FELLOWSHIP.   Sir, I say as I will do in deed.

EVERYMAN.   Then be you a good friend at need:
I have found you true here before.   230

FELLOWSHIP.   And so ye shall evermore;
For, in faith, and thou go to Hell,
I will not forsake thee by the way!

EVERYMAN.   Ye speak like a good friend; I believe you well;
I shall deserve it, and I may.

FELLOWSHIP.   I speak of no deserving, by this day.
For he that will say and nothing do
Is not worthy with good company to go;
Therefore show me the grief of your mind,
As to your friend most loving and kind.   240

EVERYMAN.   I shall show you how it is;
Commanded I am to go a journey,
A long way, hard and dangerous,
And give a strait count without delay
Before the high judge Adonai.
Wherefore I pray you, bear me company,
As ye have promised, in this journey.

FELLOWSHIP.   That is matter indeed! Promise is duty,
But, and I should take such a voyage on me,

245. *Adonai:* God.

I know it well, it should be to my pain:
  Also it make me afeard, certain. 250
  But let us take counsel here as well as we can,
  For your words would fear a strong man.
EVERYMAN. Why, ye said, If I had need,
  Ye would me never forsake, quick nor dead,
  Though it were to hell truly.
FELLOWSHIP. So I said, certainly,
  But such pleasures be set aside, thee sooth to say:
  And also, if we took such a journey,
  When should we come again? 260
EVERYMAN. Nay, never again till the day of doom.
FELLOWSHIP. In faith, then will not I come there!
  Who hath you these tidings brought?
EVERYMAN. Indeed, Death was with me here.
FELLOWSHIP. Now, by God that all hath bought,
  If Death were the messenger,
  For no man that is living to-day
  I will not go that loath journey—
  Not for the father that begat me!
EVERYMAN. Ye promised other wise, pardie. 270
FELLOWSHIP. I wot well I say so truly;
  And yet if thou wilt eat, and drink, and make good cheer,
  Or haunt to women, the lusty company,
  I would not forsake you, while the day is clear,
  Trust me verily!
EVERYMAN. Yea, thereto ye would be ready;
  To go to mirth, solace, and play,
  Your mind will sooner apply
  Than to bear me company in my long journey.
FELLOWSHIP. Now, in good faith, I will not that way. 280
  But and thou wilt murder, or any man kill,
  In that I will help thee with a good will!
EVERYMAN. O that is a simple advice indeed!
  Gentle fellow, help me in my necessity;
  We have loved long, and now I need,
  And now, gentle Fellowship, remember me.
FELLOWSHIP. Whether ye have loved me or no,
  By Saint John, I will not with thee go.
EVERYMAN. Yet I pray thee, take the labour, and do so much for me
  To bring me forward, for saint charity, 290
  And comfort me till I come without the town.
FELLOWSHIP. Nay, and thou would give me a new gown,
  I will not a foot with thee go;
  But and you had tarried I would not have left thee so.
  And as now, God speed thee in thy journey,
  For from thee I will depart as fast as I may.
EVERYMAN. Whither away, Fellowship? will you forsake me?
FELLOWSHIP. Yea, by my fay, to God I betake thee.
EVERYMAN. Farewell, good Fellowship; for this my heart is sore;
  Adieu for ever, I shall see thee no more. 300

FELLOWSHIP.   In faith, Everyman, farewell now at the end;
  For you I will remember that parting is mourning.
EVERYMAN.   Alack! shall we thus depart indeed?
  Our Lady, help, without any more comfort,
  Lo, Fellowship forsaketh me in my most need:
  For help in this world whither shall I resort?
  Fellowship herebefore with me would merry make;
  And now little sorrow for me doth he take.
  It is said, in prosperity men friends may find,
  Which in adversity be full unkind.   310
  Now whither for succour shall I flee,
  Sith that Fellowship hath forsaken me?
  To my kinsmen I will truly,
  Praying them to help me in my necessity;
  I believe that they will do so,
  For kind will creep where it may not go.
  I will go say, for yonder I see them go.
  Where be ye now, my friends and kinsmen?
KINDRED.   Here be we now at your commandment.
  Cousin, I pray you show us your intent   320
  In any wise, and not spare.
COUSIN.   Yea, Everyman, and to us declare
  If ye be disposed to go any whither,
  For wete you well, we will live and die together.
KINDRED.   In wealth and woe we will with you hold,
  For over his kin a man may be bold.
EVERYMAN.   Gramercy, my friends and kinsmen kind.
  Now shall I show you the grief of my mind:
  I was commanded by a messenger,
  That is an high king's chief officer;   330
  He bade me go a pilgrimage to my pain,
  And I know well I shall never come again;
  Also I must give a reckoning straight,
  For I have a great enemy, that hath me in wait,
  Which intendeth me for to hinder.
KINDRED.   What account is that which ye must render?
  That would I know.
EVERYMAN.   Of all my works I must show
  How I have lived and my days spent;
  Also of ill deeds, that I have used   340
  In my time, sith life was me lent;
  And of all virtues that I have refused.
  Therefore I pray you go thither with me,
  To help to make mine account, for saint charity.
COUSIN.   What, to go thither? Is that the matter?
  Nay, Everyman, I had liefer fast bread and water
  All this five year and more.
EVERYMAN.   Alas, that ever I was bore!
  For now shall I never be merry
  If that you forsake me.   350

348. *bore*: born.

KINDRED. Ah, sir; what, ye be a merry man!
  Take good heart to you, and make no moan.
  But one thing I warn you, by Saint Anne,
  As for me, ye shall go alone.
EVERYMAN. My Cousin, will you not with me go?
COUSIN. No, by our Lady; I have the cramp in my toe.
  Trust not to me, for, so God me speed,
  I will deceive you in your most need.
KINDRED. It availeth not us to tice.
  Ye shall have my maid with all my heart;   360
  She loveth to go to feasts, there to be nice,
  And to dance, and abroad to start:
  I will give her leave to help you in that journey,
  If that you and she may agree.
EVERYMAN. Now show me the very effect of your mind.
  Will you go with me, or abide behind?
KINDRED. Abide behind? yea, that I will and I may!
  Therefore farewell until another day.
EVERYMAN. How should I be merry or glad?
  For fair promises to me make,   370
  But when I have most need, they me forsake.
  I am deceived; that maketh me sad.
COUSIN. Cousin Everyman, farewell now,
  For verily I will not go with you;
  Also of mine own an unready reckoning
  I have to account; therefore I make tarrying.
  Now, God keep thee, for now I go.
EVERYMAN. Ah, Jesus, is all come hereto?
  Lo, fair words maketh fools feign;
  They promise and nothing will do certain.   380
  My kinsmen promised me faithfully
  For to abide with me steadfastly,
  And now fast away do they flee:
  Even so Fellowship promised me.
  What friend were best me of to provide?
  I lose my time here longer to abide.
  Yet in my mind a thing there is;—
  All my life I have loved riches;
  If that my good now help me might,
  He would make my heart full light.   390
  I will speak to him in this distress.—
  Where art thou, my Goods and riches?
GOODS. Who calleth me? Everyman? what haste thou hast!
  I lie here in corners, trussed and piled so high,
  And in chests I am locked so fast,
  Also sacked in bags, thou mayst see with thine eye,
  I cannot stir; in packs low I lie.
  What would ye have, lightly me say.
EVERYMAN. Come hither, Good, in all the haste thou may,
  For of counsel I must desire thee.   400

    359. *tice:* entice.

GOODS.   Sir, and ye in the world have trouble or adversity,
    That can I help you to remedy shortly.
EVERYMAN.   It is another disease that grieveth me;
    In this world it is not, I tell thee so.
    I am sent for another way to go,
    To give a straight account general
    Before the highest Jupiter of all;
    And all my life I have had joy and pleasure in thee.
    Therefore I pray thee go with me,
    For, peradventure, thou mayst before God Almighty   410
    My reckoning help to clean and purify;
    For it is said ever among,
    That money maketh all right that is wrong.
GOODS.   Nay, Everyman, I sing another song,
    I follow no man in such voyages;
    For and I went with thee
    Thou shouldst fare much the worse for me;
    For because on me thou did set thy mind,
    Thy reckoning I have made blotted and blind,
    That thine account thou cannot make truly;   420
    And that hast thou for the love of me.
EVERYMAN.   That would grieve me full sore,
    When I should come to that fearful answer.
    Up, let us go thither together.
GOODS.   Nay, not so, I am too brittle, I may not endure;
    I will follow no man one foot, be ye sure.
EVERYMAN.   Alas, I have thee loved, and had great pleasure
    All my life-days on good and treasure.
GOODS.   That is to thy damnation without lesing,
    For my love is contrary to the love everlasting.   430
    But if thou had me loved moderately during,
    As, to the poor give part of me,
    Then shouldst thou not in this dolour be,
    Nor in this great sorrow and care.
EVERYMAN.   Lo, now was I deceived or I was ware,
    And all I may wyte my spending of time.
GOODS.   What, weenest thou that I am thine?
EVERYMAN.   I had wend so.
GOODS.   Nay, Everyman, I say no;
    As for a while I was lent thee,   440
    A season thou hast had me in prosperity;
    My condition is man's soul to kill;
    If I save one, a thousand I do spill;
    Weenest thou that I will follow thee?
    Nay, from this world, not verily.
EVERYMAN.   I had wend otherwise.
GOODS.   Therefore to thy soul Good is a thief;
    For when thou art dead, this is my guise
    Another to deceive in the same wise
    As I have done thee, and all to his soul's reprief.   450

    436. *wyte:* blame.

EVERYMAN. O false Good, cursed thou be!
  Thou traitor to God, that hast deceived me,
  And caught me in thy snare.
GOODS. Marry, thou brought thyself in care,
  Whereof I am glad,
  I must needs laugh, I cannot be sad.
EVERYMAN. Ah, Good, thou hast had long my heartly love;
  I gave thee that which should be the Lord's above.
  But wilt thou not go with me in deed?
  I pray thee truth to say.   460
GOODS. No, so God me speed,
  Therefore farewell, and have good day.
EVERYMAN. O, to whom shall I make my moan
  For to go with me in that heavy journey?
  First Fellowship said he would with me gone;
  His words were very pleasant and gay,
  But afterward he left me alone.
  Then spake I to my kinsmen all in despair,
  And also they gave me words fair,
  They lacked no fair speaking,   470
  But all forsake me in the ending.
  Then went I to my Goods that I loved best,
  In hope to have comfort, but there had I least;
  For my Goods sharply did me tell
  That he bringeth many into hell.
  Then of myself I was ashamed,
  And so I am worthy to be blamed;
  Thus may I well myself hate.
  Of whom shall I now counsel take?
  I think that I shall never speed   480
  Till that I go to my Good-Deed,
  But alas, she is so weak,
  That she can neither go nor speak;
  Yet will I venture on her now.—
  My Good-Deeds, where be you?
GOOD-DEEDS. Here I lie cold in the ground;
  Thy sins hath me sore bound,
  That I cannot stir.
EVERYMAN. O, Good-Deeds, I stand in fear;
  I must you pray of counsel,   490
  For help now should come right well.
GOOD-DEEDS. Everyman, I have understanding
  That ye be summoned account to make
  Before Messias, of Jerusalem King;
  And you do by me that journey what you will I take.
EVERYMAN. Therefore I come to you, my moan to make;
  I pray you, that ye will go with me.
GOOD-DEEDS. I would full fain, but I cannot stand verily.
EVERYMAN. Why, is there anything on you fall?
GOOD-DEEDS. Yea, sir, I may thank you of all;   500

  495. *And you do by me:* If you go by me. *what:* with.

    If ye had perfectly cheered me,
    Your book of account now full ready had be.
    Look, the books of your works and deeds eke;
    Oh, see how they lie under the feet,
    To your soul's heaviness.
EVERYMAN.   Our Lord Jesus, help me!
    For one letter here I can not see.
GOOD-DEEDS.   There is a blind reckoning in time of distress!
EVERYMAN.   Good-Deeds, I pray you, help me in this need,
    Or else I am for ever damned indeed;   510
    Therefore help me to make reckoning
    Before the redeemer of all thing,
    That king is, and was, and ever shall.
GOOD-DEEDS.   Everyman, I am sorry of your fall,
    And fain would I help you, and I were able.
EVERYMAN.   Good-Deeds, your counsel I pray you give me.
GOOD-DEEDS.   That shall I do verily;
    Though that on my feet I may not go,
    I have a sister, that shall with you also,
    Called Knowledge, which shall with you abide,   520
    To help you to make that dreadful reckoning.
KNOWLEDGE.   Everyman, I will go with thee, and be thy guide,
    In thy most need to go by thy side.
EVERYMAN.   In good condition I am now in every thing,
    And am wholly content with this good thing;
    Thanked be God my Creator.
GOOD-DEEDS.   And when he hath brought thee there,
    Where thou shalt heal thee of thy smart,
    Then go you with your reckoning and your Good Deeds together
    For to make you joyful at heart   530
    Before the blessed Trinity.
EVERYMAN.   My Good-Deeds, gramercy;
    I am well content, certainly,
    With your words sweet.
KNOWLEDGE.   Now go we together lovingly,
    To Confession, that cleansing river.
EVERYMAN.   For joy I weep; I would we were there;
    But, I pray you, give me cognition
    Where dwelleth that holy man, Confession.
KNOWLEDGE.   In the house of salvation: 540
    We shall find him in that place,
    That shall us comfort by God's grace.
    Lo, this is Confession; kneel down and ask mercy,
    For he is in good conceit with God almighty.
EVERYMAN.   O glorious fountain that all uncleanness doth clarify,
    Wash from me the spots of vices unclean,
    That on me no sin may be seen;
    I come with Knowledge for my redemption,
    Repent with hearty and full contrition;
    For I am commanded a pilgrimage to take,   550
    And great accounts before God to make.

Now, I pray you, Shrift, mother of salvation,
Help my good deeds for my piteous exclamation.
CONFESSION. I know your sorrow well, Everyman;
Because with Knowledge ye come to me,
I will you comfort as well as I can,
And a precious jewel I will give thee,
Called penance, wise voider of adversity;
Therewith shall your body chastised be,
With abstinence and perseverance in God's service: 560
Here shall you receive that scourge of me,
Which is penance strong, that ye must endure,
To remember thy Saviour was scourged for thee
With sharp scourges, and suffered it patiently;
So must thou, or thou scape that painful pilgrimage;
Knowledge, keep him in this voyage,
And by that time Good-Deeds will be with thee.
But in any wise, be sure of mercy,
For your time draweth fast, and ye will saved be;
Ask God mercy, and He will grant truly, 570
When with the scourge of penance man doth him bind,
The oil of forgiveness then shall he find.
EVERYMAN. Thanked be God for his gracious work!
For now I will my penance begin;
This hath rejoiced and lighted my heart,
Though the knots be painful and hard within.
KNOWLEDGE. Everyman, look your penance that ye fulfil,
What pain that ever it to you be,
And Knowledge shall give you counsel at will,
How your accounts ye shall make clearly. 580
EVERYMAN. O eternal God, O heavenly figure,
O way of rightwiseness, O goodly vision,
Which descended down in a virgin pure
Because he would Everyman redeem,
Which Adam forfeited by his disobedience:
O blessed Godhead, elect and high-divine,
Forgive my grievous offence;
Here I cry thee mercy in this presence.
O ghostly treasure, O ransomer and redeemer
Of all the world, hope and conductor, 590
Mirror of joy, and founder of mercy,
Which illumineth heaven and earth thereby,
Hear my clamorous complaint, though it late be;
Receive my prayers; unworthy in this heavy life,
Though I be, a sinner most abominable,
Yet let my name be written in Moses' table;
O Mary, pray to the Maker of all thing,
Me for to help at my ending,
And save me from the power of my enemy,
For Death assaileth me strongly; 600
And, Lady, that I may by means of thy prayer
Of your Son's glory to be partaker,

By the means of his passion I it crave,
I beseech you, help my soul to save.—
Knowledge, give me the scourge of penance;
My flesh therewith shall give a quittance:
I will now begin, if God give me grace.

KNOWLEDGE.   Everyman, God give you time and space:
  Thus I bequeath you in the hands of our Saviour,
  Thus may you make your reckoning sure.   610

EVERYMAN.   In the name of the Holy Trinity
  My body sore punished shall be:
  Take this body for the sin of the flesh;
  Also thou delightest to go gay and fresh,
  And in the way of damnation thou did me bring;
  Therefore suffer now strokes and punishing.
  Now of penance I will wade the water clear,
  To save me from purgatory, that sharp fire.

GOOD-DEEDS.   I thank God, now I can walk and go;
  And am delivered of my sickness and woe.   620
  Therefore with Everyman I will go, and not spare;
  His good works I will help him to declare.

KNOWLEDGE.   Now, Everyman, be merry and glad;
  Your Good-Deeds cometh now; ye may not be sad;
  Now is your Good-Deeds whole and sound,
  Going upright upon the ground.

EVERYMAN.   My heart is light, and shall be evermore;
  Now will I smite faster than I did before.

GOOD-DEEDS.   Everyman, pilgrim, my special friend,
  Blessed be thou without end;   630
  For thee is prepared the eternal glory.
  Ye have me made whole and sound,
  Therefore I will bide by thee in every stound.

EVERYMAN.   Welcome, my Good-Deeds; now I hear thy voice,
  I weep for very sweetness of love.

KNOWLEDGE.   Be no more sad, but ever rejoice,
  God seeth thy living in his throne above;
  Put on this garment to thy behove,
  Which is wet with your tears,
  Or else before God you may it miss,   640
  When you to your journey's end come shall.

EVERYMAN.   Gentle Knowledge, what do you it call?

KNOWLEDGE.   It is a garment of sorrow:
  From pain it will you borrow;
  Contrition it is,
   That getteth forgiveness;
  It pleaseth God passing well.

GOOD-DEEDS.   Everyman, will you wear it for your heal?

EVERYMAN.   Now blessed be Jesu, Mary's Son!
  For now have I on true contrition.   650
  And let us go now without tarrying;

  633. *stound:* season.

Good-Deeds, have we clear our reckoning?
GOOD-DEEDS.   Yea, indeed I have it here.
EVERYMAN.   Then I trust we need not fear;
   Now, friends, let us not part in twain.
KNOWLEDGE.   Nay, Everyman, that will we not, certain.
GOOD-DEEDS.   Yet must thou lead with thee
   Three persons of great might.
EVERYMAN.   Who should they be?
GOOD-DEEDS.   Discretion and Strength they hight,   660
   And thy Beauty may not abide behind.
KNOWLEDGE.   Also ye must call to mind
   Your Five-wits as for your counsellors.
GOOD-DEEDS.   You must have them ready at all hours.
EVERYMAN.   How shall I get them hither?
KNOWLEDGE.   You must call them all together,
   And they will hear you incontinent.
EVERYMAN.   My friends, come hither and be present
   Discretion, Strength, my Five-wits, and Beauty.
BEAUTY.   Here at your will we be all ready.   670
   What will ye that we should do?
GOOD-DEEDS.   That ye would with Everyman go,
   And help him in his pilgrimage,
   Advise you, will ye with him or not in that voyage?
STRENGTH.   We will bring him all thither,
   To his help and comfort, ye may believe me.
DISCRETION.   So will we go with him all together.
EVERYMAN.   Almighty God, loved thou be,
   I give thee laud that I have hither brought
   Strength, Discretion, Beauty, and Five-wits; lack I nought;   680
   And my Good-Deeds, with Knowledge clear,
   All be in my company at my will here;
   I desire no more to my business.
STRENGTH.   And I, Strength, will by you stand in distress,
   Though thou would in battle fight on the ground.
FIVE-WITS.   And though it were through the world round,
   We will not depart for sweet nor sour.
BEAUTY.   No more will I unto death's hour,
   Whatsoever thereof befall.
DISCRETION.   Everyman, advise you first of all;   690
   Go with a good advisement and deliberation;
   We all give you virtuous monition
   That all shall be well.
EVERYMAN.   My friends, hearken what I will tell:
   I pray God reward you in his heavenly sphere.
   Now hearken, all that be here,
   For I will make my testament
   Here before you all present.
   In alms half my good I will give with my hands twain
   In the way of charity, with good intent,   700
   And the other half still shall remain

In quiet to be returned there it ought to be.
This I do in despite of the fiend of hell
To go quite out of his peril
Ever after and this day.
KNOWLEDGE.   Everyman, hearken what I say;
Go to priesthood, I you advise,
And receive of him in any wise
The holy sacrament and ointment together;
Then shortly see ye turn again hither;   710
We will all abide you here.
FIVE-WITS.   Yea, Everyman, hie you that ye ready were,
There is no emperor, king, duke, ne baron,
That of God hath commission,
As hath the least priest in the world being;
For of the blessed sacraments pure and benign,
He beareth the keys and thereof hath the cure
For man's redemption, it is ever sure;
Which God for our soul's medicine
Gave us out of his heart with great pine;   720
Here in this transitory life, for thee and me
The blessed sacraments seven there be,
Baptism, confirmation, with priesthood good,
And the sacrament of God's precious flesh and blood,
Marriage, the holy extreme unction, and penance;
These seven be good to have in remembrance,
Gracious sacraments of high divinity.
EVERYMAN.   Fain would I receive that holy body
And meekly to my ghostly father I will go.
FIVE-WITS.   Everyman, that is the best that ye can do: 730
God will you to salvation bring,
For priesthood exceedeth all other thing;
To us Holy Scripture they do teach,
And converteth man from sin heaven to reach;
God hath to them more power given,
Than to any angel that is in heaven;
With five words he may consecrate
God's body in flesh and blood to make,
And handleth his maker between his hands;
The priest bindeth and unbindeth all bands,   740
Both in earth and in heaven;
Thou ministers all the sacraments seven;
Though we kissed thy feet thou were worthy;
Thou art surgeon that cureth sin deadly:
No remedy we find under God
But all only priesthood.
Everyman, God gave priests that dignity,
And setteth them in his stead among us to be;
Thus be they above angels in degree.
KNOWLEDGE.   If priests be good it is so surely;   750
But when Jesus hanged on the cross with great smart

There he gave, out of his blessed heart,
The same sacrament in great torment:
He sold them not to us, that Lord Omnipotent.
Therefore Saint Peter the apostle doth say
That Jesu's curse hath all they
Which God their Saviour do buy or sell,
Or they for any money do take or tell.
Sinful priests giveth the sinners example bad;
Their children sitteth by other men's fires, I have heard;   760
And some haunteth women's company,
With unclean life, as lusts of lechery
These be with sin made blind.

FIVE-WITS.   I trust to God no such may we find;
Therefore let us priesthood honour,
And follow their doctrine for our souls' succour;
We be their sheep, and they shepherds be
By whom we all be kept in surety.
Peace, for yonder I see Everyman come,
Which hath made true satisfaction.   770

GOOD-DEEDS.   Methinketh it is he indeed.

EVERYMAN.   Now Jesu be our alder speed.
I have received the sacrament for my redemption,
And then mine extreme unction:
Blessed be all they that counselled me to take it!
And now, friends, let us go without longer respite;
I thank God that ye have tarried so long.
Now set each of you on this rod your hand,
And shortly follow me:
I go before, there I would be; God be our guide.   780

STRENGTH.   Everyman, we will not from you go,
Till ye have gone this voyage long.

DISCRETION.   I, Discretion, will bide by you also.

KNOWLEDGE.   And though this pilgrimage be never so strong,
I will never part you fro:
Everyman, I will be as sure by thee
As ever I did by Judas Maccabee.

EVERYMAN.   Alas, I am so faint I may not stand,
My limbs under me do fold;
Friends, let us not turn again to this land,   790
Not for all the world's gold,
For into this cave must I creep
And turn to the earth and there to sleep.

BEAUTY.   What, into this grave? alas!

EVERYMAN.   Yea, there shall you consume more and less.

BEAUTY.   And what, should I smother here?

EVERYMAN.   Yea, by my faith, and never more appear.
In this world live no more we shall,
But in heaven before the highest Lord of all.

BEAUTY.   I cross out all this; adieu by Saint John;   800
I take my cap in my lap and am gone.

772. *speed:* speed in help of all.

EVERYMAN. What, Beauty, whither will ye?
BEAUTY. Peace, I am deaf; I look not behind me,
  Not and thou would give me all the gold in thy chest.
EVERYMAN. Alas, whereto may I trust?
  Beauty goeth fast away hie;
  She promised with me to live and die.
STRENGTH. Everyman, I will thee also forsake and deny;
  Thy game liketh me not at all.
EVERYMAN. Why, then ye will forsake me all. 810
  Sweet Strength, tarry a little space.
STRENGTH. Nay, sir, by the rood of grace
  I will hie me from thee fast,
  Though thou weep till thy heart brast.
EVERYMAN. Ye would ever bide by me, ye said.
STRENGTH. Yea, I have you far enough conveyed;
  Ye be old enough, I understand,
  Your pilgrimage to take on hand;
  I repent me that I hither came.
EVERYMAN. Strength, you to displease I am to blame; 820
  Will you break promise that is debt?
STRENGTH. In faith, I care not;
  Thou art but a fool to complain,
  You spend your speech and waste your brain;
  Go thrust thee into the ground.
EVERYMAN. I had wend surer I should you have found.
  He that trusteth in his Strength
  She him deceiveth at the length.
  Both Strength and Beauty forsaketh me,
  Yet they promised me fair and lovingly. 830
DISCRETION. Everyman, I will after Strength be gone,
  As for me I will leave you alone.
EVERYMAN. Why, Discretion, will ye forsake me?
DISCRETION. Yea, in faith, I will go from thee,
  For when Strength goeth before
  I follow after evermore.
EVERYMAN. Yet, I pray thee, for the love of the Trinity,
  Look in my grave once piteously.
DISCRETION. Nay, so nigh will I not come.
  Farewell, every one! 840
EVERYMAN. O all thing faileth, save God alone;
  Beauty, Strength, and Discretion;
  For when Death bloweth his blast,
  They all run from me full fast.
FIVE-WITS. Everyman, my leave now of thee I take;
  I will follow the other, for here I thee forsake.
EVERYMAN. Alas! then may I wail and weep,
  For I took you for my best friend.
FIVE-WITS. I will no longer thee keep;
  Now farewell, and there an end. 850
EVERYMAN. O Jesu, help, all hath forsaken me!

GOOD-DEEDS.   Nay, Everyman, I will bide with thee,
  I will not forsake thee indeed;
  Thou shalt find me a good friend at need.
EVERYMAN.   Gramercy, Good-Deeds; now may I true friends see;
  They have forsaken me every one;
  I loved them better than my Good-Deeds alone.
  Knowledge, will ye forsake me also?
KNOWLEDGE.   Yea, Everyman, when ye to death do go:
  But not yet for no manner of danger.   860
EVERYMAN.   Gramercy, Knowledge, with all my heart.
KNOWLEDGE.   Nay, yet I will not from hence depart,
  Till I see where ye shall be come.
EVERYMAN.   Methinketh, alas, that I must be gone,
  To make my reckoning and my debts pay,
  For I see my time is nigh spent away.
  Take example, all ye that this do hear or see,
  How they that I loved best do forsake me,
  Except my Good-Deeds that bideth truly.
GOOD-DEEDS.   All earthly things is but vanity: 870
  Beauty, Strength, and Discretion, do man forsake,
  Foolish friends and kinsmen, that fair spake,
  All fleeth save Good-Deeds, and that am I.
EVERYMAN.   Have mercy on me, God most mighty;
  And stand by me, thou Mother and Maid, holy Mary.
GOOD-DEEDS.   Fear not, I will speak for thee.
EVERYMAN.   Here I cry God mercy.
GOOD-DEEDS.   Short our end, and minish our pain;
  Let us go and never come again.
EVERYMAN.   Into thy hands, Lord, my soul I commend;   880
  Receive it, Lord, that it be not lost;
  As thou me boughtest, so me defend,
  And save me from the fiend's boast,
  That I may appear with that blessed host
  That shall be saved at the day of doom.
  In manus tuas—of might's most
  For ever—*commendo spiritum meum*.
KNOWLEDGE.   Now hath he suffered that we all shall endure;
  The Good-Deeds shall make all sure.
  Now hath he made ending;   890
  Methinketh that I hear angels sing
  And make great joy and melody,
  Where Everyman's soul received shall be.
ANGEL.   Come, excellent elect spouse to Jesu:
  Hereabove thou shalt go
  Because of thy singular virtue:
  Now the soul is taken the body fro;
  Thy reckoning is crystal-clear.
  Now shalt thou into the heavenly sphere,
  Unto the which all ye shall come   900
  That liveth well before the day of doom.

  886. *In manus tuas*: into thy hands.   887. *commendo spiritum meum*: I commend my spirit.

DOCTOR.   This moral men may have in mind;
　Ye hearers, take it of worth, old and young,
　And forsake pride, for he deceiveth you in the end,
　And remember Beauty, Five-wits, Strength, and Discretion,
　They all at the last do Everyman forsake,
　Save his Good-Deeds, there doth he take.
　But beware, and they be small
　Before God, he hath no help at all.
　None excuse may be there for Everyman: 910
　Alas, how shall he do then?
　For after death amends may no man make,
　For then mercy and pity do him forsake.
　If his reckoning be not clear when he do come,
　God will say—*ite maledicti in ignem æternum.*
　And he that hath his account whole and sound,
　High in heaven he shall be crowned;
　Unto which place God bring us all thither
　That we may live body and soul together.
　Thereto help the Trinity,   920
　Amen, say ye, for saint Charity.

　　　　　　　THUS ENDETH THIS MORALL PLAY OF EVERYMAN.

Questions for Discussion

1. What does the prologue accomplish toward establishing the tone of the play? What advantages and disadvantages typically arise in drama or composition from an introductory statement of moral purpose? Does the allegorical (see page 502) format tend to overcome the disadvantages, or merely to emphasize them?

2. How is the Messenger successful in his attempt to involve the audience in the play's contents? How does he anticipate (like a thesis statement) the entire development of the play? In what other ways is the subject *universalized* (i.e., made applicable to all of us)? What are the universal elements in Everyman's character? More generally, is the play as relevant to the twentieth century as to the fifteenth? Why or why not?

915. *ite . . . aeternum:* go ye cursed into eternal fire.

3. How effective is the use of personification (see page 506) in *Everyman* as a device for attracting an audience's interest? What problems arise from the use of such devices? How are these difficulties compensated for? Why are such devices frequently employed in didactic (i.e., lesson teaching) writing?

4. What sort of audience must the author of *Everyman* have anticipated? In what particular ways does such an audience differ from that of a recent serious movie you may have seen? Be specific. Would you gather that the use of allegory, personification, and so on, indicates an audience automatically susceptible to moral guidance? Have you witnessed these devices in any recent movie or play? Explain.

5. How thoroughly does the anonymous author attempt to characterize his allegorical figures? Do they immediately attain any degree of humanity? Are there characters who are not strictly allegorical? Are these characters (e.g., God) presented in human terms? What do your answers to these questions suggest about the author's methods of establishing relevancy?

Suggested Theme Topics

1. Write an extensive definition of *allegory,* illustrating your definition with a discussion of allegorical methods employed in *Everyman.*

2. Discuss the use of personification in *Everyman.*

3. Write a theme delineating the moral purpose of *Everyman.* Discuss the methods employed to establish and reveal this moral purpose.

4. Write a theme in which you use personification of some abstract concept for the purpose of revealing a moral attitude.

5. Discuss a movie or television show you recently saw which, in your opinion, dealt effectively with universals, i.e., ideas and/or characters which would be equally meaningful for another audience in another age.

Richard Brinsley Sheridan

Richard Brinsley Sheridan (1751-1816), a native of Dublin, Ireland, was educated at home and in England. In his youth a long series of personal difficulties was triggered by an elopement, which led to parental disapproval and, eventually, to two duels. The resolution of these problems introduced a period of tranquility and productivity, marked especially by the production of his two most notable plays, The Rivals *(1775) and* The School for Scandal *(1777), and by his ascendancy to part-ownership and management of the Drury Lane Theatre. A moderately successful political career as member of the House of Commons and treasurer of the Navy ended in failure when Sheridan's party suddenly lost its power. This, coupled with the destruction of his theater by fire, led to the playwright's imprisonment as a debtor. Burial in Westminster Abbey followed an impoverished death.*

Satire is always directed toward a specific audience. Does this fact imply that its impact will be lost on other generations and other cultures? Note the devices by which Sheridan universalizes the content of his satiric drama.

THE SCHOOL FOR SCANDAL

CHARACTERS

SIR PETER TEAZLE
SIR OLIVER SURFACE
JOSEPH SURFACE
CHARLES SURFACE
CRABTREE
SIR BENJAMIN BACKBITE
ROWLEY
TRIP
MOSES
SNAKE
CARELESS
LADY TEAZLE
MARIA
LADY SNEERWELL
MRS. CANDOUR

Scene—London

ACT I

SCENE I

Lady Sneerwell's house.

LADY SNEERWELL *at the dressing-table*—SNAKE *drinking chocolate.*

LADY SNEER. The paragraphs, you say, Mr. Snake, were all inserted?
SNAKE. They were, madam, and as I copied them myself in a feigned hand, there can be no suspicion whence they came.
LADY SNEER. Did you circulate the reports of Lady Brittle's intrigue with Captain Boastall?
SNAKE. That is in as fine a train as your ladyship could wish,—in the common course of things, I think it must reach Mrs. Clackit's ears within four-and-twenty hours; and then, you know, the business is as good as done.
LADY SNEER. Why, truly, Mrs. Clackit has a very pretty talent, and a great deal of industry.
SNAKE. True, madam, and has been tolerably successful in her day:— to my knowledge, she has been the cause of six matches being broken off, and three sons being disinherited, of four forced elopements, as many close confinements, nine separate maintenances, and two divorces;—nay, I have more than once traced her causing a *Tête-à-Tête* in the *Town and Country Magazine*, when the parties perhaps had never seen each other's faces before in the course of their lives.
LADY SNEER. She certainly has talents, but her manner is gross.
SNAKE. 'Tis very true,—she generally designs well, has a free tongue, and a bold invention; but her coloring is too dark, and her outline often extravagant. She wants that *delicacy* of *hint*, and *mellowness* of *sneer*, which distinguish your ladyship's scandal.
LADY SNEER. Ah! you are partial, Snake.
SNAKE. Not in the least; everybody allows that Lady Sneerwell can do more with a *word* or a *look* than many can with the most labored detail, even when they happen to have a little truth on their side to support it.
LADY SNEER. Yes, my dear Snake; and I am no hypocrite to deny the satisfaction I reap from the success of my efforts. Wounded myself, in the early part of my life, by the envenomed tongue of slander, I confess I have since known no pleasure equal to the reducing others to the level of my own injured reputation.

SNAKE. Nothing can be more natural. But, Lady Sneerwell, there is one affair in which you have lately employed me, wherein, I confess, I am at a loss to guess your motives.

LADY SNEER. I conceive you mean with respect to my neighbor, Sir Peter Teazle, and his family?

SNAKE. I do; here are two young men, to whom Sir Peter has acted as a kind of guardian since their father's death; the elder possessing the most amiable character, and universally well spoken of; the youngest, the most dissipated and extravagant young fellow in the kingdom, without friends or character,—the former an avowed admirer of your ladyship, and apparently your favorite; the latter attached to Maria, Sir Peter's ward, and confessedly beloved by her. Now, on the face of these circumstances, it is utterly unaccountable to me, why you, the widow of a city knight, with a good jointure, should not close with the passion of a man of such character and expectations as Mr. Surface; and more so why you should be so uncommonly earnest to destroy the mutual attachment subsisting between his brother Charles and Maria.

LADY SNEER. Then, at once to unravel this mystery, I must inform you that love has no share whatever in the intercourse between Mr. Surface and me.

SNAKE. No!

LADY SNEER. His real attachment is to Maria, or her fortune; but, finding in his brother a favored rival, he has been obliged to mask his pretensions, and profit by my assistance.

SNAKE. Yet still I am more puzzled why you should interest yourself in his success.

LADY SNEER. Heav'ns! how dull you are! Cannot you surmise the weakness which I hitherto, through shame, have concealed even from *you?* Must I confess that Charles—that libertine, that extravagant, that bankrupt in fortune and reputation—that he it is for whom I am thus anxious and malicious, and to gain whom I would sacrifice everything?

SNAKE. Now, indeed, your conduct appears consistent; but how came you and Mr. Surface so confidential?

LADY SNEER. For our mutual interest. I have found him out a long time since—I know him to be artful, selfish, and malicious—in short, a sentimental knave.

SNAKE. Yet, Sir Peter vows he has not his equal in England—and, above all, he praises him as a man of sentiment.

LADY SNEER. True; and with the assistance of his sentiment and hypocrisy he has brought him [Sir Peter] entirely into his interest with regard to Maria.

Enter SERVANT.

SERV. Mr. Surface.

LADY SNEER. Show him up. *(Exit Servant.)* He generally calls about this time. I don't wonder at people's giving him to me for a lover.

Enter JOSEPH SURFACE.

JOS. SURF.   My dear Lady Sneerwell, how do you do to-day? Mr. Snake, your most obedient.

LADY SNEER.   Snake has just been arraigning me on our mutual attachment, but I have informed him of our real views; you know how useful he has been to us; and, believe me, the confidence is not ill placed.

JOS. SURF.   Madam, it is impossible for me to suspect a man of Mr. Snake's sensibility and discernment.

LADY SNEER.   Well, well, no compliments now;—but tell me when you saw your mistress, Maria—or, what is more material to me, your brother.

JOS. SURF.   I have not seen either since I left you; but I can inform you that they never meet. Some of your stories have taken a good effect on Maria.

LADY SNEER.   Ah, my dear Snake! the merit of this belongs to you. But do your brother's distresses increase?

JOS. SURF.   Every hour;—I am told he has had another execution in the house yesterday; in short, his dissipation and extravagance exceed any thing I ever heard of.

LADY SNEER.   Poor Charles!

JOS. SURF.   True, madam;—notwithstanding his vices, one can't help feeling for him.—Aye, poor Charles! I'm sure I wish it was in *my* power to be of any essential service to him.—For the man who does not share in the distresses of a brother, even though merited by his own misconduct, deserves—

LADY SNEER.   O lud! you are going to be moral, and forget that you are among friends.

JOS. SURF.   Egad, that's true!—I'll keep that sentiment till I see Sir Peter. However, it is certainly a charity to rescue Maria from such a libertine, who, if he is to be reclaimed, can be so only by a person of your ladyship's superior accomplishments and understanding.

SNAKE.   I believe, Lady Sneerwell, here's company coming,—I'll go and copy the letter I mentioned to you.—Mr. Surface, your most obedient. *(Exit* SNAKE.*)*

JOS. SURF.   Sir, your very devoted.—Lady Sneerwell, I am very sorry you have put any further confidence in that fellow.

LADY SNEER.   Why so?

JOS. SURF.   I have lately detected him in frequent conference with old Rowley, who was formerly my father's steward, and has never, you know, been a friend of mine.

LADY SNEER.   And do you think he would betray us?

JOS. SURF.   Nothing more likely: take my word for't, Lady Sneerwell, that fellow hasn't virtue enough to be faithful even to his own villainy.—Hah! Maria!

Enter MARIA.

LADY SNEER.   Maria, my dear, how do you do?—What's the matter?

MARIA.   Oh! there is that disagreeable lover of mine, Sir Benjamin Backbite, has just called at my guardian's, with his odious uncle, Crabtree; so I slipped out, and run hither to avoid them.

LADY SNEER. Is that all?

JOS. SURF. If my brother Charles had been of the party, ma'am, perhaps you would not have been so much alarmed.

LADY SNEER. Nay, now you are severe; for I dare swear the truth of the matter is, Maria heard *you* were here;—but, my dear, what has Sir Benjamin done, that you should avoid him so?

MARIA. Oh, he has done nothing—but 'tis for what he has said,—his conversation is a perpetual libel on all his acquaintance.

JOS. SURF. Aye, and the worst of it is, there is no advantage in not knowing him; for he'll abuse a stranger just as soon as his best friend—and his uncle's as bad.

LADY SNEER. Nay, but we should make allowance; Sir Benjamin is a wit and a poet.

MARIA. For my part, I own, madam, wit loses its respect with me, when I see it in company with malice.—What do you think, Mr. Surface?

JOS. SURF. Certainly, madam; to smile at the jest which plants a thorn in another's breast is to become a principal in the mischief.

LADY SNEER. Pshaw! there's no possibility of being witty without a little ill nature: the malice of a good thing is the barb that makes it stick.—What's your opinion, Mr. Surface?

JOS. SURF. To be sure, madam, that conversation, where the spirit of raillery is suppressed, will ever appear tedious and insipid.

MARIA. Well, I'll not debate how far scandal may be allowable; but in a man, I am sure, it is always contemptible.—We have pride, envy, rivalship, and a thousand motives to depreciate each other; but the male slanderer must have the cowardice of a woman before he can traduce one.

Enter SERVANT.

SERV. Madam, Mrs. Candour is below, and, if your ladyship's at leisure, will leave her carriage.

LADY SNEER. Beg her to walk in. *(Exit* SERVANT.*)* Now Maria, however here is a character to your taste; for, though Mrs. Candour is a little talkative, everybody allows her to be the best-natured and best sort of woman.

MARIA. Yes, with a very gross affectation of good nature and benevolence, she does more mischief than the direct malice of old Crabtree.

JOS. SURF. I'faith 'tis very true, Lady Sneerwell; whenever I hear the current running against the characters of my friends, I never think them in such danger as when Candour undertakes their defence.

LADY SNEER. Hush!—here she is!

Enter MRS. CANDOUR.

MRS. CAN. My dear Lady Sneerwell, how have you been this century?—Mr. Surface, what news do you hear?—though indeed it is no matter, for I think one hears nothing else but scandal.

JOS. SURF. Just so, indeed, madam.

MRS. CAN. Ah, Maria! child,—what, is the whole affair off between you and Charles? His extravagance, I presume—the town talks of nothing else.

MARIA. I am very sorry, ma'am, the town has so little to do.

MRS. CAN. True, true, child: but there is no stopping people's tongues.—I own I was hurt to hear it, as indeed I was to learn, from the same quarter, that your guardian, Sir Peter, and Lady Teazle have not agreed lately so well as could be wished.

MARIA. 'Tis strangely impertinent for people to busy themselves so.

MRS. CAN. Very true, child, but what's to be done? People will talk—there's no preventing it.—Why, it was but yesterday I was told that Miss Gadabout had eloped with Sir Filigree Flirt.—But, Lord! there's no minding what one hears—though, to be sure, I had this from very good authority.

MARIA. Such reports are highly scandalous.

MRS. CAN. So they are, child—shameful, shameful! But the world is so censorious, no character escapes.—Lord, now who would have suspected your friend, Miss Prim, of an indiscretion? Yet such is the ill-nature of people, that they say her uncle stopped her last week, just as she was stepping into the York Diligence with her dancing-master.

MARIA. I'll answer for't there are no grounds for the report.

MRS. CAN. Oh, no foundation in the world, I dare swear; no more, probably, than for the story circulated last month, of Mrs. Festino's affair with Colonel Cassino;—though, to be sure, that matter was never rightly cleared up.

JOS. SURF. The license of invention some people take is monstrous indeed.

MARIA. 'Tis so.—But, in my opinion, those who report such things are equally culpable.

MRS. CAN. To be sure they are; tale-bearers are as bad as the tale-makers—'tis an old observation, and a very true one—but what's to be done, as I said before? how will you prevent people from talking?—To-day, Mrs. Clackit assured me Mr. and Mrs. Honeymoon were at last become mere man and wife, like the rest of their acquaintances.—She likewise hinted that a certain widow, in the next street, had got rid of her dropsy and recovered her shape in a most surprising manner. And at the same time Miss Tattle, who was by, affirmed that Lord Buffalo had discovered his lady at a house of no extraordinary fame—and that Sir Harry Bouquet and Tom Saunter were to measure swords on a similar provocation. But, Lord, do you think I would report these things! No, no! tale-bearers, as I said before, are just as bad as tale-makers.

JOS. SURF. Ah! Mrs. Candour, if everybody had your forbearance and good nature!

MRS. CAN. I confess, Mr. Surface, I cannot bear to hear people attacked behind their backs, and when ugly circumstances come out against one's acquaintance I own I always love to think the best.—By the bye, I hope it is not true that your brother is absolutely ruined?

JOS. SURF. I am afraid his circumstances are very bad indeed, ma'am.

MRS. CAN.   Ah!—I heard so—but you must tell him to keep up his spirits—everybody almost is in the same way! Lord Spindle, Sir Thomas Splint, Captain Quinze, and Mr. Nickit—all up, I hear, within this week; so, if Charles is undone, he'll find half his acquaintances ruined too—and that, you know, is a consolation.

JOS. SURF.   Doubtless, ma'am—a very great one.

Enter SERVANT.

SERV.   Mr. Crabtree and Sir Benjamin Backbite. *(Exit Servant.)*

LADY SNEER.   So, Maria, you see your lover pursues you; positively you shan't escape.

Enter CRABTREE *and* SIR BENJAMIN BACKBITE.

CRAB.   Lady Sneerwell, I kiss your hands. Mrs. Candour, I don't believe you are acquainted with my nephew, Sir Benjamin Backbite? Egad, ma'am, he has a pretty wit, and is a pretty poet too; isn't he, Lady Sneerwell?

SIR BEN.   O fie, uncle!

CRAB.   Nay, egad it's true—I'll back him at a rebus or a charade against the best rhymer in the kingdom. Has your ladyship heard the epigram he wrote last week on Lady Frizzle's feather catching fire?—Do, Benjamin, repeat it—or the charade you made last night extempore at Mrs. Drowzie's conversazione.—Come now; your *first* is the name of a fish, your *second* a great naval commander, and—

SIR BEN.   Uncle, now—prithee—

CRAB.   I'faith, ma'am, 'twould surprise you to hear how ready he is at these things.

LADY SNEER.   I wonder, Sir Benjamin, you never publish anything.

SIR BEN.   To say truth, ma'am, 'tis very vulgar to print; and, as my little productions are mostly satires and lampoons on particular people, I find they circulate more by giving copies in confidence to the friends of the parties—however, I have some love elegies, which, when favored with this lady's smiles, I mean to give to the public.

CRAB.   'Fore heav'n, ma'am, they'll immortalize you!—you'll be handed down to posterity like Petrarch's Laura, or Waller's Sacharissa.

SIR BEN.   Yes, madam, I think you will like them, when you shall see them on a beautiful quarto page, where a neat rivulet of text shall murmur through a meadow of margin. 'Fore gad, they will be the most elegant things of their kind!

CRAB.   But, ladies, that's true—have you heard the news?

MRS. CAN.   What, sir, do you mean the report of—

CRAB.   No, ma'am, that's not it.—Miss Nicely is going to be married to her own footman.

MRS. CAN.   Impossible!

CRAB.   Ask Sir Benjamin.

SIR BEN.   'Tis very true, ma'am—everything is fixed, and the wedding liveries bespoke.

CRAB.   Yes—and they *do* say there were pressing reasons for it.

LADY SNEER. Why, I *have* heard something of this before.
MRS. CAN. It can't be—and I wonder any one should believe such a story of so prudent a lady as Miss Nicely.
SIR BEN. O lud! ma'am, that's the very reason 'twas believed at once. She has always been so *cautious* and so *reserved,* that everybody was sure there was some reason for it at bottom.
MRS. CAN. Why, to be sure, a tale of scandal is as fatal to the credit of a prudent lady of her stamp as a fever is generally to those of the strongest constitutions; but there is a sort of puny, sickly reputation that is always ailing, yet will outlive the robuster characters of a hundred prudes.
SIR BEN. True, madam, there are valetudinarians in reputation as well as constitution, who, being conscious of their weak part, avoid the least breath of air, and supply their want of stamina by care and circumspection.
MRS. CAN. Well, but this may be all a mistake. You know, Sir Benjamin, very trifling circumstances often give rise to the most injurious tales.
CRAB. That they do, I'll be sworn, ma'am. Did you ever hear how Miss Piper came to lose her lover and her character last summer at Tunbridge?—Sir Benjamin, you remember it?
SIR BEN. Oh, to be sure!—the most whimsical circumstance—
LADY SNEER. How was it, pray?
CRAB. Why, one evening, at Mrs. Ponto's assembly, the conversation happened to turn on the difficulty of breeding Nova Scotia sheep in this country. Says a young lady in company, "I have known instances of it; for Miss Letitia Piper, a first cousin of mine, had a Nova Scotia sheep that produced her twins." "What!" cries the old Dowager Lady Dundizzy (who you know is as deaf as a post), "has Miss Piper had twins?" This mistake, as you may imagine, threw the whole company into a fit of laughing. However, 'twas the next morning everywhere reported, and in a few days believed by the whole town, that Miss Letitia Piper had actually been brought to bed of a fine boy and a girl—and in less than a week there were people who could name the father, and the farm-house where the babies were put out to nurse!
LADY SNEER. Strange, indeed!
CRAB. Matter of fact, I assure you.—O lud! Mr. Surface, pray is it true that your uncle, Sir Oliver, is coming home?
JOS. SURF. Not that I know of, indeed, sir.
CRAB. He has been in the East Indies a long time. You can scarcely remember him, I believe.—Sad comfort, whenever he returns, to hear how your brother has gone on!
JOS. SURF. Charles has been imprudent, sir, to be sure; but I hope no busy people have already prejudiced Sir Oliver against him,—he may reform.
SIR BEN. To be sure he may—for my part I never believed him to be so utterly void of principle as people say—and though he has lost all his friends, I am told nobody is better spoken of by the Jews.
CRAB. That's true, egad, nephew. If the old Jewry were a ward, I believe Charles would be an alderman; no man more popular there,

'fore gad! I hear he pays as many annuities as the Irish tontine; and that, whenever he's sick, they have prayers for the recovery of his health in the Synagogue.

SIR BEN. Yet no man lives in greater splendor.—They tell me, when he entertains his friends, he can sit down to dinner with a dozen of his own securities; have a score [of] tradesmen waiting in the antechamber, and an officer behind every guest's chair. 320

JOS. SURF. This may be entertainment to you, gentlemen, but you pay very little regard to the feelings of a brother.

MARIA. Their malice is intolerable!—Lady Sneerwell, I must wish you a good morning—I'm not very well. *(Exit* MARIA.*)*

MRS. CAN. O dear! she changes color very much!

LADY SNEER. Do, Mrs. Candour, follow her—she may want assistance.

MRS. CAN. That I will, with all my soul, ma'am.—Poor dear girl! who knows what her situation may be! *(Exit* MRS. CANDOUR.*)*

LADY SNEER. 'Twas nothing but that she could not bear to hear Charles reflected on, notwithstanding their difference. 330

SIR BEN. The young lady's *penchant* is obvious.

CRAB. But, Benjamin, you mustn't give up the pursuit for that; follow her, and put her into good humor. Repeat her some of your own verses.—Come, I'll assist you.

SIR BEN. Mr. Surface, I did not mean to hurt you; but depend upon't your brother is utterly undone. *(Going.)*

CRAB. O lud, aye! undone as ever man was—can't raise a guinea. *(Going.)*

SIR BEN. And everything sold, I'm told, that was movable. *(Going.)*

CRAB. I have seen one that was at his house—not a thing left but 340 some empty bottles that were overlooked, and the family pictures, which I believe are framed in the wainscot. *(Going.)*

SIR BEN. And I am very sorry to hear also some bad stories against him. *(Going.)*

CRAB. Oh, he has done many mean things, that's certain. *(Going.)*

SIR BEN. But, however, as he's your brother—*(Going.)*

CRAB. We'll tell you all, another opportunity.

Exeunt CRABTREE *and* SIR BENJAMIN.

LADY SNEER. Ha, ha! ha! 'tis very hard for them to leave a subject they have not quite run down.

JOS. SURF. And I believe the abuse was no more acceptable to your 350 ladyship than to Maria.

LADY SNEER. I doubt her affections are farther engaged than we imagined; but the family are to be here this evening, so you may as well dine where you are, and we shall have an opportunity of observing farther;—in the meantime, I'll go and plot mischief, and you shall study sentiments.

Exeunt.

352. *doubt:* suspect.

SCENE II

Sir Peter Teazle's house.

Enter SIR PETER.

SIR PET. When an old bachelor takes a young wife, what is he to expect?—'Tis now six months since Lady Teazle made me the happiest of men—and I have been the miserablest dog ever since that ever committed wedlock! We tift a little going to church, and came to a quarrel before the bells were done ringing. I was more than once nearly choked with gall during the honeymoon, and had lost all comfort in life before my friends had done wishing me joy! Yet I chose with caution—a girl bred wholly in the country, who never knew luxury beyond one silk gown, nor dissipation above the annual gala of a race ball. Yet now she plays her part in all the extravagant fopperies of the fashion and the town, with as ready a grace as if she had never seen a bush nor a grass-plat out of Grosvenor Square! I am sneered at by my old acquaintance—paragraphed in the newspapers. She dissipates my fortune, and contradicts all my humors; yet the worst of it is, I doubt I love her, or I should never bear all this. However, I'll never be weak enough to own it.

Enter ROWLEY.

ROW. Oh! Sir Peter, your servant,—how is it with you, sir?
SIR PET. Very bad, Master Rowley, very bad;—I meet with nothing but crosses and vexations.
ROW. What can have happened to trouble you since yesterday?
SIR PET. A good question to a married man!
ROW. Nay, I'm sure your lady, Sir Peter, can't be the cause of your uneasiness.
SIR PET. Why, has anyone told you she was dead?
ROW. Come, come, Sir Peter, you love her, notwithstanding your tempers don't exactly agree.
SIR PET. But the fault is entirely hers, Master Rowley. I am, myself, the sweetest-tempered man alive, and hate a teasing temper—and so I tell her a hundred times a day.
ROW. Indeed!
SIR PET. Aye; and what is very extraordinary, in all our disputes she is always in the wrong! But Lady Sneerwell, and the set she meets at her house, encourage the perverseness of her disposition. Then, to complete my vexations, Maria, my ward, whom I ought to have the power of a father over, is determined to turn rebel too, and absolutely refuses the man whom I have long resolved on for her husband;—meaning, I suppose, to bestow herself on his profligate brother.
ROW. You know, Sir Peter, I have always taken the liberty to differ with you on the subject of these two young gentlemen. I only wish you may not be deceived in your opinion of the elder. For Charles, my life on't! he will retrieve his errors yet. Their worthy father, once

my honored master, was, at his years, nearly as wild a spark; yet, when he died, he did not leave a more benevolent heart to lament his loss.

SIR PET. You are wrong, Master Rowley. On their father's death, you know, I acted as a kind of guardian to them both, till their uncle Sir Oliver's Eastern liberality gave them an early independence; of course, no person could have more opportunities of judging of their hearts, and I was never mistaken in my life. Joseph is indeed a model for the young men of the age. He is a man of sentiment, and acts up to the sentiments he professes; but, for the other, take my word for't, if he had any grains of virtue by descent, he has dissipated them with the rest of his inheritance. Ah! my old friend, Sir Oliver, will be deeply mortified when he finds how part of his bounty has been misapplied.

ROW. I am sorry to find you so violent against the young man, because this may be the most critical period of his fortune. I came hither with news that will surprise you.

SIR PET. What! let me hear.

ROW. Sir Oliver *is* arrived, and at this moment in town.

SIR PET. How! you astonish me! I thought you did not expect him this month.

ROW. I did not; but his passage has been remarkably quick.

SIR PET. Egad, I shall rejoice to see my old friend,—'tis sixteen years since we met—we have had many a day together; but does he still enjoin us not to inform his nephews of his arrival?

ROW. Most strictly. He means, before it is known, to make some trial of their dispositions.

SIR PET. Ah! There needs no art to discover their merits—however, he shall have his way; but, pray, does he know I am married?

ROW. Yes, and will soon wish you joy.

SIR PET. What, as we drink health to a friend in a consumption! Ah, Oliver will laugh at me—we used to rail at matrimony together—but he has been steady to his text. Well, he must be at my house, though— I'll instantly give orders for his reception. But, Master Rowley, don't drop a word that Lady Teazle and I ever disagree.

ROW. By no means.

SIR PET. For I should never be able to stand Noll's jokes; so I'd have him think, Lord forgive me! that we are a very happy couple.

ROW. I understand you—but then you must be very careful not to differ while he's in the house with you.

SIR PET. Egad, and so we must—and that's impossible. Ah! Master Rowley, when an old bachelor marries a young wife, he deserves—no— the crime carries the punishment along with it.

Exeunt.

END OF ACT IST.

ACT II

SCENE I

Sir Peter Teazle's house.

Enter SIR PETER *and* LADY TEAZLE.

SIR PET. Lady Teazle, Lady Teazle, I'll not bear it!
LADY TEAZ. Sir Peter, Sir Peter, you may bear it or not, as you please; but I ought to have my own way in everything, and what's more, I *will* too.—What! though I was educated in the country, I know very well that women of fashion in London are accountable to nobody after they are married.
SIR PET. Very well, ma'am, very well,—so a husband is to have no influence, no authority?
LADY TEAZ. Authority! No, to be sure—if you wanted authority over me, you should have adopted me, and not married me; I am sure you were old enough.
SIR PET. Old enough!—aye, there it is!—Well, well, Lady Teazle, though my life may be made unhappy by your temper, I'll not be ruined by your extravagance.
LADY TEAZ. My extravagance! I'm sure I'm not more extravagant than a woman of fashion ought to be.
SIR PET. No, no, madam, you shall throw away no more sums on such unmeaning luxury. 'Slife! to spend as much to furnish your dressing-room with flowers in winter as would suffice to turn the Pantheon into a greenhouse, and give a *fête champêtre* at Christmas!
LADY TEAZ. Lord, Sir Peter, am I to blame because flowers are dear in cold weather? You should find fault with the climate, and not with me. For my part, I am sure I wish it was spring all the year round, and that roses grew under one's feet!
SIR PET. Oons! madam—if you had been born to this, I shouldn't wonder at your talking thus.—But you forget what your situation was when I married you.
LADY TEAZ. No, no, I don't; 'twas a very disagreeable one, or I should never have married *you.*
SIR PET. Yes, yes, madam, you were then in somewhat an humbler style—the daughter of a plain country squire. Recollect, Lady Teazle, when I saw you first, sitting at your tambour, in a pretty figured linen gown, with a bunch of keys by your side, your hair combed smooth over a roll, and your apartment hung round with fruits in worsted, of your own working.
LADY TEAZ. O, yes! I remember it very well, and a curious life I led— my daily occupation to inspect the dairy, superintend the poultry, make extracts from the family receipt-book, and comb my aunt Deborah's lap-dog.
SIR PET. Yes, yes, ma'am, 'twas so indeed.
LADY TEAZ. And then, you know, my evening amusements! To draw patterns for ruffles, which I had not the materials to make; to play

---

19. *Pantheon:* a London concert hall. 20. *fête champêtre:* outdoor celebration.

Pope Joan with the curate; to read a novel to my aunt; or to be stuck down to an old spinet to strum my father to sleep after a fox-chase.

SIR PET. I am glad you have so good a memory. Yes, madam, these were the recreations I took you from; but now you must have your coach—*vis-à-vis*—and three powdered footmen before your chair and, in summer, a pair of white cats to draw you to Kensington Gardens.—No recollection, I suppose, when you were content to ride double, behind the butler, on a docked coach-horse?

LADY TEAZ. No—I swear I never did that—I deny the butler and the coach-horse.

SIR PET. This, madam, was your situation—and what have I not done for you? I have made you a woman of fashion, of fortune, of rank—in short, I have made you my wife.

LADY TEAZ. Well, then, and there is but one thing more you can make me to add to the obligation—and that is—

SIR PET. My widow, I suppose?

LADY TEAZ. Hem! hem!

SIR PET. Thank you, madam—but don't flatter yourself; for though your ill-conduct may disturb my peace, it shall never break my heart, I promise you: however, I am equally obliged to you for the hint.

LADY TEAZ. Then why will you endeavor to make yourself so disagreeable to me, and thwart me in every little elegant expense?

SIR PET. 'Slife, madam, I say, had you any of these elegant expenses when you married me?

LADY TEAZ. Lud, Sir Peter! would you have me be out of the fashion?

SIR PET. The fashion, indeed! what had you to do with the fashion before you married me?

LADY TEAZ. For my part, I should think you would like to have your wife thought a woman of taste.

SIR PET. Aye—there again—taste! Zounds! madam, you had no taste when you married *me!*

LADY TEAZ. That's very true, indeed, Sir Peter! and, *after* having married you, I am sure I should never pretend to taste again! But now, Sir Peter, if we have finished our daily jangle, I presume I may go to my engagement of [at] Lady Sneerwell's?

SIR PET. Aye—there's another precious circumstance!—a charming set of acquaintance you have made there!

LADY TEAZ. Nay, Sir Peter, they are people of rank and fortune, and remarkably tenacious of reputation.

SIR PET. Yes, egad, they are tenacious of reputation with a vengeance; for they don't choose anybody should have a character but themselves! Such a crew! Ah! many a wretch has rid on a hurdle who has done less mischief than those utterers of forged tales, coiners of scandal,—and clippers of reputation.

LADY TEAZ. What! would you restrain the freedom of speech?

SIR PET. Oh! they have made you just as bad as any one of the society.

LADY TEAZ. Why, I believe I do bear a part with a tolerable grace. But I vow I have no malice against the people I abuse; when I say an ill-natured thing, 'tis out of pure good humor—and I take it for granted

---

43. *Pope Joan:* a card game. 48. *cats:* ponies. 84. *hurdle:* cart for transporting criminals to place of execution.

they deal exactly in the same manner with me. But, Sir Peter, you know you promised to come to Lady Sneerwell's too.
SIR PET. Well, well, I'll call in just to look after my own character.
LADY TEAZ. Then, indeed, you must make haste after me or you'll be too late.—So good-bye to ye. *(Exit* LADY TEAZLE.*)*
SIR PET. So—I have gained much by my intended expostulations! Yet with what a charming air she contradicts everything I say, and how pleasingly she shows her contempt of my authority! Well, though I can't make her love me, there is a great satisfaction in quarrelling with her; and I think she never appears to such advantage as when she's doing everything in her power to plague me.

Exit.

SCENE II

Lady Sneerwell's.

LADY SNEERWELL, MRS. CANDOUR, CRABTREE, SIR BENJAMIN BACKBITE, *and* JOSEPH SURFACE.

LADY SNEER. Nay, positively, we will hear it.
JOS. SURF. Yes, yes, the epigram, by all means.
SIR BEN. Plague on't, uncle! 'tis mere nonsense.
CRAB. No, no; 'fore gad, very clever for an extempore!
SIR BEN. But, ladies, you should be acquainted with the circumstance, —you must know, that one day last week, as Lady Betty Curricle was taking the dust in Hyde Park, in a sort of duodecimo phaëton, she desired me to write some verses on her ponies; upon which, I took out my pocket-book, and in one moment produced the following:

"Sure never were seen two such beautiful ponies!
Other horses are clowns, and these macaronies!
Nay, to give 'em this title I'm sure isn't wrong—
Their legs are so slim, and their tails are so long."

CRAB. There, ladies—done in the smack of a whip, and on horseback too!
JOS. SURF. A very Phœbus, mounted—indeed, Sir Benjamin.
SIR BEN. O dear sir—trifles—trifles.

Enter LADY TEAZLE *and* MARIA.

MRS. CAN. I must have a copy.
LADY SNEER. Lady Teazle, I hope we shall see Sir Peter.
LADY TEAZ. I believe he'll wait on your ladyship presently.
LADY SNEER. Maria, my love, you look grave. Come, you shall sit down to cards with Mr. Surface.
MARIA. I take very little pleasure in cards—however, I'll do as your ladyship pleases.
LADY TEAZ. *(aside).* I am surprised Mr. Surface should sit down with

7. *duodecimo:* small.

her.—I thought he would have embraced this opportunity of speaking to me before Sir Peter came.

MRS. CAN. Now, I'll die but you are so scandalous, I'll forswear your society.

LADY TEAZ. What's the matter, Mrs. Candour?

MRS. CAN. They'll not allow our friend Miss Vermilion to be handsome.

LADY SNEER. Oh, surely, she's a pretty woman.

CRAB. I am very glad you think so, ma'am.

MRS. CAN. She has a charming fresh color.

LADY TEAZ. Yes, when it is fresh put on.

MRS. CAN. O fie! I'll swear her color is natural—I have seen it come and go.

LADY TEAZ. I dare swear you have, ma'am—it goes of a night, and comes again in the morning.

MRS. CAN. Ha! ha! ha! how I hate to hear you talk so! But surely, now, her sister *is,* or *was,* very handsome.

CRAB. Who? Mrs. Evergreen?—O Lord! she's six-and-fifty if she's an hour!

MRS. CAN. Now positively you wrong her; fifty-two or fifty-three is the utmost—and I don't think she looks more.

SIR BEN. Ah! there is no judging by her looks, unless one could see her face.

LADY SNEER. Well, well, if Mrs. Evergreen *does* take some pains to repair the ravages of time, you must allow she effects it with great ingenuity; and surely that's better than the careless manner in which the widow Ochre caulks her wrinkles.

SIR BEN. Nay, now, Lady Sneerwell, you are severe upon the widow. Come, come, it is not that she paints so ill—but, when she has finished her face, she joins it on so badly to her neck, that she looks like a mended statue, in which the connoisseur may see at once that the head's modern, though the trunk's antique!

CRAB. Ha! ha! ha! Well said, nephew!

MRS. CAN. Ha! ha! ha! Well, you make me laugh, but I vow I hate you for't.—What do you think of Miss Simper?

SIR BEN. Why, she has very pretty teeth.

LADY TEAZ. Yes; and on that account, when she is neither speaking nor laughing (which very seldom happens), she never absolutely shuts her mouth, but leaves it always on a jar, as it were.

MRS. CAN. How can you be so ill-natured?

LADY TEAZ. Nay, I allow even that's better than the pains Mrs. Prim takes to conceal her losses in front. She draws her mouth till it positively resembles the aperture of a poor's-box, and all her words appear to slide out edgeways.

LADY SNEER. Very well, Lady Teazle; I see you can be a little severe.

LADY TEAZ. In defence of a friend it is but justice;—but here comes Sir Peter to spoil our pleasantry.

Enter SIR PETER TEAZLE.

SIR PET. Ladies, your most obedient—Mercy on me, here is the whole set! a character dead at every word, I suppose. *(Aside.)*
MRS. CAN. I am rejoiced you are come, Sir Peter. They have been *so* censorious. They will allow good qualities to nobody—not even good nature to our friend Mrs. Pursy.
LADY TEAZ. What, the fat dowager who was at Mrs. Codille's last night?
MRS. CAN. Nay, her bulk is her misfortune; and, when she takes such pains to get rid of it, you ought not to reflect on her. 80
LADY SNEER. That's very true, indeed.
LADY TEAZ. Yes, I know she almost lives on acids and small whey; laces herself by pulleys; and often, in the hottest noon of summer, you may see her on a little squat pony, with her hair platted up behind like a drummer's, and puffing round the Ring on a full trot.
MRS. CAN. I thank you, Lady Teazle, for defending her.
SIR PET. Yes, a good defence, truly.
MRS. CAN. But Sir Benjamin is as censorious as Miss Sallow.
CRAB. Yes, and she is a curious being to pretend to be censorious!—an 90
awkward gawky, without any one good point under heaven.
MRS. CAN. Positively you shall not be so very severe. Miss Sallow is a relation of mine by marriage, and, as for her person, great allowance is to be made; for, let me tell you, a woman labors under many disadvantages who tries to pass for a girl at six-and-thirty.
LADY SNEER. Though, surely, she is handsome still—and for the weakness in her eyes, considering how much she reads by candle-light, it is not to be wondered at.
MRS. CAN. True; and then as to her manner, upon my word I think it is particularly graceful, considering she never had the least education; 100
for you know her mother was a Welch milliner, and her father a sugar-baker at Bristol.
SIR BEN. Ah! you are both of you too good-natured!
SIR PET. Yes, damned good-natured! This their own relation! mercy on me! *(Aside.)*
SIR BEN. And Mrs. Candour is of so moral a turn she can sit for an hour to hear Lady Stucco talk sentiment.
LADY TEAZ. Nay, I vow Lady Stucco is very well with the dessert after dinner; for she's just like the French fruit one cracks for mottoes—made up of paint and proverb. 110
MRS. CAN. Well, I never will join in ridiculing a friend; and so I constantly tell my cousin Ogle, and you all know what pretensions she has to be critical in beauty.
CRAB. Oh, to be sure! she has herself the oddest countenance that ever was seen; 'tis a collection of features from all the different countries of the globe.
SIR BEN. So she has, indeed—an Irish front!
CRAB. Caledonian locks!
SIR BEN. Dutch nose!
CRAB. Austrian lip! 120
SIR BEN. Complexion of a Spaniard!
CRAB. And teeth *à la Chinoise!*

SIR BEN. In short, her face resembles a *table d'hôte* at Spa—where no two guests are of a nation—
CRAB. Or a congress at the close of a general war—wherein all the members, even to her eyes, appear to have a different interest, and her nose and chin are the only parties likely to join issue.
MRS. CAN. Ha! ha! ha!
SIR PET. Mercy on my life!—a person they dine with twice a week! *(Aside.)* 130
[LADY SNEER. Go—go—you are a couple of provoking toads.]
MRS. CAN. Nay, but I vow you shall not carry the laugh off so—for give me leave to say, that Mrs. Ogle—
SIR PET. Madam, madam, I beg your pardon—there's no stopping these good gentlemen's tongues. But when I tell *you,* Mrs. Candour, that the lady they are abusing is a particular friend of mine—I hope you'll not take her part.
LADY SNEER. Well said, Sir Peter! but you are a cruel creature—too phlegmatic yourself for a jest, and too peevish to allow wit on others.
SIR PET. Ah, madam, true wit is more nearly allied to good nature 140 than your ladyship is aware of.
LADY TEAZ. True, Sir Peter; I believe they are so near akin that they can never be united.
SIR BEN. Or rather, madam, suppose them man and wife, because one so seldom sees them together.
LADY TEAZ. But Sir Peter is such an enemy to scandal, I believe he would have it put down by parliament.
SIR PET. 'Fore heaven, madam, if they were to consider the sporting with reputation of as much importance as poaching on manors, and pass *An Act for the Preservation of Fame,* I believe many would 150 thank them for the bill.
LADY SNEER. O lud! Sir Peter; would you deprive us of our privileges?
SIR PET. Aye, madam; and then no person should be permitted to kill characters or run down reputations, but qualified old maids and disappointed widows.
LADY SNEER. Go, you monster!
MRS. CAN. But sure you would not be quite so severe on those who only report what they hear.
SIR PET. Yes, madam, I would have law merchant for them too; and in all cases of slander currency, whenever the drawer of the lie was 160 not to be found, the injured parties should have a right to come on any of the indorsers.
CRAB. Well, for my part, I believe there never was a scandalous tale without some foundation.
LADY SNEER. Come, ladies, shall we sit down to cards in the next room?

Enter SERVANT *and whispers* SIR PETER.

SIR PET. I'll be with them directly.—*(Exit* SERVANT.*)* I'll get away unperceived. *(Aside.)*
LADY SNEER. Sir Peter, you are not leaving us?

SIR PET. Your ladyship must excuse me; I'm called away by particular business—but I leave my character behind me. (*Exit* SIR PETER.)
SIR BEN. Well certainly, Lady Teazle, that lord of yours is a strange being; I could tell you some stories of him would make you laugh heartily, if he wasn't your husband.
LADY TEAZ. O pray don't mind that—come, do let's hear them.

They join the rest of the company, all talking as they are going into the next room.

JOS. SURF. (*rising with* MARIA). Maria, I see you have no satisfaction in this society.
MARIA. How is it possible I should? If to raise malicious smiles at the infirmities and misfortunes of those who have never injured us be the province of wit or humor, heaven grant me a double portion of dulness!
JOS. SURF. Yet they appear more ill-natured than they are; they have no malice at heart.
MARIA. Then is their conduct still more contemptible; for, in my opinion, nothing could excuse the intemperance of their tongues but a natural and ungovernable bitterness of mind.
JOS. SURF. But can you, Maria, feel thus for others, and be unkind to me alone? Is hope to be denied the tenderest passion?
MARIA. Why will you distress me by renewing this subject?
JOS. SURF. Ah, Maria! you would not treat me thus, and oppose your guardian, Sir Peter's will, but that I see that profligate Charles is still a favored rival.
MARIA. Ungenerously urged! But, whatever my sentiments of that unfortunate young man are, be assured I shall not feel more bound to give him up, because his distresses have lost him the regard even of a brother.

LADY TEAZLE *returns.*

JOS. SURF. Nay, but, Maria, do not leave me with a frown—by all that's honest, I swear—Gad's life, here's Lady Teazle. (*Aside.*)—You must not—no, you shall not—for, though I have the greatest regard for Lady Teazle—
MARIA. Lady Teazle!
JOS. SURF. Yet were Sir Peter to suspect—
LADY TEAZ. *(coming forward).* What's this, pray? Do you take her for me?—Child, you are wanted in the next room.—(*Exit* MARIA.) What is all this, pray?
JOS. SURF. Oh, the most unlucky circumstance in nature! Maria has somehow suspected the tender concern I have for your happiness, and threatened to acquaint Sir Peter with her suspicions, and I was just endeavoring to reason with her when you came.
LADY TEAZ. Indeed! but you seemed to adopt a very tender mode of reasoning—do you *usually* argue on your knees?
JOS. SURF. Oh, she's a child—and I thought a little bombast—but,

Lady Teazle, when are you to give me your judgment on my library, as you promised?
LADY TEAZ. No, no,—I begin to think it would be imprudent, and you know I admit you as a lover no further than *fashion* requires.
JOS. SURF. True—a mere Platonic cicisbeo, what every London wife is *entitled* to.
LADY TEAZ. Certainly, one must not be out of the fashion; however, I have so many of my country prejudices left, that, though Sir Peter's ill humor may vex me ever so, it never shall provoke me to—
JOS. SURF. The only revenge in your power. Well, I applaud your moderation.
LADY TEAZ. Go—you are an insinuating wretch! But we shall be missed—let us join the company.
JOS. SURF. But we had best not return together.
LADY TEAZ. Well, don't stay—for Maria shan't come to hear any more of your *reasoning*, I promise you. (*Exit* LADY TEAZLE.)
JOS. SURF. A curious dilemma, truly, my politics have run me into! I wanted, at first, only to ingratiate myself with Lady Teazle, that she might not be my enemy with Maria; and I have, I don't know how, become her serious lover. Sincerely I begin to wish I had never made such a point of gaining so *very good* a character, for it has led me into so many cursed rogueries that I doubt I shall be exposed at last. *(Exit.)*

SCENE III

Sir Peter's.

Enter SIR OLIVER SURFACE *and* ROWLEY.

SIR OLIV. Ha! ha! ha! and so my old friend is married, hey?—a young wife out of the country.—Ha! ha! ha!—that he should have stood bluff to old bachelor so long, and sink into a husband at last!
ROW. But you must not rally him on the subject, Sir Oliver; 'tis a tender point, I assure you, though he has been married only seven months.
SIR OLIV. Then he has been just half a year on the stool of repentance!—Poor Peter! But you say he has entirely given up Charles—never sees him, hey?
ROW. His prejudice against him is astonishing, and I am sure greatly increased by a jealousy of him with Lady Teazle, which he has been industriously led into by a scandalous society in the neighborhood, who have contributed not a little to Charles's ill name; whereas the truth is, I believe, if the lady is partial to either of them, his brother is the favorite.
SIR OLIV. Aye,—I know there are a set of malicious, prating, prudent gossips, both male and female, who murder characters to kill time, and will rob a young fellow of his good name before he has years to know the value of it,—but I am not to be prejudiced against my nephew by such, I promise you! No, no;—if Charles has done nothing

217. *cicisbeo:* fiance. 2. *bluff:* true.

false or mean, I shall compound for his extravagance.

ROW. Then, my life on't, you will reclaim him.—Ah, sir, it gives me new life to find that *your* heart is not turned against him, and that the son of my good old master has one friend, however, left.

SIR OLIV. What! shall I forget, Master Rowley, when I was at his years myself? Egad, my brother and I were neither of us very *prudent* youths—and yet, I believe, you have not seen many better men than your old master was?

ROW. Sir, 'tis this reflection gives me assurance that Charles may yet be a credit to his family.—But here comes Sir Peter.

SIR OLIV. Egad, so he does!—Mercy on me, he's greatly altered, and seems to have a settled married look! One may read husband in his face at this distance!

Enter SIR PETER TEAZLE.

SIR PET. Hah! Sir Oliver—my old friend! Welcome to England a thousand times!

SIR OLIV. Thank you, thank you, Sir Peter! and i'faith I am glad to find you well, believe me!

SIR PET. Ah! 'tis a long time since we met—sixteen years, I doubt, Sir Oliver, and many a cross accident in the time.

SIR OLIV. Aye, I have had my share—but, what! I find you are married, hey, my old boy?—Well, well, it can't be helped—and so I wish you joy with all my heart!

SIR PET. Thank you, thank you, Sir Oliver.—Yes, I have entered into the happy state—but we'll not talk of that now.

SIR OLIV. True, true, Sir Peter; old friends should not begin on grievances at first meeting. No, no, no.

ROW. (*to* SIR OLIVER). Take care, pray, sir.

SIR OLIV. Well, so one of my nephews is a wild rogue, hey?

SIR PET. Wild! Ah! my old friend, I grieve for your disappointment there—he's a lost young man, indeed; however, his brother will make you amends; Joseph is, indeed, what a youth should be—everybody in the world speaks well of him.

SIR OLIV. I am sorry to hear it—he has too good a character to be an honest fellow.—Everybody speaks well of him! Psha! then he has bowed as low to knaves and fools as to the honest dignity of genius or virtue.

SIR PET. What, Sir Oliver! do you blame him for not making enemies?

SIR OLIV. Yes, if he has merit enough to deserve them.

SIR PET. Well, well—you'll be convinced when you know him. 'Tis edification to hear him converse—he professes the noblest sentiments.

SIR OLIV. Ah, plague of his sentiments! If he salutes me with a scrap of morality in his mouth, I shall be sick directly. But, however, don't mistake me, Sir Peter; I don't mean to defend Charles's errors—but, before I form my judgment of either of them, I intend to make a trial of their hearts—and my friend Rowley and I have planned something for the purpose.

ROW. And Sir Peter shall own for once he has been mistaken.

SIR PET. Oh, my life on Joseph's honor!

SIR OLIV. Well, come, give us a bottle of good wine, and we'll drink the lad's health, and tell you our scheme. 70
SIR PET. *Allons,* then!
SIR OLIV. And don't, Sir Peter, be so severe against your old friend's son. Odds my life! I am not sorry that he has run out of the course a little; for my part, I hate to see prudence clinging to the green succors of youth; 'tis like ivy round a sapling, and spoils the growth of the tree.

Exeunt.

END OF ACT THE SECOND.

ACT III

SCENE I

Sir Peter's.

SIR PETER TEAZLE, SIR OLIVER SURFACE, *and* ROWLEY.

SIR PET. Well, then—we will see this fellow first, and have our wine afterwards. But how is this, Master Rowley? I don't see the jet of your scheme.
ROW. Why, sir, this Mr. Stanley, whom I was speaking of, is nearly related to them, by their mother; he was once a merchant in Dublin, but has been ruined by a series of undeserved misfortunes. He has applied, by letter, since his confinement, both to Mr. Surface and Charles—from the former he has received nothing but evasive promises of future service, while Charles has done all that his extravagance has left him power to do; and he is, at this time, endeavoring to raise a 10 sum of money, part of which, in the midst of his own distresses, I know he intends for the service of poor Stanley.
SIR OLIV. Ah! he is my brother's son.
SIR PET. Well, but how is Sir Oliver personally to—
ROW. Why, sir, I will inform Charles and his brother that Stanley has obtained permission to apply in person to his friends, and, as they have neither of them ever seen him, let Sir Oliver assume his character, and he will have a fair opportunity of judging at least of the benevolence of their dispositions; and believe me, sir, you will find in the youngest brother one who, in the midst of folly and dissipation, has 20 still, as our immortal bard expresses it,—

"a tear for pity, and a hand
Open as day, for melting charity."

2. *jet:* point.

SIR PET. Psha! What signifies his having an open hand or purse either, when he has nothing left to give? Well, well, make the trial, if you please; but where is the fellow whom you brought for Sir Oliver to examine, relative to Charles's affairs?

ROW. Below, waiting his commands, and no one can give him better intelligence.—This, Sir Oliver, is a friendly Jew, who, to do him justice, has done everything in his power to bring your nephew to a proper sense of his extravagance.

SIR PET. Pray let us have him in.

ROW. Desire Mr. Moses to walk upstairs.

SIR PET. But why should you suppose he will speak the truth?

ROW. Oh, I have convinced him that he has no chance of recovering certain sums advanced to Charles but through the bounty of Sir Oliver, who he knows is arrived; so that you may depend on his fidelity to his [own] interest. I have also another evidence in my power, one Snake, whom I have detected in a matter little short of forgery, and shall shortly produce to remove some of *your* prejudices, Sir Peter, relative to Charles and Lady Teazle.

SIR PET. I have heard too much on that subject.

ROW. Here comes the honest Israelite.

Enter MOSES.

—This is Sir Oliver.

SIR OLIV. Sir, I understand you have lately had great dealings with my nephew Charles.

MOS. Yes, Sir Oliver—I have done all I could for him, but he was ruined before he came to me for assistance.

SIR OLIV. That was unlucky, truly—for you have had no opportunity of showing your talents.

MOS. None at all—I hadn't the pleasure of knowing his distresses—till he was some thousands worse than nothing.

SIR OLIV. Unfortunate, indeed! But I suppose you have done all in your power for him, honest Moses?

MOS. Yes, he knows that. This very evening I was to have brought him a gentleman from the city, who doesn't know him, and will, I believe, advance him some money.

SIR PET. What, one Charles has never had money from before?

MOS. Yes; Mr. Premium, of Crutched Friars—formerly a broker.

SIR PET. Egad, Sir Oliver, a thought strikes me!—Charles, you say, doesn't know Mr. Premium?

MOS. Not at all.

SIR PET. Now then, Sir Oliver, you may have a better opportunity of satisfying yourself than by an old romancing tale of a poor relation;—go with my friend Moses, and represent Mr. Premium, and then, I'll answer for't, you will see your nephew in all his glory.

SIR OLIV. Egad, I like this idea better than the other, and I may visit Joseph afterwards, as old Stanley.

SIR PET. True—so you may.

ROW. Well, this is taking Charles rather at a disadvantage, to be sure.

However, Moses—you understand Sir Peter, and will be faithful?
MOS. You may depend upon me,—this is near the time I was to have gone.
SIR OLIV. I'll accompany you as soon as you please, Moses; but hold! I have forgot one thing—how the plague shall I be able to pass for a Jew?
MOS. There's no need—the principal is Christian.
SIR OLIV. Is he?—I'm sorry to hear it—but, then again, an't I rather too smartly dressed to look like a money-lender?
SIR PET. Not at all; 'twould not be out of character, if you went in your own carriage—would it, Moses? 80
MOS. Not in the least.
SIR OLIV. Well, but how must I talk? there's certainly some cant of usury, and mode of treating, that I ought to know.
SIR PET. Oh, there's not much to learn—the great point, as I take it, is to be exorbitant enough in your demands—hey, Moses?
MOS. Yes, that's a very great point.
SIR OLIV. I'll answer for't I'll not be wanting in that. I'll ask him eight or ten per cent on the loan, at least.
MOS. If you ask him no more than that, you'll be discovered immediately. 90
SIR OLIV. Hey! what the plague! how much then?
MOS. That depends upon the circumstances. If he appears not very anxious for the supply, you should require only forty or fifty per cent; but if you find him in great distress, and want the moneys very bad—you may ask double.
SIR PET. A good honest trade you're learning, Sir Oliver!
SIR OLIV. Truly I think so—and not unprofitable.
MOS. Then, you know, you haven't the moneys yourself, but are forced to borrow them for him of a friend. 100
SIR OLIV. Oh! I borrow it of a friend, do I?
MOS. Yes, and your friend is an unconscionable dog, but you can't help it.
SIR OLIV. My friend is an unconscionable dog, is he?
MOS. Yes, and he himself has not the moneys by him—but is forced to sell stock at a great loss.
SIR OLIV. He is forced to sell stock, is he, at a great loss, is he? Well, that's very kind of him.
SIR PET. I'faith, Sir Oliver—Mr. Premium, I mean—you'll soon be master of the trade. But, Moses! wouldn't you have him run out a little against the Annuity Bill? That would be in character, I should think. 110
MOS. Very much.
ROW. And lament that a young man now must be at years of discretion before he is suffered to ruin himself?
MOS. Aye, great pity!
SIR PET. And abuse the public for allowing merit to an act whose only object is to snatch misfortune and imprudence from the rapacious relief of usury, and give the minor a chance of inheriting his estate without being undone by coming into possession. 120

SIR OLIV. So, so—Moses shall give me further instructions as we go together.
SIR PET. You will not have much time, for your nephew lives hard by.
SIR OLIV. Oh, never fear! my tutor appears so able, that though Charles lived in the next street, it must be my own fault if I am not a complete rogue before I turn the corner.

Exeunt SIR OLIVER *and* MOSES.

SIR PET. So now I think Sir Oliver will be convinced;—you are partial, Rowley, and would have prepared Charles for the other plot.
ROW. No, upon my word, Sir Peter.
SIR PET. Well, go bring me this Snake, and I'll hear what he has to say presently.—I see Maria, and want to speak with her.—(*Exit* ROWLEY.) I should be glad to be convinced my suspicions of Lady Teazle and Charles were unjust. I have never yet opened my mind on this subject to my friend Joseph—I'm determined I will do it—*he* will give me his opinion sincerely.

Enter MARIA.

So, child, has Mr. Surface returned with you?
MARIA. No, sir—he was engaged.
SIR PET. Well, Maria, do you not reflect, the more you converse with that amiable young man, what return his partiality for you deserves?
MARIA. Indeed, Sir Peter, your frequent importunity on this subject distresses me extremely—you compel me to declare, that I know no man who has ever paid me a particular attention whom I would not prefer to Mr. Surface.
SIR PET. So—here's perverseness! No, no, Maria, 'tis Charles only whom you would prefer—'tis evident his vices and follies have won your heart.
MARIA. This is unkind, sir—you know I have obeyed you in neither seeing nor corresponding with him; I have heard enough to convince me that he is unworthy my regard. Yet I cannot think it culpable, if, while my understanding severely condemns his vices, my heart suggests some pity for his distresses.
SIR PET. Well, well, pity him as much as you please, but give your heart and hand to a worthier object.
MARIA. Never to his brother!
SIR PET. Go, perverse and obstinate! But take care, madam; you have never yet known what the authority of a guardian is—don't compel me to inform you of it.
MARIA. I can only say, you shall not have *just* reason. 'Tis true, by my father's will, I am for a short period bound to regard you as his substitute, but must cease to think you so, when you would compel me to be miserable. (*Exit* MARIA.)
SIR PET. Was ever man so crossed as I am! everything conspiring to fret me!—I had not been involved in matrimony a fortnight, before her father, a hale and hearty man, died—on purpose, I believe, for the

pleasure of plaguing me with the care of his daughter. But here comes my helpmate! She appears in great good humor. How happy I should be if I could tease her into loving me, though but a little!

Enter LADY TEAZLE.

LADY TEAZ. Lud! Sir Peter, I hope you haven't been quarrelling with Maria—it isn't using me well to be ill humored when I am not by.
SIR PET. Ah, Lady Teazle, you might have the power to make me good humored at all times.
LADY TEAZ. I am sure I wish I had—for I want you to be in charming sweet temper at this moment. Do be good humored now, and let me have two hundred pounds, will you?
SIR PET. Two hundred pounds! what, an't I to be in a good humor without paying for it! But speak to me thus, and i'faith there's nothing I could refuse you. You shall have it; but seal me a bond for the repayment.
LADY TEAZ. O, no—there—my note of hand will do as well.
SIR PET. *(kissing her hand).* And you shall no longer reproach me with not giving you an independent settlement,—I mean shortly to surprise you; but shall we always live thus, hey?
LADY TEAZ. If you please. I'm sure I don't care how soon we leave off quarrelling, provided you'll own *you* were tired first.
SIR PET. Well—then let our future contest be, who shall be most obliging.
LADY TEAZ. I assure you, Sir Peter, good nature becomes you. You look now as you did before we were married!—when you used to walk with me under the elms, and tell me stories of what a gallant you were in your youth, and chuck me under the chin, you would, and ask me if I thought I could love an old fellow, who would deny me nothing—didn't you?
SIR PET. Yes, yes, and you were as kind and attentive.
LADY TEAZ. Aye, so I was, and would always take your part, when my acquaintance used to abuse you, and turn you into ridicule.
SIR PET. Indeed!
LADY TEAZ. Aye, and when my cousin Sophy has called you a stiff, peevish old bachelor, and laughed at me for thinking of marrying one who might be my father, I have always defended you—and said, I didn't think you so ugly by any means, and that I dared say you'd make a very good sort of a husband.
SIR PET. And you prophesied right—and we shall certainly now be the happiest couple—
LADY TEAZ. And never differ again!
SIR PET. No, never!—though at the same time, indeed, my dear Lady Teazle, you must watch your temper very narrowly; for in all our little quarrels, my dear, if you recollect, my love, you always began first.
LADY TEAZ. I beg your pardon, my dear Sir Peter: indeed, you always gave the provocation.
SIR PET. Now, see, my angel! take care—*contradicting* isn't the way to keep friends.

LADY TEAZ. Then, don't *you* begin it, my love!
SIR PET. There, now! you—you are going on—you don't perceive, my life, that you are just doing the very thing which you know always makes me angry.
LADY TEAZ. Nay, you know if you will be angry without any reason—
SIR PET. There now! you want to quarrel again.
LADY TEAZ. No, I am sure I don't—but, if you will be so peevish—
SIR PET. There now! who begins first?   220
LADY TEAZ. Why, you, to be sure. I said nothing—but there's no bearing your temper.
SIR PET. No, no, madam, the fault's in your own temper.
LADY TEAZ. Aye, you are just what my cousin Sophy said you would be.
SIR PET. Your cousin Sophy is a forward, impertinent gipsy.
LADY TEAZ. You are a great bear, I'm sure, to abuse my relations.
SIR PET. Now may all the plagues of marriage be doubled on me, if ever I try to be friends with you any more!
LADY TEAZ. So much the better.   230
SIR PET. No, no, madam; 'tis evident you never cared a pin for me, and I was a madman to marry you—a pert, rural coquette, that had refused half the honest squires in the neighborhood!
LADY TEAZ. And I am sure I was a fool to marry you—an old dangling bachelor, who was single at fifty, only because he never could meet with any one who would have him.
SIR PET. Aye, aye, madam; but you were pleased enough to listen to me—*you* never had such an offer before.
LADY TEAZ. No! didn't I refuse Sir Twivy Tarrier, who everybody said would have been a better match—for his estate is just as good as   240
yours—and he has broke his neck since we have been married.
SIR PET. I have done with you, madam! You are an unfeeling, ungrateful—but there's an end of everything. I believe you capable of anything that's bad. Yes, madam, I now believe the reports relative to you and Charles, madam—yes, madam, you and Charles—are not without grounds—
LADY TEAZ. Take care, Sir Peter! you had better not insinuate any such thing! I'll not be suspected with*out cause,* I promise you.
SIR PET. Very well, madam! very well! a separate maintenance as soon as you please. Yes, madam, or a divorce! I'll make an example of my- 250
self for the benefit of all old bachelors. Let us separate, madam.
LADY TEAZ. Agreed! agreed! And now, my dear Sir Peter, we are of a mind once more, we may be the *happiest couple,* and *never differ again,* you know: ha! ha! Well, you are going to be in a passion, I see, and I shall only interrupt you—so, bye! bye! *(Exit.)*
SIR PET. Plagues and tortures! can't I make her angry neither? Oh, I am the miserablest fellow! But I'll not bear her presuming to keep her temper—no! she may break my heart, but she shan't keep her temper. *(Exit.)*

SCENE II

Charles's house.

Enter TRIP, MOSES, *and* SIR OLIVER SURFACE.

TRIP. Here, Master Moses! if you'll stay a moment, I'll try whether—what's the gentleman's name?
SIR OLIV. Mr. Moses, what *is* my name? *(Aside.)*
MOS. Mr. Premium.
TRIP. Premium—very well. *(Exit* TRIP, *taking snuff.)*
SIR OLIV. To judge by the servants, one wouldn't believe the master was ruined. But what!—sure, this was my brother's house?
MOS. Yes, sir; Mr. Charles bought it of Mr. Joseph, with the furniture, pictures, &c., just as the old gentleman left it—Sir Peter thought it a great piece of extravagance in him. 10
SIR OLIV. In my mind, the other's economy in *selling* it to him was more reprehensible by half.

Re-enter TRIP.

TRIP. My master says you must wait, gentlemen; he has company, and can't speak with you yet.
SIR OLIV. If he knew *who* it was wanted to see him, perhaps he wouldn't have sent such a message?
TRIP. Yes, yes, sir; he knows *you* are here—I didn't forget little Premium—no, no, no.
SIR OLIV. Very well—and I pray, sir, what may be your name?
TRIP. Trip, sir—my name is Trip, at your service. 20
SIR OLIV. Well, then, Mr. Trip, you have a pleasant sort of a place here, I guess.
TRIP. Why, yes—here are three or four of us pass our time agreeably enough; but then our wages are sometimes a little in arrear—and not very great either—but fifty pounds a year, and find our own bags and bouquets.
SIR OLIV. *(aside).* Bags and bouquets! halters and bastinadoes!
TRIP. But *à propos,* Moses, have you been able to get me that little bill discounted?
SIR OLIV. *(aside).* Wants to raise money, too!—mercy on me! Has his 30 distresses, I warrant, like a lord,—and affects creditors and duns.
MOS. 'Twas not to be done, indeed, Mr. Trip. *(Gives the note.)*
TRIP. Good lack, you surprise me! My friend Brush has indorsed it, and I thought when he put his mark on the back of a bill 'twas as good as cash.
MOS. No, 'twouldn't do.
TRIP. A small sum—but twenty pounds. Hark'ee, Moses, do you think you couldn't get it me by way of annuity?
SIR OLIV. *(aside).* An annuity! ha! ha! ha! a footman raise money by way of annuity! Well done, luxury, egad! 40
MOS. But you must insure your place.

TRIP. Oh, with all my heart! I'll insure my place, and my life too, if you please.
SIR OLIV. *(aside).* It's more than I would your neck.
TRIP. But then, Moses, it must be done before this d—d register takes place—one wouldn't like to have one's name made public, you know.
MOS. No, certainly. But is there nothing you could deposit?
TRIP. Why, nothing capital of my master's wardrobe has dropped lately; but I could give you a mortgage on some of his winter clothes, with equity of redemption before November—or you shall have the reversion of the French velvet, or a post-obit on the blue and silver; —these, I should think, Moses, with a few pair of point ruffles, as a collateral security—hey, my little fellow?
MOS. Well, well. *(Bell rings.)*
TRIP. Gad, I heard the bell! I believe, gentlemen, I can now introduce you. Don't forget the annuity, little Moses! This way, gentlemen, insure my place, you know.
SIR OLIV. *(aside).* If the man be a shadow of his master, this is the temple of dissipation indeed!

Exeunt.

SCENE III

CHARLES [SURFACE], CARELESS, &c., &c. *at a table with wine,* &c.

CHAS. SURF. 'Fore heaven, 'tis true!—there's the great degeneracy of the age. Many of our acquaintance have taste, spirit, and politeness; but, plague on't, they won't drink.
CARE. It is so, indeed, Charles! they give in to all the substantial luxuries of the table, and abstain from nothing but wine and wit.
CHAS. SURF. Oh, certainly society suffers by it intolerably! for now, instead of the social spirit of raillery that used to mantle over a glass of bright Burgundy, their conversation is become just like the Spa-water they drink, which has all the pertness and flatulence of champagne, without its spirit or flavor.
1 GENT. But what are *they* to do who love play better than wine?
CARE. True! there's Harry diets himself for gaming, and is now under a hazard regimen.
CHAS. SURF. Then he'll have the worst of it. What! you wouldn't train a horse for the course by keeping him from corn! For my part, egad, I am now never so successful as when I am a little merry—let me throw on a bottle of champagne, and I never lose—at least I never feel my losses, which is exactly the same thing.
2 GENT. Aye, that I believe.
CHAS. SURF. And, then, what man can pretend to be a believer in love, who is an abjurer of wine? 'Tis the test by which the lover knows his own heart. Fill a dozen bumpers to a dozen beauties, and she that floats at top is the maid that has bewitched you.

51. *post-obit:* future claim.

CARE. Now then, Charles, be honest, and give us your real favorite.
CHAS. SURF. Why, I have withheld her only in compassion to you. If I toast her, you must give a round of her peers—which is impossible—on earth.
CARE. Oh, then we'll find some canonised vestals or heathen goddesses that will do, I warrant!
CHAS. SURF. Here then, bumpers, you rogues! bumpers! Maria! Maria—*(Drink.)*
1 GENT. Maria who?
CHAS. SURF. O, damn the surname!—'tis too formal to be registered in Love's calendar—but now, Sir Toby Bumper, beware—we must have beauty superlative.
CARE. Nay, never study, Sir Toby: we'll stand to the toast, though your mistress should want an eye—and you know you have a song will excuse you.
SIR TOBY. Egad, so I have! and I'll give him the song instead of the lady. *(Sings.)*

SONG AND CHORUS

Here's to the maiden of bashful fifteen;
   Here's to the widow of fifty;
Here's to the flaunting extravagant quean,
   And here's to the housewife that's thrifty.
Chorus. Let the toast pass—
      Drink to the lass—
I'll warrant she'll prove an excuse for the glass.
Here's to the charmer whose dimples we prize;
   Now to the maid who has none, sir;
Here's to the girl with a pair of blue eyes,
   And here's to the nymph with but one, sir.
Chorus. Let the toast pass, &c.
Here's to the maid with a bosom of snow:
   Now to *her* that's as brown as a berry:
Here's to the wife with a face full of woe,
   And now for the damsel that's merry.
Chorus. Let the toast pass, &c.
For let 'em be clumsy, or let 'em be slim,
   Young or ancient, I care not a feather:
So fill a pint bumper quite up to the brim,
   —And let us e'en toast 'em together.
Chorus. Let the toast pass, &c.

ALL. Bravo! Bravo!

Enter TRIP, *and whispers* CHARLES SURFACE.

CHAS. SURF. Gentlemen, you must excuse me a little.—Careless, take the chair, will you?

CARE. Nay, prithee, Charles, what now? This is one of your peerless beauties, I suppose, has dropped in by chance?
CHAS. SURF. No, faith! To tell you the truth, 'tis a Jew and a broker, who are come by appointment.
CARE. Oh, damn it! let's have the Jew in—
1 GENT. Aye, and the broker too, by all means.
2 GENT. Yes, yes, the Jew and the broker.
CHAS. SURF. Egad, with all my heart!—Trip, bid the gentlemen walk in.—(*Exit* TRIP.) Though there's one of them a stranger, I can tell you.
CARE. Charles, let us give them some generous Burgundy, and perhaps they'll grow conscientious.
CHAS. SURF. Oh, hang 'em, no! wine does but draw forth a man's *natural* qualities; and to make *them* drink would only be to whet their knavery.

Enter TRIP, SIR OLIVER SURFACE, *and* MOSES.

CHAS. SURF. So, honest Moses; walk in, pray, Mr. Premium—that's the gentleman's name, isn't it, Moses?
MOS. Yes, sir.
CHAS. SURF. Set chairs, Trip.—Sit down, Mr. Premium.—Glasses, Trip.—Sit down, Moses.—Come, Mr. Premium, I'll give you a sentiment; here's "Success to usury!"—Moses, fill the gentleman a bumper.
MOS. Success to usury!
CARE. Right, Moses— usury is prudence and industry, and deserves to succeed.
SIR OLIV. Then here's—All the success it deserves!
CARE. No, no, that won't do! Mr. Premium, you have demurred to the toast, and must drink it in a pint bumper.
1 GENT. A pint bumper, at least.
MOS. Oh, pray, sir, consider—Mr. Premium's a gentleman.
CARE. And therefore loves good wine.
2 GENT. Give Moses a quart glass—this is mutiny, and a high contempt of the chair.
CARE. Here, now for't! I'll see justice done, to the last drop of my bottle.
SIR OLIV. Nay, pray, gentlemen—I did not expect this usage.
CHAS. SURF. No, hang it, Careless, you shan't; Mr. Premium's a stranger.
SIR OLIV. (*aside*). Odd! I wish I was well out of this company.
CARE. Plague on 'em then! if they won't drink, we'll not sit down with 'em. Come, Harry, the dice are in the next room.—Charles, you'll join us—when you have finished your business with these gentlemen?
CHAS. SURF. I will! I will!—*(Exeunt gentlemen)*. Careless!
CARE. *(returning)*. Well!
CHAS. SURF. Perhaps I may want *you.*
CARE. Oh, you know I am always ready—word, note, or bond, 'tis all the same to me. *(Exit.)*

MOS. Sir, this is Mr. Premium, a gentleman of the strictest honor and secrecy; and always performs what he undertakes. Mr. Premium, this is—

CHAS. SURF. Pshaw! have done! Sir, my friend Moses is a very honest fellow, but a little slow at expression; he'll be an hour giving us our titles. Mr. Premium, the plain state of the matter is this—I am an extravagant young fellow who want[s] money to borrow; you I take to be a prudent old fellow, who ha[s] got money to lend. I am blockhead enough to give fifty per cent sooner than not have it; and you, I presume, are rogue enough to take a hundred if you could get it. Now, sir, you see we are acquainted at once, and may proceed to business without farther ceremony.

SIR OLIV. Exceeding frank, upon my word. I see, sir, you are not a man of many compliments.

CHAS. SURF. Oh, no, sir! plain dealing in business I always think best.

SIR OLIV. Sir, I like you the better for't. However, you are mistaken in one thing—I have no money to lend, but I believe I could procure some of a friend; but then he's an unconscionable dog—isn't he, Moses? And must sell stock to accommodate you—mustn't he, Moses?

MOS. Yes, indeed! You know I always speak the truth, and scorn to tell a lie!

CHAS. SURF. Right! People that expect truth generally do. But these are trifles, Mr. Premium. What! I know money isn't to be bought without paying for't!

SIR OLIV. Well, but what security could you give? You have no land, I suppose?

CHAS. SURF. Not a mole-hill, nor a twig, but what's in beau-pots out at the window!

SIR OLIV. Nor any stock, I presume?

CHAS. SURF. Nothing but live stock—and that's only a few pointers and ponies. But pray, Mr. Premium, are you acquainted at all with any of my connections?

SIR OLIV. Why, to say truth, I am.

CHAS. SURF. Then you must know that I have a devilish rich uncle in the East Indies, Sir Oliver Surface, from whom I have the greatest expectations.

SIR OLIV. That you have a wealthy uncle, I have heard—but how your expectations will turn out is more, I believe, than you can tell.

CHAS. SURF. Oh, no!—there can be no doubt—they tell me I'm a prodigious favorite—and that he talks of leaving me everything.

SIR OLIV. Indeed! this is the first I've heard on't.

CHAS. SURF. Yes, yes, 'tis just so.—Moses knows 'tis true; don't you, Moses?

MOS. Oh, yes! I'll swear to't.

SIR OLIV. *(aside).* Egad, they'll persuade me presently I'm at Bengal.

CHAS. SURF. Now I propose, Mr. Premium, if it's agreeable to you, a post-obit on Sir Oliver's life; though at the same time the old fellow

---

139. *beau-pots:* elaborate flowerpots.

has been so liberal to me that I give you my word I should be very sorry to hear anything had happened to him.

SIR OLIV. Not more than *I* should, I assure you. But the bond you mention happens to be just the worst security you could offer me— for I might live to a hundred and never recover the principal.

CHAS. SURF. Oh, yes, you would!—the moment Sir Oliver dies, you know, you'd come on me for the money.

SIR OLIV. Then I believe I should be the most unwelcome dun you ever had in your life.

CHAS. SURF. What! I suppose you are afraid now that Sir Oliver is too good a life?

SIR OLIV. No, indeed I am not—though I have heard he is as hale and healthy as any man of his years in Christendom.

CHAS. SURF. There again you are misinformed. No, no, the climate has hurt him considerably, poor uncle Oliver. Yes, he breaks apace, I'm told—and so much altered lately that his nearest relations don't know him.

SIR OLIV. No! Ha! ha! ha! so much altered lately that his relations don't know him! Ha! ha! ha! that's droll, egad—ha! ha! ha!

CHAS. SURF. Ha! ha!—you're glad to hear that, little Premium.

SIR OLIV. No, no, I'm not.

CHAS. SURF. Yes, yes, you are—ha! ha! ha!—you know that mends your chance.

SIR OLIV. But I'm told Sir Oliver is coming over—nay, some say he is actually arrived.

CHAS. SURF. Pshaw! sure I must know better than you whether he's come or not. No, no, rely on't, he is at this moment at Calcutta, isn't he, Moses?

MOS. Oh, yes, certainly.

SIR OLIV. Very true, as you say, you must know better than I, though I have it from pretty good authority—haven't I, Moses?

MOS. Yes, most undoubted!

SIR OLIV. But, sir, as I understand you want a few hundreds immediately, is there nothing you would dispose of?

CHAS. SURF. How do you mean?

SIR OLIV. For instance, now—I have heard—that your father left behind him a great quantity of massy old plate.

CHAS. SURF. O lud! that's gone long ago— Moses can tell you how better than I can.

SIR OLIV. Good lack! all the family race-cups and corporation-bowls! *(Aside.)*—Then it was also supposed that his library was one of the most valuable and complete.

CHAS. SURF. Yes, yes, so it was—vastly too much so for a private gentleman—for my part, I was always of a communicative disposition, so I thought it a shame to keep so much knowledge to myself.

SIR OLIV. *(aside).* Mercy on me! learning that had run in the family like an heirloom!—*(Aloud.)* Pray, what are become of the books?

CHAS. SURF. You must inquire of the auctioneer, Master Premium, for I don't believe even Moses can direct you there.

MOS. I never meddle with books.

SIR OLIV. So, so, nothing of the family property left, I suppose?
CHAS. SURF. Not much, indeed; unless you have a mind to the family pictures. I have got a room full of ancestors above—and if you have a taste for old paintings, egad, you shall have 'em a bargain!
SIR OLIV. Hey! and the devil! sure, you wouldn't sell your forefathers, would you?
CHAS. SURF. Every man of 'em, to the best bidder.
SIR OLIV. What! your great-uncles and aunts?
CHAS. SURF. Aye, and my great-grandfathers and grandmothers too.
SIR OLIV. Now I give him up!—*(Aside.)*—What the plague, have you no bowels for your own kindred? Odd's life! do you take me for Shylock in the play, that you would raise money of me on your own flesh and blood?
CHAS. SURF. Nay, my little broker, don't be angry: what need *you* care, if you have your money's worth?
SIR OLIV. Well, I'll be the purchaser—I think I can dispose of the family.—*(Aside.)* Oh, I'll never forgive him this! never!

Enter CARELESS.

CARE. Come, Charles, what keeps you?
CHAS. SURF. I can't come yet. I'faith! we are going to have a sale above—here's little Premium will buy all my ancestors!
CARE. Oh, burn your ancestors!
CHAS. SURF. No, he may do that afterwards, if he pleases. Stay, Careless, we want you; egad, you shall be auctioneer—so come along with us.
CARE. Oh, have with you, if that's the case.—I can handle a hammer as well as a dice box!
SIR OLIV. Oh, the profligates!
CHAS. SURF. Come, Moses, you shall be appraiser, if we want one. —Gad's life, little Premium, you don't seem to like the business.
SIR OLIV. Oh, yes, I do, vastly! Ha! ha! yes, yes, I think it a rare joke to sell one's family by auction—ha! ha!—*(Aside.)* Oh, the prodigal!
CHAS. SURF. To be sure! when a man wants money, where the plague should he get assistance, if he can't make free with his own relations?

Exeunt.

END OF THE THIRD ACT.

ACT IV

SCENE I

Picture-room at Charles's.

Enter CHARLES SURFACE, SIR OLIVER SURFACE,
  MOSES, *and* CARELESS.

CHAS. SURF. Walk in, gentlemen, pray walk in!—here they are, the family of the Surfaces, up to the Conquest.
SIR OLIV. And, in my opinion, a goodly collection.
CHAS. SURF. Aye, aye, these are done in true spirit of portrait-painting—no volunteer grace or expression—not like the works of your modern Raphael, who gives you the strongest resemblance, yet contrives to make your own portrait independent of you; so that you may sink the original and not hurt the picture. No, no; the merit of these is the inveterate likeness—all stiff and awkward as the originals, and like nothing in human nature beside!
SIR OLIV. Ah! we shall never see such figures of men again.
CHAS. SURF. I hope not. Well, you see, Master Premium, what a domestic character I am—here I sit of an evening surrounded by my family. But come, get to your pulpit, Mr. Auctioneer—here's an old gouty chair of my grandfather's will answer the purpose.
CARE. Aye, aye, this will do. But, Charles, I have ne'er a hammer; and what's an auctioneer without his hammer?
CHAS. SURF. Egad, that's true. What parchment have we here? *(Takes down a roll.)* "Richard, heir to Thomas"—our genealogy in full. Here, Careless, you shall have no common bit of mahogany—here's the family tree for you, you rogue—this shall be your hammer, and now you may knock down my ancestors with their own pedigree.
SIR OLIV. *(aside).* What an unnatural rogue!—an *ex post facto* parricide!
CARE. Yes, yes, here's a list of your generation indeed;—faith, Charles, this is the most convenient thing you could have found for the business, for 'twill serve not only as a hammer, but a catalogue into the bargain.—But come, begin—A-going, a-going, a-going!
CHAS. SURF. Bravo, Careless! Well, here's my great uncle, Sir Richard Raviline, a marvellous good general in his day, I assure you. He served in all the Duke of Marlborough's wars, and got that cut over his eye at the battle of Malplaquet. What say you, Mr. Premium? look at him—there's a hero for you! not cut out of his feathers, as your modern clipped captains are, but enveloped in wig and regimentals, as a general should be. What do you bid?
MOS. Mr. Premium would have you speak.
CHAS. SURF. Why, then, he shall have him for ten pounds, and I am sure that's not dear for a staff-officer.
SIR OLIV. Heaven deliver me! his famous uncle Richard for ten pounds!—Very well, sir, I take him at that.

CHAS. SURF. Careless, knock down my uncle Richard.—Here, now, is a maiden sister of his, my great-aunt Deborah, done by Kneller, thought to be in his best manner, and a very formidable likeness. There she is, you see, a shepherdess feeding her flock. You shall have her for five pounds ten—the sheep are worth the money.

SIR OLIV. Ah! poor Deborah! a woman who set such a value on herself!—Five pound ten—she's mine.

CHAS. SURF. Knock down my aunt Deborah! Here, now, are two that were a sort of cousins of theirs.—You see, Moses, these pictures were done some time ago, when beaux wore wigs, and the ladies wore their own hair.

SIR OLIV. Yes, truly, head-dresses appear to have been a little lower in those days.

CHAS. SURF. Well, take that couple for the same.

MOS. 'Tis [a] good bargain.

CHAS. SURF. Careless!—This, now, is a grandfather of my mother's, a learned judge, well known on the western circuit.—What do you rate him at, Moses?

MOS. Four guineas.

CHAS. SURF. Four guineas! Gad's life, you don't bid me the price of his wig.—Mr. Premium, *you* have more respect for the woolsack; do let us knock his lordship down at fifteen.

SIR OLIV. By all means.

CARE. Gone!

CHAS. SURF. And there are two brothers of his, William and Walter Blunt, Esquires, both members of Parliament, and noted speakers; and, what's very extraordinary, I believe this is the first time they were ever bought and sold.

SIR OLIV. That's very extraordinary, indeed! I'll take them at your own price, for the honor of Parliament.

CARE. Well said, little Premium! I'll knock 'em down at forty.

CHAS. SURF. Here's a jolly fellow—I don't know what relation, but he was mayor of Manchester; take him at eight pounds.

SIR OLIV. No, no—six will do for the mayor.

CHAS. SURF. Come, make it guineas, and I'll throw you the two aldermen there into the bargain.

SIR OLIV. They're mine.

CHAS. SURF. Careless, knock down the mayor and aldermen. But, plague on't! we shall be all day retailing in this manner; do let us deal wholesale—what say you, little Premium? Give me three hundred pounds for the rest of the family in the lump.

CARE. Aye, aye, that will be the best way.

SIR OLIV. Well, well, anything to accommodate you; they are mine. But there is one portrait which you have always passed over.

CARE. What, that ill-looking little fellow over the settee?

SIR OLIV. Yes, sir, I mean that; though I don't think him so ill-looking a little fellow, by any means.

CHAS. SURF. What, that? Oh, that's my uncle Oliver! 'Twas done before he went to India.

CARE. Your uncle Oliver! Gad, then you'll never be friends, Charles.

That, now, to me, is as stern a looking rogue as ever I saw—an unforgiving eye, and a damned disinheriting countenance! an inveterate knave, depend on't. Don't you think so, little Premium?

SIR OLIV. Upon my soul, sir, I do not; I think it is as honest a looking face as any in the room, dead or alive. But I suppose your uncle Oliver goes with the rest of the lumber?

CHAS. SURF. No, hang it! I'll not part with poor Noll. The old fellow has been very good to me, and, egad, I'll keep his picture while I've a room to put it in.

SIR OLIV. The rogue's my nephew after all! *(Aside.)*—But, sir, I have somehow taken a fancy to that picture.

CHAS. SURF. I'm sorry for't, for you certainly will not have it. Oons! haven't you got enough of 'em?

SIR OLIV. I forgive him everything! *(Aside.)*—But, sir, when I take a whim in my head, I don't value money. I'll give you as much for that as for all the rest.

CHAS. SURF. Don't tease me, master broker; I tell you I'll not part with it, and there's an end on't.

SIR OLIV. How like his father the dog is!—*(Aloud.)* Well, well, I have done.—I did not perceive it before, but I think I never saw such a resemblance.—Well, sir—here is a draught for your sum.

CHAS. SURF. Why, 'tis for eight hundred pounds!

SIR OLIV. You will not let Sir Oliver go?

CHAS. SURF. Zounds! no! I tell you, once more.

SIR OLIV. Then never mind the difference; we'll balance another time. But give me your hand on the bargain; you are an honest fellow, Charles—I beg pardon, sir, for being so free.—Come, Moses.

CHAS. SURF. Egad, this is a whimsical old fellow!—but hark'ee, Premium, you'll prepare lodgings for these gentlemen.

SIR OLIV. Yes, yes, I'll send for them in a day or two.

CHAS. SURF. But hold—do now—send a genteel conveyance for them, for, I assure you, they were most of them used to ride in their own carriages.

SIR OLIV. I will, I will, for all but—Oliver.

CHAS. SURF. Aye, all but the little honest nabob.

SIR OLIV. You're fixed on that?

CHAS. SURF. Peremptorily.

SIR OLIV. A dear extravagant rogue!—Good day!—Come, Moses,—Let me hear now who dares call him profligate!

Exeunt SIR OLIVER *and* MOSES.

CARE. Why, this is the oddest genius of the sort I ever saw!

CHAS. SURF. Egad, he's the prince of brokers, I think. I wonder how the devil Moses got acquainted with so honest a fellow.—Ha! here's Rowley.—Do, Careless, say I'll join the company in a moment.

CARE. I will—but don't let that old blockhead persuade you to squander any of that money on old musty debts, or any such nonsense; for tradesmen, Charles, are the most exorbitant fellows!

CHAS. SURF. Very true, and paying them is only encouraging them.

CARE. Nothing else.
CHAS. SURF. Aye, aye, never fear.—(*Exit* CARELESS.) So! this was an odd old fellow, indeed! Let me see, two-thirds of this is mine by right—five hundred and thirty pounds. 'Fore heaven! I find one's ancestors are more valuable relations than I took 'em for!—Ladies and gentlemen, your most obedient and very grateful humble servant. 140

Enter ROWLEY.

Ha! old Rowley! egad, you are just come in time to take leave of your old acquaintance.
ROW. Yes, I heard they were going. But I wonder you can have such spirits under so many distresses.
CHAS. SURF. Why, there's the point—my distresses are so many, that I can't afford to part with my spirits; but I shall be rich and splenetic, all in good time. However, I suppose you are surprised that I am not 150 more sorrowful at parting with so many near relations; to be sure, 'tis very affecting; but, rot 'em, you see they never move a muscle, so why should I?
ROW. There's no making you serious a moment.
CHAS. SURF. Yes, faith: I am so now. Here, my honest Rowley, here, get me this changed, and take a hundred pounds of it immediately to old Stanley.
ROW. A hundred pounds! Consider only—
CHAS. SURF. Gad's life, don't talk about it! poor Stanley's wants are pressing, and, if you don't make haste, we shall have some one call 160 that has a better right to the money.
ROW. Ah! there's the point! I never will cease dunning you with the old proverb—
CHAS. SURF. "Be *just* before you're *generous*," hey!—Why, so I would if I could; but Justice is an old lame hobbling beldame, and I can't get her to keep pace with Generosity, for the soul of me.
ROW. Yet, Charles, believe me, one hour's reflection—
CHAS. SURF. Aye, aye, it's all very true; but, hark'ee, Rowley, while I have, by heaven I'll give—so, damn your economy! and now for hazard. 170

Exit.

SCENE II

The parlor.

Enter SIR OLIVER SURFACE *and* MOSES.

MOS. Well, sir, I think, as Sir Peter said, you have seen Mr. Charles in high glory; 'tis great pity he's so extravagant.
SIR OLIV. True, but he wouldn't sell my picture.
MOS. And loves wine and women so much.
SIR OLIV. But he wouldn't sell my picture!

MOS. And game[s] so deep.
SIR OLIV. But he wouldn't sell my picture. Oh, here's Rowley.

Enter ROWLEY.

ROW. So, Sir Oliver, I find you have made a purchase—
SIR OLIV. Yes, yes, our young rake has parted with his ancestors like old tapestry.
ROW. And here has he commissioned me to redeliver you part of the purchase-money—I mean, though, in your necessitous character of old Stanley.
MOS. Ah! there is the pity of all: he is so damned charitable.
ROW. And I left a hosier and two tailors in the hall, who, I'm sure, won't be paid, and this hundred would satisfy 'em.
SIR OLIV. Well, well, I'll pay his debts—and his benevolence too; but now I am no more a broker, and you shall introduce me to the elder brother as old Stanley.
ROW. Not yet awhile; Sir Peter, I know, means to call there about this time.

Enter TRIP.

TRIP. O gentlemen, I beg pardon for not showing you out; this way— Moses, a word.

Exeunt TRIP *and* MOSES.

SIR OLIV. There's a fellow for you! Would you believe it, that puppy intercepted the Jew on our coming, and wanted to raise money before he got to his master!
ROW. Indeed!
SIR OLIV. Yes, they are now planning an annuity business. Ah, Master Rowley, in my days, servants were content with the follies of their masters, when they were worn a little threadbare—but now they have their vices, like their birthday clothes, with the gloss on.

Exeunt.

SCENE III

A library in Joseph Surface's house.

JOSEPH SURFACE *and Servant.*

JOS. SURF. No letter from Lady Teazle?
SERV. No, sir.
JOS. SURF. *(aside).* I am surprised she hasn't sent, if she is prevented from coming. Sir Peter certainly does not suspect me. Yet I wish I may not lose the heiress, through the scrape I have drawn myself in with the wife; however, Charles's imprudence and bad character are great points in my favor. *(Knocking.)*

SERV. Sir, I believe that must be Lady Teazle.
JOS. SURF. Hold! See whether it is or not, before you go to the door—
I have a particular message for you, if it should be my brother.
SERV. 'Tis her ladyship, sir; she always leaves her chair at the milliner's
in the next street.
JOS. SURF. Stay, stay—draw that screen before the window—that will
do;—my opposite neighbor is a maiden lady of so curious a temper.
—*(Servant draws the screen, and exit.)* I have a difficult hand to play
in this affair. Lady Teazle has lately suspected my views on Maria;
but she must by no means be let into that secret,—at least, not till I
have her more in my power.

Enter LADY TEAZLE.

LADY TEAZ. What, sentiment in soliloquy! Have you been very
impatient now? O lud! don't pretend to look grave. I vow I couldn't
come before.
JOS. SURF. O madam, punctuality is a species of constancy, a very
unfashionable quality in a lady.
LADY TEAZ. Upon my word, you ought to pity me. Do you know that
Sir Peter is grown so ill-tempered to me of late, and so jealous of
Charles too—that's the best of the story, isn't it?
JOS. SURF. *(aside).* I am glad my scandalous friends keep that up.
LADY TEAZ. I am sure I wish he would let Maria marry him, and then
perhaps he would be convinced; don't you, Mr. Surface?
JOS. SURF. *(aside).* Indeed I do not.—Oh, certainly I do! for then my
dear Lady Teazle would also be convinced how wrong her suspicions
were of my having any design on the silly girl.
LADY TEAZ. Well, well, I'm inclined to believe you. But isn't it
provoking, to have the most ill-natured things said to one? And
there's my friend Lady Sneerwell has circulated I don't know how
many scandalous tales of me! and all without any foundation, too—
that's what vexes me.
JOS. SURF. Aye, madam, to be sure, that *is* the provoking circumstance—without foundation! yes, yes, there's the mortification,
indeed; for, when a scandalous story is believed against one, there
certainly is no comfort like the consciousness of having deserved it.
LADY TEAZ. No, to be sure—then I'd forgive their malice; but to attack
me, who am really so innocent, and who never say an ill-natured thing
of anybody—that is, of any friend—and then Sir Peter, too, to have
him so peevish, and so suspicious, when I know the integrity of my
own heart—indeed 'tis monstrous!
JOS. SURF. But, my dear Lady Teazle, 'tis your own fault if you suffer
it. When a husband entertains a groundless suspicion of his wife, and
withdraws his confidence from her, the original compact is broke,
and she owes it to the honor of her sex to endeavor to outwit him.
LADY TEAZ. Indeed! So that, if he suspects me without cause, it
follows that the best way of curing his jealousy is to give him reason
for't?
JOS. SURF. Undoubtedly—for your husband should never be deceived

in you: and in that case it becomes *you* to be frail in compliment to *his* discernment.

LADY TEAZ. To be sure, what you say is very reasonable, and when the consciousness of my own innocence—

JOS. SURF. Ah, my dear madam, there is the great mistake; 'tis this very conscious innocence that is of the greatest prejudice to you. What is it makes you negligent of forms, and careless of the world's opinion? why, the *consciousness* of your innocence. What makes you thoughtless in your conduct, and apt to run into a thousand little imprudences? why, the *consciousness* of your innocence. What makes you impatient of Sir Peter's temper and outrageous at his suspicions? why, the *consciousness* of your own innocence!

LADY TEAZ. 'Tis very true!

JOS. SURF. Now, my dear Lady Teazle, if you would but once make a trifling *faux pas,* you can't conceive how cautious you would grow—and how ready to humor and agree with your husband.

LADY TEAZ. Do you think so?

JOS. SURF. Oh, I'm sure on't; and then you would find all scandal would cease at once, for—in short, your character at present is like a person in a plethora, absolutely dying of too much health.

LADY TEAZ. So, so; then I perceive your prescription is, that I must sin in my own defence, and part with my virtue to preserve my reputation?

JOS. SURF. Exactly so, upon my credit, ma'am.

LADY TEAZ. Well, certainly this is the oddest doctrine, and the newest receipt for avoiding calumny?

JOS. SURF. An infallible one, believe me. *Prudence,* like *experience,* must be paid for.

LADY TEAZ. Why, if my understanding were once convinced—

JOS. SURF. Oh, certainly, madam, your understanding *should* be convinced. Yes, yes—heaven forbid I should persuade you to do anything you *thought* wrong. No, no, I have too much honor to desire it.

LADY TEAZ. Don't you think we may as well leave honor out of the argument?

JOS. SURF. Ah, the ill effects of your country education, I see, still remain with you.

LADY TEAZ. I doubt they do, indeed; and I will fairly own to you, that if I could be persuaded to do wrong, it would be by Sir Peter's ill-usage sooner than your honorable logic, after all.

JOS. SURF. Then, by this hand, which he is unworthy of—*(Taking her hand.)*

Re-enter Servant.

'Sdeath, you blockhead—what do you want?

SERV. I beg pardon, sir, but I thought you wouldn't choose Sir Peter to come up without announcing him.

JOS. SURF. Sir Peter!—Oons—the devil!

LADY TEAZ. Sir Peter! O lud! I'm ruined! I'm ruined!

SERV. Sir, 'twasn't I let him in.

LADY TEAZ. Oh! I'm undone! What will become of me, now, Mr. Logic?—Oh! mercy, he's on the stairs—I'll get behind here—and if ever I'm so imprudent again—*(Goes behind the screen.)*
JOS. SURF. Give me that book. *(Sits down. Servant pretends to adjust his hair.)*

Enter SIR PETER TEAZLE.

SIR PET. Aye, ever improving himself!—Mr. Surface, Mr. Surface—
JOS. SURF. Oh, my dear Sir Peter, I beg your pardon. *(Gaping, and throws away the book.)* I have been dozing over a stupid book. Well, I am much obliged to you for this call. You haven't been here, I believe, since I fitted up this room. Books, you know, are the only things I am a coxcomb in.
SIR PET. 'Tis very neat indeed. Well, well, that's proper; and you make even your screen a source of knowledge—hung, I perceive, with maps.
JOS. SURF. Oh, yes, I find great use in that screen.
SIR PET. I dare say you must—certainly—when you want to find anything in a hurry.
JOS. SURF. *(aside).* Aye, or to hide anything in a hurry either.
SIR PET. Well, I have a little private business—
JOS. SURF. You needn't stay. *(To Servant.)*
SERV. No, sir. *(Exit.)*
JOS. SURF. Here's a chair, Sir Peter—I beg—
SIR PET. Well, now we are alone, there is a subject, my dear friend, on which I wish to unburden my mind to you—a point of the greatest moment to my peace: in short, my good friend, Lady Teazle's conduct of late has made me extremely unhappy.
JOS. SURF. Indeed! I am very sorry to hear it.
SIR PET. Yes, 'tis but too plain she has not the least regard for me; but, what's worse, I have pretty good authority to suspect she must have formed an attachment to another.
JOS. SURF. You astonish me!
SIR PET. Yes! and, between ourselves, I think I have discovered the person.
JOS. SURF. How! you alarm me exceedingly.
SIR PET. Aye, my dear friend, I knew you would sympathize with me!
JOS. SURF. Yes, believe me, Sir Peter, such a discovery would hurt me just as much as it would you.
SIR PET. I am convinced of it.—Ah! it is a happiness to have a friend whom one can trust even with one's family secrets. But have you no guess who I mean?
JOS. SURF. I haven't the most distant idea. It can't be Sir Benjamin Backbite!
SIR PET. O, no! What say you to Charles?
JOS. SURF. My brother! impossible!
SIR PET. Ah, my dear friend, the goodness of your own heart misleads you—you judge of others by yourself.
JOS. SURF. Certainly, Sir Peter, the heart that is conscious of its own integrity is ever slow to credit another's treachery.

SIR PET. True; but your brother has no sentiment—you never hear him talk so.
JOS. SURF. Yet I can't but think Lady Teazle herself has too much principle—
SIR PET. Aye; but what's her principle against the flattery of a handsome, lively young fellow?
JOS. SURF. That's very true.
SIR PET. And then, you know, the difference of our ages makes it very improbable that she should have any great affection for me; and if she were to be frail, and I were to make it public, why the town would only laugh at me, the foolish old bachelor who had married a girl.
JOS. SURF. That's true, to be sure—they *would* laugh.
SIR PET. Laugh! aye, and make ballads, and paragraphs, and the devil knows what of me.
JOS. SURF. No, you must never make it public.
SIR PET. But then again—that the nephew of my old friend, Sir Oliver, should be the person to attempt such a wrong, hurts me more nearly.
JOS. SURF. Aye, there's the point. When ingratitude barbs the dart of injury, the wound has double danger in it.
SIR PET. Aye—I, that was, in a manner, left his guardian—in whose house he had been so often entertained—who never in my life denied him—my advice!
JOS. SURF. Oh, 'tis not to be credited! There *may* be a man capable of such baseness, to be sure; but, for my part, till you can give me positive proofs, I cannot but doubt it. However, if it should be proved on him, he is no longer a brother of mine! I disclaim kindred with him—for the man who can break through the laws of hospitality, and attempt the wife of his friend, deserves to be branded as the pest of society.
SIR PET. What a difference there is between you! What noble sentiments!
JOS. SURF. Yet I cannot suspect Lady Teazle's honor.
SIR PET. I am sure I wish to think well of her, and to remove all ground of quarrel between us. She has lately reproached me more than once with having made no settlement on her; and, in our last quarrel, she almost hinted that she should not break her heart if I was dead. Now, as we seem to differ in our ideas of expense, I have resolved she shall be her own mistress in that respect for the future; and, if I *were* to die, she shall find that I have not been inattentive to her interest while living. Here, my friend, are the drafts of two deeds, which I wish to have your opinion on. By one, she will enjoy eight hundred a year independent while I live; and, by the other, the bulk of my fortune after my death.
JOS. SURF. This conduct, Sir Peter, is indeed truly generous.—*(Aside.)* I wish it may not corrupt my pupil.
SIR PET. Yes, I am determined she shall have no cause to complain, though I would not have her acquainted with the latter instance of my affection yet awhile.
JOS. SURF. Nor I, if I could help it. *(Aside.)*

SIR PET. And now, my dear friend, if you please, we will talk over the situation of your hopes with Maria.
JOS. SURF. *(softly).* No, no, Sir Peter; another time, if you please.
SIR PET. I am sensibly chagrined at the little progress you seem to make in her affection.
JOS. SURF. I beg you will not mention it. What are my disappointments when your happiness is in debate! *(Softly.)*—'Sdeath, I shall be ruined every way! *(Aside.)*
SIR PET. And though you are so averse to my acquainting Lady Teazle with your passion, I am sure she's not your enemy in the affair.
JOS. SURF. Pray, Sir Peter, now oblige me. I am really too much affected by the subject we have been speaking on to bestow a thought on my own concerns. The man who is entrusted with his friend's distresses can never—

Enter Servant.

Well, sir?
SERV. Your brother, sir, is speaking to a gentleman in the street, and says he knows you are within.
JOS. SURF. 'Sdeath, blockhead—I'm not within—I'm out for the day.
SIR PET. Stay—hold—a thought has struck me—you shall be at home.
JOS. SURF. Well, well, let him up.—*(Exit Servant.)* He'll interrupt Sir Peter—however—
SIR PET. Now, my good friend, oblige me, I entreat you. Before Charles comes, let me conceal myself somewhere; then do you tax him on the point we have been talking on, and his answers may satisfy me at once.
JOS. SURF. O, fie, Sir Peter! would you have me join in so mean a trick?—to trepan my brother to?
SIR PET. Nay, you tell me you are *sure* he is innocent; if so, you do him the greatest service by giving him an opportunity to clear himself, and you will set my heart at rest. Come, you shall not refuse me; here, behind the screen will be *(Goes to the screen)*—Hey! what the devil! there seems to be *one* listener here already—I'll swear I saw a petticoat!
JOS. SURF. Ha! ha! ha! Well, this is ridiculous enough. I'll tell you, Sir Peter, though I hold a man of intrigue to be a most despicable character, yet you know, it doesn't follow that one is to be an absolute Joseph either! Hark'ee! 'tis a little French milliner, a silly rogue that plagues me—and having some character—on your coming, she ran behind the screen.
SIR PET. Ah, you rogue!—But, egad, she has overheard all I have been saying of my wife.
JOS. SURF. Oh, 'twill never go any further, you may depend on't!
SIR PET. No! then, i'faith, let her hear it out.—Here's a closet will do as well.
JOS. SURF. Well, go in then.
SIR PET. Sly rogue! sly rogue! *(Goes into the closet.)*
JOS. SURF. A very narrow escape, indeed! and a curious situation I'm

in, to part man and wife in this manner.
LADY TEAZ. *(peeping from the screen).* Couldn't I steal off?
JOS. SURF. Keep close, my angel!
SIR PET. *(peeping out).* Joseph, tax him home.
JOS. SURF. Back, my dear friend!
LADY TEAZ. *(peeping).* Couldn't you lock Sir Peter in?
JOS. SURF. Be still, my life!
SIR PET. *(peeping).* You're sure the little milliner won't blab?
JOS. SURF. In, in, my dear Sir Peter!—'Fore gad, I wish I had a key to the door.

Enter CHARLES SURFACE.

CHAS. SURF. Hollo! brother, what has been the matter? Your fellow would not let me up at first. What! have you had a Jew or a wench with you?
JOS. SURF. Neither, brother, I assure you.
CHAS. SURF. But what has made Sir Peter steal off? I thought he had been with you.
JOS. SURF. He was, brother; but, hearing *you* were coming, he did not choose to stay.
CHAS. SURF. What! was the old gentleman afraid I wanted to borrow money of him!
JOS. SURF. No, sir: but I am sorry to find, Charles, that you have lately given that worthy man grounds for great uneasiness.
CHAS. SURF. Yes, they tell me I do that to a great many worthy men. But how so, pray?
JOS. SURF. To be plain with you, brother, he thinks you are endeavoring to gain Lady Teazle's affections from him.
CHAS. SURF. Who, I? O lud! not I, upon my word.—Ha! ha! ha! so the old fellow has found out that he has got a young wife, has he?—or, what's worse, has her ladyship discovered that she has an old husband?
JOS. SURF. This is no subject to jest on, brother.—He who can laugh—
CHAS. SURF. True, true, as you were going to say—then, seriously, I never had the least idea of what you charge me with, upon my honor.
JOS. SURF. Well, it will give Sir Peter great satisfaction to hear this. *(Aloud.)*
CHAS. SURF. To be sure, I once thought the lady seemed to have taken a fancy to me; but, upon my soul, I never gave her the least encouragement. Besides, you know my attachment to Maria.
JOS. SURF. But sure, brother, even if Lady Teazle had betrayed the fondest partiality for you—
CHAS. SURF. Why, look'ee, Joseph, I hope I shall never deliberately do a dishonorable action—but if a pretty woman were purposely to throw herself in my way—and that pretty woman married to a man old enough to be her father—
JOS. SURF. Well!
CHAS. SURF. Why, I believe I should be obliged to borrow a little of your morality, that's all.—But, brother, do you know now that you

surprise me exceedingly, by naming *me* with Lady Teazle; for, faith, I alway[s] understood *you* were her favorite.

JOS. SURF. Oh, for shame, Charles! This retort is foolish.

CHAS. SURF. Nay, I swear I have seen you exchange such significant glances—

JOS. SURF. Nay, nay, sir, this is no jest—

CHAS. SURF. Egad, I'm serious! Don't you remember—one day, when I called here—

JOS. SURF. Nay, prithee, Charles—

CHAS. SURF. And found you together—

JOS. SURF. Zounds, sir, I insist—

CHAS. SURF. And another time, when your servant—

JOS. SURF. Brother, brother, a word with you!—*(Aside.)* Gad, I must stop him.

CHAS. SURF. Informed me, I say, that—

JOS. SURF. Hush! I beg your pardon, but Sir Peter has overheard all we have been saying—I knew you would clear yourself, or I should not have consented.

CHAS. SURF. How, Sir Peter! Where is he?

JOS. SURF. Softly, there! *(Points to the closet.)*

CHAS. SURF. Oh, 'fore heaven, I'll have him out.—Sir Peter, come forth!

JOS. SURF. No, no—

CHAS. SURF. I say, Sir Peter, come into court.—*(Pulls in* SIR PETER.*)* What! my old guardian!—What—turn inquisitor, and take evidence, incog.?

SIR PET. Give me your hand, Charles—I believe I have suspected you wrongfully—but you mustn't be angry with Joseph—'twas my plan!

CHAS. SURF. Indeed!

SIR PET. But I acquit you. I promise you I don't think near so ill of you as I did. What I have heard has given me great satisfaction.

CHAS. SURF. Egad, then, 'twas lucky you didn't hear any more. Wasn't it, Joseph? *(Half aside.)*

SIR PET. Ah! you would have retorted on him.

CHAS. SURF. Aye, aye, that was a joke.

SIR PET. Yes, yes, I know his honor too well.

CHAS. SURF. But you might as well have suspected him as me in this matter, for all that. Mightn't he, Joseph? *(Half aside.)*

SIR PET. Well, well, I believe you.

JOS. SURF. Would they were both out of the room!

SIR PET. And in future, perhaps, we may not be such strangers.

Enter Servant who whispers JOSEPH SURFACE.

JOS. SURF. Lady Sneerwell!—stop her by all means—*(Exit Servant.)* Gentlemen—I beg pardon—I must wait on you downstairs—here's a person come on particular business.

CHAS. SURF. Well, you can see him in another room. Sir Peter and I haven't met a long time, and I have something to say to him.

JOS. SURF. They must not be left together.—I'll send Lady Sneerwell away, and return directly.—*(Aside.)* Sir Peter, not a word of the French milliner. (*Exit* JOSEPH SURFACE.)

SIR PET. Oh! not for the world!—Ah, Charles, if you associated more with your brother, one might indeed hope for your reformation. He is a man of sentiment.—Well, there is nothing in the world so noble as a man of sentiment!

CHAS. SURF. Pshaw! he is too moral by half, and so apprehensive of his good name, as he calls it, that I suppose he would as soon let a priest into his house as a girl.

SIR PET. No, no,—come, come,—you wrong him. No, no, Joseph is no rake, but he is not such a saint in that respect either,—I have a great mind to tell him—we should have a laugh! *(Aside.)*

CHAS. SURF. Oh, hang him! he's a very anchorite, a young hermit!

SIR PET. Hark'ee—you must not abuse him; he may chance to hear of it again, I promise you.

CHAS. SURF. Why, you won't tell him?

SIR PET. No—but—this way.—*(Aside.)* Egad, I'll tell him.—Hark'ee, have you a mind to have a good laugh at Joseph?

CHAS. SURF. I should like it of all things.

SIR PET. Then, i'faith, we will!—I'll be quit with him for discovering me. *(Aside.)*—He had a girl with him when I called.

CHAS. SURF. What! Joseph? you jest.

SIR PET. Hush!—a little—French milliner—and the best of the jest is—she's in the room now.

CHAS. SURF. The devil she is!

SIR PET. Hush! I tell you. *(Points to the screen.)*

CHAS. SURF. Behind the screen! 'Slife, let's unveil her!

SIR PET. No, no, he's coming:—you shan't, indeed!

CHAS. SURF. Oh, egad, we'll have a peep at the little milliner!

SIR PET. Not for the world!—Joseph will never forgive me.

CHAS. SURF. I'll stand by you—

SIR PET. (*struggling with* CHARLES). Odds, here he is!

JOSEPH SURFACE *enters just as* CHARLES *throws down the screen.*

CHAS. SURF. Lady Teazle, by all that's wonderful!

SIR PET. Lady Teazle, by all that's horrible!

CHAS. SURF. Sir Peter, this is one of the smartest French milliners I ever saw. Egad, you seem all to have been diverting yourselves here at hide and seek—and I don't see who is out of the secret. Shall I beg your ladyship to inform me?—Not a word!—Brother, will you please to explain this matter? What! Morality dumb too!—Sir Peter, though I *found* you in the dark, perhaps you are not so now! All mute! Well—though *I* can make nothing of the affair, I suppose you perfectly understand one another; so I'll leave you to yourselves.—*(Going.)* Brother, I'm sorry to find you *have given that worthy man so much uneasiness.*—Sir Peter! there's nothing *in the world* so *noble as a man of sentiment!* (*Exit* CHARLES.*)*

They stand for some time looking at each other.

JOS. SURF. Sir Peter—notwithstanding I confess that appearances are against me—if you will afford me your patience—I make no doubt but I shall explain everything to your satisfaction.
SIR PET. If you please—
JOS. SURF. The fact is, sir, that Lady Teazle, knowing my pretensions to your ward Maria—I say, sir, Lady Teazle, being apprehensive of the jealousy of your temper—and knowing my friendship to the family—she, sir, I say—called here—in order that—I might explain those pretensions—but on your coming—being apprehensive—as I said—of your jealousy—she withdrew—and this, you may depend on't is the whole truth of the matter.
SIR PET. A very clear account, upon my word; and I dare swear the lady will vouch for every article of it.
LADY TEAZ. *(coming forward)*. For not one word of it, Sir Peter!
SIR PET. How! don't you think it worth while to agree in the lie?
LADY TEAZ. There is not one syllable of truth in what that gentleman has told you.
SIR PET. I believe you, upon my soul, ma'am!
JOS. SURF. *(aside)*. 'Sdeath, madam, will you betray me?
LADY TEAZ. Good Mr. Hypocrite, by your leave, I will speak for myself.
SIR PET. Aye, let her alone, sir; you'll find she'll make out a better story than *you*, without prompting.
LADY TEAZ. Hear me, Sir Peter!—I came here on no matter relating to your ward, and even ignorant of this gentleman's pretensions to her—but I came, seduced by his insidious arguments, at least to listen to his pretended passion, if not to sacrifice *your* honor to his baseness.
SIR PET. Now, I believe, the truth *is* coming, indeed!
JOS. SURF. The woman's mad!
LADY TEAZ. No, sir; she has recovered her senses, and your own arts have furnished her with the means.—Sir Peter, I do not expect you to credit me—but the tenderness you expressed for me, when I am sure you could not think I was a witness to it, has penetrated to my heart, and had I left the place without the shame of this discovery, my future life should have spoke[n] the sincerity of my gratitude. As for that smooth-tongue hypocrite, who would have seduced the wife of his too credulous friend, while he affected honorable addresses to his ward—I behold him now in a light so truly despicable, that I shall never again respect myself for having listened to him. *(Exit.)*
JOS. SURF. Notwithstanding all this, Sir Peter, heaven knows—
SIR PET. That you are a villain!—and so I leave you to your conscience.
JOS. SURF. You are too rash, Sir Peter; you shall hear me. The man who shuts out conviction by refusing to—
SIR PET. Oh!—

Exeunt, JOSEPH SURFACE *following and speaking.*

END OF ACT 4TH.

ACT V

SCENE i

The library in Joseph Surface's house.

Enter JOSEPH SURFACE *and Servant.*

JOS. SURF. Mr. Stanley! why should you think I would see him? you *must* know he comes to ask something.
SERV. Sir, I should not have let him in, but that Mr. Rowley came to the door with him.
JOS. SURF. Pshaw! blockhead! to suppose that I should *now* be in a temper to receive visits from poor relations!—Well, why don't you show the fellow up?
SERV. I will, sir.—Why, sir, it was not my fault that Sir Peter discovered my lady—
JOS. SURF. Go, fool! *(Exit Servant.)* Sure, Fortune never played a man of my policy such a trick before! My character with Sir Peter, my hopes with Maria, destroyed in a moment! I'm in a rare humor to listen to other people's distresses! I shan't be able to bestow even a benevolent sentiment on Stanley.—So! here he comes, and Rowley with him. I must try to recover myself—and put a little charity into my face, however. *(Exit.)*

Enter SIR OLIVER SURFACE *and* ROWLEY.

SIR OLIV. What! does he avoid us? That was he, was it not?
ROW. It was, sir—but I doubt you are come a little too abruptly—his nerves are so weak, that the sight of a poor relation may be too much for him.—I should have gone first to break you to him.
SIR OLIV. A plague of his nerves!—Yet this is he whom Sir Peter extols as a man of the most benevolent way of thinking!
ROW. As to his way of thinking, I cannot pretend to decide; for, to do him justice, he appears to have as much speculative benevolence as any private gentleman in the kingdom, though he is seldom so sensual as to indulge himself in the exercise of it.
SIR OLIV. Yet has a string of charitable sentiments, I suppose, at his fingers' ends!
ROW. Or, rather, at his tongue's end, Sir Oliver; for I believe there is no sentiment he has more faith in than that "Charity begins at home."
SIR OLIV. And his, I presume, is of that domestic sort which never stirs abroad at all.
ROW. I doubt you'll find it so;—but he's coming—I mustn't seem to interrupt you; and you know, immediately as you leave him, I come in to announce your arrival in your real character.
SIR OLIV. True; and afterwards you'll meet me at Sir Peter's.
ROW. Without losing a moment. *(Exit* ROWLEY.*)*
SIR OLIV. So! I don't like the complaisance of his features.

Re-enter JOSEPH SURFACE.

JOS. SURF. Sir, I beg you ten thousand pardons for keeping you a moment waiting—Mr. Stanley, I presume.

SIR OLIV. At your service.

JOS. SURF. Sir, I beg you will do me the honor to sit down—I entreat you, sir.

SIR OLIV. Dear sir—there's no occasion.—Too civil by half! *(Aside.)*

JOS. SURF. I have not the pleasure of knowing you, Mr. Stanley; but I am extremely happy to see you look so well. You were nearly related to my mother, I think, Mr. Stanley?

SIR OLIV. I was, sir—so nearly that my present poverty, I fear, may do discredit to her wealthy children—else I should not have presumed to trouble you.

JOS. SURF. Dear sir, there needs no apology: he that is in distress, though a stranger, has a right to claim kindred with the wealthy;—I am sure I wish *I* was one of that class, and had it in my power to offer you even a small relief.

SIR OLIV. If your uncle, Sir Oliver, were here, I should have a friend.

JOS. SURF. I wish he were, sir, with all my heart: you should not want an advocate with him, believe me, sir.

SIR OLIV. I should not *need* one—my distresses would recommend me; but I imagined his bounty had enabled *you* to become the agent of his charity.

JOS. SURF. My dear sir, you were strangely misinformed. Sir Oliver is a worthy man, a very worthy sort of man; but—avarice, Mr. Stanley, is the vice of age. I will tell you, my good sir, in confidence, what he has done for me has been a mere nothing; though people, I know, have thought otherwise, and, for my part, I never chose to contradict the report.

SIR OLIV. What! has he never transmitted you bullion! rupees! pagodas!

JOS. SURF. O dear sir, nothing of the kind! No, no; a few presents now and then—china—shawls—Congo tea—avadavats, and India[n] crackers—little more, believe me.

SIR OLIV. *(aside).* Here's gratitude for twelve thousand pounds!—Avadavats and Indian crackers!

JOS. SURF. Then, my dear sir, you have heard, I doubt not, of the extravagance of my brother; there are very few would credit what I have done for that unfortunate young man.

SIR OLIV. Not I, for one! *(Aside.)*

JOS. SURF. The sums I have lent him! Indeed I have been exceedingly to blame—it was an amiable weakness: however, I don't pretend to defend it—and now I feel it doubly culpable, since it has deprived me of the pleasure of serving *you*, Mr. Stanley, as my heart dictates.

SIR OLIV. *(aside).* Dissembler!—Then, sir, you cannot assist me?

67-68. *rupees, pagodas:* foreign coins.

JOS. SURF. At present, it grieves me to say, I cannot; but, whenever I have the ability, you may depend upon hearing from me.
SIR OLIV. I am extremely sorry—
JOS. SURF. Not more than I am, believe me; to pity, without the power to relieve, is still more painful than to ask and be denied.
SIR OLIV. Kind sir, your most obedient humble servant.
JOS. SURF. You leave me deeply affected, Mr. Stanley.—William, be ready to open the door.
SIR OLIV. O dear sir, no ceremony.
JOS. SURF. Your very obedient.
SIR OLIV. Sir, your most obsequious.
JOS. SURF. You may depend upon hearing from me, whenever I can be of service.
SIR OLIV. Sweet sir, you are too good.
JOS. SURF. In the meantime I wish you health and spirits.
SIR OLIV. Your ever grateful and perpetual humble servant.
JOS. SURF. Sir, yours as sincerely.
SIR OLIV. Now I am satisfied! *(Exit.)*
JOS. SURF. *(solus).* This is one bad effect of a good character; it invites applications from the unfortunate, and there needs no small degree of address to gain the reputation of benevolence without incurring the expense. The silver ore of pure charity is an expensive article in the catalogue of a man's good qualities; whereas the sentimental French plate I use instead of it makes just as good a show, and pays no tax.

Enter ROWLEY.

ROW. Mr. Surface, your servant—I was apprehensive of interrupting you—though my business demands immediate attention—as this note will inform you.
JOS. SURF. Always happy to see Mr. Rowley.—*(Reads.)* How! "Oliver—Surface!"—My uncle arrived!
ROW. He is, indeed—we have just parted—quite well, after a speedy voyage, and impatient to embrace his worthy nephew.
JOS. SURF. I am astonished!—William! stop Mr. Stanley, if he's not gone.
ROW. Oh! he's out of reach, I believe.
JOS. SURF. Why didn't you let me know this when you came in together?
ROW. I thought you had particular business. But I must be gone to inform your brother, and appoint him here to meet his uncle. He will be with you in a quarter of an hour.
JOS. SURF. So he says. Well, I am strangely overjoyed at his coming.—*(Aside.)* Never, to be sure, was anything so damned unlucky!
ROW. You will be delighted to see how well he looks.
JOS. SURF. Oh! I'm rejoiced to hear it.—*(Aside.)* Just at this time!
ROW. I'll tell him how impatiently you expect him.
JOS. SURF. Do, do; pray give my best duty and affection. Indeed, I cannot express the sensations I feel at the thought of seeing him.—

(*Exit* ROWLEY.) Certainly his coming just at this time is the cruellest piece of ill fortune. *(Exit.)*

SCENE II

At Sir Peter's.

Enter MRS. CANDOUR *and Maid.*

MAID. Indeed, ma'am, my lady will see nobody at present.
MRS. CAN. Did you tell her it was her friend Mrs. Candour?
MAID. Yes, madam; but she begs you will excuse her.
MRS. CAN. Do go again; I shall be glad to see her, if it be only for a moment, for I am sure she must be in great distress.—*(Exit Maid)* Dear heart, how provoking! I'm not mistress of half the circumstances! We shall have the whole affair in the newspapers, with the names of the parties at length, before I have dropped the story at a dozen houses.

Enter SIR BENJAMIN BACKBITE.

O dear Sir Benjamin! you have heard, I suppose—
SIR BEN. Of Lady Teazle and Mr. Surface—
MRS. CAN. And Sir Peter's discovery—
SIR BEN. Oh, the strangest piece of business, to be sure!
MRS. CAN. Well, I never was so surprised in my life. I am so sorry for all parties, indeed I am.
SIR BEN. Now, I don't pity Sir Peter at all—he was so extravagantly partial to Mr. Surface.
MRS. CAN. Mr. Surface! Why, 'twas with Charles Lady Teazle was detected.
SIR BEN. No such thing—Mr. Surface is the gallant.
MRS. CAN. No, no—Charles is the man. 'Twas Mr. Surface brought Sir Peter on purpose to discover them.
SIR BEN. I tell you I have it from one—
MRS. CAN. And I have it from one—
SIR BEN. Who had it from one, who had it—
MRS. CAN. From one immediately—But here's Lady Sneerwell; perhaps she knows the whole affair.

Enter LADY SNEERWELL.

LADY SNEER. So, my dear Mrs. Candour, here's a sad affair of our friend Lady Teazle!
MRS. CAN. Aye, my dear friend, who could have thought it—
LADY SNEER. Well, there's no trusting appearances; though, indeed, she was always too lively for me.
MRS. CAN. To be sure, her manners were a little too free—but she was very young!
LADY SNEER. And had, indeed, some good qualities.

MRS. CAN. So she had, indeed. But have you heard the particulars?
LADY SNEER. No; but everybody says that Mr. Surface—
SIR BEN. Aye, there, I told you—Mr. Surface was the man.
MRS. CAN. No, no, indeed—the assignation was with Charles.
LADY SNEER. With Charles! You alarm me, Mrs. Candour.
MRS. CAN. Yes, yes, he was the lover. Mr. Surface—do him justice—was only the informer.
SIR BEN. Well, I'll not dispute with you, Mrs. Candour; but, be it which it may, I hope that Sir Peter's wound will not—
MRS. CAN. Sir Peter's wound! Oh, mercy! I didn't hear a word of their fighting.
LADY SNEER. Nor I, a syllable.
SIR BEN. No! what, no mention of the duel?
MRS. CAN. Not a word.
SIR BEN. O Lord—yes, yes—they fought before they left the room.
LADY SNEER. Pray let us hear.
MRS. CAN. Aye, do oblige us with the duel.
SIR BEN. "Sir," says Sir Peter—immediately after the discovery—"you are a most ungrateful fellow."
MRS. CAN. Aye, to Charles—
SIR BEN. No, no—to Mr. Surface—"a most ungrateful fellow; and old as I am, sir," says he, "I insist on immediate satisfaction."
MRS. CAN. Aye, that must have been to Charles; for 'tis very unlikely Mr. Surface should go to fight in his house.
SIR BEN. 'Gad's life, ma'am, not at all—"giving me immediate satisfaction."—On this, madam, Lady Teazle, seeing Sir Peter in such danger, ran out of the room in strong hysterics, and Charles after her, calling out for hartshorn and water! Then, madam, they began to fight with swords—

Enter CRABTREE.

CRAB. With pistols, nephew—I have it from undoubted authority.
MRS. CAN. O Mr. Crabtree, then it is all true!
CRAB. Too true, indeed, ma'am, and Sir Peter's dangerously wounded—
SIR BEN. By a thrust of in *seconde* quite through his left side—
CRAB. By a bullet lodged in the thorax.
MRS. CAN. Mercy on me! Poor Sir Peter!
CRAB. Yes, ma'am—though Charles would have avoided the matter, if he could.
MRS. CAN. I knew Charles was the person.
SIR BEN. Oh, my uncle, I see, knows nothing of the matter.
CRAB. But Sir Peter taxed him with the basest ingratitude—
SIR BEN. That I told you, you know.
CRAB. Do, nephew, let me speak!—and insisted on an immediate—
SIR BEN. Just as I said.
CRAB. Odds life, nephew, allow others to know something too! A pair of pistols lay on the bureau (for Mr. Surface, it seems, had come the night before late from Salt-Hill, where he had been to see the Montem with a friend, who has a son at Eton), so, unluckily, the pistols were left charged.

SIR BEN. I heard nothing of this.
CRAB. Sir Peter forced Charles to take one, and they fired, it seems, pretty nearly together. Charles's shot took place, as I told you, and Sir Peter's missed; but, what is very extraordinary, the ball struck against a little bronze Pliny that stood over the chimney-piece, grazed out of the window at a right angle, and wounded the postman, who was just coming to the door with a double letter from Northamptonshire.
SIR BEN. My uncle's account is more circumstantial, I must confess; but I believe mine is the true one, for all that.
LADY SNEER. *(aside).* I am more interested in this affair than they imagine, and must have better information. (*Exit* LADY SNEERWELL.)
SIR BEN. *(after a pause looking at each other).* Ah! Lady Sneerwell's alarm is very easily accounted for.
CRAB. Yes, yes, they certainly *do* say—but that's neither here nor there.
MRS. CAN. But, pray, where is Sir Peter at present?
CRAB. Oh! they brought him home, and he is now in the house, though the servants are ordered to deny it.
MRS. CAN. I believe so, and Lady Teazle, I suppose, attending him.
CRAB. Yes, yes; I saw one of the faculty enter just before me.
SIR BEN. Hey! who comes here?
CRAB. Oh, this is he—the physician, depend on't.
MRS. CAN. Oh, certainly! it must be the physician; and now we shall know.

Enter SIR OLIVER SURFACE.

CRAB. Well, doctor, what hopes?
MRS. CAN. Aye, doctor, how's your patient?
SIR BEN. Now, doctor, isn't it a wound with a small-sword?
CRAB. A bullet lodged in the thorax, for a hundred!
SIR OLIV. Doctor! a wound with a small-sword! and a bullet in the thorax?—Oons! are you mad, good people?
SIR BEN. Perhaps, sir, you are not a doctor?
SIR OLIV. Truly, I am to thank you for my degree, if I am.
CRAB. Only a friend of Sir Peter's, then, I presume. But, sir, you must have heard of this accident?
SIR OLIV. Not a word!
CRAB. Not of his being dangerously wounded?
SIR OLIV. The devil he is!
SIR BEN. Run through the body—
CRAB. Shot in the breast—
SIR BEN. By one Mr. Surface—
CRAB. Aye, the younger.
SIR OLIV. Hey! what the plague! you seem to differ strangely in your accounts—however, you agree that Sir Peter is dangerously wounded.
SIR BEN. Oh, yes, we agree there.
CRAB. Yes, yes, I believe there can be no doubt of that.
SIR OLIV. Then, upon my word, for a person in that situation, he is

the most imprudent man alive—for here he comes, walking as if
nothing at all were the matter.

Enter SIR PETER TEAZLE.

Odds heart, Sir Peter! you are come in good time, I promise you; for
we had just *given you over.*
SIR BEN. Egad, uncle, this is the most sudden recovery!
SIR OLIV. Why, man! what do you do out of bed with a small-sword
through your body, and a bullet lodged in your thorax?
SIR PET. A small-sword and a bullet?
SIR OLIV. Aye; these gentlemen would have killed you without law
or physic, and wanted to dub me a doctor—to make me an   140
accomplice.
SIR PET. Why, what is all this?
SIR BEN. We rejoice, Sir Peter, that the story of the duel is not true,
and are sincerely sorry for your other misfortunes.
SIR PET. So, so; all over the town already. *(Aside.)*
CRAB. Though, Sir Peter, you were certainly vastly to blame to marry
at all, at your years.
SIR PET. Sir, what business is that of yours?
MRS. CAN. Though, indeed, as Sir Peter made so good a husband, he's
very much to be pitied.   150
SIR PET. Plague on your pity, ma'am! I desire none of it.
SIR BEN. However, Sir Peter, you must not mind tha laughing and
jests you will meet with on this occasion.
SIR PET. Sir, I desire to be master in my own house.
CRAB. 'Tis no uncommon case, that's one comfort.
SIR PET. I insist on being left to myself: without ceremony, I insist on
your leaving my house directly!
MRS. CAN. Well, well, we are going; and depend on't, we'll make the
best report of you we can.
SIR PET. Leave my house!   160
CRAB. And tell how hardly you have been treated.
SIR PET. Leave my house!
SIR BEN. And how patiently you bear it.
SIR PET. Fiends! vipers! furies! Oh! that their own venom would
choke them!

Exeunt MRS. CANDOUR, SIR BENJAMIN BACKBITE, CRABTREE, &c.

SIR OLIV. They are very provoking indeed, Sir Peter.

Enter ROWLEY.

ROW. I heard high words—what has ruffled you, Sir Peter?
SIR PET. Pshaw! what signifies asking? Do I ever pass a day without
my vexations?
SIR OLIV. Well, I'm not inquisitive—I come only to tell you that I have   170
seen both my nephews in the manner we proposed.

SIR PET. A precious couple they are!

ROW. Yes, and Sir Oliver is convinced that your judgment was right, Sir Peter.

SIR OLIV. Yes, I find *Joseph* is indeed the man, after all.

ROW. Yes, as Sir Peter says, he's a man of sentiment.

SIR OLIV. And acts up to the sentiments he professes.

ROW. It certainly is edification to hear him talk.

SIR OLIV. Oh, he's a model for the young men of the age! But how's this, Sir Peter? you don't join in your friend Joseph's praise, as I expected.

SIR PET. Sir Oliver, we live in a damned wicked world, and the fewer we praise the better.

ROW. What! do *you* say so, Sir Peter, who were never mistaken in your life?

SIR PET. Pshaw! plague on you both! I see by your sneering you have heard the whole affair. I shall go mad among you!

ROW. Then, to fret you no longer, Sir Peter, we are indeed acquainted with it all. I met Lady Teazle coming from Mr. Surface's, so humbled that she deigned to request me to be her advocate with you.

SIR PET. And does Sir Oliver know all too?

SIR OLIV. Every circumstance.

SIR PET. What, of the closet—and the screen, hey?

SIR OLIV. Yes, yes, and the little French milliner. Oh, I have been vastly diverted with the story! ha! ha!

SIR PET. 'Twas very pleasant.

SIR OLIV. I never laughed more in my life, I assure you: ha! ha!

SIR PET. O, vastly diverting! ha! ha!

ROW. To be sure, Joseph with his sentiments! ha! ha!

SIR PET. Yes, yes, his sentiments! ha! ha! A hypocritical villain!

SIR OLIV. Aye, and that rogue Charles to pull Sir Peter out of the closet: ha! ha!

SIR PET. Ha! ha! 'twas devilish entertaining, to be sure!

SIR OLIV. Ha! ha! Egad, Sir Peter, I should like to have seen your face when the screen was thrown down: ha! ha!

SIR PET. Yes, yes, my face when the screen was thrown down: ha! ha! Oh, I must never show my head again!

SIR OLIV. But come, come, it isn't fair to laugh at you neither, my old friend—though, upon my soul, I can't help it.

SIR PET. Oh, pray don't restrain your mirth on my account—it does not hurt me at all! I laugh at the whole affair myself. Yes, yes, I think being a standing jest for all one's acquaintances a very happy situation. O yes, and then of a morning to read the paragraphs about Mr. S——, Lady T——, and Sir P——, will be so entertaining!

ROW. Without affectation, Sir Peter, you may despise the ridicule of fools. But I see Lady Teazle going towards the next room; I am sure you must desire a reconciliation as earnestly as she does.

SIR OLIV. Perhaps my being here prevents her coming to you. Well, I'll leave honest Rowley to mediate between you; but he must bring you all presently to Mr. Surface's, where I am now returning, if not to reclaim a libertine, at least to expose hypocrisy.

SIR PET. Ah! I'll be present at your discovering yourself there with all my heart—though 'tis a vile unlucky place for discoveries!
ROW. We'll follow. (*Exit* SIR OLIVER SURFACE.)
SIR PET. She is not coming here, you see, Rowley.
ROW. No, but she has left the door of that room open, you perceive. See, she is in tears!
SIR PET. Certainly a little mortification appears very becoming in a wife! Don't you think it will do her good to let her pine a little?
ROW. Oh, this is ungenerous in you! 230
SIR PET. Well, I know not what to think. You remember, Rowley, the letter I found of hers, evidently intended for Charles!
ROW. A mere forgery, Sir Peter! laid in your way on purpose. This is one of the points which I intend *Snake* shall give you conviction on.
SIR PET. I wish I were once satisfied of that. She looks this way. What a remarkably elegant turn of the head she has! Rowley, I'll go to her.
ROW. Certainly.
SIR PET. Though, when it is known that we are reconciled, people will laugh at me ten times more!
ROW. Let them laugh, and retort their malice only by showing them 240 you are happy in spite of it.
SIR PET. I'faith, so I will! and, if I'm not mistaken, we may yet be the happiest couple in the country.
ROW. Nay, Sir Peter—he who once lays aside suspicion—
SIR PET. Hold, my dear Rowley! if you have any regard for me, never let me hear you utter anything like a sentiment—I have had enough of them to serve me the rest of my life.

Exeunt.

SCENE III

The library in Joseph Surface's house.

JOSEPH SURFACE *and* LADY SNEERWELL.

LADY SNEER. Impossible! Will not Sir Peter immediately be reconciled to Charles, and of consequence no longer oppose his union with Maria? The thought is distraction to me!
JOS. SURF. Can passion furnish a remedy?
LADY SNEER. No, nor cunning either. Oh, I was a fool, an idiot, to league with such a blunderer!
JOS. SURF. Sure, Lady Sneerwell, *I* am the greatest sufferer; yet you see I bear the accident with calmness.
LADY SNEER. Because the disappointment doesn't reach your *heart;* your *interest* only attached you to Maria. Had you felt for *her* what *I* 10 have for that ungrateful libertine, neither your temper nor hypocrisy could prevent your showing the sharpness of your vexation.
JOS. SURF. But why should your reproaches fall on *me* for this disappointment?
LADY SNEER. Are you not the cause of it? What had you to do to

bate in your pursuit of Maria to pervert Lady Teazle by the way? Had you not a sufficient field for your roguery in blinding Sir Peter, and supplanting your brother? I hate such an avarice of crimes; 'tis an unfair monopoly, and never prospers.

JOS. SURF. Well, I admit I have been to blame. I confess I deviated from the direct road of wrong, but I don't think we're so totally defeated neither.

LADY SNEER. No!

JOS. SURF. You tell me you have made a trial of Snake since we met, and that you still believe him faithful to us—

LADY SNEER. I do believe so.

JOS. SURF. And that he has undertaken, should it be necessary, to swear and prove that Charles is at this time contracted by vows and honor to your ladyship—which some of his former letters to you will serve to support?

LADY SNEER. This, indeed, might have assisted.

JOS. SURF. Come, come; it is not too late yet.—*(Knocking at the door.)* But hark! this is probably my uncle, Sir Oliver: retire to that room; we'll consult farther when he's gone.

LADY SNEER. Well! but if *he* should find you out too—

JOS. SURF. Oh, I have no fear of that. Sir Peter will hold his tongue for his own credit['s] sake—and you may depend on't I shall soon discover Sir Oliver's weak side!

LADY SNEER. I have no diffidence of your abilities—only be constant to one roguery at a time. *(Exit.)*

JOS. SURF. I will, I will! So! 'tis confounded hard, after such bad fortune, to be baited by one's confederate in evil. Well, at all events, my character is so much better than Charles's, that I certainly—hey! —what!—this is not *Sir Oliver,* but old *Stanley* again! Plague on't! that he should return to tease me just now! We shall have Sir Oliver come and find him here—and—

Enter SIR OLIVER SURFACE.

Gad's life, Mr. Stanley, why have you come back to plague me just at this time? You must not stay now, upon my word.

SIR OLIV. Sir, I hear your uncle Oliver is expected here, and though he has been so penurious to *you,* I'll try what he'll do for *me.*

JOS. SURF. Sir, 'tis impossible for you to stay now, so I must beg— Come any other time, and I promise you, you shall be assisted.

SIR OLIV. No: Sir Oliver and I must be acquainted.

JOS. SURF. Zounds, sir! then I insist on your quitting the room directly.

SIR OLIV. Nay, sir!

JOS. SURF. Sir, I insist on't!—Here, William! show this gentleman out. Since you compel me, sir—not one moment—this is such insolence! *(Going to push him out.)*

Enter CHARLES SURFACE.

CHAS. SURF. Heyday! what's the matter now? What the devil, have
   you got hold of my little broker here? Zounds, brother, don't hurt
   little Premium. What's the matter, my little fellow?
JOS. SURF. So! he has been with you, too, has he?
CHAS. SURF. To be sure he has! Why, 'tis as honest a little—But sure,
   Joseph, you have not been borrowing money too, have you?
JOS. SURF. Borrowing! no! But, brother, you know here we expect
   Sir Oliver every—
CHAS. SURF. O gad, that's true! Noll mustn't find the little broker
   here, to be sure.
JOS. SURF. Yet, *Mr. Stanley* insists—
CHAS. SURF. Stanley! why his name is *Premium*.
JOS. SURF. No, no, *Stanley*.
CHAS. SURF. No, no, *Premium*.
JOS. SURF. Well, no matter which—but—
CHAS. SURF. Aye, aye, Stanley or Premium, 'tis the same thing, as you
   say; for I suppose he goes by half [a] hundred names, besides A.B.'s
   at the coffee-houses.
JOS. SURF. Death! here's Sir Oliver at the door. *(Knocking again.)* Now
   I beg, Mr. Stanley—
CHAS. SURF. Aye, and I beg, Mr. Premium—
SIR OLIV. Gentlemen—
JOS. SURF. Sir, by heaven you shall go!
CHAS. SURF. Aye, out with him, certainly.
SIR OLIV. This violence—
JOS. SURF. 'Tis your own fault.
CHAS. SURF. Out with him, to be sure. *(Both forcing* SIR OLIVER *out.)*

Enter SIR PETER *and* LADY TEAZLE, MARIA, *and* ROWLEY.

SIR PET. My old friend, Sir Oliver—hey! What in the name of wonder!
   —Here are dutiful nephews!—assault their uncle at the first visit!
LADY TEAZ. Indeed, Sir Oliver, 'twas well we came in to rescue you.
ROW. Truly it was; for I perceive, Sir Oliver, the character of old
   Stanley was no protection to you.
SIR OLIV. Nor of Premium either: the necessities of the *former* could
   not extort a shilling from *that* benevolent gentleman; and now, egad,
   I stood a chance of faring worse than my ancestors, and being
   knocked down without being bid for.

After a pause, JOSEPH *and* CHARLES *turning to each other.*

JOS. SURF. Charles!
CHAS. SURF. Joseph!
JOS. SURF. 'Tis now complete!
CHAS. SURF. Very!
SIR OLIV. Sir Peter, my friend, and Rowley too—look on that elder
   nephew of mine. You know what he has already received from my
   bounty; and you know also how gladly I would have regarded half my
   fortune as held in trust for him—judge, then, my disappointment in

discovering him to be destitute of truth—charity—and gratitude!
SIR PET. Sir Oliver, I should be more surprised at this declaration, if I had not myself found him selfish, treacherous, and hypocritical!
LADY TEAZ. And if the gentleman pleads not guilty to these, pray let him call *me* to his character.
SIR PET. Then, I believe, we need add no more.—If he knows himself, he will consider it as the most perfect punishment that he is known to the world.
CHAS. SURF. *(aside).* If they talk this way to *Honesty,* what will they say to *me,* by and be?

SIR PETER, LADY TEAZLE, *and* MARIA *retire.*

SIR OLIV. As for that prodigal, his brother, there—
CHAS. SURF. *(aside).* Aye, now comes my turn: the damned family pictures will ruin me!
JOS. SURF. Sir Oliver!—uncle!—will you honor me with a hearing?
CHAS. SURF. *(aside).* Now if Joseph would make one of his long speeches, I might recollect myself a little.
SIR OLIV. (*to* JOSEPH SURFACE). I suppose you would undertake to justify yourself entirely?
JOS. SURF. I trust I could.
SIR OLIV. Pshaw!—Well, sir! and *you* (*to* CHARLES) could justify yourself too, I suppose?
CHAS. SURF. Not that I know of, Sir Oliver.
SIR OLIV. What!—Little Premium has been let too much into the secret, I presume?
CHAS. SURF. True, sir; but they were family secrets, and should never be mentioned again, you know.
ROW. Come, Sir Oliver, I know you cannot speak of Charles's follies with anger.
SIR OLIV. Odd's heart, no more I can—nor with gravity either. Sir Peter, do you know the rogue bargained with me for all his ancestors—sold me judges and generals by the foot—and maiden aunts as cheap as broken china.
CHAS. SURF. To be sure, Sir Oliver, I did make a little free with the family canvas, that's the truth on't. My ancestors may certainly rise in evidence against me, there's no denying it; but believe me sincere when I tell you—and upon my soul I would not say it if I was not—that if I do not appear mortified at the exposure of my follies, it is because I feel at this moment the warmest satisfaction in seeing you, my liberal benefactor.
SIR OLIV. Charles, I believe you. Give me your hand again; the ill-looking little fellow over the settee has made your peace.
CHAS. SURF. Then, sir, my gratitude to the original is still increased.
LADY TEAZ. (*pointing to* MARIA). Yet, I believe, Sir Oliver, here is one whom Charles is still more anxious to be reconciled to.
SIR OLIV. Oh, I have heard of his attachment there; and, with the young lady's pardon, if I construe right—that blush—
SIR PET. Well, child, speak your sentiments.

MARIA. Sir, I have little to say, but that I shall rejoice to hear that he is happy; for me, whatever claim I had to his affection, I willingly resign it to one who has a better title.

CHAS. SURF. How, Maria!

SIR PET. Heyday! what's the mystery now? While he appeared an incorrigible rake, you would give your hand to no one else; and now that he is likely to reform, I warrant you won't have him.

MARIA. His own heart—and Lady Sneerwell know the cause.

CHAS. SURF. Lady Sneerwell!

JOS. SURF. Brother, it is with great concern I am obliged to speak on this point, but my regard to justice compels me, and Lady Sneerwell's injuries can no longer be concealed. *(Goes to the door.)*

Enter LADY SNEERWELL.

SIR PET. So! another French milliner!—Egad, he has one in every room in the house, I suppose!

LADY SNEER. Ungrateful Charles! Well may you be surprised, and feel for the indelicate situation which your perfidy has forced me into.

CHAS. SURF. Pray, uncle, is this another plot of yours? For, as I have life, I don't understand it.

JOS. SURF. I believe, sir, there is but the evidence of one person more necessary to make it extremely clear.

SIR PET. And that person, I imagine, is Mr. Snake.—Rowley, you were perfectly right to bring him with us, and pray let him appear.

ROW. Walk in, Mr. Snake.

Enter SNAKE.

I thought his testimony might be wanted; however, it happens unluckily, that he comes to confront Lady Sneerwell, and not to support her.

LADY SNEER. Villain! Treacherous to me at last! *(Aside.)*—Speak, fellow, have *you* too conspired against me?

SNAKE. I beg your ladyship ten thousand pardons: you paid me extremely liberally for the lie in question; but I have unfortunately been offered double to speak the truth.

SIR PET. Plot and counterplot, egad—I wish your ladyship joy of the success of your negotiation.

LADY SNEER. The torments of shame and disappointment on you all!

LADY TEAZ. Hold, Lady Sneerwell—before you go, let me thank you for the trouble you and that gentleman have taken, in writing letters to me from Charles, and answering them yourself; and let me also request you to make my respects to the Scandalous College, of which you are president, and inform them, that Lady Teazle, licentiate, begs leave to return the diploma they granted her, as she leaves off practice, and kills characters no longer.

LADY SNEER. You too, madam!—provoking—insolent! May your husband live these fifty years! *(Exit.)*

SIR PET. Oons! what a fury!
LADY TEAZ. A malicious creature, indeed!
SIR PET. Hey! not for her last wish?
LADY TEAZ. Oh, no!
SIR OLIV. Well, sir, and what have you to say now?
JOS. SURF. Sir, I am so confounded, to find that Lady *Sneerwell* could be guilty of suborning Mr. *Snake* in this manner, to impose on us all, that I know not what to say; however, lest her revengeful spirit should prompt her to injure my brother, I had certainly better follow her directly. *(Exit.)*   200
SIR PET. Moral to the last drop!
SIR OLIV. Aye, and marry her, Joseph, if you can.—Oil and vinegar, egad! you'll do very well together.
ROW. I believe we have no more occasion for Mr. Snake at present.
SNAKE. Before I go, I beg pardon once for all, for whatever uneasiness I have been the humble instrument of causing to the parties present.   210
SIR PET. Well, well, you have made atonement by a good deed at last.
SNAKE. But I must request of the company, that it shall never be known.
SIR PET. Hey! what the plague! are you ashamed of having done a right thing once in your life?
SNAKE. Ah, sir,—consider I live by the badness of my character—I have nothing but my infamy to depend on! and, if it were once known that I had been betrayed into an honest action, I should lose every friend I have in the world.
SIR OLIV. Well, well—we'll not traduce you by saying anything in your praise, never fear.   220

Exit SNAKE.

SIR PET. There's a precious rogue! yet that fellow is a writer and a critic!
LADY TEAZ. See, Sir Oliver, there needs no persuasion now to reconcile your nephew and Maria.

CHARLES *and* MARIA *apart.*

SIR OLIV. Aye, aye, that's as it should be, and, egad, we'll have the wedding to-morrow morning.
CHAS. SURF. Thank you, my dear uncle.
SIR PET. What, you rogue! don't you ask the girl's consent first?
CHAS. SURF. Oh, I have done that a long time—above a minute ago— and she has looked yes.   230
MARIA. For shame, Charles!—I protest, Sir Peter, there has not been a word—
SIR OLIV. Well, then, the fewer the better—may your love for each other never know abatement.
SIR PET. And may you live as happily together as Lady Teazle and I— intend to do!
CHAS. SURF. Rowley, my old friend, I am sure you congratulate me;

and I suspect that I owe you much.
SIR OLIV. You do, indeed, Charles. 240
ROW. If my efforts to serve you had not succeeded you would have been in my debt for the attempt—but deserve to be happy—and you overpay me.
SIR PET. Aye, honest Rowley always said you would reform.
CHAS. SURF. Why as to reforming, Sir Peter, I'll make no promises, and that I take to be a proof that I intend to set about it.—But here shall be my monitor—my gentle guide.—Ah! can I leave the virtuous path those eyes illumine?

Though thou, dear maid, shouldst wa[i]ve thy *beauty's* sway,
Thou still must rule, because I *will* obey: 250
An humbled fugitive from Folly view,
No sanctuary near but *Love* and—You;

To the audience.

You can, indeed, each anxious fear remove,
For even *Scandal* dies, if *you* approve.

FINIS.

Questions for Discussion

1. In the opening dialogue between Lady Sneerwell and Snake, Sheridan makes his satiric (see page 506) purpose abundantly clear. What advantages and disadvantages arise from the author's early revelation of intention? Might the same be true of a student composition?

2. *The School for Scandal* is ordinarily classified as a comedy of manners (see page 503). What do Sheridan's choices of subject and characters indicate about the audience he anticipated? Does the nature of this audience indicate that the content of the play might have no general appeal? What does Sheridan do to overcome this problem? How successful is he?

3. Discuss Sheridan's selection of proper names. Is this an economical means of establishing character? Explain. What are its potential disadvantages?

4. Certain characters (e.g., Snake) undergo radical changes in the play's resolution. Are the characters introduced in such a way as to allow for these later alterations? Explain.

5. Did you identify with any of the characters as they were introduced? Did you sympathize with any of them? If not, what kept you from sympathizing? Did your sympathies for certain characters grow as the play progressed? If so, why? How effective is a play (or composition) in which the audience fails to identify with certain characters (or the writer)? Explain.

Suggested Theme Topics

1. Compare and contrast the satirical methods of Sheridan and Shaw.

2. Discuss *The School for Scandal* as comedy of manners.

3. Discuss the differing approaches to drama taken by the anonymous author of *Everyman* and Sheridan because of their differing audiences.

4. Discuss the effectiveness of Sheridan's selection of proper names to fit the personalities of his characters.

5. Write a theme in which you endeavor to make your readers identify with an especially embarrassing moment by showing that it might have happened to anyone.

George Bernard Shaw

George Bernard Shaw (1856-1950), a native of Ireland, is thought by many authorities to be second only to Shakespeare among English dramatists. Like many other Irish literary men, he moved to London at an early age and immediately devoted himself to writing, but without recognition or reward for almost a decade. During these early years his association with the Fabian Society was shaping a personal philosophy that was to distinguish him as thinker, social critic, reformer, and dramatist. Among his concerns—which would later become subjects for satiric treatment—were war, science, medicine, and hypocrisy (both personal and national). After a brief but successful journalistic fling, Shaw launched one of the world's most lengthy and prolific dramatic careers. His first major success was Arms and the Man *(1894); then followed (to name only a few of the most widely acclaimed)* Candida *(1898),* Caesar and Cleopatra *(1900),* The Devil's Disciple *(1900),* Man and Superman *(1903),* Major Barbara *(1905),* The Doctor's Dilemma *(1906),* Androcles and the Lion *(1913),* Pygmalion *(1914), and* Saint Joan *(1924). Shaw was awarded a Nobel Prize in 1925; but, displaying his usual unpredictable responses, he refused it. Although his creativity waned in the 1930s and '40s, Shaw never stopped writing. His last play,* Buoyant Billions *(1949), was written when he was ninety-four, only a year before his death.*

Although the intention of Arms and the Man *is obviously comic, it also contains some social commentary. In reading the play, try to deduce both the nature of the anticipated audience and the particularly human responses that Shaw sought to satirize.*

ARMS AND THE MAN

ACT I

Night. A lady's bedchamber in Bulgaria, in a small town near the Dragoman Pass, late in November in the year 1885. Through an open window with a little balcony a peak of the Balkans, wonderfully white and beautiful in the starlit snow, seems quite close at hand, though it is really miles away. The interior of the room is not like anything to be seen in the west of Europe. It is half rich Bulgarian, half cheap Viennese. Above the head of the bed, which stands against a little wall cutting off the left hand corner of the room, is a painted wooden shrine, blue and gold, with an ivory image of Christ, and a light hanging before it in a pierced metal ball suspended by three chains. The principal seat, placed towards the other side of the room and opposite the window, is a Turkish ottoman. The counterpane and hangings of the bed, the window curtains, the little carpet, and all the ornamental textile fabrics in the room are oriental and gorgeous: the paper on the walls is occidental and paltry. The washstand, against the wall on the side nearest the ottoman and window, consists of an enamelled iron basin with a pail beneath it in a painted metal frame, and a single towel on the rail at the side. The dressing table, between the bed and the window, is a common pine table, covered with a cloth of many colors, with an expensive toilet mirror on it. The door is on the side nearest the bed; and there is a chest of drawers between. This chest of drawers is also covered by a variegated native cloth; and on it there is a pile of paper backed novels, a box of chocolate creams, and a miniature easel with a large photograph of an extremely handsome officer, whose lofty bearing and magnetic glance can be felt even from the portrait. The room is lighted by a candle on the chest of drawers, and another on the dressing table with a box of matches beside it.

The window is hinged doorwise and stands wide open. Outside, a pair of wooden shutters, opening outwards, also stand open. On the balcony a young lady, intensely conscious of the romantic beauty of the night, and of the fact that her own youth and beauty are part of it, is gazing at the snowy Balkans. She is in her nightgown, well covered by a long mantle of furs, worth, on a moderate estimate, about three times the furniture of her room.

Her reverie is interrupted by her mother, CATHERINE PETKOFF, *a woman over forty, imperiously energetic, with magnificent black hair and eyes, who might be a very splendid specimen of the wife of a mountain farmer, but is determined to be a Viennese lady, and to that end wears a fashionable tea gown on all occasions.*

CATHERINE *(entering hastily, full of good news).* Raina! *(She pronounces it Rah-eena, with the stress on the ee.)* Raina! *(She goes to the bed, expecting to find* RAINA *there.)* Why, where—? (RAINA *looks into the room.*) Heavens, child! are you out in the night air instead of in your bed? Youll catch your death. Louka told me you were asleep.

RAINA *(dreamily).* I sent her away. I wanted to be alone. The stars are so beautiful! What is the matter?

CATHERINE. Such news! There has been a battle.

RAINA *(her eyes dilating).* Ah! *(She comes eagerly to* CATHERINE.*)*   10

CATHERINE. A great battle at Slivnitza! A victory! And it was won by Sergius.

RAINA *(with a cry of delight).* Ah! *(They embrace rapturously.)* Oh, mother! *(Then, with sudden anxiety)* Is father safe?

CATHERINE. Of course: he sends me the news. Sergius is the hero of the hour, the idol of the regiment.

RAINA. Tell me, tell me. How was it? *(Ecstatically)* Oh, mother! mother! mother! *(She pulls her mother down on the ottoman; and they kiss one another frantically.)*

CATHERINE *(with surging enthusiasm).* You cant guess how splendid   20 it is. A cavalry charge! think of that! He defied our Russian commanders—acted without orders—led a charge on his own responsibility—headed it himself—was the first man to sweep through their guns. Cant you see it, Raina: our gallant splendid Bulgarians with their swords and eyes flashing, thundering down like an avalanche and scattering the wretched Serbs and their dandified Austrian officers like chaff. And you! you kept Sergius waiting a year before you would be betrothed to him. Oh, if you have a drop of Bulgarian blood in your veins, you will worship him when he comes back.

RAINA. What will he care for my poor little worship after the acclamations of a whole army of heroes? But no matter: I am so happy! so proud! *(She rises and walks about excitedly.)* It proves that all our ideas were real after all.

CATHERINE *(indignantly)*. Our ideas real! What do you mean?

RAINA. Our ideas of what Sergius would do. Our patriotism. Our heroic ideals. I sometimes used to doubt whether they were anything but dreams. Oh, what faithless little creatures girls are! When I buckled on Sergius's sword he looked so noble: it was treason to think of disillusion or humiliation or failure. And yet—and yet—*(She sits down again suddenly.)* Promise me youll never tell him.

CATHERINE. Dont ask me for promises until I know what I'm promising.

RAINA. Well, it came into my head just as he was holding me in his arms and looking into my eyes, that perhaps we only had our heroic ideas because we are so fond of reading Byron and Pushkin, and because we were so delighted with the opera that season at Bucharest. Real life is so seldom like that! indeed never, as far as I knew it then. *(Remorsefully)* Only think, mother: I doubted him: I wondered whether all his heroic qualities and his soldiership might not prove mere imagination when he went into a real battle. I had an uneasy fear that he might cut a poor figure there beside all those clever officers from the Tsar's court

CATHERINE. A poor figure! Shame on you! The Serbs have Austrian officers who are just as clever as the Russians; but we have beaten them in every battle for all that.

RAINA. *(laughing and snuggling against her mother)*. Yes: I was only a prosaic little coward. Oh, to think that it was all true! that Sergius is just as splendid and noble as he looks! that the world is really a glorious world for women who can see its glory and men who can act its romance! What happiness! what unspeakable fulfilment!

They are interrupted by the entry of LOUKA, *a handsome proud girl in a pretty Bulgarian peasant's dress with double apron, so defiant that her servility to* RAINA *is almost insolent. She is afraid of* CATHERINE, *but even with her goes as far as she dares.*

LOUKA. If you please, madam, all the windows are to be closed and the shutters made fast. They say there may be shooting in the streets. (RAINA *and* CATHERINE *rise together, alarmed.*) The Serbs are being chased right back through the pass; and they say they may run into the town. Our cavalry will be after them; and our people will be ready for them, you may be sure, now theyre running away. *(She goes out on the balcony, and pulls the outside shutters to; then steps back into the room.)*

CATHERINE *(businesslike, her housekeeping instincts aroused).* I must see that everything is made safe downstairs.

RAINA. I wish our people were not so cruel. What glory is there in killing wretched fugitives?

CATHERINE. Cruel! Do you suppose they would hesitate to kill you—or worse?

RAINA *(to* LOUKA*).* Leave the shutters so that I can just close them if I hear any noise.

CATHERINE *(authoritatively, turning on her way to the door).* Oh no, dear: you must keep them fastened. You would be sure to drop off to sleep and leave them open. Make them fast, Louka.

LOUKA. Yes, madam. *(She fastens them.)*

RAINA. Don't be anxious about me. The moment I hear a shot, I shall blow out the candles and roll myself up in bed with my ears well covered.

CATHERINE. Quite the wisest thing you can do, my love. Goodnight.

RAINA. Goodnight. *(Her emotion comes back for a moment.)* Wish me joy. *(They kiss.)* This is the happiest night of my life—if only there are no fugitives.

CATHERINE. Go to bed, dear; and dont think of them. *(She goes out.)*

LOUKA *(secretly, to* RAINA*).* If you would like the shutters open, just give them a push like this *(she pushes them: they open: she pulls them to again).* One of them ought to be bolted at the bottom; but the bolt's gone.

RAINA *(with dignity, reproving her).* Thanks, Louka; but we must do what we are told. (LOUKA *makes a grimace.)* Goodnight.

LOUKA *(carelessly).* Goodnight. *(She goes out, swaggering.)*

RAINA, *left alone, takes off her fur cloak and throws it on the ottoman. Then she goes to the chest of drawers, and adores the portrait there with feelings that are beyond all expression. She does not kiss it or press it to her breast, or shew it any mark of bodily affection; but she takes it in her hands and elevates it, like a priestess.*

RAINA *(looking up at the picture).* Oh, I shall never be unworthy of you any more, my soul's hero: never, never, never. *(She replaces it reverently. Then she selects a novel from the little pile of books. She turns over the leaves dreamily; finds her page; turns the book inside out at it; and, with a happy sigh, gets into bed and prepares to read herself to sleep. But before abandoning herself to fiction, she raises her eyes once more, thinking of the blessed reality, and murmurs)* My hero! my hero!

A distant shot breaks the quiet of the night. She starts, listening; and two more shots, much nearer, follow, startling her so that she scrambles out of bed, and hastily blows out the candle on the chest of drawers. Then, putting her fingers in her ears, she runs to the dressing table, blows out the light there, and hurries back to bed in the dark, nothing being visible but the glimmer of the light in the pierced ball before the image, and the starlight seen through the slits at the top of the shutters. The firing breaks out again: there is a startling fusillade quite close at hand. Whilst it is still echoing, the shutters disappear, pulled open from without; and for an instant the rectangle of snowy starlight flashes out with the figure of a man silhouetted in black upon it. The shutters close immediately; and the room is dark again. But the silence is now broken by the sound of panting. Then there is a scratch; and the flame of a match is seen in the middle of the room.

RAINA *(crouching on the bed).* Who's there? *(The match is out instantly.)* Who's there? Who is that?

A MAN'S VOICE *(in the darkness, subduedly, but threateningly).* Sh—sh! Dont call out; or youll be shot. Be good; and no harm will happen to you. *(She is heard leaving her bed, and making for the door.)* Take care: it's no use trying to run away.

RAINA. But who—

THE VOICE *(warning).* Remember: if you raise your voice my revolver will go off. *(Commandingly.)* Strike a light and let me see you. Do you hear. *(Another moment of silence and darkness as she retreats to the chest of drawers. Then she lights a candle; and the mystery is at an end. He is a man of about 35, in a deplorable plight, bespattered with mud and blood and snow, his belt and the strap of his revolver-case keeping together the torn ruins of the blue tunic of a Serbian artillery officer. All that the candlelight and his unwashed unkempt condition make it possible to discern is that he is of middling stature and undistinguished appearance, with strong neck and shoulders, roundish obstinate looking head covered with short crisp bronze curls, clear quick eyes and good brows and mouth, hopelessly prosaic nose like that of a strong minded baby, trim soldierlike carriage and energetic manner, and with all his wits about him in spite of his desperate predicament: even with a sense of the humor of it, without, however, the least intention of trifling with it or throwing away a chance. Reckoning up what he can guess about* RAINA: *her age, her social position, her character, and the extent to which she is frightened, he continues, more politely but still most determinedly.)* Excuse my disturbing you; but you recognize my uniform? Serb! If I'm caught I shall be killed. *(Menacingly)* Do you understand that?

RAINA. Yes.

THE MAN. Well, I dont intend to get killed if I can help it. *(Still more formidably)* Do you understand that? *(He locks the door quickly but quietly.)*

RAINA *(disdainfully).* I suppose not. *(She draws herself up superbly, and looks him straight in the face, adding, with cutting emphasis)* Some soldiers, I know, are afraid to die.

THE MAN *(with grim goodhumor).* All of them, dear lady, all of them, believe me. It is our duty to live as long as we can. Now, if you raise an alarm—

RAINA *(cutting him short).* You will shoot me. How do you know that *I* am afraid to die?

THE MAN *(cunningly).* Ah; but suppose I dont shoot you, what will happen then? A lot of your cavalry will burst into this pretty room of yours and slaughter me here like a pig; for I'll fight like a demon: they shant get me into the street to amuse themselves with: I know what they are. Are you prepared to receive that sort of company in your present undress? (RAINA, *suddenly conscious of her nightgown, instinctively shrinks, and gathers it more closely about her neck. He watches her, and adds, pitilessly)* Hardly presentable, eh? *(She turns to the ottoman. He raises his pistol instantly, and cries)* Stop! *(She stops.)* Where are you going?

RAINA *(with dignified patience).* Only to get my cloak.

THE MAN *(passing swiftly to the ottoman and snatching the cloak).* A good idea! I'll keep the cloak; and youll take care that nobody comes in and sees you without it. This is a better weapon than the revolver: eh? *(He throws the pistol down on the ottoman.)*

RAINA *(revolted).* It is not the weapon of a gentleman!

THE MAN. It's good enough for a man with only you to stand between him and death. *(As they look at one another for a moment,* RAINA *hardly able to believe that even a Serbian officer can be so cynically and selfishly unchivalrous, they are startled by a sharp fusillade in the street. The chill of imminent death hushes the man's voice as he adds)* Do you hear? If you are going to bring those blackguards in on me you shall receive them as you are.

Clamor and disturbance. The pursuers in the street batter at the house door, shouting Open the door! Open the door! Wake up, will you! *A man servant's voice calls to them angrily from within* This is Major Petkoff's house: you cant come in here; *but a renewal of the clamor, and a torrent of blows on the door, end with his letting a chain down with a clank, followed by a rush of heavy footsteps and a din of triumphant yells, dominated at last by the voice of* CATHERINE, *indignantly addressing an officer with* What does this mean, sir? Do you know where you are? *The noise subsides suddenly.*

LOUKA *(outside, knocking at the bedroom door).* My lady! my lady! get up quick and open the door. If you dont they will break it down.

The fugitive throws up his head with the gesture of a man who sees that it is all over with him, and drops the manner he has been assuming to intimidate RAINA.

THE MAN *(sincerely and kindly).* No use, dear: I'm done for. *(Flinging the cloak to her)* Quick! wrap yourself up: theyre coming.

RAINA. Oh, thank you. *(She wraps herself up with intense relief.)*

THE MAN *(between his teeth).* Dont mention it.

RAINA *(anxiously).* What will you do?

THE MAN *(grimly).* The first man in will find out. Keep out of the way; and dont look. It wont last long; but it will not be nice.

(He draws his sabre and faces the door, waiting.)
RAINA *(impulsively).* I'll help you. I'll save you.
THE MAN. You cant.
RAINA. I can. I'll hide you. *(She drags him towards the window.)* Here! behind the curtains.
THE MAN *(yielding to her).* Theres just half a chance, if you keep your head.
RAINA *(drawing the curtain before him).* S-sh! *(She makes for the ottoman.)*
THE MAN *(putting out his head).* Remember—
RAINA *(running back to him).* Yes?
THE MAN. —nine soldiers out of ten are born fools.
RAINA. Oh! *(She draws the curtain angrily before him.)*
THE MAN *(looking out at the other side).* If they find me, I promise you a fight: a devil of a fight.

She stamps at him. He disappears hastily. She takes off her cloak, and throws it across the foot of the bed. Then, with a sleepy, disturbed air, she opens the door. LOUKA *enters excitedly.*

LOUKA. One of those beasts of Serbs has been seen climbing up the waterpipe to your balcony. Our men want to search for him; and they are so wild and drunk and furious. *(She makes for the other side of the room to get as far from the door as possible).* My lady says you are to dress at once, and to—*(She sees the revolver lying on the ottoman, and stops, petrified.)*
RAINA *(as if annoyed at being disturbed).* They shall not search here. Why have they been let in?
CATHERINE *(coming in hastily).* Raina, darling: are you safe? Have you seen anyone or heard anything?
RAINA. I heard the shooting. Surely the soldiers will not dare come in here?
CATHERINE. I have found a Russian officer, thank Heaven: he knows Sergius. *(Speaking through the door to someone outside)* Sir: will you come in now. My daughter will receive you.

A young Russian officer, in Bulgarian uniform, enters, sword in hand.

OFFICER *(with soft feline politeness and stiff military carriage).* Good evening, gracious lady. I am sorry to intrude; but there is a Serb hiding on the balcony. Will you and the gracious lady your mother please to withdraw whilst we search?
RAINA *(petulantly).* Nonsense, sir: you can see that there is no one on the balcony. *(She throws the shutters wide open and stands with her back to the curtain where the man is hidden, pointing to the moonlit balcony. A couple of shots are fired right under the window; and a bullet shatters the glass opposite* RAINA, *who winks and gasps, but stands her ground; whilst* CATHERINE *screams, and the officer, with a cry of* Take care! *rushes to the balcony.)*
THE OFFICER *(on the balcony, shouting savagely down to the street).*

Cease firing there, you fools: do you hear? Cease firing. damn you! *(He glares down for a moment; then turns to* RAINA, *trying to resume his polite manner.)* Could anyone have got in without your knowledge? Were you asleep?

RAINA. No: I have not been to bed.

THE OFFICER *(impatiently, coming back into the room)*. Your neighbors have their heads so full of runaway Serbs that they see them everywhere. *(Politely)* Gracious lady: a thousand pardons. Goodnight. *(Military bow, which* RAINA *returns coldly. Another to* CATHERINE, *who follows him out.)*

RAINA *closes the shutters. She turns and sees* LOUKA, *who has been watching the scene curiously.*

RAINA. Dont leave my mother, Louka, until the soldiers go away.

LOUKA *glances at* RAINA, *at the ottoman, at the curtain; then purses her lips secretively, laughs insolently, and goes out.* RAINA, *highly offended by this demonstration, follows her to the door, and shuts it behind her with a slam, locking it violently. The man immediately steps out from behind the curtain, sheathing his sabre, and closes the shutters. Then, dismissing the danger from his mind in a businesslike way, he comes affably to* RAINA.

THE MAN. A narrow shave; but a miss is as good as a mile. Dear young lady: your servant to the death. I wish for your sake I had joined the Bulgarian army instead of the other one. I am not a native Serb.

RAINA *(haughtily)*. No: you are one of the Austrians who set the Serbs on to rob us of our national liberty, and who officer their army for them. We hate them!

THE MAN. Austrian! not I. Dont hate me, dear young lady. I am a Swiss, fighting merely as a professional soldier. I joined the Serbs because they came first on the road from Switzerland. Be generous: youve beaten us hollow.

RAINA. Have I not been generous?

THE MAN. Noble! Heroic! But I'm not saved yet. This particular rush will soon pass through; but the pursuit will go on all night by fits and starts. I must take my chance to get off in a quiet interval. *(Pleasantly)* You dont mind my waiting just a minute or two, do you?

RAINA *(putting on her most genteel society manner)*. Oh, not at all. Wont you sit down?

THE MAN. Thanks. *(He sits on the foot of the bed.)*

RAINA *walks with studied elegance to the ottoman and sits down. Unfortunately she sits on the pistol, and jumps up with a shriek. The man, all nerves, shies like a frightened horse to the other side of the room.*

THE MAN *(irritably)*. Dont frighten me like that. What is it?

RAINA. Your revolver! It was staring that officer in the face all the time. What an escape!

THE MAN *(vexed at being unnecessarily terrified).* Oh, is that all?
RAINA *(staring at him rather superciliously as she conceives a poorer and poorer opinion of him, and feels proportionately more and more at her ease).* I am sorry I frightened you. *(She takes up the pistol and hands it to him.)* Pray take it to protect yourself against me.
THE MAN *(grinning wearily at the sarcasm as he takes the pistol).* No use, dear young lady: theres nothing in it. It's not loaded. *(He makes a grimace at it, and drops it disparagingly into his revolver case.)*
RAINA. Load it by all means.
THE MAN. Ive no ammunition. What use are cartridges in battle? I always carry chocolate instead; and I finished the last cake of that hours ago.
RAINA *(outraged in her most cherished ideals of manhood).* Chocolate! Do you stuff your pockets with sweets—like a schoolboy—even in the field?
THE MAN *(grinning).* Yes: isnt it contemptible? *(Hungrily)* I wish I had some now.
RAINA. Allow me. *(She sails away scornfully to the chest of drawers, and returns with the box of confectionery in her hand.)* I am sorry I have eaten them all except these. *(She offers him the box.)*
THE MAN *(ravenously).* Youre an angel! *(He gobbles the contents.)* Creams! Delicious! *(He looks anxiously to see whether there are any more. There are none: he can only scrape the box with his fingers and suck them. When that nourishment is exhausted he accepts the inevitable with pathetic goodhumor, and says, with grateful emotion)* Bless you, dear lady! You can always tell an old soldier by the inside of his holsters and cartridge boxes. The young ones carry pistols and cartridges: the old ones, grub. Thank you. *(He hands back the box. She snatches it contemptuously from him and throws it away. He shies again, as if she had meant to strike him.)* Ugh! Dont do things so suddenly, gracious lady. It's mean to revenge yourself because I frightened you just now.
RAINA *(loftily).* Frighten me! Do you know, sir, that though I am only a woman, I think I am at heart as brave as you.
THE MAN. I should think so. You havnt been under fire for three days as I have. I can stand two days without shewing it much; but no man can stand three days: I'm as nervous as a mouse. *(He sits down on the ottoman, and takes his head in his hands.)* Would you like to see me cry?
RAINA *(alarmed).* No.
THE MAN. If you would, all you have to do is to scold me just as if I were a little boy and you my nurse. If I were in camp now, theyd play all sorts of tricks on me.
RAINA *(a little moved).* I'm sorry. I wont scold you. *(Touched by the sympathy in her tone, he raises his head and looks gratefully at her: she immediately draws back and says stiffly)* You must excuse me: our soldiers are not like that. *(She moves away from the ottoman.)*
THE MAN. Oh yes they are. There are only two sorts of soldiers: old ones and young ones. Ive served fourteen years: half of your fellows never smelt powder before. Why, how is it that youve just beaten us?

Sheer ignorance of the art of war, nothing else. *(Indignantly)* I never saw anything so unprofessional.

RAINA *(ironically)*. Oh! was it unprofessional to beat you?

THE MAN. Well, come! is it professional to throw a regiment of cavalry on a battery of machine guns, with the dead certainty that if the guns go off not a horse or man will ever get within fifty yards of the fire? I couldnt believe my eyes when I saw it.

RAINA *(eagerly turning to him, as all her enthusiasm and her dreams of glory rush back on her)*. Did you see the great cavalry charge? Oh, tell me about it. Describe it to me.

THE MAN. You never saw a cavalry charge, did you?

RAINA. How could I?

THE MAN. Ah, perhaps not. No: of course not! Well, it's a funny sight. It's like slinging a handful of peas against a window pane: first one comes; then two or three close behind him; and then all the rest in a lump.

RAINA. *(her eyes dilating as she raises her clasped hands ecstatically)*. Yes, first One! the bravest of the brave!

THE MAN *(prosaically)*. Hm! you should see the poor devil pulling at his horse.

RAINA. Why should he pull at his horse?

THE MAN *(impatient of so stupid a question)*. It's running away with him, of course: do you suppose the fellow wants to get there before the others and be killed? Then they all come. You can tell the young ones by their wildness and their slashing. The old ones come bunched up under the number one guard: they know that theyre mere projectiles, and that it's no use trying to fight. The wounds are mostly broken knees, from the horses cannoning together.

RAINA. Ugh! But I dont believe the first man is a coward. I know he is a hero!

THE MAN *(goodhumoredly)*. Thats what youd have said if youd seen the first man in the charge today.

RAINA *(breathless, forgiving him everything)*. Ah, I knew it! Tell me. Tell me about him.

THE MAN. He did it like an operatic tenor. A regular handsome fellow, with flashing eyes and lovely moustache, shouting his war-cry and charging like Don Quixote at the windmills. We did laugh.

RAINA. You dared to laugh!

THE MAN. Yes; but when the sergeant ran up as white as a sheet, and told us theyd sent us the wrong ammunition, and that we couldnt fire a round for the next ten minutes, we laughed at the other side of our mouths. I never felt so sick in my life; though Ive been in one or two very tight places. And I hadnt even a revolver cartridge: only chocolate. We'd no bayonets: nothing. Of course, they just cut us to bits. And there was Don Quixote flourishing like a drum major, thinking he'd done the cleverest thing ever known, whereas he ought to be courtmartialled for it. Of all the fools ever let loose on a field of battle, that man must be the very maddest. He and his regiment simply committed suicide; only the pistol missed fire: thats all.

RAINA *(deeply wounded, but steadfastly loyal to her ideals)*. Indeed!

Would you know him again if you saw him?
THE MAN.   Shall I ever forget him!

She again goes to the chest of drawers. He watches her with a vague hope that she may have something more for him to eat. She takes the portrait from its stand and brings it to him.

RAINA.   That is a photograph of the gentleman—the patriot and hero—to whom I am betrothed.
THE MAN *(recognizing it with a shock)*.   I'm really very sorry. *(Looking at her)* Was it fair to lead me on? *(He looks at the portrait again)* Yes: thats Don Quixote: not a doubt of it. *(He stifles a laugh.)*
RAINA *(quickly)*.   Why do you laugh?
THE MAN *(apologetic, but still greatly tickled)*.   I didnt laugh, I assure you. At least I didnt mean to. But when I think of him charging the windmills and imagining he was doing the finest thing—*(He chokes with suppressed laughter.)*
RAINA *(sternly)*.   Give me back the portrait, sir.
THE MAN *(with sincere remorse)*.   Of course. Certainly. I'm really very sorry. *(He hands her the picture. She deliberately kisses it and looks him straight in the face before returning to the chest of drawers to replace it. He follows her, apologizing.)* Perhaps I'm quite wrong, you know: no doubt I am. Most likely he had got wind of the cartridge business somehow, and knew it was a safe job.
RAINA.   That is to say, he was a pretender and a coward! You did not dare say that before.
THE MAN *(with a comic gesture of despair)*.   It's no use, dear lady: I cant make you see it from the professional point of view. *(As he turns away to get back to the ottoman, a couple of distant shots threaten renewed trouble.)*
RAINA *(sternly, as she sees him listening to the shots)*.   So much the better for you!
THE MAN *(turning)*.   How?
RAINA.   You are my enemy; and you are at my mercy. What would I do if I were a professional soldier?
THE MAN.   Ah, true, dear young lady: youre always right. I know how good youve been to me: to my last hour I shall remember those three chocolate creams. It was unsoldierly; but it was angelic.
RAINA *(coldly)*.   Thank you. And now I will do a soldierly thing. You cannot stay here after what you have just said about my future husband; but I will go out on the balcony and see whether it is safe for you to climb down into the street. *(She turns to the window.)*
THE MAN *(changing countenance)*.   Down that waterpipe! Stop! Wait! I cant! I darent! The very thought of it makes me giddy. I came up it fast enough with death behind me. But to face it now in cold blood—! *(He sinks on the ottoman.)* It's no use: I give up: I'm beaten. Give the alarm. *(He drops his head on his hands in the deepest dejection.)*
RAINA *(disarmed by pity)*.   Come: dont be disheartened. *(She stoops over him almost maternally: he shakes his head.)* Oh, you are a very poor soldier: a chocolate cream soldier! Come, cheer up! it takes less

courage to climb down than to face capture: remember that.

THE MAN *(dreamily, lulled by her voice).* No: capture only means death; and death is sleep: oh, sleep, sleep, sleep, undisturbed sleep! Climbing down the pipe means doing something—exerting myself—thinking! Death ten times over first.

RAINA *(softly and wonderingly, catching the rhythm of his weariness).* Are you as sleepy as that?

THE MAN. Ive not had two hours undisturbed sleep since I joined. I havnt closed my eyes for forty-eight hours.

RAINA *(at her wit's end).* But what am I to do with you?

THE MAN *(staggering up, roused by her desperation).* Of course. I must do something. *(He shakes himself; pulls himself together; and speaks with rallied vigor and courage.)* You see, sleep or no sleep, hunger or no hunger, tired or not tired, you can always do a thing when you know it must be done. Well, that pipe must be got down: *(he hits himself on the chest)* do you hear that, you chocolate cream soldier? *(He turns to the window.)*

RAINA *(anxiously).* But if you fall?

THE MAN. I shall sleep as if the stones were a feather bed. Goodbye. *(He makes boldly for the window; and his hand is on the shutter when there is a terrible burst of firing in the street beneath.)*

RAINA *(rushing to him).* Stop! *(She seizes him recklessly, and pulls him quite round.)* Theyll kill you.

THE MAN *(coolly, but attentively).* Never mind: this sort of thing is all in my day's work. I'm bound to take my chance. *(Decisively)* Now do what I tell you. Put out the candles; so that they shant see the light when I open the shutters. And keep away from the window, whatever you do. If they see me theyre sure to have a shot at me.

RAINA *(clinging to him).* Theyre sure to see you: it's bright moonlight. I'll save you. Oh, how can you be so indifferent! You want me to save you, dont you?

THE MAN. I really dont want to be troublesome. *(She shakes him in her impatience.)* I am not indifferent, dear young lady, I assure you. But how is it to be done?

RAINA. Come away from the window. *(She takes him firmly back to the middle of the room. The moment she releases him he turns mechanically towards the window again. She seizes him and turns him back, exclaiming)* Please! *(He becomes motionless, like a hypnotized rabbit, his fatigue gaining fast on him. She releases him, and addresses him patronizingly.)* Now listen. You must trust to our hospitality. You do not yet know in whose house you are. I am a Petkoff.

THE MAN. A pet what?

RAINA *(rather indignantly).* I mean that I belong to the family of the Petkoffs, the richest and best known in our country.

THE MAN. Oh yes, of course. I beg your pardon. The Petkoffs, to be sure. How stupid of me!

RAINA. You know you never heard of them until this moment. How can you stoop to pretend!

THE MAN. Forgive me: I'm too tired to think; and the change of subject was too much for me. Dont scold me.

RAINA. I forgot. It might make you cry. *(He nods, quite seriously. She pouts and then resumes her patronizing tone.)* I must tell you that my father holds the highest command of any Bulgarian in our army. He is *(proudly)* a Major.

THE MAN *(pretending to be deeply impressed).* A Major! Bless me! Think of that!

RAINA. You shewed great ignorance in thinking that it was necessary to climb up to the balcony because ours is the only private house that has two rows of windows. There is a flight of stairs inside to get up and down by.

THE MAN. Stairs! How grand! You live in great luxury indeed, dear young lady.

RAINA. Do you know what a library is?

THE MAN. A library? A roomful of books?

RAINA. Yes. We have one, the only one in Bulgaria.

THE MAN. Actually a real library! I should like to see that.

RAINA *(affectedly).* I tell you these things to shew you that you are not in the house of ignorant country folk who would kill you the moment they saw your Serbian uniform, but among civilized people. We go to Bucharest every year for the opera season; and I have spent a whole month in Vienna.

THE MAN. I saw that, dear young lady. I saw at once that you knew the world.

RAINA. Have you ever seen the opera of Ernani?

THE MAN. Is that the one with the devil in it in red velvet, and a soldiers' chorus?

RAINA *(contemptuously).* No!

THE MAN *(stifling a heavy sigh of weariness).* Then I dont know it.

RAINA. I thought you might have remembered the great scene where Ernani, flying from his foes just as you are tonight, takes refuge in the castle of his bitterest enemy, an old Castilian noble. The noble refuses to give him up. His guest is sacred to him.

THE MAN *(quickly, waking up a little).* Have your people got that notion?

RAINA *(with dignity).* My mother and I can understand that notion, as you call it. And if instead of threatening me with your pistol as you did you had simply thrown yourself as a fugitive on our hospitality, you would have been as safe as in your father's house.

THE MAN. Quite sure?

RAINA *(turning her back on him in disgust).* Oh, it is useless to try to make you understand.

THE MAN. Dont be angry: you see how awkward it would be for me if there was any mistake. My father is a very hospitable man: he keeps six hotels; but I couldnt trust him as far as that. What about your father?

RAINA. He is away at Slivnitza fighting for his country. I answer for your safety. There is my hand in pledge of it. Will that reassure you? *(She offers him her hand.)*

THE MAN *(looking dubiously at his own hand).* Better not touch my

hand, dear young lady. I must have a wash first.
RAINA *(touched).* That is very nice of you. I see that you are a gentleman.
THE MAN *(puzzled).* Eh?
RAINA. You must not think I am surprised. Bulgarians of really good standing—people in our position—wash their hands nearly every day. So you see I can appreciate your delicacy. You may take my hand. *(She offers it again.)*
THE MAN *(kissing it with his hands behind his back).* Thanks, gracious young lady: I feel safe at last. And now would you mind breaking the news to your mother? I had better not stay here secretly longer than is necessary. 440
RAINA. If you will be so good as to keep perfectly still whilst I am away.
THE MAN. Certainly. *(He sits down on the ottoman.)*

RAINA *goes to the bed and wraps herself in the fur cloak. His eyes close. She goes to the door. Turning for a last look at him, she sees that he is dropping off to sleep.*

RAINA *(at the door).* You are not going asleep, are you? *(He murmurs inarticulately: she runs to him and shakes him.)* Do you hear? Wake up: you are falling asleep.
THE MAN. Eh? Falling aslee—? Oh no: not the least in the world: I was only thinking. It's all right: I'm wide awake. 450
RAINA *(severely).* Will you please stand up while I am away. *(He rises reluctantly.)* All the time, mind.
THE MAN *(standing unsteadily).* Certainly. Certainly: you may depend on me.

RAINA *looks doubtfully at him. He smiles weakly. She goes reluctantly, turning again at the door, and almost catching him in the act of yawning. She goes out.*

THE MAN *(drowsily).* Sleep, sleep, sleep, sleep, slee—*(The words trail off into a murmur. He wakes again with a shock on the point of falling.)* Where am I? Thats what I want to know: where am I? Must keep awake. Nothing keeps me awake except danger: remember that: *(intently)* danger, danger, danger, dan—*(trailing off again: another shock)* Wheres danger? Mus' find it. *(He starts off vaguely round the room in search of it.)* What am I looking for? Sleep—danger—dont know. *(He stumbles against the bed.)* Ah yes: now I know. All right now. I'm to go to bed, but not to sleep. Be sure not to sleep, because of danger. Not to lie down either, only sit down. *(He sits on the bed. A blissful expression comes into his face.)* Ah! *(With a happy sigh he sinks back at full length; lifts his boots into the bed with a final effort; and falls fast asleep instantly.)* 460

CATHERINE *comes in, followed by* RAINA.

RAINA *(looking at the ottoman).* He's gone! I left him here.
CATHERINE. Here! Then he must have climbed down from the—
RAINA *(seeing him).* Oh! *(She points.)*
CATHERINE *(scandalized).* Well! *(She strides to the bed,* RAINA *following until she is opposite her on the other side.)* He's fast asleep. The brute! 470
RAINA *(anxiously).* Sh!
CATHERINE *(shaking him).* Sir! *(Shaking him again, harder)* Sir!! *(Vehemently, shaking very hard)* Sir!!!
RAINA *(catching her arm).* Dont, mamma: the poor darling is worn out. Let him sleep.
CATHERINE *(letting him go, and turning amazed to* RAINA*).* The poor darling! Raina!!! *(She looks sternly at her daughter.)* The man sleeps profoundly.

ACT II

The sixth of March, 1886. In the garden of MAJOR PETKOFF's *house. It is a fine spring morning: the garden looks fresh and pretty. Beyond the paling the tops of a couple of minarets can be seen, shewing that there is a valley there, with the little town in it. A few miles further the Balkan mountains rise and shut in the landscape. Looking towards them from within the garden, the side of the house is seen on the left, with a garden door reached by a little flight of steps. On the right the stable yard, with its gateway, encroaches on the garden. There are fruit bushes along the paling and house, covered with washing spread out to dry. A path runs by the house, and rises by two steps at the corner, where it turns out of sight. In the middle, a small table, with two bent wood chairs at it, is laid for breakfast with Turkish coffee pot, cups, rolls, etc.; but the cups have been used and the bread broken. There is a wooden garden seat against the wall on the right.*

LOUKA, *smoking a cigaret, is standing between the table and the house, turning her back with angry disdain on a man servant who is lecturing her. He is a middle-aged man of cool temperament and low but clear and keen intelligence, with the complacency of the servant who values himself on his rank in servitude, and the imperturbability of the accurate calculator who has no illusions. He wears a white Bulgarian costume: jacket with embroidered border, sash, wide knickerbockers, and decorated gaiters. His head is shaved up to the crown, giving him a high Japanese forehead. His name is* NICOLA.

NICOLA. Be warned in time, Louka: mend your manners. I know the mistress. She is so grand that she never dreams that any servant could dare be disrespectful to her; but if she once suspects that you are defying her, out you go.
LOUKA. I do defy her. I will defy her. What do I care for her?
NICOLA. If you quarrel with the family, I never can marry you. It's the same as if you quarrelled with me!

LOUKA. You take her part against me, do you?

NICOLA *(sedately)*. I shall always be dependent on the good will of the family. When I leave their service and start a shop in Sofia, their custom will be half my capital: their bad word would ruin me.

LOUKA. You have no spirit. I should like to catch them saying a word against me!

NICOLA *(pityingly)*. I should have expected more sense from you, Louka. But youre young: youre young!

LOUKA. Yes; and you like me the better for it, dont you? But I know some family secrets they wouldnt care to have told, young as I am. Let them quarrel with me if they dare!

NICOLA *(with compassionate superiority)*. Do you know what they would do if they heard you talk like that?

LOUKA. What could they do?

NICOLA. Discharge you for untruthfulness. Who would believe any stories you told after that? Who would give you another situation? Who in this house would dare be seen speaking to you ever again? How long would your father be left on his little farm? *(She impatiently throws away the end of her cigaret, and stamps on it.)* Child: you dont know the power such high people have over the like of you and me when we try to rise out of our poverty against them. *(He goes close to her and lowers his voice.)* Look at me, ten years in their service. Do you think I know no secrets? I know things about the mistress that she wouldnt have the master know for a thousand levas. I know things about him that she wouldnt let him hear the last of for six months if I blabbed them to her. I know things about Raina that would break off her match with Sergius if—

LOUKA *(turning on him quickly)*. How do you know? I never told you!

NICOLA *(opening his eyes cunningly)*. So thats your little secret, is it? I thought it might be something like that. Well, you take my advice and be respectful; and make the mistress feel that no matter what you know or dont know, she can depend on you to hold your tongue and serve the family faithfully. Thats what they like; and thats how youll make most out of them.

LOUKA *(with searching scorn)*. You have the soul of a servant, Nicola.

NICOLA *(complacently)*. Yes: thats the secret of success in service.

A loud knocking with a whip handle on a wooden door is heard from the stable yard.

MALE VOICE OUTSIDE. Hollo! Hollo there! Nicola!

LOUKA. Master! back from the war!

NICOLA *(quickly)*. My word for it, Louka, the war's over. Off with you and get some fresh coffee. *(He runs out into the stable yard.)*

LOUKA *(as she collects the coffee pot and cups on the tray, and carries it into the house)*. Youll never put the soul of a servant into me.

MAJOR PETKOFF *comes from the stable yard, followed by* NICOLA. *He is a cheerful, excitable, insignificant, unpolished man of about 50, naturally unambitious except as to his income and his importance in local society, but just now greatly pleased with the military rank which the war has thrust on him as a man of consequence in his town. The fever of plucky patriotism which the Serbian attack roused in all the Bulgarians has pulled him through the war; but he is obviously glad to be home again.*

PETKOFF *(pointing to the table with his whip).* Breakfast out here, eh?
NICOLA. Yes, sir. The mistress and Miss Raina have just gone in.
PETKOFF *(sitting down and taking a roll).* Go in and say Ive come; and get me some fresh coffee.
NICOLA. It's coming, sir. *(He goes to the house door. LOUKA, with fresh coffee, a clean cup, and a brandy bottle on her tray, meets him.)* Have you told the mistress?
LOUKA. Yes: she's coming.

NICOLA *goes into the house.* LOUKA *brings the coffee to the table.*

PETKOFF. Well: the Serbs havnt run away with you, have they?
LOUKA. No, sir.
PETKOFF. Thats right. Have you brought me some cognac?
LOUKA *(putting the bottle on the table).* Here, sir.
PETKOFF. Thats right. *(He pours some into his coffee.)*

CATHERINE, *who, having at this early hour made only a very perfunctory toilet, wears a Bulgarian apron over a once brilliant but now half worn-out dressing gown, and a colored handkerchief tied over her thick black hair, comes from the house with Turkish slippers on her bare feet, looking astonishingly handsome and stately under all the circumstances.* LOUKA *goes into the house.*

CATHERINE. My dear Paul: what a surprise for us! *(She stoops over the back of his chair to kiss him.)* Have they brought you fresh coffee?
PETKOFF. Yes: Louka's been looking after me. The war's over. The treaty was signed three days ago at Bucharest; and the decree for our army to demobilize was issued yesterday.
CATHERINE *(springing erect, with flashing eyes).* Paul: have you let the Austrians force you to make peace?
PETKOFF *(submissively).* My dear: they didnt consult me. What could I do? *(She sits down and turns away from him.)* But of course we saw to it that the treaty was an honorable one. It declares peace—
CATHERINE *(outraged).* Peace!
PETKOFF *(appeasing her).* —but not friendly relations: remember that. They wanted to put that in; but I insisted on its being struck out. What more could I do?
CATHERINE. You could have annexed Serbia and made Prince Alexander Emperor of the Balkans. Thats what I would have done.
PETKOFF. I dont doubt it in the least, my dear. But I should have had to subdue the whole Austrian Empire first; and that would have kept me too long away from you. I missed you greatly.

CATHERINE *(relenting)*. Ah! *(She stretches her hand affectionately across the table to squeeze his.)*
PETKOFF. And how have you been, my dear?
CATHERINE. Oh, my usual sore throats: thats all.
PETKOFF *(with conviction)*. That comes from washing your neck every day. Ive often told you so.
CATHERINE. Nonsense, Paul!
PETKOFF *(over his coffee and cigaret)*. I dont believe in going too far with these modern customs. All this washing cant be good for the health: it's not natural. There was an Englishman at Philippopolis who used to wet himself all over with cold water every morning when he got up. Disgusting! It all comes from the English: their climate makes them so dirty that they have to be perpetually washing themselves. Look at my father! he never had a bath in his life; and he lived to be ninety-eight, the healthiest man in Bulgaria. I dont mind a good wash once a week to keep up my position; but once a day is carrying the thing to a ridiculous extreme.
CATHERINE. You are a barbarian at heart still, Paul. I hope you behaved yourself before all those Russian officers.
PETKOFF. I did my best. I took care to let them know that we have a library.
CATHERINE. Ah; but you didnt tell them that we have an electric bell in it? I have had one put up.
PETKOFF. Whats an electric bell?
CATHERINE. You touch a button; something tinkles in the kitchen; and then Nicola comes up.
PETKOFF. Why not shout for him?
CATHERINE. Civilized people never shout for their servants. Ive learnt that while you were away.
PETKOFF. Well, I'll tell you something Ive learnt too. Civilized people dont hang out their washing to dry where visitors can see it; so youd better have all that *(indicating the clothes on the bushes)* put somewhere else.
CATHERINE. Oh, thats absurd, Paul: I dont believe really refined people notice such things.
SERGIUS *(knocking at the stable gates)*. Gate, Nicola!
PETKOFF. Theres Sergius. *(Shouting)* Hollo, Nicola!
CATHERINE. Oh, dont shout, Paul: it really isnt nice.
PETKOFF. Bosh! *(He shouts louder than before)* Nicola!
NICOLA *(appearing at the house door)*. Yes, sir.
PETKOFF. Are you deaf? Dont you hear Major Saranoff knocking? Bring him round this way. *(He pronounces the name with the stress on the second syllable: Sarahnoff.)*
NICOLA. Yes, major. *(He goes into the stable yard.)*
PETKOFF. You must talk to him, my dear, until Raina takes him off our hands. He bores my life out about our not promoting him. Over my head, if you please.
CATHERINE. He certainly ought to be promoted when he marries Raina. Besides, the country should insist on having at least one native general.

PETKOFF. Yes; so that he could throw away whole brigades instead of regiments. It's no use, my dear: he hasnt the slightest chance of promotion until we're quite sure that the peace will be a lasting one.
NICOLA *(at the gate, announcing).* Major Sergius Saranoff! *(He goes into the house and returns presently with a third chair, which he places at the table. He then withdraws.)*

MAJOR SERGIUS SARANOFF, *the original of the portrait in* RAINA's *room, is a tall romantically handsome man, with the physical hardihood, the high spirit, and the susceptible imagination of an untamed mountaineer chieftain. But his remarkable personal distinctions are of a characteristically civilized type. The ridges of his eyebrows, curving with an interrogative twist round the projections at the outer corners; his jealously observant eye; his nose, thin, keen, and apprehensive in spite of the pugnacious high bridge and large nostril; his assertive chin, would not be out of place in a Parisian salon, shewing that the clever imaginative barbarian has an acute critical faculty which has been thrown into intense activity by the arrival of western civilization in the Balkans. The result is precisely what the advent of nineteenth century thought first produced in England: to wit, Byronism. By his brooding on the perpetual failure, not only of others, but of himself, to live up to his ideals; by his consequent cynical scorn for humanity; by his jejune credulity as to the absolute validity of his concepts and the unworthiness of the world in disregarding them; by his wincings and mockeries under the sting of the petty disillusions which every hour spent among men brings to his sensitive observation, he has acquired the half tragic, half ironic air, the mysterious moodiness, the suggestion of a strange and terrible history that has left nothing but undying remorse, by which Childe Harold fascinated the grandmothers of his English contemporaries. It is clear that here or nowhere is* RAINA's *ideal hero.* CATHERINE *is hardly less enthusiastic about him than her daughter, and much less reserved in shewing her enthusiasm. As he enters from the stable gate, she rises effusively to greet him.* PETKOFF *is distinctly less disposed to make a fuss about him.*

PETKOFF. Here already, Sergius! Glad to see you.
CATHERINE. My dear Sergius! *(She holds out both her hands.)*
SERGIUS *(kissing them with scrupulous gallantry).* My dear mother, if I may call you so.
PETKOFF *(drily).* Mother-in-law, Sergius: mother-in-law! Sit down; and have some coffee.
SERGIUS. Thank you: none for me. *(He gets away from the table with a certain distaste for* PETKOFF's *enjoyment of it, and posts himself with conscious dignity against the rail of the steps leading to the house.)*
CATHERINE. You look superb. The campaign has improved you, Sergius. Everybody here is mad about you. We were all wild with enthusiasm about that magnificent cavalry charge.
SERGIUS *(with grave irony).* Madam: it was the cradle and the grave of my military reputation.

CATHERINE. How so?

SERGIUS. I won the battle the wrong way when our worthy Russian generals were losing it the right way. In short, I upset their plans, and wounded their self-esteem. Two Cossack colonels had their regiments routed on the most correct principles of scientific warfare. Two major-generals got killed strictly according to military etiquette. The two colonels are now major-generals; and I am still a simple major.

CATHERINE. You shall not remain so, Sergius. The women are on your side; and they will see that justice is done you.

SERGIUS. It is too late. I have only waited for the peace to send in my resignation.

PETKOFF *(dropping his cup in his amazement)*. Your resignation!

CATHERINE. Oh, you must withdraw it!

SERGIUS *(with resolute measured emphasis, folding his arms)*. I never withdraw.

PETKOFF *(vexed)*. Now who could have supposed you were going to do such a thing?

SERGIUS *(with fire)*. Everyone that knew me. But enough of myself and my affairs. How is Raina; and where is Raina?

RAINA *(suddenly coming round the corner of the house and standing at the top of the steps in the path)*. Raina is here.

She makes a charming picture as they turn to look at her. She wears an underdress of pale green silk, draped with an overdress of thin ecru canvas embroidered with gold. She is crowned with a dainty eastern cap of gold tinsel. SERGIUS *goes impulsively to meet her. Posing regally, she presents her hand: he drops chivalrously on one knee and kisses it.*

PETKOFF *(aside to* CATHERINE, *beaming with parental pride)*. Pretty, isnt it? She always appears at the right moment.

CATHERINE *(impatiently)*. Yes: she listens for it. It is an abominable habit.

SERGIUS *leads* RAINA *forward with splendid gallantry. When they arrive at the table, she turns to him with a bend of the head: he bows; and thus they separate, he coming to his place, and she going behind her father's chair.*

RAINA *(stooping and kissing her father)*. Dear father! Welcome home!

PETKOFF *(patting her cheek)*. My little pet girl. *(He kisses her. She goes to the chair left by* NICOLA *for* SERGIUS, *and sits down.)*

CATHERINE. And so youre no longer a soldier, Sergius.

SERGIUS. I am no longer a soldier. Soldiering, my dear madam, is the coward's art of attacking mercilessly when you are strong, and keeping out of harm's way when you are weak. That is the whole secret of successful fighting. Get your enemy at a disadvantage; and never, on any account, fight him on equal terms.

PETKOFF. They wouldnt let us make a fair stand-up fight of it. However, I suppose soldiering has to be a trade like any other trade.

SERGIUS. Precisely. But I have no ambition to shine as a tradesman; so I have taken the advice of that bagman of a captain that settled the exchange of prisoners with us at Pirot, and given it up.
PETKOFF. What! that Swiss fellow? Sergius: Ive often thought of that exchange since. He over-reached us about those horses.
SERGIUS. Of course he over-reached us. His father was a hotel and livery stable keeper; and he owed his first step to his knowledge of horse-dealing. *(With mock enthusiasm)* Ah, he was a soldier: every inch a soldier! If only I had bought the horses for my regiment instead of foolishly leading it into danger, I should have been a field-marshal now!
CATHERINE. A Swiss? What was he doing in the Serbian army?
PETKOFF. A volunteer, of course: keen on picking up his profession. *(Chuckling)* We shouldnt have been able to begin fighting if these foreigners hadnt shewn us how to do it: we knew nothing about it; and neither did the Serbs. Egad! there'd have been no war without them!
RAINA. Are there many Swiss officers in the Serbian army?
PETKOFF. No. All Austrians, just as our officers were all Russians. This was the only Swiss I came across. I'll never trust a Swiss again. He humbugged us into giving him fifty ablebodied men for two hundred worn out chargers. They werent even eatable!
SERGIUS. We were two children in the hands of that consummate soldier, Major: simply two innocent little children.
RAINA. What was he like?
CATHERINE. Oh, Raina, what a silly question!
SERGIUS. He was like a commercial traveller in uniform. Bourgeois to his boots!
PETKOFF *(grinning)*. Sergius: tell Catherine that queer story his friend told us about how he escaped after Slivnitza. You remember. About his being hid by two women.
SERGIUS *(with bitter irony)*. Oh yes: quite a romance! He was serving in the very battery I so unprofessionally charged. Being a thorough soldier, he ran away like the rest of them, with our cavalry at his heels. To escape their sabres he climbed a waterpipe and made his way into the bedroom of a young Bulgarian lady. The young lady was enchanted by his persuasive commercial traveller's manners. She very modestly entertained him for an hour or so, and then called in her mother lest her conduct should appear unmaidenly. The old lady was equally fascinated; and the fugitive was sent on his way in the morning, disguised in an old coat belonging to the master of the house, who was away at the war.
RAINA *(rising with marked stateliness)*. Your life in the camp has made you coarse, Sergius. I did not think you would have repeated such a story before me. *(She turns away coldly.)*
CATHERINE *(also rising)*. She is right, Sergius. If such women exist, we should be spared the knowledge of them.
PETKOFF. Pooh! nonsense! what does it matter?
SERGIUS *(ashamed)*. No, Petkoff: I was wrong. *(To* RAINA, *with earnest humility)* I beg your pardon. I have behaved abominably.

Forgive me, Raina. *(She bows reservedly.)* And you too, madam. (CATHERINE *bows graciously and sits down. He proceeds solemnly, again addressing* RAINA) The glimpses I have had of the seamy side of life during the last few months have made me cynical; but I should not have brought my cynicism here: least of all into your presence, Raina. I–*(Here, turning to the others, he is evidently going to begin a long speech when the* MAJOR *interrupts him.)*

PETKOFF. Stuff and nonsense, Sergius! Thats quite enough fuss about nothing: a soldier's daughter should be able to stand up without flinching to a little strong conversation. *(He rises.)* Come: it's time for us to get to business. We have to make up our minds how those three regiments are to get back to Philippopolis: theres no forage for them on the Sofia route. *(He goes towards the house.)* Come along. *(*SERGIUS *is about to follow him when* CATHERINE *rises and intervenes.)*

CATHERINE. Oh, Paul, cant you spare Sergius for a few moments? Raina has hardly seen him yet. Perhaps I can help you to settle about the regiments.

SERGIUS *(protesting)*. My dear madam, impossible: you—

CATHERINE *(stopping him playfully)*. You stay here, my dear Sergius: theres no hurry. I have a word or two to say to Paul. *(*SERGIUS *instantly bows and steps back.)* Now, dear *(taking* PETKOFF's *arm)*: come and see the electric bell.

PETKOFF. Oh, very well, very well.

They go into the house together affectionately. SERGIUS, *left alone with* RAINA, *looks anxiously at her, fearing that she is still offended. She smiles, and stretches out her arms to him.*

SERGIUS *(hastening to her)*. Am I forgiven?

RAINA *(placing her hands on his shoulders as she looks up at him with admiration and worship)*. My hero! My king!

SERGIUS. My queen! *(He kisses her on the forehead.)*

RAINA. How I have envied you, Sergius! You have been out in the world, on the field of battle, able to prove yourself there worthy of any woman in the world; whilst I have had to sit at home inactive—dreaming—useless—doing nothing that could give me the right to call myself worthy of any man.

SERGIUS. Dearest: all my deeds have been yours. You inspired me. I have gone through the war like a knight in a tournament with his lady looking down at him!

RAINA. And you have never been absent from my thoughts for a moment. *(Very solemnly)* Sergius: I think we two have found the higher love. When I think of you, I feel that I could never do a base deed or think an ignoble thought.

SERGIUS. My lady and my saint! *(He clasps her reverently.)*

RAINA *(returning his embrace)*. My lord and my—

SERGIUS. Sh—sh! Let me be the worshipper, dear. You little know how unworthy even the best man is of a girl's pure passion!

RAINA. I trust you. I love you. You will never disappoint me, Sergius.

(LOUKA *is heard singing within the house. They quickly release each other.)* I cant pretend to talk indifferently before her: my heart is too full. *(*LOUKA *comes from the house with her tray. She goes to the table, and begins to clear it, with her back turned to them.)* I will get my hat; and then we can go out until lunch time. Wouldnt you like that?

SERGIUS. Be quick. If you are away five minutes, it will seem five hours. *(*RAINA *runs to the top of the steps, and turns there to exchange looks with him and wave him a kiss with both hands. He looks after her with emotion for a moment; then turns slowly away, his face radiant with the loftiest exaltation. The movement shifts his field of vision, into the corner of which there now comes the tail of* LOUKA'S *double apron. His attention is arrested at once. He takes a stealthy look at her, and begins to twirl his moustache mischievously, with his left hand akimbo on his hip. Finally, striking the ground with his heels in something of a cavalry swagger, he strolls over to the other side of the table, opposite her, and says)* Louka: do you know what the higher love is?

LOUKA *(astonished).* No, sir.

SERGIUS. Very fatiguing thing to keep up for any length of time, Louka. One feels the need of some relief after it.

LOUKA *(innocently).* Perhaps you would like some coffee, sir? *(She stretches her hand across the table for the coffee pot.)*

SERGIUS *(taking her hand).* Thank you, Louka.

LOUKA *(pretending to pull).* Oh, sir, you know I didnt mean that. I'm surprised at you!

SERGIUS *(coming clear of the table and drawing her with him).* I am surprised at myself, Louka. What would Sergius, the hero of Slivnitza, say if he saw me now? What would Sergius, the apostle of the higher love, say if he saw me now? What would the half dozen Sergiuses who keep popping in and out of this handsome figure of mine say if they caught us here? *(Letting go her hand and slipping his arm dexterously round her waist)* Do you consider my figure handsome, Louka?

LOUKA. Let me go, sir. I shall be disgraced. *(She struggles: he holds her inexorably.)* Oh, will you let go?

SERGIUS *(looking straight into her eyes).* No.

LOUKA. Then stand back where we cant be seen. Have you no common sense?

SERGIUS. Ah! thats reasonable. *(He takes her into the stableyard gateway, where they are hidden from the house.)*

LOUKA *(plaintively).* I may have been seen from the windows: Miss Raina is sure to be spying about after you.

SERGIUS *(stung: letting her go).* Take care, Louka. I may be worthless enough to betray the higher love; but do not you insult it.

LOUKA *(demurely).* Not for the world, sir, I'm sure. May I go on with my work, please, now?

SERGIUS *(again putting his arm round her).* You are a provoking little witch, Louka. If you were in love with me, would you spy out of windows on me?

LOUKA. Well, you see, sir, since you say you are half a dozen different gentlemen all at once, I should have a great deal to look after.

SERGIUS *(charmed).* Witty as well as pretty. *(He tries to kiss her.)*

LOUKA *(avoiding him).* No: I dont want your kisses. Gentlefolk are all alike: you making love to me behind Miss Raina's back; and she doing the same behind yours.

SERGIUS *(recoiling a step).* Louka!

LOUKA. It shews how little you really care.

SERGIUS *(dropping his familiarity, and speaking with freezing politeness).* If our conversation is to continue, Louka, you will please remember that a gentleman does not discuss the conduct of the lady he is engaged to with her maid.

LOUKA. It's so hard to know what a gentleman considers right. I thought from your trying to kiss me that you had given up being so particular.

SERGIUS *(turning from her and striking his forehead as he comes back into the garden from the gateway).* Devil! devil!

LOUKA. Ha! ha! I expect one of the six of you is very like me, sir; though I am only Miss Raina's maid. *(She goes back to her work at the table, taking no further notice of him.)*

SERGIUS *(speaking to himself).* Which of the six is the real man? thats the question that torments me. One of them is a hero, another a buffoon, another a humbug, another perhaps a bit of a blackguard. *(He pauses, and looks furtively at* LOUKA *as he adds, with deep bitterness)* And one, at least, is a coward: jealous, like all cowards. *(He goes to the table.)* Louka.

LOUKA. Yes?

SERGIUS. Who is my rival?

LOUKA. You shall never get that out of me, for love or money.

SERGIUS. Why?

LOUKA. Never mind why. Besides, you would tell that I told you; and I should lose my place.

SERGIUS *(holding out his right hand in affirmation).* No! on the honor of a—*(He checks himself; and his hand drops, nerveless, as he concludes sardonically)*—of a man capable of behaving as I have been behaving for the last five minutes. Who is he?

LOUKA. I dont know. I never saw him. I only heard his voice through the door of her room.

SERGIUS. Damnation! How dare you?

LOUKA *(retreating).* Oh, I mean no harm: youve no right to take up my words like that. The mistress knows all about it. And I tell you that if that gentleman ever comes here again, Miss Raina will marry him, whether he likes it or not. I know the difference between the sort of manner you and she put on before one another and the real manner.

SERGIUS *shivers as if she had stabbed him. Then, setting his face like iron, he strides grimly to her, and grips her above the elbows with both hands.*

SERGIUS. Now listen you to me.

LOUKA *(wincing).* Not so tight: youre hurting me.
SERGIUS. That doesnt matter. You have stained my honor by making me a party to your eavesdropping. And you have betrayed your mistress.
LOUKA *(writhing).* Please—
SERGIUS. That shews that you are an abominable little clod of common clay, with the soul of a servant. *(He lets her go as if she were an unclean thing, and turns away, dusting his hands of her, to the bench by the wall, where he sits down with averted head, meditating gloomily.)*
LOUKA *(whimpering angrily with her hands up her sleeves, feeling her bruised arms).* You know how to hurt with your tongue as well as with your hands. But I dont care, now Ive found out that whatever clay I'm made of, youre made of the same. As for her, she's a liar; and her fine airs are a cheat; and I'm worth six of her. *(She shakes the pain off hardily; tosses her head; and sets to work to put the things on the tray.)*

He looks doubtfully at her. She finishes packing the tray, and laps the cloth over the edges, so as to carry all out together. As she stoops to lift it, he rises.

SERGIUS. Louka! *(She stops and looks defiantly at him.)* A gentleman has no right to hurt a woman under any circumstances. *(With profound humility, uncovering his head)* I beg your pardon.
LOUKA. That sort of apology may satisfy a lady. Of what use is it to a servant?
SERGIUS *(rudely crossed in his chivalry, throws it off with a bitter laugh, and says slightingly).* Oh! you wish to be paid for the hurt? *(He puts on his shako, and takes some money from his pocket.)*
LOUKA *(her eyes filling with tears in spite of herself).* No: I want my hurt made well.
SERGIUS *(sobered by her tone).* How?

She rolls up her left sleeve; clasps her arm with the thumb and fingers of her right hand; and looks down at the bruise. Then she raises her head and looks straight at him. Finally, with a superb gesture, she presents her arm to be kissed. Amazed, he looks at her; at the arm; at her again; hesitates; and then, with shuddering intensity, exclaims Never! *and gets away as far as possible from her.*
Her arm drops. Without a word, and with unaffected dignity, she takes her tray, and is approaching the house when RAINA *returns, wearing a hat and jacket in the height of the Vienna fashion of the previous year, 1885.* LOUKA *makes way proudly for her, and then goes into the house.*

RAINA. I'm ready. Whats the matter? *(Gaily)* Have you been flirting with Louka?
SERGIUS *(hastily).* No, no. How can you think such a thing?
RAINA *(ashamed of herself).* Forgive me, dear: it was only a jest.

I am so happy to-day.

He goes quickly to her, and kisses her hand remorsefully. CATHERINE *comes out and calls to them from the top of the steps.*

CATHERINE *(coming down to them)*. I am sorry to disturb you, children; but Paul is distracted over those three regiments. He doesnt know how to send them to Philippopolis; and he objects to every suggestion of mine. You must go and help him, Sergius. He is in the library.

RAINA *(disappointed)*. But we are just going out for a walk.

SERGIUS. I shall not be long. Wait for me just five minutes. *(He runs up the steps to the door.)*

RAINA *(following him to the foot of the steps and looking up at him with timid coquetry)*. I shall go round and wait in full view of the library windows. Be sure you draw father's attention to me. If you are a moment longer than five minutes, I shall go in and fetch you, regiments or no regiments.

SERGIUS *(laughing)*. Very well. *(He goes in.)*

RAINA *watches him until he is out of her sight. Then, with a perceptible relaxation of manner, she begins to pace up and down the garden in a brown study.*

CATHERINE. Imagine their meeting that Swiss and hearing the whole story! The very first thing your father asked for was the old coat we sent him off in. A nice mess you have got us into!

RAINA *(gazing thoughtfully at the gravel as she walks)*. The little beast!

CATHERINE. Little beast! What little beast?

RAINA. To go and tell! Oh, if I had him here, I'd cram him with chocolate creams til he couldnt ever speak again!

CATHERINE. Dont talk such stuff. Tell me the truth, Raina. How long was he in your room before you came to me?

RAINA *(whisking round and recommencing her march in the opposite direction)*. Oh, I forget.

CATHERINE. You cannot forget! Did he really climb up after the soldiers were gone; or was he there when that officer searched the room?

RAINA. No. Yes: I think he must have been there then.

CATHERINE. You think! Oh, Raina! Raina! Will anything ever make you straightforward? If Sergius finds out, it will be all over between you.

RAINA *(with cool impertinence)*. Oh, I know Sergius is your pet. I sometimes wish you could marry him instead of me. You would just suit him. You would pet him, and spoil him, and mother him to perfection.

CATHERINE *(opening her eyes very widely indeed)*. Well, upon my word!

RAINA *(capriciously: half to herself)*. I always feel a longing to do or say something dreadful to him—to shock his propriety—to scandalize the five senses out of him. *(To* CATHERINE, *perversely)* I dont care whether he finds out about the chocolate cream soldier or not. I half hope he may. *(She again turns and strolls flippantly away up the path to the corner of the house.)*

CATHERINE. And what should I be able to say to your father, pray?

RAINA *(over her shoulder, from the top of the two steps).* Oh, poor father! As if he could help himself! *(She turns the corner and passes out of sight.)*

CATHERINE *(looking after her, her fingers itching).* Oh, if you were only ten years younger! *(*LOUKA *comes from the house with a salver, which she carries hanging down by her side.)* Well?

LOUKA. Theres a gentleman just called, madam. A Serbian officer.

CATHERINE *(flaming).* A Serb! And how dare he—*(checking herself bitterly)* Oh, I forgot. We are at peace now. I suppose we shall have them calling every day to pay their compliments. Well: if he is an officer why dont you tell your master? He is in the library with Major Saranoff. Why do you come to me?

LOUKA. But he asks for you, madam. And I dont think he knows who you are: he said the lady of the house. He gave me this little ticket for you. *(She takes a card out of her bosom; puts it on the salver; and offers it to* CATHERINE.*)*

CATHERINE *(reading).* "Captain Bluntschli"? Thats a German name.

LOUKA. Swiss, madam, I think.

CATHERINE *(with a bound that makes* LOUKA *jump back).* Swiss! What is he like?

LOUKA *(timidly).* He has a big carpet bag, madam.

CATHERINE. Oh Heavens! he's come to return the coat. Send him away: say we're not at home: ask him to leave his address and I'll write to him. Oh stop: that will never do. Wait! *(She throws herself into a chair to think it out.* LOUKA *waits.)* The master and Major Saranoff are busy in the library, arnt they?

LOUKA. Yes, madam.

CATHERINE *(decisively).* Bring the gentleman out here at once. *(Peremptorily)* And be very polite to him. Dont delay. Here *(impatiently snatching the salver from her):* leave that here; and go straight back to him.

LOUKA. Yes, madam *(going).*

CATHERINE. Louka!

LOUKA *(stopping).* Yes, madam.

CATHERINE. Is the library door shut?

LOUKA. I think so, madam.

CATHERINE. If not, shut it as you pass through.

LOUKA. Yes, madam *(going).*

CATHERINE. Stop! *(*LOUKA *stops.)* He will have to go that way *(indicating the gate of the stableyard).* Tell Nicola to bring his bag here after him. Dont forget.

LOUKA *(surprised).* His bag?

CATHERINE. Yes: here: as soon as possible. *(Vehemently)* Be quick! *(*LOUKA *runs into the house.* CATHERINE *snatches her apron off and* *throws it behind a bush. She then takes up the salver and uses it as a mirror, with the result that the handkerchief tied round her head follows the apron. A touch to her hair and a shake to her dressing gown make her presentable.)* Oh, how? how? how can a man be such a fool! Such a moment to select! *(LOUKA appears at the door of the house, announcing* Captain Bluntschli. *She stands aside at the top of the steps to let him pass before she goes in again. He is the man of the midnight adventure in* RAINA's *room, clean, well brushed, smartly uniformed, and out of trouble, but still unmistakably the same man. The moment* LOUKA's *back is turned,* CATHERINE *swoops on him with impetuous, urgent, coaxing appeal.)* Captain Bluntschli: I am very glad to see you; but you must leave this house at once. *(He raises his eyebrows.)* My husband has just returned with my future son-in-law; and they know nothing. If they did, the consequences would be terrible. You are a foreigner: you do not feel our national animosities as we do. We still hate the Serbs: the effect of the peace on my husband has been to make him feel like a lion baulked of his prey. If he discovers our secret, he will never forgive me; and my daughter's life will hardly be safe. Will you, like the chivalrous gentleman and soldier you are, leave at once before he finds you here?

BLUNTSCHLI *(disappointed, but philosophical).*   At once, gracious lady. I only came to thank you and return the coat you lent me. If you will allow me to take it out of my bag and leave it with your servant as I pass out, I need detain you no further. *(He turns to go into the house.)*

CATHERINE *(catching him by the sleeve).*   Oh, you must not think of going back that way. *(Coaxing him across to the stable gates)* This is the shortest way out. Many thanks. So glad to have been of service to you. Good-bye.

BLUNTSCHLI.   But my bag?

CATHERINE.   It shall be sent on. You will leave me your address.

BLUNTSCHLI.   True. Allow me. *(He takes out his card-case, and stops to write his address, keeping* CATHERINE *in an agony of impatience. As he hands her the card,* PETKOFF, *hatless, rushes from the house in a fluster of hospitality, followed by* SERGIUS.*)*

PETKOFF *(as he hurries down the steps).*   My dear Captain Bluntschli—

CATHERINE.   Oh Heavens! *(She sinks on the seat against the wall.)*

PETKOFF *(too preoccupied to notice her as he shakes* BLUNTSCHLI's *hand heartily).* Those stupid people of mine thought I was out here, instead of in the—haw!—library *(he cannot mention the library without betraying how proud he is of it).* I saw you through the window. I was wondering why you didnt come in. Saranoff is with me: you remember him, dont you?

SERGIUS *(saluting humorously, and then offering his hand with great charm of manner).*   Welcome, our friend the enemy!

PETKOFF.   No longer the enemy, happily. *(Rather anxiously)* I hope youve called as a friend, and not about horses or prisoners.

CATHERINE.   Oh, quite as a friend, Paul. I was just asking Captain Bluntschli to stay to lunch; but he declares he must go at once.

SERGIUS *(sardonically).*   Impossible, Bluntschli. We want you here badly. We have to send on three cavalry regiments to Philippopolis;

and we dont in the least know how to do it.
BLUNTSCHLI *(suddenly attentive and businesslike).* Philippopolis? The forage is the trouble, I suppose.
PETKOFF *(eagerly).* Yes: thats it. *(To* SERGIUS*)* He sees the whole thing at once.
BLUNTSCHLI. I think I can shew you how to manage that.
SERGIUS. Invaluable man! Come along! *(Towering over* BLUNTSCHLI, *he puts his hand on his shoulder and takes him to the steps,* PETKOFF *following.)*

RAINA *comes from the house as* BLUNTSCHLI *puts his foot on the first step.*

RAINA. Oh! The chocolate cream soldier!

BLUNTSCHLI *stands rigid.* SERGIUS, *amazed, looks at* RAINA, *then at* PETKOFF, *who looks back at him and then at his wife.*

CATHERINE *(with commanding presence of mind).* My dear Raina, dont you see that we have a guest here? Captain Bluntschli: one of our new Serbian friends.

RAINA *bows:* BLUNTSCHLI *bows.*

RAINA. How silly of me! *(She comes down into the center of the group, between* BLUNTSCHLI *and* PETKOFF.*)* I made a beautiful ornament this morning for the ice pudding; and that stupid Nicola has just put down a pile of plates on it and spoilt it. *(To* BLUNTSCHLI, *winningly)* I hope you didnt think that you were the chocolate cream soldier, Captain Bluntschli.
BLUNTSCHLI *(laughing).* I assure you I did. *(Stealing a whimsical glance at her)* Your explanation was a relief.
PETKOFF *(suspiciously, to* RAINA*).* And since when, pray, have you taken to cooking?
CATHERINE. Oh, whilst you were away. It is her latest fancy.
PETKOFF *(testily).* And has Nicola taken to drinking? He used to be careful enough. First he shews Captain Bluntschli out here when he knew quite well I was in the library; and then he goes downstairs and breaks Raina's chocolate soldier. He must—*(*NICOLA *appears at the top of the steps with the bag. He descends; places it respectfully before* BLUNTSCHLI; *and waits for further orders. General amazement.* NICOLA, *unconscious of the effect he is producing, looks perfectly satisfied with himself. When* PETKOFF *recovers his power of speech, he breaks out at him with)* Are you mad, Nicola?
NICOLA *(taken aback).* Sir?
PETKOFF. What have you brought that for?
NICOLA. My lady's orders, major. Louka told me that—
CATHERINE *(interrupting him).* My orders! Why should I order you to bring Captain Bluntschli's luggage out here? What are you thinking of, Nicola?

NICOLA *(after a moment's bewilderment, picking up the bag as he addresses* BLUNTSCHLI *with the very perfection of servile discretion).* I beg your pardon, captain, I am sure. *(To* CATHERINE*)* My fault, madam: I hope youll overlook it. *(He bows, and is going to the steps with the bag, when* PETKOFF *addresses him angrily.)*

PETKOFF. Youd better go and slam that bag, too, down on Miss Raina's ice pudding! *(This is too much for* NICOLA. *The bag drops from his hand almost on his master's toes, eliciting a roar of)* Begone, you butter-fingered donkey.

NICOLA *(snatching up the bag, and escaping into the house).* Yes, major.

CATHERINE. Oh, never mind, Paul: dont be angry.

PETKOFF *(blustering).* Scoundrel! He's got out of hand while I was away. I'll teach him. Infernal blackguard! The sack next Saturday! I'll clear out the whole establishment—*(He is stifled by the caresses of his wife and daughter, who hang round his neck, petting him.)*

CATHERINE ⎱ *(together).* ⎰ Now, now, now, it mustnt be angry. He meant no harm. Be good to please me, dear. I'll make another ice pudding. Sh-sh-sh-sh! Tch-ch-ch!
RAINA ⎰ ⎱ Wow, wow, wow: not on your first day at home.

PETKOFF *(yielding).* Oh well, never mind. Come, Bluntschli: let's have no more nonsense about going away. You know very well youre not going back to Switzerland yet. Until you do go back youll stay with us.

RAINA. Oh, do, Captain Bluntschli.

PETKOFF *(to* CATHERINE*).* Now, Catherine: it's of you he's afraid. Press him; and he'll stay.

CATHERINE. Of course I shall be only too delighted if *(appealingly)* Captain Bluntschli really wishes to stay. He knows my wishes.

BLUNTSCHLI *(in his driest military manner).* I am at madam's orders.

SERGIUS *(cordially).* That settles it!

PETKOFF *(heartily).* Of course!

RAINA. You see you must stay.

BLUNTSCHLI *(smiling).* Well, if I must, I must.

Gesture of despair from CATHERINE.

ACT III

In the library after lunch. It is not much of a library. Its literary equipment consists of a single fixed shelf stocked with old paper covered novels, broken backed, coffee stained, torn and thumbed; and a couple of little hanging shelves with a few gift books on them: the rest of the wall space being occupied by trophies of war and the chase. But it is a most comfortable sitting room. A row of three large windows shews a mountain panorama, just now seen in one of its friend-

liest aspects in the mellowing afternoon light. In the corner next the right hand window a square earthenware stove, a perfect tower of glistening pottery, rises nearly to the ceiling and guarantees plenty of warmth. The ottoman is like that in RAINA's room, and similarly placed; and the window seats are luxurious with decorated cushions. There is one object, however, hopelessly out of keeping with its surroundings. This is a small kitchen table, much the worse for wear, fitted as a writing table with an old canister full of pens, an eggcup filled with ink, and a deplorable scrap of heavily used pink blotting paper.

At the side of this table, which stands to the left of anyone facing the window, BLUNTSCHLI is hard at work with a couple of maps before him, writing orders. At the head of it sits SERGIUS, who is supposed to be also at work, but is actually gnawing the feather of a pen, and contemplating BLUNTSCHLI's quick, sure, businesslike progress with a mixture of envious irritation at his own incapacity and awestruck wonder at an ability which seems to him almost miraculous, though its prosaic character forbids him to esteem it. The MAJOR is comfortably established on the ottoman, with a newspaper in his hand and the tube of his hookah within easy reach. CATHERINE sits at the stove, with her back to them, embroidering. RAINA, reclining on the divan, is gazing in a daydream out at the Balkan landscape, with a neglected novel in her lap.

The door is on the same side as the stove, farther from the window. The button of the electric bell is at the opposite side, behind BLUNTSCHLI.

PETKOFF *(looking up from his paper to watch how they are getting on at the table).* Are you sure I cant help you in any way, Bluntschli?

BLUNTSCHLI *(without interrupting his writing or looking up).* Quite sure, thank you. Saranoff and I will manage it.

SERGIUS *(grimly).* Yes: we'll manage it. He finds out what to do; draws up the orders; and I sign em. Division of labor! *(BLUNTSCHLI passes him a paper.)* Another one? Thank you. *(He plants the paper squarely before him; sets his chair carefully parallel to it; and signs with his cheek on his elbow and his protruded tongue following the movements of his pen.)* This hand is more accustomed to the sword than to the pen.

PETKOFF. It's very good of you, Bluntschli: it is indeed, to let yourself be put upon in this way. Now are you quite sure I can do nothing?

CATHERINE *(in a low warning tone).* You can stop interrupting, Paul.

PETKOFF *(starting and looking round at her).* Eh? Oh! Quite right, my love: quite right. *(He takes his newspaper up again, but presently lets it drop.)* Ah, you havnt been campaigning, Catherine: you dont know how pleasant it is for us to sit here, after a good lunch, with nothing to do but enjoy ourselves. Theres only one thing I want to make me thoroughly comfortable.

CATHERINE. What is that?

PETKOFF. My old coat. I'm not at home in this one: I feel as if I were on parade.

CATHERINE. My dear Paul, how absurd you are about that old coat! It must be hanging in the blue closet where you left it.

PETKOFF. My dear Catherine, I tell you Ive looked there. Am I to believe my own eyes or not? *(CATHERINE rises and crosses the room to press the button of the electric bell.)* What are you shewing off that bell for? *(She looks at him majestically and silently resumes her chair and her needlework.)* My dear: if you think the obstinacy of your sex can make a coat out of two old dressing gowns of Raina's, your waterproof, and my mackintosh, youre mistaken. Thats exactly what the blue closet contains at present.

NICOLA *presents himself.*

CATHERINE. Nicola: go to the blue closet and bring your master's old coat here: the braided one he wears in the house.

NICOLA. Yes, madame. *(He goes out.)*

PETKOFF. Catherine.

CATHERINE. Yes, Paul?

PETKOFF. I bet you any piece of jewellery you like to order from Sofia against a week's housekeeping money that the coat isnt there.

CATHERINE. Done, Paul!

PETKOFF *(excited by the prospect of a gamble).* Come: here's an opportunity for some sport. Wholl bet on it? Bluntschli: I'll give you six to one.

BLUNTSCHLI *(imperturbably).* It would be robbing you, major. Madame is sure to be right. *(Without looking up, he passes another batch of papers to SERGIUS.)*

SERGIUS *(also excited).* Bravo, Switzerland! Major: I bet my best charger against an Arab mare for Raina that Nicola finds the coat in the blue closet.

PETKOFF *(eagerly).* Your best char—

CATHERINE *(hastily interrupting him).* Dont be foolish, Paul. An Arabian mare will cost you 50,000 levas.

RAINA *(suddenly coming out of her picturesque revery).* Really, mother, if you are going to take the jewellery, I dont see why you should grudge me my Arab.

NICOLA *comes back with the coat, and brings it to* PETKOFF, *who can hardly believe his eyes.*

CATHERINE. Where was it, Nicola?

NICOLA. Hanging in the blue closet, madame.

PETKOFF. Well, I am d—

CATHERINE *(stopping him).* Paul!

PETKOFF. I could have sworn it wasnt there. Age is beginning to tell on me. I'm getting hallucinations. *(To* NICOLA*)* Here: help me to change. Excuse me, Bluntschli. *(He begins changing coats,* NICOLA *acting as valet.)* Remember: I didnt take that bet of yours, Sergius. Youd better give Raina that Arab steed yourself, since youve roused her expectations. Eh, Raina? *(He looks round at her; but she is again*

rapt in the landscape. With a little gush of parental affection and pride, he points her out to them, and says) She's dreaming, as usual.
SERGIUS. Assuredly she shall not be the loser.
PETKOFF. So much the better for her. *I* shant come off so cheaply, I expect. *(The change is now complete. NICOLA goes out with the discarded coat.)* Ah, now I feel at home at last. *(He sits down and takes his newspaper with a grunt of relief.)*
BLUNTSCHLI *(to SERGIUS, handing a paper)*. Thats the last order.
PETKOFF *(jumping up)*. What! Finished?
BLUNTSCHLI. Finished.
PETKOFF *(with childlike envy)*. Havnt you anything for me to sign?
BLUNTSCHLI. Not necessary. His signature will do.
PETKOFF *(inflating his chest and thumping it)*. Ah well, I think weve done a thundering good day's work. Can I do anything more?
BLUNTSCHLI. You had better both see the fellows that are to take these. *(SERGIUS rises)* Pack them off at once; and shew them that Ive marked on the orders the time they should hand them in by. Tell them that if they stop to drink or tell stories—if theyre five minutes late, theyll have the skin taken off their backs.
SERGIUS *(stiffening indignantly)*. I'll say so. *(He strides to the door.)* And if one of them is man enough to spit in my face for insulting him, I'll buy his discharge and give him a pension. *(He goes out.)*
BLUNTSCHLI *(confidentially)*. Just see that he talks to them properly, major, will you?
PETKOFF *(officiously)*. Quite right, Bluntschli, quite right. I'll see to it. *(He goes to the door importantly, but hesitates on the threshold.)* By the bye, Catherine, you may as well come too. Theyll be far more frightened of you than of me.
CATHERINE *(putting down her embroidery)*. I daresay I had better. You would only splutter at them. *(She goes out, PETKOFF holding the door for her and following her.)*
BLUNTSCHLI. What an army! They make cannons out of cherry trees; and the officers send for their wives to keep discipline! *(He begins to fold and docket the papers.)*

RAINA, *who has risen from the divan, marches slowly down the room with her hands clasped behind her, and looks mischievously at him.*

RAINA. You look ever so much nicer than when we last met. *(He looks up, surprised.)* What have you done to yourself?
BLUNTSCHLI. Washed; brushed; good night's sleep and breakfast. Thats all.
RAINA. Did you get back safely that morning?
BLUNTSCHLI. Quite, thanks.
RAINA. Were they angry with you for running away from Sergius's charge?
BLUNTSCHLI *(grinning)*. No: they were glad; because theyd all just run away themselves.
RAINA *(going to the table, and leaning over it towards him)*. It must have made a lovely story for them: all that about me and my room.

BLUNTSCHLI. Capital story. But I only told it to one of them: a particular friend.
RAINA. On whose discretion you could absolutely rely?
BLUNTSCHLI. Absolutely.
RAINA. Hm! He told it all to my father and Sergius the day you exchanged the prisoners. *(She turns away and strolls carelessly across to the other side of the room.)*
BLUNTSCHLI *(deeply concerned, and half incredulous).* No! You dont mean that, do you?
RAINA *(turning, with sudden earnestness).* I do indeed. But they dont know that it was in this house you took refuge. If Sergius knew, he would challenge you and kill you in a duel.
BLUNTSCHLI. Bless me! then dont tell him.
RAINA. Please be serious, Captain Bluntschli. Can you not realize what it is to me to deceive him? I want to be quite perfect with Sergius: no meanness, no smallness, no deceit. My relation to him is the one really beautiful and noble part of my life. I hope you can understand that.
BLUNTSCHLI *(sceptically).* You mean that you wouldnt like him to find out that the story about the ice pudding was a—a—a—You know.
RAINA *(wincing).* Ah, dont talk of it in that flippant way. I lied: I know it. But I did it to save your life. He would have killed you. That was the second time I ever uttered a falsehood. *(BLUNTSCHLI rises quickly and looks doubtfully and somewhat severely at her.)* Do you remember the first time?
BLUNTSCHLI. I! No. Was I present?
RAINA. Yes; and I told the officer who was searching for you that you were not present.
BLUNTSCHLI. True. I should have remembered it.
RAINA *(greatly encouraged).* Ah, it is natural that you should forget it first. It cost you nothing: it cost me a lie! A lie!!

She sits down on the ottoman, looking straight before her with her hands clasped round her knee. BLUNTSCHLI, quite touched, goes to the ottoman with a particularly reassuring and considerate air, and sits down beside her.

BLUNTSCHLI. My dear young lady, dont let this worry you. Remember: I'm a soldier. Now what are the two things that happen to a soldier so often that he comes to think nothing of them? One is hearing people tell lies *(RAINA recoils):* the other is getting his life saved in all sorts of ways by all sorts of people.
RAINA *(rising in indignant protest).* And so he becomes a creature incapable of faith and of gratitude.
BLUNTSCHLI *(making a wry face).* Do you like gratitude? I dont. If pity is akin to love, gratitude is akin to the other thing.
RAINA. Gratitude! *(Turning on him)* If you are incapable of gratitude you are incapable of any noble sentiment. Even animals are grateful. Oh, I see now exactly what you think of me! You were not surprised to hear me lie. To you it was something I probably did every day!

every hour!! That is how men think of women. *(She paces the room tragically.)*

BLUNTSCHLI *(dubiously)*. Theres reason in everything. You said youd told only two lies in your whole life. Dear young lady: isnt that rather a short allowance? I'm quite a straightforward man myself; but it wouldnt last me a whole morning.

RAINA *(staring haughtily at him)*. Do you know, sir, that you are insulting me?

BLUNTSCHLI. I cant help it. When you strike that noble attitude and speak in that thrilling voice, I admire you; but I find it impossible to believe a single word you say.

RAINA *(superbly)*. Captain Bluntschli!

BLUNTSCHLI *(unmoved)*. Yes?

RAINA *(standing over him, as if she could not believe her senses)*. Do you mean what you said just now? Do you know what you said just now?

BLUNTSCHLI. I do.

RAINA *(gasping)*. I! I!!! *(She points to herself incredulously, meaning "I, Raina Petkoff, tell lies!" He meets her gaze unflinchingly. She suddenly sits down beside him, and adds, with a complete change of manner from the heroic to a babyish familiarity)* How did you find me out?

BLUNTSCHLI *(promptly)*. Instinct, dear young lady. Instinct, and experience of the world.

RAINA *(wonderingly)*. Do you know, you are the first man I ever met who did not take me seriously?

BLUNTSCHLI. You mean, dont you, that I am the first man that has ever taken you quite seriously?

RAINA. Yes: I suppose I do mean that. *(Cosily, quite at her ease with him)* How strange it is to be talked to in such a way! You know, Ive always gone on like that.

BLUNTSCHLI. You mean the—?

RAINA. I mean the noble attitude and the thrilling voice. *(They laugh together.)* I did it when I was a tiny child to my nurse. She believed in it. I do it before my parents. They believe in it. I do it before Sergius. He believes in it.

BLUNTSCHLI. Yes: he's a little in that line himself, isnt he?

RAINA *(startled)*. Oh! Do you think so?

BLUNTSCHLI. You know him better than I do.

RAINA. I wonder—I wonder is he? If I thought that—! *(Discouraged)* Ah, well: what does it matter? I suppose, now youve found me out, you despise me.

BLUNTSCHLI *(warmly, rising)*. No, my dear young lady, no, no, no a thousand times. It's part of your youth: part of your charm. I'm like all the rest of them: the nurse, your parents, Sergius: I'm your infatuated admirer.

RAINA *(pleased)*. Really?

BLUNTSCHLI *(slapping his breast smartly with his hand, German fashion)*. Hand aufs Herz! Really and truly.

RAINA *(very happy)*. But what did you think of me for giving you my portrait?

BLUNTSCHLI *(astonished).* Your portrait! You never gave me your portrait.

RAINA *(quickly).* Do you mean to say you never got it?

BLUNTSCHLI. No. *(He sits down beside her, with renewed interest, and says, with some complacency)* When did you send it to me?

RAINA *(indignantly).* I did not send it to you. *(She turns her head away, and adds, reluctantly)* It was in the pocket of that coat.

BLUNTSCHLI *(pursing his lips and rounding his eyes).* Oh-o-oh! I never found it. It must be there still.

RAINA *(springing up).* There still! for my father to find the first time he puts his hand in his pocket! Oh, how could you be so stupid?

BLUNTSCHLI *(rising also).* It doesnt matter: I suppose it's only a photograph: how can he tell who it was intended for? Tell him he put it there himself.

RAINA *(bitterly).* Yes: that is so clever! isnt it? *(Distractedly)* Oh! what shall I do?

BLUNTSCHLI. Ah, I see. You wrote something on it. That was rash.

RAINA *(vexed almost to tears).* Oh, to have done such a thing for you, who care no more—except to laugh at me—oh! Are you sure nobody has touched it?

BLUNTSCHLI. Well, I cant be quite sure. You see, I couldnt carry it about with me all the time: one cant take much luggage on active service.

RAINA. What did you do with it?

BLUNTSCHLI. When I got through to Pirot I had to put it in safe keeping somehow. I thought of the railway cloak room; but thats the surest place to get looted in modern warfare. So I pawned it.

RAINA. Pawned it!!!

BLUNTSCHLI. I know it doesnt sound nice; but it was much the safest plan. I redeemed it the day before yesterday. Heaven only knows whether the pawnbroker cleared out the pockets or not.

RAINA *(furious: throwing the words right into his face).* You have a low shopkeeping mind. You think of things that would never come into a gentleman's head.

BLUNTSCHLI *(phlegmatically).* Thats the Swiss national character, dear lady. *(He returns to the table.)*

RAINA. Oh, I wish I had never met you. *(She flounces away, and sits at the window fuming.)*

LOUKA *comes in with a heap of letters and telegrams on her salver, and crosses, with her bold free gait, to the table. Her left sleeve is looped up to the shoulder with a brooch, shewing her naked arm, with a broad gilt bracelet covering the bruise.*

LOUKA *(to* BLUNTSCHLI*).* For you. *(She empties the salver with a fling on to the table.)* The messenger is waiting. *(She is determined not to be civil to an enemy, even if she must bring him his letters.)*

BLUNTSCHLI *(to* RAINA*).* Will you excuse me: the last postal delivery that reached me was three weeks ago. These are the subsequent accumulations. Four telegrams: a week old. *(He opens one.)* Oho! Bad news!

RAINA *(rising and advancing a little remorsefully).* Bad news?
BLUNTSCHLI. My father's dead. *(He looks at the telegram with his lips pursed, musing on the unexpected change in his arrangements.* LOUKA *crosses herself hastily.)*
RAINA. Oh, how very sad!
BLUNTSCHLI. Yes: I shall have to start for home in an hour. He has left a lot of big hotels behind him to be looked after. *(He takes up a fat letter in a long blue envelope.)* Here's a whacking letter from the family solicitor. *(He pulls out the enclosures and glances over them.)* Great Heavens! Seventy! Two hundred! *(In a crescendo of dismay)* Four hundred! Four thousand!! Nine thousand six hundred!!! What on earth am I to do with them all?
RAINA *(timidly).* Nine thousand hotels?
BLUNTSCHLI. Hotels! nonsense. If you only knew! Oh, it's too ridiculous! Excuse me: I must give my fellow orders about starting. *(He leaves the room hastily, with the documents in his hand.)*
LOUKA *(knowing instinctively that she can annoy* RAINA *by disparaging* BLUNTSCHLI*).* He has not much heart, that Swiss. He has not a word of grief for his poor father.
RAINA *(bitterly).* Grief! A man who has been doing nothing but killing people for years! What does he care? What does any soldier care? *(She goes to the door, restraining her tears with difficulty.)*
LOUKA. Major Saranoff has been fighting too; and he has plenty of heart left. *(*RAINA*, at the door, draws herself up haughtily and goes out.)* Aha! I thought you wouldnt get much feeling out of your soldier. *(She is following* RAINA *when* NICOLA *enters with an armful of logs for the stove.)*
NICOLA *(grinning amorously at her).* Ive been trying all the afternoon to get a minute alone with you, my girl. *(His countenance changes as he notices her arm.)* Why, what fashion is that of wearing your sleeve, child?
LOUKA *(proudly).* My own fashion.
NICOLA. Indeed! If the mistress catches you, she'll talk to you. *(He puts the logs down, and seats himself comfortably on the ottoman.)*
LOUKA. Is that any reason why you should take it on yourself to talk to me?
NICOLA. Come! dont be so contrairy with me. Ive some good news for you. *(She sits down beside him. He takes out some paper money.* LOUKA*, with an eager gleam in her eyes, tries to snatch it; but he shifts it quickly to his left hand, out of her reach.)* See! a twenty leva bill! Sergius gave me that, out of pure swagger. A fool and his money are soon parted. Theres ten levas more. The Swiss gave me that for backing up the mistress's and Raina's lies about him. He's no fool, he isnt. You should have heard old Catherine downstairs as polite as you please to me, telling me not to mind the Major being a little impatient; for they knew what a good servant I was—after making a fool and a liar of me before them all! The twenty will go to our savings; and you shall have the ten to spend if youll only talk to me so as to remind me I'm a human being. I get tired of being a servant occasionally.
LOUKA. Yes: sell your manhood for 30 levas, and buy me for 10!

(Rising scornfully) Keep your money. You were born to be a servant. I was not. When you set up your shop you will only be everybody's servant instead of somebody's servant. *(She goes moodily to the table and seats herself regally in* SERGIUS's *chair.)*

NICOLA *(picking up his logs, and going to the stove).* Ah, wait til you see. We shall have our evenings to ourselves; and I shall be master in my own house, I promise you. *(He throws the logs down and kneels at the stove.)*

LOUKA. You shall never be master in mine.

NICOLA *(turning, still on his knees, and squatting down rather forlornly on his calves, daunted by her implacable disdain).* You have a great ambition in you, Louka. Remember: if any luck comes to you, it was I that made a woman of you.

LOUKA. You!

NICOLA *(scrambling up and going at her).* Yes, me. Who was it made you give up wearing a couple of pounds of false black hair on your head and reddening your lips and cheeks like any other Bulgarian girl? I did. Who taught you to trim your nails, and keep your hands clean, and be dainty about yourself, like a fine Russian lady? Me: do you hear that? me! *(She tosses her head defiantly; and he turns away, adding, more coolly)* Ive often thought that if Raina were out of the way, and you just a little less of a fool and Sergius just a little more of one, you might come to be one of my grandest customers, instead of only being my wife and costing me money.

LOUKA. I believe you would rather be my servant than my husband. You would make more out of me. Oh, I know that soul of yours.

NICOLA *(going closer to her for greater emphasis).* Never you mind my soul; but just listen to my advice. If you want to be a lady, your present behavior to me wont do at all, unless when we're alone. It's too sharp and impudent; and impudence is a sort of familiarity: it shews affection for me. And dont you try being high and mighty with me, either. Youre like all country girls: you think it's genteel to treat a servant the way I treat a stableboy. Thats only your ignorance; and dont you forget it. And dont be so ready to defy everybody. Act as if you expected to have your own way, not as if you expected to be ordered about. The way to get on as a lady is the same as the way to get on as a servant: youve got to know your place: thats the secret of it. And you may depend on me to know my place if you get promoted. Think over it, my girl. I'll stand by you: one servant should always stand by another.

LOUKA *(rising impatiently).* Oh, I must behave in my own way. You take all the courage out of me with your cold-blooded wisdom. Go and put those logs on the fire: thats the sort of thing you understand.

Before NICOLA *can retort,* SERGIUS *comes in. He checks himself a moment on seeing* LOUKA; *then goes to the stove.*

SERGIUS *(to* NICOLA*).* I am not in the way of your work, I hope.

NICOLA *(in a smooth, elderly manner).* Oh no, sir: thank you kindly. I was only speaking to this foolish girl about her habit of running up

here to the library whenever she gets a chance, to look at the books.
Thats the worst of her education, sir: it gives her habits above her
station. *(To* LOUKA*)* Make that table tidy, Louka, for the Major. *(He
goes out sedately.)*

LOUKA, *without looking at* SERGIUS, *pretends to arrange the papers on
the table. He crosses slowly to her, and studies the arrangement of her
sleeve reflectively.*

SERGIUS. Let me see: is there a mark there? *(He turns up the bracelet
and sees the bruise made by his grasp. She stands motionless, not
looking at him: fascinated, but on her guard.)* Ffff! Does it hurt?
LOUKA. Yes.
SERGIUS. Shall I cure it?
LOUKA *(instantly withdrawing herself proudly, but still not looking at
him)*. No. You cannot cure it now.
SERGIUS *(masterfully)*. Quite sure? *(He makes a movement as if to
take her in his arms.)*
LOUKA. Dont trifle with me, please. An officer should not trifle with a
servant.
SERGIUS *(indicating the bruise with a merciless stroke of his forefinger)*.
That was no trifle, Louka.
LOUKA *(flinching; then looking at him for the first time)*. Are you
sorry?
SERGIUS *(with measured emphasis, folding his arms)*. I am never sorry.
LOUKA *(wistfully)*. I wish I could believe a man could be as unlike a
woman as that. I wonder are you really a brave man?
SERGIUS *(unaffectedly, relaxing his attitude)*. Yes: I am a brave man.
My heart jumped like a woman's at the first shot; but in the charge I
found that I was brave. Yes: that at least is real about me.
LOUKA. Did you find in the charge that the men whose fathers are
poor like mine were any less brave than the men who are rich like
you?
SERGIUS *(with bitter levity)*. Not a bit. They all slashed and cursed
and yelled like heroes. Psha! the courage to rage and kill is cheap. I
have an English bull terrier who has as much of that sort of courage
as the whole Bulgarian nation, and the whole Russian nation at its
back. But he lets my groom thrash him, all the same. Thats your
soldier all over! No, Louka: your poor men can cut throats; but they
are afraid of their officers; they put up with insults and blows; they
stand by and see one another punished like children: aye, and help
to do it when they are ordered. And the officers!!! Well *(with a short
harsh laugh)* I am an officer. Oh, *(fervently)* give me the man who will
defy to the death any power on earth or in heaven that sets itself up
against his own will and conscience: he alone is the brave man.
LOUKA. How easy it is to talk! Men never seem to me to grow up:
they all have schoolboy's ideas. You dont know what true courage is.
SERGIUS *(ironically)*. Indeed! I am willing to be instructed. *(He sits on
the ottoman, sprawling magnificently.)*
LOUKA. Look at me! how much am I allowed to have my own will?

I have to get your room ready for you: to sweep and dust, to fetch and carry. How could that degrade me if it did not degrade you to have it done for you? But *(with subdued passion)* if I were Empress of Russia, above everyone in the world, then!! Ah then, though according to you I could shew no courage at all, you should see, you should see.

SERGIUS. What would you do, most noble Empress?

LOUKA. I would marry the man I loved, which no other queen in Europe has the courage to do. If I loved you, though you would be as far beneath me as I am beneath you, I would dare to be the equal of my inferior. Would you dare as much if you loved me? No: if you felt the beginnings of love for me you would not let it grow. You would not dare: you would marry a rich man's daughter because you would be afraid of what other people would say of you.

SERGIUS *(bounding up)*. You lie: it is not so, by all the stars! If I loved you, and I were the Czar himself, I would set you on the throne by my side. You know that I love another woman, a woman as high above you as heaven is above earth. And you are jealous of her.

LOUKA. I have no reason to be. She will never marry you now. The man I told you of has come back. She will marry the Swiss.

SERGIUS *(recoiling)*. The Swiss!

LOUKA. A man worth ten of you. Then you can come to me; and I will refuse you. You are not good enough for me. *(She turns to the door.)*

SERGIUS *(springing after her and catching her fiercely in his arms)*. I will kill the Swiss; and afterwards I will do as I please with you.

LOUKA *(in his arms, passive and steadfast)*. The Swiss will kill you, perhaps. He has beaten you in love. He may beat you in war.

SERGIUS *(tormentedly)*. Do you think I believe that she—she! whose worst thoughts are higher than your best ones, is capable of trifling with another man behind my back?

LOUKA. Do you think she would believe the Swiss if he told her now that I am in your arms?

SERGIUS *(releasing her in despair)*. Damnation! Oh, damnation! Mockery! mockery everywhere! everything I think is mocked by everything I do. *(He strikes himself frantically on the breast.)* Coward! liar! fool! Shall I kill myself like a man, or live and pretend to laugh at myself? *(She again turns to go.)* Louka! *(She stops near the door.)* Remember: you belong to me.

LOUKA *(turning)*. What does that mean? An insult?

SERGIUS *(commandingly)*. It means that you love me, and that I have had you here in my arms, and will perhaps have you there again. Whether that is an insult I neither know nor care: take it as you please. But *(vehemently)* I will not be a coward and a trifler. If I choose to love you, I dare marry you, in spite of all Bulgaria. If these hands ever touch you again, they shall touch my affianced bride.

LOUKA. We shall see whether you dare keep your word. And take care. I will not wait long.

SERGIUS *(again folding his arms and standing motionless in the middle of the room)*. Yes: we shall see. And you shall wait my pleasure.

BLUNTSCHLI, *much preoccupied, with his papers still in his hand, enters, leaving the door open for* LOUKA *to go out. He goes across to the table, glancing at her as he passes.* SERGIUS, *without altering his resolute attitude, watches him steadily.* LOUKA *goes out, leaving the door open.*

BLUNTSCHLI *(absently, sitting at the table as before, and putting down his papers).* Thats a remarkable looking young woman.
SERGIUS *(gravely, without moving).* Captain Bluntschli.
BLUNTSCHLI. Eh?
SERGIUS. You have deceived me. You are my rival. I brook no rivals. At six o'clock I shall be in the drilling-ground on the Klissoura road, alone, on horseback, with my sabre. Do you understand?
BLUNTSCHLI *(staring, but sitting quite at his ease).* Oh, thank you: thats a cavalry man's proposal. I'm in the artillery; and I have the choice of weapons. If I go, I shall take a machine gun. And there shall be no mistake about the cartridges this time.
SERGIUS *(flushing, but with deadly coldness).* Take care, sir. It is not our custom in Bulgaria to allow invitations of that kind to be trifled with.
BLUNTSCHLI *(warmly).* Pooh! dont talk to me about Bulgaria. You dont know what fighting is. But have it your own way. Bring your sabre along. I'll meet you.
SERGIUS *(fiercely delighted to find his opponent a man of spirit).* Well said, Switzer. Shall I lend you my best horse?
BLUNTSCHLI. No: damn your horse! thank you all the same, my dear fellow. *(*RAINA *comes in, and hears the next sentence.)* I shall fight you on foot. Horseback's too dangerous: I dont want to kill you if I can help it.
RAINA *(hurrying forward anxiously).* I have heard what Captain Bluntschli said, Sergius. You are going to fight. Why? *(*SERGIUS *turns away in silence, and goes to the stove, where he stands watching her as she continues, to* BLUNTSCHLI*)* What about?
BLUNTSCHLI. I dont know: he hasnt told me. Better not interfere, dear young lady. No harm will be done: Ive often acted as sword instructor. He wont be able to touch me; and I'll not hurt him. It will save explanations. In the morning I shall be off home; and youll never see me or hear of me again. You and he will then make it up and live happily ever after.
RAINA *(turning away deeply hurt, almost with a sob in her voice).* I never said I wanted to see you again.
SERGIUS *(striding forward).* Ha! That is a confession.
RAINA *(haughtily).* What do you mean?
SERGIUS. You love that man!
RAINA *(scandalized)* Sergius!
SERGIUS. You allow him to make love to you behind my back, just as you treat me as your affianced husband behind his. Bluntschli: you knew our relations; and you deceived me. It is for that that I call you to account, not for having received favors *I* never enjoyed.
BLUNTSCHLI *(jumping up indignantly).* Stuff! Rubbish! I have received

no favors. Why, the young lady doesnt even know whether I'm married or not.

RAINA *(forgetting herself).* Oh! *(Collapsing on the ottoman)* Are you?

SERGIUS. You see the young lady's concern, Captain Bluntschli. Denial is useless. You have enjoyed the privilege of being received in her own room, late at night—

BLUNTSCHLI *(interrupting him pepperily).* Yes, you blockhead! she received me with a pistol at her head. Your cavalry were at my heels. I'd have blown out her brains if she'd uttered a cry.

SERGIUS *(taken aback).* Bluntschli! Raina: is this true?

RAINA *(rising in wrathful majesty).* Oh, how dare you, how dare you?

BLUNTSCHLI. Apologize, man: apologize. *(He resumes his seat at the table.)*

SERGIUS *(with the old measured emphasis, folding his arms).* I never apologize!

RAINA *(passionately).* This is the doing of that friend of yours, Captain Bluntschli. It is he who is spreading this horrible story about me. *(She walks about excitedly.)*

BLUNTSCHLI. No: he's dead. Burnt alive.

RAINA *(stopping, shocked).* Burnt alive!

BLUNTSCHLI. Shot in the hip in a woodyard. Couldnt drag himself out. Your fellows' shells set the timber on fire and burnt him, with half a dozen other poor devils in the same predicament.

RAINA. How horrible!

SERGIUS. And how ridiculous! Oh, war! war! the dream of patriots and heroes! A fraud, Bluntschli. A hollow sham, like love.

RAINA *(outraged).* Like love! You say that before me!

BLUNTSCHLI. Come, Saranoff: that matter is explained.

SERGIUS. A hollow sham, I say. Would you have come back here if nothing had passed between you except at the muzzle of your pistol? Raina is mistaken about your friend who was burnt. He was not my informant.

RAINA. Who then? *(Suddenly guessing the truth)* Ah, Louka! my maid! my servant! You were with her this morning all that time after —after—Oh, what sort of god is this I have been worshipping! *(He meets her gaze with sardonic enjoyment of her disenchantment. Angered all the more, she goes closer to him, and says, in a lower, intenser tone)* Do you know that I looked out of the window as I went upstairs, to have another sight of my hero; and I saw something I did not understand then. I know now that you were making love to her.

SERGIUS *(with grim humor).* You saw that?

RAINA. Only too well. *(She turns away, and throws herself on the divan under the centre window, quite overcome.)*

SERGIUS *(cynically).* Raina: our romance is shattered. Life's a farce.

BLUNTSCHLI *(to* RAINA, *whimsically).* You see: he's found himself out now.

SERGIUS *(going to him).* Bluntschli: I have allowed you to call me a blockhead. You may now call me a coward as well. I refuse to fight you. Do you know why?

BLUNTSCHLI. No; but it doesnt matter. I didnt ask the reason when you cried on; and I dont ask the reason now that you cry off. I'm a professional soldier: I fight when I have to, and am very glad to get out of it when I havnt to. Youre only an amateur: you think fighting's an amusement.

SERGIUS *(sitting down at the table, nose to nose with him).* You shall hear the reason all the same, my professional. The reason is that it takes two men—real men—men of heart, blood and honor—to make a genuine combat. I could no more fight with you than I could make love to an ugly woman. Youve no magnetism: youre not a man: youre a machine.

BLUNTSCHLI *(apologetically).* Quite true, quite true. I always was that sort of chap. I'm very sorry.

SERGIUS. Psha!

BLUNTSCHLI. But now that youve found that life isnt a farce, but something quite sensible and serious, what further obstacle is there to your happiness?

RAINA *(rising).* You are very solicitous about my happiness and his. Do you forget his new love—Louka? It is not you that he must fight now, but his rival, Nicola.

SERGIUS. Rival!! *(bounding half across the room.)*

RAINA. Dont you know that theyre engaged?

SERGIUS. Nicola! Are fresh abysses opening? Nicola!!

RAINA *(sarcastically).* A shocking sacrifice, isnt it? Such beauty! such intellect! such modesty! wasted on a middle-aged servant man. Really, Sergius, you cannot stand by and allow such a thing. It would be unworthy of your chivalry.

SERGIUS *(losing all self-control).* Viper! Viper! *(He rushes to and fro, raging.)*

BLUNTSCHLI. Look here, Saranoff: youre getting the worst of this.

RAINA *(getting angrier).* Do you realize what he has done, Captain Bluntschli? He has set this girl as a spy on us; and her reward is that he makes love to her.

SERGIUS. False! Monstrous!

RAINA. Monstrous! *(Confronting him)* Do you deny that she told you about Captain Bluntschli being in my room?

SERGIUS. No; but—

RAINA *(interrupting).* Do you deny that you were making love to her when she told you?

SERGIUS. No; but I tell you—

RAINA *(cutting him short contemptuously).* It is unnecessary to tell us anything more. That is quite enough for us. *(She turns away from him and sweeps majestically back to the window.)*

BLUNTSCHLI *(quietly, as SERGIUS, in an agony of mortification, sinks on the ottoman, clutching his averted head between his fists).* I told you you were getting the worst of it, Saranoff.

SERGIUS. Tiger cat!

RAINA *(running excitedly to BLUNTSCHLI).* You hear this man calling me names, Captain Bluntschli?

BLUNTSCHLI. What else can he do, dear lady? He must defend himself somehow. Come *(very persuasively):* dont quarrel. What good does it do?

RAINA, *with a gasp, sits down on the ottoman, and after a vain effort to look vexedly at* BLUNTSCHLI, *falls a victim to her sense of humor, and actually leans back babyishly against the writhing shoulder of* SERGIUS.

SERGIUS.   Engaged to Nicola! Ha! ha! Ah well, Bluntschli, you are right to take this huge imposture of a world coolly.
RAINA *(quaintly to* BLUNTSCHLI, *with an intuitive guess at his state of mind).* I daresay you think us a couple of grown-up babies, dont you?
SERGIUS *(grinning savagely).*   He does: he does. Swiss civilization nursetending Bulgarian barbarism, eh?
BLUNTSCHLI *(blushing).*   Not at all, I assure you. I'm only very glad to get you two quieted. There! there! let's be pleasant and talk it over in a friendly way. Where is this other young lady?
RAINA.   Listening at the door, probably.
SERGIUS *(shivering as if a bullet had struck him, and speaking with quiet but deep indignation).* I will prove that that, at least, is a calumny. *(He goes with dignity to the door and opens it. A yell of fury bursts from him as he looks out. He darts into the passage, and returns dragging in* LOUKA, *whom he flings violently against the table, exclaiming)* Judge her, Bluntschli. You, the cool impartial man: judge the eavesdropper.

LOUKA *stands her ground, proud and silent.*

BLUNTSCHLI *(shaking his head).*   I mustnt judge her. I once listened myself outside a tent when there was a mutiny brewing. It's all a question of the degree of provocation. My life was at stake.
LOUKA.   My love was at stake. I am not ashamed.
RAINA *(contemptuously).*   Your love! Your curiosity, you mean.
LOUKA *(facing her and retorting her contempt with interest).*   My love, stronger than anything you can feel, even for your chocolate cream soldier.
SERGIUS *(with quick suspicion, to* LOUKA*).*   What does that mean?
LOUKA *(fiercely).*   It means—
SERGIUS *(interrupting her slightingly).*   Oh, I remember: the ice pudding. A paltry taunt, girl!

MAJOR PETKOFF *enters, in his shirtsleeves.*

PETKOFF.   Excuse my shirtsleeves, gentlemen. Raina: somebody has been wearing that coat of mine: I'll swear it. Somebody with a differently shaped back. It's all burst open at the sleeve. Your mother is mending it. I wish she'd make haste: I shall catch cold. *(He looks more attentively at them.)* Is anything the matter?
RAINA.   No. *(She sits down at the stove, with a tranquil air.)*

SERGIUS. Oh no. *(He sits down at the end of the table, as at first.)*
BLUNTSCHLI *(who is already seated).* Nothing. Nothing.
PETKOFF *(sitting down on the ottoman in his old place).* Thats all right. *(He notices* LOUKA.*)* Anything the matter, Louka?
LOUKA. No, sir.
PETKOFF *(genially).* Thats all right. *(He sneezes.)* Go and ask your mistress for my coat, like a good girl, will you?

NICOLA *enters with the coat.* LOUKA *makes a pretence of having business in the room by taking the little table with the hookah away to the wall near the windows.*

RAINA *(rising quickly as she sees the coat on* NICOLA's *arm).* Here it is, papa. Give it to me, Nicola; and do you put some more wood on the fire. *(She takes the coat, and brings it to the* MAJOR, *who stands up to put it on.* NICOLA *attends to the fire.)*
PETKOFF *(to* RAINA, *teasing her affectionately).* Aha! Going to be very good to poor old papa just for one day after his return from the wars, eh?
RAINA *(with solemn reproach).* Ah, how can you say that to me, father?
PETKOFF. Well, well, only a joke, little one. Come: give me a kiss. *(She kisses him.)* Now give me the coat.
RAINA. No: I am going to put it on for you. Turn your back. *(He turns his back and feels behind him with his arms for the sleeves. She dexterously takes the photograph from the pocket and throws it on the table before* BLUNTSCHLI, *who covers it with a sheet of paper under the very nose of* SERGIUS, *who looks on amazed, with his suspicions roused in the highest degree. She then helps* PETKOFF *on with his coat.)* There, dear! Now are you comfortable?
PETKOFF. Quite, little love. Thanks. *(He sits down; and* RAINA *returns to her seat near the stove.)* Oh, by the bye, Ive found something funny. Whats the meaning of this? *(He puts his hand into the picked pocket.)* Eh? Hallo! *(He tries the other pocket.)* Well, I could have sworn—! *(Much puzzled, he tries the breast pocket.)* I wonder—*(trying the original pocket)* Where can it—? *(He rises, exclaiming)* Your mother's taken it!
RAINA *(very red).* Taken what?
PETKOFF. Your photograph, with the inscription: "Raina, to her Chocolate Cream Soldier: a Souvenir." Now you know theres something more in this than meets the eye; and I'm going to find it out. *(Shouting)* Nicola!
NICOLA *(coming to him).* Sir!
PETKOFF. Did you spoil any pastry of Miss Raina's this morning?
NICOLA. You heard Miss Raina say that I did, sir.
PETKOFF. I know that, you idiot. Was it true?
NICOLA. I am sure Miss Raina is incapable of saying anything that is not true, sir.
PETKOFF. Are you? Then I'm not. *(Turning to the others)* Come: do you think I dont see it all? *(He goes to* SERGIUS, *and slaps him on the*

shoulder.) Sergius: youre the chocolate cream soldier, arnt you?
SERGIUS *(starting up).* I! A chocolate cream soldier! Certainly not.
PETKOFF. Not! *(He looks at them. They are all very serious and very conscious.)* Do you mean to tell me that Raina sends things like that to other men?
SERGIUS *(enigmatically).* The world is not such an innocent place as we used to think, Petkoff.
BLUNTSCHLI *(rising).* It's all right, Major. I'm the chocolate cream soldier. *(PETKOFF and SERGIUS are equally astonished.)* The gracious young lady saved my life by giving me chocolate creams when I was starving: shall I ever forget their flavour! My late friend Stolz told you the story at Pirot. I was the fugitive.
PETKOFF. You! *(He gasps.)* Sergius: do you remember how those two women went on this morning when we mentioned it? *(SERGIUS smiles cynically.* PETKOFF *confronts* RAINA *severely.)* Youre a nice young woman, arnt you?
RAINA *(bitterly).* Major Saranoff has changed his mind. And when I wrote that on the photograph, I did not know that Captain Bluntschli was married.
BLUNTSCHLI *(startled into vehement protest).* I'm not married.
RAINA *(with deep reproach).* You said you were.
BLUNTSCHLI. I did not. I positively did not. I never was married in my life.
PETKOFF *(exasperated).* Raina: will you kindly inform me, if I am not asking too much, which of these gentlemen you are engaged to?
RAINA. To neither of them. This young lady *(introducing* LOUKA, *who faces them all proudly)* is the object of Major Saranoff's affections at present.
PETKOFF. Louka! Are you mad, Sergius? Why, this girl's engaged to Nicola.
NICOLA. I beg your pardon, sir. There is a mistake. Louka is not engaged to me.
PETKOFF. Not engaged to you, you scoundrel! Why, you had twenty-five levas from me on the day of your betrothal; and she had that gilt bracelet from Miss Raina.
NICOLA *(with cool unction).* We gave it out so, sir. But it was only to give Louka protection. She had a soul above her station; and I have been no more than her confidential servant. I intend, as you know, sir, to set up a shop later on in Sofia; and I look forward to her custom and recommendation should she marry into the nobility. *(He goes out with impressive discretion, leaving them all staring after him.)*
PETKOFF *(breaking the silence).* Well, I am—hm!
SERGIUS. This is either the finest heroism or the most crawling baseness. Which is it, Bluntschli?
BLUNTSCHLI. Never mind whether it's heroism or baseness. Nicola's the ablest man Ive met in Bulgaria. I'll make him manager of a hotel if he can speak French and German.
LOUKA *(suddenly breaking out at* SERGIUS*).* I have been insulted by everyone here. You set them the example. You owe me an apology.

SERGIUS, *like a repeating clock of which the spring has been touched, immediately begins to fold his arms.*

BLUNTSCHLI *(before he can speak)*. It's no use. He never apologizes.
LOUKA. Not to you, his equal and his enemy. To me, his poor servant, he will not refuse to apologize.
SERGIUS *(approvingly)*. You are right. *(He bends his knee in his grandest manner.)* Forgive me.
LOUKA. I forgive you. *(She timidly gives him her hand, which he kisses.)* That touch makes me your affianced wife.
SERGIUS *(springing up)*. Ah! I forgot that.
LOUKA *(coldly)*. You can withdraw if you like.
SERGIUS. Withdraw! Never! You belong to me. *(He puts his arm about her.)*

CATHERINE *comes in and finds* LOUKA *in* SERGIUS's *arms, with all the rest gazing at them in bewildered astonishment.*

CATHERINE. What does this mean?

SERGIUS *releases* LOUKA.

PETKOFF. Well, my dear, it appears that Sergius is going to marry Louka instead of Raina. *(She is about to break out indignantly at him: he stops her by exclaiming testily)* Dont blame me: Ive nothing to do with it. *(He retreats to the stove.)*
CATHERINE. Marry Louka! Sergius: you are bound by your word to us!
SERGIUS *(folding his arms)*. Nothing binds me.
BLUNTSCHLI *(much pleased by this piece of common sense)*. Saranoff: your hand. My congratulations. These heroics of yours have their practical side after all. *(To* LOUKA*)* Gracious young lady: the best wishes of a good Republican! *(He kisses her hand, to* RAINA's *great disgust, and returns to his seat.)*
CATHERINE. Louka: you have been telling stories.
LOUKA. I have done Raina no harm.
CATHERINE *(haughtily)*. Raina!

RAINA, *equally indignant, almost snorts at the liberty.*

LOUKA. I have a right to call her Raina: she calls me Louka. I told Major Saranoff she would never marry him if the Swiss gentleman came back.
BLUNTSCHLI *(rising, much surprised)*. Hallo!
LOUKA *(turning to* RAINA*)*. I thought you were fonder of him than of Sergius. You know best whether I was right.
BLUNTSCHLI. What nonsense! I assure you, my dear Major, my dear Madame, the gracious young lady simply saved my life, nothing else. She never cared two straws for me. Why, bless my heart and soul, look at the young lady and look at me. She, rich, young, beautiful,

with her imagination full of fairy princes and noble natures and cavalry charges and goodness knows what! And I, a commonplace Swiss soldier who hardly knows what a decent life is after fifteen years of barracks and battles: a vagabond, a man who has spoiled all his chances in life through an incurably romantic disposition, a man—

SERGIUS *(starting as if a needle had pricked him and interrupting* BLUNTSCHLI *in incredulous amazement).* Excuse me, Bluntschli: what did you say had spoiled your chances in life?

BLUNTSCHLI *(promptly).* An incurably romantic disposition. I ran away from home twice when I was a boy. I went into the army instead of into my father's business. I climbed the balcony of this house when a man of sense would have dived into the nearest cellar. I came sneaking back here to have another look at the young lady when any other man of my age would have sent the coat back—

PETKOFF. My coat!

BLUNTSCHLI. —yes: thats the coat I mean—would have sent it back and gone quietly home. Do you suppose I am the sort of fellow a young girl falls in love with? Why, look at our ages! I'm thirty-four: I dont suppose the young lady is much over seventeen. *(This estimate produces a marked sensation, all the rest turning and staring at one another. He proceeds innocently)* All that adventure which was life or death to me, was only a schoolgirl's game to her—chocolate creams and hide and seek. Heres the proof! *(He takes the photograph from the table.)* Now, I ask you, would a woman who took the affair seriously have sent me this and written on it "Raina, to her Chocolate Cream Soldier: a Souvenir"? *(He exhibits the photograph triumphantly, as if it settled the matter beyond all possibility of refutation.)*

PETKOFF. Thats what I was looking for. How the deuce did it get there? *(He comes from the stove to look at it, and sits down on the ottoman.)*

BLUNTSCHLI *(to* RAINA, *complacently).* I have put everything right, I hope, gracious young lady.

RAINA *(going to the table to face him).* I quite agree with your account of yourself. You are a romantic idiot. *(*BLUNTSCHLI *is unspeakably taken aback.)* Next time, I hope you will know the difference between a schoolgirl of seventeen and a woman of twenty-three.

BLUNTSCHLI *(stupefied).* Twenty-three!

RAINA *snaps the photograph contemptuously from his hand; tears it up; throws the pieces in his face; and sweeps back to her former place.*

SERGIUS *(with grim enjoyment of his rival's discomfiture).* Bluntschli: my one last belief is gone. Your sagacity is a fraud, like everything else. You have less sense than even I!

BLUNTSCHLI *(overwhelmed).* Twenty-three! Twenty-three!! *(He considers.)* Hm! *(Swiftly making up his mind and coming to his host)* In that case, Major Petkoff, I beg to propose formally to become a suitor for your daughter's hand, in place of Major Saranoff retired.

RAINA. You dare!

BLUNTSCHLI. If you were twenty-three when you said those things to me this afternoon, I shall take them seriously.
CATHERINE *(loftily polite)*. I doubt, sir, whether you quite realize either my daughter's position or that of Major Sergius Saranoff, whose place you propose to take. The Petkoffs and the Saranoffs are known as the richest and most important families in the country. Our position is almost historical: we can go back for twenty years.
PETKOFF. Oh, never mind that, Catherine. *(To* BLUNTSCHLI*)* We should be most happy, Bluntschli, if it were only a question of your position; but hang it, you know, Raina is accustomed to a very comfortable establishment. Sergius keeps twenty horses.
BLUNTSCHLI. But who wants twenty horses? We're not going to keep a circus.
CATHERINE *(severely)*. My daughter, sir, is accustomed to a first-rate stable.
RAINA. Hush, mother: youre making me ridiculous.
BLUNTSCHLI. Oh well, if it comes to a question of an establishment, here goes! *(He darts impetuously to the table; seizes the papers in the blue envelope; and turns to* SERGIUS.*)* How many horses did you say?
SERGIUS. Twenty, noble Switzer.
BLUNTSCHLI. I have two hundred horses. *(They are amazed.)* How many carriages?
SERGIUS. Three.
BLUNTSCHLI. I have seventy. Twenty-four of them will hold twelve inside, besides two on the box, without counting the driver and conductor. How many tablecloths have you?
SERGIUS. How the deuce do I know?
BLUNTSCHLI. Have you four thousand?
SERGIUS. No.
BLUNTSCHLI. I have. I have nine thousand six hundred pairs of sheets and blankets, with two thousand four hundred eider-down quilts. I have ten thousand knives and forks, and the same quantity of dessert spoons. I have three hundred servants. I have six palatial establishments, besides two livery stables, a tea garden, and a private house. I have four medals for distinguished services; I have the rank of an officer and the standing of a gentleman; and I have three native languages. Shew me any man in Bulgaria that can offer as much!
PETKOFF *(with childish awe)*. Are you Emperor of Switzerland?
BLUNTSCHLI. My rank is the highest known in Switzerland: I am a free citizen.
CATHERINE. Then, Captain Bluntschli, since you are my daughter's choice—
RAINA *(mutinously)*. He's not.
CATHERINE *(ignoring her)*.—I shall not stand in the way of her happiness. *(*PETKOFF *is about to speak)* That is Major Petkoff's feeling also.
PETKOFF. Oh, I shall be only too glad. Two hundred horses! Whew!
SERGIUS. What says the lady?
RAINA *(pretending to sulk)*. The lady says that he can keep his tablecloths and his omnibuses. I am not here to be sold to the highest

bidder. *(She turns her back on him.)*
BLUNTSCHLI. I wont take that answer. I appealed to you as a fugitive, a beggar, and a starving man. You accepted me. You gave me your hand to kiss, your bed to sleep in, and your roof to shelter me.
RAINA. I did not give them to the Emperor of Switzerland.
BLUNTSCHLI. Thats just what I say. *(He catches her by the shoulders and turns her face-to-face with him.)* Now tell us whom you did give them to.
RAINA *(succumbing with a shy smile).* To my chocolate cream soldier.
BLUNTSCHLI *(with a boyish laugh of delight).* Thatll do. Thank you. *(He looks at his watch and suddenly becomes businesslike.)* Time's up, Major. Youve managed those regiments so well that youre sure to be asked to get rid of some of the infantry of the Timok division. Send them home by way of Lom Palanka. Saranoff: dont get married until I come back: I shall be here punctually at five in the evening on Tuesday fortnight. Gracious ladies *(his heels click)* good evening. *(He makes them a military bow, and goes.)*
SERGIUS. What a man! Is he a man?

800

Questions for Discussion

1. What does the title of *Arms and the Man* imply about the author's intent? Is there any ambiguity in the title? Does it appear to be intentional? What should be the relation of title to content in a play, story, or composition? How important is an effective title? What makes a title effective?

2. Is the tone of *Arms and the Man* essentially comic or serious? How soon is this tone established? What kinds of concrete incidents establish it? Is Bluntschli's fondness for chocolate, for instance, an economical way of indicating that he does not fit the stereotyped image of the soldier? Elaborate.

3. Does there seem to be a serious, satiric (see page 506) purpose behind Shaw's humor? What is it? To what extent is this purpose revealed by contrasts between dreams and reality (e.g., the women's romantic imaginings of war versus the unheroic actions of Bluntschli, or Raina's dreams of Sergius' gallantry versus his clownish propositioning of Louka)? Explain. Would humor seem to be an effective means of enlisting an audience's interest in a serious cause?

4. Is the satiric purpose revealed immediately or gradually? In particular, how much of the satire is conveyed through long, expository speeches? Which characters are most disposed toward this sort of exposition? Is it more noticeable in the beginning or the end of the play? Why do you suppose Shaw takes this approach?

5. Is all the humor in *Arms and the Man* satiric? Is that which appears to have no satiric purpose—particularly that which appears early in the play—irrelevant or inappropriate? Illustrate.

Suggested Theme Topics

1. Discuss *Arms and the Man* as a play of contrasts.

2. Contrast Bluntschli and the typical romantic image of the soldier.

3. Write a detailed, thoroughly illustrated elaboration of the twofold meaning of the title as it relates to Shaw's satiric purpose.

4. Delineate, with illustration, the different types of humor in *Arms and the Man*.

5. Write a theme satirizing some phase of campus life in need of reform. Make your satire either humorous or serious, but reveal your satiric purpose as gradually as possible.

Part II

MAINTAINING CREDIBILITY: THE MIDDLE

Part II

MAINTAINING CREDIBILITY: THE MIDDLE

The Latin root of the verb *cohere* means, literally, "to hold together." And the presence of coherence in a play, as in a theme, results in *unity*. If a play does not hold together, if its component scenes and character relationships do not create a unified impression, then the result is chaos and confusion for the audience. The ancient Greek dramatists saw an analogy between composing plots and the tying and untying of a knot. By this they meant that a dramatic conflict must be developed and then methodically unraveled to the delight of their audiences. But this development could not be random. In the earliest important treatise on dramatic art, Aristotle said that a tragic plot (i.e., the arrangement of actions making up the tragic play) must—since tragedy is foremost a representation of a heroic action—take precedence over such subordinate elements as character, diction, thought, spectacle, and song. In both drama and theme-writing, subordinate elements (e.g., anecdotes, digressions, interpretive commentary) must not so intrude that they draw the audience away from an awareness of the main line of development (in expository compositions, the development will be logical rather than narrative). Moreover, Aristotle supported his assertion by stating that the arrangement of parts must be orderly and that—most important for coherence—no part is justified if its presence makes no ultimate difference.

There are obviously numerous principles of arrangement that playwrights may employ. For Aristotle, the best tragedy would result from a single plot line that contained "peripety" (i.e., a reversal of the protagonist's fortune) and discovery by the protagonist of something that had previously been unknown. In 1863, a German critic, Gustav Freytag, published a treatise on dramatic technique in which he argued that the structure of a serious drama could be graphically represented by the figure of a pyramid (which corresponded to Aristotle's definition of the beginning, middle, and end). The rising slope of one side would represent the rising action, the inevitable tying of the knot; the top of the pyramid would represent the climax, the action which irrevocably—as the turning point—forced the untying of the knot; and the descending slope would represent the falling action, or resolution of the conflict. Freytag's belief that the five components of dramatic structure (introduction, rising action, climax, falling action, catastrophe) are inevitably recurring ingredients of the five-act tragedy is questionable, even if only applied to Elizabethan tragedy. Moreover, his observations, along with most categorical views, would reveal little about the structure of comedies. Of comedy, a modern critic, James Feibleman, asserts: "There is only one kind of comedy, namely, that which . . . consists in the indirect affirmation of the ideal logical order by means of the derogation of the limited orders of actuality." While this forbidding but relevant statement asserts no particular structural pattern that comedy must follow, it implies a loose chronological order in which human foibles are exposed to an audience which itself can conceive of an *ideal* order.

The classical figure of tying and untying the knot, the emphasis by Aristotle on proportion, the pyramid analogy of Freytag, the modern critic's remarks about comedy—what each of these implies is an audience potentially responsive to order, to the well-arranged placement of parts. And the principal devices by which the dramatist achieves order are often similar to those of the theme-writer. They include (1) chronology, (2) cause and effect, (3) comparison and contrast, (4) illustration, (5) definition, (6) spatial order, (7) refutation, and (8) classification. Of these, the most obvious is chronology, or time sequence, since chronological order serves as the basis of most narratives. But cause and effect, the reciprocal influence of character on plot and vice versa (i.e., Aristotle's unity of action), is equally pervasive. Likewise, the playwright frequently leads his audience to recognize similarities or contrasts in characters or events. For instance, when a character by contrast draws attention to and enhances another character, he is said to be a *foil* (e.g., Laertes is a foil to Hamlet; Shawn Keogh, in *The Playboy of the Western World*, is a foil to Christy Mahon). In *The Playboy of the Western World*, Synge obviously poses a question: What is a hero? The plot, with the richly suggestive title that constantly evolves in meaning, eventually—after examining several aspects of hero worship—furnishes a definition.

Tennessee Williams once observed: "In a play, time is arrested in the sense of being confined. By a sort of legerdemain, events are made to remain *events*, rather than being reduced so quickly to mere *occurrences*." What he means is that the dramatist, because he sifts away the inconsequential, depicts with greater intensity the essential experiences of man. The theme-writer, who similarly wishes to emphasize his organization and thus enhance the coherence of his paper, will carefully choose meaningful details and delete whatever is either inconsequential or only vaguely related. Two practical devices for assisting in establishing emphasis and order are the *jotted list* and the *outline*, the latter being a *necessary* device.

Let us assume that an instructor assigns a three-hundred-word in-class exposition and asks us to restrict the following topic to a manageable subject: "Dramatic Devices in *Hamlet*." With only an hour to write the paper, where should we begin? Obviously the key expression that must be restricted is "dramatic devices." This can be done most readily by choosing a particular device—perhaps the soliloquy. The next questions we pose are related: What about the soliloquies, and which character's soliloquies shall we consider? We remember Hamlet's soliloquies best, and after a few moments we have a subject: "The Function of Hamlet's Soliloquies." On the basis of this subject we can formulate a jotted list, a short, disorganized list of facts, thoughts, and impressions we have about our subject. From the list we shall later draw materials for casting a thesis statement and drafting an outline. The list will probably resemble this:

soliloquy—define
first soliloquy ("sullied flesh")
second soliloquy (Hecuba)
third soliloquy ("To be or not to be")
fourth soliloquy (Fortinbras and Poland)
show contemplation of death
show psychological disintegration
analogues that anticipate or recollect
show tendency to intellectualize when action is required
show lamenting a plight in which he finds himself
external events used as catalysts for action
decision to indecision
reveals mind to audience
memorable poetic effects

Within this melange of materials, we recognize entries of varying degrees and kinds of usefulness. Some entries merely remind us of the different contents of Hamlet's four soliloquies, while others relate to their function. We rapidly sift through the entries and cast our thesis statement:

Hamlet's four soliloquies display stages in the tragic hero's psychological disintegration and also contribute to the structural integrity of the work by serving as analogues of anticipation and recollection.

Now the paper can be organized in a brief, workable outline. It might resemble this:

I. Introduction (define soliloquy).
II. Revelation of Hamlet's psychological character (first and third soliloquies parallel).
   A. Both show Hamlet lamenting situation he confronts.
   B. Both show Hamlet favoring death and contemplating suicide.
   C. Both show Hamlet intellectualizing when action is required.
III. Contribution to structural integrity (second and fourth soliloquies parallel).
   A. Lament for Hecuba.
   B. Fortinbras' concept of honor.
IV. Conclusion.

Our outline is brief and, by necessity, somewhat hurried; however, an adequate three-hundred-word paper can be written from it. The length prerequisite is confining; we have four major divisions in our outline, and—if perfect symmetry were a criterion—we would need four paragraphs of seventy-five words each. However, this is not precisely the case. Introductions and conclusions are usually briefer than paragraphs in the body of the paper. On the other hand, the present necessity both to define briefly the term soliloquy and to include the thesis statement in the first paragraph will make it longer than the conclusion. Based on our outline, the paper will resemble this:

The Soliloquy and Its Function in *Hamlet*

A soliloquy is a dramatic device that provides the playwright an opportunity to reveal the mind of one of his characters. In Hamlet *the device is used on four principal occasions, and each displays a stage in the psychological disintegration of the tragic hero. Furthermore, each occasion contributes to the structural integrity of the work by serving as an analogue of either anticipation or recollection. Taken together, the four provide the most poetic passages in the play.*

The first ("0 that this too, too sullied flesh would melt . . .") and the third ("To be or not to be") soliloquies are thematically parallel in three ways: (1) both display Hamlet lamenting the situation that he confronts; (2) both show him favoring death and contemplating suicide; and (3) both reveal his tendency to intellectualize at a time when action is required. The subsequent plot does little to amplify Hamlet's character; thus the centrality of the device as a mode of characterization is obvious.

The second (Hecuba) and fourth (Fortinbras and Poland) soliloquies are similarly parallel. In each, Hamlet interprets an external and unrelated incident as being a catalyst to his long delayed action. That the players should cry for Hecuba, though she was but a fictional queen, and that Fortinbras should be willing to risk an army for nothing but honor imply to Hamlet, who has lost father, mother, lover, friends, and a kingdom, that he has been either cowardly or unthinking in continuing to delay.

Hamlet *is the tragedy of a man who could not make up his mind. The soliloquies sustain this conclusion by revealing the almost paranoiac alternations from decision to indecision. Action could not reveal this; Hamlet's mind had to be opened to the audience. The device of the soliloquy offered Shakespeare the opportunity to do so.*

William Shakespeare

William Shakespeare (1564-1616) was the object of much romantic speculation and investigation from early biographers, and certain details about his life and career were not substantiated until well into the twentieth century. A native of Stratford-on-Avon in rural central England, Shakespeare seems to have obtained a limited formal education before marrying in 1582 and then, after the birth of three children, embarking upon an acting career in London. Besides his career as actor, playwright, and theater official, he was also a poet whose sonnets are among the best known in English literature. He eventually retired to Stratford and is buried there in the Church of the Holy Trinity.

Although establishing accurate dates for Shakespeare's thirty-seven plays is impossible, numerous critics have cited the playwright's tendency to concentrate on different dramatic genres at different stages of his career. For example, nine of his ten histories—1, 2, and 3 Henry VI, Richard III, King John, Richard II, 1 and 2 Henry IV, and Henry V—were written before 1601; three of his four greatest tragedies—Othello, King Lear, and Macbeth—were written between 1604 and 1606 (the exception, Hamlet, was probably composed in 1600 or 1601); three of the best comedies—Much Ado About Nothing, As You Like It, and Twelfth Night—are dated between 1598 and 1601; and the three famous "dark" comedies—Cymbeline, Winter's Tale, and The Tempest—all come very late, between 1609 and 1611.

Maintenance of credibility in Hamlet hinges upon the protagonist's character and his frequent indecisions. Note that the unity of the play results not only from Hamlet's changes of mind and lapses in action, but also from the comparisons and contrasts that Shakespeare forces us to draw between Hamlet and other characters in the play.

HAMLET

CHARACTERS

CLAUDIUS, *king of Denmark.*
HAMLET, *son to the late, and nephew to the present king.*
POLONIUS, *lord chamberlain.*
HORATIO, *friend to Hamlet.*
LAERTES, *son to Polonius.*
VOLTIMAND
CORNELIUS
ROSENCRANTZ } *courtiers.*
GUILDENSTERN
OSRIC
A GENTLEMAN

A PRIEST.
MARCELLUS
BERNARDO } *officers.*
FRANCISCO, *a soldier.*
REYNALDO, *servant to Polonius.*
PLAYERS.
TWO CLOWNS, *grave-diggers.*
FORTINBRAS, *prince of Norway.*
A CAPTAIN.
ENGLISH AMBASSADORS.

GERTRUDE, *queen of Denmark, and mother to Hamlet.*
OPHELIA, *daughter to Polonius.*

LORDS, LADIES, OFFICERS, SOLDIERS, SAILORS, MESSENGERS,
   AND OTHER ATTENDANTS.
GHOST OF HAMLET'S FATHER.

Scene: *Denmark.*

ACT I.

SCENE I

Elsinore. A platform before the castle.

FRANCISCO *at his post. Enter to him* BERNARDO.

BER. Who's there?
FRAN. Nay, answer me: stand, and unfold yourself.
BER. Long live the king!
FRAN. Bernardo?
BER. He.
FRAN. You come most carefully upon your hour.
BER. 'Tis now struck twelve; get thee to bed, Francisco.
FRAN. For this relief much thanks: 'tis bitter cold,
  And I am sick at heart.
BER. Have you had quiet guard?
FRAN.   Not a mouse stirring.   10
BER. Well, good night.
  If you do meet Horatio and Marcellus,
  The rivals of my watch, bid them make haste.

Act I, Scene I, stage direction. *platform:* a level space on the battlements of the royal castle at Elsinore, a Danish seaport; now Helsingor. 3. *Long live the king:* evidently the password, though Horatio and Marcellus use a different one in line 15.

FRAN. I think I hear them. Stand, ho! Who 's there?

Enter HORATIO *and* MARCELLUS.

HOR. Friends to this ground.
MAR.   And liegemen to the Dane.
FRAN. Give you good night.
MAR.   O, farewell, honest soldier:
Who hath relieved you?
FRAN.   Bernardo has my place.
Give you good night. *(Exit.)*
MAR.   Holla! Bernardo!
BER.   Say,
What, is Horatio there?
HOR.   A piece of him.
BER. Welcome, Horatio: welcome, good Marcellus.   20
MAR. What, has this thing appear'd again to-night?
BER. I have seen nothing.
MAR. Horatio says 'tis but our fantasy,
And will not let belief take hold of him
Touching this dreaded sight, twice seen of us:
Therefore I have entreated him along
With us to watch the minutes of this night;
That if again this apparition come,
He may approve our eyes and speak to it.
HOR. Tush, tush, 'twill not appear.
BER.   Sit down awhile;   30
And let us once again assail your ears,
That are so fortified against our story
What we have two nights seen.
HOR.   Well, sit we down,
And let us hear Bernardo speak of this.
BER. Last night of all.
When yond same star that 's westward from the pole
Had made his course to illume that part of heaven
Where now it burns, Marcellus and myself,
The bell then beating one,—

Enter GHOST.

MAR. Peace, break thee off; look, where it comes again!   40
BER. In the same figure, like the king that 's dead.
MAR. Thou art a scholar; speak to it, Horatio.
BER. Looks it not like the king? mark it, Horatio.

---

18. *Give you:* God give you.   26. *along:* i.e., to come with him.   29. *approve:* corroborate, justify.   36. *yond same star:* probably part of the constellation of the Great Bear, since this was used to tell time by.   42. *scholar:* exorcisms were performed in Latin, which Horatio, as an educated man, would be able to speak.

HOR. Most like: it harrows me with fear and wonder.
BER. It would be spoke to.
MAR.   Question it, Horatio.
HOR. What art thou that usurp'st this time of night,
   Together with that fair and warlike form
   In which the majesty of buried Denmark
   Did sometimes march? by heaven I charge thee, speak!
MAR. It is offended.
BER.   See, it stalks away!   50
HOR. Stay! speak, speak! I charge thee, speak! *(Exit* GHOST.*)*
MAR. 'Tis gone, and will not answer.
BER. How now, Horatio! you tremble and look pale:
   Is not this something more than fantasy?
   What think you on 't?
HOR. Before my God, I might not this believe
   Without the sensible and true avouch
   Of mine own eyes.
MAR.   Is it not like the king?
HOR. As thou art to thyself:
   Such was the very armour he had on   60
   When he the ambitious Norway combated;
   So frown'd he once, when, in an angry parle,
   He smote the sledded Polacks on the ice.
   'Tis strange.
MAR. Thus twice before, and jump at this dead hour,
   With martial stalk hath he gone by our watch.
HOR. In what particular thought to work I know not;
   But in the gross and scope of my opinion,
   This bodes some strange eruption to our state.
MAR. Good now, sit down, and tell me, he that knows,   70
   Why this same strict and most observant watch
   So nightly toils the subject of the land,
   And why such daily cast of brazen cannon,
   And foreign mart for implements of war;
   Why such impress of shipwrights, whose sore task
   Does not divide the Sunday from the week;
   What might be toward, that this sweaty haste
   Doth make the night joint-labourer with the day:
   Who is''t that can inform me?
HOR.   That can I;
   At least, the whisper goes so. Our last king,   80
   Whose image even but now appear'd to us,
   Was, as you know, by Fortinbras of Norway,
   Thereto prick'd on by a most emulate pride,

---

44. *harrows:* lacerates the feelings. 45. *It . . . to:* a ghost could not speak until spoken to. 50. *stalks:* slips, moves cautiously. 65. *jump:* precisely. 68. *gross and scope:* general drift. 70. *Good now:* an expression denoting entreaty or expostulation. 72. *toils:* causes or makes to toil. *subject:* people, subjects. 73. *cast:* casting, founding. 74. *mart:* buying and selling, traffic. 75. *impress:* impressment. 83. *prick'd on:* incited. *emulate:* ambitious.

Dared to the combat; in which our valiant Hamlet—
For so this side of our known world esteem'd him—
Did slay this Fortinbras; who, by a seal'd compact,
Well ratified by law and heraldry,
Did forfeit, with his life, all those his lands
Which he stood seized of, to the conqueror:
Against the which, a moiety competent 90
Was gaged by our king; which had return'd
To the inheritance of Fortinbras,
Had he been vanquisher; as, by the same covenant,
And carriage of the article design'd,
His fell to Hamlet. Now, sir, young Fortinbras,
Of unimproved mettle hot and full,
Hath in the skirts of Norway here and there
Shark'd up a list of lawless resolutes,
For food and diet, to some enterprise
That hath a stomach in 't; which is no other— 100
As it doth well appear unto our state—
But to recover of us, by strong hand
And terms compulsatory, those foresaid lands
So by his father lost: and this, I take it,
Is the main motive of our preparations,
The source of this our watch and the chief head
Of this post-haste and romage in the land.
BER. I think it be no other but e'en so:
Well may it sort that this portentous figure
Comes armed through our watch; so like the king 110
That was and is the question of these wars.
HOR. A mote it is to trouble the mind's eye.
In the most high and palmy state of Rome,
A little ere the mightiest Julius fell,
The graves stood tenantless and the sheeted dead
Did squeak and gibber in the Roman streets:
As stars with trains of fire and dews of blood,
Disasters in the sun; and the moist star
Upon whose influence Neptune's empire stands
Was sick almost to doomsday with eclipse: 120
And even the like precurse of fear'd events,
As harbingers preceding still the fates
And prologue to the omen coming on,
Have heaven and earth together demonstrated
Unto our climatures and countrymen.—

87. *law and heraldry:* civil law and also the courts of chivalry.   90. *moiety competent:* adequate or sufficient portion.   96. *unimproved:* not turned to account.   *hot and full:* full of courage.   98. *Shark'd up:* got together in haphazard fashion.   *resolutes:* desperadoes.   99. *food and diet:* no pay but their keep.   107. *romage:* bustle, commotion.   113. *palmy state:* triumphant sovereignty.   118. *Disasters:* unfavorable aspects.   *moist star:* the moon, governing tides.   120. *sick . . . doomsday:* see Matt. 24:20; Rev. 6:12.   121. *precurse:* heralding.

But soft, behold! lo, where it comes again!

Re-enter GHOST.

I'll cross it, though it blast me. Stay, illusion!
If thou hast any sound, or use of voice,
Speak to me:
If there be any good thing to be done, 130
That may to thee do ease and grace to me,
Speak to me: *(Cock crows.)*
It thou art privy to thy country's fate,
Which, happily, foreknowing may avoid,
O, speak!
Or if thou hast uphoarded in thy life
Extorted treasure in the womb of earth,
For which, they say, you spirits oft walk in death,
Speak of it: stay, and speak! Stop it, Marcellus.
MAR. Shall I strike at it with my partisan? 140
HOR. Do, if it will not stand.
BER.   'Tis here!
HOR.   'Tis here!
MAR. 'Tis gone! *(Exit* GHOST.*)*
  We do it wrong, being so majestical,
To offer it the show of violence;
For it is, as the air, invulnerable,
And our vain blows malicious mockery.
BER. It was about to speak, when the cock crew.
HOR. And then it started like a guilty thing
Upon a fearful summons. I have heard,
The cock, that is the trumpet to the morn, 150
Doth with his lofty and shrill-sounding throat
Awake the god of day; and, at his warning,
Whether in sea or fire, in earth or air,
The extravagant and erring spirit hies
To his confine: and of the truth herein
This present object made probation.
MAR. It faded on the crowing of the cock.
Some say that ever 'gainst that season comes
Wherein our Saviour's birth is celebrated,
The bird of dawning singeth all night long: 160
And then, they say, no spirit dare stir abroad;
The nights are wholesome; then no planets strike,

127. *cross:* meet, face; thus bringing down the evil influence on the person who crosses it.   133-139. *If... it:* Horatio recites the traditional reasons why ghosts might walk. 140. *partisan:* long-handled spear with a blade having lateral projections. 147. *cock crew:* according to traditional ghost lore, spirits returned to their confines at cock crow.   154. *extravagant and erring:* wandering; both words mean the same thing. 156. *probation:* proof, trial. 162. *planets strike:* it was thought that planets were malignant and might strike travelers by night.

No fairy takes, nor witch hath power to charm,
So hallow'd and so gracious is the time.
HOR. So have I heard and do in part believe it.
But, look, the morn, in russet mantle clad,
Walks o'er the dew of yon high eastward hill:
Break we our watch up; and by my advice,
Let us impart what we have seen to-night
Unto young Hamlet; for, upon my life, 170
This spirit, dumb to us, will speak to him.
Do you consent we shall acquaint him with it,
As needful in our loves, fitting our duty?
MAR. Let 's do 't, I pray: and I this morning know
Where we shall find him most conveniently.

Exeunt.

SCENE II.

A room of state in the castle.

Enter the KING, QUEEN, HAMLET, POLONIUS, LAERTES, VOLTIMAND, CORNELIUS, LORDS, *and* ATTENDANTS.

KING. Though yet of Hamlet our dear brother's death
The memory be green, and that it us befitted
To bear our hearts in grief and our whole kingdom
To be contracted in one brow of woe,
Yet so far hath discretion fought with nature
That we with wisest sorrow think on him,
Together with remembrance of ourselves.
Therefore our sometime sister, now our queen,
The imperial jointress to this warlike state,
Have we, as 'twere with a defeated joy,— 10
With an auspicious and a dropping eye,
With mirth in funeral and with dirge in marriage,
In equal scale weighing delight and dole,—
Taken to wife: nor have we herein barr'd
Your better wisdoms, which have freely gone
With this affair along. For all, our thanks.
Now follows, that you know, young Fortinbras,
Holding a weak supposal of our worth,
Or thinking by our late dear brother's death
Our state to be disjoint and out of frame, 20
Colleagued with the dream of his advantage,
He hath not fail'd to pester us with message,
Importing the surrender of those lands

---

163. *takes:* strikes, as with a disease. 8. *sometime:* former, quondam. 9. *jointress:* dowager, wife who holds an estate settled on her to be enjoyed after her husband's death. 17. *that:* that which. 18. *weak supposal:* low estimate. 20. *disjoint:* distracted, out of joint. *frame:* order. 21. *Colleagued:* added to. *dream ... advantage:* visionary hope of success. 23. *Importing:* purporting, pertaining to.

Lost by his father, with all bonds of law,
To our most valiant brother. So much for him.
Now for ourself and for this time of meeting:
Thus much the business is: we have here writ
To Norway, uncle of young Fortinbras,—
Who, impotent and bed-rid, scarcely hears
Of this his nephew's purpose,—to suppress 30
His further gait herein; in that the levies,
The lists and full proportions, are all made
Out of his subject: and we here dispatch
You, good Cornelius, and you, Voltimand,
For bearers of this greeting to old Norway;
Giving to you no further personal power
To business with the king, more than the scope
Of these delated articles allow.
Farewell, and let your haste commend your duty.
COR.⎫
VOL.⎬ In that and all things will we show our duty. 40
KING. We doubt it nothing: heartily farewell.

Exeunt VOLTIMAND *and* CORNELIUS.

And now, Laertes, what's the news with you?
You told us of some suit; what is 't, Laertes?
You cannot speak of reason to the Dane,
And lose your voice: what wouldst thou beg, Laertes,
That shall not be my offer, not thy asking?
The head is not more native to the heart,
The hand more instrumental to the mouth,
Than is the throne of Denmark to thy father.
What wouldst thou have, Laertes?
LAER.   My dread lord, 50
Your leave and favour to return to France;
From whence though willingly I came to Denmark,
To show my duty in your coronation,
Yet now, I must confess, that duty done,
My thoughts and wishes bend again toward France
And bow them to your gracious leave and pardon.
KING. Have you your father's leave? What says Polonius?
POL. He hath, my lord, wrung from me my slow leave
By laboursome petition, and at last
Upon his will I seal'd my hard consent: 60
I do beseech you, give him leave to go.
KING. Take thy fair hour, Laertes; time be thine,

---

31. *gait:* proceeding. 33. *subject:* subjects (collectively). 38. *delated:* expressly stated. 44. *the Dane:* Danish king. 45. *lose your voice:* speak in vain. 47. *native:* closely connected, related. 48. *instrumental:* serviceable. 56. *leave and pardon:* permission to depart. 62. *Take ... hour:* enjoy the privileges of youth.

And thy best graces spend it at thy will!
But now, my cousin Hamlet, and my son,—
HAM. *(Aside).* A little more than kin, and less than kind.
KING. How is it that the clouds still hang on you?
HAM. Not so, my lord; I am too much i' the sun.
QUEEN. Good Hamlet, cast thy nighted colour off,
And let thine eye look like a friend on Denmark.
Do not for ever with thy vailed lids 70
Seek for thy noble father in the dust:
Thou know'st 'tis common; all that lives must die,
Passing through nature to eternity.
HAM. Ay, madam, it is common.
QUEEN.   If it be,
Why seems it so particular with thee?
HAM. Seems, madam! nay, it is; I know not "seems."
'Tis not alone my inky cloak, good mother,
Nor customary suits of solemn black,
Nor windy suspiration of forced breath,
No, nor the fruitful river in the eye, 80
Nor the dejected 'haviour of the visage,
Together with all forms, moods, shapes of grief,
That can denote me truly: these indeed seem,
For they are actions that a man might play:
But I have that within which passeth show;
These but the trappings and the suits of woe.
KING. 'Tis sweet and commendable in your nature, Hamlet,
To give these mourning duties to your father:
But, you must know, your father lost a father;
That father lost, lost his, and the survivor bound 90
In filial obligation for some term
To do obsequious sorrow: but to persever
In obstinate condolement is a course
Of impious stubbornness; 'tis unmanly grief;
It shows a will most incorrect to heaven,
A heart unfortified, a mind impatient,
An understanding simple and unschool'd:
For what we know must be and is as common
As any the most vulgar thing to sense,
Why should we in our peevish opposition 100

---

65. *A little . . . kind:* my relation to you has become more than kinship warrants; it has also become unnatural.   67. *I am . . . sun:* the senses seem to be: I am too much out of doors; I am too much in the sun of your grace (ironical); I am too much of a son to you. Johnson suggested an allusion to the proverb, "out of heaven's blessing into the warm sun," i.e., Hamlet is out of house and home in being deprived of the kingship.   74. *Ay . . . common:* it is common, but it hurts nevertheless; possibly a reference to the commonplace quality of the queen's remark.   78. *customary suits:* suits prescribed by custom for mourning.   79. *windy suspiration:* heavy sighing.   *forced breath:* i.e., by the distress of the heart.   93. *condolement:* sorrowing.   95. *incorrect:* untrained, uncorrected.   99. *vulgar thing:* common experience.

Take it to heart? Fie! 'tis a fault to heaven,
A fault against the dead, a fault to nature,
To reason most absurd; whose common theme
Is death of fathers, and who still hath cried,
From the first corse till he that died to-day,
"This must be so." We pray you, throw to earth
This unprevailing woe, and think of us
As of a father: for let the world take note,
You are the most immediate to our throne;
And with no less nobility of love   110
Than that which dearest father bears his son,
Do I impart toward you. For your intent
In going back to school in Wittenberg,
It is most retrograde to our desire:
And we beseech you, bend you to remain
Here, in the cheer and comfort of our eye,
Our chiefest courtier, cousin, and our son.
QUEEN. Let not thy mother lose her prayers, Hamlet:
I pray thee, stay with us; go not to Wittenberg.
HAM. I shall in all my best obey you, madam.   120
KING. Why, 'tis a loving and a fair reply:
Be as ourself in Denmark. Madam, come;
This gentle and unforced accord of Hamlet
Sits smiling to my heart: in grace whereof,
No jocund health that Denmark drinks to-day,
But the great cannon to the clouds shall tell,
And the king's rouse the heaven shall bruit again,
Re-speaking earthly thunder. Come away.

Exeunt all but HAMLET.

HAM. O, that this too too sullied flesh would melt,
Thaw and resolve itself into a dew!   130
Or that the Everlasting had not fix'd
His canon 'gainst self-slaughter! O God! God!
How weary, stale, flat and unprofitable,
Seem to me all the uses of this world!
Fie on 't! ah fie! 'tis an unweeded garden,
That grows to seed; things rank and gross in nature
Possess it merely. That it should come to this!
But two months dead: nay, not so much, not two:
So excellent a king; that was, to this,
Hyperion to a satyr; so loving to my mother   140

---

107. *unprevailing:* unavailing. 110. *nobility:* high degree. 112. *impart:* the object is apparently *love* (l. 110). 113. *Wittenberg:* famous German university founded in 1502. 114. *retrograde:* contrary. 115. *bend you:* incline yourself; imperative. 127. *rouse:* draft of liquor, bumper. *bruit again:* echo. 137. *merely:* completely, entirely. 140. *Hyperion:* god of the sun in the older regime of ancient gods; here, probably Apollo.

That he might not beteem the winds of heaven
Visit her face too roughly. Heaven and earth!
Must I remember? why, she would hang on him,
As if increase of appetite had grown
By what it fed on: and yet, within a month—
Let me not think on 't—Frailty, thy name is woman!—
A little month, or ere those shoes were old
With which she follow'd my poor father's body,
Like Niobe, all tears:—why she, even she—
O God! a beast, that wants discourse of reason,   150
Would have mourn'd longer—married with my uncle,
My father's brother, but no more like my father
Than I to Hercules: within a month:
Ere yet the salt of most unrighteous tears
Had left the flushing in her galled eyes,
She married. O, most wicked speed, to post
With such dexterity to incestuous sheets!
It is not nor it cannot come to good:
But break, my heart; for I must hold my tongue.

Enter HORATIO, MARCELLUS, *and* BERNARDO.

HOR. Hail to your lordship!
HAM.   I am glad to see you well: 160
   Horatio,—or I do forget myself.
HOR. The same, my lord, and your poor servant ever.
HAM. Sir, my good friend; I'll change that name with you:
   And what make you from Wittenberg, Horatio?
   Marcellus?
MAR. My good lord—
HAM. I am very glad to see you. Good even, sir.
   But what, in faith, make you from Wittenberg?
HOR. A truant disposition, good my lord.
HAM. I would not hear your enemy say so,   170
   Nor shall you do mine ear that violence,
   To make it truster of your own report
   Against yourself: I know you are no truant.
   But what is your affair in Elsinore?
   We'll teach you to drink deep ere you depart.
HOR. My lord, I came to see your father's funeral.
HAM. I pray thee, do not mock me, fellow-student;
   I think it was to see my mother's wedding.
HOR. Indeed, my lord, it follow'd hard upon.

---

141. *beteem:* allow.   149. *Niobe:* Tantalus' daughter, who boasted that she had more sons and daughters than Leto; for this Apollo and Artemis slew her children. She was turned into stone by Zeus on Mount Sipylus.   150. *discourse of reason:* process or faculty of reason.   157. *dexterity:* facility. *incestuous:* marriage with a deceased husband's brother is prohibited by canon law.   164. *make you:* are you doing.   179. *hard:* close.

HAM. Thrift, thrift, Horatio! the funeral baked meats 180
    Did coldly furnish forth the marriage tables.
    Would I had met my dearest foe in heaven
    Or ever I had seen that day, Horatio!
    My father!—methinks I see my father.
HOR. Where, my lord?
HAM.   In my mind's eye, Horatio.
HOR. I saw him once; he was a goodly king.
HAM. He was a man, take him for all in all,
    I shall not look upon his like again.
HOR. My lord, I think I saw him yesternight.
HAM. Saw? who? 190
HOR. My lord, the king your father.
HAM.   The king my father!
HOR. Season your admiration for a while
    With an attent ear, till I may deliver,
    Upon the witness of these gentlemen,
    This marvel to you.
HAM.   For God's love, let me hear.
HOR. Two nights together had these gentlemen,
    Marcellus and Bernardo, on their watch,
    In the dead vast and middle of the night,
    Been thus encounter'd. A figure like your father,
    Armed at point exactly, cap-a-pe, 200
    Appears before them, and with solemn march
    Goes slow and stately by them: thrice he walk'd
    By their oppress'd and fear-surprised eyes,
    Within his truncheon's length; whilst they, distill'd
    Almost to jelly with the act of fear,
    Stand dumb and speak not to him. This to me
    In dreadful secrecy impart they did;
    And I with them the third night kept the watch:
    Where, as they had deliver'd, both in time,
    Form of the thing, each word made true and good, 210
    The apparition comes: I knew your father;
    These hands are not more like.
HAM.   But where was this?
MAR. My lord, upon the platform where we watch'd.
HAM. Did you not speak to it?
HOR.   My lord, I did;
    But answer made it none: yet once methought
    It lifted up it head and did address

---

180. *baked meats:* meat pies. 182. *dearest:* direst. The adjective *dear* in Shakespeare has two different origins: O.E. *dēore,* "beloved," and O.E. *dēor,* "fierce." *Dearest* is the superlative of the second. 192. *Season your admiration:* restrain your astonishment. 200. *cap-a-pe:* from head to foot. 203. *oppress'd:* distressed. 204. *truncheon:* officer's staff. *distill'd:* softened, weakened. 205. *act:* action. 207. *dreadful:* full of fear. 216. *it:* its.

  Itself to motion, like as it would speak;
  But even then the morning cock crew loud,
  And at the sound it shrunk in haste away,
  And vanish'd from our sight.
HAM.   'Tis very strange.   220
HOR. As I do live, my honour'd lord, 'tis true;
  And we did think it writ down in our duty
  To let you know of it.
HAM. Indeed, indeed, sirs, but this troubles me.
  Hold you the watch to-night?
MAR.⎫
BER. ⎭   We do, my lord.
HAM. Arm'd, say you?
MAR.⎫
BER. ⎭ Arm'd, my lord.
HAM. From top to toe?
MAR.⎫
BER. ⎭   My lord, from head to foot.
HAM. Then saw you not his face?
HOR. O, yes, my lord; he wore his beaver up.   230
HAM. What, look'd he frowningly?
HOR. A countenance more in sorrow than in anger.
HAM. Pale or red?
HOR. Nay, very pale.
HAM.   And fix'd his eyes upon you?
HOR. Most constantly.
HAM.   I would I had been there.
HOR. It would have much amazed you.
HAM. Very like, very like. Stay'd it long?
HOR. While one with moderate haste might tell a hundred.
MAR.⎫
BER. ⎭ Longer, longer.
HOR. Not when I saw 't.
HAM.   His beard was grizzled,—no?   240
HOR. It was, as I have seen it in his life,
  A sable silver'd.
HAM.   I will watch to-night;
  Perchance 'twill walk again.
HOR.   I warrant it will.
HAM. If it assume my noble father's person,
  I'll speak to it, though hell itself should gape
  And bid me hold my peace. I pray you all,
  If you have hitherto conceal'd this sight,
  Let it be tenable in your silence still;
  And whatsoever else shall hap to-night,
  Give it an understanding, but no tongue: 250

---

230. *beaver:* visor on the helmet. 238. *tell:* count. 242. *sable:* black color. 248. *tenable:* held, contained.

I will requite your loves. So, fare you well:
Upon the platform, 'twixt eleven and twelve,
I'll visit you.
ALL.   Our duty to your honour.
HAM.   Your loves, as mine to you: farewell.

Exeunt all but HAMLET.

My father's spirit in arms! all is not well;
I doubt some foul play: would the night were come!
Till then sit still, my soul: foul deeds will rise,
Though all the earth o'erwhelm them, to men's eyes. *(Exit.)*

SCENE III.

A room in Polonius' house.

Enter LAERTES *and* OPHELIA.

LAER.   My necessaries are embark'd: farewell:
And, sister, as the winds give benefit
And convoy is assistant, do not sleep,
But let me hear from you.
OPH.   Do you doubt that?
LAER.   For Hamlet and the trifling of his favour,
Hold it a fashion and a toy in blood,
A violet in the youth of primy nature,
Forward, not permanent, sweet, not lasting,
The perfume and suppliance of a minute;
No more.
OPH.   No more but so?
LAER.   Think it no more: 10
For nature, crescent, does not grow alone
In thews and bulk, but, as this temple waxes,
The inward service of the mind and soul
Grows wide withal. Perhaps he loves you now,
And now no soil nor cautel doth besmirch
The virtue of his will: but you must fear,
His greatness weigh'd, his will is not his own;
For he himself is subject to his birth:
He may not, as unvalued persons do,
Carve for himself; for on his choice depends   20
The sanity and health of this whole state;
And therefore must his choice be circumscribed

---

3. *convoy is assistant:* means of conveyance are at hand.   6. *fashion:* custom, prevailing usage.   *toy in blood:* passing amorous fancy.   7. *primy:* in its prime.   8. *forward:* precocious.   9. *suppliance of a minute:* diversion to fill up a minute.   11. *crescent:* growing, waxing.   12. *thews:* bodily strength.   *temple:* body.   15. *soil:* blemish.   *cautel:* crafty device.   16. *virtue . . . will:* good intentions.

Unto the voice and yielding of that body
Whereof he is the head. Then if he says he loves you,
It fits your wisdom so far to believe it
As he in his particular act and place
May give his saying deed; which is no further
Than the main voice of Denmark goes withal.
Then weigh what loss your honour may sustain,
If with too credent ear you list his songs, 30
Or lose your heart, or your chaste treasure open
To his unmaster'd importunity.
Fear it, Ophelia, fear it, my dear sister,
And keep you in the rear of your affection,
Out of the shot and danger of desire.
The chariest maid is prodigal enough,
If she unmask her beauty to the moon:
Virtue itself 'scapes not calumnious strokes:
The canker galls the infants of the spring,
Too oft before their buttons be disclosed, 40
And in the morn and liquid dew of youth
Contagious blastments are most imminent.
Be wary then; best safety lies in fear:
Youth to itself rebels, though none else near.
OPH. I shall the effect of this good lesson keep,
As watchman to my heart. But, good my brother,
Do not, as some ungracious pastors do,
Show me the steep and thorny way to heaven;
Whiles, like a puff'd and reckless libertine,
Himself the primrose path of dalliance treads, 50
And recks not his own rede.
LAER.   O, fear me not.
I stay too long: but here my father comes.

Enter POLONIUS.

A double blessing is a double grace;
Occasion smiles upon a second leave.
POL. Yet here, Laertes! aboard, aboard, for shame!
The wind sits in the shoulder of your sail,
And you are stay'd for. There; my blessing with thee!
And these few precepts in thy memory
Look thou character. Give thy thoughts no tongue,
Nor any unproportion'd thought his act. 60

23. *voice and yielding:* support, approval. 27. *deed:* effect. 30. *list:* listen to. 32. *unmaster'd:* unrestrained. 36. *chariest:* most scrupulously modest. 37. *unmask... moon:* remove the mask of chastity from her beauty. 39. *The canker... spring:* the cankerworm destroys the young plants of spring. 40. *buttons:* buds. *disclosed:* opened. 42. *blastments:* blights. 47. *ungracious:* graceless. 49. *puff'd:* bloated. 50. *dalliance:* trifling, wantonness. 51. *recks:* heeds. *rede:* counsel. 53. *double:* i.e., Laertes has already bade his father good-bye. 59. *character:* write, inscribe. 60. *unproportion'd:* inordinate.

Be thou familiar, but by no means vulgar.
Those friends thou hast, and their adoption tried,
Grapple them to thy soul with hoops of steel;
But do not dull thy palm with entertainment
Of each new-hatch'd, unfledged comrade. Beware
Of entrance to a quarrel, but being in,
Bear 't that the opposed may beware of thee.
Give every man thy ear, but few thy voice;
Take each man's censure, but reserve thy judgement.
Costly thy habit as thy purse can buy, 70
But not express'd in fancy: rich, not gaudy;
For the apparel oft proclaims the man,
And they in France of the best rank and station
Are of a most select and generous chief in that.
Neither a borrower nor a lender be;
For loan oft loses both itself and friend,
And borrowing dulls the edge of husbandry.
This above all: to thine own self be true,
And it must follow, as the night the day,
Thou canst not then be false to any man. 80
Farewell: my blessing season this in thee!
LAER. Most humbly do I take my leave, my lord.
POL. The time invites you; go; your servants tend.
LAER. Farewell, Ophelia; and remember well
 What I have said to you.
OPH.   'Tis in my memory lock'd,
 And you yourself shall keep the key of it.
LAER. Farewell. *(Exit.)*
POL. What is 't, Ophelia, he hath said to you?
OPH. So please you, something touching the Lord Hamlet.
POL. Marry, well bethought: 90
 'Tis told me, he hath very oft of late
 Given private time to you; and you yourself
 Have of your audience been most free and bounteous:
 If it be so, as so 't is put on me,
 And that in way of caution, I must tell you,
 You do not understand yourself so clearly
 As it behoves my daughter and your honour.
 What is between you? give me up the truth.
OPH. He hath, my lord, of late made many tenders
 Of his affection to me. 100
POL. Affection! pooh! you speak like a green girl,
 Unsifted in such perilous circumstance.
 Do you believe his tenders, as you call them?
OPH. I do not know, my lord, what I should think.

---

64. *dull thy palm:* make yourself less sensitive to true hospitality. 65. *unfledged:* immature. 69. *censure:* judgment, opinion. 71. *express'd in fancy:* fantastical in design. 77. *husbandry:* thrift. 94. *put on:* impressed on. 102. *Unsifted:* untried.

POL. Marry, I'll teach you: think yourself a baby;
  That you have ta'en these tenders for true pay,
  Which are not sterling. Tender yourself more dearly;
  Or—not to crack the wind of the poor phrase,
  Running it thus—you'll tender me a fool.
OPH. My lord, he hath importuned me with love   110
  In honourable fashion.
POL. Ay, fashion you may call it; go to, go to.
OPH. And hath given countenance to his speech, my lord,
  With almost all the holy vows of heaven.
POL. Ay, springes to catch woodcocks. I do know,
  When the blood burns, how prodigal the soul
  Lends the tongue vows: these blazes, daughter,
  Giving more light than heat, extinct in both,
  Even in their promise, as it is a-making,
  You must not take for fire. From this time   120
  Be somewhat scanter of your maiden presence;
  Set your entreatments at a higher rate
  Than a command to parley. For Lord Hamlet,
  Believe so much in him, that he is young,
  And with a larger tether may he walk
  Than may be given you: in few, Ophelia,
  Do not believe his vows; for they are brokers,
  Not of that dye which their investments show,
  But mere implorators of unholy suits,
  Breathing like sanctified and pious bawds,   130
  The better to beguile. This is for all:
  I would not, in plain terms, from this time forth,
  Have you so slander any moment leisure,
  As to give words or talk with the Lord Hamlet.
  Look to 't, I charge you: come your ways.
OPH. I shall obey, my lord.

Exeunt.

SCENE IV.

The platform.

Enter HAMLET, HORATIO, *and* MARCELLUS.

HAM. The air bites shrewdly; it is very cold.
HOR. It is a nipping and an eager air.

---

106. *tenders:* promises to pay.   107. *sterling:* legal currency.   *Tender:* hold.   108. *crack the wind:* i.e., run it until it is broken-winded.   109. *tender ... fool:* show me a fool (for a daughter).   112. *fashion:* mere form, pretense.   115. *springs:* snares.   *woodcocks:* birds easily caught; type of stupidity.   122. *entreatments:* conversations, interviews.   123. *command to parley:* mere invitation to talk.   124. *so ... him:* this much concerning him.   126. *in few:* briefly.   127. *brokers:* go-betweens, procurers.   *investments:* clothes.   129. *implorators of:* solicitors of.   130. *Breathing:* speaking.   131. *This ... all:* these are your orders.   133. *slander:* bring disgrace or reproach upon.   2. *eager:* sharp.

HAM. What hour now?
HOR.   I think it lacks of twelve.
MAR. No, it is struck.
HOR. Indeed? I heard it not: then it draws near the season
  Wherein the spirit held his wont to walk.

A flourish of trumpets, and ordnance shot off, within.

  What does this mean, my lord?
HAM. The king doth wake to-night and takes his rouse,
  Keeps wassail, and the swaggering up-spring reels;
  And, as he drains his draughts of Rhenish down,   10
  The kettle-drum and trumpet thus bray out
  The triumph of his pledge.
HOR.   Is it a custom?
HAM. Ay, marry, is 't:
  But to my mind, though I am native here
  And to the manner born, it is a custom
  More honour'd in the breach than the observance.
  This heavy-headed revel east and west
  Makes us traduced and tax'd of other nations:
  They clepe us drunkards, and with swinish phrase
  Soil our addition; and indeed it takes   20
  From our achievements, though perform'd at height,
  The pith and marrow of our attribute.
  So, oft it chances in particular men,
  That for some vicious mole of nature in them,
  As, in their birth—wherein they are not guilty,
  Since nature cannot choose his origin—
  By the o'ergrowth of some complexion,
  Oft breaking down the pales and forts of reason,
  Or by some habit that too much o'er-leavens
  The form of plausive manners, that these men,   30
  Carrying, I say, the stamp of one defect,
  Being nature's livery, or fortune's star,—
  Their virtues else—be they as pure as grace,
  As infinite as man may undergo—
  Shall in the general censure take corruption
  From that particular fault: the dram of eale
  Doth all the noble substance of a doubt
  To his own scandal.

8. *wake:* stay awake, hold revel. *rouse:* carouse, drinking bout. 9. *wassail:* carousal. *upspring:* last and wildest dance at German merrymakings (Elze). *reels:* reels through. 10. *Rhenish:* Rhine wine. 12. *triumph . . . pledge:* his glorious achievement as a drinker. 19. *clepe:* call. *with swinish phrase:* by calling us swine. 22. *attribute:* reputation. 24. *mole of nature:* natural blemish in one's constitution. 27. *complexion:* temperament, the supposed result of the mixing of the four humors in various proportions in the body. 28. *pales:* palings (as of a fortification). 29. *o'er-leavens:* makes too light. 30. *plausive:* pleasing. 32. *nature's livery:* endowment from nature. *fortune's star:* the position in which one is placed by fortune; a reference to astrology. The two phrases are aspects of the same thing. 36-38. *the dram . . . scandal:* a famous crux; *dram of eale* has had various interpretations, the preferred one being, probably, "a dram of evil."

HOR.   Look, my lord, it comes!

Enter GHOST.

HAM.   Angels and ministers of grace defend us!
  Be thou a spirit of health or goblin damn'd,   40
  Bring with thee airs from heaven or blasts from hell,
  Be thy intents wicked or charitable,
  Thou comest in such a questionable shape
  That I will speak to thee: I'll call thee Hamlet,
  King, father, royal Dane: O, answer me!
  Let me not burst in ignorance; but tell
  Why thy canonized bones, hearsed in death,
  Have burst their cerements; why the sepulchre,
  Wherein we saw thee quietly interr'd,
  Hath oped his ponderous and marble jaws,   50
  To cast thee up again. What may this mean,
  That thou, dead corse, again in complete steel
  Revisit'st thus the glimpses of the moon,
  Making night hideous; and we fools of nature
  So horridly to shake our disposition
  With thoughts beyond the reaches of our souls?
  Say, why is this? wherefore? what should we do?

GHOST *beckons* HAMLET.

HOR.   It beckons you to go away with it,
  As if it some impartment did desire
  To you alone.
MAR.   Look, with what courteous action   60
  It waves you to a more removed ground:
  But do not go with it.
HOR.   No, by no means.
HAM.   It will not speak; then I will follow it.
HOR.   Do not, my lord.
HAM.   Why, what should be the fear?
  I do not set my life at a pin's fee;
  And for my soul, what can it do to that,
  Being a thing immortal as itself?
  It waves me forth again: I'll follow it.
HOR.   What if it tempt you toward the flood, my lord,
  Or to the dreadful summit of the cliff   70
  That beetles o'er his base into the sea,
  And there assume some other horrible form,

---

43. *questionable:* inviting question or conversation. 47. *canonized:* buried according to the canons of the church. *hearsed:* coffined. 48. *cerements:* grave-clothes. 53. *glimpses of the moon:* the earth by night. 54. *fools of nature:* persons limited in intelligence by nature. 55. *disposition:* natural constitution. 59. *impartment:* communication. 61. *removed:* remote. 71. *beetles o'er:* overhangs threateningly.

Which might deprive your sovereignty of reason
And draw you into madness? think of it:
The very place puts toys of desperation,
Without more motive, into every brain
That looks so many fathoms to the sea
And hears it roar beneath.
HAM. It waves me still.
  Go on; I'll follow thee.
MAR. You shall not go, my lord.
HAM. Hold off your hands. 80
HOR. Be ruled; you shall not go.
HAM. My fate cries out,
And makes each petty artery in this body
As hardy as the Nemean lion's nerve.
Still am I call'd. Unhand me, gentlemen.
By heaven, I'll make a ghost of him that lets me!
I say, away! Go on; I'll follow thee.

Exeunt GHOST *and* HAMLET.

HOR. He waxes desperate with imagination.
MAR. Let 's follow; 'tis not fit thus to obey him.
HOR. Have after. To what issue will this come?
MAR. Something is rotten in the state of Denmark. 90
HOR. Heaven will direct it.
MAR. Nay, let 's follow him.

Exeunt.

SCENE V.

Another part of the platform.

Enter GHOST *and* HAMLET.

HAM. Whither wilt thou lead me? speak; I'll go no further.
GHOST. Mark me.
HAM. I will.
GHOST. My hour is almost come,
  When I to sulphurous and tormenting flames
  Must render up myself.
HAM. Alas, poor ghost!
GHOST. Pity me not, but lend thy serious hearing
  To what I shall unfold.

---

73. *deprive ... reason:* take away the sovereignty of your reason. It was thought that evil spirits would sometimes assume the form of departed spirits in order to work madness in a human creature. 75. *toys of desperation:* freakish notions of suicide. 83. *Nemean lion's:* the Nemean lion was one of the monsters slain by Hercules. *nerve:* sinew, tendon. The point is that the arteries which were carrying the spirits out into the body were functioning and were as stiff and hard as the sinews of the lion. 85. *lets:* hinders. 89. *issue:* outcome. 91. *it:* i.e., the outcome.

HAM.　　　　　　Speak; I am bound to hear.
GHOST.　So art thou to revenge, when thou shalt hear.
HAM.　What?
GHOST.　I am thy father's spirit,
　Doom'd for a certain term to walk the night, 10
　And for the day confined to fast in fires,
　Till the foul crimes done in my days of nature
　Are burnt and purged away. But that I am forbid
　To tell the secrets of my prison-house,
　I could a tale unfold whose lightest word
　Would harrow up thy soul, freeze thy young blood,
　Make thy two eyes, like stars, start from their spheres,
　Thy knotted and combined locks to part
　And each particular hair to stand an end,
　Like quills upon the fretful porpentine: 20
　But this eternal blazon must not be
　To ears of flesh and blood. List, list, O, list!
　If thou didst ever thy dear father love—
HAM.　O God!
GHOST.　Revenge his foul and most unnatural murder.
HAM.　Murder!
GHOST.　Murder most foul, as in the best it is;
　But this most foul, strange and unnatural.
HAM.　Haste me to know 't, that I, with wings as swift
　As meditation or the thoughts of love, 30
　May sweep to my revenge.
GHOST.　　　　　　I find thee apt;
　And duller shouldst thou be than the fat weed
　That roots itself in ease on Lethe wharf,
　Wouldst thou not stir in this. Now, Hamlet, hear:
　'Tis given out that, sleeping in my orchard,
　A serpent stung me; so the whole ear of Denmark
　Is by a forged process of my death
　Rankly abused: but know, thou noble youth,
　The serpent that did sting thy father's life
　Now wears his crown.
HAM.　　　　　　O my prophetic soul! 40
　My uncle!
GHOST.　Ay, that incestuous, that adulterate beast,
　With witchcraft of his wit, with traitorous gifts,—
　O wicked wit and gifts, that have the power
　So to seduce!—won to his shameful lust

---

17. *spheres:* orbits. 18. *combined:* tied, bound. 19. *an end:* on end. 20. *porpentine:* porcupine. 21. *eternal blazon:* promulgation or proclamation of eternity, revelation of the hereafter. 25. *unnatural:* i.e., pertaining to fratricide. 32. *fat weed:* many suggestions have been offered as to the particular plant intended, including asphodel; probably, a general figure for plants growing along rotting wharves and piles. 33. *Lethe wharf:* bank of the river of forgetfulness in Hades. 42. *adulterate:* adulterous.

The will of my most seeming-virtuous queen:
O Hamlet, what a falling-off was there!
From me, whose love was of that dignity
That it went hand in hand even with the vow
I made to her in marriage, and to decline   50
Upon a wretch whose natural gifts were poor
To those of mine!
But virtue, as it never will be moved,
Though lewdness court it in a shape of heaven,
So lust, though to a radiant angel link'd,
Will sate itself in a celestial bed,
And prey on garbage.
But, soft! methinks I scent the morning air;
Brief let me be. Sleeping within my orchard,
My custom always of the afternoon,   60
Upon my secure hour thy uncle stole,
With juice of cursed hebenon in a vial,
And in the porches of my ears did pour
The leperous distilment; whose effect
Holds such an enmity with blood of man
That swift as quicksilver it courses through
The natural gates and alleys of the body,
And with a sudden vigour it doth posset
And curd, like eager droppings into milk,
The thin and wholesome blood: so did it mine;   70
And a most instant tetter bark'd about,
Most lazar-like, with vile and loathsome crust,
All my smooth body.
Thus was I, sleeping, by a brother's hand
Of life, of crown, of queen, at once dispatch'd:
Cut off even in the blossoms of my sin,
Unhousel'd, disappointed, unaneled,
No reckoning made, but sent to my account
With all my imperfections on my head:
O, horrible! O, horrible! most horrible!   80
If thou hast nature in thee, bear it not;
Let not the royal bed of Denmark be
A couch for luxury and damned incest.
But, howsoever thou pursuest this act,
Taint not thy mind, nor let thy soul contrive
Against thy mother aught: leave her to heaven
And to those thorns that in her bosom lodge,

61. *secure:* confident, unsuspicious. 62. *hebenon:* generally supposed to mean henbane. 64. *leperous:* causing leprosy. 68. *posset:* coagulate, curdle. 69. *eager:* sour, acid. 72. *lazar-like:* leperlike. 75. *dispatch'd:* suddenly bereft. 77. *Unhousel'd:* without having received the sacrament. *disappointed:* unready, without equipment for the last journey. *unaneled:* without having received extreme unction. 83. *luxury:* lechery. 85. *Taint... mind:* probably, deprave not thy character, do nothing except in the pursuit of a justifiable revenge.

168   Hamlet

  To prick and sting her. Fare thee well at once!
  The glow-worm shows the matin to be near,
  And 'gins to pale his uneffectual fire: 90
  Adieu, adieu! Hamlet, remember me. *(Exit.)*
HAM. O all you host of heaven! O earth! what else?
  And shall I couple hell? O, fie! Hold, hold, my heart;
  And you, my sinews, grow not instant old,
  But bear me stiffly up. Remember thee!
  Ay, thou poor ghost, while memory holds a seat
  In this distracted globe. Remember thee!
  Yea, from the table of my memory
  I'll wipe away all trivial fond records,
  All saws of books, all forms, all pressures past,   100
  That youth and observation copied there;
  And thy commandment all alone shall live
  Within the book and volume of my brain,
  Unmix'd with baser matter: yes, by heaven!
  O most pernicious woman!
  O villain, villain, smiling, damned villain!
  My tables,—meet it is I set it down,
  That one may smile, and smile, and be a villain;
  At least I 'm sure it may be so in Denmark: *(Writing.)*
  So, uncle, there you are. Now to my word;   110
  It is "Adieu, adieu! remember me."
  I have sworn 't.
MAR. }
HOR. } *(Within).* My lord, my lord,—
MAR.   *(Within).* Lord Hamlet,—
HOR.   *(Within).* Heaven secure him!
HAM. So be it!
HOR. *(Within).* Hillo, ho, ho, my lord!
HAM. Hillo, ho, ho, boy! come, bird, come.

Enter HORATIO *and* MARCELLUS.

MAR. How is 't, my noble lord?
HOR.   What news, my lord?
HAM. O, wonderful!
HOR.   Good my lord, tell it.
HAM. No; you'll reveal it.
HOR. Not I, my lord, by heaven.
MAR.   Nor I, my lord.   120
HAM. How say you, then; would heart of man once think it?
  But you'll be secret?

---

89. *matin:* morning. 90. *uneffectual fire:* cold light. 93. *couple:* add. 97. *distracted globe:* confused head. 100. *pressures:* impressions stamped. 107. *tables:* probably a small portable writing-tablet carried at the belt. 110. *word:* watchword. 115. *Hillo, ho, ho:* a falconer's call to a hawk in air.

HOR. }
MAR. }   Ay, by heaven, my lord.
HAM. There 's ne'er a villain dwelling in all Denmark
  But he 's an arrant knave.
HOR. There needs no ghost, my lord, come from the grave
  To tell us this.
HAM.   Why, right; you are i' the right;
  And so, without more circumstance at all,
  I hold it fit that we shake hands and part:
  You, as your business and desire shall point you;
  For every man has business and desire,   130
  Such as it is; and for mine own poor part,
  Look you, I'll go pray.
HOR. These are but wild and whirling words, my lord.
HAM. I'm sorry they offend you, heartily;
  Yes, 'faith, heartily.
HOR.   There 's no offence, my lord.
HAM. Yes, by Saint Patrick, but there is, Horatio,
  And much offence too. Touching this vision here,
  It is an honest ghost, that let me tell you:
  For your desire to know what is between us,
  O'ermaster 't as you may. And now, good friends,   140
  As you are friends, scholars and soldiers,
  Give me one poor request.
HOR. What is 't, my lord? we will.
HAM. Never make known what you have seen to-night.
HOR. }
MAR. } My lord, we will not.
HAM.   Nay, but swear 't.
HOR.   In faith,
  My lord, not I.
MAR.   Nor I, my lord, in faith.
HAM. Upon my sword.
MAR.   We have sworn, my lord, already.
HAM. Indeed, upon my sword, indeed.
GHOST *(Beneath).* Swear.
HAM. Ah, ha, boy! say'st thou so? art thou there, truepenny?   150
  Come on—you hear this fellow in the cellarage—
  Consent to swear.
HOR.   Propose the oath, my lord.
HAM. Never to speak of this that you have seen,
  Swear by my sword.
GHOST *(Beneath).* Swear.
HAM. Hic et ubique? then we'll shift our ground.

124. *arrant:* thoroughgoing. 136. *Saint Patrick:* St. Patrick was keeper of Purgatory and patron saint of all blunders and confusion. 138. *honest:* i.e., a real ghost and not an evil spirit. 147. *sword:* i.e., the hilt in the form of a cross. 150. *truepenny:* good old boy, or the like. 156. *Hic et ubique?:* Here and everywhere?

Come hither, gentlemen,
And lay your hands again upon my sword:
Swear by my sword,
Never to speak of this that you have heard. 160
GHOST *(Beneath).* Swear by his sword.
HAM. Well said, old mole! canst work i' the earth so fast?
A worthy pioner! Once more remove, good friends.
HOR. O day and night, but this is wondrous strange!
HAM. And therefore as a stranger give it welcome.
There are more things in heaven and earth, Horatio,
Than are dreamt of in your philosophy.
But come;
Here, as before, never, so help you mercy,
How strange or odd soe'er I bear myself, 170
As I perchance hereafter shall think meet
To put an antic disposition on,
That you, at such times seeing me, never shall,
With arms encumber'd thus, or this head-shake,
Or by pronouncing of some doubtful phrase,
As "Well, well, we know," or "We could, an if we would,"
Or "If we list to speak," or "There be, an if they might,"
Or such ambiguous giving out, to note
That you know aught of me: this not to do,
So grace and mercy at your most need help you, 180
Swear.
GHOST *(Beneath).* Swear.
HAM. Rest, rest, perturbed spirit! *(They swear.)* So, gentlemen,
With all my love I do commend me to you:
And what so poor a man as Hamlet is
May do, to express his love and friending to you,
God willing, shall not lack. Let us go in together;
And still your fingers on your lips, I pray.
The time is out of joint: O cursed spite,
That ever I was born to set it right! 190
Nay, come, let 's go together.

Exeunt.

163. *pioner:* digger, miner. 172. *antic:* fantastic. 174. *encumber'd:* folded or entwined. 178. *giving out:* profession of knowledge. *to note:* to give a sign. 186. *friending:* friendliness.

ACT II.

SCENE I.

A room in Polonius' house.

Enter POLONIUS *and* REYNALDO.

POL. Give him this money and these notes, Reynaldo.
REY. I will, my lord.
POL. You shall do marvellous wisely, good Reynaldo,
  Before you visit him, to make inquire
  Of his behaviour.
REY.   My lord, I did intend it.
POL. Marry, well said; very well said. Look you, sir,
  Inquire me first what Danskers are in Paris;
  And how, and who, what means, and where they keep,
  What company, at what expense; and finding
  By this encompassment and drift of question   10
  That they do know my son, come you more nearer
  Than your particular demands will touch it:
  Take you, as 'twere, some distant knowledge of him;
  As thus, "I know his father and his friends,
  And in part him": do you mark this, Reynaldo?
REY. Ay, very well, my lord.
POL. "And in part him; but" you may say "not well:
  But, if 't be he I mean, he 's very wild;
  Addicted so and so": and there put on him
  What forgeries you please; marry, none so rank   20
  As may dishonour him; take heed of that;
  But, sir, such wanton, wild and usual slips
  As are companions noted and most known
  To youth and liberty.
REY.   As gaming, my lord.
POL. Ay, or drinking, fencing, swearing, quarrelling,
  Drabbing: you may go so far.
REY. My lord, that would dishonor him.
POL. 'Faith, no; as you may season it in the charge.
  You must not put another scandal on him,
  That he is open to incontinency;   30
  That 's not my meaning: but breathe his faults so quaintly
  That they may seem the taints of liberty,
  The flash and outbreak of a fiery mind,

---

4. *inquire:* inquiry.   7. *Danskers: Danke* was a common variant for "Denmark"; hence "Dane."   10. *encompassment:* roundabout talking.   *drift:* gradual approach or course.   13. *Take:* assume, pretend.   19. *put on:* impute to.   25. *fencing:* indicative of the ill repute of professional fencers and fencing schools in Elizabethan times.   26. *Drabbing:* associating with immoral women.   31. *quaintly:* delicately, ingeniously.

A savageness in unreclaimed blood,
Of general assault.
REY. But, my good lord,—
POL. Wherefore should you do this?
REY. Ay, my lord,
I would know that.
POL. Marry, sir, here's my drift;
And, I believe, it is a fetch of wit:
You laying these slight sullies on my son,
As 'twere a thing a little soil'd i' the working, 40
Mark you,
Your party in converse, him you would sound,
Having ever seen in the prenominate crimes
The youth you breathe of guilty, be assured
He closes with you in this consequence;
"Good sir," or so, or "friend," or "gentleman,"
According to the phrase or the addition
Of man and country.
REY. Very good, my lord.
POL. And then, sir, does he this—he does—what was I about to say?
By the mass, I was about to say something: where did I leave? 50
REY. At "closes in the consequence," at "friend or so," and
"gentleman."
POL. At "closes in the consequence," ay, marry;
He closes thus: "I know the gentleman;
I saw him yesterday, or t' other day,
Or then, or then; with such, or such; and, as you say,
There was a' gaming; there o'ertook in 's rouse;
There falling out at tennis": or perchance,
"I saw him enter such a house of sale,"
Videlicet, a brothel, or so forth. 60
See you now;
Your bait of falsehood takes this carp of truth:
And thus do we of wisdom and of reach,
With windlasses and with assays of bias,
By indirections find directions out:
So by my former lecture and advice,
Shall you my son. You have me, have you not?
REY. My lord, I have.
POL. God be wi' you; fare you well.
REY. Good my lord!
POL. Observe his inclination in yourself. 70
REY. I shall, my lord.

---

34. *unreclaimed:* untamed. 35. *general assault:* tendency that assails all untrained youth. 45. *closes . . . consequence:* agrees with you in this conclusion. 57. *o'ertook in 's rouse:* overcome by drink. 60. *videlicet:* namely. 64. *reach:* capacity, ability. 64. *windlasses:* i.e., circuitous paths. *assays of bias:* attempts that resemble the course of the bowl, which, being weighted on one side, has a curving motion. 65. *indirections:* devious courses. *directions:* straight courses, i.e., the truth. 66. *lecture:* admonition.

POL. And let him ply his music.
REY.   Well, my lord.
POL. Farewell!

Exit REYNALDO.

Enter OPHELIA.

                        How now, Ophelia! what 's the matter?
OPH. O, my lord, my lord. I have been so affrighted!
POL. With what, i' the name of God?
OPH. My lord, as I was sewing in my closet,
  Lord Hamlet, with his doublet all unbraced;
  No hat upon his head; his stockings foul'd,
  Ungarter'd, and down-gyved to his ancle;
  Pale as his shirt; his knees knocking each other;   80
  And with a look so piteous in purport
  As if he had been loosed out of hell
  To speak of horrors,—he comes before me.
POL. Mad for thy love?
OPH.   My lord, I do not know;
  But truly, I do fear it.
POL.   What said he?
OPH. He took me by the wrist and held me hard;
  Then goes he to the length of all his arm;
  And, with his other hand thus o'er his brow,
  He falls to such perusal of my face
  As he would draw it. Long stay'd he so;   90
  At last, a little shaking of mine arm
  And thrice his head thus waving up and down,
  He raised a sigh so piteous and profound
  As it did seem to shatter all his bulk
  And end his being: that done, he lets me go:
  And, with his head over his shoulder turn'd,
  He seem'd to find his way without his eyes;
  For out o' doors he went without their helps,
  And, to the last, bended their light on me.
POL. Come, go with me: I will go seek the king.   100
  This is the very ecstasy of love,
  Whose violent property fordoes itself
  And leads the will to desperate undertakings
  As oft as any passion under heaven
  That does afflict our natures. I am sorry.
  What, have you given him any hard words of late?
OPH. No, my good lord, but, as you did command,
  I did repel his letters and denied

---

72. *ply his music:* probably to be taken literally.   76. *closet:* private chamber.   77. *doublet:* close-fitting coat.   *unbraced:* unfastened.   79. *down-gyved:* fallen to the ankles (like gyves or fetters).   94. *bulk:* body.   102. *property:* nature.   *fordoes:* destroys.

His access to me.
POL.   That hath made him mad.
I am sorry that with better heed and judgement   110
I had not quoted him: I fear'd he did but trifle,
And meant to wreck thee; but, beshrew my jealousy!
By heaven, it is as proper to our age
To cast beyond ourselves in our opinions
As it is common for the younger sort
To lack discretion. Come, go we to the king:
This must be known; which, being kept close, might move
More grief to hide than hate to utter love.

Exeunt.

SCENE II.

A room in the castle.

Enter KING, QUEEN, ROSENCRANTZ, GUILDENSTERN, *and* ATTENDANTS.

KING. Welcome, dear Rosencrantz and Guildenstern!
Moreover that we much did long to see you,
The need we have to use you did provoke
Our hasty sending. Something have you heard
Of Hamlet's transformation; so call it,
Sith nor the exterior nor the inward man
Resembles that it was. What it should be,
More than his father's death, that thus hath put him
So much from the understanding of himself,
I cannot dream of: I entreat you both,   10
That, being of so young days brought up with him,
And sith so neighbour'd to his youth and haviour,
That you vouchsafe your rest here in our court
Some little time: so by your companies
To draw him on to pleasures, and to gather,
So much as from occasion you may glean,
Whether aught, to us unknown, afflicts him thus,
That, open'd, lies within our remedy.
QUEEN. Good gentlemen, he hath much talk'd of you;
And sure I am two men there are not living   20
To whom he more adheres. If it will please you
To show us so much gentry and good will
As to expend your time with us awhile,

111. *quoted:* observed, marked. 112. *beshrew my jealousy:* curse my suspicion. 114. *cast beyond:* overshoot, miscalculate. 117-118. *might . . . love:* i.e., I might cause more grief to others by hiding the knowledge of Hamlet's love for Ophelia than hatred to me and mine by telling of it. 2. *Moreover:* besides. 11. *of . . . days:* from such early youth. 13. *vouchsafe your rest:* please to stay. 22. *gentry:* courtesy.

    For the supply and profit of our hope,
    Your visitation shall receive such thanks
    As fits a king's remembrance.
ROS.   Both your majesties
    Might, by the sovereign power you have of us,
    Put your dread pleasures more into command
    Than to entreaty.
GUIL.   But we both obey,
    And here give up ourselves, in the full bent   30
    To lay our service freely at your feet,
    To be commanded.
KING. Thanks, Rosencrantz and gentle Guildenstern.
QUEEN. Thanks, Guildenstern and gentle Rosencrantz:
    And I beseech you instantly to visit
    My too much changed son. Go, some of you,
    And bring these gentlemen where Hamlet is.
GUIL. Heavens make our presence and our practices
    Pleasant and helpful to him!
QUEEN.   Ay, amen!

Exeunt ROSENCRANTZ, GUILDENSTERN, *and some* ATTENDANTS.

Enter POLONIUS.

POL. The ambassadors from Norway, my good lord,   40
    Are joyfully return'd.
KING. Thou still hast been the father of good news.
POL. Have I, my lord? I assure my good liege,
    I hold my duty, as I hold my soul,
    Both to my God and to my gracious king:
    And I do think, or else this brain of mine
    Hunts not the trail of policy so sure
    As it hath used to do, that I have found
    The very cause of Hamlet's lunacy.
KING. O, speak of that; that do I long to hear.   50
POL. Give first admittance to the ambassadors;
    My news shall be the fruit to that great feast.
KING. Thyself do grace to them, and bring them in.

Exit POLONIUS.

    He tells me, my dear Gertrude, he hath found
    The head and source of all your son's distemper.
QUEEN. I doubt it is no other but the main;
    His father's death, and our o'erhasty marriage.
KING. Well, we shall sift him.

---

24. *supply and profit:* aid and successful outcome. 30. *in . . . bent:* to the utmost degree of our mental capacity. 52. *fruit:* dessert. 56. *main:* chief point, principal concern.

Re-enter POLONIUS, *with* VOLTIMAND *and* CORNELIUS.

                    Welcome, my good friends!
Say, Voltimand, what from our brother Norway?
VOLT. Most fair return of greetings and desires. 60
  Upon our first, he sent out to suppress
His nephew's levies; which to him appear'd
To be a preparation 'gainst the Polack;
But, better look'd into, he truly found
It was against your highness: whereat grieved,
That so his sickness, age and impotence
Was falsely borne in hand, sends out arrests
On Fortinbras; which he, in brief, obeys;
Receives rebuke from Norway, and in fine
Makes vow before his uncle never more 70
To give the assay of arms against your majesty.
Whereon old Norway, overcome with joy,
Gives him three score thousand crowns in annual fee,
And his commission to employ those soldiers,
So levied as before, against the Polack:
With an entreaty, herein further shown, *(Giving a paper.)*
That it might please you to give quiet pass
Through your dominions for this enterprise,
On such regards of safety and allowance
As therein are set down.
KING.   It likes us well; 80
  And at our more consider'd time we'll read,
Answer, and think upon this business.
Meantime we thank you for your well-took labour:
Go to your rest; at night we'll feast together:
Most welcome home!

Exeunt VOLTIMAND *and* CORNELIUS.

POL.   This business is well ended.
  My liege, and madam, to expostulate
What majesty should be, what duty is,
Why day is day, night night, and time is time,
Were nothing but to waste night, day and time.
Therefore, since brevity is the soul of wit, 90
And tediousness the limbs and outward flourishes,
I will be brief: your noble son is mad:
Mad call I it; for, to define true madness,

---

61. *our first:* opening of our audience. 67. *borne in hand:* deluded. *arrests:* orders. 71. *assay:* assault, trial (of arms). 79. *safety and allowance:* pledges of safety to the country and terms of permission for the troops to pass. 81. *consider'd:* suitable for deliberation. 90. *wit:* sound sense or judgment. 91. *flourishes:* ostentatious embellishments.

What is 't but to be nothing else but mad?
But let that go.
QUEEN.   More matter, with less art.
POL.   Madam, I swear I use no art at all.
  That he is mad, 'tis true: 'tis true 'tis pity;
And pity 'tis 'tis true: a foolish figure;
But farewell it, for I will use no art.
Mad let us grant him, then: and now remains   100
That we find out the cause of this effect,
Or rather say, the cause of this defect,
For this effect defective comes by cause:
Thus it remains, and the remainder thus.
Perpend.
I have a daughter—have while she is mine—
Who, in her duty and obedience, mark,
Hath given me this: now gather, and surmise. *(Reads.)*
"To the celestial and my soul's idol, the most beautified Ophelia,"—
That 's an ill phrase, a vile phrase; "beautified" is a vile phrase: but   110
  you shall hear. Thus: *(Reads.)*
"In her excellent white bosom, these, &c."
QUEEN. Came this from Hamlet to her?
POL. Good madam, stay awhile; I will be faithful. *(Reads.)*
     "Doubt thou the stars are fire;
      Doubt that the sun doth move;
     Doubt truth to be a liar;
      But never doubt I love.
"O dear Ophelia, I am ill at these numbers; I have not art to reckon
  my groans: but that I love thee best, O most best, believe it. Adieu.
"Thine evermore, most dear lady, whilst this machine is to him,
  HAMLET."
This, in obedience, hath my daughter shown me,   120
And more above, hath his solicitings,
As they fell out by time, by means and place,
All given to mine ear.
KING.   But how hath she
Received his love?
POL.   What do you think of me?
KING. As of a man faithful and honourable.
POL. I would fain prove so. But what might you think,
When I had seen this hot love on the wing—
As I perceived it, I must tell you that,
Before my daughter told me—what might you,
Or my dear majesty your queen here, think,   130
If I had play'd the desk or table-book,

---

95. *More . . . art:* more information with fewer rhetorical flourishes. 98. *figure:* figure of speech. 105. *Perpend:* consider. 120. *ill . . . numbers:* unskilled at writing verses. 124. *machine:* bodily frame. 126. *more above:* moreover. 127. *fell out:* occurred. 131. *play'd . . . table-book:* i.e., remained shut up, concealed his information.

Or given my heart a winking, mute and dumb,
Or look'd upon this love with idle sight;
What might you think? No, I went round to work,
And my young mistress thus I did bespeak:
"Lord Hamlet is a prince, out of thy star;
This must not be": and then I prescripts gave her,
That she should lock herself from his resort,
Admit no messengers, receive no tokens.
Which done, she took the fruits of my advice; 140
And he, repelled—a short tale to make—
Fell into a sadness, then into a fast,
Thence to a watch, thence into a weakness,
Thence to a lightness, and, by this declension,
Into the madness wherein now he raves,
And all we mourn for.
KING.   Do you think 'tis this?
QUEEN. It may be, very like.
POL. Hath there been such a time—I 'd fain know that—
  That I have positively said "'Tis so,"
  When it proved otherwise?
KING.   Not that I know. 150
POL. *(Pointing to his head and shoulder).* Take this from
  this, if this be otherwise:
  If circumstances lead me, I will find
  Where truth is hid, though it were hid indeed
  Within the centre.
KING.   How may we try it further?
POL. You know, sometimes he walks four hours together
  Here in the lobby.
QUEEN.   So he does indeed.
POL. At such a time I'll loose my daughter to him:
  Be you and I behind an arras then;
  Mark the encounter: if he love her not 160
  And be not from his reason fall'n thereon,
  Let me be no assistant for a state,
  But keep a farm and carters.
KING.   We will try it.
QUEEN. But, look, where sadly the poor wretch comes reading.
POL. Away, I do beseech you, both away:
  I'll board him presently.

---

132. *given . . . winking:* given my heart a signal to keep silent. 134. *round:* roundly, straightforwardly. 135. *bespeak:* address. 136. *out . . . star:* above you in position. 143. *watch:* state of sleeplessness. 144. *lightness:* light-headedness. *declension:* decline, deterioration. 154. *centre:* middle point of the earth. 160. *encounter:* style or manner of address, behavior. 166. *board:* accost.

Exeunt KING, QUEEN, *and* ATTENDANTS.

Enter HAMLET, *reading.*

                     O, give me leave:
How does my good Lord Hamlet?
HAM. Well, God-a-mercy.
POL. Do you know me, my lord?
HAM. Excellent well; you are a fishmonger.
POL. Not I, my lord.
HAM. Then I would you were so honest a man.
POL. Honest, my lord!
HAM. Ay, sir; to be honest, as this world goes, is to be one man picked out of ten thousand.
POL. That's very true, my lord.
HAM. For if the sun breed maggots in a dead dog, being a god kissing carrion,—Have you a daughter?
POL. I have, my lord.
HAM. Let her not walk i' the sun: conception is a blessing: but not as your daughter may conceive. Friend, look to 't.
POL. *(Aside)*. How say you by that? Still harping on my daughter: yet he knew me not at first; he said I was a fishmonger: he is far gone: and truly in my youth I suffered much extremity for love; very near this. I'll speak to him again. What do you read, my lord?
HAM. Words, words, words.
POL. What is the matter, my lord?
HAM. Between who?
POL. I mean, the matter that you read, my lord.
HAM. Slanders, sir: for the satirical rogue says here that old men have grey beards, that their faces are wrinkled, their eyes purging thick amber and plum-tree gum and that they have a plentiful lack of wit, together with most weak hams: all which, sir, though I most powerfully and potently believe, yet I hold it not honesty to have it thus set down, for yourself, sir, should be old as I am, if like a crab you could go backward.
POL. *(Aside)*. Though this be madness, yet there is method in 't. Will you walk out of the air, my lord?
HAM. Into my grave.
POL. Indeed, that is out o' the air. *(Aside)* How pregnant sometimes his replies are! a happiness that often madness hits on, which reason and sanity could not so prosperously be delivered of. I will leave him, and suddenly contrive the means of meeting between him and my daughter.—My honourable lord, I will most humbly take my leave of you.

---

171. *fishmonger:* an opprobrious expression possibly meaning "bawd," "procurer." 178-179. *god kissing carrion:* the sun god shining on a dead body. Hamlet is supposed to be reading the matter from the book he is carrying. 181. *conception:* quibble on "understanding" and "pregnancy." 183. *by:* concerning. 188. *matter:* substance. 192. *purging:* discharging. 195. *honesty:* decency. 202. *happiness:* felicity of expression. 203. *prosperously:* successfully.

HAM. You cannot, sir, take from me any thing that I will more willingly part withal: except my life, except my life, except my life.
POL. Fare you well, my lord.
HAM. These tedious old fools! 210

Enter ROSENCRANTZ *and* GUILDENSTERN.

POL. You go to seek the Lord Hamlet; there he is.
ROS. *(To* POLONIUS*).* God save you, sir! *(Exit* POLONIUS.*)*
GUIL. My honoured lord!
ROS. My most dear lord!
HAM. My excellent good friends! How dost thou, Guildenstern? Ah, Rosencrantz! Good lads, how do ye both?
ROS. As the indifferent children of the earth.
GUIL. Happy, in that we are not over-happy;
On fortune's cap we are not the very button.
HAM. Nor the soles of her shoe? 220
ROS. Neither, my lord.
HAM. Then you live about her waist, or in the middle of her favours?
GUIL. 'Faith, her privates we.
HAM. In the secret parts of fortune? O, most true; she is a strumpet. What's the news?
ROS. None, my lord, but that the world's grown honest.
HAM. Then is doomsday near: but your news is not true. Let me question more in particular: what have you, my good friends, deserved at the hands of fortune, that she sends you to prison hither?
GUIL. Prison, my lord! 230
HAM. Denmark's a prison.
ROS. Then is the world one.
HAM. A goodly one; in which there are many confines, wards and dungeons, Denmark being one o' the worst.
ROS. We think not so, my lord.
HAM. Why, then, 'tis none to you; for there is nothing either good or bad, but thinking makes it so: to me it is a prison.
ROS. Why then, your ambition makes it one; 'tis too narrow for your mind.
HAM. O God, I could be bounded in a nutshell and count myself a 240
king of infinite space, were it not that I have bad dreams.
GUIL. Which dreams indeed are ambition, for the very substance of the ambitious is merely the shadow of a dream.
HAM. A dream itself is but a shadow.
ROS. Truly, and I hold ambition of so airy and light a quality that it is but a shadow's shadow.
HAM. Then are our beggars bodies, and our monarchs and outstretched heroes the beggars' shadows. Shall we to the court? for, by my fay, I cannot reason.

217. *indifferent:* ordinary. 233. *confines:* places of confinement. 248. *fay:* faith. 249. *reason:* argue.

ROS.⎱
GUIL.⎰ We'll wait upon you. 250

HAM. No such matter: I will not sort you with the rest of my servants, for, to speak to you like an honest man, I am most dreadfully attended. But, in the beaten way of friendship, what make you at Elsinore?

ROS. To visit you, my lord; no other occasion.

HAM. Beggar that I am, I am even poor in thanks; but I thank you: and sure, dear friends, my thanks are too dear a halfpenny. Were you not sent for? Is it your own inclining? Is it a free visitation? Come, deal justly with me: come, come; nay, speak.

GUIL. What should we say, my lord? 260

HAM. Why, any thing, but to the purpose. You were sent for; and there is a kind of confession in your looks which your modesties have not craft enough to colour: I know the good king and queen have sent for you.

ROS. To what end, my lord?

HAM. That you must teach me. But let me conjure you, by the rights of our fellowship, by the consonancy of our youth, by the obligation of our ever-preserved love, and by what more dear a better proposer could charge you withal, be even and direct with me, whether you were sent for, or no? 270

ROS. *(Aside to* GUIL.*).* What say you?

HAM. *(Aside).* Nay, then, I have an eye of you.—If you love me, hold not off.

GUIL. My lord, we were sent for.

HAM. I will tell you why; so shall my anticipation prevent your discovery, and your secrecy to the king and queen moult no feather. I have of late— but wherefore I know not—lost all my mirth, forgone all custom of exercises; and indeed it goes so heavily with my disposition that this goodly frame, the earth, seems to me a sterile promontory, this most excellent canopy, the air, look you, this brave o'er- 280 hanging firmament, this majestical roof fretted with golden fire, why, it appears no other thing to me than a foul and pestilent congregation of vapours. What a piece of work is a man! how noble in reason! how infinite in faculty! in form and moving how express and admirable! in action how like an angel! in apprehension how like a god! the beauty of the world! the paragon of animals! And yet, to me what is this quintessence of dust? man delights not me: no, nor woman neither, though by your smiling you seem to say so.

ROS. My lord, there was no such stuff in my thoughts.

HAM. Why did you laugh then, when I said "man delights not me"? 290

ROS. To think, my lord, if you delight not in man, what lenten enter-

---

250. *wait upon:* accompany. 251. *sort:* class. 252-253. *dreadfully attended:* poorly provided with servants. *in the ... friendship:* as a matter of course among friends. 259. *a:* i.e., at a. 266. *conjure:* adjure, entreat. 267. *consonancy of our youth:* the fact that we are of the same age. 268. *better proposer:* one more skillful in finding proposals. 274-275. *prevent your discovery:* forestall your disclosure. 281. *fretted:* adorned. 284. *faculty:* capacity. 285. *apprehension:* understanding. 287. *quintessence:* the fifth essence of ancient philosophy, supposed to be the substance of the heavenly bodies and to be latent in all things. 291. *lenten:* meager.

tainment the players shall receive from you: we coted them on the way; and hither are they coming, to offer you service.

HAM. He that plays the king shall be welcome; his majesty shall have tribute of me; the adventurous knight shall use his foil and target; the lover shall not sigh gratis; the humorous man shall end his part in peace; the clown shall make those laugh whose lungs are tickle o' the sere; and the lady shall say her mind freely, or the blank verse shall halt for 't. What players are they?

ROS. Even those you were wont to take delight in, the tragedians of the city. 300

HAM. How chances it they travel? their residence, both in reputation and profit, was better both ways.

ROS. I think their inhibition comes by the means of the late innovation.

HAM. Do they hold the same estimation they did when I was in the city? are they so followed?

ROS. No, indeed, are they not.

HAM. How comes it? do they grow rusty?

ROS. Nay, their endeavour keeps in the wonted pace: but there is, sir, 310 an aery of children, little eyases, that cry out on the top of question, and are most tyrannically clapped for 't: these are now the fashion, and so berattle the common stages—so they call them—that many wearing rapiers are afraid of goose-quills and dare scarce come thither.

HAM. What, are they children? who maintains 'em? how are they escoted? Will they pursue the quality no longer than they can sing? will they not say afterwards, if they should grow themselves to common players—as it is most like, if their means are no better—their writers do them wrong, to make them exclaim against their own succession? 320

ROS. 'Faith, there has been much to do on both sides; and the nation holds it no sin to tarre them to controversy: there was, for a while, no money bid for argument, unless the poet and the player went to cuffs in the question.

---

292. *coted:* overtook and passed beyond. 295. *foil and target:* sword or rapier and shield. 296. *humorous man:* actor who takes the part of the humor characters. 297-298. *tickle o' the sere:* easy on the trigger. 298-299. *the lady . . . for't:* the lady (fond of talking) shall have opportunity to talk, blank verse or no blank verse. 302. *residence:* remaining in the city. 304. *inhibition:* formal prohibition (from acting plays in the city or, possibly, at court). 305. *innovation:* the allusion is either to the introduction into plays of satire on persons or to the introduction of the Children of the Revels into Blackfriars Theatre (January 1603). The actors have been forced to take to the road by two things—some "inhibition" and the rivalry of the children. 311. *aery:* nest. *eyases:* young hawks. 312. *tyrannically:* outrageously. 313. *berattle:* fill with din. 313-314. *many wearing rapiers:* many men of fashion, who were afraid to patronize the common players for fear of being satirized by the poets who wrote for the children. *goose-quills:* i.e., satire. 316. *escoted:* maintained. *no longer . . . sing:* i.e., follow the profession only until their voices change. 317-318. *common:* regular. 320. *succession:* future careers. 322. *tarre:* set on (as dogs). 323. *argument:* probably, plot for a play. 323-324. *went to cuffs:* came to blows. *question:* controversy.

HAM. Is 't possible?
GUIL. O, there has been much throwing about of brains.
HAM. Do the boys carry it away?
ROS. Ay, that they do, my lord; Hercules and his load too.
HAM. It is not very strange; for mine uncle is king of Denmark, and those that would make mows at him while my father lived, give twenty, forty, fifty, an hundred ducats a-piece for his picture in little. 'Sblood, there is something in this more than natural, if philosophy could find it out.   330

Flourish of trumpets within.

GUIL. There are the players.
HAM. Gentlemen, you are welcome to Elsinore. Your hands, come then: the appurtenance of welcome is fashion and ceremony: let me comply with you in this garb, lest my extent to the players, which, I tell you, must show fairly outward, should more appear like entertainment than yours. You are welcome: but my uncle-father and aunt-mother are deceived.   340
GUIL. In what, my dear lord?
HAM. I am but mad north-north-west: when the wind is southerly I know a hawk from a handsaw.

Re-enter POLONIUS.

POL. Well be with you, gentlemen!
HAM. Hark you, Guildenstern; and you too: at each ear a hearer: that great baby you see there is not yet out of his swaddling-clouts.
ROS. Happily he 's the second time come to them; for they say an old man is twice a child.
HAM. I will prophesy he comes to tell me of the players; mark it. You say right, sir: o' Monday morning; 'twas so indeed.   350
POL. My lord, I have news to tell you.
HAM. My lord, I have news to tell you. When Roscius was an actor in Rome,—
POL. The actors are come hither, my lord.
HAM. Buz, buz!
POL. Upon mine honour,—
HAM. Then came each actor on his ass,—
POL. The best actors in the world, either for tragedy, comedy, history, pastoral, pastoral-comical, historical-pastoral, tragical-historical, trag-

---

327. *carry it away:* win the day. 328. *Hercules...load:* regarded as an allusion to the sign of the Globe Theatre, which was Hercules bearing the world on his shoulder. 330. *mows:* grimaces. 331. *ducats:* gold coins worth 9s. 4d. *in little:* in miniature. 337. *comply:* observe the formalities of courtesy. *garb:* manner. *extent:* showing of kindness. 342. *I am...north-north-west:* I am only partly mad, i.e., in only one point of the compass. 350. *o' Monday morning:* said to mislead Polonius. 352. *Roscius:* a famous Roman actor. 357. *Then...ass:* probably a quotation, not identified.

ical-comical-historical-pastoral, scene individual, or poem unlimited: 360
Seneca cannot be too heavy, nor Plautus too light. For the law of
writ and the liberty, these are the only men.
HAM. O Jephthah, judge of Israel, what a treasure hadst thou!
POL. What a treasure had he, my lord?
HAM. Why,
"One fair daughter, and no more,
The which he loved passing well."
POL. *(Aside).* Still on my daughter.
HAM. Am I not i' the right, old Jephthah?
POL. If you call me Jephthah, my lord, I have a daughter that I love 370
passing well.
HAM. Nay, that follows not.
POL. What follows, then, my lord?
HAM. Why,
"As by lot, God wot,"
and then, you know,
"It came to pass, as most like it was,"—
the first row of the pious chanson will show you more; for look,
where my abridgement comes.

Enter four or five PLAYERS.

You are welcome, masters; welcome, all. I am glad to see thee well. 380
Welcome, good friends. O, my old friend! thy face is valanced since I
saw thee last; comest thou to beard me in Denmark? What, my young
lady and mistress! By 'r lady, your ladyship is nearer to heaven than
when I saw you last, by the altitude of a chopine. Pray God, your
voice, like a piece of uncurrent gold, be not cracked within the ring.
Masters, you are all welcome. We'll e'en to 't like French falconers,
fly at any thing we see: we'll have a speech straight: come, give us a
taste of your quality; come, a passionate speech.
FIRST PLAY. What speech, my lord?
HAM. I heard thee speak me a speech once, but it was never acted; or, 390
if it was, not above once; for the play, I remember, pleased not the
million; 'twas caviare to the general: but it was—as I received it, and
others, whose judgements in such matters cried in the top of mine—an
excellent play, well digested in the scenes, set down with as much
modesty as cunning. I remember, one said there were no sallets in the
lines to make the matter savoury, nor no matter in the phrase that

360. *scene individable:* a play observing the unity of place. *poem unlimited:* a play disregarding the unities of time and place. 361. *Seneca:* writer of Latin tragedies, a model of early Elizabethan writers of tragedy. *Plautus:* writer of Latin comedy. 363. *Jephthah . . . Israel:* a popular ballad of *Jephthah's Daughter* has been preserved in several forms. 377. *like:* probable. 378. *row:* possibly, stanza. *pious chanson:* scriptural ballad. 379. *abridgement comes:* opportunity comes for cutting short the conversation. 381. *valanced:* fringed (with a beard). 384. *chopine:* kind of shoe raised by the thickness of the heel; worn in Italy, particularly at Venice. 385. *uncurrent:* not passable as lawful coinage. *cracked within the ring:* in the center of coins were rings enclosing the sovereign's head; if the coin was cracked within this ring, it was unfit for currency. 392. *caviare to the general:* not relished by the multitude (like caviare). 393. *cried in the top of:* spoke with greater authority than. 395. *sallets:* salads; here, spicy improprieties.

might indict the author of affectation; but called it an honest method,
as wholesome as sweet, and by very much more handsome than fine.
One speech in it I chiefly loved: 'twas Aeneas' tale to Dido; and thereabout of it especially, where he speaks of Priam's slaughter: if it live   400
in your memory, begin at this line: let me see, let me see—
      "The rugged Pyrrhus, like the Hyrcanian beast,"—
it is not so:—it begins with Pyrrhus:—
"The rugged Pyrrhus, he whose sable arms,
Black as his purpose, did the night resemble
When he lay couched in the ominous horse,
Hath now this dread and black complexion smear'd
With heraldry more dismal; head to foot
Now is he total gules; horridly trick'd
With blood of fathers, mothers, daughters, sons,   410
Baked and impasted with the parching streets,
That lend a tyrannous and damned light
To their lord's murder: roasted in wrath and fire,
And thus o'er-sized with coagulate gore,
With eyes like carbuncles, the hellish Pyrrhus
Old grandsire Priam seeks."
So, proceed you.

POL. 'Fore God, my lord, well spoken, with good accent and good
discretion.

FIRST PLAY.   "Anon he finds him   420
Striking too short at Greeks; his antique sword,
Rebellious to his arm, lies where it falls,
Repugnant to command: unequal match'd,
Pyrrhus at Priam drives: in rage strikes wide;
But with the whiff and wind of his fell sword
The unnerved father falls. Then senseless Ilium,
Seeming to feel this blow, with flaming top
Stoops to his base, and with a hideous crash
Takes prisoner Pyrrhus' ear: for, lo! his sword,
Which was declining on the milky head   430
Of reverend Priam, seem'd i' the air to stick:
So, as a painted tyrant, Pyrrhus stood,
And like a neutral to his will and matter,
Did nothing.
But, as we often see, against some storm,
A silence in the heavens, the rack stand still,

---

399. *Aeneas' tale to Dido:* the lines recited by the player are imitated from Marlowe and Nashe's *Dido Queen of Carthage* (II, i, 214 ff.). They are written in such a way that the conventionality of the play within a play is raised above that of ordinary drama. 403. *Pyrrhus:* a Greek hero of the Trojan War. *Hyrcanian beast:* the tiger; see Virgil, *Aeneid*, IV, 266. 407. *ominous horse:* Trojan horse. 409. *gules:* red; a heraldic term. *trick'd:* spotted, smeared. 411. *impasted:* made into a paste. 414. *o'er-sized:* covered as with size or glue. 423. *Repugnant:* offering resistance. 424. *drives:* rushes. 426. *Then senseless Ilium:* insensible Troy. 432. *painted tyrant:* tyrant in a picture. 433. *neutral:* one indifferent. *matter:* task. 435. *against:* before. 436. *rack:* mass of clouds.

The bold winds speechless and the orb below
　　　As hush as death, anon the dreadful thunder
　　　Doth rend the region, so, after Pyrrhus' pause,
　　　Aroused vengeance sets him new a-work;　　　　　　　　　440
　　　And never did the Cyclops' hammers fall
　　　On Mars's armour forged for proof eterne
　　　With less remorse than Pyrrhus' bleeding sword
　　　Now falls on Priam.
　　　Out, out, thou strumpet, Fortune! All you gods,
　　　In general synod, take away her power;
　　　Break all the spokes and fellies from her wheel,
　　　And bowl the round nave down the hill of heaven,
　　　As low as to the fiends!"
POL. This is too long.　　　　　　　　　　　　　　　　　　　　450
HAM. It shall be to the barber's, with your beard. Prithee, say on: he's for a jig or a tale of bawdry, or he sleeps: say on: come to Hecuba.
FIRST PLAY. "But who, O, who had seen the mobled queen—"
HAM. "The mobled queen?"
POL. That's good; "mobled queen" is good.
FIRST PLAY. "Run barefoot up and down, threatening the flames
　　　With bisson rheum; a clout upon that head
　　　Where late the diadem stood, and for a robe,
　　　About her lank and all o'er-teemed loins,　　　　　　　　　460
　　　A blanket, in the alarm of fear caught up;
　　　Who this had seen, with tongue in venom steep'd,
　　　'Gainst Fortune's state would treason have pronounced:
　　　But if the gods themselves did see her then
　　　When she saw Pyrrhus make malicious sport
　　　In mincing with his sword her husband's limbs,
　　　The instant burst of clamour that she made,
　　　Unless things mortal move them not at all,
　　　Would have made milch the burning eyes of heaven,
　　　And passion in the gods."　　　　　　　　　　　　　　　　470
POL. Look, whether he has not turned his colour and has tears in 's eyes. Pray you, no more.
HAM. 'Tis well; I'll have thee speak out the rest soon. Good my lord, will you see the players well bestowed? Do you hear, let them be well used; for they are the abstract and brief chronicles of the time: after your death you were better have a bad epitaph than their ill report while you live.
POL. My lord, I will use them according to their desert.

---

439. *region:* sky.　442. *proof eterne:* eternal resistance to assault.　446. *synod:* assembly.　447. *fellies:* pieces of wood forming the rim of a wheel.　448. *nave:* hub.　452. *jig:* comic performance given at the end or in an interval of a play.　*bawdry:* indecency. 453. *Hecuba:* wife of Priam, king of Troy.　454. *mobled:* muffled.　458. *bisson rheum:* blinding tears.　*clout:* piece of cloth.　460. *o'er-teemed:* worn out with bearing children. 469. *milch:* moist with tears.　471. *turned:* changed.　475. *abstract:* summary account.

HAM. God's bodykins, man, much better: use every man after his
 desert, and who should 'scape whipping? Use them after your own   480
 honour and dignity: the less they deserve, the more merit is in your
 bounty. Take them in.
POL. Come, sirs.
HAM. Follow him, friends: we'll hear a play to-morrow. *(Exit
 POLONIUS with all the PLAYERS but the FIRST.)* Dost thou hear me,
 old friend; can you play the Murder of Gonzago?
FIRST PLAY. Ay, my lord.
HAM. We'll ha 't to-morrow night. You could, for a need, study a
 speech of some dozen or sixteen lines, which I would set down and
 insert in 't, could you not?   490
FIRST PLAY. Ay, my lord.
HAM. Very well. Follow that lord; and look you mock him not. *(Exit
 FIRST PLAYER.)* My good friends, I'll leave you till night: you are wel-
 come to Elsinore.
ROS. Good my lord!
HAM. Ay, so, God be wi' ye; *(Exeunt ROSENCRANTZ and
 GUILDENSTERN.)* Now I am alone.
 O, what a rogue and peasant slave am I!
 Is it not monstrous that this player here,
 But in a fiction, in a dream of passion,   500
 Could force his soul so to his own conceit
 That from her working all his visage wann'd,
 Tears in his eyes, distraction in 's aspect,
 A broken voice, and his whole function suiting
 With forms to his conceit? and all for nothing!
 For Hecuba!
 What 's Hecuba to him, or he to Hecuba,
 That he should weep for her? What would he do,
 Had he the motive and the cue for passion
 That I have? He would drown the stage with tears   510
 And cleave the general ear with horrid speech,
 Make mad the guilty and appal the free,
 Confound the ignorant, and amaze indeed
 The very faculties of eyes and ears.
 Yet I,
 A dull and muddy-mettled rascal, peak,
 Like John-a-dreams, unpregnant of my cause,
 And can say nothing; no, not for a king,
 Upon whose property and most dear life
 A damn'd defeat was made. Am I a coward?   520

---

479. *bodykins:* diminutive form of the oath, "by God's body." 498. *peasant:* base.
502. *wann'd:* grew pale. 504-505. *his whole . . . conceit:* his whole being responded
with forms to suit his thought. 516. *muddy-mettled:* dull-spirited. *peak:* mope, pine.
517. *John-a-dreams:* an expression occurring elsewhere in Elizabethan literature to indicate a dreamer. *unpregnant of:* not quickened by. 519. *property:* proprietorship (of
crown and life).

Who calls me villain? breaks my pate across?
Plucks off my beard, and blows it in my face?
Tweaks me by the nose? gives me the lie i' the throat,
As deep as to the lungs? who does me this?
Ha!
'Swounds, I should take it: for it cannot be
But I am pigeon-liver'd and lack gall
To make oppression bitter, or ere this
I should have fatted all the region kites
With this slave's offal: bloody, bawdy villain!   530
Remorseless, treacherous, lecherous, kindless villain!
O, vengeance!
Why, what an ass am I! This is most brave,
That I, the son of a dear father murder'd,
Prompted to my revenge by heaven and hell,
Must, like a whore, unpack my heart with words,
And fall a-cursing, like a very drab,
A scullion!
Fie upon 't! foh! About, my brain! I have heard
That guilty creatures sitting at a play   540
Have by the very cunning of the scene
Been struck so to the soul that presently
They have proclaim'd their malefactions;
For murder, though it have no tongue, will speak
With most miraculous organ. I'll have these players
Play something like the murder of my father
Before mine uncle: I'll observe his looks;
I'll tent him to the quick: if he but blench,
I know my course. The spirit that I have seen
May be the devil: and the devil hath power   550
To assume a pleasing shape; yea, and perhaps
Out of my weakness and my melancholy,
As he is very potent with such spirits,
Abuses me to damn me: I'll have grounds
More relative than this: the play 's the thing
Wherein I'll catch the conscience of the king.

Exit.

---

527. *pigeon-liver'd:* the pigeon was supposed to secrete no gall; if Hamlet, so he says, had had gall, he would have felt the bitterness of oppression, and avenged it. 529. *region kites:* kites of the air. 531. *kindless:* unnatural. 537. *drab:* prostitute. 538. *scullion:* kitchen servant. 539. *About:* about it, or turn thou right about. 548. *tent:* probe. *blench:* quail, flinch. 553. *spirits:* humors. 554. *Abuses:* deceives. 555. *relative:* closely related, definite. *this:* i.e., the ghost's story.

ACT III.

SCENE I.

A room in the castle.

Enter KING, QUEEN, POLONIUS, OPHELIA, ROSENCRANTZ, *and* GUILDENSTERN.

KING. And can you, by no drift of conference,
  Get from him why he puts on this confusion,
  Grating so harshly all his days of quiet
  With turbulent and dangerous lunacy?
ROS. He does confess he feels himself distracted;
  But from what cause he will by no means speak.
GUIL. Nor do we find him forward to be sounded,
  But, with a crafty madness, keeps aloof,
  When we would bring him on to some confession
  Of his true state.
QUEEN.   Did he receive you well? 10
ROS. Most like a gentleman.
GUIL. But with much forcing of his disposition.
ROS. Niggard of question; but, of our demands,
  Most free in his reply.
QUEEN.   Did you assay him
  To any pastime?
ROS. Madam, it so fell out, that certain players
  We o'er-raught on the way: of these we told him;
  And there did seem in him a kind of joy
  To hear of it: they are about the court,
  And, as I think, they have already order
  This night to play before him. 20
POL.   'Tis most true:
  And he beseech'd me to entreat your majesties
  To hear and see the matter.
KING. With all my heart; and it doth much content me
  To hear him so inclined.
  Good gentlemen, give him a further edge,
  And drive his purpose on to these delights.
ROS. We shall, my lord.

Exeunt ROSENCRANTZ *and* GUILDENSTERN.

KING.   Sweet Gertrude, leave us too;
  For we have closely sent for Hamlet hither,
  That he, as 'twere by accident, may here 30

1. *drift of conference:* device of conversation. 7. *forward:* willing. 12. *forcing of his disposition:* i.e., against his will. 13. *Niggard of question:* sparing of conversation. 14. *assay:* tempt, challenge. 17. *o'er-raught:* overtook. 26. *edge:* incitement. 29. *closely:* secretly.

Affront Ophelia:
Her father and myself, lawful espials,
Will so bestow ourselves that, seeing, unseen,
We may of their encounter frankly judge,
And gather by him, as he is behaved,
If 't be the affliction of his love or no
That thus he suffers for.
QUEEN. I shall obey you.
And for your part, Ophelia, I do wish
That your good beauties be the happy cause
Of Hamlet's wildness: so shall I hope your virtues   40
Will bring him to his wonted way again,
To both your honours.
OPH. Madam, I wish it may. *(Exit* QUEEN.*)*
POL. Ophelia, walk you here. Gracious, so please you,
We will bestow ourselves. *(To* OPHELIA*)* Read on this book;
That show of such an exercise may colour
Your loneliness. We are oft to blame in this,—
'Tis too much proved—that with devotion's visage
And pious action we do sugar o'er
The devil himself.
KING *(Aside).* O, 'tis too true!
How smart a lash that speech doth give my conscience!   50
The harlot's cheek, beautied with plastering art,
Is not more ugly to the thing that helps it
Than is my deed to my most painted word:
O heavy burthen!
POL. I hear him coming: let 's withdraw, my lord.

Exeunt KING *and* POLONIUS.

Enter HAMLET.

HAM. To be, or not to be: that is the question:
Whether 'tis nobler in the mind to suffer
The slings and arrows of outrageous fortune,
Or to take arms against a sea of troubles,
And by opposing end them? To die: to sleep;   60
No more; and by a sleep to say we end
The heart-ache and the thousand natural shocks
That flesh is heir to, 'tis a consummation
Devoutly to be wish'd. To die, to sleep;
To sleep: perchance to dream: ay, there 's the rub;
For in that sleep of death what dreams may come

---

31. *Affront:* confront. 32. *lawful espials:* legitimate spies. 40. *wildness:* madness.
43. *Gracious:* your grace (addressed to the king). 45. *exercise:* act of devotion. 52. *to:* compared to. *thing:* i.e., the cosmetic. 65. *rub:* obstacle, as in the game of bowls.

When we have shuffled off this mortal coil,
Must give us pause: there's the respect
That makes calamity of so long life;
For who would bear the whips and scorns of time,   70
The oppressor's wrong, the proud man's contumely,
The pangs of despised love, the law's delay,
The insolence of office and the spurns
That patient merit of the unworthy takes,
When he himself might his quietus make
With a bare bodkin? who would fardels bear,
To grunt and sweat under a weary life,
But that the dread of something after death,
The undiscover'd country from whose bourn
No traveller returns, puzzles the will   80
And makes us rather bear those ills we have
Than fly to others that we know not of?
Thus conscience does make cowards of us all;
And thus the native hue of resolution
Is sicklied o'er with the pale cast of thought,
And enterprises of great pitch and moment
With this regard their currents turn awry,
And lose the name of action.—Soft you now!
The fair Ophelia! Nymph, in thy orisons
Be all my sins remember'd.
OPH.   Good my lord,   90
How does your honour for this many a day?
HAM. I humbly thank you; well, well, well.
OPH. My lord, I have remembrances of yours,
That I have longed long to re-deliver;
I pray you, now receive them.
HAM.   No, not I;
I never gave you aught.
OPH. My honour'd lord, you know right well you did;
And, with them, words of so sweet breath composed
As made the things more rich: their perfume lost,
Take these again; for to the noble mind   100
Rich gifts wax poor when givers prove unkind.
There, my lord.

---

67. *shuffled:* sloughed, cast. *coil:* usually means "turmoil"; here, possibly, "body" (conceived of as wound about the soul like rope); *clay, soil, veil* have been suggested as emendations. 69. *of . . . life:* so long lived. 70. *time:* the world. 72. *despised:* rejected. 73. *office:* office-holders. *spurns:* insults. 75. *quietus:* acquittance; here, death. 76. *bare bodkin:* mere dagger; *bare* is sometimes understood as "unsheathed." *fardels:* burdens. 79. *bourn:* boundary. 83. *conscience:* probably, inhibition by the faculty of reason restraining the will from doing wrong. 85. *sicklied o'er:* given a sickly tinge. *cast:* shade of color. 86. *pitch:* height. 87. *regard:* respect, consideration. *currents:* courses. 89. *orisons:* prayers.

HAM. Ha, ha! are you honest?
OPH. My lord?
HAM. Are you fair?
OPH. What means your lordship?
HAM. That if you be honest and fair, your honesty should admit no discourse to your beauty.
OPH. Could beauty, my lord, have better commerce than with honesty? 110
HAM. Ay, truly; for the power of beauty will sooner transform honesty from what it is to a bawd than the force of honesty can translate beauty into his likeness: this was sometime a paradox, but now the time gives it proof. I did love you once.
OPH. Indeed, my lord, you made me believe so.
HAM. You should not have believed me; for virtue cannot so inoculate our old stock but we shall relish of it: I loved you not.
OPH. I was the more deceived.
HAM. Get thee to a nunnery: why wouldst thou be a breeder of sinners? I am myself indifferent honest; but yet I could accuse me of such things that it were better my mother had not borne me: I am very proud, revengeful, ambitious, with more offences at my beck than I have thoughts to put them in, imagination to give them shape, or time to act them in. What should such fellows as I do crawling between earth and heaven? We are arrant knaves, all; believe none of us. Go thy ways to a nunnery. Where's your father? 120
OPH. At home, my lord.
HAM. Let the doors be shut upon him, that he may play the fool no where but in 's own house. Farewell.
OPH. O, help him, you sweet heavens! 130
HAM. If thou dost marry, I'll give thee this plague for thy dowry: be thou as chaste as ice, as pure as snow, thou shalt not escape calumny. Get thee to a nunnery, go: farewell. Or, if thou wilt needs marry, marry a fool; for wise men know well enough what monsters you make of them. To a nunnery, go, and quickly too. Farewell.
OPH. O heavenly powers, restore him!
HAM. I have heard of your paintings too, well enough; God has given you one face, and you make yourselves another: you jig, you amble, and you lisp, and nick-name God's creatures, and make your wantonness your ignorance. Go to, I'll no more on 't; it hath made me mad. 140

103-108. *are you ... beauty: Honest* meaning "truthful" (l. 103) and "chaste" (l. 107), and *fair* meaning "just, honorable" (l. 105) and "beautiful" (l. 107) are not mere quibbles; the speech has the irony of a *double entendre*. 107. *your honesty:* your chastity. 108. *discourse to:* familiar intercourse with. 114. *the time:* the present age. 116. *inoculate:* graft (metaphorical). 117. *but ... it:* i.e., that we do not still have about us a taste of the old stock. 122. *beck:* command. 126. *Where's your father?:* a piece of apparently quite old stage business has Polonius stick his head out from behind the arras before this question, so that Hamlet sees him. Ophelia's lie thus convinces him of her falsity. From this point, Hamlet, under stress of deep emotion, feigns madness more violently. 134. *monsters:* an allusion to the horns of the cuckold. 138. *jig:* move with jerky motion; probably allusion to the *jig*, or song and dance, of the current stage. 139-140. *make ... ignorance:* i.e., excuse your wantonness on the ground of your ignorance.

I say, we will have no more marriages: those that are married already,
all but one, shall live; the rest shall keep as they are. To a nunnery, go.
(Exit.)
OPH. O, what a noble mind is here o'er-thrown!
  The courtier's, soldier's, scholar's, eye, tongue, sword;
  The expectancy and rose of the fair state,
  The glass of fashion and the mould of form,
  The observed of all observers, quite, quite down!
  And I, of ladies most deject and wretched,
  That suck'd the honey of his music vows,
  Now see that noble and most sovereign reason,   150
  Like sweet bells jangled, out of tune and harsh;
  That unmatch'd form and feature of blown youth
  Blasted with ecstasy: O, woe is me,
  To have seen what I have seen, see what I see!

Re-enter KING *and* POLONIUS.

KING. Love! his affections do not that way tend;
  Nor what he spake, though it lack'd form a little,
  Was not like madness. There's something in his soul,
  O'er which his melancholy sits on brood;
  And I do doubt the hatch and the disclose
  Will be some danger: which for to prevent,   160
  I have in quick determination
  Thus set it down: he shall with speed to England,
  For the demand of our neglected tribute:
  Haply the seas and countries different
  With variable objects shall expel
  This something-settled matter in his heart,
  Whereon his brains still beating puts him thus
  From fashion of himself. What think you on 't?
POL. It shall do well: but yet do I believe
  The origin and commencement of his grief   170
  Sprung from neglected love. How now, Ophelia!
  You need not tell us what Lord Hamlet said;
  We heard it all. My lord, do as you please;
  But, if you hold it fit, after the play
  Let his queen mother all alone entreat him
  To show his grief: let her be round with him;
  And I'll be placed, so please you, in the ear
  Of all their conference. If she find him not,
  To England send him, or confine him where
  Your wisdom best shall think.

---

142. *one:* i.e., the king.   145. *expectancy:* source of hope.   147. *observed . . . observers:* courted by all courtiers.   152. *blown:* blooming.   159. *disclose:* disclosure or revelation (by chipping of the shell).   165. *variable:* various.   168. *From . . . himself:* out of his natural manner.   176. *round:* plain-spoken.   178. *find:* discover the true character of.

KING.   It shall be so: 180
Madness in great ones must not unwatch'd go.

Exeunt.

SCENE II.

A hall in the castle.

Enter HAMLET *and* PLAYERS.

HAM. Speak the speech, I pray you, as I pronounced it to you, trippingly on the tongue: but if you mouth it, as many of your players do, I had as lief the town-crier spoke my lines. Nor do not saw the air too much with your hand, thus, but use all gently; for in the very torrent, tempest, and, as I may say, the whirlwind of your passion, you must acquire and beget a temperance that may give it smoothness. O, it offends me to the soul to hear a robustious periwig-pated fellow tear a passion to tatters, to very rags, to split the ears of the groundlings, who for the most part are capable of nothing but inexplicable dumb-shows and noise: I would have such a fellow whipped for o'er-   10
doing Termagant; it out-herods Herod: pray you, avoid it.

FIRST PLAY. I warrant your honour.

HAM. Be not too tame neither, but let your own discretion be your tutor: suit the action to the word, the word to the action; with this special observance, that you o'er-step not the modesty of nature: for any thing so overdone is from the purpose of playing, whose end, both at the first and now, was and is, to hold, as 't were, the mirror up to nature; to show virtue her own feature, scorn her own image, and the very age and body of the time his form and pressure. Now this overdone, or come tardy off, though it make the unskilful laugh,   20
cannot but make the judicious grieve; the censure of the which one must in your allowance o'erweigh a whole theatre of others. O, there be players that I have seen play, and heard others praise, and that highly, not to speak it profanely, that, neither having the accent of Christians nor the gait of Christian, pagan, nor man, have so strutted and bellowed that I have thought some of nature's journeymen had made men and not made them well, they imitated humanity so abominably.

---

4. *your:* indefinite use.   7. *robustious:* violent, boisterous.   *periwig-pated:* wearing a wig.   8-9. *groundings:* those who stood in the yard of the theater.   *capable of:* susceptible of being influenced by.   *inexplicable:* of no significance worth explaining.   11. *Termagant:* a god of the Saracens; a character in the St. Nicholas play, where one of his worshipers, leaving him in charge of goods, returns to find them stolen; whereupon he beats the god (or idol), which howls vociferously.   *Herod:* Herod of Jewry; character in *The Slaughter of the Innocents* and other mystery plays. The part was played with great noise and fury.   19. *very age:* actual generation.   *pressure:* stamp, impressed character.   20. *come tardy off:* inadequately done.   21. *which one:* one of whom.   26. *journeymen:* laborers not yet masters in their trade.

FIRST PLAY. I hope we have reformed that indifferently with us, sir.
HAM. O, reform it altogether. And let those that play your clowns speak no more than is set down for them; for there be of them that will themselves laugh, to set on some quantity of barren spectators to laugh too; though, in the mean time, some necessary question of the play be then to be considered: that's villanous, and shows a most pitiful ambition in the fool that uses it. Go, make you ready.

Exeunt PLAYERS.

Enter POLONIUS, ROSENCRANTZ, *and* GUILDENSTERN.

How now, my lord! will the king hear this piece of work?
POL. And the queen too, and that presently.
HAM. Bid the players make haste. *(Exit* POLONIUS.*)*
   Will you two help to hasten them?
ROS.
GUIL. } We will, my lord.

Exeunt ROSENCRANTZ *and* GUILDENSTERN.

HAM. What ho! Horatio!

Enter HORATIO.

HOR. Here, sweet lord, at your service.
HAM. Horatio, thou art e'en as just a man
   As e'er my conversation coped withal.
HOR. O, my dear lord,—
HAM.   Nay, do not think I flatter;
   For what advancement may I hope from thee
   That no revenue hast but thy good spirits,
   To feed and clothe thee? Why should the poor be flatter'd?
   No, let the candied tongue lick absurd pomp,
   And crook the pregnant hinges of the knee
   Where thrift may follow fawning. Dost thou hear?
   Since my dear soul was mistress of her choice
   And could of men distinguish her election,
   S' hath seal'd thee for herself; for thou hast been
   As one, in suffering all, that suffers nothing,
   A man that fortune's buffets and rewards
   Hast ta'en with equal thanks: and blest are those
   Whose blood and judgement are so well commeddled,
   That they are not a pipe for fortune's finger

---

29. *indifferently:* fairly, tolerably. 31. *of:* i.e., some among them. 32. *barren:* i.e., of wit. 43. *just:* honest, honorable. 49. *candied:* sugared, honeyed for the sake of flattery. 51. *thrift:* profit.

To sound what stop she please. Give me that man
That is not passion's slave, and I will wear him
In my heart's core, ay, in my heart of heart,
As I do thee.—Something too much of this.—
There is a play to-night before the king;
One scene of it comes near the circumstance
Which I have told thee of my father's death:
I prithee, when thou seest that act afoot,
Even with the very comment of thy soul
Observe mine uncle: if his occulted guilt
Do not itself unkennel in one speech,
It is a damned ghost that we have seen,
And my imaginations are as foul
As Vulcan's stithy. Give him heedful note;
For I mine eyes will rivet to his face,
And after we will both our judgements join
In censure of his seeming.
HOR.   Well, my lord:
If he steal aught the whilst this play is playing,
And 'scape detecting, I will pay the theft.
HAM. They are coming to the play; I must be idle:
Get you a place.

Danish march. A flourish. Enter KING, QUEEN, POLONIUS, OPHELIA, ROSENCRANTZ, GUILDENSTERN, *and others.*

KING. How fares our cousin Hamlet?
HAM. Excellent, i' faith; of the chameleon's dish: I eat the air, promise-crammed: you cannot feed capons so.
KING. I have nothing with this answer, Hamlet; these words are not mine.
HAM. No, nor mine now. *(To* POLONIUS*)* My lord, you played once i' the university, you say?
POL. That did I, my lord; and was accounted a good actor.
HAM. What did you enact?
POL. I did enact Julius Cæsar: I was killed i' the Capitol; Brutus killed me.
HAM. It was a brute part of him to kill so capital a calf there. Be the players ready?
ROS. Ay, my lord; they stay upon your patience.
QUEEN. Come hither, my dear Hamlet, sit by me.
HAM. No, good mother, here's metal more attractive.
POL. *(To the* KING*).* O, ho! do you mark that?
HAM. Lady, shall I lie in your lap? *(Lying down at* OPHELIA's *feet.)*

60. *stop:* hole in a wind instrument for controlling the sound. 69. *occulted:* hidden. 71. *damned:* in league with Satan. 73. *stithy:* smithy, place of *stiths* (anvils). 75. *after:* afterwards. *censure ... seeming:* judgment of his appearance or behavior. 76. *idle:* crazy, or not attending to anything serious. 82. *chameleon's dish:* chameleons were supposed to feed on air. 84. *have ... with:* make nothing of. 84-85. *are not mine:* mean nothing to me.

OPH. No, my lord.
HAM. I mean, my head upon your lap? 100
OPH. Ay, my lord.
HAM. Do you think I meant country matters?
OPH. I think nothing, my lord.
HAM. That's a fair thought to lie between maids' legs.
OPH. What is, my lord?
HAM. Nothing.
OPH. You are merry, my lord.
HAM. Who, I?
OPH. Ay, my lord.
HAM. O God, your only jig-maker. What should a man do but be 110
merry? for, look you, how cheerfully my mother looks, and my father
died within these two hours.
OPH. Nay, 'tis twice two months, my lord.
HAM. So long? Nay then, let the devil wear black, for I'll have a suit of
sables. O heavens! die two months ago, and not forgotten yet? Then
there's hope a great man's memory may outlive his life half a year:
but, by 'r lady, he must build churches, then; or else shall he suffer
not thinking on, with the hobby-horse, whose epitaph is "For, O, for,
O, the hobby-horse is forgot."

Hautboys play. The dumb-show enters.

Enter a King *and a* Queen *very lovingly; the* Queen *embracing him, and
he her. She kneels, and makes show of protestation unto him. He
takes her up, and declines his head upon her neck: lays him down
upon a bank of flowers: she, seeing him asleep, leaves him. Anon
comes in a fellow, takes off his crown, kisses it, and pours poison in
the* King's *ears, and exit. The* Queen *returns; finds the* King *dead, and
makes passionate action. The* Poisoner, *with some two or three* Mutes,
*comes in again, seeming to lament with her. The dead body is carried
away. The* Poisoner *wooes the* Queen *with gifts: she seems loath and
unwilling awhile, but in the end accepts his love. (Exeunt.)*

OPH. What means this, my lord? 120
HAM. Marry, this is miching mallecho; it means mischief.
OPH. Belike this show imports the argument of the play.

Enter PROLOGUE.

HAM. We shall know by this fellow: the players cannot keep counsel;
they'll tell all.

---

101. *country matters:* rustic behavior, with apparently some indelicate suggestion. 110. *your only:* only your. 113-114. *suit of sables:* garments trimmed with the fur of the sable, with a quibble on *sable* meaning "black." 116-117. *suffer . . . on:* undergo oblivion. 119, stage direction. *Hautboys:* wooden double-reed instruments of high pitch. 122. *show:* dumbshow. *imports:* denotes, signifies.

OPH. Will he tell us what this show meant?
HAM. Ay, or any show that you'll show him: be not you ashamed to show, he'll not shame to tell you what it means.
OPH. You are naught, you are naught: I'll mark the play.
PRO. For us, and our tragedy,
Here stooping to your clemency, 130
We beg your hearing patiently. *(Exit.)*
HAM. Is this a prologue, or the posy of a ring?
OPH. 'Tis brief, my lord.
HAM. As woman's love.

Enter two PLAYERS, King *and* Queen.

P. KING. Full thirty times hath Phœbus' cart gone round
Neptune's salt wash and Tellus' orbed ground,
And thirty dozen moons with borrow'd sheen
About the world have times twelve thirties been,
Since love our hearts and Hymen did our hands
Unite commutual in most sacred bands. 140
P. QUEEN. So many journeys may the sun and moon
Make us again count o'er ere love be done!
But, woe is me, you are so sick of late,
So far from cheer and from your former state,
That I distrust you. Yet, though I distrust,
Discomfort you, my lord, it nothing must:
For women's fear and love holds quantity;
In neither aught, or in extremity.
Now, what my love is, proof hath made you know;
And as my love is sized, my fear is so: 150
Where love is great, the littlest doubts are fear;
Where little fears grow great, great love grows there.
P. KING. 'Faith, I must leave thee, love, and shortly too;
My operant powers their functions leave to do:
And thou shalt live in this fair world behind,
Honour'd, beloved; and haply one as kind
For husband shalt thou—
P. QUEEN.   O, confound the rest!
Such love must needs be treason in my breast:
In second husband let me be accurst!
None wed the second but who kill'd the first. 160
HAM. *(Aside).* Wormwood, wormwood.
P. QUEEN. The instances that second marriage move
Are base respects of thrift, but none of love:

---

128. *naught:* naughty, wicked. 132. *posy:* motto. 136. *salt wash:* the sea. *Tellus':* Tellus was a goddess personifying the earth *(orbed ground).* 137. *borrow'd:* i.e., reflected. 139. *Hymen:* god of matrimony. 140. *commutual:* intensely mutual. 145. *distrust:* am anxious about. 147. *holds quantity:* keeps proportion between. 154. *operant:* active. *leave:* cease.

    A second time I kill my husband dead,
    When second husband kisses me in bed.
P. KING. I do believe you think what now you speak;
    But what we do determine oft we break.
    Purpose is but the slave to memory,
    Of violent birth, but poor validity:
    Which now, like fruit unripe, sticks on the tree;   170
    But fall, unshaken, when they mellow be.
    Most necessary 'tis that we forget
    To pay ourselves what to ourselves is debt:
    What to ourselves in passion we propose,
    The passion ending, doth the purpose lose.
    The violence of either grief or joy
    Their own enactures with themselves destroy:
    Where joy most revels, grief doth most lament;
    Grief joys, joy grieves, on slender accident.
    This world is not for aye, nor 'tis not strange   180
    That even our loves should with our fortunes change;
    For 'tis a question left us yet to prove,
    Whether love lead fortune, or else fortune love.
    The great man down, you mark his favourite flies;
    The poor advanced makes friends of enemies.
    And hitherto doth love on fortune tend;
    For who not needs shall never lack a friend,
    And who in want a hollow friend doth try,
    Directly seasons him his enemy.
    But, orderly to end where I begun,   190
    Our wills and fates do so contrary run
    That our devices still are overthrown;
    Our thoughts are ours, their ends none of our own:
    So think thou wilt no second husband wed;
    But die thy thoughts when thy first lord is dead.
P. QUEEN. Nor earth to me give food, nor heaven light!
    Sport and repose lock from me day and night!
    To desperation turn my trust and hope!
    An anchor's cheer in prison be my scope!
    Each opposite that blanks the face of joy   200
    Meet what I would have well and it destroy!
    Both here and hence pursue me lasting strife,
    If, once a widow, ever I be wife!
HAM. If she should break it now!
P. KING. 'Tis deeply sworn. Sweet, leave me here awhile;
    My spirits grow dull, and fain I would beguile
    The tedious day with sleep. *(Sleeps.)*
P. QUEEN.   Sleep rock thy brain;
    And never come mischance between us twain! *(Exit.)*

---

177. *enactures:* fulfillments. 180. *aye:* ever. 187. *who:* whoever. 189. *seasons:* matures, ripens. 193. *ends:* results. 199. *An anchor's:* an anchorite's. 200. *opposite:* adversary. *blanks:* causes to *blanch* or grow pale.

HAM. Madam, how like you this play?
QUEEN. The lady doth protest too much, methinks.   210
HAM. O, but she'll keep her word.
KING. Have you heard the argument? Is there no offence in 't?
HAM. No, no, they do but jest, poison in jest; no offence i' the world.
KING. What do you call the play?
HAM. The Mouse-trap. Marry, how? Tropically. This play is the image of a murder done in Vienna: Gonzago is the duke's name; his wife, Baptista: you shall see anon; 't is a knavish piece of work: but what o' that? your majesty and we that have free souls, it touches us not: let the galled jade wince, our withers are unwrung.

Enter LUCIANUS.

This is one Lucianus, nephew to the king.   220
OPH. You are as good as a chorus, my lord.
HAM. I could interpret between you and your love, if I could see the puppets dallying.
OPH. You are keen, my lord, you are keen.
HAM. It would cost you a groaning to take off my edge.
OPH. Still better, and worse.
HAM. So you must take your husbands. Begin, murderer; pox, leave thy damnable faces, and begin. Come: "the croaking raven doth bellow for revenge."
LUC. Thoughts black, hands apt, drugs fit, and time agreeing;   230
Confederate season, else no creature seeing;
Thou mixture rank, of midnight weeds collected,
With Hecate's ban thrice blasted, thrice infected,
Thy natural magic and dire property,
On wholesome life usurp immediately. *(Pours the poison into the sleeper's ears.)*
HAM. He poisons him i' the garden for 's estate. His name 's Gonzago: the story is extant, and writ in choice Italian: you shall see anon how the murderer gets the love of Gonzago's wife.
OPH. The king rises.
HAM. What, frighted with false fire!   240
QUEEN. How fares my lord?
POL. Give o'er the play.
KING. Give me some light: away!
ALL. Lights, lights, lights!

---

215. *Tropically:* figuratively. 216. *Gonzago:* in 1538 Luigi Gonzago murdered the Duke of Urbano by pouring poisoned lotion in his ears. 219. *galled jade:* horse whose hide is rubbed by saddle or harness. *withers:* the ridge above the horse's shoulder blades. *unwrung:* not wrung or twisted. 221. *chorus:* in many Elizabethan plays the action was explained by an actor known as the "chorus"; at a puppet show the actor who explained the action was known as an "interpreter," as indicated by the lines following. 227. *pox:* an imprecation. 231. *Confederate:* conspiring (to assist the murderer). 233. *Hecate:* the goddess of witchcraft. *ban:* curse. 240. *false fire:* fireworks, or a blank discharge.

Exeunt all but HAMLET *and* HORATIO.

HAM. Why, let the stricken deer go weep,
    The hart ungalled play;
  For some must watch, while some must sleep:
    So runs the world away.
Would not this, sir, and a forest of feathers—if the rest of my fortunes turn Turk with me—with two Provincial roses on my razed shoes, get me a fellowship in a cry of players, sir?   250
HOR. Half a share.
HAM. A whole one, I.
    For thou dost know, O Damon dear,
    This realm dismantled was
  Of Jove himself; and now reigns here
    A very, very—pajock.
HOR. You might have rhymed.
HAM. O good Horatio, I'll take the ghost's word for a thousand pound. Didst perceive?   260
HOR. Very well, my lord.
HAM. Upon the talk of the poisoning?
HOR. I did very well note him.
HAM. Ah, ha! Come, some music! come, the recorders!
  For if the king like not the comedy,
  Why then, belike, he likes it not, perdy.
  Come, some music!

Re-enter ROSENCRANTZ *and* GUILDENSTERN.

GUIL. Good my lord, vouchsafe me a word with you.
HAM. Sir, a whole history.
GUIL. The king, sir,—   270
HAM. Ay, sir, what of him?
GUIL. Is in his retirement marvellous distempered.
HAM. With drink, sir?
GUIL. No, my lord, rather with choler.
HAM. Your wisdom should show itself more richer to signify this to his doctor; for, for me to put him to his purgation would perhaps plunge him into far more choler.
GUIL. Good my lord, put your discourse into some frame and start not so wildly from my affair.

---

249. *this:* i.e., the play. *feathers:* allusion to the plumes which Elizabethan actors were fond of wearing. 250. *turn Turk with:* go back on. *two Provincial roses:* rosettes of ribbon like the roses of Provins near Paris, or else the roses of Provence. *razed:* cut, slashed (by way of ornament). 251. *fellowship . . . players:* partnership in a theatrical company. *cry:* pack (as of hounds). 252. *Half a share:* allusion to the custom in dramatic companies of dividing the ownership into a number of shares among the householders. 255. *dismantled:* stripped, divested. 264. *recorders:* wind instruments of the flute kind. 266. *perdy:* corruption of *par dieu.* 278. *frame:* order.

HAM. I am tame, sir: pronounce. 280
GUIL. The queen, your mother, in most great affliction of spirit, hath sent me to you.
HAM. You are welcome.
GUIL. Nay, good my lord, this courtesy is not of the right breed. If it shall please you to make me a wholesome answer, I will do your mother's commandment: if not, your pardon and my return shall be the end of my business.
HAM. Sir, I cannot.
GUIL. What, my lord?
HAM. Make you a wholesome answer; my wit's diseased: but, sir, such 290 answer as I can make, you shall command; or, rather, as you say, my mother: therefore no more, but to the matter: my mother, you say,—
ROS. Then thus she says; your behaviour hath struck her into amazement and admiration.
HAM. O wonderful son, that can so astonish a mother! But is there no sequel at the heels of this mother's admiration? Impart.
ROS. She desires to speak with you in her closet, ere you go to bed.
HAM. We shall obey, were she ten times our mother. Have you any further trade with us?
ROS. My lord, you once did love me. 300
HAM. So I do still, by these pickers and stealers.
ROS. Good my lord, what is your cause of distemper? you do, surely, bar the door upon your own liberty, if you deny your griefs to your friend.
HAM. Sir, I lack advancement.
ROS. How can that be, when you have the voice of the king himself for your succession in Denmark?
HAM. Ay, sir, but "While the grass grows,"—the proverb is something musty.

Re-enter PLAYERS *with recorders.*

O, the recorders! let me see one. To withdraw with you:—why do you 310 go about to recover the wind of me, as if you would drive me into a toil?
GUIL. O, my lord, if my duty be too bold, my love is too unmannerly.
HAM. I do not well understand that. Will you play upon this pipe?
GUIL. My lord, I cannot.
HAM. I pray you.
GUIL. Believe me, I cannot.
HAM. I do beseech you.
GUIL. I know no touch of it, my lord.
HAM. 'Tis as easy as lying: govern these ventages with your fingers and 320

285. *wholesome:* sensible.   292. *matter:* matter in hand.   301. *pickers and stealers:* hands, so called from the catechism, "to keep my hands from picking and stealing." 306. *voice:* support.   310. *withdraw:* speak in private.   311. *recover the wind:* get to the windward side.   312. *toil:* snare.   313. *if . . . unmannerly:* if I am using an unmannerly boldness, it is my love that occasions it.   320. *ventages:* stops of the recorders.

thumb, give it breath with your mouth, and it will discourse most eloquent music. Look you, these are the stops.
GUIL. But these cannot I command to any utterance of harmony; I have not the skill.
HAM. Why, look you now, how unworthy a thing you make of me! You would play upon me; you would seem to know my stops; you would pluck out the heart of my mystery; you would sound me from my lowest note to the top of my compass: and there is much music, excellent voice, in this little organ; yet cannot you make it speak. 'Sblood, do you think I am easier to be played on than a pipe? Call me what instrument you will, though you can fret me, yet you cannot play upon me. 330

Enter POLONIUS.

God bless you, sir!
POL. My lord, the queen would speak with you, and presently.
HAM. Do you see yonder cloud that's almost in shape of a camel?
POL. By the mass, and 'tis like a camel, indeed.
HAM. Methinks it is like a weasel.
POL. It is backed like a weasel.
HAM. Or like a whale?
POL. Very like a whale. 340
HAM. Then I will come to my mother by and by. They fool me to the top of my bent. I will come by and by.
POL. I will say so.
HAM. By and by is easily said. *(Exit* POLONIUS.*)*
Leave me, friends. *(Exeunt all but* HAMLET.*)*
'Tis now the very witching time of night,
When churchyards yawn and hell itself breathes out
Contagion to this world: now could I drink hot blood,
And do such bitter business as the day
Would quake to look on. Soft! now to my mother. 350
O heart, lose not thy nature; let not ever
The soul of Nero enter this firm bosom:
Let me be cruel, not unnatural:
I will speak daggers to her, but use none;
My tongue and soul in this be hypocrites;
How in my words soever she be shent,
To give them seals never, my soul, consent!

Exit.

---

328. *compass:* range of voice. 329. *organ:* musical instrument, i.e., pipe. 331. *fret:* quibble on meaning "irritate" and the piece of wood, gut, or metal which regulates the fingering. 342. *top of my bent:* limit of endurance, i.e., extent to which a bow may be bent. *by and by:* immediately. 352. *Nero:* murderer of his mother, Agrippina. 356. *shent:* rebuked. 357. *give them seals:* confirm with deeds.

SCENE III.

A room in the castle.

Enter KING, ROSENCRANTZ, *and* GUILDENSTERN.

KING. I like him not, nor stands it safe with us
  To let his madness range. Therefore prepare you;
  I your commission will forthwith dispatch,
  And he to England shall along with you:
  The terms of our estate may not endure
  Hazard so near us as doth hourly grow
  Out of his lunacies.
GUIL.   We will ourselves provide:
  Most holy and religious fear it is
  To keep those many many bodies safe
  That live and feed upon your majesty.   10
ROS. The single and peculiar life is bound,
  With all the strength and armour of the mind,
  To keep itself from noyance; but much more
  That spirit upon whose weal depend and rest
  The lives of many. The cease of majesty
  Dies not alone; but, like a gulf, doth draw
  What's near it with it: it is a massy wheel,
  Fix'd on the summit of the highest mount,
  To whose huge spokes ten thousand lesser things
  Are mortised and adjoin'd; which, when it falls,   20
  Each small annexment, petty consequence,
  Attends the boisterous ruin. Never alone
  Did the king sigh, but with a general groan.
KING. Arm you, I pray you, to this speedy voyage;
  For we will fetters put about this fear,
  Which now goes too free-footed.
ROS. }
GUIL. }   We will haste us.

Exeunt ROSENCRANTZ *and* GUILDENSTERN.

Enter POLONIUS.

POL. My lord, he's going to his mother's closet:
  Behind the arras I'll convey myself,
  To hear the process; I'll warrant she'll tax him home:
  And, as you said, and wisely was it said,   30

---

3. *dispatch:* prepare. 5. *terms:* condition, circumstances. *estate:* state. 11. *single and peculiar:* individual and private. 13. *noyance:* harm. 15. *cease:* decease. 16. *gulf:* whirlpool. 24. *Arm:* prepare. 28. *arras:* screen of tapestry placed around the walls of household apartments. *convey:* implication of secrecy; *convey* was often used to mean "steal." 29. *process:* drift, tenor. *tax him home:* reprove him severely.

'Tis meet that some more audience than a mother,
Since nature makes them partial, should o'erhear
The speech, of vantage. Fare you well, my liege:
I'll call upon you ere you go to bed,
And tell you what I know.

KING.   Thanks, dear my lord. *(Exit* POLONIUS.*)*
O, my offence is rank, it smells to heaven;
It hath the primal eldest curse upon 't,
A brother's murder. Pray can I not,
Though inclination be as sharp as will:
My stronger guilt defeats my strong intent;   40
And, like a man to double business bound,
I stand in pause where I shall first begin,
And both neglect. What if this cursed hand
Were thicker than itself with brother's blood,
Is there not rain enough in the sweet heavens
To wash it white as snow? Whereto serves mercy
But to confront the visage of offence?
And what 's in prayer but this two-fold force,
To be forestalled ere we come to fall,
Or pardon'd being down? Then I'll look up;   50
My fault is past. But, O, what form of prayer
Can serve my turn? "Forgive me my foul murder"?
That cannot be: since I am still possess'd
Of those effects for which I did the murder,
My crown, mine own ambition and my queen.
May one be pardon'd and retain the offence?
In the corrupted currents of this world
Offence's gilded hand may shove by justice,
And oft 'tis seen the wicked prize itself
Buys out the law: but 'tis not so above;   60
There is no shuffling, there the action lies
In his true nature; and we ourselves compell'd,
Even to the teeth and forehead of our faults,
To give in evidence. What then? what rests?
Try what repentance can: what can it not?
Yet what can it when one can not repent?
O wretched state! O bosom black as death!
O limed soul, that, struggling to be free,
Art more engaged! Help, angels! Make assay!
Bow, stubborn knees; and, heart with strings of steel,   70

---

33. *of vantage:* from a superior position. 39. *sharp as will:* i.e., his desire is as strong as his determination. 47. *confront:* oppose directly. 49. *forestalled:* prevented. 55. *ambition:* i.e., realization of ambition. 56. *offence:* benefit accruing from offence. 57. *currents:* courses. 58. *gilded hand:* hand offering gold as a bribe. 59. *wicked prize:* prize won by wickedness. 61. *shuffling:* escape by trickery. *lies:* is sustainable. 63. *teeth and forehead:* very face. 64. *rests:* remains. 68. *limed:* caught as with birdlime. 69. *assay:* trial.

206 Hamlet

      Be soft as sinews of the new-born babe!
      All may be well. *(Retires and kneels.)*

Enter HAMLET.

HAM.   Now might I do it pat, now he is praying;
    And now I'll do 't. And so he goes to heaven;
    And so am I revenged. That would be scann'd:
    A villain kills my father; and for that,
    I, his sole son, do this same villain send
    To heaven.
    O, this is hire and salary, not revenge.
    He took my father grossly, full of bread;   80
    With all his crimes broad blown, as flush as May;
    And how his audit stands who knows save heaven?
    But in our circumstance and course of thought,
    'Tis heavy with him: and am I then revenged,
    To take him in the purging of his soul,
    When he is fit and season'd for his passage?
    No!
    Up, sword; and know thou a more horrid hent:
    When he is drunk asleep, or in his rage,
    Or in the incestuous pleasure of his bed;   90
    At gaming, swearing, or about some act
    That has no relish of salvation in 't;
    Then trip him, that his heels may kick at heaven,
    And that his soul may be as damn'd and black
    As hell, whereto it goes. My mother stays:
    This physic but prolongs thy sickly days. *(Exit.)*
KING *(Rising).*   My words fly up, my thoughts remain below:
    Words without thoughts never to heaven go.

Exit.

SCENE IV.

The Queen's closet.

Enter QUEEN *and* POLONIUS.

POL.   He will come straight. Look you lay home to him:
    Tell him his pranks have been too broad to bear with,
    And that your grace hath screen'd and stood between

---

75. *would be scann'd:* needs to be looked into.   80. *full of bread:* allusion to Ezek. 16:49.   81. *broad blown:* in full bloom.   *flush:* lusty.   83. *in . . . course:* as we see it in our mortal situation.   86. *fit . . . passage:* i.e., reconciled to heaven by forgiveness of his sins.   88. *hent:* seizing; or more probably, occasion of seizure.   89. *drunk asleep:* in a drunken sleep.   96. *physic:* purging (by prayer).   2. *broad:* unrestrained.

Much heat and him. I'll sconce me even here.
Pray you, be round with him.
HAM. *(Within).* Mother, mother, mother!
QUEEN. I'll warrant you,
Fear me not: withdraw, I hear him coming.

POLONIUS *hides behind the arras.*

Enter HAMLET.

HAM. Now, mother, what's the matter?
QUEEN. Hamlet, thou hast thy father much offended.
HAM. Mother, you have my father much offended. 10
QUEEN. Come, come, you answer with an idle tongue.
HAM. Go, go, you question with a wicked tongue.
QUEEN. Why, how now, Hamlet!
HAM. What's the matter now?
QUEEN. Have you forgot me?
HAM. No, by the rood, not so:
You are the queen, your husband's brother's wife;
And—would it were not so!—you are my mother.
QUEEN. Nay, then, I'll set those to you that can speak.
HAM. Come, come, and sit you down; you shall not budge;
You go not till I set you up a glass
Where you may see the inmost part of you. 20
QUEEN. What wilt thou do? thou wilt not murder me?
Help, help, ho!
POL. *(Behind).* What, ho! help, help, help!
HAM. *(Drawing).* How now! a rat? Dead, for a ducat, dead!
(Makes a pass through the arras.)
POL. *(Behind).* O, I am slain! *(Falls and dies.)*
QUEEN. O me, what hast thou done?
HAM. Nay, I know not:
Is it the king?
QUEEN. O, what a rash and bloody deed is this!
HAM. A bloody deed! almost as bad, good mother,
As kill a king, and marry with his brother.
QUEEN. As kill a king!
HAM. Ay, lady, 'twas my word. 30
(Lifts up the arras and discovers POLONIUS.*)*
Thou wretched, rash, intruding fool, farewell!
I took thee for thy better: take thy fortune;
Thou find'st to be too busy is some danger.
Leave wringing of your hands: peace! sit you down,
And let me wring your heart; for so I shall,

---

4. *Much heat:* i.e., the king's anger. *sconce:* hide. 9-10. *thy father, my father:* i.e., Claudius, the elder Hamlet. 14. *rood:* cross.

If it be made of penetrable stuff,
If damned custom have not brass'd it so
That it be proof and bulwark against sense.
QUEEN. What have I done, that thou darest wag thy tongue
In noise so rude against me?
HAM.   Such an act   40
That blurs the grace and blush of modesty,
Calls virtue hypocrite, takes off the rose
From the fair forehead of an innocent love
And sets a blister there, makes marriage-vows
As false as dicers' oaths: O, such a deed
As from the body of contraction plucks
The very soul, and sweet religion makes
A rhapsody of words: heaven's face doth glow;
Yea, this solidity and compound mass,
With heated visage, as against the doom,   50
Is thought-sick at the act.
QUEEN.   Ay me, what act,
That roars so loud, and thunders in the index?
HAM. Look here, upon this picture, and on this.
The counterfeit presentment of two brothers.
See, what a grace was seated on this brow;
Hyperion's curls; the front of Jove himself;
An eye like Mars, to threaten and command;
A station like the herald Mercury
New-lighted on a heaven-kissing hill;
A combination and a form indeed,   60
Where every god did seem to set his seal,
To give the world assurance of a man:
This was your husband. Look you now, what follows:
Here is your husband; like a mildew'd ear,
Blasting his wholesome brother. Have you eyes?
Could you on this fair mountain leave to feed,
And batten on this moor? Ha! have you eyes?
You cannot call it love; for at your age
The hey-day in the blood is tame, it 's humble,
And waits upon the judgement: and what judgement   70
Would step from this to this? Sense, sure, you have,
Else could you not have motion; but sure, that sense

---

37. *brass'd:* brazened, hardened. 38. *proof:* armor. 44. *sets a blister:* brands as a harlot. 46. *contraction:* betrothal. 48. *rhapsody:* string. 49. *this ... mass:* the earth itself. 50. *doom:* Last Judgment. 51. *thought-sick:* sick with anxiety. 52. *index:* prelude or preface. 54. *counterfeit presentment:* portrayed representation; on the stage the portraits are sometimes presented as miniatures, sometimes as pictures on the wall. 56. *Hyperion:* the sun god. *front:* brow. 58. *station:* manner of standing. 62. *assurance:* pledge, guarantee. 64. *mildew'd ear:* see Gen. 41:5-7. 67. *batten:* grow fat. *moor:* barren upland. 69. *hey-day:* state of excitement. 71-72. *Sense ... motion:* sense and motion are functions of the middle or sensible soul, the possession of sense being the basis of motion.

Is apoplex'd; for madness would not err,
Nor sense to ecstasy was ne'er so thrall'd
But it reserved some quantity of choice,
To serve in such a difference. What devil was 't
That thus hath cozen'd you at hoodman-blind?
Eyes without feeling, feeling without sight,
Ears without hands or eyes, smelling sans all,
Or but a sickly part of one true sense   80
Could not so mope.
O shame! where is thy blush? Rebellious hell,
If thou canst mutine in a matron's bones,
To flaming youth let virtue be as wax,
And melt in her own fire: proclaim no shame
When the compulsive ardour gives the charge,
Since frost itself as actively doth burn
And reason pandars will.
QUEEN.   O Hamlet, speak no more:
Thou turn'st mine eyes into my very soul;
And there I see such black and grained spots   90
As will not leave their tinct.
HAM.   Nay, but to live
In the rank sweat of an enseamed bed,
Stew'd in corruption, honeying and making love
Over the nasty sty,—
QUEEN.   O, speak to me no more;
These words, like daggers, enter in mine ears;
No more, sweet Hamlet!
HAM.   A murderer and a villain;
A slave that is not twentieth part the tithe
Of your precedent lord; a vice of kings;
A cutpurse of the empire and the rule,
That from a shelf the precious diadem stole,   100
And put it in his pocket!
QUEEN.   No more!
HAM. A king of shreds and patches,—

Enter GHOST.

Save me, and hover o'er me with your wings,
You heavenly guards! What would your gracious figure?

---

73. *apoplex'd:* paralyzed. Mental derangement was of three sorts: apoplexy, ecstasy, and diabolic possession. 74. *thrall'd:* enslaved. 75. *quantity of choice:* fragment of the power to choose. 77. *cozen'd:* tricked, cheated. *hoodman-blind:* blindman's bluff. 83. *mutiny:* rebel. 86. *charge:* order, command. 88. *reason pandars will:* the normal and proper situation was one in which reason guided the will in the direction of good; here, reason is perverted and leads in the direction of evil. 90. *grained:* dyed in grain. 92. *enseamed:* loaded with grease, greased. 98. *precedent lord:* i.e., the elder Hamlet. *vice of kings:* buffoon of kings; a reference to the Vice, or clown, of the morality plays and interludes. 102. *shreds and patches:* i.e., motley, the traditional costume of the Vice.

QUEEN. Alas, he's mad!
HAM. Do you not come your tardy son to chide,
  That, lapsed in time and passion, lets go by
  The important acting of your dread command?
  O, say!
GHOST. Do not forget: this visitation   110
  Is but to whet thy almost blunted purpose.
  But, look, amazement on thy mother sits:
  O, step between her and her fighting soul:
  Conceit in weakest bodies strongest works:
  Speak to her, Hamlet.
HAM.   How is it with you, lady?
QUEEN.   Alas, how is 't with you,
  That you do bend your eye on vacancy
  And with the incorporal air do hold discourse?
  Forth at your eyes your spirits wildly peep;
  And, as the sleeping soldiers in the alarm,   120
  Your bedded hair, like life in excrements,
  Start up, and stand an end. O gentle son,
  Upon the heat and flame of thy distemper
  Sprinkle cool patience. Whereon do you look?
HAM. On him, on him! Look you, how pale he glares!
  His form and cause conjoin'd, preaching to stones,
  Would make them capable. Do not look upon me;
  Lest with this piteous action you convert
  My stern effects: then what I have to do
  Will want true colour; tears perchance for blood.   130
QUEEN. To whom do you speak this?
HAM.   Do you see nothing there?
QUEEN. Nothing at all; yet all that is I see.
HAM. Nor did you nothing hear?
QUEEN.   No, nothing but ourselves.
HAM. Why, look you there! look, how it steals away!
  My father, in his habit as he lived!
  Look, where he goes, even now, out at the portal! *(Exit* GHOST.*)*
QUEEN. This is the very coinage of your brain:
  This bodiless creation ecstasy
  Is very cunning in.
HAM.   Ecstasy!
  My pulse, as yours, doth temperately keep time,   140
  And makes as healthful music: it is not madness
  That I have utter'd: bring me to the test,

---

112. *amazement:* frenzy, distraction. 118. *incorporal:* immaterial. 121. *bedded:* laid in smooth layers. *excrements:* the hair was considered an excrement or voided part of the body. 122. *an:* on. 126. *conjoin'd:* united. 128-129. *convert...effects:* divert me from my stern duty. 130. *want true colour:* lack good reason so that (with a play on the normal sense of *colour*) I shall shed tears instead of shedding blood. 138. *ecstasy:* frenzy, state of being beside oneself.

And I the matter will re-word, which madness
Would gambol from. Mother, for love of grace,
Lay not that flattering unction to your soul,
That not your trespass, but my madness speaks:
It will but skin and film the ulcerous place,
Whiles rank corruption, mining all within,
Infects unseen. Confess yourself to heaven;
Repent what 's past; avoid what is to come; 150
And do not spread the compost on the weeds,
To make them ranker. Forgive me this my virtue;
For in the fatness of these pursy times
Virtue itself of vice must pardon beg,
Yea, curb and woo for leave to do him good.
QUEEN. O Hamlet, thou hast cleft my heart in twain.
HAM. O, throw away the worser part of it,
  And live the purer with the other half.
Good night: but go not to mine uncle's bed;
Assume a virtue, if you have it not. 160
That monster, custom, who all sense doth eat,
Of habits devil, is angel yet in this,
That to the use of actions fair and good
He likewise gives a frock or livery,
That aptly is put on. Refrain to-night,
And that shall lend a kind of easiness
To the next abstinence: the next more easy;
For use almost can change the stamp of nature,
And either . . . the devil, or throw him out
With wondrous potency. Once more, good night: 170
And when you are desirous to be bless'd,
I'll blessing beg of you. For this same lord, *(Pointing to* POLONIUS.*)*
I do repent: but heaven hath pleased it so,
To punish me with this and this with me,
That I must be their scourge and minister.
I will bestow him, and will answer well
The death I gave him. So, again, good night.
I must be cruel, only to be kind:
Thus bad begins and worse remains behind.
One word more, good lady.
QUEEN.   What shall I do? 180
HAM. Not this, by no means, that I bid you do:
  Let the bloat king tempt you again to bed;

---

143. *re-word:* repeat in words. 145. *unction:* ointment used medicinally or as a rite; suggestion that forgiveness for sin may not be so easily achieved. 148. *mining:* working under the surface. 150. *what is to come:* i.e., the sins of the future. 151. *compost:* manure. 152. *this my virtue:* this virtue of mine, i.e., in reproving you. 153. *fatness:* grossness. *pursy:* short-winded, corpulent. 155. *curb:* bow, bend the knee. 171. *be bless'd:* become blessed, i.e., repentant. 182. *bloat:* bloated.

  Pinch wanton on your cheek; call you his mouse;
  And let him, for a pair of reechy kisses,
  Or paddling in your neck with his damn'd fingers,
  Make you to ravel all this matter out,
  That I essentially am not in madness,
  But mad in craft. 'Twere good you let him know;
  For who, that's but a queen, fair, sober, wise,
  Would from a paddock, from a bat, a gib,   190
  Such dear concernings hide? who would do so?
  No, in despite of sense and secrecy,
  Unpeg the basket on the house's top,
  Let the birds fly, and, like the famous ape,
  To try conclusions, in the basket creep,
  And break your own neck down.
QUEEN. Be thou assured, if words be made of breath,
  And breath of life, I have no life to breathe
  What thou hast said to me.
HAM. I must to England; you know that?
QUEEN.   Alack,   200
  I had forgot: 'tis so concluded on.
HAM. There's letters seal'd: and my two schoolfellows,
  Whom I will trust as I will adders fang'd,
  They bear the mandate; they must sweep my way,
  And marshal me to knavery. Let it work;
  For 'tis the sport to have the enginer
  Hoist with his own petar: and 't shall go hard
  But I will delve one yard below their mines,
  And blow them at the moon: O, 'tis most sweet,
  When in one line two crafts directly meet.   210
  This man shall set me packing:
  I'll lug the guts into the neighbour room.
  Mother, good night. Indeed this counsellor
  Is now most still, most secret and most grave,
  Who was in life a foolish prating knave.
  Come, sir, to draw toward an end with you.
  Good night, mother.

Exeunt severally; HAMLET *dragging in* POLONIUS.

---

184. *reechy:* dirty, filthy.   187. *essentially:* in my essential nature.   190. *paddock:* toad. *gib:* tomcat.   191. *dear concernings:* important affairs.   195. *conclusions:* experiments.   204. *sweep my way:* clear my path.   206. *enginer:* constructor of military works, or, possibly, artilleryman.   207. *Hoist:* blown up. *petar:* defined as a small engine of war used to blow in a door or make a breach, and as a case filled with explosive materials.   210. *two crafts:* two acts of guile, with quibble on the sense of "two ships."   211. *set me packing:* set me to making schemes, set me to lugging (him), and, possibly, send me off in a hurry.   216. *draw:* come, with quibble on literal sense.

ACT IV.

SCENE I.

A room in the castle.

Enter KING, QUEEN, ROSENCRANTZ, *and* GUILDENSTERN.

KING. There 's matter in these sighs, these profound heaves:
  You must translate: 'tis fit we understand them.
  Where is your son?
QUEEN. Bestow this place on us a little while.

Exeunt ROSENCRANTZ *and* GUILDENSTERN.

  Ah, mine own lord, what have I seen to-night!
KING. What, Gertrude? How does Hamlet?
QUEEN. Mad as the sea and wind, when both contend
  Which is the mightier: in his lawless fit,
  Behind the arras hearing something stir,
  Whips out his rapier, cries, "A rat, a rat!" 10
  And, in this brainish apprehension, kills
  The unseen good old man.
KING.   O heavy deed!
  It had been so with us, had we been there:
  His liberty is full of threats to all;
  To you yourself, to us, to every one.
  Alas, how shall this bloody deed be answer'd?
  It will be laid to us, whose providence
  Should have kept short, restrain'd and out of haunt,
  This mad young man: but so much was our love,
  We would not understand what was most fit; 20
  But, like the owner of a foul disease,
  To keep it from divulging, let it feed
  Even on the pith of life. Where is he gone?
QUEEN. To draw apart the body he hath kill'd:
  O'er whom his very madness, like some ore
  Among a mineral of metals base,
  Shows itself pure; he weeps for what is done.
KING. O Gertrude, come away!
  The sun no sooner shall the mountains touch,
  But we will ship him hence: and this vile deed 30
  We must, with all our majesty and skill,
  Both countenance and excuse. Ho, Guildenstern!

---

11. *brainish:* headstrong, passionate. *apprehension:* conception, imagination. 17. *providence:* foresight. 18. *short:* i.e., on a short tether. *out of haunt:* secluded. 22. *divulging:* becoming evident. 26. *mineral:* mine.

Re-enter ROSENCRANTZ *and* GUILDENSTERN.

Friends both, go join you with some further aid:
Hamlet in madness hath Polonius slain,
And from his mother's closet hath he dragg'd him:
Go seek him out; speak fair, and bring the body
Into the chapel. I pray you, haste in this.

Exeunt ROSENCRANTZ *and* GUILDENSTERN.

Come, Gertrude, we'll call up our wisest friends;
And let them know, both what we mean to do,
And what 's untimely done   40
Whose whisper o'er the world's diameter,
As level as the cannon to his blank,
Transports his poison'd shot, may miss our name,
And hit the woundless air. O, come away!
My soul is full of discord and dismay.

Exeunt.

SCENE II.

Another room in the castle.

Enter HAMLET.

HAM. Safely stowed.
ROS. }
GUIL. } *(Within).* Hamlet! Lord Hamlet!
HAM. But soft, what noise? who calls on Hamlet? O, here
they come.

Enter ROSENCRANTZ *and* GUILDENSTERN.

ROS. What have you done, my lord, with the dead body?
HAM. Compounded it with dust, whereto 'tis kin.
ROS. Tell us where 'tis, that we may take it thence
And bear it to the chapel.
HAM. Do not believe it.
ROS. Believe what?   10
HAM. That I can keep your counsel and not mine own. Besides, to be
demanded of a sponge! what replication should be made by the son
of a king?

---

41. *diameter:* extent from side to side. 42. *level:* straight. *blank:* white spot in the center of a target. 44. *woundless:* invulnerable. 11. *keep your counsel:* Hamlet is aware of their treachery but says nothing about it. 12. *replication:* reply.

ROS. Take you me for a sponge, my lord?
HAM. Ay, sir, that soaks up the king's countenance, his rewards, his authorities. But such officers do the king best service in the end: he keeps them, like an ape an apple, in the corner of his jaw; first mouthed, to be last swallowed: when he needs what you have gleaned, it is but squeezing you, and, sponge, you shall be dry again.
ROS. I understand you not, my lord. 20
HAM. I am glad of it: a knavish speech sleeps in a foolish ear.
ROS. My lord, you must tell us where the body is, and go with us to the king.
HAM. The body is with the king, but the king is not with the body. The king is a thing—
GUIL. A thing, my lord!
HAM. Of nothing: bring me to him. Hide fox, and all after.

Exeunt.

SCENE III.

Another room in the castle.

Enter KING, *attended.*

KING. I have sent to seek him, and to find the body.
How dangerous is it that this man goes loose!
Yet must not we put the strong law on him:
He's loved of the distracted multitude,
Who like not in their judgement, but their eyes;
And where 'tis so, the offender's scourge is weigh'd,
But never the offence. To bear all smooth and even,
This sudden sending him away must seem
Deliberate pause: diseases desperate grown
By desperate appliance are relieved, 10
Or not at all.

Enter ROSENCRANTZ.

How now! what hath befall'n?
ROS. Where the dead body is bestow'd, my lord,
We cannot get from him.
KING. But where is he?
ROS. Without, my lord; guarded, to know your pleasure.
KING. Bring him before us.
ROS. Ho, Guildenstern! bring in my lord.

16. *authorities:* authoritative backing. 27. *Hide ... after:* an old signal cry in the game of hide-and-seek. 4. *distracted:* i.e., without power of forming logical judgments. 6. *scourge:* punishment. *weigh'd:* taken into consideration. 9. *Deliberate pause:* considered action.

Enter HAMLET *and* GUILDENSTERN.

KING. Now, Hamlet, where 's Polonius?
HAM. At supper.
KING. At supper! where?
HAM. Not where he eats, but where he is eaten: a certain convocation of politic worms are e'en at him. Your worm is your only emperor for diet: we fat all creatures else to fat us, and we fat ourselves for maggots: your fat king and your lean beggar is but variable service, two dishes, but to one table: that 's the end.
KING. Alas, alas!
HAM. A man may fish with the worm that hath eat of a king, and eat of the fish that hath fed of that worm.
KING. What dost thou mean by this?
HAM. Nothing but to show you how a king may go a progress through the guts of a beggar.
KING. Where is Polonius?
HAM. In heaven; send thither to see: if your messenger find him not there, seek him i' the other place yourself. But indeed, if you find him not within this month, you shall nose him as you go up the stairs into the lobby.
KING. Go seek him there. *(To some Attendants.)*
HAM. He will stay till you come. *(Exeunt Attendants.)*
KING. Hamlet, this deed, for thine especial safety,—
Which we do tender, as we dearly grieve
For that which thou hast done,—must send thee hence
With fiery quickness: therefore prepare thyself;
The bark is ready, and the wind at help,
The associates tend, and everything is bent
For England.
HAM.   For England!
KING.   Ay, Hamlet.
HAM.   Good.
KING. So is it, if thou knew'st our purposes.
HAM. I see a cherub that sees them. But, come; for England! Farewell, dear mother.
KING. Thy loving father, Hamlet.
HAM. My mother: father and mother is man and wife; man and wife is one flesh; and so, my mother. Come, for England! *(Exit.)*
KING. Follow him at foot; tempt him with speed aboard;
Delay it not; I'll have him hence to-night:
Away! for every thing is seal'd and done
That else leans on the affair: pray you, make haste.

---

21. *politic:* crafty.   23. *variable service:* a variety of dishes.   29. *progress:* royal journey of state.   39. *tender:* regard, hold dear.   51. *at foot:* close behind, at heel.

Exeunt ROSENCRANTZ *and* GUILDENSTERN.

And, England, if my love thou hold'st at aught—
As my great power thereof may give thee sense,
Since yet thy cicatrice looks raw and red
After the Danish sword, and thy free awe
Pays homage to us—thou mayst not coldly set
Our sovereign process; which imports at full,   60
By letters congruing to that effect,
The present death of Hamlet. Do it, England;
For like the hectic in my blood he rages,
And thou must cure me: till I know 'tis done,
Howe'er my haps, my joys were ne'er begun. *(Exit.)*

SCENE IV.

 A plain in Denmark.

Enter FORTINBRAS, *a* CAPTAIN, *and* SOLDIERS, *marching.*

FOR. Go, captain, from me greet the Danish king;
 Tell him that, by his license, Fortinbras
 Craves the conveyance of a promised march
 Over his kingdom. You know the rendezvous.
 If that his majesty would aught with us,
 We shall express our duty in his eye;
 And let him know so.
CAP.   I will do 't my lord.
FOR. Go softly on. *(Exeunt* FORTINBRAS *and* SOLDIERS.*)*

Enter HAMLET, ROSENCRANTZ, GUILDENSTERN, *and others.*

HAM. Good sir, whose powers are these?
CAP. They are of Norway, sir.   10
HAM. How purposed, sir, I pray you?
CAP. Against some part of Poland.
HAM. Who commands them, sir?
CAP. The nephew to old Norway, Fortinbras.
HAM. Goes it against the main of Poland, sir,
 Or for some frontier?
CAP. Truly to speak, and with no addition,
 We go to gain a little patch of ground
 That hath in it no profit but the name.
 To pay five ducats, five, I would not farm it;   20
 Nor will it yield to Norway or the Pole

---

58. *free awe:* awe still felt but no longer enforced by arms. 63. *hectic:* fever. 65. *haps:* fortunes. 2. *license:* leave. 3. *conveyance:* escort, convoy. 6. *in his eye:* in his presence. 8. *softly:* slowly. 15. *main:* country itself. 20. *farm it:* take a lease of it.

A ranker rate, should it be sold in fee.
HAM. Why, then the Polack never will defend it.
CAP. Yes, it is already garrison'd.
HAM. Two thousand souls and twenty thousand ducats
  Will not debate the question of this straw:
  This is the imposthume of much wealth and peace,
  That inward breaks, and shows no cause without
  Why the man dies. I humbly thank you, sir.
CAP. God be wi' you, sir. *(Exit.)*
ROS.   Will 't please you go, my lord?   30
HAM. I'll be with you straight. Go a little before.

Exeunt all except HAMLET.

How all occasions do inform against me,
And spur my dull revenge! What is a man,
If his chief good and market of his time
Be but to sleep and feed? a beast, no more.
Sure, he that made us with such large discourse,
Looking before and after, gave us not
That capability and god-like reason
To fust in us unused. Now, whether it be   40
Bestial oblivion, or some craven scruple
Of thinking too precisely on the event,
A thought which, quarter'd, hath but one part wisdom
And ever three parts coward, I do not know
Why yet I live to say "This thing's to do";
Sith I have cause and will and strength and means
To do 't. Examples gross as earth exhort me:
Witness this army of such mass and charge
Led by a delicate and tender prince,
Whose spirit with divine ambition puff'd
Makes mouths at the invisible event,   50
Exposing what is mortal and unsure
To all that fortune, death and danger dare,
Even for an egg-shell. Rightly to be great
Is not to stir without great argument,
But greatly to find quarrel in a straw
When honour's at the stake. How stand I then,
That have a father kill'd, a mother stain'd,
Excitements of my reason and my blood,
And let all sleep? while, to my shame, I see
The imminent death of twenty thousand men,   60
That, for a fantasy and trick of fame,

26. *debate ... straw:* settle this trifling matter. 27. *imposthume:* purulent abscess or swelling. 32. *occasions:* incidents, events. 39. *fust:* grow moldy. 45. *Sith:* since. 58. *Excitements of:* incentives to. 61. *trick:* toy, trifle.

Go to their graves like beds, fight for a plot
Whereon the numbers cannot try the cause,
Which is not tomb enough and continent
To hide the slain? O, from this time forth,
My thoughts be bloody, or be nothing worth! *(Exit.)*

SCENE V.

Elsinore. A room in the castle.

Enter QUEEN, HORATIO, *and a* GENTLEMAN.

QUEEN. I will not speak with her.
GENT. She is importunate, indeed distract:
  Her mood will needs be pitied.
QUEEN.   What would she have?
GENT. She speaks much of her father; says she hears
  There's tricks i' the world; and hems, and beats her heart;
  Spurns enviously at straws; speaks things in doubt,
  That carry but half sense: her speech is nothing,
  Yet the unshaped use of it doth move
  The hearers to collection; they yawn at it,
  And botch the words up fit to their own thoughts;   10
  Which, as her winks, and nods, and gestures yield them,
  Indeed would make one think there might be thought,
  Though nothing sure, yet much unhappily.
HOR. 'Twere good she were spoken with: for she may strew
  Dangerous conjectures in ill-breeding minds.
QUEEN. Let her come in. *(Exit HORATIO.)*
  To my sick soul, as sin's true nature is,
  Each toy seems prologue to some great amiss:
  So full of artless jealousy is guilt,
  It spills itself in fearing to be spilt.   20

Re-enter HORATIO, *with* OPHELIA.

OPH. Where is the beauteous majesty of Denmark?
QUEEN. How now, Ophelia!
OPH. *(Sings).* How should I your true love know
       From another one?
       By his cockle hat and staff,

---

62. *plot:* i.e., of ground. 64. *continent:* that which holds or contains. 5. *tricks:* deceptions. *heart:* i.e., breast. 6. *Spurns... straws:* kicks spitefully at small objects in her path. 8. *unshaped:* unformed, artless. 9. *collection:* inference. 10. *botch:* patch. 11. *yield:* deliver, bring forth (her words). 13. *much unhappily:* expressive of much unhappiness. 15. *ill-breeding minds:* minds bent on mischief. 18. *amiss:* calamity, disaster. 25. *cockle hat:* hat with cockleshell stuck in it as a sign that the wearer had been a pilgrim to the shrine of St. James of Compostella. The pilgrim's garb was a conventional disguise for lovers.

             And his sandal shoon.
QUEEN. Alas, sweet lady, what imports this song?
OPH. Say you? nay, pray you, mark.
  (Sings) He is dead and gone, lady,
          He is dead and gone;   30
        At his head a grass-green turf,
        At his heels a stone.
QUEEN. Nay, but, Ophelia,—
OPH. Pray you, mark.
  (Sings) White his shroud as the mountain snow,—

Enter KING.

QUEEN. Alas, look here, my lord.
OPH. *(Sings).* Larded all with flowers;
          Which bewept to the grave did not go
        With true-love showers.
KING. How do you, pretty lady?   40
OPH. Well, God 'ild you! They say the owl was a baker's
  daughter. Lord, we know what we are, but know not what
  we may be. God be at your table!
KING. Conceit upon her father.
OPH. Pray you, let's have no words of this; but when they ask you
  what it means, say you this:
  (Sings) To-morrow is Saint Valentine's day,
        All in the morning betime,
      And I a maid at your window,   50
        To be your Valentine.
    Then up he rose, and donn'd his clothes,
        And dupp'd the chamber-door;
    Let in the maid, that out a maid
        Never departed more.
KING. Pretty Ophelia!
OPH. Indeed, la, without an oath, I'll make an end on 't:
  (Sings) By Gis and by Saint Charity,
        Alack, and fie for shame!   60
    Young men will do 't, if they come to 't;
        By cock, they are to blame.
    Quoth she, before you tumbled me,
        You promised me to wed.
    So would I ha' done, by yonder sun,
        An thou hadst not come to my bed.
KING. How long hath she been thus?
OPH. I hope all will be well. We must be patient: but I cannot choose
  but weep, to think they should lay him i' the cold ground. My brother

---

26. *shoon:* shoes. 37. *Larded:* decorated. 41. *God 'ild:* God yield or reward. 53. *dupp'd:* opened. 59. *Gis:* Jesus. 62. *cock:* perversion of "God" in oaths.

shall know of it: and so I thank you for your good counsel. Come, 70
my coach! Good night, ladies; good night, sweet ladies; good night,
good night. *(Exit.)*
KING. Follow her close; give her good watch, I pray you.

Exit HORATIO.

O, this is the poison of deep grief: it springs
All from her father's death. O Gertrude, Gertrude,
When sorrows come, they come not single spies,
But in battalions. First, her father slain:
Next, your son gone; and he most violent author
Of his own just remove: the people muddied,
Thick and unwholesome in their thoughts and whispers, 80
For good Polonius' death: and we have done but greenly,
In hugger-mugger to inter him: poor Ophelia
Divided from herself and her fair judgement,
Without the which we are pictures, or mere beasts:
Last, and as much containing as all these,
Her brother is in secret come from France;
Feeds on his wonder, keeps himself in clouds,
And wants not buzzers to infect his ear
With pestilent speeches of his father's death;
Wherein necessity, of matter beggar'd, 90
Will nothing stick our person to arraign
In ear and ear. O my dear Gertrude, this,
Like to a murdering-piece, in many places
Gives me superfluous death.

A noise within.

QUEEN. Alack, what noise is this?
KING. Where are my Switzers? Let them guard the door.

Enter another GENTLEMAN.

What is the matter?
GENT. Save yourself, my lord:
The ocean, overpeering of his list,
Eats not the flats with more impetuous haste
Than young Laertes, in a riotous head,
O'erbears your officers. The rabble call him lord; 100
And, as the world were now but to begin,

---

81. *greenly:* foolishly. 82. *hugger-mugger:* secret haste. 87. *in clouds:* invisible. 88. *buzzers:* gossipers. 91. *nothing stick:* not hesitate. 92. *In ear and ear:* in everybody's ears. 93. *murdering-piece:* small cannon or mortar; suggestion of numerous missiles fired. 95. *Switzers:* Swiss guards, mercenaries. 97. *overpeering:* overflowing. *list:* boundary, limit.

Antiquity forgot, custom not known,
The ratifiers and props of every word,
They cry "Choose we: Laertes shall be king":
Caps, hands, and tongues, applaud it to the clouds:
"Laertes shall be king, Laertes king!"
QUEEN. How cheerfully on the false trail they cry!
  O, this is counter, you false Danish dogs!
KING. The doors are broke.

Noise within.

Enter LAERTES, *armed;* DANES *following.*

LAER. Where is this king? Sirs, stand you all without. 110
DANES. No, let 's come in.
LAER.   I pray you, give me leave.
DANES. We will, we will. *(They retire without the door.)*
LAER. I thank you: keep the door. O thou vile king,
  Give me my father!
QUEEN.   Calmly, good Laertes.
LAER. That drop of blood that 's calm proclaims me bastard,
  Cries cuckold to my father, brands the harlot
  Even here, between the chaste unsmirched brow
  Of my true mother.
KING.   What is the cause, Laertes,
  That thy rebellion looks so giant-like?
  Let him go, Gertrude; do not fear our person: 120
  There 's such divinity doth hedge a king,
  That treason can but peep to what it would,
  Acts little of his will. Tell me, Laertes,
  Why thou art thus incensed. Let him go, Gertrude.
  Speak, man.
LAER. Where is my father?
KING.   Dead.
QUEEN.   But not by him.
KING. Let him demand his fill.
LAER. How came he dead? I'll not be juggled with:
  To hell, allegiance! vows, to the blackest devil!
  Conscience and grace, to the profoundest pit! 130
  I dare damnation. To this point I stand,
  That both the worlds I give to negligence,
  Let come what comes; only I'll be revenged
  Most throughly for my father.
KING.   Who shall stay you?

---

108. *counter:* a hunting term meaning to follow the trail in a direction opposite to that which the game has taken. 123. *peep:* look. *would:* wishes to do. 132. *give to negligence:* he despises both the here and the hereafter. 134. *throughly:* thoroughly, as often.

LAER. My will, not all the world:
   And for my means, I'll husband them so well,
   They shall go far with little.
KING.   Good Laertes,
   If you desire to know the certainty
   Of your dear father's death, is 't writ in your revenge,
   That, swoopstake, you will draw both friend and foe,   140
   Winner and loser?
LAER. None but his enemies.
KING.   Will you know them then?
LAER. To his good friends thus wide I'll ope my arms;
   And like the kind life-rendering pelican,
   Repast them with my blood.
KING.   Why, now you speak
   Like a good child and a true gentleman.
   That I am guiltless of your father's death,
   And am most sensibly in grief for it,
   It shall as level to your judgement 'pear
   As day does to your eye.
DANES *(Within)*. Let her come in.   150
LAER. How now! what noise is that?

Re-enter OPHELIA.

   O heat, dry up my brains! tears seven times salt,
   Burn out the sense and virtue of mine eye!
   By heaven, thy madness shall be paid with weight,
   Till our scale turn the beam. O rose of May!
   Dear maid, kind sister, sweet Ophelia!
   O heavens! is 't possible, a young maid's wits
   Should be as mortal as an old man's life?
   Nature is fine in love, and where 'tis fine,
   It sends some precious instance of itself   160
   After the thing it loves.
OPH. *(Sings)*. They bore him barefaced on the bier;
         Hey non nonny, nonny, hey nonny;
         And in his grave rain'd many a tear:—
   Fare you well, my dove!
LAER. Hadst thou thy wits, and didst persuade revenge,
   It could not move thus.
OPH. *(Sings)*. You must sing a-down a-down,
         An you call him a-down-a.
   O, how the wheel becomes it! It is the false steward, that stole his   170
   master's daughter.

---

135. *My will:* he will not be stopped except by his own will. 140. *swoopstake:* literally, drawing the whole stake at once, i.e., indiscriminately. 144. *pelican:* reference to the belief that the pelican feeds its young with its own blood. 152. *heat:* probably the heat generated by the passion of grief. 170. *false steward:* the story is unknown.

LAER. This nothing 's more than matter.
OPH. There 's rosemary, that 's for remembrance; pray, love,
remember: and there is pansies, that 's for thoughts.
LAER. A document in madness, thoughts and remembrance fitted.
OPH. There 's fennel for you, and columbines: there 's rue for you; and
here 's some for me: we may call it herb of grace o' Sundays: O, you
must wear your rue with a difference. There 's a daisy: I would give
you some violets, but they withered all when my father died: they
say he made a good end,— 180
(Sings) For bonny sweet Robin is all my joy.
LAER. Thought and affliction, passion, hell itself,
She turns to favour and to prettiness.
OPH. *(Sings).* And will he not come again?
And will he not come again?
No, no, he is dead:
Go to thy death-bed:
He never will come again.

His beard was as white as snow,
All flaxen was his poll: 190
He is gone, he is gone,
And we cast away moan:
God ha' mercy on his soul!
And of all Christian souls, I pray God. God be wi' ye. *(Exit.)*
LAER. Do you see this, O God?
KING. Laertes, I must commune with your grief,
Or you deny me right. Go but apart,
Make choice of whom your wisest friends you will,
And they shall hear and judge 'twixt you and me:
If by direct or by collateral hand 200
They find us touch'd, we will our kingdom give,
Our crown, our life, and all that we call ours,
To you in satisfaction; but if not,
Be you content to lend your patience to us,
And we shall jointly labour with your soul
To give it due content.
LAER.   Let this be so;
His means of death, his obscure funeral—
No trophy, sword, nor hatchment o'er his bones,
No noble rite nor formal ostentation—

---

173. *rosemary:* used as a symbol of remembrance both at weddings and at funerals.
174. *pansies:* emblems of love and courtship; cf. French *pensées.* 175. *document:* piece of instruction or lesson. 176. *fennel:* emblem of flattery. 178. *daisy:* emblem of dissembling, faithlessness. 179. *violets:* emblems of faithfulness. 181. *For . . . joy:* possibly a line from a Robin Hood ballad. 182. *Thought:* melancholy thought. 190. *poll:* head. 192. *cast away:* shipwrecked. 197. *right:* my rights. 200. *collateral:* indirect. 201. *touch'd:* implicated. 208. *hatchment:* tablet displaying the armorial bearings of a deceased person.

Cry to be heard, as 'twere from heaven to earth,   210
  That I must call 't in question.
    KING.   So you shall;
  And where the offence is let the great axe fall.
  I pray you, go with me.

Exeunt.

SCENE VI.

Another room in the castle.

Enter HORATIO *and a* SERVANT.

HOR. What are they that would speak with me?
SERV. Sailors, sir: they say they have letters for you.
HOR. Let them come in. *(Exit* SERVANT.*)*
  I do not know from what part of the world
  I should be greeted, if not from lord Hamlet.

Enter SAILORS.

FIRST SAIL. God bless you, sir.
HOR. Let him bless thee too.
FIRST SAIL. He shall, sir, an 't please him. There 's a letter for you,
  sir; it comes from the ambassador that was bound for England; if your
  name be Horatio, as I am let to know it is.   10
HOR. *(Reads).* "Horatio, when thou shalt have overlooked this, give
  these fellows some means to the king: they have letters for him. Ere
  we were two days old at sea, a pirate of very warlike appointment
  gave us chase. Finding ourselves too slow of sail, we put on a compelled valour, and in the grapple I boarded them: on the instant they
  got clear of our ship; so I alone became their prisoner. They have
  dealt with me like thieves of mercy: but they knew what they did; I
  am to do a good turn for them. Let the king have the letters I have
  sent; and repair thou to me with as much speed as thou wouldst fly
  death. I have words to speak in thine ear will make thee dumb; yet   20
  are they much too light for the bore of the matter. These good
  fellows will bring thee where I am. Rosencrantz and Guildenstern
  hold their course for England: of them I have much to tell thee.
  Farewell.
  "He that thou knowest thine, HAMLET."
  Come, I will make you way for these your letters;
  And do 't the speedier, that you may direct me
  To him from whom you brought them.

Exeunt.

12. *means:* means of access. 21. *bore:* caliber, importance.

226 Hamlet

SCENE VII.

Another room in the castle.

Enter KING *and* LAERTES.

KING. Now must your conscience my acquittance seal
   And you must put me in your heart for friend,
   Sith you have heard, and with a knowing ear,
   That he which hath your noble father slain
   Pursued my life.
LAER.   It well appears: but tell me
   Why you proceeded not against these feats,
   So criminal and so capital in nature,
   As by your safety, wisdom, all things else,
   You mainly were stirr'd up.
KING.   O, for two special reasons;
   Which may to you, perhaps, seem much unsinew'd,   10
   But yet to me they are strong. The queen his mother
   Lives almost by his looks; and for myself—
   My virtue or my plague, be it either which—
   She's so conjunctive to my life and soul,
   That, as the star moves not but in his sphere,
   I could not but by her. The other motive,
   Why to a public count I might not go,
   Is the great love the general gender bear him;
   Who, dipping all his faults in their affection,
   Would, like the spring that turneth wood to stone,   20
   Convert his gyves to graces; so that my arrows,
   Too slightly timber'd for so loud a wind,
   Would have reverted to my bow again,
   And not where I had aim'd them.
LAER. And so have I a noble father lost;
   A sister driven into desperate terms,
   Whose worth, if praises may go back again,
   Stood challenger on mount of all the age
   For her perfections: but my revenge will come.   30
KING. Break not your sleeps for that: you must not think
   That we are made of stuff so flat and dull
   That we can let our beard be shook with danger

---

1. *conscience:* knowledge that this is true.   7. *capital:* punishable by death.   9. *mainly:* greatly.   10. *unsinew'd:* weak.   14. *conjunctive:* conformable (the next line suggesting planetary conjunction).   15. *sphere:* the hollow sphere in which, according to Ptolemaic astronomy, the planets were supposed to move.   17. *count:* account, reckoning.   18. *general gender:* common people.   20. *spring:* i.e., one heavily charged with lime.   21. *gyves:* fetters; here, faults or, possibly, punishments inflicted (on him).   22. *slightly timber'd:* light.   *loud:* strong.   26. *terms:* state, condition.   27. *go back:* i.e., to Ophelia's former virtues.   28. *of all the age:* qualifies *challenger* and not *mount.*

And think it pastime. You shortly shall hear more:
I loved your father, and we love ourself;
And that, I hope, will teach you to imagine—

Enter a MESSENGER.

How now! what news?
MESS. Letters, my lord, from Hamlet:
This to your majesty; this to the queen.
KING. From Hamlet! who brought them?
MESS. Sailors, my lord, they say; I saw them not:
They were given me by Claudio; he received them 40
Of him that brought them.
KING. Laertes, you shall hear them.
Leave us. *(Exit* MESSENGER.*)*
(Reads) "High and mighty, You shall know I am set naked on your
kingdom. To-morrow shall I beg leave to see your kingly eyes: when
I shall, first asking your pardon thereunto, recount the occasion of
my sudden and more strange return.   "HAMLET."
What should this mean? Are all the rest come back?
Or is it some abuse, and no such thing?
LAER. Know you the hand?
KING. 'Tis Hamlet's character. "Naked!"
And in a postscript here, he says "alone." 50
Can you advise me?
LAER. I'm lost in it, my lord. But let him come;
It warms the very sickness in my heart,
That I shall live and tell him to his teeth,
"Thus didst thou."
KING. If it be so, Laertes—
As how should it be so? how otherwise?—
Will you be ruled by me?
LAER. Ay, my lord;
So you will not o'errule me to a peace.
KING. To thine own peace. If he be now return'd,
As checking at his voyage, and that he means 60
No more to undertake it, I will work him
To an exploit, now ripe in my device,
Under the which he shall not choose but fall:
And for his death no wind of blame shall breathe,
But even his mother shall uncharge the practice
And call it accident.
LAER. My lord, I will be ruled;
The rather, if you could devise it so.

---

40. *Claudio:* this character does not appear in the play. 44. *naked:* unprovided (with retinue). 49. *abuse:* deception. 61. *checking at:* used in falconry of a hawk's leaving the quarry to fly at a chance bird. 66. *uncharge the practice:* not object to the stratagem.

    That I might be the organ.
KING.   It falls right.
    You have been talk'd of since your travel much,
    And that in Hamlet's hearing, for a quality
    Wherein, they say, you shine: your sum of parts
    Did not together pluck such envy from him
    As did that one, and that, in my regard,
    Of the unworthiest siege.
LAER.   What part is that, my lord?
KING. A very riband in the cap of youth,
    Yet needful too; for youth no less becomes
    The light and careless livery that it wears
    Than settled age his sables and his weeds,
    Importing health and graveness. Two months since,
    Here was a gentleman of Normandy:—
    I've seen myself, and served against, the French,
    And they can well on horseback: but this gallant
    Had witchcraft in 't; he grew unto his seat;
    And to such wondrous doing brought his horse,
    As had he been incorpsed and demi-natured
    With the brave beast: so far he topp'd my thought,
    That I, in forgery of shapes and tricks,
    Come short of what he did.
LAER.   A Norman was 't?
KING. A Norman.
LAER. Upon my life, Lamond.
KING.   The very same.
LAER. I know him well: he is the brooch indeed
    And gem of all the nation.
KING. He made confession of you,
    And gave you such a masterly report
    For art and exercise in your defence
    And for your rapier most especial,
    That he cried out, 'twould be a sight indeed,
    If one could match you: the scrimers of their nation,
    He swore, had neither motion, guard, nor eye,
    If you opposed them. Sir, this report of his
    Did Hamlet so envenom with his envy
    That he could nothing do but wish and beg
    Your sudden coming o'er, to play with him.
    Now, out of this,—
LAER.   What out of this, my lord?

---

69. *organ:* agent, instrument.   74. *siege:* rank.   78. *sables:* rich garments.   82. *can well:* are skilled.   85. *incorpsed and demi-natured:* of one body and nearly of one nature (like the centaur).   86. *topp'd:* surpassed.   87. *forgery:* invention.   90. *brooch:* jewel, ornament.   92. *confession:* report.   94. *art and exercise:* skillful exercise.   *defense:* science of defense in sword practice.   98. *scrimers:* fencers.   103. *play:* fence.

KING. Laertes, was your father dear to you?
  Or are you like the painting of a sorrow,
  A face without a heart?
LAER.   Why ask you this?
KING. Not that I think you did not love your father;
  But that I know love is begun by time;
  And that I see, in passages of proof, 110
  Time qualifies the spark and fire of it.
  There lives within the very flame of love
  A kind of wick or snuff that will abate it;
  And nothing is at a like goodness still;
  For goodness, growing to a plurisy,
  Dies in his own too much: that we would do,
  We should do when we would; for this "would" changes
  And hath abatements and delays as many
  As there are tongues, are hands, are accidents;
  And then this "should" is like a spendthrift sigh, 120
  That hurts by easing. But, to the quick o' the ulcer:—
  Hamlet comes back: what would you undertake,
  To show yourself your father's son in deed
  More than in words?
LAER.   To cut his throat i' the church.
KING. No place, indeed, should murder sanctuarize;
  Revenge should have no bounds. But, good Laertes,
  Will you do this, keep close within your chamber.
  Hamlet return'd shall know you are come home:
  We'll put on those shall praise your excellence
  And set a double varnish on the fame 130
  The Frenchman gave you, bring you in fine together
  And wager on your heads: he, being remiss,
  Most generous and free from all contriving,
  Will not peruse the foils; so that, with ease,
  Or with a little shuffling, you may choose
  A sword unbated, and in a pass of practice
  Requite him for your father.
LAER.   I will do 't:
  And, for that purpose, I'll anoint my sword.
  I bought an unction of a mountebank,
  So mortal that, but dip a knife in it, 140
  Where it draws blood no cataplasm so rare,

---

110. *passages of proof:* proved instances. 115. *plurisy:* excess, plethora. 116. *in his own too much:* of its own excess. 118. *abatements:* diminutions. 119. *accidents:* occurrences, incidents. 120. *spendthrift:* an allusion to the belief that each sigh cost the heart a drop of blood. 121. *quick o' the ulcer:* heart of the difficulty. 125. *sanctuarize:* protect from punishment; allusion to the right of sanctuary with which certain religious places were invested. 131. *in fine:* in the end. 136. *unbated:* not blunted, having no button. *pass of practice:* treacherous thrust. 139. *mountebank:* quack doctor. 141. *cataplasm:* plaster or poultice.

    Collected from all simples that have virtue
    Under the moon, can save the thing from death
    That is but scratched withal: I'll touch my point
    With this contagion, that, if I gall him slightly,
    It may be death.
KING.   Let 's further think of this;
    Weigh what convenience both of time and means
    May fit us to our shape: if this should fail,
    And that our drift look through our bad performance,
    'Twere better not assay'd: therefore this project   150
    Should have a back or second, that might hold,
    If this should blast in proof. Soft! let me see:
    We'll make a solemn wager on your cunnings:
    I ha 't:
    When in your motion you are hot and dry—
    As make your bouts more violent to that end—
    And that he calls for drink, I'll have prepared him
    A chalice for the nonce, whereon but sipping,
    If he by chance escape your venom'd stuck,
    Our purpose may hold there.

Enter QUEEN.

                    How now, sweet queen!   160
QUEEN. One woe doth tread upon another's heel,
  So fast they follow: your sister 's drown'd, Laertes.
LAER. Drown'd! O, where?
QUEEN. There is a willow grows aslant a brook,
  That shows his hoar leaves in the glassy stream;
  There with fantastic garlands did she make
  Of crow-flowers, nettles, daisies, and long purples
  That liberal shepherds give a grosser name,
  But our cold maids do dead men's fingers call them:
  There, on the pendent boughs her coronet weeds   170
  Clambering to hang, an envious sliver broke;
  When down her weedy trophies and herself
  Fell in the weeping brook. Her clothes spread wide;
  And, mermaid-like, awhile they bore her up:
  Which time she chanted snatches of old tunes;
  As one incapable of her own distress,

---

142. *simples:* herbs. 143. *Under the moon:* i.e., when collected by moonlight to add to their medicinal value. 145. *gall:* graze, wound. 148. *shape:* part we propose to act. 149. *drift... performance:* intention be disclosed by our bungling. 152. *blast in proof:* burst in the test (like a cannon). 157. *chalice:* cup. *for the nonce:* for such an occasion. 158. *stuck:* thrust (from *stoccado*). 163. *willow:* for its significance of forsaken love. 164. *hoar:* white (i.e., on the underside). 166. *crow-flowers:* buttercups. 167. *liberal:* probably, free-spoken. 169. *coronet:* made into a chaplet. 170. *sliver:* branch. 171. *weedy:* i.e., of plants. 175. *incapable:* lacking capacity to apprehend.

Or like a creature native and indued
Unto that element: but long it could not be
Till that her garments, heavy with their drink,
Pull'd the poor wretch from her melodious lay   180
To muddy death.
LAER.   Alas then, she is drown'd?
QUEEN.   Drown'd, drown'd.
LAER.   Too much of water hast thou, poor Ophelia,
   And therefore I forbid my tears: but yet
   It is our trick; nature her custom holds,
   Let shame say what it will: when these are gone,
   The woman will be out. Adieu, my lord:
   I have a speech of fire, that fain would blaze,
   But that this folly douts it. *(Exit.)*
KING.   Let's follow, Gertrude:
   How much I had to do to calm his rage!   190
   Now fear I this will give it start again;
   Therefore let 's follow.

Exeunt.

ACT V.

SCENE I.

A churchyard.

Enter two CLOWNS, *with spades, &c.*

FIRST CLO.   Is she to be buried in Christian burial that wilfully seeks her own salvation?
SEC. CLO.   I tell thee she is; and therefore make her grave straight: the crowner hath sat on her, and finds it Christian burial.
FIRST CLO.   How can that be, unless she drowned herself in her own defence?
SEC. CLO.   Why, 'tis found so.
FIRST CLO.   It must be "se offendendo"; it cannot be else. For here lies the point: if I drown myself wittingly, it argues an act: and an act hath three branches; it is, to act, to do, and to perform: argal, she   10
drowned herself wittingly.

---

176. *indued:* endowed with qualities fitting her for living in water.   185. *trick:* way.
186-187. *when ... out:* when my tears are all shed, the woman in me will be satisfied.
189. *douts:* does out, extinguishes.   Act V, Scene I, stage direction. *Clowns:* the word *clown* was used to denote peasants as well as humorous characters; here applied to the rustic type of clown.   4. *crowner:* coroner.   8. *se offendendo:* for *se defendendo*, term used in verdicts of justifiable homicide.   10. *three branches:* parody of legal phraseology. *argal:* corruption of *ergo*, therefore.

SEC. CLO. Nay, but hear you, goodman delver,—
FIRST CLO. Give me leave. Here lies the water; good: here stands the man; good: if the man go to this water, and drown himself, it is, will he, nill he, he goes,—mark you that; but if the water come to him and drown him, he drowns not himself: argal, he that is not guilty of his own death shortens not his own life.
SEC. CLO. But is this law?
FIRST CLO. Ay, marry, is 't; crowner's quest law.
SEC. CLO. Will you ha' the truth on 't? If this had not been a gentle-woman, she should have been buried out o' Christian burial.
FIRST CLO. Why, there thou say'st: and the more pity that great folk should have countenance in this world to drown or hang themselves, more than their even Christian. Come, my spade. There is no ancient gentlemen but gardeners, ditchers, and grave-makers: they hold up Adam's profession.
SEC. CLO. Was he a gentleman?
FIRST CLO. A' was the first that ever bore arms.
SEC. CLO. Why, he had none.
FIRST CLO. What, art a heathen? How dost thou understand the Scripture? The Scripture says "Adam digged": could he dig without arms? I'll put another question to thee: if thou answerest me not to the purpose, confess thyself—
SEC. CLO. Go to.
FIRST CLO. What is he that builds stronger than either the mason, the shipwright, or the carpenter?
SEC. CLO. The gallows-maker; for that frame outlives a thousand tenants.
FIRST CLO. I like thy wit well, in good faith: the gallows does well; but how does it well? it does well to those that do ill: now thou dost ill to say the gallows is built stronger than the church: argal, the gallows may do well to thee. To 't again, come.
SEC. CLO. "Who builds stronger than a mason, a shipwright, or a carpenter?"
FIRST CLO. Ay, tell me that, and unyoke.
SEC. CLO. Marry, now I can tell.
FIRST CLO. To 't.
SEC. CLO. Mass, I cannot tell.

Enter HAMLET *and* HORATIO, *at a distance.*

FIRST CLO. Cudgel thy brains no more about it, for your dull ass will not mend his pace with beating; and, when you are asked this question next, say "a grave-maker": the houses that he makes last till doomsday. Go, get thee in, and fetch me a stoup of liquor. *(Exit*

---

12. *delver:* digger.   19. *crowner's quest:* coroner's inquest.   22. *there thou say'st:* that's right.   23. *countenance:* privilege.   24. *even:* fellow.   25. *hold up:* maintain, continue.
33. *confess thyself:* "and be hanged" completes the proverb.   48. *Mass:* by the Mass.
52. *stoup:* two-quart measure.

SEC. CLOWN. *He digs, and sings.)*
  In youth, when I did love, did love,
    Methought it was very sweet,
  To contract, O, the time, for, ah, my behove,
    O, methought, there was nothing meet.
HAM. Has this fellow no feeling of his business, that he sings at grave-making?
HOR. Custom hath made it in him a property of easiness.   60
HAM. 'Tis e'en so: the hand of little employment hath the daintier sense.
FIRST CLO. *(Sings).*
  But age, with his stealing steps,
    Hath claw'd me in his clutch,
  And hath shipped me into the land,
    As if I had never been such. *(Throws up a skull.)*
HAM. That skull had a tongue in it, and could sing once: how the knave jowls it to the ground, as if it were Cain's jaw-bone, that did the first murder! It might be the pate of a politician, which this ass   70
now o'er-reaches; one that would circumvent God, might it not?
HOR. It might, my lord.
HAM. Or of a courtier; which could say "Good morrow, sweet lord! How dost thou, good lord?" This might be my lord such-a-one, that praised my lord such-a-one's horse, when he meant to beg it; might it not?
HOR. Ay, my lord.
HAM. Why, e'en so: and now my Lady Worm's; chapless, and knocked about the mazzard with a sexton's spade: here's fine revolution, an we had the trick to see 't. Did these bones cost no more the breeding,   80
but to play at loggats with 'em? mine ache to think on 't.
FIRST CLO. *(Sings).*
  A pick-axe, and a spade, a spade,
    For and a shrouding sheet:
  O, a pit of clay for to be made
    For such a guest is meet. *(Throws up another skull.)*
HAM. There's another: why may not that be the skull of a lawyer? Where be his quiddities now, his quillets, his cases, his tenures, and his tricks? why does he suffer this rude knave now to knock him about the sconce with a dirty shovel, and will not tell him of his   90
action of battery? Hum! This fellow might be in 's time a great buyer of land, with his statutes, his recognizances, his fines, his double

---

55. *behove:* benefit. 60. *property of easiness:* a peculiarity that now is easy. 69. *jowls:* dashes. 70. *politician:* schemer, plotter. 78. *chapless:* having no lower jaw. 79. *mazzard:* head. *revolution:* change, alteration. 81. *loggats:* a game in which six sticks are thrown to lie as near as possible to a stake fixed in the ground, or block of wood on a floor. 83. *For and:* and moreover. 88. *quiddities:* subtleties, quibbles. *quillets:* verbal niceties, subtle distinctions. *tenures:* the holding of a piece of property or office or the conditions or period of such holding. 90. *sconce:* head. 92. *statutes, recognizances:* legal terms connected with the transfer of land.

vouchers, his recoveries: is this the fine of his fines, and the recovery of his recoveries, to have his fine pate full of fine dirt? will his vouchers vouch him no more of his purchases, and double ones too, than the length and breadth of a pair of indentures? The very conveyances of his lands will hardly lie in this box; and must the inheritor himself have no more, ha?

HOR. Not a jot more, my lord.

HAM. Is not parchment made of sheep-skins? 100

HOR. Ay, my lord, and of calf-skins too.

HAM. They are sheep and calves which seek out assurance in that. I will speak to this fellow. Whose grave's this, sirrah?

FIRST CLO. Mine, sir.

(Sings) O, a pit of clay for to be made
For such a guest is meet.

HAM. I think it be thine, indeed; for thou liest in 't.

FIRST CLO. You lie out on 't, sir, and therefore it is not yours: for my part, I do not lie in 't, and yet it is mine.

HAM. Thou dost lie in 't, to be in 't and say it is thine: 'tis for the 110 dead, not for the quick; therefore thou liest.

FIRST CLO. 'Tis a quick lie, sir; 'twill away again, from me to you.

HAM. What man dost thou dig it for?

FIRST CLO. For no man, sir.

HAM. What woman, then?

FIRST CLO. For none, neither.

HAM. Who is to be buried in 't?

FIRST CLO. One that was a woman, sir; but, rest her soul, she's dead.

HAM. How absolute the knave is! we must speak by the card, or equivocation will undo us. By the Lord, Horatio, these three years I have 120 taken note of it; the age is grown so picked that the toe of the peasant comes so near the heel of the courtier, he galls his kibe. How long hast thou been a grave-maker?

FIRST CLO. Of all the days i' the year, I came to 't that day that our last king Hamlet overcame Fortinbras.

HAM. How long is that since?

FIRST CLO. Cannot you tell that? every fool can tell that: it was the very day that young Hamlet was born; he that is mad, and sent into England.

HAM. Ay, marry, why was he sent into England? 130

FIRST CLO. Why, because he was mad: he shall recover his wits there; or, if he do not, it 's no great matter there.

---

93. *vouchers:* persons called on to warrant a tenant's title. *recoveries:* process for transfer of entailed estate. *fine:* the four uses of this word are (1) end, (2) legal process, (3) elegant, (4) small. 96. *indentures:* conveyances or contracts. 97. *inheritor:* possessor, owner. 101. *calf-skins:* suggestive of stupidity. 102. *assurance in that:* safety in legal parchments. 111. *quick:* living. 119. *absolute:* positive, decided. *by the card:* with precision, i.e., by the mariner's card on which the points of the compass were marked. 119-120. *equivocation:* ambiguity in the use of terms. 121. *picked:* refined, fastidious. 122. *kibe:* chilblain.

HAM. Why?
FIRST CLO. 'Twill not be seen in him there; there the men are as mad as he.
HAM. How came he mad?
FIRST CLO. Very strangely, they say.
HAM. How strangely?
FIRST CLO. Faith, e'en with losing his wits.
HAM. Upon what ground? 140
FIRST CLO. Why, here in Denmark: I have been sexton here, man and boy, thirty years.
HAM. How long will a man lie i' the earth ere he rot?
FIRST CLO. I' faith, if he be not rotten before he die—as we have many pocky corses now-a-days, that will scarce hold the laying in—he will last you some eight year or nine year: a tanner will last you nine year.
HAM. Why he more than another?
FIRST CLO. Why, sir, his hide is so tanned with his trade, that he will keep out water a great while, and your water is a sore decayer of your whoreson dead body. Here 's a skull now hath lain you i' th' earth 150 three and twenty years.
HAM. Whose was it?
FIRST CLO. A whoreson mad fellow's it was: whose do you think it was?
HAM. Nay, I know not.
FIRST CLO. A pestilence on him for a mad rogue! a' poured a flagon of Rhenish on my head once. This same skull, sir, was Yorick's skull, the king's jester.
HAM. This?
FIRST CLO. E'en that. 160
HAM. Let me see. *(Takes the skull.)* Alas, poor Yorick! I knew him, Horatio: a fellow of infinite jest, of most excellent fancy: he hath borne me on his back a thousand times; and now, how abhorred in my imagination it is! my gorge rises at it. Here hung those lips that I have kissed I know not how oft. Where be your gibes now? your gambols? your songs? your flashes of merriment, that were wont to set the table on a roar? Not one now, to mock your own grinning? quite chap-fallen? Now get you to my lady's chamber, and tell her, let her paint an inch thick, to this favour she must come; make her laugh at that. Prithee, Horatio, tell me one thing. 170
HOR. What 's that, my lord?
HAM. Dost thou think Alexander looked o' this fashion i' the earth?
HOR. E'en so.
HAM. And smelt so? pah! *(Puts down the skull.)*
HOR. E'en so, my lord.
HAM. To what base uses we may return, Horatio! Why may not imagination trace the noble dust of Alexander, till he find it stopping a bung-hole?

143. *thirty years:* this statement with that in line 160 shows Hamlet's age to be thirty years. 146. *pocky:* rotten, diseased.

HOR. 'Twere to consider too curiously, to consider so.
HAM. No, faith, not a jot; but to follow him thither with modesty   180
    enough, and likelihood to lead it: as thus: Alexander died, Alexander
    was buried, Alexander returneth into dust; the dust is earth; of earth
    we make loam; and why of that loam, whereto he was converted,
    might they not stop a beer-barrel?
    Imperious Cæsar, dead and turn'd to clay,
    Might stop a hole to keep the wind away:
    O, that that earth, which kept the world in awe,
    Should patch a wall to expel the winter's flaw!
    But soft! but soft! aside: here comes the king,

Enter PRIESTS, *&c. in procession; the Corpse of* OPHELIA, LAERTES
and MOURNERS, *following;* KING, QUEEN, *their trains, &c.*

    The queen, the courtiers: who is this they follow?   190
    And with such maimed rites? This doth betoken
    The corse they follow did with desperate hand
    Fordo it own life: 'twas of some estate.
    Couch we awhile, and mark. *(Retiring with* HORATIO.*)*
LAER. What ceremony else?
HAM.   That is Laertes,
    A very noble youth: mark.
LAER. What ceremony else?
FIRST PRIEST. Her obsequies have been as far enlarged
    As we have warranty: her death was doubtful;
    And, but that great command o'ersways the order,   200
    She should in ground unsanctified have lodged
    Till the last trumpet; for charitable prayers,
    Shards, flints and pebbles should be thrown on her:
    Yet here she is allow'd her virgin crants,
    Her maiden strewments and the bringing home
    Of bell and burial.
LAER. Must there no more be done?
FIRST PRIEST.   No more be done:
    We should profane the service of the dead
    To sing a requiem and such rest to her
    As to peace-parted souls.
LAER.   Lay her i' the earth: 210
    And from her fair and unpolluted flesh

---

179. *curiously:* minutely.   183. *loam:* clay paste for brickmaking.   185. *Imperious:* imperial.   188. *flaw:* gust of wind.   193. *Fordo:* destroy.   *it:* its.   194. *Couch:* hide, lurk.   198. *enlarged:* extended, referring to the fact that suicides are not given full burial rites.   203. *Shards:* broken bits of pottery.   204. *crants:* garlands customarily hung upon the biers of unmarried women.   205. *strewments:* traditional strewing of flowers.   205-206. *bringing . . . burial:* strictly, the bridal procession from the church; applied to a maid's funeral.   210. *peace-parted:* allusion to the text, "Lord, now lettest thou thy servant depart in peace."

May violets spring! I tell thee, churlish priest,
A ministering angel shall my sister be,
When thou liest howling.
HAM.   What, the fair Ophelia!
QUEEN. Sweets to the sweet: farewell! *(Scattering flowers.)*
I hoped thou shouldst have been my Hamlet's wife;
I thought thy bride-bed to have deck'd, sweet maid,
And not have strew'd thy grave.
LAER.   O, treble woe
Fall ten times treble on that cursed head,
Whose wicked deed thy most ingenious sense   220
Deprived thee of! Hold off the earth awhile,
Till I have caught her once more in mine arms:

Leaps into the grave.

Now pile your dust upon the quick and dead,
Till of this flat a mountain you have made,
To o'ertop old Pelion, or the skyish head
Of blue Olympus.
HAM. *(Advancing).*   What is he whose grief
  Bears such an emphasis? whose phrase of sorrow
  Conjures the wandering stars, and makes them stand
  Like wonder-wounded hearers? This is I,
  Hamlet the Dane. *(Leaps into the grave.)*
LAER.   The devil take thy soul! *(Grappling with him.)*   230
HAM. Thou pray'st not well.
  I prithee, take thy fingers from my throat;
  For, though I am not splenitive and rash,
  Yet have I in me something dangerous,
  Which let thy wiseness fear: hold off thy hand.
KING. Pluck them asunder.
QUEEN.   Hamlet, Hamlet!
ALL. Gentleman,—
HOR.   Good my lord, be quiet.

The Attendants part them, and they come out of the grave.

HAM. Why, I will fight with him upon this theme
  Until my eyelids will no longer wag.
QUEEN. O my son, what theme?   240
HAM. I loved Ophelia: forty thousand brothers
  Could not, with all their quantity of love,
  Make up my sum. What wilt thou do for her?

---

214. *howling:* i.e., in hell.   220. *ingenious sense:* probably, reason (as the most ingenious of the senses).   225. *Pelion:* Olympus, Pelion, and Ossa are mountains in the north of Thessaly.   228. *wandering stars:* planets.   233. *splenitive:* quick-tempered.   239. *wag:* move (not used ludicrously).

KING. O, he is mad, Laertes.
QUEEN. For love of God, forbear him.
HAM. 'Swounds, show me what thou 'lt do:
  Woo 't weep? woo 't fight? woo 't fast? woo 't tear thyself?
  Woo 't drink up eisel? eat a crocodile?
  I'll do 't. Dost thou come here to whine?
  To outface me with leaping in her grave?   250
  Be buried quick with her, and so will I:
  And, if thou prate of mountains, let them throw
  Millions of acres on us, till our ground,
  Singeing his pate against the burning zone,
  Make Ossa like a wart! Nay, an thou 'lt mouth,
  I'll rant as well as thou.
QUEEN.   This is mere madness:
  And thus awhile the fit will work on him;
  Anon, as patient as the female dove,
  When that her golden couplets are disclosed,
  His silence will sit drooping.
HAM.   Hear you, sir;   260
  What is the reason that you use me thus?
  I loved you ever: but it is no matter;
  Let Hercules himself do what he may,
  The cat will mew and dog will have his day. *(Exit.)*
KING. I pray you, good Horatio, wait upon him.

Exit HORATIO.

(To LAERTES*)* Strengthen your patience in our last night's speech;
We'll put the matter to the present push.
Good Gertrude, set some watch over your son.
This grave shall have a living monument:
An hour of quiet shortly shall we see;   270
Till then, in patience our proceeding be.

Exeunt.

SCENE II.

A hall in the castle.

Enter HAMLET *and* HORATIO.

HAM. So much for this, sir: now shall you see the other;
  You do remember all the circumstance?
HOR. Remember it, my lord!

---

246. *'Swounds:* oath, "God's wounds." 247. *Woo 't:* wilt thou. 248. *eisel:* vinegar.
266. *in:* by recalling. 267. *present push:* immediate test. 269. *living:* lasting; also refers (for Laertes' benefit) to the plot against Hamlet.

HAM. Sir, in my heart there was a kind of fighting,
   That would not let me sleep: methought I lay
   Worse than the mutines in the bilboes. Rashly,
   And praised be rashness for it, let us know,
   Our indiscretion sometimes serves us well,
   When our deep plots do pall: and that should teach us
   There 's a divinity that shapes our ends, 10
   Rough-hew them how we will,—
HOR.   That is most certain.
HAM. Up from my cabin,
   My sea-gown scarf'd about me, in the dark
   Groped I to find out them; had my desire,
   Finger'd their packet, and in fine withdrew
   To mine own room again; making so bold,
   My fears forgetting manners, to unseal
   Their grand commission; where I found, Horatio,—
   O royal knavery!—an exact command,
   Larded with many several sorts of reasons 20
   Importing Denmark's health and England's too,
   With, ho! such bugs and goblins in my life,
   That, on the supervise, no leisure bated,
   No, not to stay the grinding of the axe,
   My head should be struck off.
HOR.   Is 't possible?
HAM. Here 's the commission: read it at more leisure.
   But wilt thou hear me how I did proceed?
HOR. I beseech you.
HAM. Being thus be-netted round with villanies,—
   Ere I could make a prologue to my brains, 30
   They had begun the play—I sat me down,
   Devised a new commission, wrote it fair:
   I once did hold it, as our statists do,
   A baseness to write fair and labour'd much
   How to forget that learning, but, sir, now
   It did me yeoman's service: wilt thou know
   The effect of what I wrote?
HOR.   Ay, good my lord.
HAM. An earnest conjuration from the king,
   As England was his faithful tributary,
   As love between them like the palm might flourish, 40
   As peace should still her wheaten garland wear

6. *mutines:* mutineers. *bilboes:* shackles. *Rashly:* goes with line 12. 9. *pall:* fail. 15. *Finger'd:* pilfered, filched. 20. *Larded:* interspersed. 22. *such . . . life:* such imaginary dangers if I were allowed to live, or such exaggeration of the actual facts of life. 23. *supervise:* perusal. *leisure bated:* delay allowed. 30-31. *prologue . . . play:* i.e., before I could begin to think, my mind had made its decision. 33. *statists:* statesmen. 34. *fair:* in a clear hand. 36. *yeoman's:* i.e., faithful. 41. *wheaten garland:* symbol of peace.

      And stand a comma 'tween their amities,
      And many such-like "As"es of great charge,
      That, on the view and knowing of these contents,
      Without debatement further, more or less,
      He should the bearers put to sudden death,
      Not shriving-time allow'd.
HOR.   How was this seal'd?
HAM. Why, even in that was heaven ordinant.
      I had my father's signet in my purse,
      Which was the model of that Danish seal;
      Folded the writ up in form of the other,
      Subscribed it, gave 't the impression, placed it safely,
      The changeling never known. Now, the next day
      Was our sea-fight; and what to this was sequent
      Thou know'st already.
HOR. So Guildenstern and Rosencrantz go to 't.
HAM. Why, man, they did make love to this employment;
      They are not near my conscience; their defeat
      Does by their own insinuation grow:
      'Tis dangerous when the baser nature comes
      Between the pass and fell incensed points
      Of mighty opposites.
HOR.   Why, what a king is this!
HAM. Does it not, thinks 't thee, stand me now upon—
      He that hath kill'd my king and whored my mother,
      Popp'd in between the election and my hopes,
      Thrown out his angle for my proper life,
      And with such cozenage—is 't not perfect conscience,
      To quit him with this arm? and is 't not to be damn'd,
      To let this canker of our nature come
      In further evil?
HOR. It must be shortly known to him from England
      What is the issue of the business there.
HAM. It will be short: the interim is mine;
      And a man's life 's no more than to say "One."
      But I am very sorry, good Horatio,
      That to Laertes I forgot myself;
      For, by the image of my cause, I see
      The portraiture of his: I'll court his favours:
      But, sure, the bravery of his grief did put me
      Into a towering passion.
HOR.   Peace! who comes here?

---

43. *"As"es:* probably the "whereases" of a formal document, with play on the word *ass.* *charge:* import, and burden.   47. *shriving-time:* time for absolution.   48. *ordinant:* directing.   54. *sequent:* subsequent.   59. *insinuation:* interference.   61. *pass:* thrust. *fell incensed:* fiercely angered.   63. *stand:* become incumbent.   65. *election:* the Danish throne was filled by election.   66. *angle:* fishhook.   67. *cozenage:* trickery.   69. *canker:* ulcer, or possibly the worm which destroys buds and leaves.   79. *bravery:* bravado.

Enter OSRIC.

OSR. Your lordship is right welcome back to Denmark.
HAM. I humbly thank you, sir. Dost know this water-fly?
HOR. No, my good lord.
HAM. Thy state is the more gracious; for 'tis a vice to know him. He hath much land, and fertile: let a beast be lord of beasts, and his crib shall stand at the king's mess: 'tis a chough; but, as I say, spacious in the possession of dirt.
OSR. Sweet lord, if your lordship were at leisure, I should impart a thing to you from his majesty.
HAM. I will receive it, sir, with all diligence of spirit. Put your bonnet to his right use; 'tis for the head.
OSR. I thank your lordship, it is very hot.
HAM. No, believe me, 'tis very cold; the wind is northerly.
OSR. It is indifferent cold, my lord, indeed.
HAM. But yet methinks it is very sultry and hot for my complexion.
OSR. Exceedingly, my lord; it is very sultry,—as 'twere,—I cannot tell how. But, my lord, his majesty bade me signify to you that he has laid a great wager on your head: sir, this is the matter,—
HAM. I beseech you, remember—*(*HAMLET *moves him to put on his hat.)*
OSR. Nay, good my lord; for mine ease, in good faith. Sir, here is newly come to court Laertes; believe me, an absolute gentleman, full of most excellent differences, of very soft society and great showing: indeed, to speak feelingly of him, he is the card or calendar of gentry, for you shall find in him the continent of what part a gentleman would see.
HAM. Sir, his definement suffers no perdition in you; though, I know, to divide him inventorially would dizzy the arithmetic of memory, and yet but yaw neither, in respect of his quick sail. But, in the verity of extolment, I take him to be a soul of great article; and his infusion of such dearth and rareness, as, to make true diction of him, his semblable is his mirror; and who else would trace him, his umbrage, nothing more.

---

82. *water-fly:* vain or busily idle person. 85. *lord of beasts:* cf. Gen. 1:26, 28. 85-86. *his crib . . . mess:* he shall eat at the king's table, i.e., be one of the group of persons (usually four) constituting a *mess* at a banquet. 86. *chough:* probably, chattering jackdaw; also explained as *chuff,* provincial boor or churl. 94. *indifferent:* somewhat. 99. *remember:* i.e., remember thy courtesy; conventional phrase for "be covered." 100. *mine ease:* conventional reply declining the invitation of "remember thy courtesy." 102. *differences:* distinguishing qualities. *soft:* gentle. *showing:* distinguished appearance. 103. *feelingly:* with just perception. *card:* chart, map. *gentry:* good breeding. 106. *definement:* definition. *perdition:* loss, diminution. 107. *divide him inventorially:* i.e., enumerate his graces. 108. *yaw:* to move unsteadily (of a ship). 109. *article:* moment or importance. *infusion:* infused temperament, character imparted by nature. 110. *dearth and rareness:* rarity. *diction:* description in words. 110-111. *semblable:* like, match. 111. *trace:* follow. *umbrage:* shadow.

OSR. Your lordship speaks most infallibly of him.
HAM. The concernancy, sir? why do we wrap the gentleman in our more rawer breath?
OSR. Sir?
HOR. Is 't not possible to understand in another tongue? You will do 't, sir, really.
HAM. What imports the nomination of this gentleman?
OSR. Of Laertes? 120
HOR. His purse is empty already; all 's golden words are spent.
HAM. Of him, sir.
OSR. I know you are not ignorant—
HAM. I would you did, sir; yet, in faith, if you did, it would not much approve me. Well, sir?
OSR. You are not ignorant of what excellence Laertes is—
HAM. I dare not confess that, lest I should compare with him in excellence; but, to know a man well, were to know himself.
OSR. I mean, sir, for his weapon; but in the imputation laid on him by them, in his meed he 's unfellowed. 130
HAM. What 's his weapon?
OSR. Rapier and dagger.
HAM. That 's two of his weapons: but, well.
OSR. The king, sir, hath wagered with him six Barbary horses: against the which he has imponed, as I take it, six French rapiers and poniards, with their assigns, as girdle, hangers, and so: three of the carriages, in faith, are very dear to fancy, very responsive to the hilts, most delicate carriages, and of very liberal conceit.
HAM. What call you the carriages?
HOR. I knew you must be edified by the margent ere you had done. 140
OSR. The carriages, sir, are the hangers.
HAM. The phrase would be more german to the matter, if we could carry cannon by our sides: I would it might be hangers till then. But, on: six Barbary horses against six French swords, their assigns, and three liberal-conceited carriages; that 's the French bet against the Danish. Why is this "imponed," as you call it?
OSR. The king, sir, hath laid, that in a dozen passes between yourself and him, he shall not exceed you three hits: he hath laid on twelve for nine; and it would come to immediate trial, if your lordship would vouchsafe the answer. 150
HAM. How if I answer "no"?
OSR. I mean, my lord, the opposition of your person in trial.
HAM. Sir, I will walk here in the hall: if it please his majesty, 't is the

---

114. *concernancy:* import. 115. *breath:* speech. 117. *Is't . . . tongue?:* probably, can you not understand your jargon when somebody else uses it? 119. *nomination:* naming. 125. *approve:* commend. 128. *but . . . himself:* but to know a man as excellent were to know Laertes. 129. *imputation:* reputation. 130. *meed:* merit. 135. *he has imponed:* he has wagered. 136. *hangers:* straps on the sword belt from which the sword hung. 137. *dear to fancy:* fruitfully made. 138. *delicate:* i.e., in workmanship. *liberal conceit:* elaborate design. 140. *margent:* margin of a book, place for explanatory notes. 142. *german:* germain, appropriate.

breathing time of day with me; let the foils be brought, the gentleman
willing, and the king hold his purpose, I will win for him an I can; if
not, I will gain nothing but my shame and the odd hits.

OSR. Shall I re-deliver you e'en so?

HAM. To this effect, sir; after what flourish your nature will.

OSR. I commend my duty to your lordship.

HAM. Yours, yours. *(Exit* OSRIC.*)* He does well to commend it himself; there are no tongues else for 's turn.

HOR. This lapwing runs away with the shell on his head.

HAM. He did comply with his dug, before he sucked it. Thus has he—and many more of the same breed that I know the drossy age dotes on—only got the tune of the time and out of an habit of encounter; a kind of yesty collection, which carries them through and through the most fann'd and winnowed opinions; and do but blow them to their trial, the bubbles are out.

Enter a LORD.

LORD. My lord, his majesty commended him to you by young Osric, who brings back to him, that you attend him in the hall: he sends to know if your pleasure hold to play with Laertes, or that you will take longer time.

HAM. I am constant to my purposes; they follow the king's pleasure: if his fitness speaks, mine is ready; now or whensoever, provided I be so able as now.

LORD. The king and queen and all are coming down.

HAM. In happy time.

LORD. The queen desires you to use some gentle entertainment to Laertes before you fall to play.

HAM. She well instructs me. *(Exit* LORD.*)*

HOR. You will lose this wager, my lord.

HAM. I do not think so; since he went into France, I have been in continual practice; I shall win at the odds. But thou wouldst not think how ill all 's here about my heart: but it is no matter.

HOR. Nay, good my lord,—

HAM. It is but foolery; but it is such a kind of gain-giving, as would perhaps trouble a woman.

HOR. If your mind dislike any thing, obey it: I will forestal their repair hither, and say you are not fit.

HAM. Not a whit, we defy augury: there 's a special providence in the fall of a sparrow. If it be now, 'tis not to come; if it be not to come, it will be now; if it be not now, yet it will come: the readiness is all:

---

154. *breathing time:* exercise period. 163. *did comply with his dug:* paid compliment to his mother's breast. 164. *drossy:* frivolous. 165. *tune:* temper, mood. *habit of encounter:* demeanor of social intercourse. 166. *yesty:* frothy. 167-168. *blow . . . out:* i.e., put them to the test, and their ignorance is exposed. 177. *In happy time:* a phrase of courtesy. 183. *at the odds:* with the balance of advantage in my favor. 186. *gain-giving:* misgiving.

since no man has aught of what he leaves, what is 't to leave betimes?
Let be.

Enter KING, QUEEN, LAERTES, LORDS, OSRIC, *and* ATTENDANTS *with foils, &c.*

KING. Come, Hamlet, come, and take this hand from me.

The KING *puts* LAERTES' *hand into* HAMLET'*s.*

HAM. Give me your pardon, sir: I 've done you wrong;
But pardon 't, as you are a gentleman.
This presence knows,
And you must needs have heard, how I am punish'd
With sore distraction. What I have done,   200
That might your nature, honour and exception
Roughly awake, I here proclaim was madness.
Was 't Hamlet wrong'd Laertes? Never Hamlet:
If Hamlet from himself be ta'en away,
And when he 's not himself does wrong Laertes,
Then Hamlet does it not, Hamlet denies it.
Who does it, then? His madness: if 't be so,
Hamlet is of the faction that is wrong'd;
His madness is poor Hamlet's enemy.
Sir, in this audience,   210
Let my disclaiming from a purposed evil
Free me so far in your most generous thoughts,
That I have shot mine arrow o'er the house,
And hurt my brother.
   LAER.   I am satisfied in nature,
Whose motive, in this case, should stir me most
To my revenge: but in my terms of honour
I stand aloof; and will no reconcilement,
Till by some elder masters, of known honour,
I have a voice and precedent of peace,
To keep my name ungored. But till that time,   220
I do receive your offer'd love like love,
And will not wrong it.
   HAM.   I embrace it freely;
And will this brother's wager frankly play.
Give us the foils. Come on.
   LAER.   Come, one for me.
   HAM. I'll be your foil, Laertes: in mine ignorance
Your skill shall, like a star i' the darkest night,
Stick fiery off indeed.

---

198. *presence:* royal assembly.   201. *exception:* disapproval.   219. *voice:* authoritative pronouncement.   225. *foil:* quibble on the two senses, "background which sets something off," and "blunted rapier for fencing."   227. *Stick fiery off:* stand out brilliantly.

LAER.   You mock me, sir.
HAM. No, by this hand.
KING. Give them the foils, young Osric. Cousin Hamlet,
  You know the wager?
HAM.   Very well, my lord;   230
  Your grace hath laid the odds o' the weaker side.
KING. I do not fear it; I have seen you both:
  But since he is better'd, we have therefore odds.
LAER. This is too heavy, let me see another.
HAM. This likes me well. These foils have all a length?

They prepare to play.

OSR. Ay, my good lord.
KING. Set me the stoups of wine upon that table.
  If Hamlet give the first or second hit,
  Or quit in answer of the third exchange,
  Let all the battlements their ordnance fire;   240
  The king shall drink to Hamlet's better breath;
  And in the cup an union shall he throw,
  Richer than that which four successive kings
  In Denmark's crown have worn. Give me the cups;
  And let the kettle to the trumpet speak,
  The trumpet to the cannoneer without,
  The cannons to the heavens, the heavens to earth,
  "Now the king drinks to Hamlet." Come, begin:
  And you, the judges, bear a wary eye.
HAM. Come on, sir.
LAER.   Come, my lord.

They play.

HAM.   One.
LAER.   No.
HAM.   Judgement.   250
OSR. A hit, a very palpable hit.
LAER.   Well; again.
KING. Stay; give me drink. Hamlet, this pearl is thine;
  Here's to thy health.

Trumpets sound, and cannon shot off within.

                  Give him the cup.
HAM. I'll play this bout first; set it by awhile.
  Come. *(They play.)* Another hit; what say you?
LAER. A touch, a touch, I do confess 't.
KING. Our son shall win.

242. *union:* pearl. 245. *kettle:* kettledrum.

QUEEN. He's fat, and scant of breath.
  Here, Hamlet, take my napkin, rub thy brows:
  The queen carouses to thy fortune, Hamlet.
HAM. Good madam!
KING. Gertrude, do not drink. 260
QUEEN. I will, my lord; I pray you, pardon me.
KING *(Aside).* It is the poison'd cup: it is too late.
HAM. I dare not drink yet, madam; by and by.
QUEEN. Come, let me wipe thy face.
LAER. My lord, I'll hit him now.
KING. I do not think 't.
LAER. *(Aside).* And yet 'tis almost 'gainst my conscience.
HAM. Come, for the third, Laertes: you but dally;
  I pray you, pass with your best violence;
  I am afeard you make a wanton of me.
LAER. Say you so? come on. 270

They play.

OSR. Nothing, neither way.
LAER. Have at you now!

LAERTES *wounds* HAMLET; *then, in scuffling, they change rapiers, and*
  HAMLET *wounds* LAERTES.

KING. Part them; they are incensed.
HAM. Nay, come, again.

The QUEEN *falls.*

OSR. Look to the queen there, ho!
HOR. They bleed on both sides. How is it, my lord?
OSR. How is 't, Laertes?
LAER. Why, as a woodcock to mine own springe, Osric;
  I am justly kill'd with mine own treachery.
HAM. How does the queen?
KING. She swounds to see them bleed.
QUEEN. No, no, the drink, the drink,—O my dear
  Hamlet,—
The drink, the drink! I am poison'd. *(Dies.)* 280
HAM. O villany! Ho! let the door be lock'd:
  Treachery! Seek it out.
LAER. It is here, Hamlet: Hamlet, thou art slain;
  No medicine in the world can do thee good;
  In thee there is not half an hour of life;
  The treacherous instrument is in thy hand,

---

259. *carouses:* drinks a toast. 269. *wanton:* spoiled child. 276. *woodcock:* as type of stupidity or as decoy. *springe:* trap, snare. 278. *swounds:* swoons.

Unbated and envenom'd: the foul practice
Hath turn'd itself on me; lo, here I lie,
Never to rise again: thy mother 's poison'd:
I can no more: the king, the king 's to blame. 290
HAM. The point envenom'd too!
Then, venom, to thy work. *(Stabs the KING.)*
ALL. Treason! treason!
KING. O, yet defend me, friends; I am but hurt.
HAM. Here, thou incestuous, murderous, damned Dane,
Drink off this potion. Is thy union here?
Follow my mother.

KING *dies.*

LAER. He is justly served;
It is a poison temper'd by himself.
Exchange forgiveness with me, noble Hamlet:
Mine and my father's death come not upon thee,
Nor thine on me! *(Dies.)* 300
HAM. Heaven make thee free of it! I follow thee.
I am dead, Horatio. Wretched queen, adieu!
You that look pale and tremble at this chance,
That are but mutes or audience to this act,
Had I but time—as this fell sergeant, death,
Is strict in his arrest—O, I could tell you—
But let it be. Horatio, I am dead;
Thou livest; report me and my cause aright
To the unsatisfied.
HOR. Never believe it: 310
I am more an antique Roman than a Dane:
Here 's yet some liquor left.
HAM. As thou 'rt a man,
Give me the cup: let go; by heaven, I'll have 't.
O God! Horatio, what a wounded name,
Things standing thus unknown, shall live behind me!
If thou didst ever hold me in thy heart,
Absent thee from felicity awhile,
And in this harsh world draw thy breath in pain,
To tell my story.

March afar off, and shot within.

What warlike noise is this?
OSR. Young Fortinbras, with conquest come from Poland, 320
To the ambassadors of England gives
This warlike volley.

---

287. *Unbated:* not blunted with a button. 298. *temper'd:* mixed. 305. *mutes:* performers in a play who speak no words. 306. *sergeant:* sheriff's officer.

HAM.　　　　　　O, I die, Horatio;
　　The potent poison quite o'er-crows my spirit:
　　I cannot live to hear the news from England;
　　But I do prophesy the election lights
　　On Fortinbras: he has my dying voice;
　　So tell him, with the occurrents, more and less,
　　Which have solicited. The rest is silence. *(Dies.)*
HOR.　Now cracks a noble heart. Good night, sweet prince;
　　And flights of angels sing thee to thy rest!　　　　　　330
　　Why does the drum come hither?

March within.

Enter FORTINBRAS, *the* ENGLISH AMBASSADORS, *and others.*

FORT.　Where is this sight?
HOR.　　　　　　What is it ye would see?
　　If aught of woe or wonder, cease your search.
FORT.　This quarry cries on havoc. O proud death,
　　What feast is toward in thine eternal cell,
　　That thou so many princes at a shot
　　So bloodily hast struck?
FIRST AMB.　　　　The sight is dismal;
　　And our affairs from England come too late:
　　The ears are senseless that should give us hearing,
　　To tell him his commandment is fulfill'd,　　　　　　340
　　That Rosencrantz and Guildenstern are dead:
　　Where should we have our thanks?
HOR.　　　　　Not from his mouth,
　　Had it the ability of life to thank you:
　　He never gave commandment for their death.
　　But since, so jump upon this bloody question,
　　You from the Polack wars, and you from England,
　　Are here arrived, give order that these bodies
　　High on a stage be placed to the view;
　　And let me speak to the yet unknowing world
　　How these things came about: so shall you hear　　　　350
　　Of carnal, bloody, and unnatural acts,
　　Of accidental judgements, casual slaughters,
　　Of deaths put on by cunning and forced cause,
　　And, in this upshot, purposes mistook
　　Fall'n on the inventors' heads: all this can I
　　Truly deliver.
FORT.　　　　Let us haste to hear it,

---

323. *o'er-crows:* triumphs over.　327. *occurrents:* events, incidents.　328. *solicited:* moved, urged.　334. *quarry:* heap of dead.　*cries on havoc:* indicates merciless slaughter.　335. *eternal:* used to express extreme abhorrence.　342. *his mouth:* i.e., the king's.　348. *stage:* platform.　351-355. *Of carnal . . . heads:* the words bear detailed reference to the tragic issues of the play.

    And call the noblest to the audience.
    For me, with sorrow I embrace my fortune:
    I have some rights of memory in this kingdom,
    Which now to claim my vantage doth invite me.   360
HOR. Of that I shall have also cause to speak,
    And from his mouth whose voice will draw on more:
    But let this same be presently perform'd,
    Even while men's minds are wild; lest more mischance,
    On plots and errors, happen.
FORT.   Let four captains
    Bear Hamlet, like a soldier, to the stage;
    For he was likely, had he been put on,
    To have proved most royal: and, for his passage,
    The soldiers' music and the rites of war
    Speak loudly for him.   370
    Take up the bodies: such a sight as this
    Becomes the field, but here shows much amiss.
    Go, bid the soldiers shoot.

A dead march. Exeunt, bearing off the dead bodies; after which a peal of ordnance is shot off.

Questions for Discussion

1. Does Shakespeare follow Aristotle's advice (see pages 142-143) concerning the predominance of plot over character in tragic drama? Explain. Might one argue that plot and character in *Hamlet* are so mutually reliant on each other that they cannot be separately discussed? For example, might one contend that the development of Hamlet's character (particularly his indecision) provides impetus for the plot? Elaborate.

2. Might one argue that the *structure* of *Hamlet* is also governed by its hero's character development? Shakespeare's other great tragedies —*Macbeth, Othello,* and *King Lear*—all follow the pyramidal structure described in the introduction to this section (see page 142). Is the same true of *Hamlet*? Explain. Do your answers to this question

---

359. *of memory:* traditional, remembered.   362. *draw on more:* lead more to speak.
367. *On:* on account of or, possibly, on top of, in addition to.   368. *passage:* death.
372. *field:* i.e., of battle.

suggest that once a writer knows the rules he can occasionally violate them? Can you think of a situation in which this might be applied to your own writing?

3. Is the sequence of *Hamlet* chronological? Elaborate. Could Shakespeare have presented his story in any sequence other than chronological without damaging its structure? Does a composition student appear to have more options regarding methods of organization than playwrights have? Why or why not?

4. Do the scenes of comic relief (e.g., the "Alas, poor Yorick" scene) disrupt the organization and mood of the play, or do they intensify the tragic mood by briefly establishing a contrasting comic atmosphere? Explain and illustrate.

5. Shakespeare was writing for an essentially middle-class English audience. Is there anything in *Hamlet,* despite its noble characters and foreign setting, which might appeal especially to English playgoers? To middle-class playgoers? Are there elements which might appeal to any given audience of any given age? For instance?

Suggested Theme Topics

1. Discuss the relative importance of characterization and plot in *Hamlet.*

2. Summarize the plot of *Hamlet,* employing an expository mode of expression (rather than chronological) in such a way as to emphasize Hamlet's seeming indecision about killing the king.

3. Discuss Shakespeare's use of comic relief in *Hamlet.* Elaborate on its appropriateness or inappropriateness to the playwright's generally serious purpose.

4. Write a description of *Hamlet* as a tragedy. Pay special attention to setting and subject matter.

5. Analyze the structure of *Hamlet* as either illustrating or violating Freytag's rules for structuring tragic drama discussed in the introduction to this section.

Douglas Turner Ward

Douglas Turner Ward (1931-   ) was born on a Louisiana plantation and grew up in New Orleans. After arriving in New York City in 1948, he worked as an apprentice journalist and enrolled in Paul Mann's Actors' Workshop. He is a successful actor and has appeared in such plays as The Iceman Cometh, A Raisin in the Sun, *and* One Flew over the Cuckoo's Nest. *Mr. Ward's first produced plays,* Happy Ending *and* Day of Absence, *were presented at the St. Marks Playhouse and received the Vernon Rice Drama Award and the 1966 Obie Award. In 1966 Mr. Ward called for the establishment of a Negro-oriented theater that would provide opportunities for blacks in all areas of theatrical production, that is, in playwriting, directing, technical theater, and acting. That dream was realized in the Negro Ensemble Company, which had its first highly successful season in 1968 under the leadership of Mr. Ward and Robert Hooks.*

Day of Absence *displays Ward's disdain for the trappings of concrete reality and, at the same time, reveals a striking continuity in plot and coherence in characterization and theme. The comedy results from hyperbolic characterizations and implausible plot; beneath it is a serious theme. In that contrast—the use of comedy to make serious statements and ultimately to reform—we have a classic example of theatrical satire.*

DAY OF ABSENCE: A SATIRICAL FANTASY

The time is now.
Play opens in unnamed Southern town of medium population on a somnolent cracker morning—meaning no matter the early temperature, it's gonna get hot. The hamlet is just beginning to rouse itself from the sleepy lassitude of night.

Notes on production: No scenery is necessary—only actors shifting in and out on an almost bare stage and freezing into immobility as focuses change or blackouts occur.
Play is conceived for performance by a Negro cast, a reverse minstrel show done in white face. Logically, it might also be performed by whites—at their own risk. If any producer is faced with choosing between opposite hues, author strongly suggests: "Go 'long wit the blacks—besides all else, they need the work more."

If acted by the latter, race members are urged to go for broke, yet cautioned not to ham it up too broadly. In fact—it just might be more effective if they aspire to serious tragedy. Only qualification needed for Caucasian casting is that the company fit a uniform pattern—insipid white.

Before any horrifying discrimination doubts arise, I hasten to add that a bona fide white actor should be cast as the ANNOUNCER in all productions, likewise a Negro thespian in pure native black as RASTUS. This will truly subvert any charge that the production is unintegrated.

All props, except essential items (chairs, brooms, rags, mop, debris) should be imaginary (phones, switchboard, mikes, eating utensils, food, etc.). Actors should indicate their presence through mime.

The cast of characters develops as the play progresses. In the interest of economical casting, actors should double or triple in roles wherever possible.

Production concept: This is a red-white-and-blue play—meaning that the entire production should be designed around the basic color scheme of our patriotic trinity. Lighting should illustrate, highlight, and detail time, action, and mood—opening scenes stage-lit with white rays of morning, transforming to panic reds of afternoon, flowing into ominous blues of evening. Costuming should be orchestrated around the same color scheme. In addition, subsidiary usage of grays, khakis, yellows, pinks, and patterns of stars and bars should be employed. All actors (ANNOUNCERS and RASTUS excepted, of course) should wear white shoes or sneakers, and all women characters clothed in knee-length frocks should wear white stockings. Blond wigs, both for males and females, can be used in selected instances. Makeup should have uniform consistency, with individual touches thrown in to enhance personal identity.

Sample models of makeup and costuming:
MARY: *Kewpie-doll face, ruby-red lips painted to valentine pursing, moon-shaped rough circles implanted on each cheek, blond wig of fat flowing ringlets, dazzling ankle-length snow-white nightie.*
MAYOR: *Seersucker white ensemble, ten-gallon hat, red string tie, and blue belt.*
CLEM: *Khaki pants, bareheaded, and blond.*
LUKE: *Blue work jeans, strawhatted.*
CLUB WOMAN: *Yellow dress patterned with symbols of Dixie, gray hat.*
CLAN: *A veritable, riotous advertisement of red-white-and-blue combinations with stars and bars tossed in.*
PIOUS: *White ministerial garb with black cleric's collar topping his snow-white shirt.*
OPERATORS: *All in red with different color wigs.*
All other characters should be carefully defined through costuming which typifies their identify.

Scene: Street.

Time: Early morning.

CLEM *(sitting under a sign suspended by invisible wires and bold-printed with the lettering:* "STORE"*).* Morning, Luke ...
LUKE *(sitting a few paces away under an identical sign).* Morning, Clem ...
CLEM. Gon be a hot day.
LUKE. Looks that way ...
CLEM. Might rain though ...
LUKE. Might.
CLEM. Hope it does ...
LUKE. Me too ...
CLEM. Farmers could use a little wet spell for a change ... How's the Missis?
LUKE. Same.
CLEM. 'N the kids?
LUKE. Them too ... How's yourns?
CLEM. Fine, thank you ... *(They both lapse into drowsy silence, waving lethargically from time to time at imaginary passersby.)* Hi, Joe ...
LUKE. Joe ...
CLEM. How'd it go yesterday, Luke?
LUKE. Fair.
CLEM. Same wit me ... Business don't seem to git no better or no worse. Guess we in a rut, Luke, don't it 'pear that way to you?—Morning, Ma'm.
LUKE. Morning ...
CLEM. Tried display, sales, advertisement, stamps—everything—yet merchandising stumbles 'round in the same old groove. ... But—that's better than plunging downwards, I reckon.
LUKE. Guess it is.
CLEM. Morning, Bret. How's the family? ... That's good.
LUKE. Bret—
CLEM. Morning, Sue.
LUKE. How do, Sue.
CLEM *(starting after her).* Fine hunk of woman.
LUKE. Sure is.
CLEM. Wonder if it's any good?
LUKE. Bet it is.
CLEM. Sure like to find out!
LUKE. So would I.
CLEM. You ever try?
LUKE. Never did ...
CLEM. Morning, Gus ...
LUKE. Howdy, Gus.
CLEM. Fine, thank you. *(They lapse into silence again.* CLEM *rouses himself slowly, begins to look around quizzically.)* Luke ... ?

LUKE. Huh?
CLEM. Do you . . . er, er—feel anything—funny . . . ?
LUKE. Like what?
CLEM. Like . . . er—something—strange?
LUKE. I dunno . . . haven't thought about it.
CLEM. I mean . . . like something's wrong—outta place, unusual?
LUKE. I don't know . . . What you got in mind?
CLEM. Nothing . . . just that—just that—like somp'um's outta kilter. I got a funny feeling somp'um's not up to snuff. Can't figger out what it is . . .
LUKE. Maybe it's in your haid . . .
CLEM. No, not like that . . . Like somp'um's happened—or happening—gone haywire, loony.
LUKE. Well, don't worry 'bout it, it'll pass.
CLEM. Guess you right *(attempts return to somnolence but doesn't succeed)*. I'm sorry, Luke, but you sure you don't feel nothing peculiar . . . ?
LUKE *(slightly irked)*. Toss it out your mind, Clem! We got a long day ahead of us. If something's wrong, you'll know 'bout it in due time. No use worrying about it 'till it comes and if it's coming, it will. Now, relax!
CLEM. All right, you right . . . Hi, Margie . . .
LUKE. Marge.
CLEM *(unable to control himself)*. Luke, I don't give a damn what you say. Somp'um's topsy-turvy, I just know it!
LUKE *(increasingly irritated)*. Now look here, Clem—it's a bright day, it looks like it's gon git hotter. You say the wife and kids are fine and the business is no better or no worse? Well, what else could be wrong? . . . If somp'um's gon happen, it's gon happen anyway and there ain't a damn fool thing you kin do to stop it! So you ain't helping me, yourself or nobody else by thinking 'bout it. It's not gon be no better or no worse when it gits here. It'll come to you when it gits ready to come and it's gon be the same whether you worry about it or not. So stop letting it upset you! *(LUKE settles back in his chair. CLEM does likewise. LUKE shuts his eyes. After a few moments, they reopen. He forces them shut again. They reopen in greater curiosity. Finally, he rises slowly to an upright position in the chair, looks around frowningly. Turns slowly to CLEM.)* Clem? . . . You know something? . . . Somp'um is peculiar . . .
CLEM *(vindicated)*. I knew it, Luke! I jist knew it! Ever since we been sitting here, I been having that feeling!

(Scene is blacked out abruptly. Lights rise on another section of the stage where a young couple lie in bed under an invisible wire-suspension sign lettered "HOME." Loud, insistent sounds of baby yells are heard. JOHN, the husband, turns over trying to ignore the cries; MARY, the wife, is undisturbed. JOHN's efforts are futile; the cries continue until they cannot be denied. He bolts upright, jumps out of bed, and disappears offstage. Returns quickly and tries to rouse MARY.)

JOHN. Mary . . . *(Nudges her, pushes her, yells into her ear, but she fails to respond)* Mary, get up . . . Get up!
MARY. Ummm . . . *(Shrugs away, still sleeping.)*
JOHN. GET UP!
MARY. Ummmmmmmmm!
JOHN. Don't you hear the baby's bawling? . . . NOW GET UP!
MARY *(mumbling drowsily).* What baby . . . whose baby . . . ?
JOHN. Yours!
MARY. Mine? That's ridiculous . . . what'd you say . . . ? Somebody's baby bawling? . . . How could that be so? *(Hearing screams)* Who's crying? Somebody's crying! . . . What's crying? . . . *Where's Lula?*
JOHN. I don't know. You better get up.
MARY. That's outrageous! . . . What time is it?
JOHN. Late 'nuff! Now rise up!
MARY. You must be joking . . . I'm sure I still have four or five hours' sleep in store—even more after that head-splittin' blowout last night . . . *(Tumbles back under covers.)*
JOHN. Nobody told you to gulp those last six bourbons—
MARY. Don't tell me how many bourbons to swallow, not after you guzzled the whole stinking bar! . . . Get up? . . . You must be cracked . . . Where's Lula? She must be here, she always is . . .
JOHN. Well, she ain't here yet, so get up and muzzle that brat before she does drive me cuckoo!
MARY *(springing upright, finally realizing gravity of situation).* Whaddaya mean Lula's not here? She's always here, she must be here . . . Where else kin she be? She supposed to be . . . She just can't *not* be here—call her!

(Blackout as JOHN *rushes offstage. Scene shifts to a trio of* TELEPHONE OPERATORS *perched on stools before imaginary switchboards. Chaos and bedlam are taking place to the sound of buzzes. Effect of following dialogue should simulate rising pandemonium.)*

FIRST OPERATOR. The line is busy—
SECOND OPERATOR. Line is busy—
THIRD OPERATOR. Is busy—
FIRST OPERATOR. Doing best we can—
SECOND OPERATOR. Having difficulty—
THIRD OPERATOR. Soon as possible—
FIRST OPERATOR. Just one moment—
SECOND OPERATOR. Would you hold on—
THIRD OPERATOR. Awful sorry, madam—
FIRST OPERATOR. Would you hold on, please—
SECOND OPERATOR. Just a second, please—
THIRD OPERATOR. Please hold on, please—
FIRST OPERATOR. The line is busy.
SECOND OPERATOR. The line is busy—
THIRD OPERATOR. The line is busy—
FIRST OPERATOR. Doing best we can—
SECOND OPERATOR. Hold on, please—

THIRD OPERATOR. Can't make connections—
FIRST OPERATOR. Unable to put it in—
SECOND OPERATOR. Won't plug through—
THIRD OPERATOR. Sorry, madam—
FIRST OPERATOR. If you'd wait a moment—
SECOND OPERATOR. Doing best we can—
THIRD OPERATOR. Sorry—
FIRST OPERATOR. One moment—
SECOND OPERATOR. Just a second—
THIRD OPERATOR. Hold on—
FIRST OPERATOR. *Yes—*
SECOND OPERATOR. *Stop it!—*
THIRD OPERATOR. *How do I know—*
FIRST OPERATOR. *You another one!*
SECOND OPERATOR. *Hold on, Dammit!*
THIRD OPERATOR. *Up yours, too!*
FIRST OPERATOR. *The line is busy—*
SECOND OPERATOR. *The line is busy—*
THIRD OPERATOR. *The line is busy—*

(The switchboard clamors a cacaphony of buzzes as OPERATORS *plug connections with the frenzy of a Chaplin movie. Their replies degenerate into a babble of gibberish. At the height of frenzy, the* SUPERVISOR *appears.)*

SUPERVISOR. *What's the snarl-up?*
FIRST OPERATOR. Everybody calling at the same time, Ma'am!
SECOND OPERATOR. Board can't handle it!
THIRD OPERATOR. Like everybody in big New York City is trying to squeeze a call through to lil ole us!
SUPERVISOR. God! . . . Somp'um terrible musta happened! . . . Buzz the emergency frequency hookup to the Mayor's office and find out what the hell's going on!

(Scene blacks out quickly to CLEM *and* LUKE.*)*

CLEM *(something slowly dawning on him).* Luke . . . ?
LUKE. Yes, Clem?
CLEM *(eyes roving around in puzzlement).* Luke . . . ?
LUKE *(irked).* I said what, Clem!
CLEM. Luke . . . ? Where—where is—the—the—?
LUKE. The *what?*
CLEM. Nigras . . . ?
LUKE. What . . . ?
CLEM. Nigras . . . Where is the Nigras, where is they, Luke . . . ? *All the Nigras!* . . . I don't see no Nigras . . . !
LUKE. Whatcha mean . . . ?
CLEM *(agitatedly).* Luke there ain't a darkey in sight . . . . And if you remember, we ain't seen a nappy hair all morning . . . The Nigras, Luke! We ain't laid eyes on nary a coon this whole morning!

LUKE. You must be crazy or something, Clem!
CLEM. Think about it, Luke, we been sitting here for an hour or more —try and recollect if you remember seeing jist *one* go by!
LUKE *(confused)*. I don't recall ... But ... but there musta been some ... The heat musta got you, Clem! How in hell could that be so?
CLEM *(triumphantly)*. Just think, Luke! ... Look around ya ... Now, every morning mosta people walkin 'long this street is colored. They's strolling by going to work, they's waiting for the buses, they's sweeping sidewalks, cleaning stores, starting to shine shoes and wetting the mops—Right? ... Well, look around you, Luke—Where is they? *(*LUKE *paces up and down, checking.)* I told you, Luke, they ain't nowheres to be seen.
LUKE. This ... this ... some kind of holiday for 'em—or something?
CLEM. I don't know, Luke ... but ... but what I do know is they ain't here'n we haven't seen a solitary one ... It's scarifying, Luke ... !
LUKE. Well ... Maybe they's jist standing 'n walking and shining on other streets—Let's go look!

(Scene blacks out to JOHN *and* MARY. *Baby cries are as insistent as ever.)*

MARY *(at end of patience)*. Smother it!
JOHN *(beyond his)*. That's a hell of a thing to say 'bout your own child! You should know what to do to hush her up!
MARY. Why don't you try?
JOHN. You had her!
MARY. You shared in borning her!
JOHN. Possibly not!
MARY. Why, you lousy—!
JOHN. What good is a mother who can't shut up her own daughter?
MARY. I told you she yells louder every time I try to lay hands on her —Where's Lula? Didn't you call her?
JOHN. I told you I can't get the call through!
MARY. Try agin—
JOHN. It's no use! I tried numerous times and can't even git through to the switchboard. You've got to quiet her down yourself. *(Firmly)* Now, go in there and clam her up 'fore I lose my patience! *(*MARY *exits. Soon, we hear the yells increase. She rushes back in.)*
MARY. She won't let me touch her, just screams louder!
JOHN. Probably wet 'n soppy!
MARY. Yes! Stinks something awful! Phooooey! I can't stand that filth and odor!
JOHN. That's why she's screaming! Needs her didee changed—go change it!
MARY. How you 'spect me to when I don't know how? Suppose I faint?
JOHN. Well let her blast away. I'm getting outta here.
MARY. You can't leave me here like this!

JOHN. Just watch me! ... See this nice split-level cottage, peachy furniture, multicolored T.V., hi-fi set n' the rest? ... Well, how you think I scraped 'em together while you curled up on your fat lil fanny? ... By gitting outta here—not only *on time* ... but *earlier!*— Beating a frantic crew of nice young executives to the punch—gitting there fustest with the mostest brown-nosing you ever saw! Now if I goof one day—just ONE DAY!—you reckon I'd stay ahead? NO! ... There'd be a wolf pack trampling over my prostrate body, racing to replace my smiling face against the boss's left rump! ... *No, mam!* I'm zooming outta here on time, just as I always have, and what's more—you gon fix me some breakfast. *I'm hungry!*
MARY. But—
JOHN. No buts about it! *(Flash blackout as he gags on a mouthful of coffee.)* What you trying to do, STRANGLE ME? *(Jumps up and starts putting on jacket.)*
MARY *(sarcastically).* What did you expect?
JOHN *(in biting fury).* That you could possibly boil a pot of water, toast a few slices of bread and fry a coupler eggs! ... It was a mistaken assumption!
MARY. So they aren't as good as Lula's!
JOHN. That is an overstatement. Your efforts don't result in anything that could possibly be digested by man, mammal, or insect! ... When I married you, I thought I was fairly acquainted with your faults and weaknesses—I chalked 'em up to human imperfection ... But now I know I was being extremely generous, overoptimistic and phenomenally deluded!—You have no idea how useless you really are!
MARY. Then why'd you marry me?
JOHN. Decoration!
MARY. You shoulda married Lula!
JOHN. I might've if it wasn't 'gainst the segregation law! ... But for the sake of my home, my child and my sanity, I will even take a chance on sacrificing my slippery grip on the status pole and drive by her shanty to find out whether she or someone like her kin come over here and prevent some ultimate disaster. *(Storms toward door, stopping abruptly at exit)* Are you sure you kin make it to the bathroom wit'out Lula backing you up?

(Blackout. Scene shifts to MAYOR's *office where a cluttered desk stands center stage amid paper debris.)*

MAYOR *(striding determinedly toward desk; stopping midway, bellowing).* Woodfence! ... Woodfence! ... Woodfence! *(Receiving no reply, completes distance to desk)* Jack-son! ... Jackson!
JACKSON *(entering worriedly).* Yes, sir ... ?
MAYOR. Where's Vice-Mayor Woodfence, that no-good brother-in-law of mine?
JACKSON. Hasn't come in yet, sir.
MAYOR. *Hasn't come in?* ... Damn bastard! Knows we have a crucial conference. Soon as he staggers through that door, tell him to shoot in here! *(Angrily focusing on his disorderly desk and littered*

surroundings) And git Mandy here to straighten up this mess—Rufus too! You know he shoulda been waiting to knock dust off my shoes soon as I step in. Get 'em in here! ... What's the matter wit them lazy Nigras? ... Already had to dress myself because of J. C., fix my own coffee without May-Belle, drive myself to work 'counta Bubber, feel my old bag's tits after Sapphi—*Never Mind!*—Git 'em in here—*Quick!*

JACKSON *(meekly)*. They aren't ... they aren't here, sir ...

MAYOR. Whaddaya mean they aren't here? Find out where they at. We got important business, man! You can't run a town wit laxity like this. Can't allow things to git snafued jist because a bunch of lazy Nigras been out gitting drunk and living it up all night! Discipline, man, discipline!

JACKSON. That's what I'm trying to tell you, sir ... they didn't come in, can't be found ... none of 'em.

MAYOR. Ridiculous, boy! Scare 'em up and tell 'em scoot here in a hurry befo' I git mad and fire the whole goddamn lot of 'em!

JACKSON. But we can't find 'em, sir.

MAYOR. Hogwash! Can't nobody in this office do anything right? Do I hafta handle every piddling little matter myself? Git me their numbers, I'll have 'em here befo' you kin shout to—

(THREE MEN *burst into room.)*

ONE. Henry—they vanished!
TWO. Disappeared into thin air!
THREE. Gone wit'out a trace!
TWO. Not a one on the street!
THREE. In the house!
ONE. On the job!
MAYOR. Wait a minute! ... Hold your water! Calm down—!
ONE. But they've gone, Henry—GONE! All of 'em!
MAYOR. What the hell you talking 'bout? Gone? Who's gone—?
ONE. The Nigras, Henry! They gone!
MAYOR. Gone? ... Gone where?
TWO. That's what we trying to tell ya—they just disappeared! The Nigras have disappeared, swallowed up, vanished! All of 'em! Every last one!
MAYOR. Has everybody 'round here gone batty? ... That's impossible, how could the Nigras vanish?
THREE. Beats me, but it's happened!
MAYOR. You mean a whole town of Nigras just evaporated like that—poof!—overnight?
ONE. Right!
MAYOR. Y'all must be drunk! Why, half this town is colored. How could they just sneak out?
TWO. Don't ask me, but there ain't one in sight!
MAYOR. Simmer down 'n put it to me easy-like.
ONE. Well ... I first suspected somp'um smelly when Sarah Jo didn't show up this morning and I couldn't reach her—

TWO. Dorothy Jane didn't 'rive at my house—
THREE. Georgia Mae wasn't at mine neither—and SHE sleeps in!
ONE. When I reached the office, I realized I hadn't seen nary one Nigra all morning! Nobody else had either—Wait a minute—Henry, have you?
MAYOR. Now that you mention it . . . no, I haven't . . .
ONE. They gone, Henry . . . Not a one on the street, not a one in our homes, not a single, last living one to be found nowheres in town. What we gon' do?
MAYOR *(thinking)*. Keep heads on your shoulders 'n put clothes on your back . . . They can't be far . . . Must be 'round somewheres . . . Probably playing hide 'n seek, that's it! . . . *Jackson!*
JACKSON. Yessir?
MAYOR. Immediately mobilize our Citizens Emergency Distress Committee!—order a fleet of sound trucks to patrol streets urging the population to remain calm—situation's not as bad as it looks—everything's under control! Then, have another squadron of squawk buggies drive slowly through all Nigra alleys, ordering them to come out wherever they are. If that don't git 'em, organize a vigilante search squad to flush 'em outta hiding! But most important of all, track down that lazy goldbricker Woodfence and tell him to git on top of the situation! By God, we'll find 'em even if we hafta dig 'em outta the ground!

(Blackout. Scene shifts back to JOHN *and* MARY *a few hours later. A funereal solemnity pervades their mood.)*

JOHN. Walked up to the shack, knocked on door, didn't git no answer. Hollered: "Lula? Lula . . . ?"—not a thing. Went 'round the side, peeped in window—nobody stirred. Next door—nobody there. Crossed other side of street and banged on five or six other doors— not a colored person could be found! Not a man, neither woman or child—not even a black dog could be seen, smelt or heard for blocks around . . . They've gone, Mary.
MARY. What does it all mean, John?
JOHN. I don't know, Mary . . .
MARY. I always had Lula, John. Never missed a day at my side . . . That's why I couldn't accept your wedding proposal until I was sure you'd welcome me and her together as a package. How am I gonna git through the day? Baby don't know *me*, I ain't acquainted wit *it*. I've never lifted cover off pot, swung a mop or broom, dunked a dish or even pushed a dustrag. I'm lost wit'out Lula, I need her, John, I need her. *(Begins to weep softly.* JOHN *pats her consolingly.)*
JOHN. Courage, honey . . . Everybody in town is facing the same dilemma. We mustn't crack up . . .

(Blackout. Scene shifts back to MAYOR's *office later in day. Atmosphere and tone resembles a wartime headquarters at the front.* MAYOR *is perched on ladder checking over huge map.)*

INDUSTRIALIST. Half the day is gone already, Henry. On behalf of the factory owners of this town, you've got to bail us out! Seventy-five percent of all production is paralyzed. With the Nigra absent, men are waiting for machines to be cleaned, floors to be swept, crates lifted, equipment delivered and bathrooms deodorized. Why, restrooms and toilets are so filthy until they not only cannot be sat in, but it's virtually impossible to get within hailing distance because of the stench!
MAYOR. Keep your shirt on, Jeb—
BUSINESSMAN. Business is even in worse condition, Henry. The volume of goods moving 'cross counters has slowed down to a trickle—almost negligible. Customers are not only not purchasing—but the absence of handymen, porters, sweepers, stockmovers, deliverers and miscellaneous dirty-work doers is disrupting the smooth harmony of marketing!
CLUBWOMAN. Food poisoning, severe indigestitis, chronic diarrhea, advanced diaper chafings and a plethora of unsanitary household disasters dangerous to life, limb and property! . . . As a representative of the Federation of Ladies' Clubs, I must sadly report that unless the trend is reversed, a complete breakdown in family unity is imminent . . . Just as homosexuality and debauchery signaled the fall of Greece and Rome, the downgrading of Southern Bellesdom might very well prophesy the collapse of our indigenous institutions . . . . Remember—it has always been pure, delicate, lily-white images of Dixie femininity which provided backbone, inspiration and ideology for our male warriors in their defense against the onrushing black horde. If our gallant men are drained of this worship and idolatry—God knows! The cause won't be worth a Confederate nickel!
MAYOR *(jumping off ladder)*. Stop this panicky defeatism, y'all hear me! All machinery at my disposal is being utilized. I assure you wit great confidence the damage will soon repair itself—Cheerful progress reports are expected any moment now—Wait! See, here's Jackson . . . Well, Jackson?
JACKSON. As of now, sir, all efforts are fruitless. Neither hide nor hair of them has been located. We have not unearthed a single one in our shack-to-shack search. Not a single one has heeded our appeal. Scoured every creek and cranny inside their hovels, turning furniture upside down and inside out, breaking down walls and tearing through ceilings. We made determined efforts to discover where'bouts of our faithful Uncle Toms and informers—but even they have vanished without a trace . . . Searching squads are on the verge of panic and hysteria, sir, wit hotheads among 'em campaigning for scorched earth policies. Nigras on a whole lack cellars, but there's rising sentiment favoring burning to find out whether they're underground-dug in!
MAYOR. Absolutely counter such foolhardy suggestions! Suppose they are tombed in? We'd only accelerate the gravity of the situation using incendiary tactics! Besides, when they're rounded up where will we put 'em if we've already burned up their shacks—*in our own bedrooms?*
JACKSON. I agree, sir, but the mood of the crowd is becoming irrational. In anger and frustration, they's forgetting their original purpose was to *find* the Nigras!

MAYOR. At all costs! Stamp out all burning proposals! Must prevent extremist notions from gaining ascendancy. Git wit it . . . Wait—'n for Jehovah's sake, find out where the hell is that trifling slacker, *Woodfence!*
COURIER *(rushing in).* Mr. Mayor! . . . We've found some! We've found some!
MAYOR *(excitedly).* Where?
COURIER. In the—in the—*(Can't catch breath).*
MAYOR *(impatiently).* Where, man? Where?
COURIER. In the colored wing of the city hospital!
MAYOR. The hos—? The hospital! I shoulda known! How could those helpless, crippled, cut and shot Nigras disappear from a hospital? Should thought of that! . . . Tell me more, man!
COURIER. I—I didn't wait, sir . . . I—I ran in to report soon as I heard—
MAYOR. Well git back on the phone, you idiot! Don't you know what this means?
COURIER. Yes, sir. *(Races out.)*
MAYOR. Now we gitting somewhere! . . . Gentlemen, if one sole Nigra is among us, we're well on the road to rehabilitation! Those Nigras in the hospital must know somp'um 'bout the others where'bouts . . . Scat back to your colleagues, boost up their morale and inform 'em that things will zip back to normal in a jiffy! *(They start to file out, then pause to observe the* COURIER *re-entering dazedly.)* Well . . . ? Well, man . . . ? What's the matter wit you, ninny? Tell me what else was said!
COURIER. They all . . . they all . . . they all in a—in a—a coma, sir . . .
MAYOR. They all in a what . . . ?
COURIER. In a coma, sir . . .
MAYOR. Talk sense, man! . . . Whaddaya mean, they all in a coma?
COURIER. Doctor says every last one of the Nigras are jist laying in bed . . . *still* . . . not moving . . . neither live or dead . . . laying up there in a coma . . . every last one of 'em . . .
MAYOR *(sputters, then grabs phone).* Get me Confederate Memorial . . . Put me through to the Staff Chief . . . YES, this is the Mayor . . . Sam? . . . What's this I hear? . . . But how could they be in a coma, Sam? . . . You don't know! Well, what the hell you think the city's paying you for! You've got 'nuff damn hacks and quacks there to find out! . . . How could it be somp'um unknown? You mean Nigras know somp'um 'bout drugs your damn butchers don't? . . . Well, what the crap good are they? . . . All right, all right, I'll be calm. . . . Now, tell me . . . Uh huh, uh huh . . . Well, can't you give 'em some injections or somp'um . . . ?—You did . . . uh huh . . . *Did you try a lil rough treatment?*—that too, huh . . . All right, Sam, keep trying . . . *(Puts phone down deliberately, continuing absently.)* Can't wake 'em up. Just lay there. Them that's sick won't git no sicker, them that's half-well won't git no better, babies that's due won't be born and them that's come won't show no life. Nigras wit cuts won't bleed and them which need blood won't be transfused . . . He say dying Nigras is even refusing to pass away! *(Is silently perplexed for a moment, then suddenly breaks into action.)* Jackson? . . . Call up the

police—*the jail!* Find out what's going on there! Them Nigras are captives! If there's one place we got darkies under control, it's there! Them sonsabitches too onery to act right either for colored or white! *(JACKSON exits.)* Keep your fingers crossed, citizens, them Nigras in jail are the most important Nigras we got!

(All hands are raised conspicuously aloft, fingers prominently crossed. Seconds tick by. Soon JACKSON *returns crestfallen.)*

JACKSON. Sheriff Bull says they don't know whether they still on premises or not. When they went to rouse Nigra jailbirds this morning, cell block doors refused to swing open. Tried everything—even exploded dynamite charges—but it just wouldn't budge ... Then they hoisted guards up to peep through barred windows, but couldn't see good 'nuff to tell whether Nigras was inside or not. Finally, gitting desperate, they power-hosed the cells wit water but had to cease 'cause Sheriff Bull said he didn't wanta jeopardize drowning the Nigras since it might spoil his chance of shipping a record load of cotton pickers to the State Penitentiary for cotton-snatching jubilee ... Anyway—they ain't heard a Nigra-squeak all day.

MAYOR. That so ... ? *What 'bout trains 'n busses passing through?* There must be some dinges riding through?

JACKSON. We checked ... not a one on board.

MAYOR. Did you hear whether any other towns lost their Nigras?

JACKSON. Things are status quo everywhere else.

MAYOR *(angrily).* Then what they picking on us for?

COURIER *(rushing in).* Mr. Mayor! Your sister jist called—*hysterical!* She says Vice-Mayor Woodfence went to bed wit her last night, but when she woke up this morning he was gone! Been missing all day!

MAYOR. Could Nigras be holding him hostage?

COURIER. No, sir. Besides him—investigations reveal that dozens or more prominent citizens—two City Council members, the chairman of the Junior Chamber of Commerce, our City College All-Southern halfback, the chairlady of the Daughters of the Confederate Rebellion, Miss Cotton Sack Festival of the Year and numerous other miscellaneous nobodies—are absent wit'out leave. Dangerous evidence points to the conclusion that they been infiltrating!

MAYOR. Infiltrating?

COURIER. Passing all along!

MAYOR. *What?*

COURIER. Secret Nigras all the while!

MAYOR. *Naw!*

*(*CLUBWOMAN *keels over in faint.* JACKSON, BUSINESSMAN *and* INDUSTRIALIST *begin to eye each other suspiciously.)*

COURIER. Yessir!
MAYOR. *Passing?*
COURIER. Yessir!
MAYOR. *Secret Nig–?*

COURIER. Yessir!

MAYOR *(momentarily stunned to silence).* The dirty mongrelizers! ... Gentlemen, this is a grave predicament indeed ... It pains me to surrender priority of our states rights credo, but it is my solemn task and frightening duty to inform you that we have no other recourse but to seek outside help for deliverance.

(Blackout. Lights rise again on Huntley-Brinkley-Murrow-Severeid-Cronkite-Reasoner-type ANNOUNCER *grasping a hand-held microphone [imaginary] a few hours later. He is vigorously, excitedly mouthing his commentary, but no sound escapes his lips. During this dumb, wordless section of his broadcast, a bedraggled assortment of figures marching with picket signs occupies his attention. On their picket signs are inscribed various appeals and slogans.* "CINDY LOU UNFAIR TO BABY JOE" ... "CAP'N SAM MISS BIG BOY" ... "RETURN LIL BLUE TO MARS JIM" ... "INFORMATION REQUESTED BOUT MAMMY GAIL" ... "BOSS NATHAN PROTEST TO FAST LEROY." *Trailing behind the* MARCHERS, *forcibly isolated, is a* WOMAN *dressed in widow black holding a placard which reads:* "WHY DIDN'T YOU TELL US—YOUR DEFILED WIFE AND 11 ABSENT MONGRELS.")

ANNOUNCER *(who has been silently mouthing his delivery during the picketing procession, is suddenly heard as if caught in the midst of commentary).* Factories standing idle from the loss of nonessential workers. Stores remaining shuttered from the absconding of uncrucial personnel. Fruit, vegetables and other edible foodstuffs rotting in warehouses, with uncollected garbage threatening pestilence and pollution ... Also, each second somewheres in this former utopia below the Mason and Dixon, dozens of decrepit old men and women usually tended by faithful nurses and servants are popping off like flies—abandoned by sons, daughters and grandchildren whose refusal to provide these doddering souls with bedpans and other soothing necessities results in their hasty, nasty, messy departures ...

An equally wretched fate lurks in wait for juveniles of the town as hundreds of new born infants HUNGER for the comforting embraces of devoted nannies while being forced to endure the presence of strange parents ...

But most critically affected of all by this complete drought of Afro-American resources are policemen and other public safety guardians denied their daily quota of Negro arrests. One officer known affectionately as "Two-a-Day-Pete" because of his unblemished record of TWO Negro headwhippings per day has already been carted off to the County Insane Asylum—strait jacketed, screaming and biting, unable to withstand the shock of having his spotless slate sullied by interruption ... It is feared that similar attacks are soon expected among municipal judges prevented for the first time in years of distinguished bench-sitting from sentencing one single Negro to corrective institutions ...

Ladies and gentlemen, as you trudge in from the joys and headaches of workday chores and dusk begins to descend on this sleepy

Southern hamlet, we *repeat*—today—before early morning dew had dried upon magnolia blossoms, your comrade citizens of this lovely Dixie village awoke to the realization that some—pardon me! not some but *all*—of their Negroes were missing... Absent, vamoosed, departed, at bay, fugitive, away, gone and so far unretrieved...
    In order to dispel your incredulity, gauge the temper of your suffering compatriots and just possibly prepare you for the likelihood of an equally nightmarish eventuality, we have gathered a cross section of this city's most distinguished leaders for exclusive interviews... First, Mr. Council Clan, grand dragoon of this area's most active civic organizations and staunch bellwether of the political opposition... Mr. Clan, how do you *account* for this incredible disappearance?

CLAN. A *plot*, plain and simple, that's what it is, as plain as the corns on your feet!

ANNOUNCER. Whom would you consider responsible?

CLAN. I could go on all night.

ANNOUNCER. Cite a few.

CLAN. Too numerous.

ANNOUNCER. Just one?

CLAN. Name names when time comes.

ANNOUNCER. Could you be referring to native Negroes?

CLAN. Ever try quaranteening lepers from their spots?

ANNOUNCER. Their organizations?

CLAN. Could you slice a nose off a mouth and still keep a face?

ANNOUNCER. Commies?

CLAN. Would you lop off a titty from a chest and still have a breast?

ANNOUNCER. Your city government?

CLAN. Now you talkin'!

ANNOUNCER. State administration?

CLAN. Warming up!

ANNOUNCER. Federal?

CLAN. Kin a blind man see?

ANNOUNCER. The Court?

CLAN. Is a pig clean?

ANNOUNCER. Clergy?

CLAN. Do a polecat stink?!

ANNOUNCER. Well, Mr. Clan, with this massive complicity, how do you think the plot could've been prevented from succeeding?

CLAN. If I'da been in office, it never woulda happened.

ANNOUNCER. Then you're laying major blame at the doorstep of the present administration?

CLAN. Damn tooting!

ANNOUNCER. But from your oft-expressed views, Mr. Clan, shouldn't you and your followers be delighted at the turn of events? After all— isn't it one of the main policies of your society to *drive* the Negroes away? *Drive* 'em back where they came from?

CLAN. Drivvve, boy! Driiiivvve! That's right!... When we say so and not befo'. Ain't supposed to do nothing 'til we tell 'em. Got to stay put until we exercise our God-given right to tell 'em when to git!

ANNOUNCER. But why argue if they've merely jumped the gun? Why

not rejoice at this premature purging of undesirables?
CLAN.   The time ain't ripe yet, boy . . . The time ain't ripe yet.
ANNOUNCER.   Thank you for being so informative, Mr. Clan—Mrs. Aide? Mrs. Aide? Over here, Mrs. Aide . . . Ladies and gentlemen, this city's Social Welfare Commissioner, Mrs. Handy Anna Aide . . . Mrs. Aide, with all your freeloading Negroes seemingly AWOL, haven't developments alleviated the staggering demands made upon your Welfare Department? Reduction of relief requests, elimination of case loads, removal of chronic welfare dependents, et cetera?
AIDE.   Quite the contrary. Disruption of our pilot projects among Nigras saddles our white community with extreme hardship . . . You see, historically, our agencies have always been foremost contributors to the Nigra Git-A-Job movement. We pioneered in enforcing social welfare theories which oppose coddling the fakers. We strenuously believe in helping Nigras help themselves by participating in meaningful labor. "Relief is Out, Work is In," is our motto. We place them as maids, cooks, butlers, and breast-feeders, cesspool-diggers, wash-basin maintainers, shoeshine boys, and so on—mostly on a volunteer self-work basis.
ANNOUNCER.   Hired at prevailing salaried rates, of course?
AIDE.   God forbid! Money is unimportant. Would only make 'em worse. Our main goal is to improve their ethical behavior. "Rehabilitation Through Positive Participation" is another motto of ours. All unwed mothers, loose-living malingering fathers, bastard children and shiftless grandparents are kept occupied through constructive muscle therapy. This provides 'em with less opportunity to indulge their pleasure-loving amoral inclinations.
ANNOUNCER.   They volunteer to participate in these pilot projects?
AIDE.   Heavens no! They're notorious shirkers. When I said the program is voluntary, I meant white citizens in overwhelming majorities do the volunteering. Placing their homes, offices, appliances and persons at our disposal for use in "Operation Uplift" . . . We would never dare place such a decision in the hands of the Nigra. It would never get off the ground! No, they have no choice in the matter. "Work or Starve" is the slogan we use to stimulate their awareness of what's good for survival.
ANNOUNCER.   And a good one it is. Thank you, Mrs. Aide, and good luck . . . Rev? . . . Rev? . . . Ladies and gentlemen, this city's foremost spiritual guidance counselor, Reverend Reb Pious . . . How does it look to you, Reb Pious?
PIOUS *(continuing to gaze skyward).*   It's in *His* hands, son, it's in *His* hands.
ANNOUNCER.   How would you assess the disappearance, from a moral standpoint?
PIOUS.   An immoral act, son, morally wrong and ethically indefensible. A perversion of Christian principles to be condemned from every pulpit of this nation.
ANNOUNCER.   Can you account for its occurrence after the many decades of the Church's missionary activity among them?
PIOUS.   It's basically a reversion of the Nigra to his deep-rooted

primitivism ... Now, at last, you can understand the difficulties of the Church in attempting to anchor God's kingdom among ungratefuls. It's a constant, unrelenting, no-holds-barred struggle against Satan to wrestle away souls locked in his possession for countless centuries! Despite all our aid, guidance, solace and protection, Old Beezlebub still retains tenacious grips upon the Nigras' childish loyalty—comparable to the lure of bright flames to an infant.

ANNOUNCER. But actual physical departure, Reb Pious? How do you explain that?

PIOUS. Voodoo, my son, voodoo ... With Satan's assist, they have probably employed some heathen magic which we cultivated, sophisticated Christians know absolutely nothing about. However, before long we are confident about counteracting this evil witch-doctory and triumphing in our Holy Savior's name. At this perilous juncture, true believers of all denominations are participating in joint, 'round-the-clock observances, offering prayers for our Master's swiftiest intercession. I'm optimistic about the outcome of His intervention ... Which prompts me—if I may, sir—to offer these words of counsel to our delinquent Nigras ... I say to you without rancor or vengeance, quoting a phrase of one of your greatest prophets, Booker T. Washington: "Return your buckets to where they lay and all will be forgiven."

ANNOUNCER. A very inspirational appeal, Reb Pious. I'm certain they will find the tug of its magnet sincerity irresistible. Thank you, Reb Pious ... All in all—as you have witnessed, ladies and gentlemen—this town symbolizes the face of disaster, suffering as severe a prostration as any city wrecked, ravaged and devastated by the holocaust of war. A vital, lively, throbbing organism brought to a screeching halt by the strange enigma of the missing Negroes ...

We take you now to offices of the one man into whose hands has been thrust the final responsibility of rescuing this shuddering metropolis from the precipice of destruction ... We give you the honorable Mayor, Henry R. E. Lee ... Hello, Mayor Lee.

MAYOR *(jovially)*. Hello, Jack.

ANNOUNCER. Mayor Lee, we have just concluded interviews with some of your city's leading spokesmen. If I may say so, sir, they don't sound too encouraging about the situation.

MAYOR. Nonsense, Jack! The situation's as well in hand as it could be under the circumstances. Couldn't be better in hand. Underneath every dark cloud, Jack, there's always a ray of sunlight, ha, ha, ha.

ANNOUNCER. Have you discovered one, sir?

MAYOR. Well, Jack, I'll tell you ... Of course we've been faced wit a little crisis, but look at it like this—we've faced 'em befo': Sherman marched through Georgia—*once!* Lincoln freed the slaves—*momentarily!* Carpetbaggers even put Nigras in the Governor's mansion, state legislature, Congress and the Senate of the United States. But what happened? Ole Dixie bounced right on back up ... At this moment the Supreme Court's trying to put Nigras in our schools and the Nigra has got it in his haid to put hisself everywhere ... But what you spect gon happen? Ole Dixie will kangaroo back even higher. Southern courage, fortitude, chivalry and superiority always wins out. . . . SHUCKS! We'll have us some Nigras befo' daylight is gone!

ANNOUNCER. Mr. Mayor, I hate to introduce this note, but in an earlier interview one of your chief opponents, Mr. Clan, hinted at your own complicity in the affair—

MAYOR. *A lot of poppycock!* Clan is politicking! I've beaten him four times outta four and I'll beat him four more times outta four! This is no time for partisan politics! What we need now is level-headedness and across-the-board unity. This typical, rash, mealy-mouth, shooting-off-at-the-lip of Clan and his ilk proves their insincerity, and voters will remember that in the next election! Won't you, voters? *(Has risen to the height of campaign oratory.)*

ANNOUNCER. Mr. Mayor! . . . Mr. Mayor! . . . Please—

MAYOR. I tell you, I promise you—

ANNOUNCER. *Please, Mr. Mayor!*

MAYOR. Huh? . . . Oh—yes, carry on.

ANNOUNCER. Mr. Mayor, your cheerfulness and infectious good spirits lead me to conclude that startling new developments warrant fresh-found optimism. What concrete, declassified information do you have to support your claim that Negroes will reappear before nightfall?

MAYOR. Because we are presently awaiting the payoff of a masterful five-point supra-recovery program which can't help but reap us a bonanza of Nigras 'fore sundown! . . . First: Exhaustive efforts to pinpoint the where'bouts of our own missing darkies continue to zero in on the bull's-eye . . . Second: The President of the United States, following an emergency cabinet meeting, has designated us the prime disaster area of the century—National Guard is already on the way . . . Third: In an unusual, but bold, maneuver we have appealed to the NAACP 'n all other Nigra conspirators to help us git to the bottom of the vanishing act . . . Fourth: We have exercised our nonreciprocal option and requested that all fraternal Southern states express their solidarity by lending us some of their Nigras temporarily on credit . . . Fifth and foremost: We have already gotten consent of the Governor to round up all stray, excess and incorrigible Nigras to be shipped to us under escort of the state militia . . . That's why we've stifled pessimism and are brimming wit confidence that this full-scale concerted mobilization will ring down a jackpot of jigaboos 'fore light vanishes from sky!

ANNOUNCER. Congratulations! What happens if it fails?

MAYOR. Don't even think *that!* Absolutely no reason to suspect it will . . . *(Peers over shoulder, then whispers confidentially while placing hand over mouth by* ANNOUNCER's *imaginary mike)* But speculating on the dark side of your question—if we don't turn up some by nightfall, it may be all over. The harm has already been done. You see the South has always been glued together by the uninterrupted presence of its darkies. No telling how unstuck we might git if things keep on like they have—Wait a minute, it musta paid off already! Mission accomplished 'cause here's Jackson 'head a time wit the word . . . Well, Jackson, what's new?

JACKSON. Situation on the home front remains static, sir—can't uncover scent or shadow. The NAACP and all other Nigra front groups 'n plotters deny any knowledge or connection wit the missing Nigras. Maintained this even after appearing befo' a Senate Emergency Investigating Committee which subpoenaed 'em to Washington posthaste and threw 'em in jail for contempt. A handful of Nigras who agreed to make spectacular appeals for ours to come back to us have themselves mysteriously disappeared. But, worst news of all, sir, is our sister cities and counties, inside and outside the state, have changed their minds, fallen back on their promises and refused to lend us any Nigras, claiming they don't have 'nuff for themselves.

MAYOR. What 'bout Nigras promised by the Governor?

JACKSON. Jailbirds and vagrants escorted here from chain gangs and other reservations either revolted and escaped en route or else vanished mysteriously on approaching our city limits . . . Deterioration rapidly escalates, sir. Estimates predict we kin hold out only one more hour before overtaken by anarchistic turmoil . . . Some citizens seeking haven elsewheres have already fled, but on last report were being forcibly turned back by armed sentinels in other cities who wanted no parts of 'em—claiming they carried a jinx.

MAYOR. That bad, huh?

JACKSON. Worse, sir . . . we've received at least five reports of plots on your life.

MAYOR. What?—We've gotta act quickly then!

JACKSON. Run out of ideas, sir.

MAYOR. Think harder, boy!

JACKSON. Don't have much time, sir. One measly hour, then all hell gon break loose.

MAYOR. Gotta think of something drastic, Jackson!

JACKSON. I'm dry, sir.

MAYOR. Jackson! Is there any planes outta here in the next hour?

JACKSON. All transportation's been knocked out, sir.

MAYOR. I thought so!

JACKSON. What were you contemplating, sir?

MAYOR. Don't ask me what I was contemplating! I'm still boss 'round here! Don't forgit it!

JACKSON. Sorry, sir.

MAYOR. Hold the wire! . . . Wait a minute . . . ! Waaaaait a minute—*goddammit!* All this time crapping 'round, diddling and fotsing wit puny lil solutions—all the while neglecting our ace in the hole, our trump card! Most potent weapon for digging Nigras outta the woodpile? All the while right befo' our eyes! . . . Ass! Why didn't you remind me?

JACKSON. What is it, sir?

MAYOR. *Me—That's what! Me!* a personal appeal from ME! *Directly to them!* . . . Although we wouldn't let 'em march to the polls and express their affection for me through the ballot box, we've always known I'm held highest in their esteem. A direct address from their beloved Mayor! . . . If they's anywheres close within the sound of my voice, they'll shape up! Or let us know by a sign they's ready to.

JACKSON. You sure *that'll* turn the trick, sir?

MAYOR. As sure as my ancestors befo' me who knew that when they puckered their lips to whistle, ole Sambo was gonna come a-lickey-splitting to answer the call! . . . That same chips-down blood courses through these Confederate gray veins of Henry R. E. Lee ! ! !

ANNOUNCER. I'm delighted to offer our network's facilities for such a crucial public interest address, sir. We'll arrange immediately for your appearance on an international hookup, placing you in widest proximity to contact them wherever they may be.

MAYOR. Thank you, I'm very grateful . . . Jackson, regrease the machinery and set wheels in motion. Inform townspeople what's being done. Tell 'em we're all in this together. The next hour is countdown. I demand absolute cooperation, citywide silence and inactivity. I don't want the Nigras frightened if they's nearby. This is the most important hour in the town's history. Tell 'em if one single Nigra shows up during the hour of decision, victory is within sight. I'm gonna git 'em that one—maybe all! Hurry and crack to it!

(ANNOUNCER rushes out, followed by JACKSON.
Blackout. Scene reopens, with MAYOR seated, eyes front, spotlight illuminating him in semidarkness. Shadowy figures stand in the background, prepared to answer phones or aid in any other manner.
MAYOR waits patiently until "Go" signal is given.)

MAYOR *(voice combining elements of confidence, tremolo and gravity).* Good evening . . . Despite the fact that millions of you wonderful people throughout the nation are viewing and listening to this momentous broadcast—and I thank you for your concern and sympathy in this hour of our peril—I primarily want to concentrate my attention and address these remarks solely for the benefit of our departed Nigra friends who may be listening somewheres in our far-flung land to the sound of my voice . . . If you are—it is with heartfelt emotion and fond memories of our happy association that I ask—"Where are you . . . ?"

Your absence has left a void in the bosom of every single man, woman and child of our great city. I tell you—you don't know what it means for us to wake up in the morning and discover that your cheerful, grinning, happy-go-lucky faces are missing! . . . From the depths of my heart, I can meekly, humbly suggest what it means to me personally . . . You see—the one face I will never be able to erase from my memory is the face—not of my Ma, not of Pa, neither wife or child—but the image of the first woman I came to love so well when just a wee lad—the vision of the first human I laid clear sight on at childbirth—the profile—better yet the full face of my dear old . . . Jemimah—God rest her soul . . . Yes! My dear ole mammy, wit her round black moonbeam gleaming down upon me in the crib, teeth shining, blood-red bandana standing starched, peaked and proud, gazing down on me affectionately as she crooned me a Southern lullaby . . . Oh! It's a memorable picture I will eternally cherish in permanent treasure chambers of my heart, now and forever always . . .

Well, if this radiant image can remain so infinitely vivid to me all these many years after her unfortunate demise in the po' folks' home —*think* of the misery the rest of us must be suffering after being *freshly* denied your soothing presence!

We need ya. If you kin hear me, just contact this station 'n I will welcome you back personally. Let me just tell you that since you eloped, nothing has been the same. How could it? You're part of us, you belong to us. Just give us a sign and we'll be contented that all is well . . .

Now if you've skipped away on a little fun fest, we understand, ha, ha. We know you like a good time and we don't begrudge it to ya. Hell—er, er, we like a good time ourselves—who doesn't . . . In fact, think of all the good times we've had together, huh? We've had some real fun, you and us, yesiree! . . . Nobody knows better than you and I what fun we've had together. You singing us those old Southern coon songs and dancing those Nigra jigs and us clapping, prodding 'n spurring you on! Lots of fun, huh? . . . *Oh boy!* The times we've had together . . . If you've snucked away for a bit of fun by yourself, we'll go 'long wit ya—long as you let us know where you at so we won't be worried about you . . .

We'll go 'long wit you long as you don't take the joke too far. I'll admit a joke is a joke and you've played a *lulu!* . . . I'm warning you, we can't stand much more horsing 'round from you! Business is business 'n fun is fun! You've had your fun so now let's get down to business! Come on back, *you hear me!*

If you been hoodwinked by agents of some foreign government, I've been authorized by the President of these United States to inform you that this liberty-loving Republic is prepared to rescue you from their clutches. Don't pay no 'tention to their sireen songs and atheistic promises! You better off under our control and you know it! . . . If you been bamboozled by rabble-rousing nonsense of your own so-called leaders, we prepared to offer some protection. Just call us up! Just give us a sign! . . . Come on, give us a sign . . . give us a sign—even a teeny weeny one . . . ? *(Glances around checking on possible communications. A bevy of headshakes indicate no success.* MAYOR *returns to address with desperate fervor.)*

Now look—you don't know what you doing! If you persist in this disobedience, you know all too well the consequences! We'll track you to the end of the earth, beyond the galaxy, across the stars! We'll capture you and chastise you with all the vengeance we command! 'N you know only too well how stern we kin be when double-crossed! The city, the state and the entire nation will crucify you for this unpardonable defiance! *(Checks again)* No call . . . ? No sign . . . ? Time is running out! Deadline slipping past! They gotta respond! They gotta! *(Resuming)* Listen to me! I'm begging y'all, you've gotta come back . . . ! Look, George! *(Waves dirty rag aloft)* I brought the rag you wax the car wit . . . Remember, George . . . ? Don't this bring back memories, George, of all the days you spent shining that automobile to shimmering perfection . . . ? And you, Rufus! . . . Here's the polish and the brush! . . . 'Member, Rufus? . . . Remember the happy mornings you spent popping this rag and whisking this brush so furiously 'till it created music that was sympho-nee to the ear . . . ? And you—*Mandy?* . . . Here's the wastebasket you didn't dump this morning. I saved it just for you! . . . *Look,* all y'all out there . . . *(Signals and a three-person procession parades one after the other before the imaginary camera.)*

DOLL WOMAN *(brandishing a crying baby [doll] as she strolls past and exits).* She's been crying ever since you left, Caldonia . . .

MOP MAN *(flashing mop).* It's been waiting in the same corner, Buster . . .

BRUSH MAN *(flagging toilet brush).* It's been dry ever since you left, Washington . . .

MAYOR *(jumping in on the heels of the last exit).* Don't these things mean anything to y'all? By God! Are your memories so short? Is there nothing sacred to ya . . . Please come back, for my sake, please! All of you—even you questionable ones! I promise no harm will be done to you! Revenge is disallowed! We'll forgive everything! Just come on back and I'll git down on my knees—*(Immediately drops to knees)* I'll be kneeling in the middle of Dixie Avenue to kiss the first shoe of the first one to show up . . . I'll smooch any other spot you request . . . Erase this nightmare 'n we'll concede any demand you make, just come on back—please? . . . *Pleeeeeeze!*

VOICE *(shouting).* Time!

MAYOR *(remaining on knees, frozen in a pose of supplication. After a brief, deadly silence, he whispers almost inaudibly.)* They wouldn't answer . . . they wouldn't answer . . .

(Blackout as bedlam erupts offstage. Total blackness holds during a sufficient interval where offstage sound effects create the illusion of complete pandemonium, followed by a diminution which trails off into an expressionistic simulation of a city coming to a stricken standstill: industrial machinery clanks to halt, traffic blares to silence, etc. . . . The stage remains dark and silent for a long moment, then lights rise again on the ANNOUNCER.)

ANNOUNCER. A pitiful sight, ladies and gentlemen. Soon after his unsuccessful appeal, Mayor Lee suffered a vicious pummeling from the mob and barely escaped with his life. National guardsmen and state militia were impotent in quelling the fury of a town venting its frustration in an orgy of destruction—a frenzy of rioting, looting and all other aberrations of a town gone berserk . . . Then—suddenly—as if a magic wand had been waved, madness evaporated and something more frightening replaced it: submission . . .

Even whimpering ceased. The city: exhausted, benumbed—Slowly its occupants slinked off into shadows, and by midnight the town was occupied exclusively by zombies. The fight and life had been drained out . . . Pooped . . . Hope ebbed away as completely as the beloved, absent Negroes . . . As our crew packed gear and crept away silently, we treaded softly—as if we were stealing away from a mausoleum . . . The face of a defeated city.

Blackout.

Lights rise slowly at the sound of rooster crowing, signaling the approach of a new day, the next morning. Scene is same as opening of play. CLEM *and* LUKE *are huddled over dazedly, trancelike. They remain so for a long count. Finally, a figure drifts on stage, shuffling slowly.*

LUKE *(gazing in silent fascination at the approaching figure).* Clem . . . ? Do you see what I see or am I dreaming . . . ?

CLEM. It's a . . . a Nigra, ain't it, Luke . . . ?

LUKE. Sure looks like one, Clem—but we better make sure—eyes could be playing tricks on us . . . Does he still look like one to you, Clem?

CLEM. He still does, Luke—but I'm scared to believe—

LUKE. Why . . . ? It looks like Rastus, Clem!

CLEM. Sure does, Luke . . . but we better not jump to no hasty conclusion . . .

LUKE *(in timid softness).* That you, Rastus . . . ?

RASTUS *(Stepin Fetchit, Willie Best, Nicodemus, Butterfly McQueen and all the rest rolled into one).* Why . . . howdy . . . Mr. Luke . . . Mr. Clem . . .

CLEM. It is him, Luke! It is him!

LUKE. Rastus?

RASTUS. Yas . . . sah?

LUKE. Where was you yesterday?

RASTUS *(very, very puzzled).* Yes . . . ter . . . day? . . . Yester . . . day . . . ? Why . . . right . . . here . . . Mr. Luke . . .

LUKE. No you warn't, Rastus, don't lie to me! Where was you yestiddy?

RASTUS. Why . . . I'm sure I was . . . Mr. Luke . . . Remember . . . I made . . . that . . . delivery for you . . .

LUKE. That was *Monday*, Rastus, yestiddy was *Tuesday*.

RASTUS. Tues . . . day . . . ? You don't say . . . Well , . . well . . . well . . .

LUKE. Where was you 'n all the other Nigras yesterday, Rastus?

RASTUS. I . . . thought . . . yestiddy . . . was . . . Monday, Mr. Luke—I coulda swore it . . . ! . . . See how . . . things . . . kin git all mixed up? . . . I coulda swore it . . .

LUKE. *Today* is *Wednesday*, Rastus. Where was you *Tuesday*?

RASTUS. Tuesday . . . huh? That's somp'um . . . I . . . don't remember . . . missing . . . a day . . . Mr. Luke . . . but I guess you right . . .

LUKE. Then where was you?

RASTUS. Don't rightly know, Mr. Luke. I didn't know I had skipped a day—But that jist goes to show you how time kin fly, don't it, Mr. Luke . . . Uuh, uuh, uuh . . . *(He starts shuffling off, scratching head, a flicker of a smile playing across his lips.* CLEM *and* LUKE *gaze dumbfoundedly as he disappears.)*

LUKE *(eyes sweeping around in all directions).* Well . . . There's the

others, Clem... Back jist like they useta be... Everything's same as always...
CLEM. Is it... Luke...?

(Slow fade.)

CURTAIN

Questions for Discussion

1. In his production notes Ward asserts that the play requires no scenery, that the production "should be designed around the basic color scheme of our patriotic trinity" (red, white, and blue), and that the play is conceived as "a reverse minstrel show done in white face." Together these assertions suggest that the coherence of the play will not depend on realistic techniques, or verisimilitude in presentation. How then is the play coherent? In theme? Through the rhetoric of comparison and contrast? Explain.

2. Are the characters in the play individuals or types? Explain. Do the method of characterization and the coherence of plot in any way resemble *Everyman?* Explain. Why does Ward suggest (in the production notes) that a Caucasian cast should "fit a uniform pattern—insipid white"?

3. How strongly established are the cause-and-effect relationships in *Day of Absence?* For instance, to what extent are the Mayor's actions the result of political expediency?

4. Clem and Luke appear in both the opening and closing scenes of the play. Do they function like the frame for a picture; that is, do they focus attention on what is presented within? Explain. Is the Announcer also a dramatic device? What function does he serve?

5. Satire differs from ridicule in that its purpose is to reform. Mr. Ward calls his play "A Satirical Fantasy." Is the designation accurate? Explain.

Suggested Theme Topics

1. Discuss the coherence of *Day of Absence,* with special reference to structural matters such as sequence and character relationships.

2. Defend or refute the assertion that the play embodies ridicule, not satire.

3. Discuss Ward's use of special effects (as described in his production notes) as an effective or ineffective method of theatrical presentation.

4. Discuss the role of humor in characterization in *Day of Absence*.

5. Write a theme in which you recount seriously an implausible sequence of events in order to depict some idiosyncrasy or flaw in human behavior.

Part III

ACHIEVING RESOLUTION: THE END

Part III

ACHIEVING RESOLUTION: THE END

The conclusion of a play, like that of a theme, serves several purposes. It should tie all loose ends together, reemphasize the pervading idea, and convince the audience that something has been resolved, not that the author has simply run out of anything further to say. If the conclusion adds irrelevant or unnecessary details, if it introduces a new idea that has not been developed in the body of the play, or if it wanders about aimlessly without recapitulating anything, then nothing has been resolved and the playwright has not availed himself of a final opportunity to demonstrate his fulfillment of all the obligations generated by the dramatic conflict of his play.

In establishing the relevance of all that has gone before, the conclusion should proceed naturally from the body of the play. For example, consider the concluding scene (Act V, Scene 12) of Ben Jonson's *Volpone*. At the beginning of the scene, Volpone clutches his final two opportunities to escape exposure (i.e., to silence Voltore and to again enlist Mosca's aid). When Mosca completes the circle by turning on his master, there is no hope. Volpone removes his disguise, thereby exposing all the avarice—including his own—that surrounds him; thus, "the knot is now undone by miracle." Alluding directly to all that has preceded in the play, the court pronounces its damning judgment on all those whose only emotion is greed. Likewise, the conclusion of a theme should both *recall the entire body* and *emphasize the main point or points*. Let us assume, for example, that the following paragraph, after an appropriate introduction, comprises the body of a theme:

> *One of the major differences I noted between Kingsboro and New York resulted from mere size. Kingsboro has a population of only four thousand, and most of the citizens belong to the same social, economic, and religious groups. Since the people there have common interests (e.g., farming, food prices, and the "social" at one of the protestant churches), there is a real sense of oneness. Nobody argues about politics, religion, or civil rights—since there are no Republicans, nonprotestants, or minority groups in the population. New York is different. Because of its size, there can be no sense of unity; because of its numerous political, religious, and ethnic groups, various disagreements must*

> *become matters of topical conversation. Just as noticeable as these differences resulting from size, however, are other differences resulting from attitudes—especially attitudes toward minor infractions of the law. In Kingsboro, if one parks overtime he has to pay a quarter fine; if he parks on a yellow line, the policeman (who probably recognizes his car) will call and tell him to move it. In New York, overtime meter parking leads to a $5.00 fine, and parking on a yellow line leads to a $15.00 fine and, perhaps, having the car towed away by a police wrecker. Another difference, perhaps the most prominent one, concerns variety of entertainment. In Kingsboro, there are two movies, occasional school plays, eight bridge groups, and high school athletic events. These would seem dull fare to the New Yorker, who has Broadway, innumerable movies, museums, lectures, concerts, and athletic events of every kind.*

Such a full paragraph, about 250 words long, will require a brief concluding paragraph, which may read as follows:

> *In conclusion, the differences between small towns and cities are principally those that result either from size or from attitudes. Size implies a population of diverse backgrounds, impersonal relationships, and varied entertainments. On the other hand, smallness implies unity, personal relationships, and less diverse entertainment.*

This brief statement is a reminder of the writer's points of emphasis, not just a rehashing of what has come before.

The tone of the conclusion must ordinarily be consistent with the body of the play or theme. For example, the opening action of Christopher Fry's *A Phoenix Too Frequent*, where Dynamene (with mock exaggeration) metaphorically compares her dead husband to a ship, projects a tone of comic irony:

> *He was the ship. He had such a deck, Doto,*
> *Such a white, scrubbed deck. Such a stern prow,*
> *Such a proud stern, so slim from port to starboard.*
> *If ever you meet a man with such fine masts*
> *Give your life to him, Doto. The figurehead*
> *Bore his own features, so serene in the brow*
> *And hung with a little seaweed. O Virilius,*
> *My husband, you have left a wake in my soul.*
> *You cut the glassy water with a diamond keel.*
> *I must cry again.*

Because this tone is maintained throughout the play, the farcical resolution—where Dynamene observes that the dead Virilius may become an instrument for Tegeus-Chromis' escape—does not appear unnaturally ludicrous. Likewise, in theme-writing the conclusion should usually embody the same tone as the rest of the paper. To close a serious paper with a flippant conclusion will likely distract the reader, destroy credibility, and cast doubt on the writer's sincerity—although it is possible for a skillful writer to permit a comic tone to deepen as the theme progresses, concluding with acknowledgment of his issue's serious side. Such a resolution must, however, be carefully foreshadowed.

One device by which the playwright frequently concludes his play might be called "completing the cycle." This denotes a situation in which the concluding scene (perhaps the final resolution) recalls through character relationship or situation or setting the opening scene. Likewise, in theme-writing the "completed cycle" often provides an incremental repetition serving as an effective conclusion. If a graphic image, an unusual event, or a cleverly worded or memorable phrase appears in the introduction, it may—after the subject has been developed—be repeated in the conclusion. Note, for example, the following introduction and conclusion for a paper on the subject of modern and older baseball:

> Introduction: *The home run, synthetic turf, Vitalis ad, relief pitcher, and television set are all part of the baseball world of today, and this world is far different from the world of that sport's infant days. This change implies not only the particular character of the modern player, but also a difference in the modern spectator....*
>
> Conclusion: *During baseball's infant days, the spectator expected long pitching duels, fistfights, tobacco-chewing marathons, and vicious sliding plays at second and home. But all this is over; the fan today is more staid. He can only be enticed to the park by Bat Day or Helmet Day. The rest of the time he combats the heat by staying away from the park, watching television in an air-conditioned living room, and granting a mild nostalgia to the good old days.*

In this example the conclusion simply repeats the introductory proposition, but in more specific terms (since the validity of the premise has been illustrated concretely in the body of the theme).

The playwright must use his conclusion *to convince the audience that something has been resolved.* In other words, it must finally become apparent in the play that all the preceding actions come together to make a coherent statement. Consider, for example, the closing scene (Part 3, Scene 4) of Eugene O'Neill's *Desire Under the Elms.* Here Cabot, who has seldom questioned either his own judgment or way of life, suddenly must face the truth. He has misjudged both Eben and Abbie, and he has nothing—not even any money—that will permit him to escape the life he has built. Also, in this scene Eben comes himself to recognize that he shares the responsibility for Abbie's crime, as well as that their common desire—or lust—has brought events to their present state.

In theme-writing, too, the conclusion must clarify what has been resolved or explained. The following suggestions take cognizance of the most common pitfalls in concluding paragraphs:

1. Avoid advertising your concluding paragraph. Since the reader can plainly see that nothing else follows, such expressions as these are superfluous: "And so I bring my paper to a close . . ."; "Having reached the end of my paper, I would like to say . . ."; "Last but not least, I . . ."; etc.

2. Avoid a conclusion that suggests you simply became weary with composing or ran out of time. It is difficult to end a paper with a bang, but—if you do not—remember that your whimper will be the last impression that a reader has of you.

3. Include a summary for a long paper. If the composition is longer than four-hundred words, the summary should comprise most of the concluding paragraph.

4. Unless you are consciously "completing the cycle," avoid using the same diction and sentence structure in the conclusion that you used in the introduction. The conclusion should be more emphatic if you wish to demonstrate to the reader that you have written with conviction.

5. If you have been criticising something, avoid ending your paper with a negative point. Let the final paragraph contain a positive statement or suggestion.

6. Avoid ending your paper with a qualification. If you have written an argumentative paper and there is a major point of view that contrasts with yours, you should have countered it in the body of your paper. For example, here is a poor conclusion:

I admit that there may be other reasons for the low batting averages on modern baseball teams. But, as I have demonstrated, the high pay that comes with hitting home runs is the major factor. Of course, modern pitchers may be better too.

7. Avoid ending your paper with an apology, such as:

If the library hours had been more convenient, I might have been able to do more research on this subject.

Ben Jonson

Ben Jonson (1573-1637) was a bricklayer, soldier, and actor before turning to writing. His reputation as poet and dramatist is surpassed among Renaissance figures only by Shakespeare and (possibly) Marlowe.

Jonson's first dramatic success was The Case Is Altered *(1598), followed later in the same year by* Every Man in His Humour. *Attacks on these and other comedies caused him to undertake tragedy as a dramatic mode, the most notable results being two companion pieces,* Sejanus *(1603) and* Catiline's Conspiracy *(1611). Fortunately, however, he continued to write comedies, including* Volpone *(1606),* The Silent Woman *(1609), and* The Alchemist *(1610). In addition, Jonson and Inigo Jones collaborated on a series of highly successful court masques during this period. Jonson's influence and creativity continued to ascend until approximately 1625, when he began a long period of debt, illness, and kingly disfavor. The waning of his physical circumstances was matched by a comparable decline in his artistic success, but he never stopped writing and was working on a comedy,* The Sad Shepherd, *when he died. Jonson's body lies in Westminster Abbey.*

Throughout Volpone, *the playwright mingles comic and serious commentary on the depravity of mankind. Decide if the resolution indicates a judgment as to whether or not man's depravity is likely to prevail in a given situation over his more praiseworthy characteristics. In reaching this decision, note how Jonson represents various human types—or perversions—by caricaturing them as animals.*

VOLPONE: OR, THE FOX

CHARACTERS

VOLPONE, *a Magnifico*
MOSCA, *his Parasite*
VOLTORE, *an Advocate*
CORBACCIO, *an old Gentleman*
CORVINO, *a Merchant*
BONARIO, *a young Gentleman, [son to Corbaccio]*
[SIR] POLITIC WOULD-BE, *a Knight*
PEREGRINE, *a Gentleman Traveller*
NANO, *a Dwarf*
CASTRONE, *an Eunuch*

ANDROGYNO, *a Hermaphrodite*
GREGE *[or Mob]*
COMMANDADORI, *Officers [of Justice]*
MERCATORI, *three Merchants*
AVOCATORI, *four Magistrates*
NOTARIO, *the Register*
SERVITORE, *a Servant*
FINE MADAME WOULD-BE, *the Knight's Wife*
CELIA, *[Corvino] the Merchant's Wife*
[TWO WAITING-] WOMEN

The Scene:—Venice

THE ARGUMENT

V olpone, childless, rich, feigns sick, despairs,
O ffers his state to hopes of several heirs,
L ies languishing: his parasite receives
P resents of all, assures, deludes; then weaves
O ther cross-plots, which ope themselves, are told.
N ew tricks for safety are sought; they thrive: when, bold,
E ach tempts th' other again, and all are sold.

PROLOGUE

Now, luck yet send us, and a little wit
  Will serve to make our play hit;
According to the palates of the season,
  Here is rhyme, not empty of reason.
This we were bid to credit from our poet,
  Whose true scope, if you would know it,
In all his poems still hath been this measure,
  To mix profit with your pleasure;
And not as some, whose throats their envy failing,
  Cry hoarsely, "All he writes is railing": 10
And when his plays come forth, think they can flout them,
  With saying, he was a year about them.
To these there needs no lie, but this his creature,
  Which was two months since no feature:
And though he dares give them five lives to mend it,
  'T is known, five weeks fully penn'd it,
From his own hand, without a coadjutor,
  Novice, journeyman, or tutor.
Yet thus much I can give you as a token
  Of his play's worth, no eggs are broken, 20
Nor quaking custards with fierce teeth affrighted,

Wherewith your rout are so delighted;
Nor hales he in a gull, old ends reciting,
  To stop gaps in his loose writing;
With such a deal of monstrous and forc'd action,
  As might make Bethlem a faction:
Nor made he his play for jests stol'n from each table,
  But makes jests to fit his fable;
And so presents quick comedy refin'd,
  As best critics have design'd; 30
The laws of time, place, persons he observeth,
  From no needful rule he swerveth.
All gall and copperas from his ink he draineth,
  Only a little salt remaineth,
Wherewith he'll rub your cheeks, till, red with laughter,
  They shall look fresh a week after.

ACT I

SCENE I

A Room in Volpone's House.

VOLPONE, MOSCA

[VOLP.] Good morning to the day; and next, my gold!
  Open the shrine, that I may see my saint.

MOSCA *withdraws the rear-stage curtain, and discovers piles of gold, plate, jewels, etc.*

Hail the world's soul, and mine! More glad than is
The teeming earth to see the long'd-for sun
Peep through the horns of the celestial Ram,
Am I, to view thy splendour dark'ning his;
That lying here, amongst my other hoards,
Show'st like a flame by night, or like the day
Struck out of chaos, when all darkness fled
Unto the centre. O thou son of Sol, 10
But brighter than thy father, let me kiss,
With adoration, thee, and every relic
Of sacred treasure in this blessed room.
Well did wise poets, by thy glorious name,
Title that age which they would have the best;
Thou being the best of things, and far transcending
All style of joy, in children, parents, friends,

---

23. *old ends:* scraps of old plays.   26. *Bethlem:* Bedlam, the hospital for the insane.
33. *copperas:* vitriol.   10. *centre:* i.e., of the earth.

Or any other waking dream on earth.
Thy looks when they to Venus did ascribe,
They should have given her twenty thousand Cupids; 20
Such are thy beauties and our loves! Dear saint,
Riches, the dumb god, that giv'st all men tongues,
That canst do nought, and yet mak'st men do all things;
The price of souls; even hell, with thee to boot,
Is made worth heaven. Thou art virtue, fame,
Honour, and all things else. Who can get thee,
He shall be noble, valiant, honest, wise—
MOS. And what he will, sir. Riches are in fortune
A greater good than wisdom is in nature.
VOLP. True, my beloved Mosca. Yet I glory 30
More in the cunning purchase of my wealth,
Than in the glad possession, since I gain
No common way; I use no trade, no venter;
I wound no earth with ploughshares, fat no beasts
To feed the shambles; have no mills for iron,
Oil, corn, or men, to grind 'em into powder;
I blow no subtle glass, expose no ships
To threat'nings of the furrow-faced sea;
I turn no moneys in the public bank,
No usure private.
MOS.   No, sir, nor devour 40
Soft prodigals. You shall ha' some will swallow
A melting heir as glibly as your Dutch
Will pills of butter, and ne'er purge for it;
Tear forth the fathers of poor families
Out of their beds, and coffin them alive
In some kind clasping prison, where their bones
May be forthcoming, when the flesh is rotten:
But your sweet nature doth abhor these courses;
You loathe the widow's or the orphan's tears
Should wash your pavements, or their piteous cries 50
Ring in your roofs, and beat the air for vengeance.
VOLP. Right, Mosca; I do loathe it.
MOS.   And, besides, sir,
You are not like the thresher that doth stand
With a huge flail, watching a heap of corn,
And, hungry, dares not taste the smallest grain,
But feeds on mallows, and such bitter herbs;
Nor like the merchant, who hath fill'd his vaults
With Romagnía, and rich Candian wines,
Yet drinks the lees of Lombard's vinegar:
You will not lie in straw, whilst moths and worms 60
Feed on your sumptuous hangings and soft beds;

31. *purchase:* acquisition. 33. *venter:* investment, speculation. 49. *loathe:* i.e., loathe that. 58. *Romagnía:* Rumney, Greek.

You know the use of riches, and dare give now
From that bright heap, to me, your poor observer,
Or to your dwarf, or your hermaphrodite,
Your eunuch, or what other household trifle
Your pleasure allows maint'nance—
VOLP.   Hold thee, Mosca,
Take of my hand; thou strik'st on truth in all,
And they are envious term thee parasite.
Call forth my dwarf, my eunuch, and my fool,
And let 'em make me sport. *(Exit* MOS.*)*
    What should I do,   70
But cocker up my genius, and live free
To all delights my fortune calls me to?
I have no wife, no parent, child, ally,
To give my substance to; but whom I make
Must be my heir; and this makes men observe me:
This draws new clients daily to my house,
Women and men of every sex and age,
That bring me presents, send me plate, coin, jewels,
With hope that when I die (which they expect
Each greedy minute) it shall then return   80
Tenfold upon them; whilst some, covetous
Above the rest, seek to engross me whole,
And counter-work the one unto the other,
Contend in gifts, as they would seem in love:
All which I suffer, playing with their hopes,
And am content to coin 'em into profit,
And look upon their kindness, and take more,
And look on that; still bearing them in hand,
Letting the cherry knock against their lips,
And draw it by their mouths, and back again.—   90
How now!

SCENE II

The Same.

NANO, ANDROGYNO, CASTRONE, VOLPONE, MOSCA

[NAN.] Now, room for fresh gamesters, who do will you to know,
   They do bring you neither play nor university show;
   And therefore do intreat you that whatsoever they rehearse,
   May not fare a whit the worse, for the false pace of the verse.
   If you wonder at this, you will wonder more ere we pass,
   For know, here is inclos'd the soul of Pythagoras,

---

63. *observer:* servant, obsequious follower. 68. *term:* i.e., who call. 71. *cocker up:* pamper. 75. *observe:* be obsequious to. 82. *engross:* monopolize. 88. *bearing... hand:* deceiving them. 6. *here:* i.e., in Androgyno.

That juggler divine, as hereafter shall follow;
Which soul, fast and loose, sir, came first from Apollo,
And was breath'd into Aethalides, Mercurius his son,
Where it had the gift to remember all that ever was done. 10
From thence it fled forth, and made quick transmigration
To goldy-lock'd Euphorbus, who was kill'd in good fashion,
At the siege of old Troy, by the cuckold of Sparta.
Hermotimus was next (I find it in my charta),
To whom it did pass, where no sooner it was missing,
But with one Pyrrhus of Delos it learn'd to go a-fishing;
And thence did it enter the sophist of Greece.
From Pythagore, she went into a beautiful piece,
Hight Aspasia, the meretrix; and the next toss of her
Was again of a whore she became a philosopher, 20
Crates the cynic, as itself doth relate it:
Since kings, knights, and beggars, knaves, lords, and fools gat it,
Besides ox and ass, camel, mule, goat, and brock,
In all which it hath spoke, as in the cobbler's cock.
But I come not here to discourse of that matter,
Or his one, two, or three, or his great oath, BY QUATER!
His musics, his trigon, his golden thigh,
Or his telling how elements shift; but I
Would ask, how of late thou hast suffer'd translation,
And shifted thy coat in these days of reformation. 30
AND. Like one of the reform'd, a fool, as you see,
    Counting all old doctrine heresy.
NAN. But not on thine own forbid meats hast thou venter'd?
AND. On fish, when first a Carthusian I enter'd.
NAN. Why, then thy dogmatical silence hath left thee?
AND. Of that an obstreperous lawyer bereft me.
NAN. O wonderful change, when sir lawyer forsook thee!
    For Pythagore's sake, what body then took thee?
AND. A good dull moyle.
NAN.   And how! by that means
    Thou wert brought to allow of the eating of beans? 40
AND. Yes.
NAN. But from the moyle into whom didst thou pass?
AND. Into a very strange beast, by some writers call'd an ass;
    By others a precise, pure, illuminate brother
    Of those devour flesh, and sometimes one another;
    And will drop you forth a libel, or a sanctifi'd lie,
    Betwixt every spoonful of a nativity-pie.
NAN. Now quit thee, for heaven, of that profane nation,
    And gently report thy next transmigration.

9. *Aethalides:* one of the Argonauts. 13. *cuckold:* Menelaus. 14. *charta:* paper. 19. *Hight:* called. *meretrix:* harlot. 23. *brock:* badger. 26. *Quater:* the tetractys, a geometrical figure which represented the number ten as the triangle of four, by which the Pythagoreans swore. 27. *trigon:* triangular lyre. 31. *one . . . reform'd:* a Protestant. 39. *moyle:* mule. 44. *precise . . . brother:* a Puritan. 45. *those:* those who. 47. *nativity-pie:* Christmas pie.

AND. To the same that I am.
NAN.   A creature of delight,
  And, what is more than a fool, an hermaphrodite! 50
  Now, pray thee, sweet soul, in all thy variation,
  Which body wouldst thou choose to take up thy station?
AND. Troth, this I am in: even here would I tarry.
NAN. 'Cause here the delight of each sex thou canst vary?
AND. Alas, those pleasures be stale and forsaken;
  No, 't is your fool wherewith I am so taken,
  The only one creature that I can call blessed;
  For all other forms I have prov'd most distressed.
NAN. Spoke true, as thou wert in Pythagoras still.
  This learned opinion we celebrate will, 60
  Fellow eunuch, as behooves us, with all our wit and art,
  To dignify that whereof ourselves are so great and special a part.
VOLP. Now, very, very pretty! Mosca, this
  Was thy invention?
MOS.   If it please my patron,
  Not else.
VOLP. It doth, good Mosca.
MOS.   Then it was, sir.

NANO *and* CASTRONE *sing.*

SONG

Fools, they are the only nation
Worth men's envy or admiration;
Free from care or sorrow-taking,
Selves and others merry making:
All they speak or do is sterling. 70
Your fool he is your great man's dearling,
And your ladies' sport and pleasure;
Tongue and bauble are his treasure.
E'en his face begetteth laughter,
And he speaks truth free from slaughter;
He 's the grace of every feast,
And sometimes the chiefest guest;
Hath his trencher and his stool,
When wit waits upon the fool.
  O, who would not be 80
  He, he, he?

One knocks without.

VOLP. Who 's that? Away! Look, Mosca.
MOS. Fool, begone!

---

75. *free from slaughter:* with impunity.

Exeunt NANO, CAST., *and* ANDRO.

     'T is Signior Voltore, the advocate;
I know him by his knock.
VOLP.   Fetch me my gown,
 My furs and night-caps; say my couch is changing
 And let him entertain himself awhile
 Without i' th' gallery. *(Exit* MOSCA.*)* Now, now my clients
 Begin their visitation! Vulture, kite,
 Raven, and gorcrow, all my birds of prey,
 That think me turning carcase, now they come: 90
 I am not for 'em yet.

Re-enter MOSCA, *with the gown, etc.*

     How now! the news?
MOS. A piece of plate, sir.
VOLP.   Of what bigness?
MOS.   Huge,
 Massy, and antique, with your name inscrib'd,
 And arms engraven.
VOLP.   Good! and not a fox
 Stretch'd on the earth, with fine delusive sleights,
 Mocking a gaping crow? ha, Mosca!
MOS.   Sharp, sir.
VOLP. Give me my furs. *(Puts on his sick dress.)*
     Why dost thou laugh so, man?
MOS. I cannot choose, sir, when I apprehend
 What thoughts he has without now, as he walks:
 That this might be the last gift he should give,   100
 That this would fetch you; if you died to-day,
 And gave him all, what he should be to-morrow;
 What large return would come of all his venters;
 How he should worshipp'd be, and reverenc'd;
 Ride with his furs, and foot cloths; waited on
 By herds of fools and clients; have clear way
 Made for his moyle, as letter'd as himself;
 Be call'd the great and learned advocate:
 And then concludes, there 's nought impossible.
VOLP. Yes, to be learned, Mosca.
MOS.   O, no: rich   110
 Implies it. Hood an ass with reverend purple,
 So you can hide his two ambitious ears,
 And he shall pass for a cathedral doctor.
VOLP. My caps, my caps, good Mosca.
 Fetch him in.
MOS. Stay, sir; your ointment for your eyes.
VOLP.   That 's true;

---

89. *gorcrow:* carrion crow. 112. *ambitious:* mobile.

>   Dispatch, dispatch: I long to have possession
>   Of my new present.
> MOS. That, and thousands more,
>   I hope to see you lord of.
> VOLP. Thanks, kind Mosca.
> MOS. And that, when I am lost in blended dust,
>   And hundred such as I am, in succession—   120
> VOLP. Nay, that were too much, Mosca.
> MOS. You shall live
>   Still to delude these harpies.
> VOLP. Loving Mosca!
> 'T is well: my pillow now, and let him enter.

Exit MOSCA.

> Now, my feign'd cough, my phthisic, and my gout,
> My apoplexy, palsy, and catarrhs,
> Help, with your forced functions, this my posture,
> Wherein, this three year, I have milk'd their hopes.
> He comes; I hear him—Uh! *(coughing)* uh! uh! uh! O—

SCENE III

The Same.

MOSCA, VOLTORE, VOLPONE

> [MOS.] You still are what you were, sir. Only you,
>   Of all the rest, are he commands his love,
>   And you do wisely to preserve it thus,
>   With early visitation, and kind notes
>   Of your good meaning to him, which, I know,
>   Cannot but come most grateful. Patron! sir!
>   Here's Signior Voltore is come—
> VOLP. *(Faintly).* What say you?
> MOS. Sir, Signior Voltore is come this morning
>   To visit you.
> VOLP. I thank him.
> MOS. And hath brought
>   A piece of antique plate, bought of St. Mark,   10
>   With which he here presents you.
> VOLP. He is welcome.
>   Pray him to come more often.
> MOS. Yes.
> VOLT. What says he?
> MOS. He thanks you, and desires you see him often.
> VOLP. Mosca.

2. *he:* the one who. 10. *of St. Mark:* at a goldsmith's in St. Mark's Square.

MOS. My patron!
VOLP. Bring him near, where is he?
  I long to feel his hand.
MOS. The plate is here, sir.
VOLT. How fare you, sir?
VOLP. I thank you, Signior Voltore;
  Where is the plate? mine eyes are bad.
VOLT. *(Putting it into his hands).* I'm sorry
  To see you still thus weak.
MOS. *(Aside).* That he is not weaker.
VOLP. You are too munificent.
VOLT. No, sir; would to heaven
  I could as well give health to you, as that plate! 20
VOLP. You give, sir, what you can; I thank you. Your love
  Hath taste in this, and shall not be unanswer'd:
  I pray you see me often.
VOLT. Yes, I shall, sir.
VOLP. Be not far from me.
MOS. Do you observe that, sir?
VOLP. Hearken unto me still; it will concern you.
MOS. You are a happy man, sir; know your good.
VOLP. I cannot now last long—
MOS. *(Aside).* You are his heir, sir.
VOLT. *(Aside).* Am I?
VOLP. I feel me going: Uh! uh! uh! uh!
  I am sailing to my port. Uh! uh! uh! uh!
  And I am glad I am so near my haven. 30
MOS. Alas, kind gentleman! Well, we must all go—
VOLT. But, Mosca—
MOS. Age will conquer.
VOLT. Pray thee, hear me;
  Am I inscrib'd his heir for certain?
MOS. Are you!
  I do beseech you, sir, you will vouchsafe
  To write me i' your family. All my hopes
  Depend upon your worship: I am lost
  Except the rising sun do shine on me.
VOLT. It shall both shine, and warm thee, Mosca.
MOS. Sir,
  I am a man that have not done your love
  All the worst offices: here I wear your keys, 40
  See all your coffers and your caskets lock'd,
  Keep the poor inventory of your jewels,
  Your plate, and moneys; am your steward, sir,
  Husband your goods here.
VOLT. But am I sole heir?
MOS. Without a partner, sir: confirm'd this morning:

35. *write . . . family:* enroll me among your servants.

        The wax is warm yet, and the ink scarce dry
        Upon the parchment.
    VOLT.   Happy, happy me!
        By what good chance, sweet Mosca?
    MOS.   Your desert, sir;
        I know no second cause.
    VOLT.   Thy modesty
        Is loath to know it; well, we shall requite it.   50
    MOS.   He ever lik'd your course, sir; that first took him.
        I oft have heard him say how he admir'd
        Men of your large profession, that could speak
        To every cause, and things mere contraries,
        Till they were hoarse again, yet all be law;
        That, with most quick agility, could turn,
        And return; make knots, and undo them;
        Give forked counsel; take provoking gold
        On either hand, and put it up; these men,
        He knew, would thrive with their humility.   60
        And, for his part, he thought he should be blest
        To have his heir of such a suff'ring spirit,
        So wise, so grave, of so perplex'd a tongue,
        And loud withal, that would not wag, nor scarce
        Lie still, without a fee; when every word
        Your worship but lets fall, is a cecchine!—

    Another knocks.

        Who's that? one knocks; I would not have you seen, sir.
        And yet—pretend you came and went in haste;
        I'll fashion an excuse—and, gentle sir,
        When you do come to swim in golden lard,   70
        Up to the arms in honey, that your chin
        Is borne up stiff with fatness of the flood,
        Think on your vassal; but remember me:
        I ha' not been your worst of clients.
    VOLT.   Mosca!—
    MOS.   When will you have your inventory brought, sir?
        Or see a copy of the will?—Anon!
        I'll bring 'em to you, sir. Away, begone,
        Put business i' your face. *(Exit* VOLTORE.*)*
    VOLP.   Excellent Mosca!
        Come hither, let me kiss thee.
    MOS.   Keep you still, sir.
        Here is Corbaccio.
    VOLP.   Set the plate away: 80
        The vulture's gone, and the old raven's come.

---

59. *put it up:* pocket it. 66. *cecchine:* a Venetian gold coin (sequin) worth over two dollars.

SCENE IV

The Same.

MOSCA, CORBACCIO, VOLPONE

[MOS.]   Betake you to your silence, and your sleep.
   Stand there and multiply. *(Putting the plate to the rest.)*
      Now shall we see
   A wretch who is indeed more impotent
   Than this can feign to be; yet hopes to hop
      Over his grave.

Enter CORBACCIO

                  Signior Corbaccio!
   You 're very welcome, sir.
CORB.   How does your patron?
MOS. Troth, as he did, sir; no amends.
CORB.   What! mends he?
MOS. No, sir: he is rather worse.
CORB.   That 's well. Where is he?
MOS. Upon his couch, sir, newly fall'n asleep.
CORB. Does he sleep well?
MOS.   No wink, sir, all this night,
   Nor yesterday; but slumbers.
CORB.   Good! he should take
   Some counsel of physicians: I have brought him
   An opiate here, from mine own doctor.
MOS. He will not hear of drugs.
CORB.   Why? I myself
   Stood by while 't was made, saw all th' ingredients;
   And know it cannot but most gently work:
   My life for his, 't is but to make him sleep.
VOLP. *(Aside).* Ay, his last sleep, if he would take it.
MOS.   Sir,
   He has no faith in physic.
CORB.   Say you, say you?
MOS. He has no faith in physic: he does think
   Most of your doctors are the greater danger,
   And worse disease, t' escape. I often have
   Heard him protest that your physician
   Should never be his heir.
CORB.   Nor I his heir?
MOS. Not your physician, sir.
CORB.   O, no, no, no,
   I do not mean it.
MOS.   No, sir, nor their fees
   He cannot brook: he says they flay a man
   Before they kill him.

10

20

CORB.   Right, I do conceive you.
MOS.   And then they do it by experiment;
   For which the law not only doth absolve 'em,   30
   But gives them great reward: and he is loath
   To hire his death so.
CORB.   It is true, they kill
   With as much license as a judge.
MOS.   Nay, more;
   For he but kills, sir, where the law condemns,
   And these can kill him too.
CORB.   Ay, or me;
   Or any man. How does his apoplex?
   Is that strong on him still?
MOS.   Most violent.
   His speech is broken, and his eyes are set,
   His face drawn longer than 't was wont—
CORB.   How! how!
   Stronger than he was wont?
MOS.   No, sir; his face   40
   Drawn longer than 't was wont.
CORB.   O, good!
MOS.   His mouth
   Is ever gaping, and his eyelids hang.
CORB.   Good.
MOS.   A freezing numbness stiffens all his joints,
   And makes the colour of his flesh like lead.
CORB.   'T is good.
MOS.   His pulse beats slow, and dull.
CORB.   Good symptoms still.
MOS.   And from his brain—
CORB.   Ha? How? Not from his brain?
MOS.   Yes, sir, and from his brain—
CORB.   I conceive you; good.
MOS.   Flows a cold sweat, with a continual rheum,
   Forth the resolved corners of his eyes.
CORB.   Is 't possible? Yet I am better, ha!   50
   How does he with the swimming of his head?
MOS.   O, sir, 't is past the scotomy; he now
   Hath lost his feeling, and hath left to snort:
   You hardly can perceive him, that he breathes.
CORB.   Excellent, excellent! sure I shall outlast him:
   This makes me young again, a score of years.
MOS.   I was a-coming for you, sir.
CORB.   Has he made his will?
   What has he giv'n me?
MOS.   No, sir.
CORB.   Nothing! ha?

49. *resolved:* weeping.   52. *scotomy:* dizziness.   53. *left:* ceased.

MOS. He has not made his will, sir.
CORB. Oh, oh, oh!
What then did Voltore, the lawyer, here?
MOS. He smelt a carcase, sir, when he but heard
My master was about his testament;
As I did urge him to it for your good—
CORB. He came unto him, did he? I thought so.
MOS. Yes, and presented him this piece of plate.
CORB. To be his heir?
MOS. I do not know, sir.
CORB. True:
I know it too.
MOS. *(Aside).* By your own scale, sir.
CORB. Well,
I shall prevent him yet. See, Mosca, look,
Here I have brought a bag of bright cecchines,
Will quite weigh down his plate.
MOS. *(Taking the bag).* Yea, marry, sir.
This is true physic, this your sacred medicine;
No talk of opiates to this great elixir!
CORB. 'T is *aurum palpabile,* if not *potabile.*
MOS. It shall be minister'd to him in his bowl.
CORB. Ay, do, do, do.
MOS. Most blessed cordial!
This will recover him.
CORB. Yes, do, do, do.
MOS. I think it were not best, sir.
CORB. What?
MOS. To recover him.
CORB. O, no, no, no; by no means.
MOS. Why, sir, this
Will work some strange effect, if he but feel it.
CORB. 'T is true, therefore forbear; I 'll take my venter:
Give me 't again.
MOS. At no hand: pardon me:
You shall not do yourself that wrong, sir. I
Will so advise you, you shall have it all.
CORB. How?
MOS. All, sir; 't is your right, your own; no man
Can claim a part: 't is yours without a rival,
Decreed by destiny.
CORB. How, how, good Mosca?
MOS. I 'll tell you, sir. This fit he shall recover,—
CORB. I do conceive you.
MOS. And on first advantage
Of his gain'd sense, will I re-importune him

67. *scale:* standard. 73. *aurum: aurum palpabile* is gold which can be felt; *aurum potabile* (drinkable gold) was regarded as a sovereign remedy of great efficacy. 81. *At no hand:* by no means.

Unto the making of his testament: 90
And show him this. *(Pointing to the money.)*
CORB.   Good, good.
MOS.   'T is better yet,
If you will hear, sir.
CORB.   Yes, with all my heart.
MOS. Now would I counsel you, make home with speed;
There, frame a will; whereto you shall inscribe
My master your sole heir.
CORB.   And disinherit
My son?
MOS. O, sir, the better: for that colour
Shall make it much more taking.
CORB.   O, but colour?
MOS. This will, sir, you shall send it unto me.
Now, when I come to enforce, as I will do,
Your cares, your watchings, and your many prayers, 100
Your more than many gifts, your this day's present,
And last, produce your will; where, without thought,
Or least regard, unto your proper issue,
A son so brave, and highly meriting,
The stream of your diverted love hath thrown you
Upon my master, and made him your heir;
He cannot be so stupid, or stone-dead,
But out of conscience and mere gratitude—
CORB. He must pronounce me his?
MOS.   'T is true.
CORB.   This plot
Did I think on before.
MOS.   I do believe it. 110
CORB. Do you not believe it?
MOS.   Yes, sir.
CORB.   Mine own project.
MOS. Which, when he hath done, sir—
CORB.   Publish'd me his heir?
MOS. And you so certain to survive him—
CORB.   Ay.
MOS. Being so lusty a man—
CORB.   'T is true.
MOS.   Yes, sir—
CORB. I thought on that too. See, how he should be
The very organ to express my thoughts!
MOS. You have not only done yourself a good—
CORB. But multipli'd it on my son.
MOS.   'T is right, sir.
CORB. Still, my invention.
MOS.   'Las, sir! heaven knows,

96. *colour:* pretence. 103. *proper issue:* own child.

```
        It hath been all my study, all my care,                    120
        (I e'en grow gray withal,) how to work things—
CORB.   I do conceive, sweet Mosca.
MOS.              You are he
        For whom I labour here.
CORB.             Ay, do, do, do:
        I 'll straight about it. (Going.)
MOS. (Aside).   Rook go with you, raven!
CORB.   I know thee honest.
MOS.              You do lie, sir!
CORB.             And—
MOS.    Your knowledge is no better than your ears, sir.
CORB.   I do not doubt to be a father to thee.
MOS.    Nor I to gull my brother of his blessing.
CORB.   I may ha' my youth restor'd to me; why not?
MOS.    Your worship is a precious ass!
CORB.             What sayst thou?                                 130
MOS.    I do desire your worship to make haste, sir.
CORB.   'T is done, 't is done; I go. (Exit.)
VOLP.             O, I shall burst!
        Let out my sides, let out my sides—
MOS.              Contain
        Your flux of laughter, sir: you know this hope
        Is such a bait, it covers any hook.
VOLP.   O, but thy working, and thy placing it!
        I cannot hold; good rascal, let me kiss thee:
        I never knew thee in so rare a humour.
MOS.    Alas, sir, I but do as I am taught;
        Follow your grave instructions; give 'em words;            140
        Pour oil into their ears, and send them hence.
VOLP.   'T is true, 't is true. What a rare punishment
        Is avarice to itself!
MOS.              Ay, with our help, sir.
VOLP.   So many cares, so many maladies,
        So many fears attending on old age.
        Yea, death so often call'd on, as no wish
        Can be more frequent with 'em, their limbs faint,
        Their senses dull, their seeing, hearing, going,
        All dead before them; yea, their very teeth,
        Their instruments of eating, failing them:                 150
        Yet this is reckon'd life! Nay, here was one.
        Is now gone home, that wishes to live longer!
        Feels not his gout, nor palsy; feigns himself
        Younger by scores of years, flatters his age
        With confident belying it, hopes he may
        With charms like Aeson, have his youth restor'd;
```

124. *Rook . . . you:* may you be rooked, or cheated. 128. *gull:* cheat. 140. *give 'em words:* deceive them. 148. *going:* faculty of walking.

And with these thoughts so battens, as if fate
Would be as easily cheated on as he,
And all turns air! Who 's that there, now? a third!

Another knocks.

MOS. Close, to your couch again; I hear his voice. 160
    It is Corvino, our spruce merchant.
VOLP. *(Lies down as before).*   Dead.
MOS. Another bout, sir, with your eyes *(anointing them).*
    Who 's there?

SCENE V

The Same.

MOSCA, CORVINO, VOLPONE

    Signior Corvino! come most wish'd for! O,
How happy were you, if you knew it, now!
CORV. Why? what? wherein?
MOS.   The tardy hour is come, sir.
CORV. He is not dead?
MOS.   Not dead, sir, but as good;
    He knows no man.
CORV.   How shall I do then?
MOS.   Why, sir?
CORV. I have brought him here a pearl.
MOS.   Perhaps he has
So much remembrance left as to know you, sir:
He still calls on you; nothing but your name
Is in his mouth. Is your pearl orient, sir?
CORV. Venice was never owner of the like. 10
VOLP. *(Faintly).* Signior Corvino!
MOS.   Hark!
VOLP.   Signior Corvino.
MOS. He calls you; step and give it him.—He 's here, sir.
    And he has brought you a rich pearl.
CORV.   How do you, sir?
Tell him it doubles the twelfth carat.
MOS.   Sir,
He cannot understand, his hearing 's gone;
And yet it comforts him to see you—
CORV.   Say
I have a diamond for him, too.
MOS.   Best show 't, sir;
Put it into his hand: 't is only there

---

8. *still:* continually. 9. *orient:* of the finest quality.

He apprehends: he has his feeling yet.
See how he grasps it!
CORV.   'Las, good gentleman!
How pitiful the sight is!
MOS.   Tut, forget, sir.
The weeping of an heir should still be laughter
Under a visor.
CORV.   Why, am I his heir?
MOS. Sir, I am sworn, I may not show the will
Till he be dead; but here has been Corbaccio,
Here has been Voltore, here were others too,
I cannot number 'em, they were so many;
All gaping here for legacies: but I,
Taking the vantage of his naming you,
(Signior Corvino! Signior Corvino!) took
Paper, and pen, and ink, and there I ask'd him
Whom he would have his heir? Corvino. Who
Should be executor? Corvino. And
To any question he was silent to,
I still interpreted the nods he made,
Through weakness, for consent: and sent home th' others,
Nothing bequeath'd them, but to cry and curse.
CORV. O, my dear Mosca. *(They embrace.)* Does he not perceive us?
MOS. No more than a blind harper. He knows no man,
No face of friend, nor name of any servant,
Who 't was that fed him last, or gave him drink:
Not those he hath begotten, or brought up,
Can he remember.
CORV.   Has he children?
MOS.   Bastards,
Some dozen, or more, that he begot on beggars,
Gypsies, and Jews, and black-moors, when he was drunk.
Knew you not that, sir? 't is the common fable,
The dwarf, the fool, the eunuch, are all his;
He 's the true father of his family,
In all save me:—but he has giv'n 'em nothing.
CORV. That 's well, that 's well! Art sure he does not hear us?
MOS. Sure, sir! why, look you, credit your own sense. *(Shouts in VOLP.'s ear.)*
The pox approach, and add to your diseases,
If it would send you hence the sooner, sir,
For your incontinence, it hath deserv'd it
Throughly and throughly, and the plague to boot!—
You may come near, sir.—Would you would once close
Those filthy eyes of yours, that flow with slime
Like two frog-pits; and those same hanging cheeks,
Cover'd with hide instead of skin—Nay, help, sir—
That look like frozen dish-clouts set on end!

---

59. *sir:* to Corvino.

CORV. Or like an old smok'd wall, on which the rain
Ran down in streaks!
MOS. Excellent, sir! speak out:
You may be louder yet; a culverin
Discharged in his ear would hardly bore it.
CORV. His nose is like a common sewer, still running.
MOS. 'T is good! And what his mouth?
CORV. A very draught.
MOS. O, stop it up—
CORV. By no means.
MOS. Pray you, let me:
Faith I could stifle him rarely with a pillow
As well as any woman that should keep him.
CORV. Do as you will; but I 'll begone.
MOS. Be so; 70
It is your presence makes him last so long.
CORV. I pray you use no violence.
MOS. No, sir! why?
Why should you be thus scrupulous, pray you, sir?
CORV. Nay, at your discretion.
MOS. Well, good sir, be gone.
CORV. I will not trouble him now to take my pearl.
MOS. Pooh! nor your diamond. What a needless care
Is this afflicts you? Is not all here yours?
Am not I here, whom you have made? your creature,
That owe my being to you?
CORV. Grateful Mosca!
Thou art my friend, my fellow, my companion, 80
My partner, and shalt share in all my fortunes.
MOS. Excepting one.
CORV. What 's that?
MOS. Your gallant wife, sir. *(Exit* CORV.*)*
Now is he gone: we had no other means
To shoot him hence but this.
VOLP. My divine Mosca!
Thou hast to-day outgone thyself. Who 's there? *(Another knocks.)*
I will be troubled with no more. Prepare
Me music, dances, banquets, all delights;
The Turk is not more sensual in his pleasures
Than will Volpone. *(Exit* MOS.*)* Let me see; a pearl!

---

63. *culverin:* small cannon. 69. *keep:* nurse.

A diamond! plate! cecchines! Good morning's purchase. 90
Why, this is better than rob churches, yet;
Or fat, by eating, once a month, a man—

Re-enter MOSCA

    Who is 't?
MOS.   The beauteous Lady Would-be, sir,
  Wife to the English knight, Sir Politic Would-be,
  (This is the style, sir, is directed me,)
  Hath sent to know how you have slept to-night,
  And if you would be visited?
VOLP.   Not now:
  Some three hours hence.
MOS.   I told the squire so much.
VOLP. When I am high with mirth and wine; then, then:
  'Fore heaven, I wonder at the desperate valour 100
  Of the bold English, that they dare let loose
  Their wives to all encounters!
MOS.   Sir, this knight
  Had not his name for nothing, he is *politic*,
  And knows, howe'er his wife affect strange airs,
  She hath not yet the face to be dishonest:
  But had she Signior Corvino's wife's face—
VOLP. Has she so rare a face?
MOS.   O, sir, the wonder,
  The blazing star of Italy! a wench
  O' the first year, a beauty ripe as harvest!
  Whose skin is whiter than a swan all over, 110
  Than silver, snow, or lilies; a soft lip,
  Would tempt you to eternity of kissing!
  And flesh that melteth in the touch to blood!
  Bright as your gold, and lovely as your gold!
VOLP. Why had not I known this before?
MOS.   Alas, sir,
  Myself but yesterday discover'd it.
VOLP. How might I see her?
MOS.   O, not possible;
  She 's kept as warily as is your gold;
  Never does come abroad, never takes air
  But at a windore. All her looks are sweet, 120
  As the first grapes or cherries, and are watch'd
  As near as they are.
VOLP.   I must see her.
MOS.   Sir,
  There is a guard of ten spies thick upon her,

---

90. *purchase:* booty. 92. *fat:* fatten. 98. *squire:* messenger. 120. *windore:* window. 122. *near:* closely.

All his whole household; each of which is set
Upon his fellow, and have all their charge,
When he goes out, when he comes in, examin'd.
VOLP. I will go see her, though but at her windore.
MOS. In some disguise then.
VOLP.   That is true; I must
Maintain mine own shape still the same: we 'll think.

Exeunt.

ACT II

SCENE I

St. Mark's Place, before Corvino's House.

[SIR] POLITIC WOULD-BE, PEREGRINE

[SIR P.] Sir, to a wise man, all the world 's his soil:
  It is not Italy, nor France, nor Europe,
  That must bound me, if my fates call me forth.
  Yet I protest, it is no salt desire
  Of seeing countries, shifting a religion,
  Nor any disaffection to the state
  Where I was bred, and unto which I owe
  My dearest plots, hath brought me out, much less
  That idle, antique, stale, grey-headed project
  Of knowing men's minds and manners, with Ulysses!
  But a peculiar humour of my wife's
  Laid for this height of Venice, to observe,
  To quote, to learn the language, and so forth—
  I hope you travel, sir, with license?
PER.   Yes.
SIR P. I dare the safelier converse—How long, sir,
  Since you left England?
PER.   Seven weeks.
SIR P.   So lately!
  You ha' not been with my lord ambassador?
PER. Not yet, sir.
SIR P. Pray you, what news, sir, vents our climate?
  I heard last night a most strange thing reported
  By some of my lord's followers, and I long
  To hear how 't will be seconded.
PER.   What was 't, sir?

---

4. *salt:* inordinate. 12. *height:* meridian. 13. *quote:* make note of. 14. *license:* Englishmen of rank required a royal license to leave the country. 18. *our climate:* England.

SIR P. Marry, sir, of a raven that should build
In a ship royal of the king's.
PER. *(Aside).*   This fellow,
Does he gull me, trow? or is gull'd? Your name, sir?
SIR P. My name is Politic Would-be.
PER. *(Aside).*   O, that speaks him.
A knight, sir?
SIR P.   A poor knight, sir.
PER.   Your lady
Lies here in Venice, for intelligence
Of tires and fashions, and behaviour,
Among the courtesans? The fine Lady Would-be?
SIR P. Yes, sir; the spider and the bee oft-times   30
Suck from one flower.
PER.   Good Sir Politic,
I cry you mercy; I have heard much of you:
'T is true, sir, of your raven.
SIR P.   On your knowledge?
PER. Yes, and your lion's whelping in the Tower.
SIR P. Another whelp!
PER.   Another, sir.
SIR P.   Now heaven!
What prodigies be these? The fires at Berwick!
And the new star! These things concurring, strange,
And full of omen! Saw you those meteors?
PER. I did, sir.
SIR P.   Fearful! Pray you, sir, confirm me,
Were there three porcpisces seen above the bridge,   40
As they give out?
PER.   Six, and a sturgeon, sir.
SIR P. I am astonish'd.
PER.   Nay, sir, be not so;
I 'll tell you a greater prodigy than these.
SIR P.   What should these things portend?
PER.   The very day
(Let me be sure) that I put forth from London,
There was a whale discover'd in the river,
As high as Woolwich, that had waited there,
Few know how many months, for the subversion
Of the Stode fleet.
SIR P.   Is 't possible? Believe it,
'T was either sent from Spain, or the archduke's: 50
Spinola's whale, upon my life, my credit!
Will they not leave these projects? Worthy sir,

---

27. *Lies:* stays. 35. *whelp:* a lion was born in the Tower of London on August 5, 1604, and another on February 26, 1606. 40. *porcpisces:* porpoises. 49. *Stode:* Hanseatic town near Hamburg. 51. *Spinola:* a contemporary Spanish general, known as the inventor of fantastic military engines. 52. *leave ... projects:* give up these plots.

Some other news.
PER. Faith, Stone the fool is dead,
And they do lack a tavern fool extremely.
SIR P. Is Mass Stone dead?
PER. He 's dead, sir; why, I hope
You thought him not immortal?—*(Aside.)* O, this knight,
Were he well known, would be a precious thing
To fit our English stage: he that should write
But such a fellow, should be thought to feign
Extremely, if not maliciously.
SIR P. Stone dead! 60
PER. Dead.—Lord! how deeply, sir, you apprehend it!
He was no kinsman to you?
SIR P. That I know of.
Well! that same fellow was an unknown fool.
PER. And yet you knew him, it seems?
SIR P. I did so. Sir,
I knew him one of the most dangerous heads
Living within the state, and so I held him.
PER. Indeed, sir?
SIR P. While he liv'd, in action.
He has receiv'd weekly intelligence,
Upon my knowledge, out of the Low Countries,
For all parts of the world, in cabbages; 70
And those dispens'd again to ambassadors,
In oranges, musk-mellons, apricots,
Lemons, pome-citrons, and such-like; sometimes
In Colchester oysters, and your Selsey cockles.
PER. You make me wonder.
SIR P. Sir, upon my knowledge.
Nay, I've observ'd him, at your public ordinary,
Take his advertisement from a traveller,
A conceal'd statesman, in a trencher of meat;
And instantly, before the meal was done,
Convey an answer in a tooth-pick.
PER. Strange! 80
How could this be, sir?
SIR P. Why, the meat was cut
So like his character, and so laid as he
Must easily read the cipher.
PER. I have heard,
He could not read, sir.
SIR P. So 't was given out,
In policy, by those that did employ him:
But he could read, and had your languages.
And to 't, as sound as noddle—

---

55. *Mass:* master. 62. *That:* not that. 76. *ordinary:* tavern. 77. *advertisement:* information. 87. *to 't:* in addition.

PER.   I have heard, sir,
   That your baboons were spies, and that they were
   A kind of subtle nation near to China.
SIR P. Ay, ay, your Mamaluchi. Faith, they had   90
   Their hand in a French plot or two; but they
   Were so extremely giv'n to women, as
   They made discovery of all: yet I
   Had my advices here, on Wednesday last,
   From one of their own coat, they were return'd,
   Made their relations, as the fashion is,
   And now stand fair for fresh employment.
PER. *(Aside).*   Heart!
   This Sir Pol will be ignorant of nothing.—
   It seems, sir, you know all.
SIR P.   Not all, sir; but
   I have some general notions. I do love   100
   To note and to observe: though I live out,
   Free from the active torrent, yet I 'd mark
   The currents and the passages of things
   For mine own private use; and know the ebbs
   And flows of state.
PER.   Believe it, sir, I hold
   Myself in no small tie unto my fortunes,
   For casting me thus luckily upon you,
   Whose knowledge, if your bounty equal it,
   May do me great assistance, in instruction
   For my behaviour, and my bearing, which   110
   Is yet so rude and raw.
SIR P.   Why? came you forth
   Empty of rules for travel?
PER.   Faith, I had
   Some common ones, from out that vulgar grammar,
   Which he that cri'd Italian to me, taught me.
SIR P. Why, this it is that spoils all our brave bloods,
   Trusting our hopeful gentry unto pedants,
   Fellows of outside, and mere bark. You seem
   To be a gentleman of ingenuous race:—
   I not profess it, but my fate hath been
   To be, where I have been consulted with,   120
   In this high kind, touching some great men's sons,
   Persons of blood and honour.—
PER.   Who be these, sir?

---

95. *coat:* kind. 96. *relations:* reports. 106. *tie:* obligation. 114. *cri'd:* spoke.

SCENE II

The Same.

MOSCA, POLITIC, PEREGRINE, VOLPONE, NANO, GREGE

[MOS.] Under that windore, there 't must be. The same.
SIR P. Fellows, to mount a bank. Did your instructor
  In the dear tongues never discourse to you
  Of the Italian mountebanks?
PER.   Yes, sir.
SIR P.   Why,
  Here shall you see one.
PER.   They are quacksalvers,
  Fellows that live by venting oils and drugs.
SIR P. Was that the character he gave you of them?
PER. As I remember.
SIR P.   Pity his ignorance.
  They are the only knowing men of Europe!
  Great general scholars, excellent physicians,   10
  Most admir'd statesmen, profess'd favourites
  And cabinet counsellors to the greatest princes;
  The only languag'd men of all the world!
PER. And, I have heard, they are most lewd impostors;
  Made all of terms and shreds; no less beliers
  Of great men's favours, than their own vile medicines;
  Which they will utter upon monstrous oaths;
  Selling that drug for twopence, ere they part,
  Which they have valu'd at twelve crowns before.
SIR P. Sir, calumnies are answer'd best with silence.   20
  Yourself shall judge.—Who is it mounts, my friends?
MOS. Scoto of Mantua, sir.
SIR P.   Is 't he? Nay, then
  I 'll proudly promise, sir, you shall behold
  Another man than has been phant'sied to you.
  I wonder yet, that he should mount his bank,
  Here in this nook, that has been wont t' appear
  In face of the Piazza!—Here he comes.

Enter VOLPONE, *disguised as a mountebank Doctor, and followed by a crowd of people*

VOLP. Mount, zany. *(To* NANO.*)*
GREGE. Follow, follow, follow, follow, follow.
SIR P. See how the people follow him! he 's a man   30
  May write ten thousand crowns in bank here. Note,

Scene II, stage direction. *Grege:* a mob of people. 2. *bank:* platform, bench. 3. *dear tongues:* difficult languages. 6. *venting:* dispensing. 14. *lewd:* ignorant. 17. *utter:* sell. 22. *Scoto:* an Italian juggler, then in England. 24. *phant'sied:* represented. 28. *zany:* buffoon.

VOLPONE *mounts the stage.*

Mark but his gesture:—I do use to observe
The state he keeps in getting up.
PER.   'T is worth it, sir.
VOLP. "Most noble gentlemen, and my worthy patrons! It may seem strange that I, your Scoto Mantuano, who was ever wont to fix my bank in face of the public Piazza, near the shelter of the Portico to the Procuratia, should now, after eight months' absence from this illustrious city of Venice, humbly retire myself into an obscure nook of the Piazza."
SIR P. Did not I now object the same?
PER.   Peace, sir.   40
VOLP. "Let me tell you: I am not, as your Lombard proverb saith, cold on my feet; or content to part with my commodities at a cheaper rate than I accustom'd: look not for it. Nor that the calumnious reports of that impudent detractor, and shame to our profession (Alessandro Buttone, I mean), who gave out, in public, I was condemn'd *a' sforzato* to the galleys, for poisoning the Cardinal Bembo's cook, hath at all attach'd, much less dejected me. No, no, worthy gentlemen; to tell you true, I cannot endure to see the rabble of these ground *ciarlitani,* that spread their cloaks on the pavement, as if they meant to do feats of activity, and then come in lamely, with their mouldy tales out of Boccaccio, like stale Tabarin, the fabulist: some of them discoursing their travels, and of their tedious captivity in the Turks' galleys, when, indeed, were the truth known, they were the Christians' galleys, where very temporately they eat bread, and drunk water, as a wholesome penance, enjoin'd them by their confessors, for base pilferies."
SIR P. Note but his bearing, and contempt of these.
VOLP. "These turdy-facy-nasty-paty-lousy-fartical rogues, with one poor groat's-worth of unprepar'd antimony, finely wrapp'd up in several *scartoccios,* are able, very well, to kill their twenty a week,   60
and play; yet these meagre, starv'd spirits, who have half stopp'd the organs of their minds with earthy oppilations, want not their favourers among your shrivell'd salad-eating artisans, who are overjoy'd that they may have their half-pe'rth of physic; though it purge 'em into another world, 't makes no matter."
SIR P. Excellent! ha' you heard better language, sir?
VOLP. "Well, let 'em go. And, gentlemen, honourable gentlemen, know, that for this time, our bank, being thus remov'd from the clamours of the *canaglia* shall be the scene of pleasure and delight; for I have nothing to sell, little or nothing to sell."   70
SIR P. I told you, sir, his end.

---

46. *a' sforzato:* with hard labor (Ital.). 49. *ciarlitani:* petty impostors. 51. *Tabarin:* member of an Italian strolling company that visited France in 1570. *fabulist:* professional storyteller. 60. *scartoccios:* waste papers. 62. *oppilations:* obstructions. 69. *canaglia:* rabble.

PER.   You did so, sir.
VOLP. "I protest, I, and my six servants, are not able to make of this precious liquor so fast as it is fetch'd away from my lodging by gentlemen of your city; strangers of the terra firma; worshipful merchants; ay, and senators too: who, ever since my arrival, have detained me to their uses, by their splendidous liberalities. And worthily; for, what avails your rich man to have his magazines stuff'd with *moscadelli*, or of the purest grape, when his physicians prescribe him, on pain of death, to drink nothing but water cocted with anise-seeds? O health! health! the blessing of the rich! the riches of the poor! who can buy thee at too dear a rate, since there is no enjoying this world without thee? Be not then so sparing of your purses, honourable gentlemen, as to abridge the natural course of life—" 80
PER. You see his end?
SIR P.   Ay, is 't not good?
VOLP. "For when a humid flux, or catarrh, by the mutability of air, falls from your head into an arm or shoulder, or any other part; take you a ducat, or your cecchine of gold, and apply to the place affected: see what good effect it can work. No, no, 't is this blessed *unguento*, this rare extraction, that hath only power to disperse all malignant humours, that proceed either of hot, cold, moist, or windy causes—" 90
PER. I would he had put in dry too.
SIR P.   Pray you observe.
VOLP. "To fortify the most indigest and crude stomach, ay, were it of one that, through extreme weakness, vomited blood, applying only a warm napkin to the place, after the unction and fricace;—for the *vertigine* in the head, putting but a drop into your nostrils, likewise behind the ears; a most sovereign and approved remedy; the *mal caduco*, cramps, convulsions, paralyses, epilepsies, *tremor cordia*, retired nerves, ill vapours of the spleen, stoppings of the liver, the stone, the strangury, *hernia ventosa, iliaca passio;* stops a *dysenteria* immediately; easeth the torsion of the small guts; and cures *melancholia hypocondriaca*, being taken and applied, according to my printed receipt. For *(Pointing to his bill and his glass.)* this is the physician, this the medicine; this counsels, this cures; this gives the direction, this works the effect; and, in sum, both together may be term'd an abstract of the theoric and practic in the Aesculapian art. 'T will cost you eight crowns. And,—Zan Fritada, pray thee sing a verse extempore in honour of it." 100
SIR P. How do you like him, sir?
PER.   Most strangely, I!
SIR P. Is not his language rare?
PER.   But alchemy, 110

74. *terra firma:* mainland. 77-78. *moscadelli:* sweet wines. 79. *cocted:* boiled. 89. *unguento:* ointment. 95. *fricace:* rubbing. 96. *vertigine:* giddiness. This speech gives a list of diseases which could be cured by Scoto's Oil. Jonson often used strings of technical words to give an air of authenticity to a particular scene. 110. *But:* except (in).

I never heard the like; or Broughton's books.

NANO *sings.*

SONG

Had old Hippocrates, or Galen,
That to their books put med'cines all in,
But known this secret, they had never
(Of which they will be guilty ever)
Been murderers of so much paper,
Or wasted many a hurtless taper;
No Indian drug had e'er been famed,
Tobacco, sassafras not named;
Ne yet of guacum one small stick, sir,   120
Nor Raymund Lully's great elixir.
Ne had been known the Danish Gonswart,
Or Paracelsus, with his long sword.

PER. All this, yet, will not do; eight crowns is high.
VOLP. "No more.—Gentlemen, if I had but time to discourse to you the miraculous effects of this my oil, surnamed *oglio del Scoto;* with the countless catalogue of those I have cured of th' aforesaid, and many more diseases; the patents and privileges of all the princes and commonwealths of Christendom; or but the depositions of those that appear'd on my part, before the signiory of the Sanitá and most   130
learned College of Physicians; where I was authorized, upon notice taken of the admirable virtues of my medicaments, and mine own excellency in matter of rare and unknown secrets, not only to disperse them publicly in this famous city, but in all the territories, that happily joy under the government of the most pious and magnificent states of Italy. But may some other gallant fellow say, 'O, there be divers that make profession to have as good, and as experimented receipts as yours.' Indeed, very many have assay'd, like apes, in imitation of that, which is really and essentially in me, to make of this oil; bestow'd great cost in furnaces, stills, alembics, continual fires, and   140
preparation of the ingredients (as indeed there goes to it six hundred several simples, besides some quantity of human fat, for the conglutination, which we buy of the anatomists), but when these practitioners come to the last decoction, blow, blow, puff, puff, and all flies in fumo: ha, ha, ha! Poor wretches! I rather pity their folly and indiscretion, than their loss of time and money; for those may be recovered by industry: but to be a fool born, is a disease incurable.

"For myself, I always from my youth have endeavour'd to get the

---

111. *Broughton:* an eccentric theologian of the time. 120. *guacum:* a resinous drug.
121. *Lully:* a famous medieval alchemist. 122. *Conswart:* Gansfort, a Westphalian scholar of the fifteenth century. 142. *simples:* herbs. 145. *fumo:* smoke.

rarest secrets, and book them, either in exchange, or for money; I
spared nor cost nor labour, where anything was worthy to be learned. 150
And, gentlemen, honourable gentlemen, I will undertake, by virtue
of chymical art, out of the honourable hat that covers your head, to
extract the four elements; that is to say, the fire, air, water, and earth,
and return you your felt without burn or stain. For, whilst others
have been at the *ballo,* I have been at my book; and am now past the
craggy paths of study, and come to the flowery plains of honour and
reputation."

SIR P. I do assure you, sir, that is his aim.
VOLP. "But to our price—"
PER.   And that withal, Sir Pol.
VOLP. "You all know, honourable gentlemen, I never valu'd this   160
ampulla, or vial, at less than eight crowns; but for this time, I am
content to be depriv'd of it for six; six crowns is the price, and less in
courtesy I know you cannot offer me; take it or leave it, howsoever,
both it and I am at your service. I ask you not as the value of the
thing, for then I should demand of you a thousand crowns, so the
Cardinals Montalto, Fernese, the great Duke of Tuscany, my gossip,
with divers other princes, have given me; but I despise money. Only
to show my affection to you, honourable gentlemen, and your illus-
trous state here, I have neglected the messages of these princes, mine
own offices, fram'd my journey hither, only to present you with the   170
fruits of my travels.—Tune your voices once more to the touch of
your instruments, and give the honourable assembly some delightful
recreation."

PER. What monstrous and most painful circumstance
Is here, to get some three or four gazettes,
Some threepence i' the whole! for that 't will come to.

NANO *sings.*

SONG

You that would last long, list to my song,
Make no more coil, but buy of this oil.
Would you be ever fair and young?
Stout of teeth, and strong of tongue?   180
Tart of palate? quick of ear?
Sharp of sight? of nostril clear?
Moist of hand? and light of foot?
Or, I will come nearer to 't,
Would you live free from all diseases?
Do the act your mistress pleases,
Yet fright all aches from your bones?
Here 's a med'cine for the nones.

---

155. *ballo:* an Italian game of ball.   166. *gossip:* familiar friend.   170. *offices:* duties.
174. *circumstance:* beating about the bush.   175. *gazettes:* small Venetian coins.   178.
coil: disturbance.   187. *aches:* pronounced "aitches."   188. *nones:* occasion.

VOLP. "Well, I am in a humour at this time to make a present of the
small quantity my coffer contains; to the rich in courtesy, and to the   190
poor for God's sake. Wherefore now mark: I ask'd you six crowns;
and six crowns, at other times, you have paid me; you shall not give
me six crowns, nor five, nor four, nor three, nor two, nor one; nor
half a ducat; no, nor a *moccinigo.* Sixpence it will cost you, or six
hundred pound—expect no lower price, for, by the banner of my
front, I will not bate a *bagatine.*—That I will have, only, a pledge of
your loves, to carry something from amongst you, to show I am not
contemn'd by you. Therefore, now, toss your handkerchiefs, cheerfully, cheerfully; and be advertised, that the first heroic spirit that
deigns to grace me with a handkerchief, I will give it a little remem-   200
brance of something beside, shall please it better than if I had presented it with a double pistolet."
PER. Will you be that heroic spark, Sir Pol?

CELIA, *at the window, throws down her handkerchief.*

O, see! the windore has prevented you.
VOLP. "Lady, I kiss your bounty; and for this timely grace you have
done your poor Scoto of Mantua, I will return you, over and above
my oil, a secret of that high and inestimable nature, shall make you
forever enamour'd on that minute, wherein your eye first descended
on so mean, yet not altogether to be despis'd, an object. Here is a
powder conceal'd in this paper, of which, if I should speak to the   210
worth, nine thousand volumes were but as one page, that page as a
line, that line as a word; so short is this pilgrimage of man (which
some call life) to the expressing of it. Would I reflect on the price?
Why, the whole world were but as an empire, that empire as a province, that province as a bank, that bank as a private purse to the purchase of it. I will only tell you; it is the powder that made Venus a
goddess (given her by Apollo), that kept her perpetually young,
clear'd her wrinkles, firm'd her gums, fill'd her skin, colour'd her hair;
from her deriv'd to Helen, and at the sack of Troy unfortunately lost:
till now, in this our age, it was as happily recover'd, by a studious   220
antiquary, out of some ruins of Asia, who sent a moiety of it to the
court of France (but much sophisticated), wherewith the ladies there
now colour their hair. The rest, at this present, remains with me;
extracted to a quintessence: so that, wherever it but touches, in
youth it perpetually preserves, in age restores the complexion; seats
your teeth, did they dance like virginal jacks, firm as a wall: makes
them white as ivory, that were black as—"

---

194. *moccinigo:* a Venetian coin worth less than twenty cents. 196. *bagatine:* a small Italian coin. 202. *pistolet:* a Spanish gold coin. 204. *prevented:* anticipated. 226. *virginal jacks:* pieces of wood which make the quills pluck the strings of a virginal.

SCENE III

The Same.

CORVINO, POLITIC, PEREGRINE

[CORV.] Spite o' the devil, and my shame! come down here;
Come down!—No house but mine to make your scene?
Signior Flaminio, will you down, sir? down?
What, is my wife your Franciscina, sir?
No windores on the whole Piazza, here,
To make your properties, but mine? but mine?

He beats away the mountebank, &c.

Heart! ere to-morrow I shall be new christen'd,
And called the Pantalone di Besogniosi,
About the town.
PER.   What should this mean, Sir Pol?
SIR P. Some trick of state, believe it; I will home.   10
PER. It may be some design on you.
SIR P.   I know not.
I'll stand upon my guard.
PER.   It is your best, sir.
SIR P. This three weeks, all my advices, all my letters,
They have been intercepted.
PER.   Indeed, sir!
 Best have a care.
SIR P.   Nay, so I will.
PER.   This knight,
I may not lose him, for my mirth, till night.

Exeunt.

SCENE IV

A Room in Volpone's House.

VOLPONE, MOSCA

[VOLP.] O, I am wounded!
MOS.   Where, sir?
VOLP.   Not without;
Those blows were nothing: I could bear them ever.
But angry Cupid, bolting from her eyes,
Hath shot himself into me like a flame;

---

3. *Flaminio:* Flaminio Scala, leader of a famous company of actors.   4. *Franciscina:* a stock character, a flirtatious servant-girl.   8. *Pantalone di Besogniosi:* a stock humorous character (literally, "fool of beggars").

Where now he flings about his burning heat,
As in a furnace an ambitious fire
Whose vent is stopp'd. The fight is all within me.
I cannot live, except thou help me, Mosca;
My liver melts, and I, without the hope
Of some soft air from her refreshing breath,
Am but a heap of cinders.
MOS.   'Las, good sir,
Would you had never seen her!
VOLP.   Nay, would thou
Hadst never told me of her!
MOS.   Sir, 't is true;
I do confess I was unfortunate,
And you unhappy; but I 'm bound in conscience,
No less than duty, to effect my best
To your release of torment, and I will, sir.
VOLP. Dear Mosca, shall I hope?
MOS.   Sir, more than dear,
I will not bid you to despair of aught
Within a human compass.
VOLP.   O, there spoke
My better angel. Mosca, take my keys,
Gold, plate, and jewels, all 's at thy devotion;
Employ them how thou wilt: nay, coin me too:
So thou in this but crown my longings, Mosca.
MOS. Use but your patience.
VOLP.   So I have.
MOS.   I doubt not
To bring success to your desires.
VOLP.   Nay, then,
I not repent me of my late disguise.
MOS. If you can horn him, sir, you need not.
VOLP.   True:
Besides, I never meant him for my heir.
Is not the colour o' my beard and eyebrows
To make me known?
MOS.   No jot.
VOLP.   I did it well.
MOS. So well, would I could follow you in mine,
With half the happiness! and yet I would
Escape your epilogue.
VOLP.   But were they gull'd
With a belief that I was Scoto?
MOS.   Sir,
Scoto himself could hardly have distinguish'd!
I have not time to flatter you now; we 'll part:
And as I prosper, so applaud my art.

Exeunt.

28. *horn him:* make him a cuckold.   34. *epilogue:* i.e., the beating from Corvino.

SCENE V

A Room in Corvino's House.

CORVINO, CELIA, SERVITORE

[CORV.]   Death of mine honour, with the city's fool!
   A juggling, tooth-drawing, prating mountebank!
   And at a public windore! where, whilst he,
   With his strain'd action, and his dole of faces,
   To his drug-lecture draws your itching ears,
   A crew of old, unmarri'd, noted lechers,
   Stood leering up like satyrs: and you smile
   Most graciously, and fan your favours forth,
   To give your hot spectators satisfaction!
   What, was your mountebank their call? their whistle?   10
   Or were you enamour'd on his copper rings,
   His saffron jewel, with the toad-stone in 't,
   Or his embroid'red suit, with the cope-stitch,
   Made of a hearse cloth? or his old tilt-feather?
   Or his starch'd beard! Well, you shall have him, yes!
   He shall come home, and minister unto you
   The fricace for the mother. Or, let me see,
   I think you 'd rather mount; would you not mount?
   Why, if you 'll mount, you may; yes, truly, you may!
   And so you may be seen, down to the foot.   20
   Get you a cittern, Lady Vanity,
   And be a dealer with the virtuous man;
   Make one. I 'll but protest myself a cuckold,
   And save your dowry. I 'm a Dutchman, I!
   For if you thought me an Italian,
   You would be damn'd ere you did this, you whore!
   Thou 'dst tremble to imagine that the murder
   Of father, mother, brother, all thy race,
   Should follow, as the subject of my justice.
CEL.   Good sir, have patience.
CORV.   What couldst thou propose   30
   Less to thyself, than in this heat of wrath,
   And stung with my dishonour, I should strike
   This steel unto thee, with as many stabs
   As thou wert gaz'd upon with goatish eyes?

---

4. *dole of faces:* grimaces.   12. *toad-stone:* the jewel supposed to be found in the toad's head.   14. *tilt-feather:* discarded plume from the tilt-yard.   17. *mother:* hysteria.   18. *mount:* join the mountebanks.   21. *cittern:* guitar.   30. *propose:* expect.

CEL. Alas, sir, be appeas'd! I could not think
My being at the windore should more now
Move your impatience than at other times.
CORV. No! not to seek and entertain a parley
With a known knave, before a multitude!
You were an actor with your handkerchief, 40
Which he most sweetly kiss'd in the receipt,
And might, no doubt, return it with a letter,
And point the place where you might meet; your sister's,
Your mother's, or your aunt's might serve the turn.
CEL. Why, dear sir, when do I make these excuses,
Or ever stir abroad, but to the church?
And that so seldom—
CORV.   Well, it shall be less;
And thy restraint before was liberty,
To what I now decree: and therefore mark me.
First, I will have this bawdy light damm'd up; 50
And till 't be done, some two or three yards off,
I'll chalk a line; o'er which if thou but chance
To set thy desp'rate foot, more hell, more horror,
More wild remorseless rage shall seize on thee,
Than on a conjuror that had heedless left
His circle's safety ere his devil was laid.
Then here's a lock which I will hang upon thee,
And, now I think on 't, I will keep thee backwards;
Thy lodging shall be backwards: thy walks backwards;
Thy prospect, all be backwards; and no pleasure, 60
That thou shalt know but backwards: nay, since you force
My honest nature, know, it is your own,
Being too open, makes me use you thus:
Since you will not contain your subtle nostrils
In a sweet room, but they must snuff the air
Of rank and sweaty passengers. *(Knock within.)* One knocks.
Away, and be not seen, pain of thy life;
Nor look toward the windore; if thou dost—
Nay, stay, hear this—let me not prosper, whore,
But I will make thee an anatomy, 70
Dissect thee mine own self, and read a lecture
Upon thee to the city, and in public.
Away!—*(Exit* CELIA.*)*

Enter SERVANT

        Who's there?
SER.   'T is Signior Mosca, sir.

---

58. *backwards:* in the back of the house. 66. *passengers:* passersby. 70. *anatomy:* corpse for dissection.

SCENE VI

The Same.

CORVINO, MOSCA

[CORV.] Let him come in. His master 's dead; there 's yet
  Some good to help the bad.—My Mosca, welcome!
  I guess your news.
MOS.   I fear you cannot, sir.
CORV. Is 't not his death?
MOS.   Rather the contrary.
CORV. Not his recovery?
MOS.   Yes, sir.
CORV.   I am curs'd,
  I am bewitch'd, my crosses meet to vex me.
  How? how? how? how?
MOS.   Why, sir, with Scoto's oil;
  Corbaccio and Voltore brought of it,
  Whilst I was busy in an inner room—
CORV. Death! that damn'd mountebank! but for the law   10
  Now, I could kill the rascal: 't cannot be
  His oil should have that virtue. Ha' not I
  Known him a common rogue, come fiddling in
  To th' *osteria,* with a tumbling whore,
  And, when he has done all his forc'd tricks, been glad
  Of a poor spoonful of dead wine, with flies in 't?
  It cannot be. All his ingredients
  Are a sheep's gall, a roasted bitch's marrow,
  Some few sod earwigs, pounded caterpillars,
  A little capon's grease, and fasting spittle: 20
  I know 'em to a dram.
MOS.   I know not, sir;
  But some on 't, there, they pour'd into his ears,
  Some in his nostrils, and recover'd him;
  Applying but the fricace.
CORV.   Pox o' that fricace!
MOS. And since, to seem the more officious
  And flatt'ring of his health, there, they have had,
  At extreme fees, the college of physicians
  Consulting on him, how they might restore him;
  Where one would have a cataplasm of spices,
  Another a flay'd ape clapp'd to his breast,   30
  A third would ha' it a dog, a fourth an oil,
  With wild cats' skins: at last, they all resolv'd
  That to preserve him, was no other means
  But some young woman must be straight sought out,

---

14. *osteria:* inn.   19. *sod:* boiled.   29. *cataplasm:* poultice.

Lusty, and full of juice, to sleep by him;
And to this service most unhappily,
And most unwillingly am I now employ'd,
Which here I thought to pre-acquaint you with,
For your advice, since it concerns you most;
Because I would not do that thing might cross   40
Your ends, on whom I have my whole dependence, sir;
Yet, if I do it not they may delate
My slackness to my patron, work me out
Of his opinion; and there all your hopes,
Venters, or whatsoever, are all frustrate!
I do but tell you, sir. Besides, they are all
Now striving who shall first present him; therefore—
I could entreat you, briefly conclude somewhat;
Prevent 'em if you can.
CORV.   Death to my hopes,
This is my villainous fortune! Best to hire   50
Some common courtesan.
MOS.   Ay. I thought on that, sir;
But they are all so subtle, full of art—
And age again doting and flexible,
So as—I cannot tell—we may, perchance,
Light on a quean may cheat us all.
CORV.   'T is true.
MOS. No, no: it must be one that has no tricks, sir,
Some simple thing, a creature made unto it;
Some wench you may command. Ha' you no kinswoman?
Gods so—Think, think, think, think, think, think, think, sir.
One o' the doctors offer'd there his daughter.   60
CORV. How!
MOS.   Yes, Signior Lupo, the physician.
CORV. His daughter!
MOS.   And a virgin, sir. Why, alas,
He knows the state of 's body, what it is:
That nought can warm his blood, sir, but a fever;
Nor any incantation raise his spirit:
A long forgetfulness hath seiz'd that part.
Besides, sir, who shall know it? Some one or two—
CORV. I pray thee give me leave. *(Walks aside.)* If any man
But I had had this luck—The thing in 't self,
I know, is nothing.—Wherefore should not I   70
As well command my blood and my affections
As this dull doctor? In the point of honour,
The cases are all one of wife and daughter.
MOS. *(Aside).* I hear him coming.
CORV.   She shall do 't: 't is done.

---

42. *delate:* report (an evil action). 55. *quean:* jade, hussy. 74. *coming:* i.e., into my trap.

Slight! if this doctor, who is not engag'd,
Unless 't be for his counsel, which is nothing,
Offer his daughter, what should I, that am
So deeply in? I will prevent him. Wretch!
Covetous wretch!—Mosca, I have determin'd.

MOS. How, sir?

CORV.   We 'll make all sure. The party you wot of   80
Shall be mine own wife, Mosca.

MOS.   Sir, the thing,
But that I would not seem to counsel you,
I should have motion'd to you, at the first:
And make your count, you have cut all their throats.
Why, 't is directly taking a possession!
And in his next fit, we may let him go.
'T is but to pull the pillow from his head,
And he is throttled: 't had been done before
But for your scrupulous doubts.

CORV.   Ay, a plague on 't,
My conscience fools my wit! Well, I 'll be brief,   90
And so be thou, lest they should be before us.
Go home, prepare him, tell him with what zeal
And willingness I do it: swear it was
On the first hearing, as thou mayst do, truly,
Mine own free motion.

MOS.   Sir, I warrant you,
I'll so possess him with it, that the rest
Of his starv'd clients shall be banish'd all;
And only you receiv'd. But come not, sir,
Until I send, for I have something else
To ripen for your good, you must not know 't.   100

CORV. But do not you forget to send now.

MOS.   Fear not. *(Exit.)*

SCENE VII

The Same.

CORVINO, CELIA

[CORV.] Where are you, wife? My Celia! wife!

Enter CELIA

        —What, blubbering?
Come, dry those tears. I think thou thought'st me in earnest;
Ha! by this light I talk'd so but to try thee:

---

83. *motion'd:* proposed. 84. *make your count:* be sure. *cut...throats:* outdone them all.

    Methinks, the lightness of the occasion
    Should ha' confirm'd thee. Come, I am not jealous.
CEL. No?
CORV.   Faith I am not, I, nor never was;
    It is a poor unprofitable humour.
    Do not I know, if women have a will,
    They 'll do 'gainst all the watches o' the world.
    And that the fiercest spies are tam'd with gold?   10
    Tut, I am confident in thee, thou shalt see 't;
    And see, I 'll give thee cause too, to believe it.
    Come kiss me. Go, and make thee ready straight,
    In all thy best attire, thy choicest jewels,
    Put 'em all on, and, with 'em, thy best look:
    We are invited to a solemn feast,
    At old Volpone's, where it shall appear
    How far I am free from jealousy or fear.

Exeunt.

ACT III

SCENE I

A Street.

MOSCA

MOS. I fear I shall begin to grow in love
    With my dear self, and my most prosp'rous parts,
    They do so spring and burgeon; I can feel
    A whimsy i' my blood: I know not how,
    Success hath made me wanton. I could skip
    Out of my skin now, like a subtle snake,
    I am so limber. O! your parasite
    Is a most precious thing, dropp'd from above,
    Not bred 'mongst clods and clodpoles, here on earth.
    I muse, the mystery was not made a science,   10
    It is so liberally profess'd! Almost
    All the wise world is little else, in nature,
    But parasites or sub-parasites. And yet
    I mean not those that have your bare town-art,
    To know who 's fit to feed 'em; have no house,
    No family, no care, and therefore mould
    Tales for men's ears, to bait that sense; or get
    Kitchen-invention, and some stale receipts

---

10. *mystery:* profession. 17. *sense:* i.e., love of gossip.

To please the belly, and the groin; nor those,
With their court dog-tricks, that can fawn and fleer, 20
Make their revenue out of legs and faces,
Echo my lord, and lick away a moth:
But your fine elegant rascal, that can rise
And stoop, almost together, like an arrow;
Shoot through the air as nimbly as a star;
Turn short as doth a swallow; and be here,
And there, and here, and yonder, all at once;
Present to any humour, all occasion;
And change a visor swifter than a thought!
This is the creature had the art born with him; 30
Toils not to learn it, but doth practise it
Out of most excellent nature: and such sparks
Are the true parasites, others but their zanies.

SCENE II

The Same.

MOSCA, BONARIO

MOS. Who's this? Bonario, old Corbaccio's son?
  The person I was bound to seek. Fair sir,
  You are happ'ly met.
BON.   That cannot be by thee.
MOS. Why, sir?
BON.   Nay, pray thee know thy way, and leave me:
  I would be loath to interchange discourse
  With such a mate as thou art.
MOS.   Courteous sir,
  Scorn not my poverty.
BON.   Not I, by heaven;
  But thou shalt give me leave to hate thy baseness.
MOS. Baseness!
BON.   Ay; answer me, is not thy sloth
  Sufficient argument? thy flattery? 10
  Thy means of feeding?
MOS.   Heaven be good to me!
  These imputations are too common, sir,
  And eas'ly stuck on virtue when she's poor.
  You are unequal to me, and howe'er
  Your sentence may be righteous, yet you are not,
  That, ere you know me, thus proceed in censure:
  St. Mark bear witness 'gainst you, 't is inhuman. *(Weeps.)*
BON. *(Aside).* What! does he weep? the sign is soft and good:

---

21. *legs and faces:* bows and smirks. 29. *visor:* expression. 6. *mate:* fellow. 14. *unequal:* unjust.

   I do repent me that I was so harsh.
MOS. 'T is true, that, sway'd by strong necessity,   20
  I am enforc'd to eat my careful bread
  With too much obsequy; 't is true, beside,
  That I am fain to spin mine own poor raiment
  Out of my mere observance, being not born
  To a free fortune: but that I have done
  Base offices, in rending friends asunder,
  Dividing families, betraying counsels,
  Whisp'ring false lies, or mining men with praises,
  Train'd their credulity with perjuries,
  Corrupted chastity, or am in love   30
  With mine own tender ease, but would not rather
  Prove the most rugged and laborious course,
  That might redeem my present estimation,
  Let me here perish, in all hope of goodness.
BON. *(Aside).* This cannot be a personated passion.—
  I was to blame, so to mistake thy nature;
  Pray thee forgive me: and speak out thy business.
MOS. Sir, it concerns you; and though I may seem
  At first to make a main offence in manners,
  And in my gratitude unto my master,   40
  Yet for the pure love which I bear all right,
  And hatred of the wrong, I must reveal it.
  This very hour your father is in purpose
  To disinherit you—
BON.   How!
MOS.   And thrust you forth,
  As a mere stranger to his blood: 't is true, sir.
  The work no way engageth me, but as
  I claim an interest in the general state
  Of goodness and true virtue, which I hear
  T' abound in you; and for which mere respect,
  Without a second aim, sir, I have done it.   50
BON. This tale hath lost thee much of the late trust
  Thou hadst with me; it is impossible.
  I know not how to lend it any thought,
  My father should be so unnatural.
MOS. It is a confidence that well becomes
  Your piety; and form'd, no doubt, it is
  From your own simple innocence: which makes
  Your wrong more monstrous and abhorr'd. But, sir,
  I now will tell you more. This very minute,
  It is, or will be doing; and if you   60
  Shall be but pleas'd to go with me, I 'll bring you,
  I dare not say where you shall see, but where
  Your ear shall be a witness of the deed;

---

24. *observance:* service. 29. *Train'd:* lured.

Hear yourself written bastard, and profess'd
The common issue of the earth.
BON.   I'm maz'd!
MOS.   Sir, if I do it not, draw your just sword,
And score your vengeance on my front and face;
Mark me your villain: you have too much wrong,
And I do suffer for you, sir. My heart
Weeps blood in anguish—
BON.   Lead; I follow thee.   70

Exeunt.

SCENE III

A Room in Volpone's House.

VOLPONE, NANO, ANDROGYNO, CASTRONE

[VOLP.]   Mosca stays long, methinks.—Bring forth your sports,
And help to make the wretched time more sweet.
NAN.   "Dwarf, fool, and eunuch, well met here we be.
A question it were now, whether of us three,
Being all the known delicates of a rich man,
In pleasing him, claim the precedency can?"
CAS.   "I claim for myself."
AND.   "And so doth the fool."
NAN.   "'T is foolish indeed: let me set you both to school.
First for your dwarf, he's little and witty,
And everything, as it is little, is pretty;   10
Else why do men say to a creature of my shape,
So soon as they see him, 'It's a pretty little ape'?
And why a pretty ape, but for pleasing imitation
Of greater men's action, in a ridiculous fashion?
Beside, this feat body of mine doth not crave
Half the meat, drink, and cloth, one of your bulks will have.
Admit your fool's face be the mother of laughter,
Yet, for his brain, it must always come after:
And though that do feed him, it's a pitiful case,
His body is beholding to such a bad face."   20

One knocks.

VOLP.   Who's there? My couch; away! look, Nano, see!
(Exeunt AND. *and* CAS.*)*
Give me my caps first—go, inquire. *(Exit* NANO.*)* Now, Cupid
Send it be Mosca, and with fair return!

---

4. *whether:* which.   5. *delicates:* favorites, pets.   15. *feat:* neatly formed.

NAN. *(Within).*   It is the beauteous madam—
VOLP.   Would-be—is it?
NAN.   The same.
VOLP.   Now torment on me! Squire her in:
  For she will enter, or dwell here for ever.
  Nay, quickly, that my fit were past! *(Retires to his couch.)* I fear
  A second hell too, that my loathing this
  Will quite expel my appetite to the other:
  Would she were taking now her tedious leave.   30
  Lord, how it threats me what I am to suffer!

SCENE IV

The Same.

LADY [POLITIC WOULD-BE], VOLPONE, NANO, 2 WOMEN

[LADY P.]   I thank you, good sir. Pray you signify
  Unto your patron I am here.—This band
  Shows not my neck enough.—I trouble you sir;
  Let me request you bid one of my women
  Come hither to me. In good faith, I am dress'd
  Most favourably to-day! It is no matter:
  'T is well enough.

Enter 1 WAITING-WOMAN

              Look, see these petulant things,
  How they have done this!
VOLP. *(Aside).*   I do feel the fever
  Ent'ring in at mine ears; O, for a charm,
  To fright it hence!
LADY P.   Come nearer: is this curl   10
  In his right place, or this? Why is this higher
  Than all the rest? You ha' not wash'd your eyes yet!
  Or do they not stand even i' your head?
  Where 's your fellow? call her. *(Exit 1 WOMAN.)*
NAN.   Now, St. Mark
  Deliver us! anon she 'll beat her women,
  Because her nose is red.

Re-enter 1 *with* 2 WOMAN

LADY P.   I pray you view
  This tire, forsooth: are all things apt, or no?
1 WOM.   One hair a little here sticks out, forsooth.
LADY P.   Does 't so, forsooth! and where was your dear sight,

17. *tire:* headdress.

368   Volpone

  When it did so, forsooth! What now! bird-ey'd?   20
  And you, too? Pray you, both approach and mend it.
  Now, by that light I muse you 're not asham'd!
  I, that have preach'd these things so oft unto you,
  Read you the principles, argu'd all the grounds,
  Disputed every fitness, every grace,
  Call'd you to counsel of so frequent dressings—
NAN. *(Aside).* More carefully than of your fame or honour.
LADY P. Made you acquainted what an ample dowry
  The knowledge of these things would be unto you,
  Able alone to get you noble husbands   30
  At your return: and you thus to neglect it!
  Besides, you seeing what a curious nation
  Th' Italians are, what will they say of me?
  "The English lady cannot dress herself."
  Here 's a fine imputation to our country!
  Well, go your ways, and stay i' the next room.
  This fucus was too coarse too; it 's no matter.—
  Good sir, you 'll give 'em entertainment?

Exeunt NANO *and* WAITING-WOMEN.

VOLP. The storm comes toward me.
LADY P. *(Goes to the couch).*   How does my Volpone!
VOLP. Troubl'd with noise, I cannot sleep; I dreamt   40
  That a strange fury ent'red now my house,
  And, with the dreadful tempest of her breath,
  Did cleave my roof asunder.
LADY P.   Believe me, and I
  Had the most fearful dream, could I remember 't—
VOLP. *(Aside).* Out on my fate! I have given her the occasion
  How to torment me: she will tell me hers.
LADY P. Methought the golden mediocrity,
  Polite, and delicate—
VOLP.   O, if you do love me,
  No more: I sweat, and suffer, at the mention
  Of any dream; feel how I tremble yet.   50
LADY P. Alas, good soul! the passion of the heart.
  Seed-pearl were good now, boil'd with syrup of apples,
  Tincture of gold, and coral, citron-pills,
  Your elecampane root, myrobalanes—
VOLP. Ay me, I have ta'en a grasshopper by the wing!
LADY P. Burnt silk and amber. You have muscadel
  Good i' the house—
VOLP.   You will not drink, and part?

20. *bird-ey'd:* shortsighted or keen-eyed (in derision). 32. *curious:* fastidious. 37. *fucus:* rouge. 52-54. *Seed-pearl ... myrobalanes:* remedies for melancholy. 55. *grasshopper:* an ancient proverb holds that the tighter grasshoppers are held by the wings the louder they scream.

LADY P. No, fear not that. I doubt we shall not get
   Some English saffron, half a dram would serve;
   Your sixteen cloves, a little musk, dried mints;   60
   Bugloss, and barley-meal—
VOLP. *(Aside).*   She's in again!
   Before I feign'd diseases, now I have one.
LADY P. And these appli'd with a right scarlet cloth.
VOLP. *(Aside).* Another flood of words! a very torrent!
LADY P. Shall I, sir, make you a poultice?
VOLP.   No, no, no.
   I'm very well, you need prescribe no more.
LADY P. I have a little studied physic; but now
   I'm all for music, save, i' the forenoons,
   An hour or two for painting. I would have
   A lady, indeed, t' have all letters and arts,   70
   Be able to discourse, to write, to paint,
   But principal, as Plato holds, your music
   (And so does wise Pythagoras, I take it,)
   Is your true rapture: when there is concent
   In face, in voice, and clothes: and is, indeed,
   Our sex's chiefest ornament.
VOLP.   The poet
   As old in time as Plato, and as knowing,
   Says that your highest female grace is silence.
LADY P. Which o' your poets? Petrarch, or Tasso, or Dante?
   Guarini? Ariosto? Aretine?   80
   Cieco di Hadria? I have read them all.
VOLP. *(Aside).* Is everything a cause to my destruction?
LADY P. I think I ha' two or three of 'em about me.
VOLP. *(Aside).* The sun, the sea, will sooner both stand still
   Than her eternal tongue! nothing can scape it
LADY P. Here's *Pastor Fido*—
VOLP. *(Aside).*   Profess obstinate silence;
   That's now my safest.
LADY P.   All our English writers,
   I mean such as are happy in th' Italian,
   Will deign to steal out of this author, mainly;
   Almost as much as from Montagnié: 90
   He has so modern and facile a vein,
   Fitting the time, and catching the court-ear!
   Your Petrarch is more passionate, yet he,
   In days of sonnetting, trusted 'em with much:
   Dante is hard, and few can understand him.
   But for a desperate wit, there's Aretine;
   Only his pictures are a little obscene—
   You mark me not.

74. *concent:* harmony. 86. *Pastor Fido: The Faithful Shepherd,* Guarini's pastoral drama.

VOLP. Alas, my mind 's perturb'd.
LADY P. Why, in such cases, we must cure ourselves,
  Make use of our philosophy—
VOLP. Oh me! 100
LADY P. And as we find our passions do rebel,
  Encounter 'em with reason, or divert 'em.
  By giving scope unto some other humour
  Of lesser danger: as, in politic bodies,
  There 's nothing more doth overwhelm the judgment,
  And clouds the understanding, than too much
  Settling and fixing, and, as 't were, subsiding
  Upon one object. For the incorporating
  Of these same outward things, into that part
  Which we call mental, leaves some certain faeces 110
  That stop the organs, and, as Plato says,
  Assassinates our knowledge.
VOLP. *(Aside).* Now, the spirit
  Of patience help me!
LADY P. Come, in faith, I must
  Visit you more a days; and make you well:
  Laugh and be lusty.
VOLP. *(Aside).* My good angel save me!
LADY P. There was but one sole man in all the world
  With whom I e'er could sympathize; and he
  Would lie you, often, three, four hours together
  To hear me speak; and be sometime so rapt,
  As he would answer me quite from the purpose, 120
  Like you, and you are like him, just. I 'll discourse,
  An 't be but only, sir, to bring you asleep,
  How we did spend our time and loves together,
  For some six years.
VOLP. Oh, oh, oh, oh, oh, oh!
LADY P. For we were *coaetanei,* and brought up—
VOLP. Some power, some fate, some fortune rescue me!

SCENE V

The Same.

MOSCA, LADY [POLITIC WOULD-BE], VOLPONE

[MOS.] God save you, madam!
LADY P. Good sir.
VOLP. Mosca! welcome,
  Welcome to my redemption.
MOS. Why, sir?
VOLP. Oh,

---

114. *more a days:* more frequently.   125. *coaetanei:* equals in age.

Rid me of this my torture, quickly, there;
My madam with the everlasting voice:
The bells, in time of pestilence, ne'er made
Like noise or were in that perpetual motion!
The Cock-pit comes not near it. All my house,
But now, steam'd like a bath with her thick breath,
A lawyer could not have been heard; nor scarce
Another woman, such a hail of words   10
She has let fall. For hell's sake, rid her hence.
MOS. Has she presented?
VOLP.   Oh, I do not care;
  I 'll take her absence upon any price,
  With any loss.
MOS.   Madam—
LADY P.   I ha' brought your patron
  A toy, a cap here, of mine own work.
MOS.   'T is well.
  I had forgot to tell you I saw your knight
  Where you would little think it.—
LADY P.   Where?
MOS.   Marry,
  Where yet, if you make haste, you may apprehend him,
  Rowing upon the water in a gondole,
  With the most cunning courtesan of Venice.   20
LADY P. Is 't true?
MOS.   Pursue 'em, and believe your eyes:
  Leave me to make your gift.

Exit LADY P. *hastily.*

            I knew 't would take:
  For, lightly, they that use themselves most license,
  Are still most jealous.
VOLP.   Mosca, hearty thanks
  For thy quick fiction, and delivery of me.
  Now to my hopes, what sayst thou?

Re-enter LADY P. WOULD-BE

LADY P.   But do you hear, sir?—
VOLP. Again! I fear a paroxysm.
LADY P.   Which way
  Row'd they together?
MOS.   Toward the Rialto.
LADY P. I pray you lend me your dwarf.
MOS. I pray you take him. *(Exit* LADY P.*)*   30
  Your hopes, sir, are like happy blossoms, fair,

---

12. *presented:* made a present.   23. *lightly:* commonly.

And promise timely fruit, if you will stay
　　　But the maturing; keep you at your couch,
　　　Corbaccio will arrive straight, with the will;
　　　When he is gone, I 'll tell you more. *(Exit.)*
　VOLP.　　　　　　My blood,
　　　My spirits are return'd; I am alive:
　　　And, like your wanton gamester at primero,
　　　Whose thought had whisper'd to him, not go less,
　　　Methinks I lie, and draw—for an encounter.

SCENE VI

　　The Same.

　MOSCA, BONARIO

　[MOS.]　Sir, here conceal'd *(opening a door)* you may hear all. But,
　　　pray you,
　　　Have patience, sir; *(One knocks.)* the same 's your father knocks:
　　　I am compell'd to leave you. *(Exit.)*
　BON.　　　　　　Do so.—Yet
　　　Cannot my thought imagine this a truth. *(Goes in.)*

SCENE VII

　　The Same.

　MOSCA, CORVINO, CELIA, BONARIO, VOLPONE

　[MOS.]　Death on me! you are come too soon! what meant you?
　　　Did not I say I would send?
　CORV.　　　　　　Yes, but I fear'd
　　　You might forget it, and then they prevent us.
　MOS.　Prevent! *(Aside.)* Did e'er man haste so for his horns?
　　　A courtier would not ply it so for a place.
　　　—Well, now there is no helping it, stay here;
　　　I 'll presently return. *(Exit.)*
　CORV.　　　　　　Where are you, Celia?
　　　You know not wherefore I have brought you hither?
　CEL.　Not well, except you told me.
　CORV.　　　　　　Now I will:
　　　Hark hither. *(They retire to one side.)*

　Re-enter MOSCA

　MOS.　　　Sir, your father hath sent word, *(To* BONARIO.*)*　　　10

---

37. *primero:* a card game.　38. *go:* wager.　39. *draw:* "draw" and "encounter" are terms in primero, but Volpone also plays on his position. His couch is on the inner stage, and the curtain is drawn before him as the scene closes.

It will be half an hour ere he come;
And therefore, if you please to walk the while
Into that gallery—at the upper end,
There are some books to entertain the time:
And I'll take care no man shall come unto you, sir.
BON. Yes, I will stay there.—*(Aside.)* I do doubt this fellow. *(Exit.)*
MOS. There; he is far enough; he can hear nothing:
And for his father, I can keep him off.

Draws the curtains before VOLPONE's *couch*

CORV. Nay, now, there is no starting back, and therefore,
  Resolve upon it: I have so decreed.
  It must be done. Nor would I move 't afore,
  Because I would avoid all shifts and tricks,
  That might deny me.
CEL.   Sir, let me beseech you,
  Affect not these strange trials; if you doubt
  My chastity, why, lock me up for ever;
  Make me the heir of darkness. Let me live
  Where I may please your fears, if not your trust.
CORV. Believe it, I have no such humour, I.
  All that I speak I mean; yet I am not mad;
  Not horn-mad, see you? Go to, show yourself
  Obedient, and a wife.
CEL.   O heaven!
CORV.   I say it,
  Do so.
CEL. Was this the train?
CORV.   I've told you reasons;
  What the physicians have set down; how much
  It may concern me; what my engagements are;
  My means, and the necessity of those means
  For my recovery: wherefore, if you be
  Loyal and mine, be won, respect my venture.
CEL. Before your honour?
CORV.   Honour! tut, a breath:
  There's no such thing in nature; a mere term
  Invented to awe fools. What is my gold
  The worse for touching, clothes for being look'd on?
  Why, this's no more. An old decrepit wretch,
  That has no sense, no sinew; takes his meat
  With others' fingers: only knows to gape
  When you do scald his gums; a voice, a shadow;
  And what can this man hurt you?
CEL. *(Aside).*   Lord! what spirit
  Is this hath ent'red him?

32. *train:* plot.

CORV. And for your fame,
That's such a jig: as if I would go tell it,
Cry it on the Piazza! Who shall know it
But he that cannot speak it, and this fellow, 50
Whose lips are i' my pocket? Save yourself,
(If you'll proclaim 't, you may,) I know no other
Should come to know it.
CEL. Are heaven and saints then nothing?
Will they be blind or stupid?
CORV. How!
CEL. Good sir,
Be jealous still, emulate them; and think
What hate they burn with toward every sin.
CORV. I grant you: if I thought it were a sin
I would not urge you. Should I offer this
To some young Frenchman, or hot Tuscan blood
That had read Aretine, conn'd all his prints, 60
Knew every quirk within lust's labyrinth,
And were profess'd critic in lechery;
And I would look upon him, and applaud him,
This were a sin: but here, 't is contrary,
A pious work, mere charity for physic,
And honest polity, to assure mine own.
CEL. O heaven! canst thou suffer such a change?
VOLP. Thou art mine honour, Mosca, and my pride,
My joy, my tickling, my delight! Go bring 'em.
MOS. *(Advancing).* Please you draw near, sir.
CORV. Come on, what— 70
You will not be rebellious? By that light—
MOS. Sir, Signior Corvino, here, is come to see you.
VOLP. Oh!
MOS. And hearing of the consultation had,
So lately, for your health, is come to offer,
Or rather, sir, to prostitute—
CORV. Thanks, sweet Mosca.
MOS. Freely, unask'd, or unintreated—
CORV. Well.
MOS. As the true fervent instance of his love,
His own most fair and proper wife; the beauty
Only of price in Venice—
CORV. 'T is well urg'd.
MOS. To be your comfortress, and to preserve you. 80
VOLP. Alas, I am past, already! Pray you, thank him
For his good care and promptness; but for that,
'T is a vain labour e'en to fight 'gainst heaven;
Applying fire to a stone—uh, uh, uh, uh! *(Coughing.)*
Making a dead leaf grow again. I take

48. *jig:* farce.   79. *Only of price:* unparalleled.

    His wishes gently, though; and you may tell him
    What I have done for him: marry, my state is hopeless.
    Will him to pray for me; and t' use his fortune
    With reverence when he comes to 't.
MOS.   Do you hear, sir?
    Go to him with your wife.
CORV.   Heart of my father!
    Wilt thou persist thus? Come, I pray thee, come.
    Thou seest 't is nothing, Celia. By this hand
    I shall grow violent. Come, do 't, I say.
CEL.   Sir, kill me, rather: I will take down poison,
    Eat burning coals, do anything—
CORV.   Be damn'd!
    Heart, I will drag thee hence home by the hair;
    Cry thee a strumpet through the streets; rip up
    Thy mouth unto thine ears; and slit thy nose,
    Like a raw rochet!—Do not tempt me; come,
    Yield, I am loath—Death! I will buy some slave
    Whom I will kill, and bind thee to him alive;
    And at my windore hang you forth, devising
    Some monstrous crime, which I, in capital letters,
    Will eat into thy flesh with aquafortis,
    And burning cor'sives, on this stubborn breast.
    Now, by the blood thou hast incens'd, I 'll do 't!
CEL.   Sir, what you please, you may; I am your martyr.
CORV.   Be not thus obstinate, I ha' not deserv'd it:
    Think who it is intreats you. Pray thee, sweet;—
    Good faith, thou shalt have jewels, gowns, attires,
    What thou wilt think, and ask. Do but go kiss him.
    Or touch him but. For my sake. At my suit—
    This once. No! not! I shall remember this.
    Will you disgrace me thus? Do you thirst my undoing?
MOS.   Nay, gentle lady, be advis'd.
CORV.   No, no.
    She has watch'd her time. God's precious, this is scurvy,
    'T is very scurvy; and you are—
MOS.   Nay, good sir.
CORV.   An arrant locust—by heaven, a locust!—
    Whore, crocodile, that hast thy tears prepar'd,
    Expecting how thou 'lt bid 'em flow—
MOS.   Nay, pray you, sir!
    She will consider.
CEL.   Would my life would serve
    To satisfy—
CORV.   'Sdeath! if she would but speak to him,
    And save my reputation, 't were somewhat;
    But spitefully to affect my utter ruin!

---

99. *rochet:* a fish of a red color.   104. *aquafortis:* nitric acid.

MOS. Ay, now you have put your fortune in her hands.
Why i' faith, it is her modesty, I must quit her.
If you were absent, she would be more coming;
I know it: and dare undertake for her.
What woman can before her husband? Pray you,
Let us depart and leave her here.
CORV.   Sweet Celia,   130
Thou may'st redeem all yet; I'll say no more:
If not, esteem yourself as lost. Nay, stay there. *(Exit with* MOSCA.*)*
CEL. O God, and his good angels! whither, whither,
Is shame fled human breasts? that with such ease,
Men dare put off your honours, and their own?
Is that, which ever was a cause of life,
Now plac'd beneath the basest circumstance,
And modesty an exile made, for money?
VOLP. Ay, in Corvino, and such earth-fed minds, *(He leaps off from
    his couch.)*
That never tasted the true heaven of love.   140
Assure thee, Celia, he that would sell thee,
Only for hope of gain, and that uncertain,
He would have sold his part of Paradise
For ready money, had he met a cope-man.
Why art thou maz'd to see me thus riviv'd?
Rather applaud thy beauty's miracle;
'T is thy great work, that hath, not now alone,
But sundry times rais'd me, in several shapes,
And, but this morning, like a mountebank,
To see thee at thy windore: ay, before   150
I would have left my practice, for thy love,
In varying figures, I would have contended
With the blue Proteus, or the horned flood.
Now art thou welcome.
CEL.   Sir!
VOLP.   Nay, fly me not,
Nor let thy false imagination
That I was bed-rid, make thee think I am so:
Thou shalt not find it. I am now as fresh,
As hot, as high, and in as jovial plight
As, when, in that so celebrated scene,
At recitation of our comedy,   160
For entertainment of the great Valois,
I acted young Antinous; and attracted
The eyes and ears of all the ladies present,
T' admire each graceful gesture, note, and footing. *(Sings.)*

---

126. *quit:* excuse, acquit.   128. *undertake:* promise.   144. *cope-man:* chapman, merchant.   151. *practice:* plotting.   153. *horned flood:* the ocean.   161. *entertainment:* for Henri III of France at Venice in 1574.

SONG

Come, my Celia, let us prove
While we can, the sports of love,
Time will not be ours for ever,
He, at length, our good will sever;
Spend not then his gifts in vain:
Suns that set may rise again; 170
But if once we lose this light,
'T is with us perpetual night.
Why should we defer our joys?
Fame and rumour are but toys.
Cannot we delude the eyes
Of a few poor household spies?
Or his easier ears beguile,
Thus removed by our wile?
'T is no sin love's fruits to steal,
But the sweet thefts to reveal: 180
To be taken, to be seen,
These have crimes accounted been.

CEL. Some serene blast me, or dire lightning strike
   This my offending face!
VOLP.   Why droops my Celia?
Thou hast, in place of a base husband found
A worthy lover: use thy fortune well,
With secrecy and pleasure. See, behold,
What thou art queen of; not in expectation,
As I feed others: but possess'd and crown'd.
See, here, a rope of pearl; and each more orient 190
Than that the brave Aegyptian queen carous'd:
Dissolve and drink 'em. See, a carbuncle,
May put out both the eyes of our St. Mark;
A diamond would have bought Lollia Paulina,
When she came in like star-light, hid with jewels
That were the spoils of provinces; take these
And wear, and lose 'em; yet remains an earring
To purchase them again, and this whole state.
A gem but worth a private patrimony
Is nothing; we will eat such at a meal. 200
The heads of parrots, tongues of nightingales,
The brains of peacocks, and of estriches,
Shall be our food, and, could we get the phœnix,
Though nature lost her kind, she were our dish.
CEL. Good sir, these things might move a mind affected
   With such delights; but I, whose innocence

---

183. *serene:* mildew. 194. *Lollia Paulina:* a Roman heiress. 204. *Though . . . kind:* though this unique bird became thereby extinct.

Is all I can think wealthy, or worth th' enjoying,
And which, once lost, I have nought to lose beyond it,
Cannot be taken with these sensual baits:
If you have conscience—

VOLP. 'T is the beggar's virtue; 210
If thou hast wisdom, hear me, Celia.
Thy baths shall be the juice of July-flowers,
Spirit of roses, and of violets,
The milk of unicorns, and panthers' breath
Gather'd in bags, and mix'd with Cretan wines.
Our drink shall be prepared gold and amber;
Which we will take until my roof whirl round
With the vertigo: and my dwarf shall dance,
My eunuch sing, my fool make up the antic,
Whilst we, in changed shapes, act Ovid's tales, 220
Thou, like Europa now, and I like Jove,
Then I like Mars, and thou like Erycine:
So of the rest, till we have quite run through,
And wearied all the fables of the gods.
Then will I have thee in more modern forms,
Attired like some sprightly dame of France,
Brave Tuscan lady, or proud Spanish beauty;
Sometimes unto the Persian sophy's wife;
Or the grand signior's mistress; and for change,
To one of our most artful courtesans, 230
Or some quick Negro, or cold Russian;
And I will meet thee in as many shapes:
Where we may so transfuse our wand'ring souls
Out at our lips, and score up sums of pleasures, *(Sings.)*

That the curious shall not know
How to tell them as they flow;
And the envious, when they find
What their number is, be pin'd.

CEL. If you have ears that will be pierc'd—or eyes
That can be open'd—a heart may be touch'd— 240
Or any part that yet sounds man about you—
If you have touch of holy saints—or heaven—
Do me the grace to let me scape:—if not,
Be bountiful and kill me. You do know,
I am a creature, hither ill betray'd,
By one whose shame I would forget it were:
If you will deign me neither of these graces,
Yet feed your wrath, sir, rather than your lust,
(It is a vice comes nearer manliness,)

---

219. *antic:* grotesque pageant. 222. *Erycine:* Venus. 228. *sophy:* Shah. 229. *grand signior:* Sultan. 240. *may:* that may.

    And punish that unhappy crime of nature,   250
    Which you miscall my beauty: flay my face,
    Or poison it with ointments for seducing
    Your blood to this rebellion. Rub these hands
    With what may cause an eating leprosy,
    E'en to my bones and marrow: anything
    That may disfavour me, save in my honour—
    And I will kneel to you, pray for you, pay down
    A thousand hourly vows, sir, for your health;
    Report, and think you virtuous—
VOLP.   Think me cold,
    Frozen, and impotent, and so report me?   260
    That I had Nestor's hernia, thou wouldst think.
    I do degenerate, and abuse my nation,
    To play with opportunity thus long;
    I should have done the act, and then have parley'd.
    Yield, or I 'll force thee. *(Seizes her.)*
CEL.   O! just God!
VOLP.   In vain—
BON.   Forbear, foul ravisher! libidinous swine! *(He leaps out from*
    where MOSCA *had plac'd him.)*
    Free the forc'd lady, or thou diest, impostor.
    But that I 'm loath to snatch thy punishment
    Out of the hand of justice, thou shouldst yet
    Be made the timely sacrifice of vengeance,   270
    Before this altar and this dross, thy idol.—
    Lady, let 's quit the place, it is the den
    Of villainy; fear nought, you have a guard:
    And he ere long shall meet his just reward.

Exeunt BON. *and* CEL.

VOLP.   Fall on me, roof, and bury me in ruin!
    Become my grave, that wert my shelter! O!
    I am unmask'd, unspirited, undone,
    Betray'd to beggary, to infamy—

SCENE VIII

    The Same.

MOSCA, VOLPONE

[MOS.] Where shall I run, most wretched shame of men,
    To beat out my unlucky brains?
VOLP.   Here, here.
    What! dost thou bleed?
MOS.   O, that his well-driv'n sword
    Had been so courteous to have cleft me down
    Unto the navel, ere I liv'd to see

My life, my hopes, my spirits, my patron, all
Thus desperately engaged by my error!
VOLP. Woe on thy fortune!
MOS.   And my follies, sir.
VOLP. Th' hast made me miserable.
MOS.   And myself, sir.
Who would have thought he would have hearken'd so?   10
VOLP. What shall we do?
MOS.   I know not; if my heart
Could expiate the mischance, I 'd pluck it out.
Will you be pleas'd to hang me, or cut my throat?
And I 'll requite you, sir. Let 's die like Romans,
Since we have liv'd like Grecians.

They knock without.

VOLP.   Hark! who 's there?
I hear some footing; officers, the saffi,
Come to apprehend us! I do feel the brand
Hissing already at my forehead; now
Mine ears are boring.
MOS.   To your couch, sir, you.
Make that place good, however. *(VOLPONE lies down as before.)*
     Guilty men   20
Suspect what they deserve still. Signior Corbaccio!

SCENE IX

The Same.

CORBACCIO, MOSCA, *(later)* VOLTORE, VOLPONE *(on his couch)*

[CORB.] Why, how now, Mosca?
MOS.   O, undone, amaz'd, sir.
Your son, I know not by what accident,
Acquainted with your purpose to my patron,
Touching your will, and making him your heir,
Ent'red our house with violence, his sword drawn,
Sought for you, call'd you wretch, unnatural,
Vow'd he would kill you.
CORB.   Me!
MOS.   Yes, and my patron.
CORB. This act shall disinherit him indeed:
Here is the will.
MOS.   'T is well, sir.
CORB.   Right and well:
Be you as careful now for me.

---

14. *like Romans:* i.e., by suicide. 15. *like Grecians:* luxuriously. 16. *saffi:* bailiffs.

Enter VOLTORE *behind*

MOS.　　　　　　　　My life, sir,　　　　　　　　　10
　Is not more tender'd; I am only yours.
CORB.　How does he? Will he die shortly, think'st thou?
MOS.　　　　　I fear
　He'll outlast May.
CORB.　　　　　To-day?
MOS.　　　　　　　No, last out May, sir.
CORB.　Couldst thou not gi' him a dram?
MOS.　　　　　　O, by no means, sir.
CORB.　Nay, I'll not bid you.
VOLT. *(Coming forward)*.　This is a knave, I see.
MOS. *(Aside, seeing* VOLT.*)*.　How! Signior Voltore! did he hear me?
VOLT.　　　　　Parasite!
MOS.　Who's that?—O, sir, most timely welcome—
VOLT.　　　　　Scarce,
　To the discovery of your tricks, I fear.
　You are his, *only?* And mine also, are you not?
MOS.　Who? I, sir!
VOLT.　　　　　You, sir. What device is this　　　　20
　About a will?
MOS.　　　　　A plot for you, sir.
VOLT.　　　　　Come,
　Put not your foists upon me; I shall scent 'em.
MOS.　Did you not hear it?
VOLT.　　　　　Yes, I hear Corbaccio
　Hath made your patron there his heir.
MOS.　　　　　'T is true,
　By my device, drawn to it by my plot.
　With hope—
VOLT.　　　　　Your patron should reciprocate?
　And you have promis'd?
MOS.　　　　　For your good I did, sir.
　Nay, more, I told his son, brought, hid him here,
　Where he might hear his father pass the deed;
　Being persuaded to it by this thought, sir,　　　30
　That the unnaturalness, first, of the act,
　And then his father's oft disclaiming in him,
　(Which I did mean t' help on), would sure enrage him
　To do some violence upon his parent,
　On which the law should take sufficient hold,
　And you be stated in a double hope.
　Truth be my comfort, and my conscience,
　My only aim was to dig you a fortune

11. *tender'd:* cared for.　22. *foists:* deceits.

Out of these two old rotten sepulchres—
VOLT. I cry thee mercy, Mosca.
MOS.   —Worth your patience,   40
And your great merit, sir. And see the change!
VOLT. Why, what success?
MOS.   Most hapless! you must help, sir.
Whilst we expected th' old raven, in comes
Corvino's wife, sent hither by her husband—
VOLT. What, with a present?
MOS.   No, sir, on visitation;
(I 'll tell you how anon;) and staying long,
The youth he grows impatient, rushes forth,
Seizeth the lady, wounds me, makes her swear
(Or he would murder her, that was his vow)
T' affirm my patron to have done her rape: 50
Which how unlike it is, you see! and hence,
With that pretext he 's gone, t' accuse his father,
Defame my patron, defeat you—
VOLT.   Where 's her husband?
Let him be sent for straight.
MOS.   Sir, I 'll go fetch him.
VOLT. Bring him to the Scrutineo.
MOS.   Sir, I will.
VOLT. This must be stopp'd.
MOS.   O you do nobly, sir.
Alas, 't was labour'd all, sir, for your good;
Nor was there want of counsel in the plot:
But Fortune can, at any time, o'erthrow
The projects of a hundred learned clerks, sir.   60
CORB. *(Listening).* What 's that?
VOLT.   Wilt please you, sir, to go along?

Exit CORBACCIO, *followed by* VOLTORE.

MOS. Patron, go in, and pray for our success.
VOLP. *(Rising from his couch).* Need makes devotion: heaven your
labour bless!

Exeunt.

40. *cry ... mercy:* beg your pardon.   55. *Scrutineo:* Senate House.

ACT IV

SCENE I

A Street.

POLITIC, PEREGRINE

[SIR P.]   I told you, sir, it was a plot; you see
   What observation is! You mention'd me
   For some instructions: I will tell you, sir,
   (Since we are met here in this height of Venice,)
   Some few particulars I have set down,
   Only for this meridian, fit to be known
   Of your crude traveller; and they are these.
   I will not touch, sir, at your phrase, or clothes,
   For they are old.
PER.   Sir, I have better.
SIR P.   Pardon,
   I meant, as they are themes.
PER.   O, sir, proceed: 10
   I'll slander you no more of wit, good sir.
SIR P.   First, for your garb, it must be grave and serious,
   Very reserv'd and lock'd; not tell a secret
   On any terms, not to your father; scarce
   A fable, but with caution: make sure choice
   Both of your company and discourse; beware
   You never speak a truth—
PER.   How!
SIR P.   Not to strangers,
   For those be they you must converse with most;
   Others I would not know, sir, but at distance
   So as I still might be a saver in 'em: 20
   You shall have tricks else pass'd upon you hourly.
   And then, for your religion, profess none,
   But wonder at the diversity of all;
   And, for your part, protest, were there no other
   But simply the laws o' th' land, you could content you.
   Nick Machiavel and Monsieur Bodin, both
   Were of this mind. Then must you learn the use
   And handling of your silver fork at meals,
   The metal of your glass; (these are main matters
   With your Italian;) and to know the hour   30
   When you must eat your melons and your figs.
PER.   Is that a point of state too?

---

10. *themes:* subjects to discuss.   13. *lock'd:* reticent.   26. *Bodin:* a French writer on politics (1530-1596).

SIR P. Here it is:
  For your Venetian, if he see a man
  Preposterous in the least, he has him straight;
  He has; he strips him. I 'll acquaint you, sir.
  I now have liv'd here 't is some fourteen months:
  Within the first week of my landing here,
  All took me for a citizen of Venice,
  I knew the forms so well—
PER. *(Aside).* And nothing else.
SIR P. I had read Contarene, took me a house, 40
  Dealt with my Jews to furnish it with movables—
  Well, if I could but find one man, one man
  To mine own heart, whom I durst trust, I would—
PER. What, what, sir?
SIR P. Make him rich; make him a fortune:
  He should not think again. I would command it.
PER. As how?
SIR P. With certain projects that I have;
  Which I may not discover.
PER. *(Aside).* If I had
  But one to wager with, I would lay odds now,
  He tells me instantly.
SIR P. One is, and that
  I care not greatly who knows, to serve the state 50
  Of Venice with red herrings for three years,
  And at a certain rate, from Rotterdam,
  Where I have correspondence. There 's a letter,
  Sent me from one o' th' states, and to that purpose:
  He cannot write his name, but that 's his mark.
PER. He is a chandler?
SIR P. No, a cheesemonger.
  There are some other too with whom I treat
  About the same negotiation;
  And I will undertake it: for 't is thus.
  I 'll do 't with ease, I have cast it all. Your hoy 60

---

40. *Contarene:* Gasparo Contarini (1483-1542), cardinal, diplomatist, and writer on Venice. 45. *think:* i.e., about money. 60. *cast:* calculated. *hoy:* small sloop.

Carries but three men in her, and a boy;
And she shall make me three returns a year:
So if there come but one of three, I save;
If two, I can defalk:—but this is now,
If my main project fail.
PER.   Then you have others?
SIR P. I should be loath to draw the subtle air
Of such a place, without my thousand aims.
I 'll not dissemble, sir: where'er I come,
I love to be considerative; and 't is true,
I have at my free hours thought upon   70
Some certain goods unto the state of Venice,
Which I do call my Cautions; and, sir, which
I mean, in hope of pension, to propound
To the Great Council, then unto the Forty,
So to the Ten. My means are made already—
PER. By whom?
SIR P.   Sir, one that though his place be obscure,
Yet he can sway, and they will hear him. He 's
A *commandadore.*
PER.   What! a common sergeant?
SIR P. Sir, such as they are, put it in their mouths,
What they should say, sometimes; as well as greater: 80
I think I have my notes to show you— *(Searching his pockets.)*
PER.   Good sir.
SIR P. But you shall swear unto me, on your gentry,
Not to anticipate—
PER.   I, sir!
SIR P.   Nor reveal
A circumstance—My paper is not with me.
PER. O, but you can remember, sir.
SIR P.   My first is
Concerning tinder-boxes. You must know,
No family is here without its box.
Now, sir, it being so portable a thing,
Put case, that you or I were ill affected
Unto the state, sir; with it in our pockets,   90
Might not I go into the Arsenal,
Or you? come out again, and none the wiser?
PER. Except yourself, sir.
SIR P.   Go to, then. I therefore
Advertise to the state, how fit it were
That none but such as were known patriots,
Sound lovers of their country, should be suffer'd
T' enjoy them in their houses; and even those
Seal'd at some office, and at such a bigness

---

64. *defalk:* make a reduction. 69. *considerative:* thoughtful. 89. *Put case:* suppose.

    As might not lurk in pockets.
PER.   Admirable!
SIR P.   My next is, how t' inquire, and be resolv'd
    By present demonstration, whether a ship,
    Newly arriv'd from Soria, or from
    Any suspected part of all the Levant,
    Be guilty of the plague: and where they use
    To lie out forty, fifty days, sometimes,
    About the Lazaretto, for their trial;
    I'll save that charge and loss unto the merchant,
    And in an hour clear the doubt.
PER.   Indeed, sir!
SIR P.   Or—I will lose my labour.
PER.   My faith, that's much.
SIR P.   Nay, sir, conceive me. 'T will cost me, in onions,
    Some thirty livres—
PER.   Which is one pound sterling.
SIR P.   Beside my waterworks: for this I do, sir.
    First, I bring in your ship 'twixt two brick walls;
    But those the state shall venter. On the one
    I strain me a fair tarpaulin, and in that
    I stick my onions, cut in halves; the other
    Is full of loopholes, out at which I thrust
    The noses of my bellows; and those bellows
    I keep, with waterworks, in perpetual motion,
    Which is the easiest matter of a hundred.
    Now, sir, your onion, which doth naturally
    Attract th' infection, and your bellows blowing
    The air upon him, will show instantly,
    By his chang'd colour, if there be contagion;
    Or else remain as fair as at the first.
    Now 't is known, 't is nothing.
PER.   You are right, sir.
SIR P.   I would I had my note.
PER.   Faith, so would I:
    But you ha' done well for once, sir.
SIR P.   Were I false,
    Or would be made so, I could show you reasons
    How I could sell this state now to the Turk,
    Spite of their galleys, or their—*(Examining his papers.)*
PER.   Pray you, Sir Pol.
SIR P.   I have 'em not about me.
PER.   That I fear'd.
    They are there, sir?
SIR P.   No, this is my diary,
    Wherein I note my actions of the day.

---

102. *Soria:* Syria. 106. *Lazaretto:* building or ship used for quarantine. 111. *livres:* French coins. 114. *venter:* invest in. 115. *strain:* stretch.

PER. Pray you, let's see, sir. What is here? "*Notandum: (Reads.)*
A rat had gnawn my spur-leathers; notwithstanding,
I put on new, and did go forth; but first
I threw three beans over the threshold. *Item,*
I went and bought two toothpicks, whereof one
I burst immediately, in a discourse   140
With a Dutch merchant, 'bout *ragion' del stato.*
From him I went and paid a *moccinigo*
For piecing my silk stockings; by the way
I cheapen'd sprats; and at St. Mark's I urin'd."
'Faith these are politic notes!
SIR P.   Sir, I do slip
No action of my life, thus, but I quote it.
PER. Believe me, it is wise!
SIR P.   Nay, sir, read forth.

SCENE II

The Same.

LADY [POLITIC WOULD-BE], NANO, WOMEN, [SIR] POLITIC, PEREGRINE

[LADY P.] Where should this loose knight be, trow? Sure he's hous'd.
NAN. Why, then he's fast.
LADY P.   Ay, he plays both with me.
I pray you stay. This heat will do more harm
To my complexion than his heart is worth.
(I do not care to hinder, but to take him.)
How it comes off! *(Rubbing her cheeks.)*
1 WOM.   My master's yonder.
LADY P.   Where?
2 WOM.   With a young gentleman.
LADY P.   That same's the party:
In man's apparel! Pray you, sir, jog my knight:
I will be tender to his reputation,
However he demerit.
SIR P. *(Seeing her).*   My lady!
PER.   Where?   10
SIR P. 'T is she indeed, sir; you shall know her. She is,
Were she not mine, a lady of that merit,
For fashion and behaviour; and for beauty
I durst compare—
PER.   It seems you are not jealous,
That dare commend her.
SIR P.   Nay, and for discourse—
PER. Being your wife, she cannot miss that.

---

141. *ragion' del stato:* politics.   144. *cheapen'd:* bargained for.   2. *both:* i.e., fast and loose.

SIR P. *(Introducing* PER.*).* Madam,
  Here is a gentleman, pray you, use him fairly;
  He seems a youth, but he is—
LADY P.   None?
SIR P.   Yes, one
  Has put his face as soon into the world—
LADY P. You mean, as early? But to-day?
SIR P.   How 's this?   20
LADY P. Why, in this habit, sir; you apprehend me.
  Well, Master Would-be, this doth not become you;
  I had thought the odour, sir, of your good name
  Had been more precious to you; that you would not
  Have done this dire massácre on your honour;
  One of your gravity, and rank besides!
  But knights, I see, care little for the oath
  They make to ladies; chiefly their own ladies.
SIR P. Now, by my spurs, the symbol of my knighthood—
PER. *(Aside).* Lord, how his brain is humbled for an oath!   30
SIR P. I reach you not.
LADY P.   Right, sir, your polity
  May bear it through thus. Sir, a word with you. *(To* PER.*)*
  I would be loath to contest publicly
  With any gentlewoman, or to seem
  Froward, or violent, as the courtier says;
  It comes too near rusticity in a lady,
  Which I would shun by all means: and however
  I may deserve from Master Would-be, yet
  T' have one fair gentlewoman thus be made
  The unkind instrument to wrong another,   40
  And one she knows not, ay, and to persever;
  In my poor judgment, is not warranted
  From being a solecism in our sex,
  If not in manners.
PER.   How is this!
SIR P.   Sweet madam,
  Come nearer to your aim.
LADY P.   Marry, and will, sir.
  Since you provoke me with your impudence,
  And laughter of your light land-siren here,
  Your Sporus, your hermaphrodite—
PER.   What 's here?
  Poetic fury and historic storms!
SIR P. The gentleman, believe it, is of worth   50
  And of our nation.
LADY P.   Ay, your Whitefriars nation.
  Come, I blush for you, Master Would-be, I;

31. *reach:* understand. 51. *Whitefriars:* a part of London where malefactors were immune from arrest.

          And am asham'd you should ha' no more forehead
          Than thus to be the patron, or St. George,
          To a lewd harlot, a base fricatrice,
          A female devil, in a male outside.
SIR P.   Nay,
   An you be such a one, I must bid adieu
   To your delights. The case appears too liquid. *(Exit.)*
LADY P. Ay, you may carry 't clear, with your state-face!
   But for your carnival concupiscence,   60
   Who here is fled for liberty of conscience,
   From furious persecution of the marshal,
   Her will I disc'ple.
PER.   This is fine, i' faith!
   And do you use this often? Is this part
   Of your wit's exercise, 'gainst you have occasion?
   Madam—
LADY P. Go to, sir.
PER.   Do you hear me, lady?
   Why, if your knight have set you to beg shirts,
   Or to invite me home, you might have done it
   A nearer way by far.
LADY P.   This cannot work you
   Out of my snare.
PER.   Why, am I in it, then?   70
   Indeed your husband told me you were fair,
   And so you are; only your nose inclines,
   That side that's next the sun, to the queen-apple.
LADY P. This cannot be endur'd by any patience.

                          SCENE III

              The Same.

MOSCA, LADY [POLITIC WOULD-BE], PEREGRINE

[MOS.] What's the matter, madam?
LADY P.   If the senate
   Right not my quest in this, I will protest 'em
   To all the world no aristocracy.
MOS. What is the injury, lady?
LADY P.   Why, the callet
   You told me of, here I have ta'en disguis'd.
MOS. Who? this! what means your ladyship? The creature
   I mention'd to you is apprehended now,
   Before the senate; you shall see her—
LADY P.   Where?

---

53. *forehead:* sense of shame. 55. *fricatrice:* prostitute. 58. *liquid:* clear. 63. *disc'ple:* discipline, punish. 73. *queen-apple:* this apple is red on the side toward the sun. 4. *callet:* wanton.

MOS. I'll bring you to her. This young gentleman,
  I saw him land this morning at the port.   10
LADY P. Is't possible! how has my judgment wander'd?
  Sir, I must, blushing, say to you, I have err'd;
  And plead your pardon.
PER.   What, more changes yet!
LADY P. I hope you ha' not the malice to remember
  A gentlewoman's passion. If you stay
  In Venice here, please you to use me, sir—
MOS. Will you go, madam?
LADY P.   Pray you, sir, use me; in faith,
  The more you see me the more I shall conceive
  You have forgot our quarrel.

Exeunt LADY WOULD-BE, MOSCA, NANO, *and* WAITING-WOMEN

PER.   This is rare!
  Sir Politic Would-be? No, Sir Politic Bawd,   20
  To bring me thus acquainted with his wife!
  Well, wise Sir Pol, since you have practis'd thus
  Upon my freshman-ship, I'll try your salt-head,
  What proof it is against a counter-plot. *(Exit.)*

SCENE IV

The Scrutineo.

VOLTORE, CORBACCIO, CORVINO, MOSCA

[VOLT.] Well, now you know the carriage of the business,
  Your constancy is all that is requir'd
  Unto the safety of it.
MOS.   Is the lie
  Safely convey'd amongst us? Is that sure?
  Knows every man his burden?
CORV.   Yes.
MOS.   Then shrink not.
CORV. But knows the advocate the truth?
MOS.   O, sir,
  By no means; I devis'd a formal tale,
  That salv'd your reputation. But be valiant, sir.
CORV. I fear no one but him, that this his pleading
  Should make him stand for a co-heir—
MOS.   Co-halter!   10
  Hang him; we will but use his tongue, his noise,
  As we do croaker's here.

23. *salt-head:* the opposite of "freshman." 1. *carriage:* purpose, conduct. 4. *convey'd:* communicated. 5. *burden:* the refrain he has to sing. 12. *croaker's:* Corbaccio's.

CORV. Ay, what shall he do?
MOS. When we ha' done, you mean?
CORV. Yes.
MOS. Why, we 'll think;
  Sell him for mummia: he 's half dust already.—
  Do not you smile, to see this buffalo, *(To* VOLTORE.*)*
  How he doth sport it with his head? *(Aside.)* I should,
  If all were well and past.—Sir, only you *(To* CORBACCIO.*)*
  Are he that shall enjoy the crop of all,
  And these not know for whom they toil.
CORB. Ay, peace.
MOS. But you shall eat it. *(Aside.)* Much!—Worshipful sir, *(To*   20
  CORVINO, *then to* VOLTORE *again.)*
  Mercury sit upon your thund'ring tongue,
  Or the French Hercules, and make your language
  As conquering as his club, to beat along,
  As with a tempest, flat, our adversaries:
  But much more yours, sir.
VOLT. Here they come, ha' done.
MOS. I have another witness, if you need, sir,
  I can produce.
VOLT. Who is it?
MOS. Sir, I have her.

SCENE V

The Same.

4 AVOCATORI, BONARIO, CELIA, VOLTORE, CORBACCIO, CORVINO, MOSCA, NOTARIO, COMMANDADORI

[1 AVOC.] The like of this the senate never heard of.
2 AVOC. 'T will come most strange to them when we report it.
4 AVOC. The gentlewoman has been ever held
  Of unreproved name.
3 AVOC. So the young man.
4 AVOC. The more unnatural part that of his father.
2 AVOC. More of the husband.
1 AVOC. I not know to give
  His act a name, it is so monstrous!
4 AVOC. But the impostor, he is a thing created
  T' exceed example!
1 AVOC. And all after-times!
2 AVOC. I never heard a true voluptuary   10
  Describ'd but him.

---

14. *mummia:* a drug supposed to be derived from mummies. 15. *buffalo:* horned beast. 20. *Much:* i.e., much chance you have of doing so! 22. *French Hercules:* Ogmius, a symbol of eloquence.

3 AVOC.   Appear yet those were cited?
NOT. All but the old magnifico, Volpone.
1 AVOC. Why is not he here?
MOS.   Please your fatherhoods,
  Here is his advocate: himself 's so weak,
  So feeble—
4 AVOC.   Who are you?
BON.   His parasite,
  His knave, his pandar. I beseech the court
  He may be forc'd to come, that your grave eyes
  May bear strong witness of his strange impostures.
VOLT. Upon my faith and credit with your virtues,
  He is not able to endure the air.   20
2 AVOC. Bring him, however.
3 AVOC.   We will see him.
4 AVOC.   Fetch him.
VOLT. Your fatherhoods' fit pleasures be obey'd; *(Exeunt* OFFICERS.*)*
  But sure, the sight will rather move your pities
  Than indignation. May it please the court,
  In the mean time, he may be heard in me.
  I know this place most void of prejudice,
  And therefore crave it, since we have no reason
  To fear our truth should hurt our cause.
3 AVOC.   Speak free.
VOLT. Then know, most honour'd fathers, I must now
  Discover to your strangely abused ears,   30
  The most prodigious and most frontless piece
  Of solid impudence, and treachery,
  That ever vicious nature yet brought forth
  To shame the state of Venice. This lewd woman,
  That wants no artificial looks or tears
  To help the vizor she has now put on,
  Hath long been known a close adulteress
  To that lascivious youth there; not suspected,
  I say, but known, and taken in the act
  With him; and by this man, the easy husband,   40
  Pardon'd; whose timeless bounty makes him now
  Stand here, the most unhappy, innocent person,
  That ever man's own goodness made accus'd.
  For these, not knowing how to owe a gift
  Of that dear grace, but with their shame; being plac'd
  So above all powers of their gratitude,
  Began to hate the benefit; and in place
  Of thanks, devise t' extirp the memory
  Of such an act: wherein I pray your fatherhoods
  To observe the malice, yea, the rage of creatures   50
  Discover'd in their evils: and what heart

---

31. *frontless:* shameless.   41. *timeless:* untimely.   44. *owe:* own.

Such take, ev'n from their crimes:—but that anon
Will more appear.—This gentleman, the father,
Hearing of this foul fact, with many others,
Which daily struck at his too tender ears,
And griev'd in nothing more than that he could not
Preserve himself a parent (his son's ills
Growing to that strange flood), at last decreed
To disinherit him.
1 AVOC.   These be strange turns!
2 AVOC. The young man's fame was ever fair and honest.   60
VOLT. So much more full of danger is his vice,
That can beguile so, under shade of virtue.
But, as I said, my honour'd sires, his father
Having this settled purpose, by what means
To him betray'd, we know not, and this day
Appointed for the deed; that parricide,
I cannot style him better, by confederacy
Preparing this his paramour to be there,
Ent'red Volpone's house (who was the man,
Your fatherhoods must understand, design'd   70
For the inheritance), there sought his father:—
But with what purpose sought he him, my lords?
I tremble to pronounce it, that a son
Unto a father, and to such a father,
Should have so foul, felonious intent!
It was to murder him: when being prevented
By his more happy absence, what then did he?
Not check his wicked thoughts; no, now new deeds;
(Mischief doth ever end where it begins)
An act of horror, fathers! He dragg'd forth   80
The aged gentleman that had there lien bed-rid
Three years and more, out of his innocent couch,
Naked upon the floor; there left him; wounded
His servant in the face; and with this strumpet,
The stale to his forg'd practice, who was glad
To be so active,—(I shall here desire
Your fatherhoods to note but my collections,
As most remarkable,—) thought at once to stop
His father's ends, discredit his free choice
In the old gentleman, redeem themselves,   90
By laying infamy upon this man,
To whom, with blushing, they should owe their lives.
1 AVOC. What proofs have you of this?
BON.   Most honour'd fathers,
I humbly crave there be no credit given

---

54. *fact:* deed. 79. *Mischief . . . begins:* mischief, once begun, always fulfills itself. (Modern editors change "ever" to "never.") 85. *stale:* stalking horse. 87. *collections:* evidences.

To this man's mercenary tongue.
2 AVOC. Forbear.
BON. His soul moves in his fee.
3 AVOC. O, sir.
BON. This fellow,
For six sols more would plead against his Maker.
1 AVOC. You do forget yourself.
VOLT. Nay, nay, grave fathers,
Let him have scope: can any man imagine
That he will spare his accuser, that would not   100
Have spar'd his parent?
1 AVOC. Well, produce your proofs.
CEL. I would I could forget I were a creature.
VOLT. Signior Corbaccio!

CORBACCIO *comes forward.*

4 AVOC. What is he?
VOLT. The father.
2 AVOC. Has he had an oath?
NOT. Yes.
CORB. What must I do now?
NOT. Your testimony 's crav'd.
CORB. Speak to the knave?
I 'll ha' my mouth first stopp'd with earth; my heart
Abhors his knowledge: I disclaim in him.
1 AVOC. But for what cause?
CORB. The mere portent of nature!
He is an utter stranger to my loins.
BON. Have they made you to this?
CORB. I will not hear thee,   110
Monster of men, swine, goat, wolf, parricide!
Speak not, thou viper.
BON. Sir, I will sit down,
And rather wish my innocence should suffer
Than I resist the authority of a father.
VOLT. Signior Corvino!

CORVINO *comes forward.*

2 AVOC. This is strange.
1 AVOC. Who 's this?
NOT. The husband.
4 AVOC. Is he sworn?
NOT. He is.
3 AVOC. Speak then.

97. *sols:* small coins, sous.   107. *disclaim in:* disown.   110. *made:* prepared.

CORV. This woman, please your fatherhoods, is a whore,
  Of most hot exercise, more than a partridge,
  Upon record—
1 AVOC.   No more.
CORV.   Neighs like a jennet.
NOT. Preserve the honour of the court.
CORV.   I shall,   120
  And modesty of your most reverend ears.
  And yet I hope that I may say, these eyes
  Have seen her glu'd unto that piece of cedar,
  That fine well timber'd gallant: and that here
  The letters may be read, thorough the horn,
  That make the story perfect.
MOS.   Excellent! sir.
CORV. *(Aside to* MOSCA*).* There is no shame in this now, is there?
MOS.   None.
CORV. Or if I said, I hop'd that she were onward
  To her damnation, if there be a hell   130
  Greater than whore and woman, a good Catholic
  May make the doubt.
3 AVOC.   His grief hath made him frantic.
1 AVOC. Remove him hence.
2 AVOC.   Look to the woman.

She swoons.

CORV.   Rare
  Prettily feign'd again!
4 AVOC.   Stand from about her.
1 AVOC. Give her the air.
3 AVOC.   What can you say? *(To* MOSCA.*)*
MOS.   My wound,
  May 't please your wisdoms, speaks for me, receiv'd
  In aid of my good patron, when he miss'd
  His sought-for father, when that well-taught dame
  Had her cue giv'n her to cry out, "A rape!"
BON. O most laid impudence! Fathers—
3 AVOC.   Sir, be silent;
  You had your hearing free, so must they theirs.   140
2 AVOC. I do begin to doubt th' imposture here.
4 AVOC. This woman has too many moods.
VOLT.   Grave fathers,
  She is a creature of a most profess'd
  And prostituted lewdness.
CORV.   Most impetuous,
  Unsatisfi'd, grave fathers!
VOLT.   May her feignings

---

125. *horn:* of a hornbook and of a cuckold.   139. *laid:* carefully contrived.

Not take your wisdoms: but this day she baited
A stranger, a grave knight, with her loose eyes,
And more lascivious kisses. This man saw 'em
Together on the water, in a gondola.
MOS. Here is the lady herself, that saw 'em too, 150
Without; who then had in the open streets
Pursu'd them, but for saving her knight's honour.
1 AVOC. Produce that lady.
2 AVOC.   Let her come. *(Exit* MOSCA.*)*
4 AVOC.   These things,
They strike with wonder.
3 AVOC.   I am turn'd a stone.

SCENE VI

The Same.

MOSCA, LADY [POLITIC WOULD-BE], AVOCATORI, &c.

MOS. Be resolute, madam.
LADY P.   Ay, this same is she.

(Pointing to CELIA.*)*

Out, thou chameleon harlot! now thine eyes
Vie tears with the hyena. Dar'st thou look
Upon my wronged face? I cry your pardons,
I fear I have forgettingly trangress'd
Against the dignity of the court—
2 AVOC.   No, madam:
LADY P. And been exorbitant—
1 AVOC.   You have not, lady.
4 AVOC. These proofs are strong.
LADY P.   Surely, I had no purpose
To scandalize your honours, or my sex's.
3 AVOC. We do believe it.
LADY P.   Surely you may believe it. 10
2 AVOC. Madam, we do.
LADY P.   Indeed you may; my breeding
Is not so coarse—
4 AVOC. We know it.
LADY P.   To offend
With pertinacy—
3 AVOC.   Lady—
LADY P.   Such a presence!
No surely.
1 AVOC. We well think it.
LADY P.   You may think it.
1 AVOC. Let her o'ercome. What witnesses have you
To make good your report?

BON. Our consciences.
CEL. And heaven, that never fails the innocent.
4 AVOC. These are no testimonies.
BON. Not in your courts,
  Where multitude and clamour overcomes.
1 AVOC. Nay, then you do wax insolent.

VOLPONE *is brought in, as impotent*

VOLT. Here, here,
  The testimony comes that will convince,
  And put to utter dumbness their bold tongues!
  See here, grave fathers, here's the ravisher,
  The rider on men's wives, the great impostor,
  The grand voluptuary! Do you not think
  These limbs should affect venery? or these eyes
  Covet a concubine? Pray you, mark these hands;
  Are they not fit to stroke a lady's breasts?
  Perhaps he doth dissemble!
BON. So he does.
VOLT. Would you ha' him tortur'd?
BON. I would have him prov'd.
VOLT. Best try him then with goads, or burning irons;
  Put him to the strappado: I have heard
  The rack hath cur'd the gout; faith, give it him,
  And help him of a malady; be courteous.
  I'll undertake, before these honour'd fathers,
  He shall have yet as many left diseases,
  As she has known adulterers, or thou strumpets.
  O, my most equal hearers, if these deeds,
  Acts of this bold and most exorbitant strain,
  May pass with suff'rance, what one citizen
  But owes the forfeit of his life, yea, fame,
  To him that dares traduce him? Which of you
  Are safe, my honour'd fathers? I would ask,
  With leave of your grave fatherhoods, if their plot
  Have any face or colour like to truth?
  Or if, unto the dullest nostril here,
  It smell not rank, and most abhorred slander?
  I crave your care of this good gentleman,
  Whose life is much endanger'd by their fable;
  And as for them, I will conclude with this,
  That vicious persons, when they're hot, and flesh'd
  In impious acts, their constancy abounds:
  Damn'd deeds are done with greatest confidence.
1 AVOC. Take 'em to custody, and sever them.
2 AVOC. 'T is pity two such prodigies should live.

32. *strappado:* a cruel form of torture. 38. *equal:* impartial.

398 Volpone

1 AVOC. Let the old gentleman be return'd with care.

Exeunt OFFICERS *with* VOLPONE.

    I'm sorry our credulity wrong'd him.
4 AVOC. These are two creatures!
3 AVOC.   I have an earthquake in me.
2 AVOC. Their shame, ev'n in their cradles, fled their faces.
4 AVOC. You 've done a worthy service to the state, sir,   60
  In their discovery. *(To* VOLT.*)*
1 AVOC.   You shall hear, ere night,
  What punishment the court decrees upon 'em.
VOLT. We thank your fatherhoods.

Exeunt AVOCAT., NOT., *and* OFFICERS *with* BONARIO *and* CELIA.

            How like you it?
MOS.   Rare.
  I'd ha' your tongue, sir, tipp'd with gold for this;
  I 'd ha' you be the heir to the whole city;
  The earth I 'd have want men ere you want living:
  They 're bound to erect your statue in St. Mark's.
  Signior Corvino, I would have you go
  And show yourself that you have conquer'd.
CORV.   Yes.
MOS. It was much better that you should profess   70
  Yourself a cuckold thus, than that the other
  Should have been prov'd.
CORV.   Nay, I consider'd that:
  Now it is her fault.
MOS.   Then it had been yours.
CORV. True; I do doubt this advocate still.
MOS.   I' faith,
  You need not, I dare ease you of that care.
CORV. I trust thee, Mosca. *(Exit.)*
MOS.   As your own soul, sir.
CORB.   Mosca!
MOS. Now for your business, sir.
CORB.   How! ha' you business?
MOS. Yes, yours, sir.
CORB.   O, none else?
MOS.   None else, not I.
CORB. Be careful, then.
MOS.   Rest you with both your eyes, sir.
CORB. Dispatch it.
MOS.   Instantly.
CORB.   And look that all,   80

---

79. *Rest . . . eyes:* leave the matter to me.

Whatever, be put in, jewels, plate, moneys,
Household stuff, bedding, curtains.
MOS.   Curtain-rings, sir:
Only the advocate's fee must be deducted.
CORB. I 'll pay him now; you 'll be too prodigal.
MOS. Sir, I must tender it.
CORB.   Two cecchines is well.
MOS. No, six, sir.
CORB.   'T is too much.
MOS.   He talk'd a great while;
You must consider that, sir.
CORB.   Well, there 's three—
MOS. I 'll give it him.
CORB. Do so, and there 's for thee. *(Exit.)*
MOS. *(Aside).* Bountiful bones! What horrid strange offence
Did he commit 'gainst nature, in his youth,   90
Worthy this age?—You see, sir, *(to* VOLT.*)* how I work
Unto your ends; take you no notice.
VOLT.   No,
I'll leave you.
MOS.   All is yours, the devil and all,
Good advocate!—Madam, I 'll bring you home.
LADY P. No, I 'll go see your patron.
MOS.   That you shall not:
I 'll tell you why. My purpose is to urge
My patron to reform his will, and for
The zeal you 've shown to-day, whereas before
You were but third or fourth, you shall be now
Put in the first; which would appear as begg'd   100
If you were present. Therefore—
LADY P. You shall sway me.

Exeunt.

ACT V

SCENE I

Volpone's House.

VOLPONE

Well, I am here, and all this brunt is past.
I ne'er was in dislike with my disguise
Till this fled moment: here 't was good, in private;

1. *brunt:* crisis.

But in your public,—*cave* whilst I breathe.
'Fore God, my left leg 'gan to have the cramp,
And I apprehended straight some power had struck me
With a dead palsy. Well! I must be merry,
And shake it off. A many of these fears
Would put me into some villainous disease,
Should they come thick upon me: I'll prevent 'em. 10
Give me a bowl of lusty wine, to fright
This humour from my heart. *(He drinks.)* Hum, hum, hum!
'T is almost gone already; I shall conquer.
Any device now of rare ingenious knavery,
That would possess me with a violent laughter,
Would make me up again. So, so, so, so! *(Drinks again.)*
This heat is life; 't is blood by this time:—Mosca!

SCENE II

The Same.

MOSCA, VOLPONE, *[and later]* NANO, CASTRONE

[MOS.]   How now, sir? Does the day look clear again?
   Are we recover'd, and wrought out of error,
   Into our way, to see our path before us?
   Is our trade free once more?
VOLP.   Exquisite Mosca!
MOS.   Was it not carri'd learnedly?
VOLP.   And stoutly:
   Good wits are greatest in extremities.
MOS.   It were a folly beyond thought to trust
   Any grand act unto a cowardly spirit.
   You are not taken with it enough, methinks.
VOLP.   O, more than if I had enjoy'd the wench: 10
   The pleasure of all woman-kind 's not like it.
MOS.   Why, now you speak, sir. We must here be fix'd;
   Here we must rest; this is our masterpiece;
   We cannot think to go beyond this.
VOLP.   True,
   Thou hast play'd thy prize, my precious Mosca.
MOS.   Nay, sir,
   To gull the court—
VOLP.   And quite divert the torrent
   Upon the innocent.
MOS.   Yes, and to make
   So rare a music out of discords—
VOLP.   Right.
   That yet to me 's the strangest, how th' hast borne it!

4. *cave:* beware.

    That these, being so divided 'mongst themselves,   20
    Should not scent somewhat, or in me or thee,
    Or doubt their own side.
MOS.   True, they will not see 't.
    Too much light blinds 'em, I think. Each of 'em
    Is so possess'd and stuff'd with his own hopes
    That anything unto the contrary,
    Never so true, or never so apparent,
    Never so palpable, they will resist it—
VOLP. Like a temptation of the devil.
MOS.   Right, sir.
    Merchants may talk of trade, and your great signiors
    Of land that yields well; but if Italy   30
    Have any glebe more fruitful than these fellows,
    I am deceiv'd. Did not your advocate rare?
VOLP. O—"My most honour'd fathers, my grave fathers,
    Under correction of your fatherhoods,
    What face of truth is here? If these strange deeds
    May pass, most honour'd fathers"—I had much ado
    To forbear laughing.
MOS.   'T seem'd to me, you sweat, sir.
VOLP. In troth, I did a little.
MOS.   But confess, sir,
    Were you not daunted?
VOLP.   In good faith, I was
    A little in a mist, but not dejected;   40
    Never but still myself.
MOS.   I think it, sir.
    Now, so truth help me, I must needs say this, sir,
    And out of conscience for your advocate,
    He has taken pains, in faith, sir, and deserv'd,
    (In my poor judgment, I speak it under favour,
    Not to contrary you, sir,) very richly—
    Well—to be cozen'd.
VOLP.   Troth, and I think so too,
    By that I heard him in the latter end.
MOS. O, but before, sir: had you heard him first
    Draw it to certain heads, then aggravate,   50
    Then use his vehement figures—I look'd still
    When he would shift a shirt; and doing this
    Out of pure love, no hope of gain—
VOLP.   'T is right.
    I cannot answer him, Mosca, as I would,
    Not yet; but for thy sake, at thy entreaty,
    I will begin, e'en now—to vex 'em all,
    This very instant.

---

31. *glebe:* soil.   32. *rare:* finely.   48. *latter end:* conclusion of his speech.   50. *aggravate:* emphasize.   52. *shift a shirt:* because of the violence of his gestures.

MOS. Good sir.
VOLP. Call the dwarf
  And eunuch forth.
MOS. Castrone, Nano!

Enter CASTRONE *and* NANO

NANO. Here.
VOLP. Shall we have a jig now?
MOS. What you please, sir.
VOLP. Go,
  Straight give out about the streets, you two, 60
  That I am dead; do it with constancy,
  Sadly, do you hear? Impute it to the grief
  Of this late slander.

Exeunt CAST. *and* NANO.

MOS. What do you mean, sir?
VOLP. O,
  I shall have instantly my Vulture, Crow,
  Raven, come flying hither, on the news,
  To peck for carrion, my she-wolf, and all,
  Greedy, and full of expectation—
MOS. And then to have it ravish'd from their mouths!
VOLP. 'T is true. I will ha' thee put on a gown,
  And take upon thee, as thou wert mine heir; 70
  Show 'em a will. Open that chest, and reach
  Forth one of those that has the blanks; I 'll straight
  Put in thy name.
MOS. It will be rare, sir. *(Gives him a paper.)*
VOLP. Ay,
  When they e'en gape, and find themselves deluded—
MOS. Yes.
VOLP. And thou use them scurvily! Dispatch,
  Get on thy gown.
MOS. *(Putting on a gown).* But what, sir, if they ask
  After the body?
VOLP. Say, it was corrupted.
MOS. I 'll say it stunk, sir; and was fain to have it
  Coffin'd up instantly, and sent away.
VOLP. Anything; what thou wilt. Hold, here 's my will. 80
  Get thee a cap, a count-book, pen and ink,
  Papers afore thee; sit as thou wert taking
  An inventory of parcels. I 'll get up
  Behind the curtain, on a stool, and hearken:
  Sometime peep over, see how they do look,
  With what degrees their blood doth leave their faces.
  O, 't will afford me a rare meal of laughter!

62. *sadly:* seriously.

MOS.   Your advocate will turn stark dull upon it.
VOLP. It will take off his oratory's edge.
MOS.   But your clarissimo, old roundback, he   90
  Will crump you like a hog-louse, with the touch.
VOLP. And what Corvino?
MOS.   O, sir, look for him,
  To-morrow morning, with a rope and a dagger,
  To visit all the streets; he must run mad.
  My lady too, that came into the court
  To bear false witness for your worship—
VOLP.   Yes,
  And kiss'd me 'fore the fathers, when my face
  Flow'd all with oils—
MOS.   And sweat, sir. Why, your gold
  Is such another med'cine, it dries up
  All those offensive savours: it transforms   100
  The most deformed, and restores 'em lovely,
  As 't were the strange poetical girdle. Jove
  Could not invent t' himself a shroud more subtle
  To pass Acrisius' guards. It is the thing
  Makes all the world her grace, her youth, her beauty.
VOLP. I think she loves me.
MOS.   Who? The lady, sir?
  She 's jealous of you.
VOLP.   Dost thou say so?

Knocking within.

MOS.   Hark.
  There 's some already.
VOLP.   Look.
MOS.   It is the Vulture;
  He has the quickest scent.
VOLP.   I 'll to my place,
  Thou to thy posture. *(Goes to upper stage.)*
MOS.   I am set.
VOLP.   But, Mosca,   110
  Play the artificer now, torture 'em rarely.

SCENE III

The Same.

VOLTORE, MOSCA, CORBACCIO, CORVINO, LADY [POLITIC
  WOULD-BE], VOLPONE

[VOLT.]   How now, my Mosca?

---

90. *clarissimo:* Corbaccio.   91. *crump you:* curl up.   102. *girdle:* "cestus" (Jonson's note), the girdle of Venus.   104. *Acrisius:* father of Danae.   111. *artificer:* artist.

MOS. *(Writing).* "Turkey carpets, nine—"
VOLT. Taking an inventory! that is well.
MOS. "Two suits of bedding, tissue—"
VOLT. Where's the will?
　Let me read that the while.

Enter SERVANTS *with* CORBACCIO *in a chair*

CORB. So, set me down,
　And get you home. *(Exeunt* SERVANTS.*)*
VOLT. Is he come now, to trouble us?
MOS. "Of cloth of gold, two more—"
CORB. Is it done, Mosca?
MOS. "Of several vellets, eight—"
VOLT. I like his care.
CORB. Dost thou not hear?

Enter CORVINO

CORV. Ha! is the hour come, Mosca?
VOLP. Ay, now they muster.

VOLPONE *peeps from behind a traverse.*

CORV. What does the advocate here, 10
　Or this Corbaccio?
CORB. What do these here?

Enter LADY POL. WOULD-BE

LADY P. Mosca!
　Is his thread spun?
MOS. "Eight chests of linen—"
VOLP. O,
　My fine Dame Would-be, too!
CORV. Mosca, the will,
　That I may show it these, and rid 'em hence.
MOS. "Six chests of diaper, four of damask."—There. *(Gives them the
　will carelessly, over his shoulder.)*
CORB. Is that the will?
MOS. "Down-beds, and bolsters—"
VOLP. Rare!
　Be busy still. Now they begin to flutter:
　They never think of me. Look, see, see, see!
　How their swift eyes run over the long deed,
　Unto the name, and to the legacies, 20

---

4. *tissue:* of rich fabric.　8. *vellets:* velvets.　15. *diaper:* a fabric with a woven pattern.

What is bequeath'd them there—
MOS.   "Ten suits of hangings—"
VOLP. Ay, i' their garters, Mosca. Now their hopes
  Are at the gasp.
VOLT.   Mosca the heir!
CORB.   What 's that?
VOLP. My advocate is dumb; look to my merchant,
  He 's heard of some strange storm, a ship is lost,
  He faints; my lady will swoon. Old glazen-eyes,
  He hath not reach'd his despair yet.
CORB.   All these
  Are out of hope; I 'm, sure, the man. *(Takes the will.)*
CORV.   But, Mosca—
MOS. "Two cabinets—"
CORV.   Is this in earnest?
MOS.   "One
  Of ebony—"
CORV.   Or do you but delude me?
MOS. "The other, mother of pearl."—I am very busy,
  Good faith, it is a fortune thrown upon me—
  "Item, one salt of agate"—not my seeking.
LADY P. Do you hear, sir?
MOS.   "A perfum'd box"—Pray you, forbear,
  You see I am troubled—"made of an onyx—"
LADY P.   How!
MOS. To-morrow or next day, I shall be at leisure
  To talk with you all.
CORV.   Is this my large hope's issue?
LADY P. Sir, I must have a fairer answer.
MOS.   Madam!
Marry, and shall: pray you, fairly quit my house.
Nay, raise no tempest with your looks; but hark you,
Remember what your ladyship off'red me
To put you in an heir; go to, think on 't:
And what you said e'en your best madams did
For maintenance; and why not you? Enough.
Go home, and use the poor Sir Pol, your knight, well,
For fear I tell some riddles; go, be melancholic.

Exit LADY WOULD-BE.

VOLP. O, my fine devil!
CORV.   Mosca, pray you a word.
MOS. Lord! will not you take your dispatch hence yet?
  Methinks, of all, you should have been th' example.
  Why should you stay here? With what thought, what promise?
  Hear you; do not you know, I know you an ass,

---

22. *Ay . . . garters:* playing on "hangings."   33. *salt:* salt cellar.

And that you would most fain have been a wittol,
If fortune would have let you? that you are
A declar'd cuckold, on good terms? This pearl,
You 'll say, was yours? right: this diamond?
I 'll not deny 't, but thank you. Much here else?
It may be so. Why, think that these good works
May help to hide your bad. I 'll not betray you;
Although you be but extraordinary,
And have it only in title, it sufficeth: 60
Go home, be melancholic too, or mad.

Exit CORVINO.

VOLP. Rare Mosca! how his villainy becomes him!
VOLT. Certain he doth delude all these for me.
CORB. Mosca the heir!
VOLP.   O, his four eyes have found it.
CORB. I 'm cozen'd, cheated, by a parasite-slave;
Harlot, th' hast gull'd me.
MOS.   Yes, sir. Stop your mouth,
Or I shall draw the only tooth is left.
Are not you he, that filthy covetous wretch,
With the three legs, that here, in hope of prey,
Have, any time this three year, snuff'd about, 70
With your most grov'ling nose, and would have hir'd
Me to the pois'ning of my patron, sir?
Are not you he that have to-day in court
Profess'd the disinheriting of your son?
Perjur'd yourself? Go home, and die, and stink;
If you but croak a syllable, all comes out:
Away, and call your porters! *(Exit* CORBACCIO.*)* Go, go, stink.
VOLP. Excellent varlet!
VOLT.   Now, my faithful Mosca,
I find thy constancy—
MOS.   Sir!
VOLT.   Sincere.
MOS. *(Writing)*.   "A table
Of porphyry"—I marle you 'll be thus troublesome. 80
VOLT. Nay, leave off now, they are gone.
MOS.   Why, who are you?
What! who did send for you? O, cry you mercy,
Reverend sir! Good faith, I am griev'd for you,
That any chance of mine should thus defeat
Your (I must needs say) most deserving travails:
But I protest, sir, it was cast upon me,
And I could almost wish to be without it,
But that the will o' th' dead must be observ'd.

52. *wittol:* a willing cuckold.   66. *Harlot:* fellow (orginally used only of males).
80. *marle:* marvel.

Marry, my joy is that you need it not;
You have a gift, sir, (thank your education),
Will never let you want, while there are men,
And malice, to breed causes. Would I had
But half the like, for all my fortune, sir!
If I have any suits, as I do hope,
Things being so easy and direct, I shall not,
I will make bold with your obstreperous aid,—
Conceive me, for your fee, sir. In mean time,
You that have so much law, I know ha' the conscience
Not to be covetous of what is mine.
Good sir, I thank you for my plate; 't will help
To set up a young man. Good faith, you look
As you were costive; best go home and purge, sir. *(Exit* VOLTORE.*)*
VOLP. *(Comes down).*   Bid him eat lettuce well. My witty mischief
Let me embrace thee. O that I could now
Transform thee to a Venus!—Mosca, go,
Straight take my habit of clarissimo,
And walk the streets; be seen, torment 'em more:
We must pursue, as well as plot. Who would
Have lost this feast?
MOS.   I doubt it will lose them.
VOLP. O, my recovery shall recover all.
That I could now but think on some disguise
To meet 'em in, and ask 'em questions:
How I would vex 'em still at every turn!
MOS. Sir, I can fit you.
VOLP.   Canst thou?
MOS.   Yes, I know
One o' the *commandadori*, sir, so like you;
Him will I straight make drunk, and bring you his habit.
VOLP. A rare disguise, and answering thy brain!
O, I will be a sharp disease unto 'em.
MOS. Sir, you must look for curses—
VOLP.   Till they burst;
The Fox fares ever best when he is curs'd.

Exeunt.

SCENE IV

A Hall in Sir Politic's House.

PEREGRINE, 3 MERCATORI, *[later]* WOMAN, POLITIC

[PER.]   Am I enough disguis'd?
1 MER.   I warrant you.

---

92. *causes:* lawsuits.   102. *costive:* constipated.   103. *eat lettuce:* to cure his complexion.

408 Volpone

PER.   All my ambition is to fright him only.
2 MER. If you could ship him away, 't were excellent.
3 MER. To Zant, or to Aleppo!
PER.   Yes, and ha' his
  Adventures put i' th' Book of Voyages,
  And his gull'd story regist'red for truth.
  Well, gentlemen, when I am in a while,
  And that you think us warm in our discourse,
  Know your approaches.
1 MER.   Trust it to our care.

Exeunt MERCHANTS

Enter WAITING-WOMAN

PER. Save you, fair lady! Is Sir Pol within?   10
WOM. I do not know, sir.
PER.   Pray you, say unto him,
  Here is a merchant, upon earnest business,
  Desires to speak with him.
WOM.   I will see, sir. *(Exit.)*
PER.   Pray you.
  I see the family is all female here.

Re-enter WAITING-WOMAN

WOM. He says, sir, he has weighty affairs of state,
  That now require him whole; some other time
  You may possess him.
PER.   Pray you, say again,
  If those require him whole, these will exact him,
  Whereof I bring him tidings. *(Exit* WOM.*)* What might be
  His grave affair of state now! How to make   20
  Bolognian sausages here in Venice, sparing
  One o' th' ingredients?

Re-enter WAITING-WOMAN

WOM.   Sir, he says, he knows
  By your word "tidings," that you are no statesman,
  And therefore wills you stay.
PER.   Sweet, pray you, return him,
  I have not read so many proclamations,
  And studied them for words, as he has done—
  But—here he deigns to come. *(Exit* WOMAN.*)*

---

4. *Zant:* Zacynthus, a Greek island.   5. *Book of Voyages:* Hakluyt's *Principle Navigations, Voyages, etc.* (2nd ed., 1598-1600).   18. *exact:* bring to an end, finish utterly (Latinism).   24. *return:* answer.

Enter SIR POLITIC

SIR P. Sir, I must crave
  Your courteous pardon. There hath chanc'd to-day
  Unkind disaster 'twixt my lady and me;
  And I was penning my apology,
  To give her satisfaction, as you came now.
PER. Sir, I am griev'd I bring you worse disaster:
  The gentleman you met at th' port to-day,
  That told you he was newly arriv'd—
SIR P. Ay, was
  A fugitive punk?
PER. No, sir, a spy set on you:
  And he has made relation to the senate,
  That you profess'd to him to have a plot
  To sell the State of Venice to the Turk.
SIR P. O me!
PER. For which warrants are sign'd by this time,
  To apprehend you, and to search your study
  For papers—
SIR P. Alas, sir, I have none, but notes
  Drawn out of play-books—
PER. All the better, sir.
SIR P. And some essays. What shall I do?
PER. Sir, best
  Convey yourself into a sugar-chest;
  Or, if you could lie round, a frail were rare;
  And I could send you aboard.
SIR P. Sir, I but talk'd so,
  For discourse sake merely. *(They knock without.)*
PER. Hark! they are there.
SIR P. I am a wretch, a wretch!
PER. What will you do, sir?
  Ha' you ne'er a currant-butt to leap into?
  They 'll put you to the rack; you must be sudden.
SIR P. Sir, I have an ingine—
3 MER. *(Within).* Sir Politic Would-be!
2 MER. *(Within).* Where is he?
SIR P. That I have thought upon before time.
PER. What is it?
SIR P. I shall ne'er endure the torture.
  Marry, it is, sir, of a tortoise-shell,
  Fitted for these extremities: pray you, sir, help me.
  Here I 've a place, sir, to put back my legs,
  Please you to lay it on, sir, *(Lies down while* PER. *places the shell
    upon him.)*—with this cap,
  And my black gloves. I 'll lie, sir, like a tortoise,

---

35. *punk:* prostitute. 45. *frail:* rush basket. 49. *currant-butt:* wine-cask. 51. *ingine:* contrivance.

Till they are gone.
PER. And call you this an ingine?
SIR P. Mine own device.—Good sir, bid my wife's women 60
To burn my papers.

They rush in.

1 MER. Where's he hid?
3 MER. We must,
And will sure find him.
2 MER. Which is his study?
1 MER. What
Are you, sir?
PER. I'm a merchant, that came here
To look upon this tortoise.
3 MER. How!
1 MER. St. Mark!
What beast is this?
PER. It is a fish.
2 MER. Come out here!
PER. Nay, you may strike him, sir, and tread upon him,
He'll bear a cart.
1 MER. What, to run over him?
PER. Yes.
3 MER. Let's jump upon him.
2 MER. Can he not go?
PER. He creeps.
1 MER. Let's see him creep.
PER. No, good sir, you will hurt him.
2 MER. Heart, I'll see him creep, or prick his guts. 70
3 MER. Come out here!
PER. Pray you, sir, creep a little.
1 MER. Forth.
2 MER. Yet further.
PER. Good sir!—Creep.
2 MER. We'll see his legs.

They pull off the shell and discover him.

3 MER. Gods so, he has garters!
1 MER. Ay, and gloves!
2 MER. Is this
Your fearful tortoise?
PER. *(Discovering himself).* Now, Sir Pol, we are even;
For your next project I shall be prepar'd:
I am sorry for the funeral of your notes, sir.
1 MER. 'T were a rare motion to be seen in Fleet-street.

77. *motion:* exhibition.

2 MER. Ay, i' the Term.
1 MER. Or Smithfield, in the fair.
3 MER. Methinks 't is but a melancholic sight.
PER. Farewell, most politic tortoise!

Exeunt PER. *and* MERCHANTS. *Re-enter* WAITING-WOMAN

SIR P. Where 's my lady? 80
  Knows she of this?
WOM. I know not, sir.
SIR P. Enquire.—
  O, I shall be the fable of all feasts,
The freight of the gazetti, ship-boys' tale;
And, which is worst, even talk for ordinaries.
WOM. My lady 's come most melancholic home,
  And says, sir, she will straight to sea, for physic.
SIR P. And I, to shun this place and clime for ever,
  Creeping with house on back, and think it well
To shrink my poor head in my politic shell.

Exeunt.

SCENE V

A Room in Volpone's House.

VOLPONE, MOSCA. *The first in the habit of a Commandadore: the other, of a Clarissimo*

[VOLP.] Am I then like him?
MOS. O, sir, you are he;
  No man can sever you.
VOLP. Good.
MOS. But what am I?
VOLP. 'Fore heaven, a brave clarissimo; thou becom'st it!
  Pity thou wert not born one.
MOS. *(Aside).* If I hold
  My made one, 't will be well.
VOLP. I 'll go and see
  What news first at the court. *(Exit.)*
MOS. Do so. My Fox
  Is out on his hole, and ere he shall re-enter,
I 'll make him languish in his borrow'd case,
Except he come to composition with me.—
Androgyno, Castrone, Nano!

---

78. *fair:* Bartholomew Fair. 83. *gazetti:* newspapers. 2. *sever:* distinguish. 8. *case:* skin. 9. *composition:* terms, agreement.

Enter ANDROGYNO, CASTRONE, *and* NANO

ALL. Here. 10
MOS. Go, recreate yourselves abroad; go, sport.—*(Exeunt.)*
   So, now I have the keys, and am possess'd.
   Since he will needs be dead afore his time,
   I 'll bury him, or gain by him: I 'm his heir,
   And so will keep me, till he share at least.
   To cozen him of all, were but a cheat
   Well plac'd; no man would construe it a sin:
   Let his sport pay for 't. This is call'd the Fox-trap. *(Exit.)*

SCENE VI

   A Street.

CORBACCIO, CORVINO, *[later]* VOLPONE

[CORB.] They say the court is set.
CORV.   We must maintain
   Our first tale good, for both our reputations.
CORB. Why, mine 's no tale: my son would there have kill'd me.
CORV. That 's true, I had forgot:—mine is, I 'm sure.
   But for your will, sir.
CORB.   Ay, I 'll come upon him
   For that hereafter, now his patron 's dead.

Enter VOLPONE

VOLP. Signior Corvino! and Corbaccio! sir,
   Much joy unto you.
CORV.   Of what?
VOLP.   The sudden good
   Dropp'd down upon you—
CORB.   Where?
VOLP.   And none knows how,
   From old Volpone, sir.
CORB.   Out, arrant knave!   10
VOLP. Let not your too much wealth, sir, make you furious.
CORB. Away, thou varlet.
VOLP.   Why, sir?
CORB.   Dost thou mock me?
VOLP. You mock the world, sir; did you not change wills?
CORB. Out, harlot!
VOLP.   O! belike you are the man,
   Signior Corvino? Faith, you carry it well;
   You grow not mad withal; I love your spirit:
   You are not over-leaven'd with your fortune.

You should ha' some would swell now, like a wine-fat,
With such an autumn.—Did he gi' you all, sir?
CORB. Avoid, you rascal!
VOLP.   Troth, your wife has shown
Herself a very woman; but you are well,
You need not care, you have a good estate,
To bear it out, sir, better by this chance:
Except Corbaccio have a share.
CORB.   Hence, varlet.
VOLP. You will not be a'known, sir; why, 't is wise.
Thus do all gamesters, at all games, dissemble:
No man will seem to win. *(Exeunt* CORVINO *and* CORBACCIO.*)*
  Here comes my Vulture,
Heaving his beak i' the air, and snuffing.

SCENE VII

The Same.

VOLTORE, VOLPONE

[VOLT.] Outstripp'd thus, by a parasite! a slave,
Would run on errands, and make legs for crumbs!
Well, what I 'll do—
VOLP.   The court stays for your worship.
I e'en rejoice, sir, at your worship's happiness,
And that it fell into so learned hands,
That understand the fing'ring—
VOLT.   What do you mean?
VOLP. I mean to be a suitor to your worship,
For the small tenement, out of reparations,
That, at the end of your long row of houses,
By the Piscaria: it was, in Volpone's time,
Your predecessor, ere he grew diseas'd,
A handsome, pretty, custom'd bawdy-house
As any was in Venice, none disprais'd;
But fell with him: his body and that house
Decay'd together.
VOLT.   Come, sir, leave your prating.
VOLP. Why, if your worship give me but your hand
That I may ha' the refusal, I have done.
'T is a mere toy to you, sir; candle-rents;
As your learn'd worship knows—
VOLT.   What do I know?
VOLP. Marry, no end of your wealth, sir; God decrease it!
VOLT. Mistaking knave! what, mock'st thou my misfortune? *(Exit.)*
VOLP. His blessing on your heart, sir; would 't were more!—
Now to my first again, at the next corner. *(Exit.)*

18. *wine-fat:* wine-vat. 19. *autumn:* harvest. 25. *a'known:* acknown (will not confess it). 8. *reparations:* repair. 10. *Piscaria:* fish-market. 12. *custom'd:* well-frequented.

SCENE VIII

Another Street.

CORBACCIO, CORVINO *(MOSCA passant), [later]* VOLPONE

[CORB.] See, in our habit! see the impudent varlet!
CORV.   That I could shoot mine eyes at him, like gun-stones!

Enter VOLPONE

VOLP. But is this true, sir, of the parasite?
CORB. Again, t' afflict us! monster!
VOLP.   In good faith, sir,
  I 'm heartily griev'd, a beard of your grave length
  Should be so over-reach'd. I never brook'd
  That parasite's hair; methought his nose should cozen:
  There still was somewhat in his look, did promise
  The bane of a clarissimo.
CORB.   Knave—
VOLP.   Methinks
  Yet you, that are so traded i' the world,   10
  A witty merchant, the fine bird, Corvino,
  That have such moral emblems on your name,
  Should not have sung your shame, and dropp'd your cheese,
  To let the Fox laugh at your emptiness.
CORV. Sirrah, you think the privilege of the place,
  And your red saucy cap, that seems to me
  Nail'd to your jolt-head with those two cecchines,
  Can warrant your abuses; come you hither:
  You shall perceive, sir, I dare beat you; approach.
VOLP. No haste, sir, I do know your valour well,   20
  Since you durst publish what you are, sir.
CORV.   Tarry,
  I 'd speak with you.
VOLP.   Sir, sir, another time—
CORV. Nay, now.
VOLP.   O God, sir! I were a wise man,
  Would stand the fury of a distracted cuckold.

MOSCA walks by 'em.

CORB. What, come again!
VOLP.   Upon 'em, Mosca; save me.
CORB. The air 's infected where he breathes.
CORV.   Let 's fly him.

Scene VIII, stage directions. *passant:* walking across the stage. 1. *habit:* that of clarissimo. 2. *gun-stones:* cannonballs. 17. *jolt-head:* blockhead.

Exeunt CORV. *and* CORB.

VOLP. Excellent basilisk! turn upon the Vulture.

SCENE IX

The Same.

VOLTORE, MOSCA, VOLPONE

[VOLT.] Well, flesh-fly, it is summer with you now;
  Your winter will come on.
MOS.   Good advocate,
  'Pray thee not rail, nor threaten out of place, thus;
  Thou 'lt make a solecism, as madam says.
  Get you a biggin more; your brain breaks loose. *(Exit.)*
VOLT. Well sir.
VOLP.   Would you ha' me beat the insolent slave,
  Throw dirt upon his first good clothes?
VOLT.   This same
  Is doubtless some familiar.
VOLP.   Sir, the court,
  In troth, stays for you. I am mad, a mule, 10
  That never read Justinian, should get up,
  And ride an advocate. Had you no quirk
  To avoid gullage, sir, by such a creature?
  I hope you do but jest; he has not done 't:
  This 's but confederacy to blind the rest.
  You are the heir?
VOLT.   A strange, officious,
  Troublesome knave! thou dost torment me.
VOLP.   I know—
  It cannot be, sir, that you should be cozen'd;
  'T is not within the wit of man to do it;
  You are so wise, so prudent; and 't is fit
  That wealth and wisdom still should go together. 20

Exeunt.

SCENE X

The Scrutineo.

4 AVOCATORI, NOTARIO, COMMANDADORI, BONARIO, CELIA, CORBACCIO, CORVINO, *[later]* VOLTORE, VOLPONE

[1 AVOC.] Are all the parties here?

---

27. *basilisk:* a mythical beast who killed by a look. 5. *biggin:* lawyer's cap. 8. *familiar:* demon.

NOT.　　　　　　　All but the advocate.
2 AVOC.　And here he comes.

Enter VOLTORE *and* VOLPONE

1 AVOC.　Then bring 'em forth to sentence.
VOLT.　O, my most honour'd fathers, let your mercy
　Once win upon your justice, to forgive—
　I am distracted—
VOLP. *(Aside).*　What will he do now?
VOLT.　　　　　　　O,
　I know not which t' address myself to first;
　Whether your fatherhoods, or these innocents—
CORV. *(Aside).*　Will he betray himself?
VOLT.　　　　　　Whom equally
　I have abus'd, out of most covetous ends—
CORV. *(Aside).*　The man is mad!
CORB. *(Aside).*　　What's that?
CORV. *(Aside).*　　He is possess'd.　　　　　　　　10
VOLT.　For which, now struck in conscience, here I prostrate
　Myself at your offended feet, for pardon.
1, 2 AVOC.　Arise.
CEL.　　　　　O heaven, how just thou art!
VOLP.　　　　　I'm caught
　I' mine own noose—
CORV. *(To* CORBACCIO*).*　Be constant, sir; nought now
　Can help but impudence.
1 AVOC.　　　　　Speak forward.
COM.　　　　　　Silence!
VOLT.　It is not passion in me, reverend fathers,
　But only conscience, conscience, my good sires,
　That makes me now tell truth. That parasite,
　That knave, hath been the instrument of all.
1 AVOC.　Where is that knave? Fetch him.
VOLP.　　　　　I go. *(Exit.)*
CORV.　　　　　　Grave fathers,　　　　　　　　　20
　This man's distracted; he confess'd it now:
　For, hoping to be old Volpone's heir,
　Who now is dead—
3 AVOC.　　　　　How!
2 AVOC.　　　　　Is Volpone dead?
CORV.　Dead since, grave fathers—
BON.　　　　　O sure vengeance!
1 AVOC.　　　　　Stay,
　Then he was no deceiver?
VOLT.　　　　　O no, none:
　The parasite, grave fathers.
CORV.　　　　　He does speak
　Out of mere envy, 'cause the servant's made
　The thing he gap'd for. Please your fatherhoods,

This is the truth, though I 'll not justify
The other, but he may be some-deal faulty. 30
VOLT. Ay, to your hopes, as well as mine, Corvino:
But I 'll use modesty. Pleaseth your wisdoms,
To view these certain notes, and but confer them;
As I hope favour, they shall speak clear truth.
CORV. The devil has ent'red him!
BON.   Or bides in you.
4 AVOC. We have done ill, by a public officer
To send for him, if he be heir.
2 AVOC.   For whom?
4 AVOC. Him that they call the parasite.
3 AVOC.   'T is true,
He is a man of great estate, now left.
4 AVOC. Go you, and learn his name, and say the court 40
Entreats his presence here, but to the clearing
Of some few doubts. *(Exit* NOTARY.*)*
2 AVOC.   This same 's a labyrinth!
1 AVOC. Stand you unto your first report?
CORV.   My state,
My life, my fame—
BON. *(Aside)*.   Where is 't?
CORV.   Are at the stake.
1 AVOC. Is yours so too?
CORB.   The advocate 's a knave,
And has a forked tongue—
2 AVOC.   Speak to the point.
CORB. So is the parasite too.
1 AVOC.   This is confusion.
VOLT. I do beseech your fatherhoods, read but those— *(Giving them papers.)*
CORV. And credit nothing the false spirit hath writ:
It cannot be but he is possess'd, grave fathers. 50

Exeunt.

SCENE XI

A Street.

VOLPONE, *[later]* NANO, ANDROGYNO, CASTRONE

[VOLP.] To make a snare for mine own neck and run
My head into it, wilfully! with laughter!
When I had newly scap'd, was free and clear,
Out of mere wantonness! O, the dull devil
Was in this brain of mine when I devis'd it,

---

32. *modesty:* moderation.   33. *confer:* compare.

And Mosca gave it second; he must now
Help to sear up this vein, or we bleed dead.

Enter NANO, ANDROGYNO, *and* CASTRONE

How now! Who let you loose? Whither go you now?
What, to buy gingerbread, or to drown kitlings?
NAN. Sir, Master Mosca call'd us out of doors,   10
And bid us all go play, and took the keys.
AND. Yes.
VOLP.   Did Master Mosca take the keys? Why, so!
I 'm farther in. These are my fine conceits!
I must be merry, with a mischief to me!
What a vile wretch was I, that could not bear
My fortune soberly? I must ha' my crochets,
And my conundrums! Well, go you, and seek him:
His meaning may be truer than my fear.
Bid him, he straight come to me to the court;
Thither will I, and, if 't be possible,   20
Unscrew my advocate, upon new hopes:
When I provok'd him, then I lost myself.

SCENE XII

The Scrutineo.

AVOCATORI, &c.

[1 AVOC.] These things can ne'er be reconcil'd. He here *(Showing the papers.)*
Professeth that the gentleman was wrong'd,
And that the gentlewoman was brought thither,
Forc'd by her husband, and there left.
VOLT.   Most true.
CEL. How ready is heaven to those that pray!
1 AVOC. But that
Volpone would have ravish'd her, he holds
Utterly false, knowing his impotence.
CORV. Grave fathers, he 's possess'd; again, I say,
Possess'd: nay, if there be possession, and
Obsession, he has both.
3 AVOC.   Here comes our officer.   10

Enter VOLPONE

VOLP. The parasite will straight be here, grave fathers.

16. *crochets:* whimsical fancies.

4 AVOC. You might invent some other name, sir varlet.
3 AVOC. Did not the notary meet him?
VOLP.   Not that I know.
4 AVOC. His coming will clear all.
2 AVOC.   Yet it is misty.
VOLT. May 't please your fatherhoods—

VOLPONE *whispers the* ADVOCATE.

VOLP.   Sir, the parasite
  Will'd me to tell you that his master lives;
  That you are still the man; your hopes the same;
  And this was only a jest—
VOLT.   How?
VOLP.   Sir, to try
  If you were firm, and how you stood affected.
VOLT. Art sure he lives?
VOLP.   Do I live, sir?
VOLT.   O me!   20
  I was too violent.
VOLP.   Sir, you may redeem it.
  They said you were possess'd; fall down, and seem so:
  I 'll help to make it good. *(*VOLTORE *falls.)* God bless the man!—
  Stop your wind hard, and swell—See, see, see, see!
  He vomits crooked pins! His eyes are set,
  Like a dead hare's hung in a poulter's shop!
  His mouth 's running away! Do you see, signior?
  Now 't is in his belly.
CORV. *(Aside).*   Ay, the devil!
VOLP. Now in his throat.
CORV. *(Aside).*   Ay, I perceive it plain.
VOLP. 'T will out, 't will out! stand clear. See where it flies,   30
  In shape of a blue toad, with a bat's wings!
  Do not you see it, sir?
CORB.   What? I think I do.
CORV. 'T is too manifest.
VOLP.   Look! he comes t' himself!
VOLT. Where am I?
VOLP. Take good heart, the worst is past, sir.
  You 're dispossess'd.
1 AVOC.   What accident is this!
2 AVOC. Sudden and full of wonder!
3 AVOC.   If he were
  Possess'd, as it appears, all this is nothing.
CORV. He has been often subject to these fits.
1 AVOC. Show him that writing:—do you know it, sir?
VOLP. *(Whispers* VOLT.*).* Deny it, sir, forswear it; know it not.   40
VOLT. Yes, I do know it well, it is my hand;
  But all that it contains is false.

BON. O practice!
2 AVOC. What maze is this!
1 AVOC. Is he not guilty then,
  Whom you there name the parasite?
VOLT. Grave fathers,
  No more than his good patron, old Volpone.
4 AVOC. Why, he is dead.
VOLT. O no, my honour'd fathers,
  He lives—
1 AVOC. How! lives?
VOLT. Lives.
2 AVOC. This is subtler yet!
3 AVOC. You said he was dead.
VOLT. Never.
3 AVOC. You said so.
CORV. I heard so.
4 AVOC. Here comes the gentleman; make him way.

Enter MOSCA

3 AVOC. A stool.
4 AVOC. *(Aside).* A proper man; and were Volpone dead, 50
  A fit match for my daughter.
3 AVOC. Give him way.
VOLP. *(Aside to* MOS.*).* Mosca, I was a'most lost; the advocate
  Had betray'd all; but now it is recover'd;
  All 's o' the hinge again—Say I am living.
MOS. What busy knave is this!—Most reverend fathers,
  I sooner had attended your grave pleasures,
  But that my order for the funeral
  Of my dear patron did require me—
VOLP. *(Aside).* Mosca!
MOS. Whom I intend to bury like a gentleman.
VOLP. *(Aside).* Ay, quick, and cozen me of all.
2 AVOC. Still stranger! 60
  More intricate!
1 AVOC. And come about again!
4 AVOC. *(Aside).* It is a match, my daughter is bestow'd.
MOS. *(Aside to* VOLP.*).* Will you gi' me half?
VOLP. First I 'll be hang'd.
MOS. I know
  Your voice is good, cry not so loud.
1 AVOC. Demand
  The advocate.—Sir, did not you affirm
  Volpone was alive?
VOLP. Yes, and he is;
  This gent'man told me so.—*(Aside to* MOS.*)* Thou shalt have half.

42. *practice:* conspiracy. 60. *quick:* alive.

MOS. Whose drunkard is this same? Speak, some that know him:
 I never saw his face.—*(Aside to* VOLP.*)* I cannot now
 Afford it you so cheap.
VOLP.   No!
1 AVOC.   What say you?
VOLT. The officer told me.
VOLP.   I did, grave fathers,
 And will maintain he lives, with mine own life,
 And that this creature *(points to* MOS.*)* told me. *(Aside.)*—I was born
 With all good stars my enemies.
MOS.   Most grave fathers,
 If such an insolence as this must pass
 Upon me, I am silent: 't was not this
 For which you sent, I hope.
2 AVOC.   Take him away.
VOLP. Mosca!
3 AVOC.   Let him be whipp'd.
VOLP. *(Aside).*   Wilt thou betray me?
 Cozen me?
3 AVOC.   And taught to bear himself
 Toward a person of his rank.
4 AVOC.   Away.

The OFFICERS *seize* VOLPONE.

MOS. I humbly thank your fatherhoods.
VOLP.   Soft, soft: *(Aside.)* Whipp'd!
 And lose all that I have! If I confess,
 It cannot be much more.
4 AVOC.   Sir, are you married?
VOLP. *(Aside).* They 'll be alli'd anon; I must be resolute;
 The Fox shall here uncase.

He puts off his disguise.

MOS. *(Aside).*   Patron!
VOLP.   Nay, now
 My ruins shall not come alone; your match
 I 'll hinder sure: my substance shall not glue you,
 Nor screw you into a family.
MOS. *(Aside).*   Why, patron!
VOLP. I am Volpone, and this is my knave; *(Pointing to* MOSCA.*)*
 This *(To* VOLT.*)*, his own knave; this *(to* CORB.*)*, avarice's fool;
 This *(To* CORV.*)*, a chimera of wittol, fool, and knave:
 And, reverend fathers, since we all can hope
 Nought but a sentence, let 's not now despair it.

85. *uncase:* remove his skin. 91. *chimera:* a monster composed of the parts of various animals.

You hear me brief.
CORV. May it please your fatherhoods—
COM. Silence.
1 AVOC. The knot is now undone by miracle.
2 AVOC. Nothing can be more clear.
3 AVOC. Or can more prove
  These innocent.
1 AVOC. Give 'em their liberty.
BON. Heaven could not long let such gross crimes be hid.
2 AVOC. If this be held the highway to get riches,
  May I be poor!
3 AVOC. This 's not the gain, but torment. 100
1 AVOC. These possess wealth, as sick men possess fevers,
  Which trulier may be said to possess them.
2 AVOC. Disrobe that parasite.
CORV. [AND] MOS. Most honour'd fathers—
1 AVOC. Can you plead aught to stay the course of justice?
  If you can, speak.
CORV. [AND] VOLT. We beg favour.
CEL. And mercy.
1 AVOC. You hurt your innocence, suing for the guilty.
  Stand forth; and first the parasite. You appear
  T' have been the chiefest minister, if not plotter,
  In all these lewd impostures, and now, lastly,
  Have with your impudence abus'd the court, 110
  And habit of a gentleman of Venice,
  Being a fellow of no birth or blood:
  For which our sentence is, first, thou be whipp'd;
  Then live perpetual prisoner in our galleys.
VOLP. I thank you for him.
MOS. Bane to thy wolfish nature!
1 AVOC. Deliver him to the saffi. *(MOSCA is carried out.)* Thou,
    Volpone,
  By blood and rank a gentleman, canst not fall
  Under like censure; but our judgment on thee
  Is, that thy substance all be straight confiscate
  To the hospital of the *Incurabili:* 120
  And since the most was gotten by imposture,
  By feigning lame, gout, palsy, and such diseases,
  Thou art to lie in prison, cramp'd with irons,
  Till thou be'st sick and lame indeed. Remove him. *(He is taken from
    the Bar.)*
VOLP. This is called mortifying of a Fox.
1 AVOC. Thou, Voltore, to take away the scandal
  Thou hast giv'n all worthy men of thy profession,
  Art banish'd from their fellowship, and our state.
  Corbaccio!—bring him near. We here possess

110. *abus'd:* imposed upon.

Thy son of all thy state, and confine thee
To the monastery of San Spirito;
Where, since thou knew'st not how to live well here,
Thou shalt be learn'd to die well.
CORB.   Ha! what said he?
COM.   You shall know anon, sir.
1 AVOC.   Thou, Corvino, shalt
Be straight embark'd from thine own house, and row'd
Round about Venice, through the Grand Canal
Wearing a cap, with fair long ass's ears,
Instead of horns! and so to mount, a paper
Pinn'd on thy breast, to the *berlina*.
CORV.   Yes.
And have mine eyes beat out with stinking fish,
Bruis'd fruit, and rotten eggs—'t is well. I 'm glad
I shall not see my shame yet.
1 AVOC.   And to expiate
Thy wrongs done to thy wife, thou art to send her
Home to her father, with her dowry trebled:
And these are all your judgments.
ALL.   Honour'd fathers—
1 AVOC.   Which may not be revok'd. Now you begin,
When crimes are done and past, and to be punish'd,
To think what your crimes are. Away with them!
Let all that see these vices thus rewarded,
Take heart, and love to study 'em. Mischiefs feed
Like beasts, till they be fat, and then they bleed.

Exeunt.

VOLPONE *(comes forward).* "The seasoning of a play is the applause.
Now, though the Fox be punish'd by the laws,
He yet doth hope, there is no suff'ring due,
For any fact which he hath done 'gainst you;
If there be, censure him; here he doubtful stands.
If not, fare jovially, and clap your hands." *(Exit.)*

THE END

130. *state:* estate.   139. *berlina:* pillory.

Questions for Discussion

1. Does there appear to be a serious moral purpose underlying the comedy of *Volpone?* If so, how early and in what ways is this purpose revealed (see I, iv, 142-145)? Does the underlying seriousness damage the comic tone? Does the resolution uphold the author's moral? If so, how? How effective is comedy likely to be as a tool for making a serious point in a student composition? What dangers are involved?

2. Are the villains too severely punished at the play's resolution to maintain the comic atmosphere? In other words, is the resolution inconsistent with the rest of the play? Explain. Are there earlier scenes (e.g., the attempted rape of Celia) in which the characters' actions appear too villainous to be comic? Discuss.

3. Is the tone made inconsistent by the mixture of poetry and prose? What seems to be the author's purpose in mixing the forms? Does the form, whether prose or poetry, vary according to speaker and situation? Illustrate. Why do you suppose the final scenes are entirely written in poetry? Does the necessity for tying all loose ends together in a play or a theme require a degree of consistency in the conclusion not strictly necessary in earlier sections?

4. Does *Volpone* seem to have two parallel plot lines? If so, in what sense are they parallel? Might, for instance, Sir Politic Would-be and Peregrine be described as foils for Volpone and Mosca? What are the similarities and differences in the characters? Are the two plots resolved simultaneously or separately? Are they given equal attention in the play's resolution? Might Jonson's methods in these respects lend some insight into handling the resolution of a comparison-contrast composition? Does it seem essential or wise, for instance, to wait until the conclusion to demonstrate the essence of the contrast?

5. Given the characters' names, can we assume that Jonson's intent is allegorical (see page 502) in the manner of *Everyman?* If not, what are the differences in method and emphasis? Whether or not the characters in *Volpone* are allegorical, could they be described as types? How does Jonson's handling of his characters affect the interrelationships of plot, theme, and characterization?

Suggested Theme Topics

1. Delineate the moral purpose of *Volpone,* concentrating on its revelation through comic methods.

2. Compare and contrast Jonson's use of proper names with that in either *Everyman* or *The School for Scandal*.

3. Trace the parallel plot lines in *Volpone*, showing their relationship to characterization.

4. Discuss Jonson's idea of justice as defined by the resolution of *Volpone*. Comment on the resolution as either appropriate or inappropriate to the total content.

5. Write a theme comparing and contrasting the methods of two classroom teachers, emphasizing the contrasts throughout your theme and summarizing them in your conclusion so as to indicate why they are significant enough to deserve your attention.

Eugene O'Neill

Eugene O'Neill (1888-1953), the son of actor James O'Neill, was educated in a series of boarding schools and briefly at Princeton and Harvard. His departure from college initiated five years of inactivity, ended by a breakdown necessitating a period of recuperation in a tuberculosis sanatorium. His career as playwright began in 1914 with his involvement in George Pierce Baker's "47 Workshop." O'Neill was awarded a Pulitzer Prize for his first full-length play, Beyond the Horizon *(1920). His ensuing dramatic output, certainly the finest ever produced by an American, was prolific and varied; his most widely praised achievements include* The Emperor Jones *(1921),* The Hairy Ape *(1922),* The Great God Brown *(1926),* The Iceman Cometh *(1946),* Ah, Wilderness *(1932),* Mourning Becomes Electra *(1931), and the posthumous* Long Day's Journey into Night *(1956). Altogether O'Neill was awarded four Pulitzer prizes and a Nobel Prize.*

The resolution of Desire Under the Elms *(1924) certainly embodies tragic effects, but it also recalls the tradition of the English morality play, such as* Everyman. *Note that the characters in O'Neill's play allude by their names to certain Old Testament families. This quality, along with the obvious parallels in plot with the Oedipus story, serve together to foreshadow an inevitable tragic conclusion.*

DESIRE UNDER THE ELMS

CHARACTERS

EPHRAIM CABOT
SIMEON
PETER } his sons
EBEN
ABBIE PUTNAM
YOUNG GIRL, TWO FARMERS, THE FIDDLER, A SHERIFF,
 AND OTHER FOLK FROM THE NEIGHBORING FARMS.

The action of the entire play takes place in, and immediately outside of, the Cabot farmhouse in New England, in the year 1850. The south end of the house faces front to a stone wall with a wooden gate at center opening on a country road. The house is in good condition but in need of paint. Its walls are a sickly grayish, the green of the shutters faded. Two enormous elms are on each side of the house. They bend their trailing branches down over the roof. They appear to protect and at the same time subdue. There is a sinister maternity in their aspect, a crushing, jealous absorption. They have developed from their intimate contact with the life of man in the house an appalling humanness. They brood oppressively over the house. They are like exhausted women resting their sagging breasts and hands and hair on its roof, and when it rains their tears trickle down monotonously and rot on the shingles.

There is a path running from the gate around the right corner of the house to the front door. A narrow porch is on this side. The end wall facing us has two windows in its upper story, two larger ones on the floor below. The two upper are those of the father's bedroom and that of the brothers. On the left, ground floor, is the kitchen—on the right, the parlor, the shades of which are always drawn down.

PART 1

SCENE 1

Exterior of the farmhouse. It is sunset of a day at the beginning of summer in the year 1850. There is no wind and everything is still. The sky above the roof is suffused with deep colors, the green of the elms glows, but the house is in shadow, seeming pale and washed out by contrast.

A door opens and EBEN CABOT *comes to the end of the porch and stands looking down the road to the right. He has a large bell in his hand and this he swings mechanically, awakening a deafening clangor. Then he puts his hands on his hips and stares up at the sky. He sighs with a puzzled awe and blurts out with halting appreciation.*

EBEN. God! Purty! *(His eyes fall and he stares about him frowningly. He is twenty-five, tall and sinewy. His face is well-formed, good-looking, but its expression is resentful and defensive. His defiant, dark eyes remind one of a wild animal's in captivity. Each day is a cage in which he finds himself trapped but inwardly unsubdued. There is a fierce repressed vitality about him. He has black hair, mustache, a thin curly trace of beard. He is dressed in rough farm clothes.*

He spits on the ground with intense disgust, turns and goes back into the house.)

SIMEON *and* PETER *come in from their work in the fields. They are tall men, much older than their half-brother (*SIMEON *is thirty-nine and* PETER *thirty-seven), built on a squarer, simpler model, fleshier in body, more bovine and homelier in face, shrewder and more practical. Their shoulders stoop a bit from years of farm work. They clump heavily along in their clumsy thick-soled boots caked with earth.*

Their clothes, their faces, hands, bare arms and throats are earth-stained. They smell of earth. They stand together for a moment in front of the house and, as if with the one impulse, stare dumbly up at the sky, leaning on their hoes. Their faces have a compressed, unresigned expression. As they look upward, this softens.

SIMEON *(grudgingly).* Purty.
PETER. Ay-eh.
SIMEON *(suddenly).* Eighteen year ago.
PETER. What?
SIMEON. Jenn. My woman. She died.
PETER. I'd fergot.
SIMEON. I rec'lect—now an' agin. Makes it lonesome. She'd hair long's a hoss' tail—an' yaller like gold!
PETER. Waal—she's gone. *(This with indifferent finality—then after a pause)* They's gold in the West, Sim.
SIMEON *(still under the influence of sunset—vaguely).* In the sky?
PETER. Waal—in a manner o' speakin'—thar's the promise. *(Growing excited)* Gold in the sky—in the West—Golden Gate—Californi-a!—Goldest West!—fields o' gold!
SIMEON *(excited in his turn).* Fortunes layin' just atop o' the ground waitin' t' be picked! Solomon's mines, they says! *(For a moment they continue looking up at the sky—then their eyes drop.)*
PETER *(with sardonic bitterness).* Here—it's stones atop o' the ground—stones atop o' stones—makin' stone walls—year atop o' year—him 'n' yew 'n' me 'n' then Eben—makin' stone walls fur him to fence us in!
SIMEON. We've wuked. Give our strength. Give our years. Plowed 'em under in the ground—*(he stamps rebelliously)*—rottin'—makin' soil for his crops! *(A pause.)* Waal—the farm pays good for here-abouts.
PETER. If we plowed in Californi-a, they'd be lumps o' gold in the furrow!
SIMEON. Californi-a's t'other side o' earth, a'most. We got t' calc'late—
PETER *(after a pause).* 'Twould be hard fur me, too, to give up what we've 'arned here by our sweat. *(A pause,* EBEN *sticks his head out of the dining-room window, listening.)*
SIMEON. Ay-eh. *(A pause.)* Mebbe—he'll die soon.
PETER *(doubtfully).* Mebbe.
SIMEON. Mebbe—fur all we knows—he's dead now.
PETER. Ye'd need proof.
SIMEON. He's been gone two months—with no word.
PETER. Left us in the fields an evenin' like this. Hitched up an' druv off into the West. That's plum onnateral. He hain't never been off this farm 'ceptin t' the village in thirty year or more, not since he married Eben's maw. *(A pause. Shrewdly)* I calc'late we might git him declared crazy by the court.
SIMEON. He skinned 'em too slick. He got the best o' all on 'em. They'd never b'lieve him crazy. *(A pause.)* We got t' wait—till he's under ground.
EBEN *(with a sardonic chuckle).* Honor thy father! *(They turn, startled, and stare at him. He grins, then scowls.)* I pray he's died.

(They stare at him. He continues matter-of-factly.) Supper's ready.
SIMEON AND PETER *(together).* Ay-eh.
EBEN *(gazing up at the sky).* Sun's downin' purty.
SIMEON AND PETER *(together).* Ay-eh. They's gold in the West.
EBEN. Ay-eh. *(Pointing)* Yonder atop o' the hill pasture, ye mean?
SIMEON AND PETER *(together).* In Californi-a!
EBEN. Hunh? *(Stares at them indifferently for a second, then drawls)* Waal—supper's gittin' cold. *(He turns back into kitchen.)*
SIMEON *(startled—smacks his lips).* I air hungry!
PETER *(sniffing).* I smells bacon!
SIMEON *(with hungry appreciation).* Bacon's good!
PETER *(in same tone).* Bacon's bacon! *(They turn, shouldering each other, their bodies bumping and rubbing together as they hurry clumsily to their food, like two friendly oxen toward their evening meal. They disappear around the right corner of house and can be heard entering the door.)*

CURTAIN

SCENE 2

The color fades from the sky. Twilight begins. The interior of the kitchen is now visible. A pine table is at center, a cook-stove in the right rear corner, four rough wooden chairs, a tallow candle on the table. In the middle of the rear wall is fastened a big advertising poster with a ship in full sail and the word "California" in big letters. Kitchen utensils hang from nails. Everything is neat and in order but the atmosphere is of a men's camp kitchen rather than that of a home. Places for three are laid. EBEN *takes boiled potatoes and bacon from the stove and puts them on the table, also a loaf of bread and a crock of water.* SIMEON *and* PETER *shoulder in, slump down in their chairs without a word.* EBEN *joins them. The three eat in silence for a moment, the two elder as naturally unrestrained as beasts of the field,* EBEN *picking at his food without appetite, glancing at them with a tolerant dislike.*

SIMEON *(suddenly turns to* EBEN*).* Looky here! Ye'd oughtn't t' said that, Eben.
PETER. 'Twa'n't righteous.
EBEN. What?
SIMEON. Ye prayed he'd died.
EBEN. Waal—don't yew pray it? *(A pause.)*
PETER. He's our Paw.
EBEN *(violently).* Not mine!
SIMEON *(dryly).* Ye'd not let no one else say that about yer Maw! Ha! *(He gives one abrupt sardonic guffaw.* PETER *grins.)*
EBEN *(very pale).* I meant—I hain't his'n—I hain't like him—he hain't me!
PETER *(dryly).* Wait till ye've growed his age!

EBEN *(intensely)*. I'm Maw—every drop o' blood! *(A pause. They stare at him with indifferent curiosity.)*
PETER *(reminiscently)*. She was good t' Sim 'n' me. A good Stepmaw's scurse.
SIMEON. She was good t' everyone.
EBEN *(greatly moved, gets to his feet and makes an awkward bow to each of them—stammering)*. I be thankful t'ye. I'm her—her heir. *(He sits down in confusion.)*
PETER *(after a pause—judicially)*. She was good even t' him.
EBEN *(fiercely)*. An' fur thanks he killed her!
SIMEON *(after a pause)*. No one never kills nobody. It's allus somethin'. That's the murderer.
EBEN. Didn't he slave Maw t' death?
PETER. He slaved himself t' death. He's slaved Sim 'n' me 'n' yew t' death—on'y none o' us hain't died—yit.
SIMEON. It's somethin'—drivin' him—t' drive us!
EBEN *(vengefully)*. Waal—I hold him t' jedgment! *(Then scornfully)* Somethin'! What's somethin'?
SIMEON. Dunno.
EBEN *(sardonically)*. What's drivin' yew to Californi-a, mebbe? *(They look at him in surprise.)* Oh, I've heerd ye! *(Then, after a pause)* But ye'll never go t' the gold fields!
PETER *(assertively)*. Mebbe!
EBEN. Whar'll ye git the money?
PETER. We kin walk. It's an a'mighty ways—Californi-a—but if yew was t' put all the steps we've walked on this farm end t' end we'd be in the moon!
EBEN. The Injuns'll skulp ye on the plains.
SIMEON *(with grim humor)*. We'll mebbe make 'em pay a hair fur a hair!
EBEN *(decisively)*. But t'ain't that. Ye won't never go because ye'll wait here fur yer share o' the farm, thinkin' allus he'll die soon.
SIMEON *(after a pause)*. We've a right.
PETER. Two-thirds belongs t' us.
EBEN *(jumping to his feet)*. Ye've no right! She wa'n't yewr Maw! It was her farm! Didn't he steal it from her? She's dead. It's my farm.
SIMEON *(sardonically)*. Tell that t' Paw—when he comes! I'll bet ye a dollar he'll laugh—fur once in his life. Ha! *(He laughs himself in one single mirthless bark.)*
PETER *(amused in turn, echoes his brother)*. Ha!
SIMEON *(after a pause)*. What've ye got held agin us, Eben? Year after year it's skulked in yer eye—somethin'.
PETER. Ay-eh.
EBEN. Ay-eh. They's somethin'. *(Suddenly exploding)* Why didn't ye never stand between him 'n' my Maw when he was slavin' her to her grave—t' pay her back fur the kindness she done t' yew? *(There is a long pause. They stare at him in surprise.)*
SIMEON. Waal—the stock'd got t' be watered.
PETER. 'R they was woodin' t' do.
SIMEON. 'R plowin'.

PETER. 'R hayin'.
SIMEON. 'R spreadin' manure.
PETER. 'R weedin'.
SIMEON. 'R prunin'.
PETER. 'R milkin'.
EBEN *(breaking in harshly).* An' makin' walls—stone atop o' stone—makin' walls till yer heart's a stone ye heft up out o' the way o' growth onto a stone wall t' wall in yer heart!
SIMEON *(matter-of-factly).* We never had no time t' meddle.
PETER *(to EBEN).* Yew was fifteen afore yer Maw died—an' big fur yer age. Why didn't ye never do nothin'?
EBEN *(harshly).* They was chores t' do, wa'n't they? *(A pause—then slowly)* It was on'y arter she died I come to think o' it. Me cookin' —doin' her work—that made me know her, suffer her sufferin'—she'd come back t' help—come back t' bile potatoes—come back t' fry bacon—come back t' bake biscuits—come back all cramped up t' shake the fire, an' carry ashes, her eyes weepin' an' bloody with smoke an' cinders same's they used t' be. She still comes back—stands by the stove thar in the evenin'—she can't find it nateral sleepin' an' restin' in peace. She can't git used t' bein' free—even in her grave.
SIMEON. She never complained none.
EBEN. She'd got too tired. She'd got too used t' bein' too tired. That was what he done. *(With vengeful passion)* An' sooner'r later, I'll meddle. I'll say the thin's I didn't say then t' him! I'll yell 'em at the top o' my lungs. I'll see t' it my Maw gits some rest an' sleep in her grave! *(He sits down again, relapsing into a brooding silence. They look at him with a queer indifferent curiosity.)*
PETER *(after a pause).* Whar in tarnation d'ye s'pose he went, Sim?
SIMEON. Dunno. He druv off in the buggy, all spick an' span, with the mare all breshed an' shiny, druv off clackin' his tongue an' wavin' his whip. I remember it right well. I was finishin' plowin', it was spring an' May an' sunset, an' gold in the West, an' he druv off into it. I yells "Whar ye goin', Paw?" an' he hauls up by the stone wall a jiffy. His old snake's eyes was glitterin' in the sun like he'd been drinkin' a jugful an' he says with a mule's grin: "Don't ye run away till I come back!"
PETER. Wonder if he knowed we was wantin' fur Californi-a?
SIMEON. Mebbe. I didn't say nothin' and he says, lookin' kinder queer an' sick: "I been hearin' the hens cluckin' an' the roosters crowin' all the durn day. I been listenin' t' the cows lowin' an' everythin' else kickin' up till I can't stand it no more. It's spring an' I'm feelin' damned," he says. "Damned like an old bare hickory tree fit on'y fur burnin'," he says. An' then I calc'late I must've looked a mite hopeful, fur he adds real spry and vicious: "But don't git no fool idee I'm dead. I've sworn t' live a hundred an' I'll do it, if on'y t' spite yer sinful greed! An' now I'm ridin' out t' learn God's message t' me in the spring, like the prophets done. An' yew git back t' yer plowin'," he says. An' he druv off singin' a hymn. I thought he was drunk—'r I'd stopped him goin'.
EBEN *(scornfully).* No, ye wouldn't! Ye're scared o' him. He's stronger

—inside—than both o' ye put together!

PETER *(sardonically).* An' yew—be yew Samson?

EBEN. I'm gittin' stronger. I kin feel it growin' in me—growin' an' growin'—till it'll bust out—! *(He gets up and puts on his coat and a hat. They watch him, gradually breaking into grins.* EBEN *avoids their eyes sheepishly.)* I'm goin' out fur a spell—up the road.

PETER. T' the village?

SIMEON. T' see Minnie?

EBEN *(defiantly).* Ay-eh!

PETER *(jeeringly).* The Scarlet Woman!

SIMEON. Lust—that's what's growin' in ye!

EBEN. Waal—she's purty!

PETER. She's been purty fur twenty year!

SIMEON. A new coat o' paint'll make a heifer out of forty.

EBEN. She hain't forty!

PETER. If she hain't, she's teeterin' on the edge.

EBEN *(desperately).* What d'yew know—

PETER. All they is . . . Sim knew her—an' then me arter—

SIMEON. An' Paw kin tell yew somethin' too! He was fust!

EBEN. D'ye mean t' say he . . . ?

SIMEON *(with a grin).* Ay-eh! We air his heirs in everythin'!

EBEN *(intensely).* That's more to it! That grows on it! It'll bust soon! *(Then violently)* I'll go smash my fist in her face! *(He pulls open the door in rear violently.)*

SIMEON *(with a wink at* PETER—*drawlingly).* Mebbe—but the night's wa'm—purty—by the time ye git thar mebbe ye'll kiss her instead!

PETER. Sart'n he will! *(They both roar with coarse laughter.* EBEN *rushes out and slams the door—then the outside front door—comes around the corner of the house and stands still by the gate, staring up at the sky.)*

SIMEON *(looking after him).* Like his Paw.

PETER. Dead spit an' image!

SIMEON. Dog'll eat dog!

PETER. Ay-eh. *(Pause. With yearning)* Mebbe a year from now we'll be in Californi-a.

SIMEON. Ay-eh. *(A pause. Both yawn.)* Let's git t'bed. *(He blows out the candle. They go out door in rear.* EBEN *stretches his arms up to the sky—rebelliously.)*

EBEN. Waal—thar's a star, an' somewhar's they's him, an' here's me, an' thar's Min up the road—in the same night. What if I does kiss her? She's like t'night, she's soft 'n' wa'm, her eyes kin wink like a star, her mouth's wa'm, her arms're wa'm, she smells like a wa'm plowed field, she's purty . . . Ay-eh! By God A'mighty she's purty, an' I don't give a damn how many sins she's sinned afore mine or who's she's sinned 'em with, my sin's as purty as any one on 'em! *(He strides off down the road to the left.)*

SCENE 3

It is the pitch darkness just before dawn. EBEN *comes in from the left and goes around to the porch, feeling his way, chuckling bitterly and cursing half-aloud to himself.*

EBEN. The cussed old miser! *(He can be heard going in the front door. There is a pause as he goes upstairs, then a loud knock on the bedroom door of the brothers.)* Wake up!
SIMEON *(startedly).* Who thar?
EBEN *(pushing open the door and coming in, a lighted candle in his hand. The bedroom of the brothers is revealed. Its ceiling is the sloping roof. They can stand upright only close to the center dividing wall of the upstairs.* SIMEON *and* PETER *are in a double bed, front.* EBEN'S *cot is to the rear.* EBEN *has a mixture of silly grin and vicious scowl on his face).* I be!
PETER *(angrily).* What in hell's-fire . . . ?
EBEN. I got news fur ye! Ha! *(He gives one abrupt sardonic guffaw.)*
SIMEON *(angrily).* Couldn't ye hold it 'til we'd got our sleep?
EBEN. It's nigh sunup. *(Then explosively)* He's gone an' married agen!
SIMEON AND PETER *(explosively).* Paw?
EBEN. Got himself hitched to a female 'bout thirty-five—an' purty, they says . . .
SIMEON *(aghast).* It's a durn lie!
PETER. Who says?
SIMEON. They been stringin' ye!
EBEN. Think I'm a dunce, do ye? The hull village says. The preacher from New Dover, he brung the news—told it t'our preacher—New Dover, that's whar the old loon got himself hitched—that's whar the woman lived—
PETER *(no longer doubting—stunned).* Waal . . . !
SIMEON *(the same).* Waal . . . !
EBEN *(sitting down on a bed—with vicious hatred).* Ain't he a devil out o' hell? It's jest t' spite us—the damned old mule!
PETER *(after a pause).* Everythin'll go t' her now.
SIMEON. Ay-eh. *(A pause—dully)* Waal—if it's done—
PETER. It's done us. *(Pause—then persuasively)* They's gold in the fields o' Californi-a, Sim. No good a-stayin' here now.
SIMEON. Jest what I was a-thinkin'. *(Then with decision)* S'well fust's last! Let's light out and git this mornin'.
PETER. Suits me.
EBEN. Ye must like walkin'.
SIMEON *(sardonically).* If ye'd grow wings on us we'd fly thar!
EBEN. Ye'd like ridin' better—on a boat, wouldn't ye? *(Fumbles in his pocket and takes out a crumpled sheet of foolscap)* Waal, if ye sign this ye kin ride on a boat. I've had it writ out an' ready in case ye'd ever go. It says fur three hundred dollars t' each ye agree yewr shares o' the farm is sold t' me. *(They look suspiciously at the paper. A pause.)*
SIMEON *(wonderingly).* But if he's hitched agen—

PETER. An' whar'd yew git that sum o' money, anyways?
EBEN *(cunningly).* I know whar it's hid. I been waitin'—Maw told me. She knew whar it lay fur years, but she was waitin' . . . It's her'n—the money he hoarded from her farm an' hid from Maw. It's my money by rights now.
PETER. Whar's it hid?
EBEN *(cunningly).* Whar yew won't never find it without me. Maw spied on him—'r she'd never knowed. *(A pause. They look at him suspiciously, and he at them.)* Waal, is it fa'r trade?
SIMEON. Dunno.
PETER. Dunno.
SIMEON *(looking at window).* Sky's grayin'.
PETER. Ye better start the fire, Eben.
SIMEON. An' fix some vittles.
EBEN. Ay-eh. *(Then with a forced jocular heartiness)* I'll git ye a good one. If ye're startin' t' hoof it t' Californi-a ye'll need somethin' that'll stick t' yer ribs. *(He turns to the door, adding meaningly)* But ye kin ride on a boat if ye'll swap. *(He stops at the door and pauses. They stare at him.)*
SIMEON *(suspiciously).* Whar was ye all night?
EBEN *(defiantly).* Up t' Min's. *(Then slowly)* Walkin' thar, fust I felt 's if I'd kiss her; then I got a-thinkin' o' what ye'd said o' him an' her an' I says, I'll bust her nose fur that! Then I got t' the village an' heerd the news an' I got madder'n hell an' run all the way t' Min's not knowin' what I'd do—*(He pauses—then sheepishly but more defiantly)* Waal—when I seen her, I didn't hit her—nor I didn't kiss her nuther—I begun t' beller like a calf an' cuss at the same time, I was so durn mad —an' she got scared—an' I jest grabbed holt an' tuk her! *(Proudly)* Yes, sirree! I tuk her. She may've been his'n—an' your'n, too—but she's mine now!
SIMEON *(dryly).* In love, air yew?
EBEN *(with lofty scorn).* Love! I don't take no stock in sech slop!
PETER *(winking at* SIMEON*).* Mebbe Eben's aimin' t' marry, too.
SIMEON. Min'd make a true faithful he'pmeet! *(They snicker.)*
EBEN. What do I care fur her—'ceptin' she's round an' wa'm? The p'int is she was his'n—an' now she belongs t' me! *(He goes to the door— then turns—rebelliously.)* An' Min hain't sech a bad un. They's worse'n Min in the world, I'll bet ye! Wait'll we see this cow the Old Man's hitched t'! She'll beat Min, I got a notion! *(He starts to go out.)*
SIMEON *(suddenly).* Mebbe ye'll try t' make her your'n, too?
PETER. Ha! *(He gives a sardonic laugh of relish at this idea.)*
EBEN *(spitting with disgust).* Her—here—sleepin' with him—stealin' my Maw's farm! I'd as soon pet a skunk 'r kiss a snake! *(He goes out. The two stare after him suspiciously. A pause. They listen to his steps receding.)*
PETER. He's startin' the fire.
SIMEON. I'd like t' ride t' Californi-a—but—
PETER. Min might o' put some scheme in his head.
SIMEON. Mebbe it's all a lie 'bout Paw marryin'. We'd best wait an' see the bride.

PETER. An' don't sign nothin' till we does!
SIMEON. Nor till we've tested it's good money! *(Then with a grin)* But if Paw's hitched we'd be sellin' Eben somethin' we'd never git nohow!
PETER. We'll wait an' see. *(Then with sudden vindictive anger)* An' till he comes, let's yew 'n' me not wuk a lick, let Eben tend to thin's if he's a mind t', let's us jest sleep an' eat an' drink likker, an' let the hull damned farm go t' blazes!
SIMEON *(excitedly)*. By God, we've 'arned a rest! We'll play rich fur a change. I hain't a-goin' to stir outa bed till breakfast's ready.
PETER. An' on the table!
SIMEON *(after a pause—thoughtfully)*. What d' ye calc'late she'll be like—our new Maw? Like Eben thinks?
PETER. More'n likely.
SIMEON *(vindictively)*. Waal—I hope she's a she-devil that'll make him wish he was dead an' livin' in the pit o' hell fur comfort!
PETER *(fervently)*. Amen!
SIMEON *(imitating his father's voice)*. "I'm ridin' out t' learn God's message t' me in the spring like the prophets done," he says. I'll bet right then an' thar he knew plumb well he was goin' whorin', the stinkin' old hypocrite!

SCENE 4

Same as Scene 2—shows the interior of the kitchen with a lighted candle on table. It is gray dawn outside. SIMEON *and* PETER *are just finishing their breakfast.* EBEN *sits before his plate of untouched food, brooding frowningly.*

PETER *(glancing at him rather irritably)*. Lookin' glum don't help none.
SIMEON *(sarcastically)*. Sorrowin' over his lust o' the flesh!
PETER *(with a grin)*. Was she yer fust?
EBEN *(angrily)*. None o' yer business. *(A pause.)* I was thinkin' o' him. I got a notion he's gittin' near—I kin feel him comin' on like yew kin feel malaria chill afore it takes ye.
PETER. It's too early yet.
SIMEON. Dunno. He'd like t' catch us nappin'—just t' have somethin' t' hoss us 'round over.
PETER *(mechanically gets to his feet.* SIMEON *does the same)*. Waal —let's git t' wuk. *(They both plod mechanically toward the door before they realize. Then they stop short.)*
SIMEON *(grinning)*. Ye're a cussed fool, Pete—and I be wuss! Let him see we hain't wukin'! We don't give a durn!
PETER *(as they go back to the table)*. Not a damned durn! It'll serve t' show him we're done with him. *(They sit down again.* EBEN *stares from one to the other with surprise.)*
SIMEON *(grins at him)*. We're aimin' t' start bein' lilies o' the field.
PETER. Nary a toil 'r spin 'r lick o' wuk do we put in!
SIMEON. Ye're sole owner—till he comes—that's what ye wanted. Waal, ye got t' be sole hand, too.

PETER. The cows air bellerin'. Ye better hustle at the milkin'.
EBEN *(with excited joy)*. Ye mean ye'll sign the paper?
SIMEON *(dryly)*. Mebbe.
PETER. Mebbe.
SIMEON. We're considerin'. *(Peremptorily)* Ye better git t' wuk.
EBEN *(with queer excitement)*. It's Maw's farm agen! It's my farm! Them's my cows! I'll milk my durn fingers off fur cows o' mine! *(He goes out door in rear, they stare after him indifferently.)*
SIMEON. Like his Paw.
PETER. Dead spit 'n' image!
SIMEON. Waal—let dog eat dog! *(EBEN comes out of front door and around the corner of the house. The sky is beginning to grow flushed with sunrise. EBEN stops by the gate and stares around him with glowing, possessive eyes. He takes in the whole farm with his embracing glance of desire.)*
EBEN. It's purty! It's damned purty! It's mine! *(He suddenly throws his head back boldly and glares with hard, defiant eye at the sky.)* Mine, d'ye hear? Mine! *(He turns and walks quickly off left, rear, toward the barn. The two brothers light their pipes.)*
SIMEON *(putting his muddy boots up on the table, tilting back his chair, and puffing defiantly)*. Waal—this air solid comfort—fur once.
PETER. Ay-eh. *(He follows suit. A pause. Unconsciously they both sigh.)*
SIMEON *(suddenly)*. He never was much o' a hand at milkin', Eben wa'n't.
PETER *(with a snort)*. His hands air like hoofs! *(A pause.)*
SIMEON. Reach down the jug thar! Let's take a swaller. I'm feelin' kind o' low.
PETER. Good idee! *(He does so—gets two glasses—they pour out drinks of whisky.)* Here's t' the gold in Californi-a!
SIMEON. An' luck t' find it! *(They drink—puff resolutely—sigh—take their feet down from the table.)*
PETER. Likker don't 'pear t' sot right.
SIMEON. We hain't used t' it this early. *(A pause. They become very restless.)*
PETER. Gittin' close in this kitchen.
SIMEON *(with immense relief)*. Let's git a breath o' air. *(They arise briskly and go out rear—appear around house and stop by the gate. They stare up at the sky with a numbed appreciation.)*
PETER. Purty!
SIMEON. Ay-eh. Gold's t' the East now.
PETER. Sun's startin' with us fur the Golden West.
SIMEON *(staring around the farm, his compressed face tightened, unable to conceal his emotion)*. Waal—it's our last mornin'—mebbe.
PETER *(the same)*. Ay-eh.
SIMEON *(stamps his foot on the earth and addresses it desperately)*. Waal—ye've thirty year o' me buried in ye—spread out over ye—blood an' bone an' sweat—rotted away—fertilizin' ye—richin' yer soul—prime manure, by God, that's what I been t' ye!
PETER. Ay-eh! An' me!

SIMEON. An' yew, Peter. *(He sighs—then spits.)* Waal—no use'n cryin' over spilt milk.
PETER. They's gold in the West—an' freedom, mebbe. We been slaves t' stone walls here.
SIMEON *(defiantly).* We hain't nobody's slaves from this out—nor no thin's slaves nuther. *(A pause—restlessly)* Speakin' o' milk, wonder how Eben's managin'?
PETER. I s'pose he's managin'.
SIMEON. Mebbe we'd ought t' help—this once.
PETER. Mebbe. The cows knows us.
SIMEON. An' likes us. They don't know him much.
PETER. An' the hosses, an' pigs, an' chickens. They don't know him much.
SIMEON. They knows us like brothers—an' likes us! *(Proudly)* Hain't we raised 'em t' be fust-rate, number one prize stock?
PETER. We hain't—not no more.
SIMEON *(dully).* I was fergittin'. *(Then resignedly)* Waal, let's go help Eben a spell an' git waked up.
PETER. Suits me. *(They are starting off down left, rear, for the barn when* EBEN *appears from there hurrying toward them, his face excited.)*
EBEN *(breathlessly).* Waal—har they be! The old mule an' the bride! I seen 'em from the barn down below at the turnin'.
PETER. How could ye tell that far?
EBEN. Hain't I as far-sight as he's near-sight? Don't I know the mare 'n' buggy, an' two people settin' in it? Who else . . . ? An' I tell ye I kin feel 'em a-comin', too! *(He squirms as if he had the itch.)*
PETER *(beginning to be angry).* Waal—let him do his own unhitchin'!
SIMEON *(angry in his turn).* Let's hustle in an' git our bundles an' be a-goin' as he's a-comin'. I don't want never t' step inside the door agen arter he's back. *(They both start back around the corner of the house.* EBEN *follows them.)*
EBEN *(anxiously).* Will ye sign it afore ye go?
PETER. Let's see the color o' the old skinflint's money an' we'll sign. *(They disappear left. The two brothers clump upstairs to get their bundles.* EBEN *appears in the kitchen, runs to the window, peers out, comes back and pulls up a strip of flooring in under stove, takes out a canvas bag and puts it on table, then sets the floorboard back in place. The two brothers appear a moment after. They carry old carpet bags.)*
EBEN *(puts his hand on bag guardingly).* Have ye signed?
SIMEON *(shows paper in his hand).* Ay-eh. *(Greedily)* Be that the money?
EBEN *(opens bag and pours out pile of twenty-dollar gold pieces).* Twenty-dollar pieces—thirty on 'em. Count 'em. *(PETER does so, arranging them in stacks of five, biting one or two to test them.)*
PETER. Six hundred. *(He puts them in bag and puts it inside his shirt carefully.)*
SIMEON *(handing paper to* EBEN*).* Har ye be.
EBEN *(after a glance, folds it carefully and hides it under his shirt—gratefully).* Thank yew.

PETER. Thank yew fur the ride.
SIMEON. We'll send ye a lump o' gold fur Christmas. *(A pause.* EBEN *stares at them and they at him.)*
PETER *(awkwardly).* Waal—we're a-goin'.
SIMEON. Comin' out t' the yard?
EBEN. No. I'm waitin' in here a spell. *(Another silence. The brothers edge awkwardly to the door in rear—then turn and stand.)*
SIMEON. Waal—good-by.
PETER. Good-by.   100
EBEN. Good-by. *(They go out. He sits down at the table, faces the stove and pulls out the paper. He looks from it to the stove. His face, lighted up by the shaft of sunlight from the window, has an expression of trance. His lips move. The two brothers come out to the gate.)*
PETER *(looking off toward barn).* Thar he be—unhitchin'.
SIMEON *(with a chuckle).* I'll bet ye he's riled!
PETER. An' thar she be.
SIMEON. Let's wait 'n' see what our new Maw looks like.
PETER *(with a grin).* An' give him our partin' cuss!
SIMEON *(grinning).* I feel like raisin' fun. I feel light in my head an' feet.
PETER. Me, too. I feel like laffin' till I'd split up the middle.
SIMEON. Reckon it's the likker?   110
PETER. No. My feet feel itchin' t' walk an' walk—an' jump high over thin's—an'....
SIMEON. Dance? *(A pause.)*
PETER *(puzzled).* It's plumb onnateral.
SIMEON *(a light coming over his face).* I calc'late it's 'cause school's out. It's holiday. Fur once we're free!
PETER *(dazedly).* Free?
SIMEON. The halter's broke—the harness is busted—the fence bars is down—the stone walls air crumblin' an' tumblin'! We'll be kickin' up an' tearin' away down the road!   120
PETER *(Drawing a deep breath—oratorically).* Anybody that wants this stinkin' old rock-pile of a farm kin hev it. 'Tain't our'n, no sirree!
SIMEON *(takes the gate off its hinges and puts it under his arm).* We harby 'bolishes shet gates an' open gates, an' all gates, by thunder!
PETER. We'll take it with us fur luck an' let 'er sail free down some river.
SIMEON *(as a sound of voices comes from left, rear).* Har they comes! *(The two brothers congeal into two stiff, grim-visaged statues.)*
EPHRAIM CABOT *and* ABBIE PUTNAM *come in.* CABOT *is seventy-five, tall and gaunt, with great, wiry, concentrated power, but stoop-shouldered from toil. His face is as hard as if it were hewn out of a boulder, yet there is a weakness in it, a petty pride in its own narrow strength. His eyes are small, close together, and extremely near-sighted, blinking continually in the effort to focus on objects, their stare having a straining, ingrowing quality. He is dressed in his dismal black Sunday suit.* ABBIE *is thirty-five, buxom, full of vitality. Her round face is pretty but marred by its rather gross sensuality. There is strength and obstinacy in her jaw, a hard determination in her eyes,*

and about her whole personality the same unsettled, untamed, desperate quality which is so apparent in EBEN.)
CABOT *(as they enter—a queer strangled emotion in his dry cracking voice).* Har we be t' hum, Abbie.
ABBIE *(with lust for the word).* Hum! *(Her eyes gloating on the house without seeming to see the two stiff figures at the gate.)* It's purty—purty! I can't b'lieve it's r'ally mine.
CABOT *(sharply).* Yewr'n? Mine! *(He stares at her penetratingly. She stares back. He adds relentingly.)* Our'n—mebbe! It was lonesome too long. I was growin' old in the spring. A hum's got t' hev a woman.
ABBIE *(her voice taking possession).* A woman's got t' hev a hum!
CABOT *(nodding uncertainly).* Ay-eh. *(Then irritably)* Whar be they? Ain't thar nobody about—'r wukin'—'r' nothin'?
ABBIE *(sees the brothers. She returns their stare of cold appraising contempt with interest—slowly).* Thar's two men loafin' at the gate an' starin' at me like a couple o' strayed hogs.
CABOT *(straining his eyes).* I kin see 'em—but I can't make out....
SIMEON. It's Simeon.
PETER. It's Peter.
CABOT *(exploding).* Why hain't ye wukin'?
SIMEON *(dryly).* We're waitin' t' welcome ye hum—yew an' the bride!
CABOT *(confusedly).* Huh? Waal—this be yer new Maw, boys. *(She stares at them and they at her.)*
SIMEON *(turns away and spits contemptuously).* I see her!
PETER *(spits also).* An' I see her!
ABBIE *(with the conqueror's conscious superiority).* I'll go in an' look at *my* house. *(She goes slowly around to porch.)*
SIMEON *(with a snort).* *Her* house!
PETER *(calls after her).* Ye'll find Eben inside. Ye better not tell him it's *yewr* house.
ABBIE *(mouthing the name).* Eben. *(Then quietly)* I'll tell Eben.
CABOT *(with a contemptuous sneer).* Ye needn't heed Eben. Eben's a dumb fool—like his Maw—soft an' simple!
SIMEON *(with his sardonic burst of laughter).* Ha! Eben's a chip o' yew—spit 'n' image—hard 'n' bitter's a hickory tree! Dog'll eat dog. He'll eat ye yet, old man!
CABOT *(commandingly).* Ye git t' wuk!
SIMEON *(as* ABBIE *disappears in house—winks at* PETER *and says tauntingly).* So that thar's our new Maw, be it? Whar in hell did ye dig her up? *(He and* PETER *laugh.)*
PETER. Ha! Ye'd better turn her in the pen with the other sows. *(They laugh uproariously, slapping their thighs.)*
CABOT *(so amazed at their effrontery that he stutters in confusion).* Simeon! Peter! What's come over ye? Air ye drunk?
SIMEON. We're free, old man—free o' yew an' the hull damned farm! *(They grow more and more hilarious and excited.)*
PETER. An' we're startin' out fur the gold fields o' Californi-a!
SIMEON. Ye kin take this place an' burn it!
PETER. An' bury it—fur all we cares!
SIMEON. We're free, old man! *(He cuts a caper.)*

PETER. Free! *(He gives a kick in the air.)*
SIMEON *(in a frenzy)*. Whoop!
PETER. Whoop! *(They do an absurd Indian war dance about the old man who is petrified between rage and the fear that they are insane.)*
SIMEON. We're free as Injuns! Lucky we don't sculp ye!
PETER. An' burn yer barn an' kill the stock!
SIMEON. An' rape yer new woman! Whoop! *(He and PETER stop their dance, holding their sides, rocking with wild laughter.)*
CABOT *(edging away)*. Lust fur gold—fur the sinful, easy gold o' Californi-a! It's made ye mad!
SIMEON *(tauntingly)*. Wouldn't ye like us to send ye back some sinful gold, ye old sinner?
PETER. They's gold besides what's in Californi-a! *(He retreats back beyond the vision of the old man and takes the bag of money and flaunts it in the air above his head, laughing.)*
SIMEON. And sinfuller, too!
PETER. We'll be voyagin' on the sea! Whoop! *(He leaps up and down.)*
SIMEON. Livin' free! Whoop! *(He leaps in turn.)*
CABOT *(suddenly roaring with rage)*. My cuss on ye!
SIMEON. Take our'n in trade fur it! Whoop!
CABOT. I'll hev ye both chained up in the asylum!
PETER. Ye old skinflint! Good-by!
SIMEON. Ye old blood sucker! Good-by!
CABOT. Go afore I . . . !
PETER. Whoop! *(He picks a stone from the road. SIMEON does the same.)*
SIMEON. Maw'll be in the parlor.
PETER. Ay-eh! One! Two!
CABOT *(frightened)*. What air ye . . . ?
PETER. Three! *(They both throw, the stones hitting the parlor window with a crash of glass, tearing the shade.)*
SIMEON. Whoop!
PETER. Whoop!
CABOT *(in a fury now, rushing toward them)*. If I kin lay hands on ye—I'll break yer bones fur ye! *(But they beat a capering retreat before him, SIMEON with the gate still under his arm. CABOT comes back, panting with impotent rage. Their voices as they go off take up the song of the gold-seekers to the old tune of "Oh, Susannah!")*

"I jumped aboard the Liza ship,
And traveled on the sea,
And every time I thought of home
I wished it wasn't me!
Oh! Californi-a,
That's the land fur me!
I'm off to Californi-a!
With my wash bowl on my knee."

In the meantime, the window of the upper bedroom on right is raised and ABBIE *sticks her head out. She looks down at* CABOT—*with a sigh of relief.*

ABBIE. Waal—that's the last o' them two, hain't it? *(He doesn't answer. Then in possessive tones)* This here's a nice bedroom, Ephraim. It's a r'al nice bed. Is it my room, Ephraim?
CABOT *(grimly—without looking up).* Our'n! *(She cannot control a grimace of aversion and pulls back her head slowly and shuts the window. A sudden horrible thought seems to enter* CABOT'S *head.)* They been up to somethin'! Mebbe—mebbe they've pizened the stock —'r somethin'! *(He almost runs off down toward the barn. A moment later the kitchen door is slowly pushed open and* ABBIE *enters. For a moment she stands looking at* EBEN. *He does not notice her at first. Her eyes take him in penetratingly with a calculating appraisal of his strength as against hers. But under this her desire is dimly awakened by his youth and good looks. Suddenly he becomes conscious of her presence and looks up. Their eyes meet. He leaps to his feet, glowering at her speechlessly.)*
ABBIE *(in her most seductive tones which she uses all through this scene).* Be you—Eben? I'm Abbie—*(She laughs.)* I mean, I'm yer new Maw.
EBEN *(viciously).* No, damn ye!
ABBIE *(as if she hadn't heard—with a queer smile).* Yer Paw's spoke a lot o' yew. . . .
EBEN. Ha!
ABBIE. Ye mustn't mind him. He's an old man. *(A long pause. They stare at each other.)* I don't want t' pretend playin' Maw t' ye, Eben. *(Admiringly)* Ye're too big an' too strong fur that. I want t' be frens with ye. Mebbe with me fur a fren ye'd find ye'd like livin' here better. I kin make it easy fur ye with him, mebbe. *(With a scornful sense of power)* I calc'late I kin get him t' do most anythin' fur me.
EBEN *(with bitter scorn).* Ha! *(They stare again,* EBEN *obscurely moved, physically attracted to her—in forced stilted tones)* Yew kin go t' the devil!
ABBIE *(calmly).* If cussin' me does ye good, cuss all ye've a mind t'. I'm all prepared t' have ye agin me—at fust. I don't blame ye nuther. I'd feel the same at any stranger comin' t' take my Maw's place. *(He shudders. She is watching him carefully.)* Yew must've cared a lot fur yewr Maw, didn't ye? My Maw died afore I'd growed. I don't remember her none. *(A pause.)* But yew won't hate me long, Eben. I'm not the wust in the world—an' yew an' me've got a lot in common. I kin tell that by lookin' at ye. Waal—I've had a hard life, too—oceans o' trouble an' nuthin' but wuk fur reward. I was a orphan early an' had t' wuk fur others in other folks' hums. Then I married an' he turned out a drunken spreer an' so he had to wuk fur others an' me too agen in other folks' hums, an' the baby died, an' my husband got sick an' died too, an' I was glad sayin' now I'm free fur once, on'y I diskivered right away all I was free fur was t' wuk agen in other folks' hums, doin' other folks' wuk till I'd most give up hope o' ever doin' my own wuk in my own hum, an' then your Paw come. . . .
*(*CABOT *appears returning from the barn. He comes to the gate and*

looks down the road the brothers have gone. A faint strain of their retreating voices is heard: "Oh, Californi-a! That's the place for me." He stands glowering, his fist clenched, his face grim with rage.)

EBEN *(fighting against his growing attraction and sympathy—harshly).* An' bought yew—like a harlot! *(She is stung and flushes angrily. She has been sincerely moved by the recital of her troubles. He adds furiously:)* An' the price he's payin' ye—this farm—was my Maw's, damn ye!—an' mine now!

ABBIE *(with a cool laugh of confidence).* Yewr'n? We'll see 'bout that! *(Then strongly)* Waal—what if I did need a hum? What else'd I marry an old man like him fur?

EBEN *(maliciously).* I'll tell him ye said that!

ABBIE *(smiling).* I'll say ye're lyin' a-purpose—an' he'll drive ye off the place!

EBEN. Ye devil!

ABBIE *(defying him).* This be my farm—this be my hum—this be my kitchen—!

EBEN *(furiously, as if he were going to attack her).* Shut up, damn ye!

ABBIE *(walks up to him—a queer coarse expression of desire in her face and body—slowly).* An' upstairs—that be my bedroom—an' my bed! *(He stares into her eyes, terribly confused and torn. She adds softly:)* I hain't bad nor mean—'ceptin' fur an enemy—but I got t' fight fur what's due me out o' life, if I ever 'spect t' git it. *(Then putting her hand on his arm—seductively)* Let's yew 'n' me be frens, Eben.

EBEN *(stupidly—as if hypnotized).* Ay-eh. *(Then furiously flinging off her arm)* No, ye durned old witch! I hate ye! *(He rushes out the door.)*

ABBIE *(looks after him smiling satisfiedly—then half to herself, mouthing the word).* Eben's nice. *(She looks at the table, proudly.)* I'll wash up *my* dishes now. *(EBEN appears outside, slamming the door behind him. He comes around corner, stops on seeing his father, and stands staring at him with hate.)*

CABOT *(raising his arms to heaven in the fury he can no longer control).* Lord God o' Hosts, smite the undutiful sons with Thy wust cuss!

EBEN *(breaking in violently).* Yew 'n' yewr God! Allus cussin' folks—allus naggin' 'em!

CABOT *(oblivious to him—summoningly).* God o' the old! God o' the lonesome!

EBEN *(mockingly).* Naggin' His sheep t' sin! T' hell with yewr God! *(CABOT turns. He and EBEN glower at each other.)*

CABOT *(harshly).* So it's yew. I might've knowed it. *(Shaking his finger threateningly at him)* Blasphemin' fool! *(Then quickly)* Why hain't ye t' wuk?

EBEN. Why hain't yew? They've went. I can't wuk it all alone.

CABOT *(contemptuously).* Nor noways! I'm wuth ten o' ye yit, old's I be! Ye'll never be more'n half a man! *(Then, matter-of-factly)* Waal—let's git t' the barn. *(They go. A last faint note of the "Californi-a" song is heard from the distance. ABBIE is washing her dishes.)*

CURTAIN

PART 2

SCENE 1

The exterior of the farmhouse, as in Part 1—a hot Sunday afternoon two months later. ABBIE, *dressed in her best, is discovered sitting in a rocker at the end of the porch. She rocks listlessly, enervated by the heat, staring in front of her with bored, half-closed eyes.*

EBEN *sticks his head out of his bedroom window. He looks around furtively and tries to see—or hear—if anyone is on the porch, but although he has been careful to make no noise, Abbie has sensed his movement. She stops rocking, her face grows animated and eager, she waits attentively.* EBEN *seems to feel her presence, he scowls back his thoughts of her and spits with exaggerated disdain—then withdraws back into the room.* ABBIE *waits, holding her breath as she listens with passionate eagerness for every sound within the house.*

EBEN *comes out. Their eyes meet. His falter, he is confused, he turns away and slams the door resentfully. At this gesture,* ABBIE *laughs tantalizingly, amused but at the same time piqued and irritated. He scowls, strides off the porch to the path and starts to walk past her to the road with a grand swagger of ignoring her existence. He is dressed in his store suit, spruced up, his face shines from soap and water.* ABBIE *leans forward on her chair, her eyes hard and angry now, and, as he passes her, gives a sneering, taunting chuckle.*

EBEN *(stung—turns on her furiously).* What air yew cacklin' 'bout?
ABBIE *(triumphant).* Yew!
EBEN. What about me?
ABBIE. Ye look all slicked up like a prize bull.
EBEN *(with a sneer).* Waal—ye hain't so durned purty yerself, be ye? *(They stare into each other's eyes, his held by hers in spite of himself, hers glowingly possessive. Their physical attraction becomes a palpable force quivering in the hot air.)*
ABBIE *(softly).* Ye don't mean that, Eben. Ye may think ye mean it, mebbe, but ye don't. Ye can't. It's agin nature, Eben. Ye been fightin' yer nature ever since the day I come—tryin' t' tell yerself I hain't purty t'ye. *(She laughs a low humid laugh without taking her eyes from his. A pause—her body squirms desirously—she murmurs languorously.)* Hain't the sun strong an' hot? Ye kin feel it burnin' into the earth—Nature—makin' thin's grow—bigger 'n' bigger—burnin' inside ye—makin' ye want t' grow—into somethin' else—till ye're jined with it—an' it's yourn—but it owns ye, too—an' makes ye grow bigger—like a tree—like them elums—*(She laughs again softly, holding his eyes. He takes a step toward her, compelled against his will.)* Nature'll beat ye, Eben. Ye might's well own up t' it fust 's last.
EBEN *(trying to break from her spell—confusedly).* If Paw'd hear ye goin' on.... *(Resentfully)* But ye've made such a damned idjit out o' the old devil...! *(ABBIE laughs.)*
ABBIE. Waal—hain't it easier fur yew with him changed softer?
EBEN *(defiantly).* No. I'm fightin' him—fightin' yew—fightin' fur

10

20

Maw's rights t' her hum! *(This breaks her spell for him. He glowers at her.)* An' I'm onto ye. Ye hain't foolin' me a mite. Ye're aimin' t' swaller up everythin' an' make it your'n. Waal, you'll find I'm a heap sight bigger hunk nor yew kin chew! *(He turns from her with a sneer.)*

ABBIE *(trying to regain her ascendancy—seductively).* Eben!

EBEN. Leave me be! *(He starts to walk away.)*

ABBIE *(more commandingly).* Eben!

EBEN *(stops—resentfully).* What d'ye want?

ABBIE *(trying to conceal a growing excitement).* Whar air ye goin'?

EBEN *(with malicious nonchalance).* Oh—up the road a spell.

ABBIE. T' the village?

EBEN *(airily).* Mebbe.

ABBIE *(excitedly).* T' see that Min, I s'pose?

EBEN. Mebbe.

ABBIE *(weakly).* What d'ye want t' waste time on her fur?

EBEN *(revenging himself now—grinning at her).* Ye can't beat Nature, didn't ye say? *(He laughs and again starts to walk away.)*

ABBIE *(bursting out).* An ugly old hake!

EBEN *(with a tantalizing sneer).* She's purtier'n yew be!

ABBIE. That every wuthless drunk in the country has....

EBEN *(tauntingly).* Mebbe—but she's better'n yew. She owns up fa'r 'n' squar' t' her doin's.

ABBIE *(furiously).* Don't ye dare compare....

EBEN. She don't go sneakin' an' stealin'—what's mine.

ABBIE *(savagely seizing on his weak point).* Your'n? Yew mean—my farm?

EBEN. I mean the farm yew sold yerself fur like any other old whore—my farm!

ABBIE *(stung—fiercely).* Ye'll never live t' see the day when even a stinkin' weed on it'll belong t' ye! *(Then in a scream)* Git out o' my sight! Go on t' yer slut—disgracin' yer Paw 'n' me! I'll git yer Paw t' horsewhip ye off the place if I want t'! Ye're only livin' here 'cause I tolerate ye! Git along! I hate the sight o' ye! *(She stops, panting and glaring at him.)*

EBEN *(returning her glance in kind).* An' I hate the sight o' yew! *(He turns and strides off up the road. She follows his retreating figure with concentrated hate. Old* CABOT *appears coming up from the barn. The hard, grim expression of his face has changed. He seems in some queer way softened, mellowed. His eyes have taken on a strange, incongruous dreamy quality. Yet there is no hint of physical weakness about him—rather he looks more robust and younger.* ABBIE *sees him and turns away quickly with unconcealed aversion. He comes slowly up to her.)*

CABOT *(mildly).* War yew an' Eben quarrelin' agen?

ABBIE *(shortly).* No.

CABOT. Ye was talkin' a'mighty loud. *(He sits down on the edge of porch.)*

ABBIE *(snappishly).* If ye heered us they hain't no need askin' questions.

CABOT. I didn't hear what ye said.

ABBIE *(relieved)*. Waal—it wa'n't nothin' t' speak on.
CABOT *(after a pause)*. Eben's queer.
ABBIE *(bitterly)*. He's the dead spit 'n' image o' yew!
CABOT *(queerly interested)*. D'ye think so, Abbie? *(After a pause, ruminatingly)* Me 'n' Eben's allus fit 'n' fit. I never could b'ar him noways. He's so thunderin' soft—like his Maw.
ABBIE *(scornfully)*. Ay-eh! 'Bout as soft as yew be!
CABOT *(as if he hadn't heard)*. Mebbe I been too hard on him.
ABBIE *(jeeringly)*. Waal—ye're gettin' soft now—soft as slop! That's what Eben was sayin'.
CABOT *(his face instantly grim and ominous)*. Eben was sayin'? Waal, he'd best not do nothin' t' try me 'r he'll soon diskiver.... *(A pause. She keeps her face turned away. His gradually softens. He stares up at the sky.)* Purty, hain't it?
ABBIE *(crossly)*. I don't see nothin' purty.
CABOT. The sky. Feels like a wa'm field up thar.
ABBIE *(sarcastically)*. Air yew aimin' t' buy up over the farm too? *(She snickers contemptuously.)*
CABOT *(strangely)*. I'd like t' own my place up thar. *(A pause.)* I'm gittin' old, Abbie, I'm gittin' ripe on the bough. *(A pause. She stares at him mystified. He goes on.)* It's allus lonesome cold in the house— even when it's bilin' hot outside. Hain't yew noticed?
ABBIE. No.
CABOT. It's wa'm down t' the barn—nice smellin' an' wa'm—with the cows. *(A pause.)* Cows is queer.
ABBIE. Like yew?
CABOT. Like Eben. *(A pause.)* I'm gittin' t' feel resigned t' Eben—jest as I got t' feel 'bout his Maw. I'm gittin' t' learn to b'ar his softness— jest like her'n. I calc'late I c'd a'most take t' him—if he wa'n't sech a dumb fool! *(A pause.)* I s'pose it's old age a-creepin' in my bones.
ABBIE *(indifferently)*. Waal—ye hain't dead yet.
CABOT *(roused)*. No, I hain't, yew bet—not by a hell of a sight—I'm sound 'n' tough as hickory! *(Then moodily)* But arter three score and ten the Lord warns ye t' prepare. *(A pause.)* That's why Eben's come in my head. Now that his cussed sinful brothers is gone their path t' hell, they's no one left but Eben.
ABBIE *(resentfully)*. They's me, hain't they? *(Agitatedly)* What's all this sudden likin' ye tuk to Eben? Why don't ye say nothin' 'bout me? Hain't I yer lawful wife?
CABOT *(simply)*. Ay-eh. Ye be. *(A pause—he stares at her desirously —his eyes grow avid—then with a sudden movement he seizes her hands and squeezes them, declaiming in a queer camp meeting preacher's tempo:)* Yew air my Rose o' Sharon! Behold, yew air fair; yer eyes air doves; yer lips air like scarlet; yer two breasts air like two fawns; yer navel be like a round goblet; yer belly be like a heap o' wheat.... *(He covers her hand with kisses. She does not seem to notice. She stares before her with hard angry eyes.)*
ABBIE *(jerking her hands away—harshly)*. So ye're plannin' t' leave the farm t' Eben, air ye?
CABOT *(dazedly)*. Leave...? *(Then with resentful obstinacy)* I hain't a-givin' it t' no one!

ABBIE *(remorselessly).* Ye can't take it with ye.
CABOT *(thinks a moment—then reluctantly).* No, I calc'late not. *(After a pause—with a strange passion)* But if I could, I would, by the Etarnal! 'R if I could, in my dyin' hour, I'd set it afire an' watch it burn—this house an' every ear o' corn an' every tree down t' the last blade o' hay! I'd sit an' know it was all a-dying with me an' no one else'd ever own what was mine, what I'd made out o' nothin' with my own sweat 'n' blood! *(A pause—then he adds with a queer affection.)* 'Ceptin' the cows. Them I'd turn free.
ABBIE *(harshly).* An' me?
CABOT *(with a queer smile).* Ye'd be turned free, too.
ABBIE *(furiously).* So that's the thanks I git fur marryin' ye—t' have ye change kind to Eben who hates ye, an' talk o' turnin' me out in the road.
CABOT *(hastily).* Abbie! Ye know I wa'n't . . .
ABBIE *(vengefully).* Just let me tell ye a thing or two 'bout Eben. Whar's he gone? T' see that harlot, Min! I tried fur t' stop him. Disgracin' yew an' me—on the Sabbath, too!
CABOT *(rather guiltily).* He's a sinner—natoral-born. It's lust eatin' his heart.
ABBIE *(enraged beyond endurance—wildly vindictive).* An' his lust fur me! Kin ye find excuses fur that?
CABOT *(stares at her—after a dead pause).* Lust—fur yew?
ABBIE *(defiantly).* He was tryin' t' make love t' me—when ye heerd us quarrelin'.
CABOT *(stares at her—then a terrible expression of rage comes over his face—he springs to his feet shaking all over).* By the A'mighty God—I'll end him!
ABBIE *(frightened now for* EBEN*).* No! Don't ye!
CABOT *(violently).* I'll git the shotgun an' blow his soft brains t' the top o' them elums!
ABBIE *(throwing her arms around him).* No, Ephraim!
CABOT *(pushing her away violently).* I will, by God!
ABBIE *(in a quieting tone).* Listen, Ephraim. 'Twa'n't nothin' bad—on'y a boy's foolin'—'twa'n't meant serious—jest jokin' an' teasin'. . . .
CABOT. Then why did ye say—lust?
ABBIE. It must hev sounded wusser'n I meant. An' I was mad at thinkin'—ye'd leave him the farm.
CABOT *(quieter but still grim and cruel).* Waal then, I'll horsewhip him off the place if that much'll content ye.
ABBIE *(reaching out and taking his hand).* No. Don't think o' me! Ye mustn't drive him off. 'Tain't sensible. Who'll ye get to help ye on the farm? They's no one hereabouts.
CABOT *(considers this—then nodding his appreciation).* Ye got a head on ye. *(Then irritably)* Waal, let him stay. *(He sits down on the edge of the porch. She sits beside him. He murmurs contemptuously:)* I oughtn't git riled so—at that 'ere fool calf. *(A pause.)* But har's the p'int. What son o' mine'll keep on here t' the farm—when the Lord does call me? Simeon an' Peter air gone t' hell—an' Eben's follerin' 'em.

ABBIE. They's me.
CABOT. Ye're on'y a woman.
ABBIE. I'm yewr wife.
CABOT. That hain't me. A son is me—my blood—mine. Mine ought t' git mine. An' then it's still mine—even though I be six foot under. D'ye see?
ABBIE *(giving him a look of hatred).* Ay-eh. I see. *(She becomes very thoughtful, her face growing shrewd, her eyes studying* CABOT *craftily.)*
CABOT. I'm gittin' old—ripe on the bough. *(Then with a sudden forced reassurance)* Not but what I hain't a hard nut t' crack even yet—an' fur many a year t' come! By the Eternal, I kin break most o' the young fellers' backs at any kind o' work any day o' the year!
ABBIE *(suddenly).* Mebbe the Lord'll give *us* a son.
CABOT *(turns and stares at her eagerly).* Ye mean—a son—t' me 'n' yew?
ABBIE *(with a cajoling smile).* Ye're a strong man yet, hain't ye? 'Tain't noways impossible, be it? We know that. Why d'ye stare so? Hain't ye never thought o' that afore? I been thinkin' o' it all along. Ay-eh—an' I been prayin' it'd happen, too.
CABOT *(his face growing full of joyous pride and a sort of religious ecstasy).* Ye been prayin', Abbie?—fur a son?—t' us?
ABBIE. Ay-eh. *(With a grim resolution)* I want a son now.
CABOT *(excitedly clutching both of her hands in his).* It'd be the blessin' o' God, Abbie—the blessin' o' God A'mighty on me—in my old age—in my lonesomeness! They hain't nothin' I wouldn't do fur ye then, Abbie. Ye'd hev on'y t' ask it—anythin' ye'd a mind t'!
ABBIE *(interrupting).* Would ye will the farm t' me then—t' me an' it . . . ?
CABOT *(vehemently).* I'd do anythin' ye axed, I tell ye! I swar it! May I be everlastin' damned t' hell if I wouldn't! *(He sinks to his knees pulling her down with him. He trembles all over with the fervor of his hopes.)* Pray t' the Lord agen, Abbie. It's the Sabbath! I'll jine ye! Two prayers air better nor one. "An' God hearkened unto Rachel"! An' God hearkened unto Abbie! Pray, Abbie! Pray fur him to hearken! *(He bows his head, mumbling. She pretends to do likewise but gives him a side glance of scorn and triumph.)*

SCENE 2

*About eight in the evening. The interior of the two bedrooms on the top floor is shown—*EBEN *is sitting on the side of his bed in the room on the left. On account of the heat he has taken off everything but his undershirt and pants. His feet are bare. He faces front, brooding moodily, his chin propped on his hands, a desperate expression on his face.*

In the other room CABOT *and* ABBIE *are sitting side by side on the edge of their bed, an old four-poster with feather mattress. He is in his night shirt, she in her nightdress. He is still in the queer, excited mood into which the notion of a son has thrown him. Both rooms are lighted dimly and flickeringly by tallow candles.*

CABOT. The farm needs a son.

ABBIE. I need a son.

CABOT. Ay-eh. Sometimes ye air the farm an' sometimes the farm be yew. That's why I clove t' ye in my lonesomeness. *(A pause. He pounds his knee with his fist.)* Me an' the farm has got t' beget a son!

ABBIE. Ye'd best go t' sleep. Ye're gittin' thin's all mixed.

CABOT *(with an impatient gesture).* No, I hain't. My mind's clear's a well. Ye don't know me, that's it. *(He stares hopelessly at the floor.)*

ABBIE *(indifferently).* Mebbe. *(In the next room* EBEN *gets up and paces up and down distractedly.* ABBIE *hears him. Her eyes fasten on the intervening wall with concentrated attention.* EBEN *stops and stares. Their hot glances seem to meet through the wall. Unconsciously he stretches out his arms for her and she half rises. Then aware, he mutters a curse at himself and flings himself face downward on the bed, his clenched fists above his head, his face buried in the pillow.* ABBIE *relaxes with a faint sigh but her eyes remain fixed on the wall; she listens with all her attention for some movement from* EBEN.*)*

CABOT *(suddenly raises his head and looks at her—scornfully).* Will ye ever know me—'r will any man 'r woman? *(Shaking his head)* No. I calc'late 't wa'n't t' be. *(He turns away.* ABBIE *looks at the wall. Then, evidently unable to keep silent about his thoughts, without looking at his wife, he puts out his hand and clutches her knee. She starts violently, looks at him, sees he is not watching her, concentrates again on the wall and pays no attention to what he says.)* Listen, Abbie. When I come here fifty odd year ago—I was jest twenty an' the strongest an' hardest ye ever seen—ten times as strong an' fifty times as hard as Eben. Waal—this place was nothin' but fields o' stones. Folks laughed when I tuk it. They couldn't know what I knowed. When ye kin make corn sprout out o' stones, God's livin' in yew! They wa'n't strong enuf fur that! They reckoned God was easy. They laughed. They don't laugh no more. Some died hereabouts. Some went West an' died. They're all under ground—fur follerin' arter an easy God. God hain't easy. *(He shakes his head slowly.)* An' I growed hard. Folks kept allus sayin' he's a hard man like 'twas sinful t' be hard, so's at last I said back at 'em: Waal then, by thunder, ye'll git me hard an' see how ye like it! *(Then suddenly)* But I give in t' weakness once. 'Twas arter I'd been here two year. I got weak—despairful—they was so many stones. They was a party leavin', givin' up, goin' West. I jined 'em. We tracked on 'n' on. We come t' broad medders, plains, whar the soil was black an' rich as gold. Nary a stone. Easy. Ye'd on'y to plow an' sow an' then set an' smoke yer pipe an' watch thin's grow. I could o' been a rich man—but somethin' in me fit me an' fit me—the voice o' God sayin': "This hain't wuth nothin' t' Me. Get ye back t' hum!" I got afeerd o' that voice an' I lit out back t' hum here, leavin' my claim an' crops t' whoever'd a mind t' take 'em. Ay-eh. I actoolly give up what was rightful mine! God's hard, not easy! God's in the stones! Build my church on a rock—out o' stones an' I'll be in them! That's what He meant t' Peter! *(He sighs heavily—a pause.)* Stones. I picked 'em up an' piled 'em into walls. Ye kin read the years o' my life in them walls, every day a hefted stone, climbin' over the hills up and down, fencin' in the fields that was mine, whar I'd made thin's grow out o' nothin'—like the will o' God, like the servant o' His hand. It wa'n't easy. It was hard an' He made me hard fur it. *(He pauses.)* All the time I kept gittin' lonesomer. I tuk a wife. She bore Simeon an' Peter. She was a good woman. She wuked hard. We was married twenty year. She never knowed me. She helped but she never knowed what she was helpin'. I was allus lonesome. She died. After that it wa'n't so lonesome fur a spell. *(A pause.)* I lost count o' the years. I had no time t' fool away countin' 'em. Sim an' Peter helped. The farm growed. It was all mine! When I thought o' that I didn't feel lonesome. *(A pause.)* But ye can't hitch yer mind t' one thin' day an' night. I tuk another wife—Eben's Maw. Her folks was contestin' me at law over my deeds t' the farm—my farm! That's why Eben keeps a'talkin' his fool talk o' this bein' his Maw's farm. She bore Eben. She was purty—but soft. She tried t' be hard. She couldn't. She never knowed me nor nothin'. It was lonesomer 'n hell with her. After a matter o' sixteen odd years, she died. *(A pause.)* I lived with the boys. They hated me 'cause I was hard. I hated them 'cause they was soft. They coveted the farm without knowin' what it meant. It made me bitter 'n wormwood. It aged me—them coveting what I'd made fur mine. Then this spring the call come—the voice o' God cryin' in my wilderness, in my lonesomeness—t' go out an' seek an' find! *(Turning to her with strange passion)* I sought ye an' I found ye! Yew air my Rose o' Sharon! Yer eyes air like. . . . *(She has turned a blank face, resentful eyes to his. He stares at her for a moment—then harshly)* Air ye any the wiser fur all I've told ye?

ABBIE *(confusedly).* Mebbe.

CABOT *(pushing her away from him—angrily).* Ye don't know nothin' —nor never will. If ye don't hev a son t' redeem ye . . . *(This in a tone of cold threat.)*

ABBIE *(resentfully).* I've prayed, hain't I?

CABOT *(bitterly).* Pray agen—fur understandin'!

ABBIE *(a veiled threat in her tone).* Ye'll have a son out o' me, I promise ye.

CABOT. How kin ye promise?

ABBIE. I got second-sight mebbe. I kin foretell. *(She gives a queer smile.)*

CABOT. I believe ye have. Ye give me the chills sometimes. *(He shivers.)* It's cold in this house. It's oneasy. They's thin's pokin' about in the dark—in the corners. *(He pulls on his trousers, tucking in his night shirt, and pulls on his boots.)*

ABBIE *(surprised).* Whar air ye goin'?

CABOT *(queerly).* Down whar it's restful—whar it's warm—down t' the barn. *(Bitterly)* I kin talk t' the cows. They know. They know the farm an' me. They'll give me peace. *(He turns to go out the door.)*

ABBIE *(a bit frightenedly).* Air ye ailin' tonight, Ephraim?

CABOT. Growin'. Growin' ripe on the bough. *(He turns and goes, his boots clumping down the stairs.* EBEN *sits up with a start, listening.* ABBIE *is conscious of his movement and stares at the wall.* CABOT *comes out of the house around the corner and stands by the gate, blinking at the sky. He stretches up his hands in a tortured gesture.)* God A'mighty, call from the dark! *(He listens as if expecting an answer. Then his arms drop, he shakes his head and plods off toward the barn.* EBEN *and* ABBIE *stare at each other through the wall.* EBEN *sighs heavily and* ABBIE *echoes it. Both become terribly nervous, uneasy. Finally* ABBIE *gets up and listens, her ear to the wall. He acts as if he saw every move she was making, he becomes resolutely still. She seems driven into a decision—goes out the door in rear determinedly. His eyes follow her. Then as the door of his room is opened softly, he turns away, waits in an attitude of strained fixity.* ABBIE *stands for a second staring at him, her eyes burning with desire. Then with a little cry she runs over and throws her arms about his neck, she pulls his head back and covers his mouth with kisses. At first, he submits dumbly; then he puts his arms about her neck and returns her kisses, but finally, suddenly aware of his hatred, he hurls her away from him, springing to his feet. They stand speechless and breathless, panting like two animals.)*

ABBIE *(at last—painfully).* Ye shouldn't, Eben—ye shouldn't—I'd make ye happy!

EBEN *(harshly).* I don't want t' be happy—from yew!

ABBIE *(helplessly).* Ye do, Eben! Ye do! Why d'ye lie?

EBEN *(viciously).* I don't take t'ye, I tell ye! I hate the sight o' ye!

ABBIE *(with an uncertain troubled laugh).* Waal, I kissed ye anyways—an' ye kissed back—yer lips was burnin'—ye can't lie 'bout that! *(Intensely)* If ye don't care, why did ye kiss me back—why was yer lips burnin'?

EBEN *(wiping his mouth).* It was like pizen on 'em *(Then tauntingly)* When I kissed ye back, mebbe I thought 'twas someone else.

ABBIE *(wildly).* Min?

EBEN. Mebbe.

ABBIE *(torturedly).* Did ye go t' see her? Did ye r'ally go? I thought ye mightn't. Is that why ye throwed me off jest now?

EBEN *(sneeringly).* What if it be?

ABBIE *(raging).* Then ye're a dog, Eben Cabot!

EBEN *(threateningly).* Ye can't talk that way t' me!

ABBIE *(with a shrill laugh).* Can't I? Did ye think I was in love with ye —a weak thin' like yew? Not much! I on'y wanted ye fur a purpose o' my own—an' I'll hev ye fur it yet 'cause I'm stronger'n yew be!

EBEN *(resentfully).* I knowed well it was on'y part o' yer plan t' swaller everythin'!

ABBIE *(tauntingly).* Mebbe!

EBEN *(furious).* Git out o' my room!

ABBIE. This air my room an' ye're on'y hired help!

EBEN *(threateningly).* Git out afore I murder ye!

ABBIE *(quite confident now).* I hain't a mite afeerd. Ye want me, don't ye? Yes, ye do! An' yer Paw's son'll never kill what he wants! Look at yer eyes! They's lust fur me in 'em, burnin' 'em up! Look at yer lips now! They're tremblin' an' longin' t' kiss me, an' yer teeth t' bite *(He is watching her now with a horrible fascination. She laughs a crazy triumphant laugh.)* I'm a-goin' t' make all o' this hum my hum! They's one room hain't mine yet, but it's a-goin' t' be tonight. I'm a-goin' down now an' light up! *(She makes him a mocking bow.)* Won't ye come courtin' me in the best parlor, Mister Cabot?

EBEN *(staring at her—horribly confused—dully).* Don't ye dare! It hain't been opened since Maw died an' was laid out thar! Don't ye . . . ! *(But her eyes are fixed on his so burningly that his will seems to wither before hers. He stands swaying toward her helplessly.)*

ABBIE *(holding his eyes and putting all her will into her words as she backs out the door).* I'll expect ye afore long, Eben.

EBEN *(stares after her for a while, walking toward the door. A light appears in the parlor window. He murmurs).* In the parlor? *(This seems to arouse connotations for he comes back and puts on his white shirt, collar, half ties the tie mechanically, puts on coat, takes his hat, stands barefooted looking about him in bewilderment, mutters wonderingly:)* Maw! Whar air yew? *(Then goes slowly toward the door in rear.)*

SCENE 3

A few minutes later. The interior of the parlor is shown. A grim, repressed room like a tomb in which the family has been interred alive. ABBIE *sits on the edge of the horsehair sofa. She has lighted all the candles and the room is revealed in all its preserved ugliness. A change has come over the woman. She looks awed and frightened now, ready to run away.*

The door is opened and EBEN *appears. His face wears an expression of obsessed confusion. He stands staring at her, his arms hanging disjointedly from his shoulders, his feet bare, his hat in his hand.*

ABBIE *(after a pause—with a nervous, formal politeness).* Won't ye set?

EBEN *(dully).* Ay-eh. *(Mechanically he places his hat carefully on the floor near the door and sits stiffly beside her on the edge of the sofa. A pause. They both remain rigid, looking straight ahead with eyes full of fear.)*

ABBIE. When I fust came in—in the dark—they seemed somethin' here.

EBEN *(simply).* Maw.

ABBIE. I kin still feel—somethin'. . . .

EBEN. It's Maw.

ABBIE. At fust I was feered o' it. I wanted t' yell an' run. Now—since yew come—seems like it's growin' soft an' kind t' me. *(Addressing the air—queerly)* Thank yew.

EBEN. Maw allus loved me.

ABBIE. Mebbe it knows I love yew too. Mebbe that makes it kind t' me.

EBEN *(dully).* I dunno. I should think she'd hate ye.

ABBIE *(with certainty).* No. I kin feel it don't—not no more.

EBEN. Hate ye fur stealin' her place—here in her hum—settin' in her parlor whar she was laid—*(He suddenly stops, staring stupidly before him.)*

ABBIE. What is it, Eben?

EBEN *(in a whisper).* Seems like Maw didn't want me t' remind ye.

ABBIE *(excitedly).* I knowed, Eben! It's kind t' me! It don't b'ar me no grudges fur what I never knowed an' couldn't help!

EBEN. Maw b'ars him a grudge.

ABBIE. Waal, so does all o' us.

EBEN. Ay-eh. *(With passion)* I does, by God!

ABBIE *(taking one of his hands in hers and patting it).* Thar! Don't git riled thinkin' o' him. Think o' yer Maw who's kind t' us. Tell me about yer Maw, Eben.

EBEN. They hain't nothin' much. She was kind. She was good.

ABBIE *(putting one arm over his shoulder. He does not seem to notice—passionately).* I'll be kind an' good t' ye!

EBEN. Sometimes she used t' sing fur me.

ABBIE. I'll sing fur ye!

EBEN. This was her hum. This was her farm.

ABBIE. This is my hum! This is my farm!

EBEN. He married her t' steal 'em. She was soft an' easy. He couldn't 'preciate her.

ABBIE. He can't 'preciate me!

EBEN. He murdered her with his hardness.

ABBIE. He's murderin' me!

EBEN. She died. *(A pause.)* Sometimes she used to sing fur me. *(He bursts into a fit of sobbing.)*

ABBIE *(both her arms around him—with wild passion).* I'll sing fur ye! I'll die fur ye! *(In spite of her overwhelming desire for him, there is a sincere maternal love in her manner and voice—a horribly frank mixture of lust and mother love.)* Don't cry, Eben! I'll take yer Maw's place! I'll be everythin' she was t' ye! Let me kiss ye, Eben! *(She pulls his head around. He makes a bewildered pretense of resistance. She is tender.)* Don't be afeered! I'll kiss ye pure, Eben—same 's if I was a Maw t' ye—an' ye kin kiss me back 's if yew was my son—my boy—sayin' good-night t' me! Kiss me, Eben. *(They kiss in restrained fashion. Then suddenly wild passion overcomes her. She kisses him lustfully again and again and he flings his arms about her and returns her kisses. Suddenly, as in the bedroom, he frees himself from her violently and springs to his feet. He is trembling all over, in a strange state of terror. ABBIE strains her arms toward him with fierce pleading.)* Don't ye leave me, Eben! Can't ye see it hain't enuf—lovin' ye like a Maw—can't ye see it's got t' be that an' more—much more—a hundred times more—fur me t' be happy—fur yew t' be happy?

EBEN *(to the presence he feels in the room).* Maw! Maw! What d'ye want? What air ye tellin' me?

ABBIE. She's tellin' ye t' love me. She knows I love ye an' I'll be good t' ye. Can't ye feel it? Don't ye know? She's tellin' ye t' love me, Eben!

EBEN. Ay-eh. I feel—mebbe she—but—I can't figger out—why—when ye've stole her place—here in her hum—in the parlor whar she was—

ABBIE *(fiercely).* She knows I love ye!

EBEN *(his face suddenly lighting up with a fierce triumphant grin).*

I see it! I sees why. It's her vengeance on him—so's she kin rest quiet in her grave!

ABBIE *(wildly).* Vengeance o' God on the hull o' us! What d'we give a durn? I love ye, Eben! God knows I love ye! *(She stretches out her arms for him.)*

EBEN *(throws himself on his knees beside the sofa and grabs her in his arms—releasing all his pent-up passion).* An' I love yew, Abbie!—now I kin say it! I been dyin' fur want o' ye—every hour since ye come! I love ye! *(Their lips meet in a fierce, bruising kiss.)*

SCENE 4

Exterior of the farmhouse. It is just dawn. The front door at right is opened and EBEN *comes out and walks around to the gate. He is dressed in his working clothes. He seems changed. His face wears a bold and confident expression, he is grinning to himself with evident satisfaction. As he gets near the gate, the window of the parlor is heard opening and the shutters are flung back and* ABBIE *sticks her head out. Her hair tumbles over her shoulders in disarray, her face is flushed, she looks at* EBEN *with tender, languorous eyes and calls softly.*

ABBIE. Eben. *(As he turns—playfully)* Jest one more kiss afore ye go. I'm goin' to miss ye fearful all day.

EBEN. An' me yew, ye kin bet! *(He goes to her. They kiss several times. He draws away, laughingly.)* Thar. That's enuf, hain't it? Ye won't hev none left fur next time.

ABBIE. I got a million o' 'em left fur yew! *(Then a bit anxiously)* D'ye r'ally love me, Eben?

EBEN *(emphatically).* I like ye better'n any gal I ever knowed! That's gospel!

ABBIE. Likin' hain't lovin'.

EBEN. Waal then—I love ye. Now air yew satisfied?

ABBIE. Ay-eh, I be. *(She smiles at him adoringly.)*

EBEN. I better git t' the barn. The old critter's liable t' suspicion an' come sneakin' up.

ABBIE *(with a confident laugh).* Let him! I kin allus pull the wool over his eyes. I'm goin' t' leave the shutters open and let in the sun 'n' air. This room's been dead long enuf. Now it's goin' t' be my room!

EBEN *(frowning).* Ay-eh.

ABBIE *(hastily).* I meant—our room.

EBEN. Ay-eh.

ABBIE. We made it our'n last night, didn't we? We give it life—our lovin' did. *(A pause.)*

EBEN *(with a strange look).* Maw's gone back t' her grave. She kin sleep now.

ABBIE. May she rest in peace! *(Then tenderly rebuking)* Ye oughtn't t' talk o' sad thin's—this mornin'.

EBEN. It jest come up in my mind o' itself.

ABBIE. Don't let it. *(He doesn't answer. She yawns.)* Waal, I'm a-goin' t' steal a wink o' sleep. I'll tell the Old Man I hain't feelin' pert. Let him git his own vittles.

EBEN. I see him comin' from the barn. Ye better look smart an' git upstairs.

ABBIE. Ay-eh. Good-by. Don't fergit me. *(She throws him a kiss. He grins—then squares his shoulders and awaits his father confidently. CABOT walks slowly up from the left, staring up at the sky with a vague face.)*

EBEN *(jovially)*. Mornin', Paw. Star-gazin' in daylight?

CABOT. Purty, hain't it?

EBEN *(looking around him possessively)*. It's a durned purty farm.

CABOT. I mean the sky.

EBEN *(grinning)*. How d'ye know? Them eyes o' your'n can't see that fur. *(This tickles his humor and he slaps his thigh and laughs.)* Ho-ho! That's a good un!

CABOT *(grimly sarcastic)*. Ye're feelin' right chipper, hain't ye? Whar'd ye steal the likker?

EBEN *(good-naturedly)*. 'Tain't likker. Jest life. *(Suddenly holding out his hand—soberly)* Yew 'n' me is quits. Let's shake hands.

CABOT *(suspiciously)*. What's come over ye?

EBEN. Then don't. Mebbe it's jest as well. *(A moment's pause.)* What's come over me? *(Queerly)* Didn't ye feel her passin'—goin' back t' her grave?

CABOT *(dully)*. Who?

EBEN. Maw. She kin rest now an' sleep content. She's quits with ye.

CABOT *(confusedly)*. I rested. I slept good—down with the cows. They know how t' sleep. They're teachin' me.

EBEN *(suddenly jovial again)*. Good fur the cows! Waal—ye better git t' work.

CABOT *(grimly amused)*. Air yew bossin' me, ye calf?

EBEN *(beginning to laugh)*. Ay-eh! I'm bossin' yew! Ha-ha-ha! see how ye like it! Ha-ha-ha! I'm the prize rooster o' this roost. Ha-ha-ha! *(He goes off toward the barn laughing.)*

CABOT *(looks after him with scornful pity)*. Soft-headed. Like his Maw. Dead spit 'n' image. No hope in him! *(He spits with contemptuous disgust.)* A born fool! *(Then matter-of-factly)* Waal—I'm gittin' peckish. *(He goes toward door.)*

CURTAIN

PART 3

SCENE 1

A night in late spring the following year. The kitchen and the two bedrooms upstairs are shown. The two bedrooms are dimly lighted by a tallow candle in each. EBEN *is sitting on the side of the bed in his* room, his chin propped on his fists, his face a study of the struggle he is making to understand his conflicting emotions. The noisy laughter and music from below where a kitchen dance is in progress annoy and distract him. He scowls at the floor.

In the next room a cradle stands beside the double bed.

In the kitchen all is festivity. The stove has been taken down to give more room to the dancers. The chairs, with wooden benches added, have been pushed back against the walls. On these are seated, squeezed in tight against one another, farmers and their wives and their young folks of both sexes from the neighboring farms. They are all chattering and laughing loudly. They evidently have some secret joke in common. There is no end of winking, of nudging, of meaning nods of the head toward CABOT who, in a state of extreme hilarious excitement increased by the amount he has drunk, is standing near the rear door where there is a small keg of whisky and serving drinks to all the men. In the left corner, front, dividing the attention with her husband, ABBIE is sitting in a rocking chair, a shawl wrapped about her shoulders. She is very pale, her face is thin and drawn, her eyes are fixed anxiously on the open door in rear as if waiting for someone.

The musician is tuning up his fiddle, seated in the far right corner. He is a lanky young fellow with a long, weak face. His pale eyes blink incessantly and he grins about him slyly with a greedy malice.

ABBIE *(suddenly turning to a young girl on her right).* Whar's Eben?
YOUNG GIRL *(eying her scornfully).* I dunno, Mrs. Cabot. I hain't seen Eben in ages. *(Meaningly)* Seems like he's spent most o' his time t' hum since yew come.
ABBIE *(vaguely).* I tuk his Maw's place.
YOUNG GIRL. Ay-eh. So I heerd. *(She turns away to retell this bit of gossip to her mother sitting next to her.* ABBIE *turns to her left to a big stoutish middle-aged man whose flushed face and staring eyes show the amount of "likker" he has consumed.)*
ABBIE. Ye hain't seen Eben, hev ye?
MAN. No, I hain't. *(Then he adds with a wink)* If yew hain't, who would?
ABBIE. He's the best dancer in the county. He'd ought t' come an' dance.
MAN *(with a wink).* Mebbe he's doin' the dutiful an' walkin' the kid t' sleep. It's a boy, hain't it?
ABBIE *(nodding vaguely).* Ay-eh—born two weeks back—purty's a picter.
MAN. They all is—t' their Maws. *(Then in a whisper, with a nudge and a leer)* Listen, Abbie—if ye ever git tired o' Eben, remember me! Don't fergit now! *(He looks at her uncomprehending face for a second—then grunts disgustedly.)* Waal—guess I'll likker agin. *(He goes over and joins* CABOT *who is arguing noisily with an old farmer over cows. They all drink.)*
ABBIE *(this time appealing to nobody in particular).* Wonder what Eben's a-doin'? *(Her remark is repeated down the line with many a*

guffaw and titter until it reaches the fiddler. He fastens his blinking eyes on ABBIE.)

FIDDLER *(raising his voice).* Bet I kin tell ye, Abbie, what Eben's doin'! He's down t' the church offerin' up prayers o' thanksgivin'. *(They all titter expectantly.)*

MAN. What fur? *(Another titter.)*

FIDDLER. 'Cause unto him a—*(he hesitates just long enough)*—brother is born! *(a roar of laughter. They all look from* ABBIE *to* CABOT. *She is oblivious, staring at the door.* CABOT, *although he hasn't heard the words, is irritated by the laughter and steps forward, glaring about him. There is an immediate silence.)*

CABOT. What're ye all bleatin' about—like a flock o' goats? Why don't ye dance, damn ye? I axed ye here t' dance—t' eat, drink an' be merry—an' thar ye set cacklin' like a lot o' wet hens with the pip! Ye've swilled my likker an' guzzled my vittles like hogs, hain't ye? Then dance fur me, can't ye? That's fa'r an' squar', hain't it? *(A grumble of resentment goes around but they are all evidently in too much awe of him to express it openly.)*

FIDDLER *(slyly).* We're waitin' fur Eben. *(A suppressed laugh.)*

CABOT *(with a fierce exultation).* T'hell with Eben! Eben's done fur now! I got a new son! *(His mood switching with drunken suddenness)* But ye needn't t' laugh at Eben, none o' ye! He's my blood, if he be a dumb fool. He's better nor any o' yew! He kin do a day's work a'most up t' what I kin—an' that'd put any o' yew pore critters t' shame!

FIDDLER. An' he kin do a good night's work, too! *(A roar of laughter.)*

CABOT. Laugh, ye damn fools! Ye're right jist the same, Fiddler. He kin work day an' night too, like I kin, if need be!

OLD FARMER *(from behind the keg where he is weaving drunkenly back and forth—with great simplicity).* They hain't many t' touch ye, Ephraim—a son at seventy-six. That's a hard man fur ye! I be on'y sixty-eight an' I couldn't do it. *(A roar of laughter in which* CABOT *joins uproariously.)*

CABOT *(slapping him on the back).* I'm sorry fur ye, Hi. I'd never suspicion sech weakness from a boy like yew!

OLD FARMER. An' I never reckoned yew had it in ye nuther, Ephraim. *(There is another laugh.)*

CABOT *(suddenly grim).* I got a lot in me—a hell of a lot—folks don't know on. *(Turning to the* FIDDLER*)* Fiddle 'er up, durn ye! Give 'em somethin' t' dance t'! What air ye, an ornament? Hain't this a celebration? Then grease yer elbow an' go it!

FIDDLER *(seizes a drink which the* OLD FARMER *holds out to him and downs it).* Here goes! *(He starts to fiddle* "Lady of the Lake." *Four young fellows and four girls form in two lines and dance a square dance. The* FIDDLER *shouts directions for the different movements, keeping his words in the rhythm of the music and interspersing them with jocular personal remarks to the dancers themselves. The people seated along the walls stamp their feet and clap their hands in unison.* CABOT *is especially active in this respect. Only* ABBIE *remains apathetic, staring at the door as if she were alone in a silent room.)*

FIDDLER. Swing your partner t' the right! That's it, Jim! Give her a b'ar hug! Her Maw hain't lookin'. *(Laughter.)* Change partners! That suits ye, don't it, Essie, now ye got Reub afore ye? Look at her redden up, will ye! Waal, life is short an' so's love, as the feller says. *(Laughter.)*

CABOT *(excitedly, stamping his foot).* Go it, boys! Go it, gals!

FIDDLER *(with a wink at the others).* Ye're the spryest seventy-six ever I sees, Ephraim! Now if ye'd on'y good eye-sight . . . ! *(Suppressed laughter. He gives* CABOT *no chance to retort but roars.)* Promenade! Ye're walkin' like a bride down the aisle, Sarah! Waal, while they's life they's allus hope. I've heerd tell. Swing your partner to the left! Gosh A'mighty, look at Johnny Cook high-steppin'! They hain't goin' t' be much strength left fur howin' in the corn lot t'morrow. *(Laughter.)*

CABOT. Go it! Go it! *(Then suddenly, unable to restrain himself any longer, he prances into the midst of the dancers, scattering them, waving his arms about wildly.)* Ye're all hoofs! Git out o' my road! Give me room! I'll show ye dancin'. Ye're all too soft! *(He pushes them roughly away. They crowd back toward the walls, muttering, looking at him resentfully.)*

FIDDLER *(jeeringly).* Go it, Ephraim! Go it! *(He starts "Pop Goes the Weasel," increasing the tempo with every verse until at the end he is fiddling crazily as fast as he can go.)*

CABOT *(starts to dance, which he does very well and with tremendous vigor. Then he begins to improvise, cuts incredibly grotesque capers, leaping up and cracking his heels together, prancing around in a circle with body bent in an Indian war dance, then suddenly straightening up and kicking as high as he can with both legs. He is like a monkey on a string. And all the while he intersperses his antics with shouts and derisive comments).* Whoop! Here's dancin' fur ye! Whoop! See that! Seventy-six, if I'm a day! Hard as iron yet! Beatin' the young 'uns like I allus done! Look at me! I'd invite ye t' dance on my hundredth birthday on'y ye'll all be dead by then. Ye're a sickly generation! Yer hearts air pink, not red! Yer veins is full o' mud an' water! I be the on'y man in the county! Whoop! See that! I'm a Injun! I've killed Injuns in the West afore ye was born—an' skulped 'em too! They's a arrer wound on my backside I c'd show ye! The hull tribe chased me. I outrun 'em all—with the arrer stuck in me! An' I tuk vengeance on 'em. Ten eyes fur an eye, that was my motter! Whoop! Look at me! I kin kick the ceilin' off the room! Whoop!

FIDDLER *(stops playing—exhaustedly).* God A'mighty, I got enuf. Ye got the devil's strength in ye.

CABOT *(delightedly).* Did I beat yew, too? Wa'al, ye played smart. Hev a swig. *(He pours whisky for himself and* FIDDLER. *They drink. The others watch* CABOT *silently with cold, hostile eyes. There is a dead pause. The* FIDDLER *rests.* CABOT *leans against the keg, panting, glaring around him confusedly. In the room above,* EBEN *gets to his feet and tiptoes out the door in rear, appearing a moment later in the other bedroom. He moves silently, even frightenedly, toward the cradle and stands there looking down at the baby. His face is as vague* as his reactions are confused, but there is a trace of tenderness, of interested discovery. At the same moment that he reaches the cradle, ABBIE *seems to sense something. She gets up weakly and goes to* CABOT.)

ABBIE. I'm goin' up t' the baby.

CABOT *(with real solicitude).* Air ye able fur the stairs? D'ye want me t' help ye, Abbie?

ABBIE. No. I'm able. I'll be down agen soon.

CABOT. Don't ye git wore out! He needs ye, remember—our son does! *(He grins affectionately, patting her on the back. She shrinks from his touch.)*

ABBIE *(dully).* Don't—tech me. I'm goin'—up. *(She goes.* CABOT *looks after her. A whisper goes around the room.* CABOT *turns. It ceases. He wipes his forehead streaming with sweat. He is breathing pantingly.)*

CABOT. I'm a-goin' out t' git fresh air. I'm feelin' a mite dizzy. Fiddle up thar! Dance, all o' ye! Here's likker fur them as wants it. Enjoy yerselves. I'll be back. *(He goes, closing the door behind him.)*

FIDDLER *(sarcastically).* Don't hurry none on our account! *(A suppressed laugh. He imitates* ABBIE.*)* Whar's Eben? *(More laughter.)*

A WOMAN *(loudly).* What's happened in this house is plain as the nose on yer face! *(*ABBIE *appears in the doorway upstairs and stands looking in surprise and adoration at* EBEN *who does not see her.)*

A MAN. Ssshh! He's li'ble t' be listenin' at the door. That'd be like him. *(Their voices die to an intensive whispering. Their faces are concentrated on this gossip. A noise as of dead leaves in the wind comes from the room.* CABOT *has come out from the porch and stands by the gate, leaning on it, staring at the sky blinkingly.* ABBIE *comes across the room silently.* EBEN *does not notice her until quite near.)*

EBEN *(starting).* Abbie!

ABBIE. Ssshh! *(She throws her arms around him. They kiss—then bend over the cradle together.)* Ain't he purty?—dead spit 'n' image o' yew!

EBEN *(pleased).* Air he? I can't tell none.

ABBIE. E-zactly like!

EBEN *(frowningly).* I don't like this. I don't like lettin' on what's mine's his'n. I been doin' that all my life. I'm gittin' t' the end o' b'arin' it!

ABBIE *(putting her finger on his lips).* We're doin' the best we kin. We got t' wait. Somethin's bound t' happen. *(She puts her arms around him.)* I got t' go back.

EBEN. I'm goin' out. I can't b'ar it with the fiddle playin' an' the laughin'.

ABBIE. Don't git feelin' low. I love ye, Eben. Kiss me. *(He kisses her. They remain in each other's arms.)*

CABOT *(at the gate, confusedly).* Even the music can't drive it out—somethin'. Ye kin feel it droppin' off the elums, climbin' up the roof, sneakin' down the chimney, pokin' in the corners! They's no peace in houses, they's no rest livin' with folks. Somethin's always livin' with ye. *(With a deep sigh)* I'll go t' the barn an' rest a spell. *(He goes wearily toward the barn.)*

FIDDLER *(tuning up).* Let's celebrate the old skunk gittin' fooled! We kin have some fun now he's went. *(He starts to fiddle "Turkey in the Straw." There is real merriment now. The young folks get up to dance.)*

SCENE 2

A half hour later—exterior— EBEN *is standing by the gate looking up at the sky, an expression of dumb pain bewildered by itself on his face.* CABOT *appears, returning from the barn, walking wearily, his eyes on the ground. He sees* EBEN *and his whole mood immediately changes. He becomes excited, a cruel, triumphant grin comes to his lips, he strides up and slaps* EBEN *on the back. From within comes the whining of the fiddle and the noise of stamping feet and laughing voices.*

CABOT. So har ye be!
EBEN *(startled, stares at him with hatred for a moment—then dully).* Ay-eh.
CABOT *(surveying him jeeringly).* Why hain't ye been in t' dance? They was all axin' fur ye.
EBEN. Let 'em ax!
CABOT. They's a hull passel o' purty gals.
EBEN. T' hell with 'em!
CABOT. Ye'd ought t' be marryin' one o' 'em soon.
EBEN. I hain't marryin' no one.
CABOT. Ye might 'arn a share o' a farm that way.
EBEN *(with a sneer).* Like yew did, ye mean? I hain't that kind.
CABOT *(stung).* Ye lie! 'Twas yer Maw's folks aimed t' steal my farm from me.
EBEN. Other folks don't say so. *(After a pause—defiantly)* An' I got a farm, anyways!
CABOT *(derisively).* Whar?
EBEN *(stamps a foot on the ground).* Har!
CABOT *(throws his head back and laughs coarsely).* Ho-ho! Ye hev, hev ye? Waal, that's a good un!
EBEN *(controlling himself—grimly).* Ye'll see!
CABOT *(stares at him suspiciously, trying to make him out—a pause—then with scornful confidence).* Ay-eh. I'll see. So'll ye. It's ye that's blind—blind as a mole underground. *(*EBEN *suddenly laughs, one short sardonic bark: "Ha." A pause.* CABOT *peers at him with renewed suspicion.)* Whar air ye hawin' 'bout? *(*EBEN *turns away without answering.* CABOT *grows angry.)* God A'mighty, yew air a dumb dunce! They's nothin' in that thick skull o' your'n but noise—like a empty keg it be! *(*EBEN *doesn't seem to hear—* CABOT'S *rage grows.)* Yewr farm! God A'mighty! If ye wa'n't a born donkey ye'd know ye'll never own stick nor stone on it, specially now arter him bein' born. It's his'n, I tell ye—his'n arter I die—but I'll live a hundred jest t' fool ye all—an' he'll be growed then—yewr age a'most! *(*EBEN *laughs again his sardonic "Ha." This drives* CABOT *into a fury.)* Ha? Ye think ye kin git 'round that someways, do ye? Waal, it'll be her'n,

too—Abbie's—ye won't git 'round her—she knows yer tricks—she'll be too much fur ye—she wants the farm her'n—she was afeerd o' ye—she told me ye was sneakin' 'round tryin' t' make love t' her t' git her on yer side ... ye ... ye mad fool, ye! *(He raises his clenched fists threateningly.)*

EBEN *(is confronting him choking with rage).* Ye lie, ye old skunk! Abbie never said no sech thing!

CABOT *(suddenly triumphant when he sees how shaken* EBEN *is).* She did. An' I says, I'll blow his brains t' the top o' them elums—an' she says no, that hain't sense, who'll ye git t' help ye on the farm in his place—an' then she says yew'n me ought t' have a son—I know we kin, she says—an' I says, if we do, ye kin have anythin' I've got ye've a mind t'. An' she says, I wants Eben cut off so's this farm'll be mine when ye die! *(With terrible gloating)* An' that's what's happened, hain't it? An' the farm's her'n! An' the dust o' the road—that's you'rn! Ha! Now who's hawin'?

EBEN *(has been listening, petrified with grief and rage—suddenly laughs wildly and brokenly).* Ha-ha-ha! So that's her sneakin' game—all along!—like I suspicioned at fust—t' swaller it all—an' me, too ... ! *(Madly)* I'll murder her! *(He springs toward the porch but* CABOT *is quicker and gets in between.)*

CABOT. No, ye don't!

EBEN. Git out o' my road! *(He tries to throw* CABOT *aside. They grapple in what becomes immediately a murderous struggle. The old man's concentrated strength is too much for* EBEN. CABOT *gets one hand on his throat and presses him back across the stone wall. At the same moment,* ABBIE *comes out on the porch. With a stifled cry she runs toward them.)*

ABBIE. Eben! Ephraim! *(She tugs at the hand on* EBEN'S *throat.)* Let go, Ephraim! Ye're chokin' him!

CABOT *(removes his hand and flings* EBEN *sideways full length on the grass, gasping and choking. With a cry,* ABBIE *kneels beside him, trying to take his head on her lap, but he pushes her away.* CABOT *stands looking down with fierce triumph).* Ye needn't t've fret, Abbie, I wa'n't aimin' t' kill him. He hain't wuth hangin' fur—not by a hell of a sight! *(More and more triumphantly)* Seventy-six an' him not thirty yit—an' look whar he be fur thinkin' his Paw was easy! No, by God, I hain't easy! An' him upstairs, I'll raise him t' be like me! *(He turns to leave them.)* I'm goin' in an' dance!—sing an' celebrate! *(He walks to the porch—then turns with a great grin.)* I don't calc'late it's left in him, but if he gits pesky, Abbie, ye jest sing out. I'll come a-runnin' an' by the Etarnal, I'll put him across my knee an' birch him! Ha-ha-ha! *(He goes into the house laughing. A moment later his loud "whoop" is heard.)*

ABBIE *(tenderly).* Eben. Air ye hurt? *(she tries to kiss him but he pushes her violently away and struggles to a sitting position.)*

EBEN *(gaspingly).* T'hell—with ye!

ABBIE *(not believing her ears).* It's me, Eben—Abbie—don't ye know me?

EBEN *(glowering at her with hatred).* Ay-eh—I know ye—now! *(He suddenly breaks down, sobbing weakly.)*

ABBIE *(fearfully)*. Eben—what's happened t' ye—why did ye look at me 's if ye hated me?

EBEN *(violently, between sobs and gasps)*. I do hate ye! Ye're a whore—a damn trickin' whore!

ABBIE *(shrinking back horrified)*. Eben! Ye don't know what ye're sayin'!

EBEN *(scrambling to his feet and following her—accusingly)*. Ye're nothin' but a stinkin' passel o' lies! Ye've been lyin' t' me every word ye spoke, day an' night, since we fust—done it. Ye've kept sayin' ye loved me....

ABBIE *(frantically)*. I do love ye! *(She takes his hand but he flings hers away.)*

EBEN *(unheeding)*. Ye've made a fool o' me—a sick, dumb fool—a-purpose! Ye've been on'y playin' yer sneakin', stealin' game all along—gittin' me t' lie with ye so's ye'd hev a son he'd think was his'n, an' makin' him promise he'd give ye the farm and let me eat dust, if ye did git him a son! *(Staring at her with anguished, bewildered eyes)* They must be a devil livin' in ye! 'Tain't human t' be as bad as that be!

ABBIE *(stunned—dully)*. He told yew...?

EBEN. Hain't it true? It hain't no good in yew lyin'.

ABBIE *(pleadingly)*. Eben, listen—ye must listen—it was long ago—afore we done nothin'—yew was scornin' me—goin' t' see Min—when I was lovin' ye—an' I said it t' him t' git vengeance on ye!

EBEN *(unheedingly. With tortured passion)*. I wish ye was dead! I wish I was dead along with ye afore this come! *(Ragingly)* But I'll git my vengeance too! I'll pray Maw t' come back t' help me—t' put her cuss on yew an' him!

ABBIE *(brokenly)*. Don't ye, Eben! Don't ye! *(She throws herself on her knees before him, weeping.)* I didn't mean t' do bad t'ye! Fergive me, won't ye?

EBEN *(not seeming to hear her—fiercely)*. I'll git squar' with the old skunk—an' yew! I'll tell him the truth 'bout the son he's so proud o'! Then I'll leave ye here t' pizen each other—with Maw comin' out o' her grave at nights—an' I'll go t' the gold fields o' Californi-a whar Sim an' Peter be!

ABBIE *(terrified)*. Ye won't—leave me? Ye can't!

EBEN *(with fierce determination)*. I'm a-goin', I tell ye! I'll git rich thar an' come back an' fight him fur the farm he stole—an' I'll kick ye both out in the road—t' beg an' sleep in the woods—an' yer son along with ye—t' starve an' die! *(He is hysterical at the end.)*

ABBIE *(with a shudder—humbly)*. He's yewr son, too, Eben.

EBEN *(torturedly)*. I wish he never was born! I wish he'd die this minit! I wish I'd never sot eyes on him! It's him—yew havin' him—a purpose t' steal—that's changed everythin'!

ABBIE *(gently)*. Did ye believe I loved ye—afore he come?

EBEN. Ay-eh—like a dumb ox!

ABBIE. An' ye don't believe no more?

EBEN. B'lieve a lyin' thief! Ha!

ABBIE *(shudders—then humbly)*. An did ye r'ally love me afore?

EBEN *(brokenly)*. Ay-eh—an' ye was trickin' me!
ABBIE. An' ye don't love me now! 120
EBEN *(violently)*. I hate ye, I tell ye!
ABBIE. An' ye're truly goin' West—goin' t' leave me—all account o' him being born?
EBEN. I'm a-goin' in the mornin'—or may God strike me t' hell!
ABBIE *(after a pause—with a dreadful cold intensity—slowly)*. If that's what his comin's done t' me—killin' yewr love—takin' yew away—my on'y joy—the on'y joy I've ever knowed—like heaven t' me—purtier'n heaven—then I hate him, too, even if I be his Maw!
EBEN *(bitterly)*. Lies! Ye love him! He'll steal the farm fur ye! *(Brokenly)* But 'tain't the farm so much—not no more—it's yew 130 foolin' me—gittin' me t' love ye—lyin' yew loved me—jest t' git a son t' steal!
ABBIE *(distractedly)*. He won't steal! I'd kill him fust! I do love ye! I'll prove t' ye . . . !
EBEN *(harshly)*. Tain't no use lyin' no more. I'm deaf t' ye! *(He turns away.)* I hain't seein' ye agen. Good-by!
ABBIE *(pale with anguish)*. Hain't ye even goin' t' kiss me—not once—arter all we loved?
EBEN *(in a hard voice)*. I hain't wantin' t' kiss ye never agen! I'm wantin' t' forgit I ever sot eyes on ye! 140
ABBIE. Eben!—ye mustn't—wait a spell—I want t' tell ye . . .
EBEN. I'm a-goin' in t' git drunk. I'm a-goin' t' dance.
ABBIE *(clinging to his arm—with passionate earnestness)*. If I could make it—'s if he'd never come up between us—if I could prove t' ye I wa'n't schemin' t' steal from ye—so's everythin' could be jest the same with us, lovin' each other jest the same, kissin' an' happy the same's we've been happy afore he come—if I could do it—ye'd love me agen, wouldn't ye? Ye'd kiss me agen? Ye wouldn't never leave me, would ye?
EBEN *(moved)*. I calc'late not. *(Then shaking her hand off his arm—* 150 *with a bitter smile)* But ye hain't God, be ye?
ABBIE *(exultantly)*. Remember ye've promised! *(Then with strange intensity)* Mebbe I kin take back one thin' God does!
EBEN *(peering at her)*. Ye're gittin' cracked, hain't ye? *(Then going towards door)* I'm a-goin' t' dance.
ABBIE *(calls after him intensely)*. I'll prove t' ye! I'll prove I love ye better'n. . . . *(He goes in the door, not seeming to hear. She remains standing where she is, looking after him—then she finishes desperately:)* Better'n everythin' else in the world!

SCENE 3

Just before dawn in the morning—shows the kitchen and CABOT'S *bedroom. In the kitchen, by the light of a tallow candle on the table,* EBEN *is sitting, his chin propped on his hands, his drawn face blank and expressionless. His carpetbag is on the floor beside him. In the bedroom, dimly lighted by a small whale-oil lamp,* CABOT *lies asleep.*

ABBIE *is bending over the cradle, listening, her face full of terror yet with an undercurrent of desperate triumph. Suddenly, she breaks down and sobs, appears about to throw herself on her knees beside the cradle; but the old man turns restlessly, groaning in his sleep, and she controls herself, and shrinking away from the cradle with a gesture of horror, backs swiftly toward the door in rear and goes out. A moment later she comes into the kitchen and, running to* EBEN, *flings her arms about his neck and kisses him wildly. He hardens himself, he remains unmoved and cold, he keeps his eyes straight ahead.*

ABBIE *(hysterically).* I done it, Eben! I told ye I'd do it! I've proved I love ye—better'n everythin'—so's ye can't never doubt me no more!
EBEN *(dully).* Whatever ye done, it hain't no good now.
ABBIE *(wildly).* Don't ye say that! Kiss me, Eben, won't ye? I need ye t' kiss me arter what I done! I need ye t' say ye love me!
EBEN *(kisses her without emotion—dully).* That's fur good-by. I'm a-goin' soon.
ABBIE. No! No! Ye won't go—not now!
EBEN *(going on with his own thoughts).* I been a-thinkin'—an' I hain't goin' t' tell Paw nothin'. I'll leave Maw t' take vengeance on ye. If I told him, the old skunk'd jest be stinkin' mean enuf to take it out on that baby. *(His voice showing emotion in spite of him)* An' I don't want nothin' bad t' happen t' him. He hain't t' blame fur yew. *(He adds with a certain queer pride:)* An' he looks like me! An' by God, he's mine! An' some day I'll be a-comin' back an' ... !
ABBIE *(too absorbed in her own thoughts to listen to him—pleadingly).* They's no cause fur ye t' go now—they's no sense—it's all the same's it was—they's nothin' come b'tween us now—arter what I done!
EBEN *(something in her voice arouses him. He stares at her a bit frightenedly).* Ye look mad, Abbie. What did ye do?
ABBIE. I—I killed him, Eben.
EBEN *(amazed).* Ye killed him?
ABBIE *(dully).* Ay-eh.
EBEN *(recovering from his astonishment—savagely).* An' serves him right! But we got t' do somethin' quick t' make it look s'if the old skunk'd killed himself when he was drunk. We kin prove by 'em all how drunk he got.
ABBIE *(wildly).* No! No! Not him! *(Laughing distractedly)* But that's what I ought t' done, hain't it? I oughter killed him instead! Why didn't ye tell me?
EBEN *(appalled).* Instead? What d'ye mean?
ABBIE. Not him.
EBEN *(his face grown ghastly).* Not—not that baby!
ABBIE *(dully).* Ay-eh!
EBEN *(falls to his knees as if he'd been struck—his voice trembling with horror).* Oh, God A'mighty! A'mighty God! Maw, whar was ye, why didn't ye stop her?
ABBIE *(simply).* She went back t' her grave that night we fust done it, remember? I hain't felt her about since. *(A pause.* EBEN *hides his head in his hands, trembling all over as if he had the ague. She goes*

on dully:) I left the piller over his little face. Then he killed himself. He stopped breathin'. *(She begins to weep softly.)*

EBEN *(rage beginning to mingle with grief).* He looked like me. He was mine, damn ye!

ABBIE *(slowly and brokenly).* I didn't want t' do it. I hated myself fur doin' it. I loved him. He was so purty—dead spit 'n' image o' yew. But I loved yew more—an' yew was goin' away—far off whar I'd never see ye agen, never kiss ye, never feel ye pressed agin me agen—an' ye said ye hated me fur havin' him—ye said ye hated him an' wished he was dead—ye said if it hadn't been fur him comin' it'd be the same's afore between us.

EBEN *(unable to endure this, springs to his feet in a fury, threatening her, his twitching fingers seeming to reach out for her throat).* Ye lie! I never said—I never dreamed ye'd—I'd cut off my head afore I'd hurt his finger!

ABBIE *(piteously, sinking on her knees).* Eben, don't ye look at me like that—hatin' me—not after what I done fur ye—fur us—so's we could be happy agen—

EBEN *(furiously now).* Shut up, or I'll kill ye! I see yer game now—the same old sneakin' trick—ye're aimin' t' blame me fur the murder ye done!

ABBIE *(moaning—putting her hands over her ears).* Don't ye, Eben! Don't ye! *(She grasps his legs.)*

EBEN *(his mood suddenly changing to horror, shrinks away from her).* Don't ye tech me! Ye're pizen! How could ye—t' murder a pore little critter—Ye must've swapped yer soul t' hell! *(Sudden raging)* Ha! I kin see why ye done it! Not the lies ye jest told—but 'cause ye wanted t' steal agen—steal the last thin' ye'd left me—my part o' him—no, the hull o' him—ye saw he looked like me—ye knowed he was all mine—an' ye couldn't b'ar it—I know ye! Ye killed him fur bein' mine! *(All this has driven him almost insane. He makes a rush past her for the door—then turns—shaking both fists at her, violently.)* But I'll take vengeance now! I'll git the Sheriff! I'll tell him everythin'! Then I'll sing "I'm off to Californi-a!" an' go—gold—Golden Gate—gold sun—fields o' gold in the West! *(This last he half shouts, half croons incoherently, suddenly breaking off passionately.)* I'm a-goin' fur the Sheriff t' come an' git ye! I want ye tuk away, locked up from me! I can't stand t' luk at ye! Murderer an' thief 'r not, ye still tempt me! I'll give ye up t' the Sheriff! *(He turns and runs out, around the corner of house, panting and sobbing, and breaks into a swerving sprint down the road.)*

ABBIE *(struggling to her feet, runs to the door, calling after him).* I love ye, Eben! I love ye! *(She stops at the door weakly, swaying, about to fall.)* I don't care what ye do—if ye'll on'y love me agen— *(She falls limply to the floor in a faint.)*

SCENE 4

About an hour later. Same as Scene 3. Shows the kitchen and CABOT'S *bedroom. It is after dawn. The sky is brilliant with the sunrise. In the* kitchen, ABBIE *sits at the table, her body limp and exhausted, her head bowed down over her arms, her face hidden. Upstairs,* CABOT *is still asleep but awakens with a start. He looks toward the window and gives a snort of surprise and irritation—throws back the covers and begins hurriedly pulling on his clothes. Without looking behind him, he begins talking to* ABBIE *whom he supposes beside him.*

CABOT. Thunder 'n' lightnin', Abbie! I hain't slept this late in fifty year! Looks 's if the sun was full riz a'most. Must've been the dancin' an' likker. Must be gittin' old. I hope Eben's t'wuk. Ye might've tuk the trouble t' rouse me, Abbie. *(He turns—sees no one there—surprised.)* Waal—whar air she? Gittin' vittles, I calc'late. *(He tiptoes to the cradle and peers down—proudly)* Mornin', sonny. Purty's a picter! Sleepin' sound. He don't beller all night like most o' 'em. *(He goes quietly out the door in rear—a few moments later enters kitchen—sees* ABBIE*—with satisfaction)* So thar ye be. Ye got any vittles cooked?

ABBIE *(without moving).* No.

CABOT *(coming to her, almost sympathetically).* Ye feelin' sick?

ABBIE. No.

CABOT *(pats her on shoulder. She shudders).* Ye'd best lie down a spell. *(Half jocularly)* Yer son'll be needin' ye soon. He'd ought t' wake up with a gnashin' appetite, the sound way he's sleepin'.

ABBIE *(shudders—then in a dead voice).* He ain't never goin' to wake up.

CABOT *(jokingly).* Takes after me this mornin'. I ain't slept so late in . . .

ABBIE. He's dead.

CABOT *(stares at her—bewilderedly).* What . . .

ABBIE. I killed him.

CABOT *(stepping back from her—aghast).* Air ye drunk—'r crazy—'r . . . !

ABBIE *(suddenly lifts her head and turns on him—wildly).* I killed him, I tell ye! I smothered him. Go up an' see if ye don't b'lieve me! *(*CABOT *stares at her a second, then bolts out the rear door, can be heard bounding up the stairs, and rushes into the bedroom and over to the cradle.* ABBIE *has sunk back lifelessly into her former position.* CABOT *puts his hand down on the body in the crib. An expression of fear and horror comes over his face.)*

CABOT *(shrinking away—tremblingly).* God A'mighty! God A'mighty. *(He stumbles out the door—in a short while returns to the kitchen—comes to* ABBIE, *the stunned expression still on his face—hoarsely)* Why did ye do it? Why? *(As she doesn't answer, he grabs her violently by the shoulder and shakes her.)* I ax ye why ye done it! Ye'd better tell me'r . . . !

ABBIE *(gives him a furious push which sends him staggering back and springs to her feet—with wild rage and hatred).* Don't ye dare tech me! What right hev ye t' question me 'bout him? He wa'n't yewr son! Think I'd have a son by yew? I'd die fust! I hate the sight o' ye an' allus did! It's yew I should've murdered, if I'd had good sense! I hate ye! I love Eben. I did from the fust. An' he was Eben's son—mine an' Eben's—not your'n!

CABOT *(stands looking at her dazedly—a pause—finding his words with an effort—dully).* That was it—what I felt—pokin' round the corners—while ye lied—holdin' yerself from me—sayin' ye'd a'ready conceived—*(He lapses into crushed silence—then with a strange emotion)* He's dead, sart'n. I felt his heart. Pore little critter! *(He blinks back one tear, wiping his sleeve across his nose.)*

ABBIE *(hysterically).* Don't ye! Don't ye! *(She sobs unrestrainedly.)*

CABOT *(with a concentrated effort that stiffens his body into a rigid line and hardens his face into a stony mask—through his teeth to himself).* I got t' be—like a stone—a rock o' jedgment! *(A pause. He gets complete control over himself—harshly)* If he was Eben's, I be glad he air gone! An' mebbe I suspicioned it all along. I felt they was somethin' onnateral—somewhars—the house got so lonesome—an' cold—drivin' me down t' the barn—t' the beasts o' the field. . . . Ay-eh. I must've suspicioned—somethin'. Ye didn't fool me—not altogether, leastways—I'm too old a bird—growin' ripe on the bough. . . . *(He becomes aware he is wandering, straightens again, looks at* ABBIE *with a cruel grin.)* So ye'd liked t' hev murdered me 'stead o' him, would ye? Waal, I'll live to a hundred! I'll live t' see ye hung! I'll deliver ye up t' the jedgment o' God an' the law! I'll git the Sheriff now. *(Starts for the door.)*

ABBIE *(dully).* Ye needn't. Eben's gone fur him.

CABOT *(amazed).* Eben—gone fur the Sheriff?

ABBIE. Ay-eh.

CABOT. T' inform agen ye?

ABBIE. Ay-eh.

CABOT *(considers this—a pause—then in a hard voice).* Waal, I'm thankful fur him savin' me the trouble. I'll git t' wuk. *(He goes to the door—then turns—in a voice full of strange emotion)* He'd ought t' been my son, Abbie. Ye'd ought t' loved me. I'm a man. If ye'd loved me, I'd never told no Sheriff on ye no matter what ye did, if they was t' brile me alive!

ABBIE *(defensively).* They's more to it nor yew know, makes him tell.

CABOT *(dryly).* Fur yewr sake, I hope they be. *(He goes out—comes around to the gate—stares up at the sky. His control relaxes. For a moment he is old and weary. He murmurs despairingly:)* God A'mighty, I be lonesomer'n ever! *(He hears running footsteps from the left, immediately is himself again.* EBEN *runs in, panting exhaustedly, wild-eyed and mad looking. He lurches through the gate.* CABOT *grabs him by the shoulder.* EBEN *stares at him dumbly.)* Did ye tell the Sheriff?

EBEN *(nodding stupidly).* Ay-eh.

CABOT *(gives him a push away that sends him sprawling—laughing with withering contempt).* Good fur ye! A prime chip o' yer Maw ye be! *(He goes toward the barn, laughing harshly.* EBEN *scrambles to his feet. Suddenly* CABOT *turns—grimly threatening)* Git off this farm when the Sheriff takes her—or, by God, he'll have t' come back an' git me fur murder, too! *(He stalks off.* EBEN *does not appear to have heard him. He runs to the door and comes into the kitchen.* ABBIE *looks up with a cry of anguished joy.* EBEN *stumbles over and throws himself on his knees beside her—sobbing brokenly.)*

EBEN. Fergive me!

ABBIE *(happily).* Eben! *(She kisses him and pulls his head over against her breast.)*

EBEN. I love ye! Fergive me!

ABBIE *(ecstatically).* I'd fergive ye all the sins in hell fur sayin' that! *(She kisses his head, pressing it to her with a fierce passion of possession.)*

EBEN *(brokenly).* But I told the Sheriff. He's comin' fur ye!

ABBIE. I kin b'ar what happens t' me—now!

EBEN. I woke him up. I told him. He says, wait 'til I git dressed. I was waiting. I got to thinkin' o' yew. I got to thinkin' how I'd loved ye. It hurt like somethin' was bustin' in my chest an' head. I got t' cryin'. I knowed sudden I loved ye yet, an' allus would love ye!

ABBIE *(caressing his hair—tenderly).* My boy, hain't ye?

EBEN. I begun t' run back. I cut across the fields an' through the woods. I thought ye might have time t' run away—with me—an' ...

ABBIE *(shaking her head).* I got t' take my punishment—t' pay fur my sin.

EBEN. Then I want t' share it with ye.

ABBIE. Ye didn't do nothin'.

EBEN. I put it in yer head. I wisht he was dead! I as much as urged ye t' do it!

ABBIE. No. It was me alone!

EBEN. I'm as guilty as yew be! He was the child o' our sin.

ABBIE *(lifting her head as if defying God).* I don't repent that sin! I hain't askin' God t' fergive that!

EBEN. Nor me—but it led up t' the other—an' the murder ye did, ye did 'count o' me—an' it's my murder, too, I'll tell the Sheriff—an' if ye deny it, I'll say we planned it t'gether—an' they'll all b'lieve me, fur they suspicion everythin' we've done, an' it'll seem likely an' true to 'em. An' it is true—way down. I did help ye—somehow.

ABBIE *(laying her head on his—sobbing).* No! I don't want yew t' suffer!

EBEN. I got t' pay fur my part o' the sin! An' I'd suffer wuss leavin' ye, goin' West, thinkin' o' ye day an' night, bein' out when yew was in—*(lowering his voice)*—'r bein' alive when yew was dead. *(A pause.)* I want t' share with ye, Abbie—prison 'r death 'r hell 'r anythin'! *(He looks into her eyes and forces a trembling smile.)* If I'm sharin' with ye, I won't feel lonesome, leastways.

ABBIE *(weakly).* Eben! I won't let ye! I can't let ye!

EBEN *(kissing her—tenderly).* Ye can't he'p yerself. I got ye beat fur once!

ABBIE *(forcing a smile—adoringly).* I hain't beat—s'long's I got ye!

EBEN *(hears the sound of feet outside).* Ssshh! Listen! They've come t' take us!

ABBIE. No, it's him. Don't give him no chance to fight ye, Eben. Don't say nothin'—no matter what he says. An' I won't neither. *(It is*

CABOT. *He comes up from the barn in a great state of excitement and strides into the house and then into the kitchen.* EBEN *is kneeling beside* ABBIE, *his arm around her, hers around him. They stare straight ahead.)*

CABOT *(stares at them, his face hard. A long pause—vindictively).* Ye make a slick pair o' murderin' turtle doves! Ye'd ought t' be both hung on the same limb an' left thar t' swing in the breeze an' rot—a warnin' t' old fools like me t' b'ar their lonesomeness alone—an' fur young fools like ye t' hobble their lust. *(A pause. The excitement returns to his face, his eyes snap, he looks a bit crazy.)* I couldn't work today. I couldn't take no interest. T' hell with the farm! I'm leavin' it! I've turned the cows an' other stock loose! I've druv 'em into the woods whar they kin be free! By freein' 'em, I'm freein' myself! I'm quittin' here today! I'll set fire t' house an' barn an' watch 'em burn, an' I'll leave yer Maw t' haunt the ashes, an' I'll will the fields back t' God, so that nothin' human kin never touch 'em! I'll be a-goin' to Californi-a—t' jine Simeon an' Peter—true sons o' mine if they be dumb fools—an' the Cabots'll find Solomon's Mines t'gether! *(He suddenly cuts a mad caper.)* Whoop! What was the song they sung? "Oh, Californi-a! That's the land fur me." *(He sings this—then gets on his knees by the floor-board under which the money was hid.)* An' I'll sail thar on one o' the finest clippers I kin find! I've got the money! Pity ye didn't know whar this was hidden so's ye could steal... *(He has pulled up the board. He stares—feels—stares again. A pause of dead silence. He slowly turns, slumping into a sitting position on the floor, his eyes like those of a dead fish, his face the sickly green of an attack of nausea. He swallows painfully several times—forces a weak smile at last.)* So—ye did steal it!

EBEN *(emotionlessly).* I swapped it t' Sim an' Peter fur their share o' the farm—t' pay their passage t' Californi-a.

CABOT *(with one sardonic)* Ha! *(He begins to recover. Gets slowly to his feet—strangely)* I calc'late God give it to 'em—not yew! God's hard, not easy! Mebbe they's easy gold in the West but it hain't God's gold. It hain't fur me. I kin hear His voice warnin' me agen t' be hard an' stay on my farm. I kin see his hand usin' Eben t' steal t' keep me from weakness. I kin feel I be in the palm o' His hand, His fingers guidin' me. *(A pause—then he mutters sadly:)* It's a-goin' t' be lonesomer now than ever it war afore—an' I'm gittin' old, Lord—ripe on the bough.... *(Then stiffening)* Waal—what d'ye want? God's lonesome, hain't He? God's hard an' lonesome! *(A pause. The* SHERIFF *with two men comes up the road from the left. They move cautiously to the door. The* SHERIFF *knocks on it with the butt of his pistol.)*

SHERIFF. Open in the name o' the law! *(They start.)*

CABOT. They've come fur ye. *(He goes to the rear door.)* Come in, Jim! *(The three men enter.* CABOT *meets them in doorway.)* Jest a minit, Jim. I got 'em safe here. *(The* SHERIFF *nods. He and his companions remain in the doorway.)*

EBEN *(suddenly calls).* I lied this mornin', Jim. I helped her to do it. Ye kin take me, too.

ABBIE *(brokenly).* No!

CABOT. Take 'em both. *(He comes forward—stares at* EBEN *with a trace of grudging admiration.)* Purty good—fur yew! Waal, I got t' round up the stock. Good-by.   160
EBEN. Good-by.
ABBIE. Good-by. *(CABOT turns and strides past the men—comes out and around the corner of the house, his shoulders squared, his face stony, and stalks grimly toward the barn. In the meantime the* SHERIFF *and men have come into the room.)*
SHERIFF *(embarrassedly)*. Waal—we'd best start.
ABBIE. Wait. *(Turns to* EBEN.*)* I love ye, Eben.
EBEN. I love ye, Abbie. *(They kiss. The three men grin and shuffle embarrassedly.* EBEN *takes* ABBIE'S *hand. They go out the door in rear, the men following, and come from the house, walking hand in hand to the gate.* EBEN *stops there and points to the sunrise sky.)* Sun's a-risin'. Purty, hain't it?
ABBIE. Ay-eh. *(They both stand for a moment looking up raptly in attitudes strangely aloof and devout.)*
SHERIFF *(looking around at the farm enviously—to his companion)*. It's a jim-dandy farm, no denyin'. Wished I owned it!

CURTAIN
THE END

Questions for Discussion

1. Can you, in retrospect, locate the point at which the conclusion of *Desire Under the Elms* becomes inevitable? Is it the moment when Abbie arrives, or the seduction scene (Part 2, Scene 3)? Or could one argue that the family's history foreshadows a tragic resolution even before Abbie's appearance? Substantiate whichever viewpoint you assume. Would you describe that point as the climax (see pages 142, 503) of the play? Explain.

2. Some critics have argued that the author set out to create a study of human greed and then became preoccupied with human lust instead, thus leaving a disjointed effect. Does this charge seem justified? Does the emphasis, for instance, shift from Ephraim to Eben as the play progresses? If so, is this shift harmful? How might a shift in emphasis be constructively executed in a student composition?

3. Also related to the problems raised in the second question, Simeon and Peter disappear from the farm—and hence from the play—in Part 1. Does this indicate that their presence is irrelevant in the first place, or inessential to the eventual resolution? Why or why not? Do they enhance our understanding of Ephraim's character? Of Eben's? Explain.

4. How much does the physical setting (e.g., the elms, the stone wall, etc.) contribute to the mood of impending doom? In what ways? Do these symbols recur throughout the play? Illustrate. How would you describe the overall atmosphere (see page 502) of the play?

5. What appear to be some of the problems involved in creating a modern tragedy? In particular, how have audiences' concerns changed since Shakespeare's time? How do these problems manifest themselves in *Desire Under the Elms?* Has O'Neill elevated his subject to the level of tragedy? If so, who is the tragic hero and why? If not, why does he appear to have failed? In what ways does the play more closely resemble a morality play such as *Everyman?* Consider particularly the names of characters and the mythic overtones of the plot.

Suggested Theme Topics

1. Discuss, with illustrations from various sections of the play, the importance of setting in *Desire Under the Elms.*

2. Write a chronological analysis of Ephraim Cabot's character, indicating his growing or waning importance to the developing plot.

3. Compare and contrast *Volpone* and *Desire Under the Elms* as studies in human greed.

4. Compare and contrast *Hamlet* and *Desire Under the Elms* as tragedies.

5. Write a theme dealing with some series of current events in which you deliberately and obviously shift your emphasis at some point without destroying the coherence or altering the tone of your essay.

Christopher Fry

Christopher Fry (1907-   ), born in Bristol, England, was a teacher, actor, editor, and director before World War II. Since the war he has devoted full time to writing and translating plays. Chief practitioner of what otherwise has generally been a dying (or at least dormant) form, the verse drama, Fry has been equally successful with religious plays (e.g., The Boy with a Cart, *1939;* The Firstborn, *1946; and* A Sleep of Prisoners, *1951) and comedies (e.g.,* A Phoenix Too Frequent, *1946;* The Lady's Not for Burning, *1949;* Venus Observed, *1950; and* The Dark Is Light Enough, *1954). Jean Anouilh and Jean Giraudoux are among the French playwrights successfully translated by Fry into English.*

The plot of A Phoenix Too Frequent *is resolved by a series of comic reversals upon the original premise. Note how these reversals sustain the overall atmosphere (see page 502) created by the exaggerated comic dialogue that characterizes most of the play.*

A PHOENIX TOO FREQUENT

CHARACTERS

DYNAMENE
DOTO
TEGEUS-CHROMIS

Scene: The tomb of Virilius, near Ephesus; night.

Note: The story was got from Jeremy Taylor who had it from Petronius.

The curtain rises on a stage in almost total darkness. The set is an underground tomb, and the only light at first comes from a very low dim flame in an oil lamp. As the light from the lamp and the starry sky overhead increases, the shape and furniture of the tomb are gradually perceived. The stage is semicircular, and the up stage walls, R. and L., are masked by plain curtains or drapes, hung in folds. Down R. is the only entrance, an arched doorway, leading down to stage level by a

Petronius: ancient Roman writer, author of the *Satyricon.*

flight of stone steps. Down C. *is a stone or marble plinth, resembling the lowest part of a classic column. On top of this stands a simple stone urn. Down* L. *is a fairly large plinth or other similar base on which lies a stone coffin. Up* C. *is a "flat" extending from the stage floor up to the top of the set. Cut into this, and large enough to show a person passing by, is a sort of simple framework or grill. The stage set has no roof or covering and above this, very dimly lighted, is the suggestion of a sky at night, with a slight shimmering from the starry sky. Above the top of the curtains or drapes, between* U. C. *and* L. C., *there is a cut-out or stencil-like suggestion of the branches of two or three trees, and from these a further suggestion of six soldiers who have been hanged from the branches. The night sky should be extended over the rest of the set as seen to the right. The entrance to the tomb is so arranged as to permit a suggestion of starlight or moonlight. A rock, large enough to be used as a stool, is down* R. *below the lowest of the steps leading to the door.*

A few seconds after the rise of the curtain DOTO *is seen standing by the lamp, which is placed on the top step leading from the entrance right.* DYNAMENE *leans on the* R. *of the coffin plinth.*

DOTO. Nothing but the harmless day gone into black
Is all the dark is. And so what's my trouble?
Demons is so much wind. Are so much wind.
I've plenty to fill my thoughts. All that I ask
Is don't keep turning men over in my mind,
Venerable Aphrodite. I've had my last one
And thank you. I thank thee. He smelt of sour grass
And was likeable. He collected ebony quoits.
(An owl hoots near at hand.)
O Zeus! O some god or other, where is the oil?
(Rises, goes U. S.*)*
Fire's from Prometheus. *(Back to lamp.)* I thank thee. If I
Mean to die I'd better see what I'm doing.
(She fills the lamp with oil. The flame burns up brightly and shows
   DYNAMENE, *beautiful and young, leaning asleep beside a bier.)*
Honestly, I would rather have to sleep
With a bald bee-keeper who was wearing his boots
Than spend more days fasting and thirsting and crying
In a tomb. I shouldn't have said that. Pretend
I didn't hear myself. But life and death
Is cat and dog in this double-bed of a world.
My master, my poor master, was a man
Whose nose was as straight as a little buttress,
And now he has taken it into Elysium
Where it won't be noticed among all the other straightness.
(The owl cries again and wakens DYNAMENE.*)*
Oh, them owls. Those owls. It's woken her. *(Crosses* L.*)*
DYNAMENE. Ah! I'm breathless. I caught up with the ship
But it spread its wings, creaking a cry of *Dew,*
Dew! and flew figurehead foremost into the sun.

DOTO. How crazy, madam.
DYNAMENE.   Doto, draw back the curtains.
  I'll take my barley-water.
DOTO.   We're not at home
  Now, madam. It's the master's tomb.
DYNAMENE.   Of course!
  Oh, I'm wretched. Already I have disfigured
  My vigil. My cynical eyelids have soon dropped me
  In a dream.
DOTO.   But then it's possible *(Kneels to* DYNAMENE.*),*
    madam, you might
  Find yourself in bed with him again
  In a dream, madam. Was he on the ship?
DYNAMENE. He was the ship.
DOTO.   Oh. That makes it different.
DYNAMENE. He was the ship. He had such a deck, Doto,
  Such a white, scrubbed deck. Such a stern prow,
  Such a proud stern, so slim from port to starboard.
  If ever you meet a man with such fine masts
  Give your life to him, Doto. The figurehead
  Bore his own features, so serene in the brow
  And hung with a little seaweed. O Virilius,
  My husband, you have left a wake in my soul.
  You cut the glassy water with a diamond keel.
  I must cry again.
DOTO.   What, when you mean to join him?
  Don't you believe he will be glad to see you, madam?
  Thankful to see you, I should imagine, among
  Them shapes and shades; all shapes of shapes and all
  Shades of shades, from what I've heard. I know
  I shall feel odd at first with Cerberus,
  Sop or no sop. Still, I know how you feel, madam.
  You think he may find a temptation in Hades.
  I shouldn't worry. It would help him to settle down.
  *(*DYNAMENE *weeps.)*
  It would only be *fun,* madam. He couldn't go far
  With a shade.
DYNAMENE.   He was one of the coming men.
  He was certain to have become the most well-organized provost
  The town has known, once they had made him provost.
  He was so punctual, you could regulate
  The sun by him. He made the world succumb
  To his daily revolution of habit. But who,
  In the world he has gone to, will appreciate that?
  O poor Virilius! To be a coming man
  Already gone—it must be distraction.
  Why did you leave me walking about our ambitions
  Like a cat in the ruins of a house? Promising husband,
  Why did you insult me by dying? Virilius,
  Now I keep no flower, except in the vase

Of the tomb.
DOTO.   O poor madam! O poor master!
   I presume so far as to cry somewhat for myself
   As well. I know you won't mind, madam. It's two
   Days not eating makes me think of my uncle's
   Shop in the country, where he has a hardware business,   70
   Basins, pots, ewers, and alabaster birds.
   He makes you die of laughing. O madam,
   Isn't it sad?

(They both weep.)

DYNAMENE.   How could I have allowed you
   To come and die of my grief? Doto, it puts
   A terrible responsibility on me. Have you
   No grief of your own you could die of?
DOTO.   Not really, madam.
DYNAMENE.   Nothing?
DOTO.   Not really. They was all one to me.
   Well, all but two was all one to me. And they,
   Strange enough, was two who kept recurring.
   I could never be sure if they had gone for good
   Or not; and so that kept things cheerful, madam.   80
   One always gave a wink before he deserted me,
   The other slapped me as it were behind, madam;
   Then they would be away for some months.
DYNAMENE.   Oh, Doto,
   What an unhappy life you were having to lead.
DOTO. Yes, I'm sure. But never mind, madam,
   It seemed quite lively then. And now I know
   It's what you say; life is more big than a bed
   And full of miracles and mysteries like
   One man made for one woman, etcetera, etcetera.
   Lovely. I feel sung, madam, by a baritone   90
   In mixed company with everyone pleased.
   And so I had to come with you here, madam,
   For the last sad chorus of me. It's all
   Fresh to me. Death's a new interest in life,
   If it doesn't disturb you, madam, to have me crying.
   It's because of us not having breakfast again.
   And the master, of course. And the beautiful world.
   And you crying too, madam. Oh—Oh!
DYNAMENE. I can't forbid your crying; but you must cry
   On the other side of the tomb. I'm becoming confused.   100
   (DOTO rises, walks over R.)
   This is my personal grief and my sacrifice
   Of self, solus. Right over there, darling girl.
DOTO. What here?
DYNAMENE.   Now, if you wish, you may cry, Doto.
   (Rises and goes U. S.*)*

But our tears are very different. For me
The world is all with Charon, all, all,
Even the metal and plume of the rose garden,
And the forest where the sea fumes overhead
In vegetable tides, and particularly
The entrance to the warm baths in Arcite Street
Where we first met;—all!—the sun itself 110
Trails an evening hand in the sultry river
Far away down by Acheron. I am lonely,
Virilius. *(Sits on* U. S. *end of coffin plinth.)* Where is the punctual eye
And where is the cautious voice which made
Balance-sheets sound like Homer and Homer sound
Like balance-sheets? The precision of limbs, the amiable
Laugh, the exact festivity? Gone from the world.
You were the peroration of nature, Virilius.
You explained everything to me, even the extremely
Complicated gods. You wrote them down 120
In seventy columns. Dear curling calligraphy!
Gone from the world, once and for all. And I taught you
(Rises.)
In your perceptive moments to appreciate me.
You said I was harmonious, Virilius,
Moulded and harmonious, little matronal
Ox-eye, your package. *(Moves* R. *in circular move.)* And then I
  would walk
Up and down largely, as it were making my own
Sunlight. *(Back to coffin.)* What a mad blacksmith *(Moves* R.*)*
  creation is
Who blows his furnaces until the stars fly upward
And iron Time is hot and politicians glow 130
And bulbs and roots sizzle into hyacinth
And orchis, and the sand puts out the lion,
Roaring yellow, and oceans bud with porpoises,
Blenny, tunny and the almost unexisting
Blindfish; throats are cut, the masterpiece
Looms out of labor; nations and rebellions
Are spat out to hang on the wind—*(Back to* D. S. *end of plinth.)* and
  all is gone
In one Virilius, wearing his office tunic,
Checking the pence column as he went.
Where's animation now? What is there that stays 140
To dance? The eye of the one-eyed world is out. *(Kneels at coffin.*
  She weeps.)
DOTO. I shall try to grieve a little, too.
It would take lessons, I imagine, to do it out loud
For long. If I could only remember
Any one of those fellows without wanting to laugh.
Hopeless, I am. Now those good pair of shoes
I gave away without thinking, that's a different—
Well, I've cried enough about *them,* I suppose.

Poor madam, poor master.

(TEGEUS *comes through the gate to the top of the steps.*)

TEGEUS. What's your trouble?
DOTO. Oh!
Oh! Oh, a man. I thought for a moment it was something
With harm in it. Trust a man to be where it's dark.
What is it? Can't you sleep?
TEGEUS. Now, listen—
DOTO. Hush!
Remember you're in the grave. You must go away.
Madam is occupied.
TEGEUS. What, here?
DOTO. Becoming
Dead. We both are.
TEGEUS. What's going on here?
DOTO. Grief.
Are you satisfied now?
TEGEUS. Less and less. Do you know
What the time is?
DOTO. I'm not interested.
We've done with all that. Go away. Be a gentleman.
If we can't be free of men in a grave
Death's a dead loss.
TEGEUS. It's two in the morning. All
I ask is what are women doing down here
At two in the morning?
DOTO. Can't you see she's crying?
Or is she sleeping again? Either way
She's making arrangements to join her husband.
TEGEUS. Where?
DOTO. Good god, in the Underworld, dear man. Haven't you learnt
About life and death?
TEGEUS. In a manner, yes; in a manner;
The rudiments. So the lady means to die?
DOTO. For love; beautiful, curious madam.
TEGEUS. Not curious;
I've had thoughts like it. Death is a kind of love.
Not anything I can explain.
DOTO. You'd better come in
And sit down. *(Sits C., R. side.)*
TEGEUS. I'd be grateful. *(Sits R. on stool.)*
DOTO. Do. It will be my last
Chance to have company, in the flesh.
TEGEUS. Do you mean
You're going too?
DOTO. Oh, certainly I am.
Not anything I can explain.
It all started with madam saying a man

Was two men really, and I'd only noticed one,
One each, I mean. It seems he has a soul
As well as his other troubles. And I like to know
What I'm getting with a man. I'm inquisitive,
I suppose you'd call me.
TEGEUS. It takes some courage.
DOTO. Well, yes
And no. I'm fond of change.
TEGEUS. Would you object
To have me eating my supper here? *(Takes food out.)*
DOTO. Be careful
Of the crumbs. We don't want a lot of squeaking mice
Just when we're dying.
TEGEUS. What a sigh she gave then. *(Rises.)*
Down the air like a slow comet.
And now she's all dark again. Mother of me.
How long has this been going on?
DOTO. Two days.
It should have been three by now, but at first
Madam had difficulty with the Town Council. They said
They couldn't have a tomb used as a private residence.
But madam told them she wouldn't be eating here,
Only suffering, and they thought that would be all right.
TEGEUS. Two of you. Marvellous. *(Sits.)* Who would have said
I should ever have stumbled on anything like this?
Do you have to cry? Yes, I suppose so. It's all
Quite reasonable.
DOTO. Your supper and your knees.
That's what's making me cry. I can't bear sympathy
And they're sympathetic.
TEGEUS. Please eat a bit of something.
I've no appetite left.
DOTO. And see her go ahead of me?
Wrap it up; put it away. You sex of wicked beards!
It's no wonder you have to shave off your black souls
Every day as they push through your chins.
I'll turn my back on you. It means utter
Contempt. Eat? Utter contempt. Oh, little new rolls!
(To R. end of C. plinth.)
TEGEUS. Forget it, forget it; please forget it. Remember
I've had no experience of this kind of thing before.
(Rises, crosses L. to back of DOTO.)
Indeed I'm as sorry as I know how to be. *(Puts food down.)* Ssh,
We'll disturb her. She sighed again. O Zeus,
It's terrible! Asleep, and still sighing.
Mourning has made a warren in her spirit,
All that way below. Ponos! the heart

211. *Ponos:* pain.

Is the devil of a medicine.
DOTO.   And I don't intend
To turn round.
TEGEUS.   I understand how you must feel.
Would it be—have you any objection
To my having a drink? I have a little wine here.
And, you probably see how it is: grief's in order,
(To R. *end of plinth.)*
And death's in order, and women—I can usually
Manage that too; but not all three together
At this hour of the morning. So you'll excuse me.
(U. S. to get drink.)
How about you? It would make me more comfortable   220
If you'd take a smell of it.
DOTO.   One for the road?
TEGEUS.   One for the road. *(Pours drinks.)*
DOTO.   It's the dust in my throat. The tomb
Is so dusty. Thanks, I will. *(Takes drink.)* There's no point in dying
Of everything, simultaneous. *(Rises.)*
TEGEUS.   It's lucky
I brought two bowls. I was expecting to keep
A drain for my relief when he comes in the morning.
DOTO.   Are you on duty? *(To* TEGEUS R.*)*
TEGEUS.   Yes.
DOTO.   It looks like it.
TEGEUS.   Well,
Here's your good health.
DOTO.   What good is that going to do me?
Here's to an easy crossing and not too much waiting
About on the bank. Do you have to tremble like that?   230
TEGEUS.   The idea—I can't get used to it.
DOTO.   For a member
Of the forces, you're peculiarly queasy. *(An owl hoots.)* I wish
Those owls were in Hades—oh, no; let them stay where they are.
Have you never had nothing to do with corpses before?
TEGEUS.   I've got six of them outside.
DOTO.   Morpheus, that's plenty.
What are they doing here?
TEGEUS.   Hanging.
DOTO.   Hanging?
TEGEUS.   On trees.
Five plane trees and a holly. The holly-berries
Are just reddening. Another drink?
DOTO.   Why not?
TEGEUS.   It's from Samos. Here's—
DOTO.   All right. Let's just drink it.
—How did they get in that predicament?   240
TEGEUS.   The sandy-haired fellow said *(To bannister.)* we should
    collaborate
With everybody; the little man said he wouldn't

Collaborate with anybody; the old one
Said that the Pleiades weren't sisters but cousins
And anyway were manufactured in Lacedaemon.
The fourth said that we hanged men for nothing.
The other two said nothing. Now they hang
About at the corner of the night, they're present
And absent, horribly obsequious to every
Move in the air, and yet they keep me standing   250
For five hours at a stretch.
DOTO.   The wine has gone
Down to my knees. *(Sits R. end of plinth.)*
TEGEUS.   And up to your cheeks. You're looking
Fresher. If only—
DOTO.   Madam? She never would.
Shall I ask her? *(Half rises.)*
TEGEUS.   No; no, don't dare, don't breathe it.
(Crosses L. behind, sits on L. side of plinth.)
This is privilege, to come so near
To what is undeceiving and uncorrupt
And undivided; this is the clear fashion
For all souls, a ribbon to bind the unruly
Curls of living, a faith, a hope, Zeus
Yes, a fine thing. I am human, and this   260
Is human fidelity, and we can be proud
And unphilosophical.
DOTO.   I need to dance
But I haven't the use of my legs.
TEGEUS.   No, no, don't dance,
Or, at least, only inwards; don't dance; cry
Again. We'll put a moat of tears
Round her bastion of love, and save
The world. It's something, it's more than something,
It's regeneration, to see how a human cheek
Can become as pale as a pool.
DOTO.   Do you love me, handsome?
TEGEUS. To have found life, after all, unambiguous!   270
DOTO. Did you say Yes?
TEGEUS.   Certainly; just now I love all men. *(Rises.)*
DOTO. So do I.
TEGEUS.   And the world is a good creature again.
I'd begun to see it as mildew, verdigris,
Rust, woodrot, or as though the sky had uttered
An oval twirling blasphemy with occasional vistas
In country districts. I was within an ace
Of volunteering for overseas service. Despair
Abroad can always nurse pleasant thoughts of home.
Integrity, by god!
DOTO.   I love all the world *(Rises.)*
And the movement of the apple in your throat.   280
So shall you kiss me? It would be better, I should think,

    To go moistly to Hades.
TEGEUS.   Hers is the way,
    Luminous with sorrow.
DOTO.   Then I'll take
    (To helmet, by bannister R.)
    Another little swiggy. I love all men,
    Everybody, even you, and I'll pick you
    Some outrageous honeysuckle for your helmet,
    If only it lived here. Pardon.
DYNAMENE.   Doto. Who is it?

(TEGEUS crosses R. to about.)

DOTO.   Honeysuckle, madam. *(Crosses L. in front.)* Because of the
    bees.
    Go back to sleep, madam.
DYNAMENE.   What person is it?
DOTO.   Yes, I see what you mean, madam. It's a kind of   290
    Corporal talking to his soul, on a five-hour shift,
    Madam, with six bodies. He's been having his supper.
    (Crossing L. to DOTO and taking her U. S.)
TEGEUS.   I'm going. It's terrible that we should have disturbed her.
DOTO.   He was delighted to see you so sad, madam.
    It has stopped him going abroad.
DYNAMENE.   One with six bodies?
    A messenger, a guide to where we go.
    (TEGEUS brings DOTO down and crosses R.)
    It is possible he has come to show us the way
    Out of these squalid suburbs of life, a shade,
    A gorgon, who has come swimming up, against
    The falls of my tears (for which in truth he would need   300
    Many limbs) to guide me to Virilius.
    I shall go quietly. *(Behind plinth and R. to TEGEUS.)*
TEGEUS.   I do assure you—
    Such clumsiness, such a vile and unforgivable
    Intrusion. I shall obliterate myself
    Immediately.
DOTO.   Oblit—oh, what a pity
    To oblit. Pardon. Don't let him, the nice fellow.
    (Sits L. end plinth.)
DYNAMENE.   Sir: your other five bodies: where are they?
TEGEUS.   Madam—
    Outside; I have them outside. On trees.
DYNAMENE.   Quack!
TEGEUS.   What do I reply?
DYNAMENE.   Quack, charlatan!
    (TEGEUS retreats back R. to stove.)
    You've never known the gods. You came to mock me.   310
    Doto, this never was a gorgon, never.
    Nor a gentleman either. He's completely spurious.

Admit it, you creature. Have you even a feather
Of the supernatural in your system? Have you?
(Sits R. end of plinth.)
TEGEUS.   Some of my relations—
DYNAMENE.   Well?
TEGEUS.   Are dead, I think;
That is to say I have connexions—*(Sits stone R.)*
DYNAMENE.   Connexions
With pickpockets. It's a shameless imposition.
Does the army provide you with no amusements?
If I were still of the world, and not cloistered
In a colorless landscape of winter thought
Where the approaching Spring is desired oblivion,
I should write sharply to your commanding officer.
It should be done, it should be done. If my fingers
Weren't so cold I would do it now. But they are,
Horribly cold. *(She rises and moves U. S.)* And why should insolence matter
When my color of life is unreal, a blush on death,
A partial mere diaphane? I don't know
Why it should matter. *(Down to plinth.)* Oafish, non-commissioned
Young man! The boots of your conscience will pinch for ever
If life's dignity has any self-protection.
Oh, I have to sit down. *(Sits R. end of plinth.)* The tomb's going round.
DOTO.   Oh, madam, don't give over. I can't remember *(Rises.)*
When things were so lively. He looks marvellously
Marvellously uncomfortable. Go on, madam.
Can't you, madam? Oh, madam, don't you feel up to it?
(Crosses R. in front of TEGEUS.)
There, do you see her, you acorn-chewing infantryman?
You've made her cry, you square-bashing barbarian.
TEGEUS *(Crosses L. behind and sits L. end plinth).*
O history, my private history, why
Was I led here? What stigmatism has got
Into my stars? Why wasn't it my brother?
He has a tacit misunderstanding with everybody
And washes in it. Why wasn't it my mother?
She makes a collection of other people's tears
And dries them all. *(Rises, crosses R. to foot of steps.)* Let them forget I came;
And lie in the terrible black crystal of grief
Which held them, before I broke it. Outside, Tegeus.
DOTO.   Hey, I don't think so, I shouldn't say so. Come *(To* TEGEUS.*)*
Down again, uniform. Do you think you're going
To half kill an unprotected lady and then
Back out upwards? Do you think you can leave her like this?
TEGEUS.   Yes, yes, I'll leave her. O directorate of gods,
How can I? Beauty's bit is between my teeth.
She has added another torture to me. Bottom

Of Hades' bottom.
DOTO.   Madam, Madam, the corporal
Has some wine here. It will revive you, madam.
And then you can go at him again, madam.
TEGEUS *(Moving down to* DYNAMENE*).*
It's the opposite of everything you've said,
I swear. I swear by Horkos and the Styx,
I swear by the nine acres of Tityos,
I swear the Hypnotic oath, by all the Titans—   360
By Koeos, Krios, Iapetos, Kronos, and so on—
By the three Hekatoncheires, by the insomnia
Of Tisiphone, by Jove, by jove, and the dew
On the feet of my boyhood, I am innocent
Of mocking you. Am I a Salmoneus
That, seeing such a flame of sorrow—
DYNAMENE.   You needn't
Labor to prove your secondary education.
Perhaps I jumped to a wrong conclusion, perhaps
I was hasty.
DOTO.   How easy to swear if you're properly educated.
Wasn't it pretty, madam? Pardon.
DYNAMENE.   If I misjudged you   370
I apologize, I apologize. Will you please leave us?
You were wrong to come here. In a place of mourning
Light itself is a trespasser; nothing can have
The right of entrance except those natural symbols
Of mortality, the jabbing, funeral, sleek—
With-omen raven, the death-watch beetle which mocks
Time: particularly, I'm afraid, the spider
(Watching spider on floor moving L. of coffin.)
Weaving his home with swift self-generated
Threads of slaughter; and, of course, the worm.
I wish it could be otherwise. Oh dear,   380
They aren't easy to live with.
DOTO *(Crossing* L. *to* DYNAMENE*).*
                Not even a *little* wine, madam?
DYNAMENE. Here, Doto?
DOTO.   Well, on the steps perhaps,
Except it's so draughty.
DYNAMENE.   Doto! Here?
DOTO.   No, madam;
I quite see.
DYNAMENE. I might be wise to strengthen myself
In order to fast again; it would make me abler
For grief. I will breathe a little of it, Doto.
(Crosses, sits on L. *end of plinth.)*
DOTO. Thank god. Where's the bottle? *(Gets bottle from* R.*)*

360. *Hypnotic oath:* directed toward Hypnos, the Greek god of sleep.

DYNAMENE *(Picking up bowl, which has been left on plinth).*
   What an exquisite bowl.
TEGEUS.   Now that it's peacetime we have pottery classes.
DYNAMENE.   You made it yourself?
TEGEUS.   Yes. Do *(To* DYNAMENE.*)* you see   390
   the design?
   The corded god, tied also by the rays
   Of the sun, and the astonished ship erupting
   Into vines and vine-leaves, inverted pyramids
   Of grapes, the uplifted hands of the men (the raiders),
   And here the headlong sea, itself almost
   Venturing into leaves and tendrils, and Proteus
   With his beard braiding the wind, and this
   Held by other hands is a drowned sailor—
DYNAMENE.   Always, always.
DOTO *(Pouring drink).*   Hold the bowl steady, madam.
   Pardon.
DYNAMENE.   Doto, have you been drinking? *(Rising.)*
DOTO.   Here, madam?   400
   I coaxed some a little way towards my mouth, madam,
   But I scarcely swallowed except because I had to. The hiccup
   Is from no breakfast, madam, and not meant to be funny.

   (Gives bowl to DOTO *and breaks L. to coffin.)*

DYNAMENE.   You may drink this too. Oh, how the inveterate body,
   Even when cut from the heart, insists on leaf,
   Puts out, with a separate meaningless will,
   Fronds to intercept the thankless sun.
   How it does, oh, how it does. And how it confuses
   The nature of the mind.
TEGEUS.   Yes, yes, the confusion;
   (Sits L. end of plinth.)
   That's something I understand better than anything.   410
DYNAMENE *(Turning to* TEGEUS*).*
   When the thoughts would die, the instincts will set sail
   For life. And when the thoughts are alert for life
   The instincts will rage to be destroyed on the rocks.
   (Turning toward coffin.)
   To Virilius it was not so; his brain was an ironing-board
   For all crumpled indecision: and I follow him,
   The hawser of my world. You don't belong here,
   You see; you don't belong here at all.
TEGEUS *(Rising, crossing L. to* DYNAMENE*).*
                            If only
   I did. If only you knew the effort it costs me

400. *Pardon:* i.e., pardon my hiccough.

>   To mount those steps again into an untrustworthy,
>   Unpredictable, unenlightened night,   420
>   And turn my back on—on a state of affairs,
>   I can only call it a vision, a hope, a promise,
>   A—*(Backing toward steps.)* By that I mean loyalty, enduring passion,
>   Unrecking bravery and beauty all in one.
>
> DOTO. He means you, or you and me; or me, madam.
> TEGEUS. It only remains for me to thank you, and to say
> >   That whatever awaits me and for however long
> >   I may be played by this poor musician, existence,
> >   Your person and sacrifice will leave their trace
> >   As clear upon me as the shape of the hills   430
> > *(Quick move to bottom of steps.)*
> >   Around my birthplace. Now I must leave you to your husband.
> DOTO. Oh! You, madam.
> DYNAMENE.   I'll tell you what I will do.
> *(Crossing R. to TEGEUS.)*
> >   I will drink with you to the memory of my husband,
> >   Because I have been curt, because you are kind,
> >   And because I'm extremely thirsty. And then we will say
> >   Good-bye and part to go to our opposite corruptions,
> >   The world and the grave.
> *(She takes bowl and moves L. to C. DOTO moves R., takes bottle.)*
> TEGEUS.   The climax to the vision.
> *(He takes bowl, goes to DYNAMENE.)*
> DYNAMENE *(Drinking).* My husband, and all he stood for.
> TEGEUS.   Stands for.
> DYNAMENE.   Stands for.
> TEGEUS. Your husband.
> DOTO.   The master. *(Sits on rock, R.)*
> DYNAMENE.   How good it is,
> >   How it sings to the throat, purling with summer.   440
> TEGEUS. It has a twin nature, winter and warmth in one,
> >   Moon and meadow. Do you agree?
> DYNAMENE.   Perfectly;
> >   A cold bell sounding in a golden month.
> TEGEUS. Crystal in harvest.
> DYNAMENE.   Perhaps a nightingale
> >   Sobbing among the pears.
> TEGEUS.   In an old autumnal midnight.
> DOTO. Grapes.—Pardon. There's some more here.
> TEGEUS.   Plenty.
> >   I drink to the memory of your husband.
> DYNAMENE.   My husband.
> DOTO.   The master.
> DYNAMENE. He was careless in his choice of wines. *(Sits L. end.)*
> TEGEUS.   And yet
> >   Rendering to living its rightful poise is not
> >   Unimportant. *(Placing his foot on R. end of plinth.)*
> DYNAMENE.   A mystery's in the world   450

Where a little liquid, with flavor, quality, and fume
Can be as no other, can hint and flute our senses
As though a music played in harvest hollows
And a movement was in the swathes of our memory.
(Putting her arm on TEGEUS' *knee.)*
Why should scent, why should flavor come
With such wings upon us? Parsley, for instance.
(Realizing what she is doing, and taking away her arm.)
TEGEUS. Seaweed.
DYNAMENE. Lime trees.
DOTO. Horses.
TEGEUS. Fruit in the fire.
DYNAMENE. Do I know your name?
TEGEUS. Tegeus. *(Sitting* R. *end.)*
DYNAMENE. That's very thin for you,
 It hardly covers your bones. Something quite different,
 Altogether other. I shall think of it presently.
TEGEUS. Darker vowels, perhaps.
DYNAMENE. Yes, certainly darker vowels. 460
 And your consonants should have a slight angle,
 And a certain temperature. Do you know what I mean?
 It will come to me.
TEGEUS. Now *your* name—
DYNAMENE. It is nothing
 To any purpose. I'll be to you the She
 In the tomb. You have the air of a natural-historian
 As though you were accustomed to handling birds' eggs,
 Or tadpoles, or putting labels on moths. You see?
 The genius of dumb things, that they are nameless.
 Have I found the seat of the weevil in human brains?
 Our names. They make us broody; we sit and sit 470
 To hatch them into reputation and dignity.
 And then they set upon us and become despair,
 Guilt and remorse. We go where they lead. We dance
 Attendance on something wished upon us by the wife
 Of our mother's physician. But insects meet and part
 And put the woods about them, fill the dusk
 And freckle the light and go and come without
 A name among them, without the wish of a name
 And very pleasant too. Did I interrupt you?
TEGEUS. I forget. We'll have no names then.
DYNAMENE. I should like 480
 You to have a name, I don't know why; a small one
 To fill out the conversation.
TEGEUS. I should like
 You to have a name too, if only for something
 To remember. Have you still some wine in your bowl?
DYNAMENE. Not altogether.
TEGEUS. We haven't come to the end
 By several inches. Did I splash you?

DYNAMENE.   It doesn't matter.
   Well, here's to my husband's name.
TEGEUS.   Your husband's name.
DOTO.   The master.
DYNAMENE.   It was kind of you to come.
TEGEUS.   It was more than coming. I followed my future here,
   As we all do if we're sufficiently inattentive   490
   And don't vex ourselves with questions; or do I mean
   Attentive? If so, attentive to what? Do I sound
   Incoherent?
DYNAMENE.   You're wrong. There isn't a future here,
   Not here, not for you.
TEGEUS.   Your name's Dynamene.
DYNAMENE.   Who—Have I been utterly irreverent? Are you—
   Who made you say that? Forgive me the question,
   But are you dark or light? I mean which shade
   (Rising, going behind plinth to DYNAMENE.*)*
   Of the supernatural? Or if neither, what prompted you?
TEGEUS.   Dynamene—
DYNAMENE.   No, but I'm sure you're the friend of nature,
   It must be so, I think I see little Phoebuses
   Rising and setting in your eyes.
DOTO.   They're not little Phoebuses,   500
   They're hoodwinks, madam. Your name is on your brooch.
   No little Phoebuses tonight.
DYNAMENE.   That's twice. *(Moving away* U. S. L.*)*
   You've played me a trick. Oh, I know practical jokes
   Are common on Olympus, but haven't we at all
   Developed since the gods were born? Are gods
   And men both to remain immortal adolescents?
   How tiresome it all is.
TEGEUS *(Moving* U. S. *to* DYNAMENE*).*
                      It was you, each time,
   Who said I was supernatural. When did I say so?
   *(*DYNAMENE *moves down,* TEGEUS *follows.)*
   You're making me into whatever you imagine   510
   And then you blame me because I can't live up to it.
DYNAMENE.   I shall call you Chromis. It has a breadlike sound.
   I think of you as a crisp loaf.
TEGEUS.   And now
   You'll insult me because I'm not sliceable.
   (Crossing R., *sitting* L. *end of plinth.)*
DYNAMENE.   I think drinking is harmful to our tempers.
TEGEUS.   If I seem to be frowning, that is only because
   I'm looking directly into your light: I must look
   Angrily, or shut my eyes.
DYNAMENE.   Shut them.—*(Moving* R.*)* Oh,
   You have eyelashes! A new perspective of you.
   Is that how you look when you sleep?

(Flood creeps on from outside.)

TEGEUS.   My jaw drops down.   520
DYNAMENE.   Show me how.
TEGEUS.   Like this.
DYNAMENE.   It makes an irresistible
  Moron of you. Will you waken now? *(Crossing R. behind.)*
  It's morning; I see a thin dust of daylight
  Blowing on to the steps.
TEGEUS.   Already? *(Rising.)* Dynamene,
  You're tricked again. This time by the moon.
DYNAMENE.   Oh, well,
  Moon's daylight, then. Doto is asleep.
TEGEUS.   Doto
  Is asleep.
DYNAMENE.   Chromis, what made you walk about
  (Moving down, sitting R. end of plinth.)
  In the night? What, I wonder, made you not stay
  Sleeping wherever you slept? Was it the friction
  Of the world on your mind? Those two are difficult   530
  To make agree. Chromis—now try to learn
  To answer your name. I won't say Tegeus.
TEGEUS.   And I
  Won't say Dynamene.
DYNAMENE.   Not?
TEGEUS.   It makes you real.
  Forgive me, a terrible thing has happened. *(Breaks L.)* Shall I
  Say it and perhaps destroy myself for you?
  Forgive me first, or, more than that, forgive
  Nature who winds her furtive stream all through
  Our reason. Do you forgive me?
DYNAMENE.   I'll forgive
  Anything, if it's the only way I can know
  What you have to tell me.
TEGEUS *(Turning to* DYNAMENE, *head down).*
              I felt us to be alone;   540
  Here in a grave, separate from any life,
  I and the only one of beauty, the only
  Persuasive key to all my senses, *(Head up.)*
  In spite of my having lain day after day
  And pored upon the sepals, corolla, stamen, and bracts
  Of the yellow bog-iris. Then my body ventured
  A step towards interrupting your perfection of purpose
  And my own renewed faith in human nature.
  Would you have believed that possible?
DYNAMENE.   I have never
  Been greatly moved by the yellow bog-iris. Alas,   550
  It's as I said. This place is for none but the spider,
  Raven and worms, not for a living man.

TEGEUS. It has been a place of blessing to me. It will always
   Play in me, a fountain of confidence
   When the world is arid. But I know it is true
   I have to leave it, and though it withers my soul
   I must let you make your journey.
   (Moving R., behind, to go.)
DYNAMENE.   No.
TEGEUS.   Not true?
DYNAMENE.   We can talk of something quite different.
TEGEUS.   Yes, we can!
   Oh, yes, we will! Is it your opinion *(Moving L. behind.)*
   That no one believes who hasn't learned to doubt?   560
   Or, another thing, if we persuade ourselves
   To one particular Persuasion, become Sophist,
   Stoic, Platonist, anything whatever,
   Would you say that there must be areas of soul
   Lying unproductive therefore, or dishonored
   Or blind?
DYNAMENE.   No, I don't know.
TEGEUS.   No. It's impossible
   To tell. Dynamene, if only I had *(Sitting L. end of plinth.)*
   Two cakes of pearl-barley and hydromel
   I could see you to Hades, leave you with your husband
   And come back to the world.
DYNAMENE.   Ambition, I suppose,   570
   Is an appetite particular to man. *(Turning away from* TEGEUS.*)*
   What is your definition?
TEGEUS.   The desire to find
   A reason for living.
DYNAMENE.   But then, suppose it leads,
   As often, one way or another, it does, to death.
TEGEUS.   Then that may be life's reason. Oh, but how
   Could I bear to return, Dynamene? The earth's
   Daylight would be my grave if I had left you
   In that unearthly night.
DYNAMENE.   O Chromis—*(Turning to* TEGEUS.*)*
TEGEUS.   Tell me,
   (Turning away to avoid kissing her.)
   What is your opinion of Progress? Does it, for example,
   Exist? Is there ever progression without retrogression?   580
   Therefore is it not true that mankind
   Can more justly be said increasingly to Gress?
   As the material improves, the craftsmanship deteriorates
   And honor and virtue remain the same. I love you,
   Dynamene.
DYNAMENE.   Would you consider we go round and round?
TEGEUS.   We concertina, I think; taking each time
   A larger breath, so that the farther we go out
   The farther we have to go in.
DYNAMENE.   There'll come a time

When it will be unbearable to continue.
TEGEUS. Unbearable.
DYNAMENE. Perhaps we had better have something
   To eat. *(TEGEUS rises, crosses R. behind to get roll.)* The wine has
   made your eyes so quick
   I am breathless beside them. It *is*
   Your eyes, I think; or your intelligence
   Holding my intelligence up above you
   Between its hands. Or the cut of your uniform.
TEGEUS. Here's *(Crosses L. behind.)* a new roll with honey. In the
   gods' names
   Let's sober ourselves. *(Handing roll to DYNAMENE.)*
DYNAMENE. As soon as possible.
TEGEUS. Have you
   Any notion of algebra? *(Sitting on floor L., front of plinth.)*
DYNAMENE. We'll discuss you, Chromis.
   We will discuss you, till you're nothing but words.
TEGEUS. I? There is nothing, of course, I would rather discuss,
   Except—if it would be no intrusion—you, Dynamene.
DYNAMENE. No, you couldn't want to. But your birthplace, Chromis,
   With the hills that placed themselves in you for ever
   As you say, where was it?
TEGEUS. My father's farm at Pyxa.
DYNAMENE. There? Could it be there?
TEGEUS. I was born in the hills
   Between showers, a quarter of an hour before milking time.
   Do you know Pyxa? It stretches to the crossing of two
   Troublesome roads, and buries its back in beechwood,
   From which come the white owls of our nights
   And the mulling and cradling of doves in the day.
   I attribute my character to those shadows
   And heavy roots; and my interest in music
   To the sudden melodious escape of the young river
   Where it breaks from nosing through the cresses and kingcups.
   That's honestly so.
DYNAMENE. You used to climb about
   Among the windfallen tower of Phrasidemus
   Looking for bees' nests.
TEGEUS. What? When have I
   Said so?
DYNAMENE. Why, all the children did.
TEGEUS. Yes: but, in the name of light, how do you *know* that?
DYNAMENE. I played there once, on holiday.
TEGEUS *(Rising)*. O Klotho,
   Lachesis and Atropos!
DYNAMENE. It's the strangest chance:
   I may have seen, for a moment, your boyhood.
TEGEUS. I may
   Have seen something like an early flower

Something like a girl. *(Kneeling on floor to* DYNAMENE.*)* If I only
   could remember how I must
Have seen you. Were you after the short white violets?
Maybe I blundered past you, taking your look,
And scarcely acknowledged how a star
Ran through me, to live in the brooks of my blood for ever.
Or I saw you playing at hiding in the cave
Where the ferns are and the water drips. *(Rising.)*   630
DYNAMENE.   I was quite plain and fat and I was usually
   Hitting someone. I wish I could remember you.
   I'm envious of the days and children who saw you
   Then. It is curiously a little painful
   Not to share your past.
TEGEUS.   How did it come
   Our stars could mingle for an afternoon
   So long ago, and then forget us or tease us
   Or helplessly look on the dark high seas
   Of our separation, while time drank
   The golden hours? What hesitant fate is that?   640
DYNAMENE *(Rising, going* U. S.*).*
   Time? Time? Why—how old are we?
TEGEUS.   Young,
   Thank both our mothers, but still we're older than tonight
   And so older than we should be. Wasn't I born
   In love with what, only now, I have grown to meet?
   I'll tell you something else. I was born entirely
   For this reason. I was born to fill a gap
   In the world's experience, which had never known
   Chromis loving Dynamene.
DYNAMENE *(Down-stage on* R.*).*
                        You are so
Excited, poor Chromis. What is it? Here you are   650
   With a woman who has wept away all claims
   To appearance, unbecoming in her oldest clothes,
   With not a trace of liveliness, a drab
   Of melancholy, entirely shadow without
   A smear of sun. Forgive me if I tell you
   That you fall easily into superlatives.
TEGEUS.   Very well. I'll say nothing, then. I'll fume
   With feeling. *(Turning away.)*
DYNAMENE.   Now you go to the extreme. Certainly
   You must speak. You may have more to say. Besides
   You might let your silence run away with you
   And not say something that you should. And how   660
   Should I answer you then? Chromis, you boy,
   I can't look away from you. You use
   The lamplight and the moon so skilfully,
   So arrestingly, in and around your furrows.
   A humorous ploughman goes whistling to a team
   Of sad sorrow, to and fro in your brow

    And over your arable cheek. Laugh for me. Have you
    Cried for women, ever?
TEGEUS.   In looking about for you.
    But I have recognized them for what they were.
DYNAMENE.   What were they?
TEGEUS *(Standing on* L. *end of plinth).*
                          Never you: never, although   670
    They could walk with bright distinction into all men's
    Longest memories, never you, by a hint
    Or a faint quality, or at least not more
    Than reflectively, stars lost and uncertain
    In the sea, compared with the shining salt, the shiners,
    The galaxies, the clusters, the bright grain whirling
    Over the black threshing-floor of space.
    Will you make some effort to believe that?
DYNAMENE.   No, no effort.
    It lifts me and carries me. It may be wild
    But it comes to me with a charm, like trust indeed,   680
    And eats out of my heart, dear Chromis,
    Absurd, disconcerting Chromis. You make me
    Feel I wish I could look my best for you.
    I wish, at least, that I could believe myself
    To be showing some beauty for you, to put in the scales
    (Looking out front.)
    Between us. But they dip to you, they sink
    With masculine victory.
TEGEUS.   Eros, no! No! *(Getting down.)*
    If this is less than your best, then never, in my presence,
    Be more than your less: never! If you should bring
    More to your mouth or to your eyes, a moisture   690
    Or a flake of light, anything, anything fatally
    More, perfection would fetch her unsparing rod
    Out of pickle to flay me, and what would have been love
    Will be the end of me. O Dynamene,
    Let me unload something of my lips' longing
    On to yours receiving. Oh, when I cross
    Like this the hurt of the little space between us
    I come a journey from the wrenching ice
    To walk in the sun. That is the feeling.
DYNAMENE.   Chromis,   700
    Where am I going? No, don't answer. It's death
    I desire, not you. *(Crossing* L.)
TEGEUS.   Where is the difference? Call me
    Death instead of Chromis. I'll answer to anything.
    It's desire all the same, of death in me, or me
    In death, but Chromis either way. Is it so?
    Do you not love me, Dynamene?
DYNAMENE.   How could it happen?
    I'm going to my husband. I'm too far on the way
    To admit myself to life again. Love's in Hades.

TEGEUS. Also here. *(Crosses* L. *on* DYNAMENE'S L.*)* And here are we,
   not there
   In Hades. Is your husband expecting you?
DYNAMENE. Surely, surely. *(Turning away, looking at coffin.)*
TEGEUS.   Not necessarily. I,   710
   If I had been your husband, *(*DYNAMENE *turns away from coffin.)*
      would never dream
   Of expecting you. I should remember your body
   Descending stairs in the floating light, but not
   *(*TEGEUS *crosses to her* R.*)*
   Descending in Hades. I should say "I have left
   My wealth warm on the earth, and, hell, earth needs it."
   "Was all I taught her of love," I should say, "so poor
   That she will leave her flesh and become shadow?"
   "Wasn't our love for each other" (I should continue)
   "Infused with life, and life infused with our love?
   Very well; repeat me in love, repeat me in life,   720
   And let me sing in your blood for ever."
DYNAMENE. Stop, stop, I shall be dragged apart!
   (To C. *stage in front of plinth.)*
   Why should the fates do everything to keep me
   From dying honorably? They must have got
   Tired of honor in Elysium. Chromis, it's terrible
   To be susceptible to two conflicting norths.
   I have the constitution of a whirlpool.
   Am I actually twirling, or is it just sensation?
TEGEUS. You're still; still as the darkness.
DYNAMENE.   What appears
   Is so unlike what is. And what is madness   730
   To those who only observe, is often wisdom
   To those to whom it happens.
TEGEUS.   Are we compelled
   To go into all this? *(Following* DYNAMENE.*)*
DYNAMENE.   Why, how could I return
   To my friends? Am I to be an entertainment?
TEGEUS. That's for tomorrow. Tonight I need to kiss you,
   Dynamene. Let's see what the whirlpool does
   Between my arms; let it whirl on my breast. O love,
   Come in.
DYNAMENE.   I am there before I reach you; my body
   Only follows to join my longing which
   Is holding you already.—Now I am   740
   All one again. *(They kiss.)*
TEGEUS.   I feel as the gods feel:
   This is their sensation of life, not a man's:
   Their suspension of immortality, to enrich
   Themselves with time. O life, O death, O body,
   O spirit, O Dynamene.
DYNAMENE.   O all
   In myself; it so covets all in you,

My care, my Chromis. Then I shall be
Creation.
TEGEUS.   You have the skies already;
   Out of them you are buffeting me with your gales
   Of beauty. Can we be made of dust, as they tell us?   750
   What! dust with dust releasing such a light
   And such an apparition of the world
   Within one body? A thread of your hair has stung me.
   Why do you push me away?
DYNAMENE.   There's so much metal
   About you. Do I have to be imprisoned
   In an armoury?
TEGEUS.   Give your hand to the buckles and then
   To me.
DYNAMENE.   Don't help; I'll do them all myself. *(She undoes his armor.)*
TEGEUS.   O time and patience! I want you back again.
DYNAMENE.   We have a lifetime. O Chromis, think, think
   Of that. And even unfastening a buckle   760
   Is loving. And not easy. Very well,
   You can help me. *(TEGEUS sits L. side of plinth. DYNAMENE kneels by him.)* Chromis, what zone of miracle
   Did you step into to direct you in the dark
   To where I waited, not knowing I waited?
TEGEUS.   I saw
   The lamplight. That was only the appearance
   Of some great gesture in the bed of fortune.
   I saw the lamplight.
DYNAMENE.   But here? So far from life?
   What brought you near enough to see lamplight?
TEGEUS.   Zeus,
   That reminds me.
DYNAMENE.   What is it, Chromis?
TEGEUS.   I'm on duty. *(Rises.)*
DYNAMENE.   Is it warm enough to do without your greaves?   770
TEGEUS.   Darling loom of magic, I must go back
   To take a look at those boys. The whole business
   Of guard had gone out of my mind.
DYNAMENE.   What boys, my heart?
TEGEUS.   My six bodies.
DYNAMENE.   Chromis, not that joke
   Again.
TEGEUS.   No joke, sweet. Today our city
   Held a sextuple hanging. I'm minding the bodies
   Until five o'clock. Already I've been away
   For half an hour.
DYNAMENE.   What can they do, poor bodies,
   In half an hour, or half a century?
   You don't really mean to go?
TEGEUS.   Only to make   780

My conscience easy. Then, Dynamene,
No cloud can rise on love, no hovering thought
Fidget, and the night will be only to *us*.
DYNAMENE.   But if every half-hour—
TEGEUS.   Hush, *(Sits.)* smile of my soul,
My sprig, my sovereign: this is to hold your eyes,
I sign my lips on them both: this is to keep
Your forehead—do you feel the claim of my kiss
Falling into your thought? And now your throat
Is a white branch and my lips two singing birds—
They are coming to rest. Throat, remember me   790
Until I come back in five minutes. Over all
Here is my parole: I give it to your mouth
To give me again before it's dry. I promise:
Before it's dry, or not long after. *(Rising.)*
DYNAMENE.   Run, *(Rising.)*
Run all the way. You needn't be afraid of stumbling.
There's plenty of moon. The fields are blue. Oh, wait,
(TEGEUS crosses R. to her.)
Wait! My darling. No, not now: it will keep
Until I see you; I'll have it here at my lips. *(Crosses to him.)*
Hurry.
TEGEUS.   So long, my haven.
DYNAMENE.   Hurry, hurry! *(Exit TEGEUS.)*
DOTO.   Yes, madam, hurry; of course. Are we there   800
Already? How nice. Death doesn't take
Any doing at all. We were gulped into Hades
As easy as an oyster.
DYNAMENE.   Doto!
DOTO.   Hurry, hurry,
Yes, madam.—But they've taken out all my bones.
(Trying to stand.)
I haven't a bone left. I'm a Shadow: wonderfully shady
In the legs. We shall have to sit out eternity, madam,
If they've done the same to you.
DYNAMENE.   You'd better wake up.
If you can't go to sleep again, you'd better wake up.
Oh dear.—We're still alive, Doto, do you hear me?
DOTO.   You must speak for yourself, madam. I'm quite dead.   810
I'll tell you how I know. I feel
Invisible. *(Crossing L. with a birdlike movement to coffin.)* I'm a
   wraith, madam; I'm only
Waiting to be wafted.
DYNAMENE *(Moving L. to behind plinth).*
                  If only you *would* be.
Do you see where you are? Look. Do you see?
DOTO.   Yes. You're right, madam. We're still alive.
Isn't it enough to make you swear?
Here we are, dying to be dead,
And where does it get us?

DYNAMENE. Perhaps you should try to die
In some other place. Yes! Perhaps the air here
Suits you too well. You were sleeping very heavily. 820
DOTO. And all the time you alone and dying.
I shouldn't have. Has the corporal been long gone,
Madam?
DYNAMENE. He came and went, came and went,
You know the way. *(Breaking R.)*
DOTO. Very well I do. And went
He should have, come he should never. Oh dear, he must
Have disturbed you, madam.
DYNAMENE. He could be said
To've disturbed me. Listen; I have something to say to you.
DOTO. I expect so, madam. Maybe I *could* have kept him out
But men are in before I wish they wasn't.
I think quickly enough, but I get behindhand 830
With what I ought to be saying. It's a kind of stammer
In my way of life, madam.
DYNAMENE. I have been unkind,
I have sinfully wronged you, Doto. *(Crossing L. to DOTO.)*
DOTO. Never, madam.
DYNAMENE. Oh, yes. I was letting you die with me, Doto, without
Any fair reason. I was drowning you
In grief that wasn't yours. That was wrong, Doto.
DOTO. But I haven't got anything against dying, madam.
I may *like* the situation, as far as I like
Any situation, madam. Now if you'd said mangling,
A lot of mangling, I might have thought twice about staying. 840
We all have our dislikes, madam.
DYNAMENE. I'm asking you
To leave me, Doto, at once, as quickly as possible,
Now, before—now, Doto, and let me forget
My bad mind which confidently expected you
To companion me to Hades. Now good-bye,
Good-bye. *(Pushing DOTO toward entrance.)*
DOTO. No, it's not good-bye at all. *(Moving L. again.)*
I shouldn't know another night of sleep, wondering
How you got on, or what I was missing, come to that.
I should be anxious about you, too. When you belong
To an upper class, the netherworld might come strange. 850
Now I was born nether, madam, though not
As nether as some. No, it's not good-bye, madam.
(Sitting L. end of plinth.)
DYNAMENE. Oh, Doto, go; you must, you must! And if I seem
Without gratitude, forgive me. It isn't so,
(Crossing L. to DOTO.)
It is far, far from so. But I can only
Regain my peace of mind if I know you're gone.
(Looking anxiously toward entrance.)
DOTO. Besides, look at the time, madam. Where should I go

At three in the morning? Even if I was to think
Of going; and think of it I never shall.
DYNAMENE.   Think of the unmatchable world, Doto.
DOTO.   I do
Think of it, madam. And when I think of it, what
Have I thought? Well, it depends, madam.
DYNAMENE.   I insist,
Obey me! At once! Doto!
DOTO.   Here I sit.
DYNAMENE.   What shall I do with you?
(Moving behind plinth to entrance.)
DOTO.   Ignore me, madam.
I know my place. I shall die quite unobtrusive.
(Relaxing on plinth.)
Oh, look, the corporal's forgotten to take his equipment.
DYNAMENE.   Could he be so careless?
DOTO.   I shouldn't hardly have thought so.
Poor fellow. They'll go and deduct it off his credits.
I suppose, madam, I suppose he couldn't be thinking
Of coming back?
DYNAMENE.   He'll think of these. He will notice
He isn't wearing them. He'll come; he is sure to come.
(Looking out of entrance.)
DOTO.   Oh.
DYNAMENE.   I know he will.
DOTO.   Oh, oh.
Is that all for tonight, madam? May I go now, madam? *(Rising.)*
DYNAMENE.   Doto! Will you?
DOTO.   Just you try to stop me, madam.
Sometimes going is a kind of instinct with me.
I'll leave death to some other occasion.
(Crossing L. to entrance.)
DYNAMENE.   Do,
Doto. Any other time. Now you must hurry.
I won't delay you from life another moment.
Oh, Doto, good-bye.
DOTO.   Good-bye. Life is unusual,
Isn't it, madam? Remember me to Cerberus.
(Re-enter TEGEUS. DOTO *passes him on the steps.
As she goes.)* You left something behind. Ye gods, what a moon!
DYNAMENE.   Chromis, it's true; my lips are hardly dry.
Time runs again; the void is space again;
Space has life again; Dynamene has Chromis.
TEGEUS.   It's over. *(Sitting on rock* R. *of entrance.)*
DYNAMENE.   Chromis, you're sick. As white as wool.
(By his side.)
Come, you covered the distance too quickly.
Rest in my arms; get your breath again.
TEGEUS.   I've breathed one night too many. Why did I see you,
Why in the name of life did I see you?

860

870

880

DYNAMENE.   Why?
  Weren't we gifted with each other? O heart,   890
  What do you mean?
TEGEUS.   I mean that joy is nothing
  But the parent of doom. Why should I have found
  Your constancy such balm to the world and yet
  Find, by the same vision, its destruction
  A necessity? We're set upon by love
  To make us incompetent to steer ourselves,
  To make us docile to fate. I should have known:
  Indulgences, not fulfilment, is what the world
  Permits us.
DYNAMENE. Chromis, is this intelligible?
  Help me to follow you. What did you meet in the fields   900
  To bring about all this talk? Do you still love me?
TEGEUS. What good will it do us? I've lost a body.
DYNAMENE.   A body?
  One of the six? Well, it isn't with them you propose
  To love me; and you couldn't keep it for ever.
  Are we going to allow a body that isn't there
  To come between us?
TEGEUS.   But I'm responsible for it.
  I have to account for it in the morning. *(Crossing* L. *to* L. *side of
    plinth.)* Surely
  You see, Dynamene, the horror we're faced with?
  The relatives have had time to cut him down
  And take him away for burial. It means   910
  A court martial. No doubt about the sentence.
  I shall take the place of the missing man.
  To be hanged, Dynamene! Hanged, Dynamene!
  (Head on hands.)
DYNAMENE. No; it's monstrous! Your life is yours, Chromis.
  (Crossing to him.)
TEGEUS. Anything but. That's why I have to take it.
  At the best we live our lives on loan,
  At the worst in chains. And I was never born
  To have life. Then for what? To be had by it,
  And so are we all. But I'll make it what it is,
  By making it nothing.
DYNAMENE.   Chromis, you're frightening me.   920
  What are you meaning to do?
TEGEUS.   I have to die,
  Dance of my heart, I have to die, to die,
  To part us, to go to my sword and let it part us.
  I'll have my free will even if I'm compelled to it.
  I'll kill myself. *(Reaching for his sword.)*
DYNAMENE.   Oh, no! No, Chromis!
  (Taking sword, and backing L. *to coffin,* TEGEUS *follows.)*
  It's all unreasonable—no such horror
  Can come of a pure accident. Have you hanged?

How can they hang you for simply not being somewhere?
How can they hang you for losing a dead man?
They must have wanted to lose him, or they wouldn't   930
Have hanged him. No, you're scaring yourself for nothing
And making me frantic.
  TEGEUS.   It's section six, paragraph
Three in the Regulations. That's my doom.
I've read it for myself. And, by my doom,
Since I have to die, let me die here, in love,
Promoted by your kiss to tower, in dying,
High above my birth. For god's sake let me die
On a wave of life, Dynamene, with an action
I can take some pride in. How could I settle to death
Knowing that you last saw me stripped and strangled   940
On a holly tree? Demoted first and then hanged!
(Moving R. to her.)
  DYNAMENE. Am I supposed to love the corporal. *(Moving further down L.)*
Or you? It's you I love, from head to foot
And out to the ends of your spirit. What shall I do
If you die? How could I follow you? I should find you
Discussing me with my husband, comparing your feelings,
Exchanging reactions. Where should I put myself?
Or am I to live on alone, or find in life
Another source of love, in memory
Of Virilius and of you?
  TEGEUS.   Dynamene, *(Crossing L. to her.)*   950
Not that! Since everything in the lives of men
Is brief to indifference, let our love at least
Echo and perpetuate itself uniquely
As long as time allows you. Though you go
To the limit of age, it won't be far to contain me.
  DYNAMENE. It will seem like eternity ground into days and days.
  TEGEUS. Can I be certain of you, for ever?
  DYNAMENE.   But, Chromis,
Surely you said—
  TEGEUS.   Surely we have sensed
Our passion to be greater than mortal? Must I
Die believing it is dying with me?
  DYNAMENE.   Chromis,   960
You must never die, never! It would be
An offence against truth.
  TEGEUS.   I cannot live to be hanged.
It would be an offence against life. Give me my sword,
Dynamene. O Hades, when you look pale
You take the heart out of me. I could die
Without a sword by seeing you suffer. Quickly!
Give me my heart back again with your lips
And I'll live the rest of my ambitions
In a last kiss.

DYNAMENE. Oh, no, no, no! *(Crossing R. to in front of plinth.)*
   Give my blessing to your desertion of me?
   Never, Chromis, never. Kiss you and then
   Let you go? Love you, for death to have you?
   Am I to be made the fool of courts martial?
   Who are they who think they can discipline souls
   Right off the earth? What discipline is that?
   Chromis, love is the only discipline
   And we're the disciples of love. I hold you to that:
   Hold you, hold you. *(Breaking L. to him.)*
TEGEUS. We have no chance. It's determined
   In section six, paragraph three, of the Regulations.
   That has more power than love. It can snuff the great
   Candles of creation. It makes me able
   To do the impossible, to leave you, to go from the light
   That keeps you.
DYNAMENE. No!
TEGEUS. O dark, it does. Good-bye,
   My memory of earth, my dear most dear
   Beyond every expectation. I was wrong
   To want you to keep our vows existent
   In the vacuum that's coming. It would make you
   A heaviness to the world, when you should be,
   As you are, a form of light. *(They kiss.* TEGEUS *takes sword from her, crosses to R. C.)* Dynamene, turn
   Your head away. I'm going to let my sword
   Solve all the riddles. *(He is about to fall on sword.)*
DYNAMENE. Chromis, I have it! I know!
   Virilius will help you.
TEGEUS. Virilius?
DYNAMENE. My husband. He can be the other body.
TEGEUS. Your husband can?
DYNAMENE. He has no further use
   For what he left of himself to lie with us here.
   Is there any reason why he shouldn't hang
   On your holly tree? Better, far better, he,
   Than you who are still alive, and surely better
   Than *idling* into corruption?
TEGEUS. Hang your husband?
   Dynamene, it's terrible, horrible.
DYNAMENE. How little you can understand. I loved
   His life not his death. And now we can give his death
   The power of life. Not horrible: wonderful!
   Isn't it so? That I should be able to feel
   He moves again in the world, accomplishing
   Our welfare? It's more than my grief could do.
TEGEUS. What can I say?
DYNAMENE. That you love me; as I love him
(Crosses to him.)
   And you. Let's celebrate your safety then.

Where's the bottle? *(Takes bowl which has been at back of plinth.)*
  There's some wine unfinished in this bowl.
I'll share it with you. Now forget the fear   1010
We were in; look at me, Chromis. Come away
From the pit you nearly dropped us in. My darling,
  I give you Virilius. *(She drinks, passes bowl to* TEGEUS.*)*
TEGEUS.   Virilius. *(He drinks.)*
  And all that follows.
DOTO *(On the steps, with the bottle).*   The master. Both the masters.

                              CURTAIN

                                                Questions for Discussion

1. There are some startling reversals in the resolution of *A Phoenix Too Frequent,* from Dynamene's original determination to die with her husband and Doto's determination to die with her mistress. Does Fry make any attempt to make these turnabouts credible? What factors hasten the women's reversals? Why is Doto's more sudden than Dynamene's? Is Dynamene's made somewhat plausible by her gradual revelation of Virilius' personality and character?

2. What is the nature of Tegeus' change in character? What are its motivations? Are they plausible? Explain. Are they more or less gradual than Dynamene's? Explain.

3. How much of the ironic tone is established and maintained by Fry's use of verse? What are the particular characteristics of Fry's verse that make it especially suitable to the ironic content? Does the irony arise more from the verse *form* or the *diction*? Illustrate. How important in drama or composition is diction toward establishing a tone? Illustrate with two or three neutral statements that acquire ironic effect through minor changes in diction.

4. What are some other ways in which Fry foreshadows his ironic ending? For example, are the numerous allusions to classical mythology (use your dictionary to familiarize yourself with names not already familiar) in keeping with the flowery, metaphorical diction? If so, how? What seems to be Fry's general intent? Are the allusions and the diction suitable to the content? Why would any playwright

or composition student wish to create a conflict between his subject matter and the terms in which he expresses it? What is the overall effect in *A Phoenix Too Frequent*?

5. Dynamene's solution to Tegeus' problem (and her own) is, on the surface, fairly gruesome. In fact the setting of the entire play—an underground tomb overlooked by several hanging bodies—is itself gruesome. Did you react to the setting and to Dynamene's final forsaking of Virilius as one might be expected to react? If not, why not? How does Fry go about transforming a macabre setting and situation into comic terms? Illustrate.

Suggested Theme Topics

1. Write a character sketch of either Dynamene or Tegeus, showing the several gradual stages of change in the character.

2. Write a character sketch of Doto, emphasizing the aspects of her character which make her sudden change of mind seem plausible.

3. Analyze Fry's use of elevated diction and allusion for comic effect.

4. Discuss Fry's ironic use of setting.

5. Write an ironic theme on any subject, establishing the irony through selection of deliberately inappropriate diction.

Glossary

Absurdist Drama   A post-World War II European and American drama that espouses the themes of man's hopelessness and despair. Though the dramatists associated with the term *theater of the absurd* are too consciously individualistic to be called a school or movement, they (e.g., Samuel Beckett, Eugene Ionesco, Jack Gelber, Arthur Kopit, Edward Albee) are similar both in theme and dramaturgy. Their primary themes are the impossibility of communication, the bankruptcy of ideals, the failures of tradition to counter man's uncertainties, and the limitations and failures of a traditional approach to life. In defining the condition of man, Ionesco said: "Absurd is that which is devoid of purpose." By rebelling against traditional stage devices, situations, and dialogue, and by employing absurd situations, paradoxes, striking images, and illogical actions, these playwrights claim to reveal more honestly the human condition.

Allegory   A literary work in which all or most characters, actions, and aspects of setting represent symbolically abstract qualities, values, or ideas. For example, in *Everyman* Good Deeds and Death are both characters and abstractions, and the dramatic action obviously represents the Christian doctrine of salvation.

Antagonist   The force or character in conflict with the protagonist (or hero).

Anticlimax   A dramatic situation which, after suggesting that forces in conflict will reach a conclusion or come into open conflict, ends indecisively.

Aside   A dramatic convention in which a character's words are directed not to other characters on the stage but to the theater audience. Frequently, asides are brief comments which interpret the character's reaction to a situation or to something said by another character.

Atmosphere (Mood)   The overall feeling generated by a part or the totality of a dramatic production (including costumes, scenery, and lighting as well as dialogue and action). For example, the opening scene of Shakespeare's *Hamlet*—where the apprehensive guards recall a fearful situation—creates an ominous atmosphere that is also mysterious.

Catastrophe   The point in a play—usually near the end—where the conflict is resolved by one force (or character) irrevocably triumphing over another.

Character Foil   See *Foil*.

Characterization   The ability of the playwright to successfully create imaginary characters. In evaluating this ability, one would consider such matters as clarity, consistency, function, and effect (i.e., whether or not the character elicits audience interest).

Climax   See pages 142-143. The point (eliciting greatest audience interest and response) at which a character—usually the protagonist—reaches the decision, comes to the new awareness, or commits the action toward which all that has preceded (i.e., the rising action) has been directed; thus, the point at which the rising action will begin to fall.

Comedy   An inclusive term used to designate a play with a happy ending that is meant primarily to amuse. While precise distinctions between comedy and other dramatic forms are not always clear, the following are recurrent characteristics of comedy: (1) witty and humorous dialogue; (2) the presence of uncomplicated characters who possess common vices or virtues; (3) the presence of characters whose language, action, or personality is incongruous to the situations in which they are placed; (4) the presence of a few basic plots—usually involving the pursuit of fortune, love, fame, or happiness—which usually include startling reversals, chance confrontations, or elaborate intrigue; and (5) a happy resolution that finds the protagonist in some way triumphant.

Comedy of Humors (Humours)   A term used to denote a type of early English comedy, especially the kind written by Ben Jonson and George Chapman. During the medieval period and Renaissance, the term *humors* referred to the four fluids (blood, phlegm, yellow bile, and black bile) contained in the human body. It was then thought that a proper balance of those fluids would produce a healthy body and temperament, whereas an imbalance would result in the dominance of a single character trait. Thus, in the Comedy of Humors, a character's actions—his entire life—are determined by a single bias or whim of character (i.e., a "humor"). These "humors" may be, for example, jealousy, greed, lechery, etc.

Comedy of Manners   A type of comedy, most popular during the Restoration and eighteenth century (though it was later rejuvenated by Oscar Wilde and Noel Coward), that concerned the social views, conventions, manners, language, and fashions of a glittering, highly sophisticated society. In the dramas of such playwrights as Etherege, Congreve, Wycherley, Sheridan, and Goldsmith, this type of comedy usually involved intrigues (frequently amorous), witty dialogue, and satire (frequently directed at the inept person who unsuccessfully attempted to crash into or pass himself off as being a member of the sophisticated set).

Comic Relief   See *Subplot*.

Confidant (Fem., Confidante)   A device character, not himself seriously involved in the dramatic plot, who contributes to the play's exposition by serving as a sounding board for the protagonist. Usually he is a friend, acquaintance, or relative to whom the protagonist reveals his motives, plans, and/or actions.

Conflict An aspect of plot, frequently its most essential ingredient, that depicts the opposition of the play's protagonist by some other character, characters, or force. The playwright usually attempts to direct the audience's interest toward the central conflict.

Crux An unsolved question on which a literary interpretation may rest.

Dialogue The conversation of characters in a play. These conversations may be realistic (as in most modern drama) or conventional (as in the miniature essays that comprise the dialogue of *Everyman* or the poetic speeches delivered by the major characters in Elizabethan drama).

Domestic Tragedy A type of tragedy that rejected both the traditional conventions of character (i.e., a protagonist, usually historical, of high political or social rank) and plot (i.e., high politics or noble quests) associated with classical tragedy. The characters in domestic tragedy were drawn rather from the contemporary lower or middle classes, and the plots concerned domestic situations and problems of topical interest. Though the term is frequently limited to a few Elizabethan plays, it has also been used to designate a revival in the eighteenth century and to characterize much modern drama.

Dramatic Conventions Those conventions (or devices) employed by the playwright or director to induce an audience to accept as real what he knows to be an imitation. For example, a scene or act break must be thought to represent whatever period of time the plot requires; the stage itself must be thought to represent whatever the setting of the play may be; and such devices as *asides* and *soliloquies* must be thought to reveal the processes of a character's mind.

Dramatic Irony See *Irony*.

Dramatic Structure See pages 142-144.

Elizabethan Tragedy (Romantic Tragedy) When applied to such playwrights as Marlowe and Shakespeare, the term denotes a type of tragedy —sometimes called romantic tragedy—that rebelled against certain Aristotelian concepts. For example, romantic tragedy may include subplots for comic relief (thus violating Aristotle's unity of action), and the protagonist—unlike those described by Aristotle—may be a villain, as is Shakespeare's Macbeth. Unlike classical tragedy, which—though not prescribed by Aristotle himself—largely recognized the unities of place and time, the plots of Elizabethan tragedies often widely vary geographical setting from scene to scene and embody large amounts of time, perhaps months or years. Likewise, Elizabethan tragedy did not recognize classical decorum, or standards of propriety (involving such things as murder or death on the stage). Nevertheless, the protagonist was always a person of high station whose downfall would affect those below his station.

Epilogue   A brief closing section to a play, usually spoken directly to the audience by an actor or actress.

Exposition   In drama, the introductory section that introduces characters, establishes setting and tone, and provides the details necessary for understanding the action.

Expressionism   A term which, as applied to art, drama, poetry, and fiction, has received so many definitions that it seldom conveys a precise meaning. Generally, it suggests a play that sacrifices external reality (verisimilitude) in favor of certain symbols, images, lighting, and stage devices by which the playwright hopes to render "inner experience," or psychological states.

Farce   A term that originally denoted comic interludes interpolated into religious plays and later any light, short, humorous play (as distinguished from a full-length comedy). Today the term denotes a type of comedy that features improbable or incongruous actions or situations, flat and ridiculous characters, broad and obvious (or coarse) humor, and exaggerated horseplay (e.g., chases, escapes, confrontations).

Foil (Character Foil)   See page 143.

Irony (Dramatic Irony)   A literary tone that emerges when a character speaks or acts without certain information that the audience possesses. The tone results largely from the audience's recognition that the character would speak or act differently if he possessed the information that it has.

Melodrama   A type of drama that makes constant emotional appeals on the audience, develops a sensational plot (frequently containing bizarre circumstances and chance events) with characters who are either obscurely or implausibly motivated, draws clear distinction between the good characters (of whom the protagonist is usually one) and the thoroughly evil villains, ends with poetic justice, and employs unusually elaborate elements (e.g., music, weird sound or lighting effects) to induce excitement and suspense.

Mood   See *Atmosphere*.

Morality Play   A type of late medieval poetic drama (*Everyman* is the best known example) which—by employing an elaborate allegory—instructs an audience in the religious life. The original morality plays placed a character allegorically named Man, who sought salvation, into a maze of personified abstractions represented primarily by the Seven Moral Virtues (faith, hope, love, prudence, justice, fortitude, and temperance) and the Seven Deadly Sins (pride, envy, wrath, sloth, avarice, gluttony, and lust) of medieval theology. Gradually, the term has come to denote a play which employs allegorical techniques to deal with a character who seeks to come to terms with a single moral imperfection.

Naturalism A term which, when applied to drama, suggests a late nineteenth-century revolt against the well-made play and toward the "truth" of scientific determinism. Usually the characters in naturalistic drama are totally governed by their heredity, environment, or personal psychology or physiology. Thus, since these characters lack free will, their actions are interpreted as being essentially amoral.

Personification Endowment of abstract concepts—such as death, virtue, etc.—with human characteristics.

Plot A series of related actions, usually building to and falling from a conflict, that comprise the organizational plan for an imitation of human events. In drama there may be a single plot, two interrelated plots of equal importance, or a main plot with one or more subplots. For a play to have unity, both the relationships of actions that comprise individual plots and the connection between various plots must be apparent to the audience.

Poetic Drama Plays written in verse and designed to be acted (as opposed to *closet drama,* i.e., drama written to be read but not presented on the stage).

Prologue A brief introduction to a play written either by the playwright or (especially in the eighteenth century) by someone else. In English drama, the prologue characteristically comprises a group of lines spoken by a member of the cast before the action of the play has begun. While the lines frequently deal directly with the play, prologues are sometimes more discursive and deal with other matters.

Protagonist The main character in a play.

Reversal A point in a dramatic plot, either preceding or following the climax, where the protagonist's position changes for better or for worse.

Romantic Tragedy See *Elizabethan tragedy.*

Satire In drama, the term implies the use of wit or humor for the purpose of changing and reforming individuals or institutions. In proposing reform, the term is distinct from either personal abuse or sarcasm.

Soliloquy A speech delivered by a character who is alone; thus a dramatic convention for revealing the thoughts, motives, and/or psychology of a character. The soliloquy is usually longer and more complex than the aside.

Subplot A secondary plot, consuming less space, that presents an action in addition to the main plot in the play. Usually it is connected to the main plot by one or more characters who appear in both. The subplot may serve as a comparison or contrast (i.e., a foil) for the main plot; it may introduce a new or supporting theme; or it may furnish "comic relief" (i.e., a lighter tone that relieves the tension of the main plot).

Theme The dominant idea, usually an abstract concept, that is presented concretely in the play. While numerous playwrights have presented such themes as the failures of inordinate pride or the moral bankruptcy of the ardent materialist, one should not assume that every play contains a didactic (i.e., lesson-teaching) theme. Thus, *theme* is not a synonym for moral or message or lesson.

Tone The attitude (e.g., solemn, cheerful, serious, intimate) expressed by the playwright toward his subject (or theme), his audience, or both.

Thesis Play A play which illustrates and poses a solution for a social problem. This type of drama is sometimes called *didactic drama* or *propaganda play*.

Tragedy An inclusive term used to designate a serious play that, on most occasions, chronicles the downfall of a protagonist. While tragedy may take many forms (see *Domestic tragedy* and *Elizabethan tragedy*), the most common definition is that provided by Aristotle. For him tragedy "is an imitation of an action that is serious, complete, and of a certain magnitude; in language embellished with each kind of artistic ornament . . . ; in the form of action, not of narrative; through pity and fear effecting the proper purgation" of the audience's emotions. Thus the protagonist moves from fortune to failure through some flaw in character or error in judgment with which the audience can identify. Obviously, Elizabethan romantic tragedy and domestic tragedy constituted a revolt from Aristotelian principles, and modern tragedies tend to depict the psychological abnormalities rather than errors or character flaws that bring about human failure.

Tragicomedy In the strictest sense, a drama in which the plot and conflict appear tragic but the happy resolution suggests a comedy. However, the definition has been extended to include a play in which a comic plot ends tragically or even to include any play blending tragic and comic elements.

Well-Made Play An artificial and obvious play that is cleverly plotted and neatly resolved with nothing left unexplained. The term is sometimes used in an uncomplimentary sense because it suggests slickness rather than profundity.